T0137296

Lecture Notes of the Institute for Computer Sciences, Social Informatics and Telecommunications Engineering 467

More information about this series at https://link.springer.com/bookseries/8197

Mian Ahmad Jan · Fazlullah Khan (Eds.)

Application of Big Data, Blockchain, and Internet of Things for Education Informatization

Second EAI International Conference, BigIoT-EDU 2022
Virtual Event, July 29–31, 2022
Proceedings, Part III

Editors
Mian Ahmad Jan 🆔
Department of Computer Science
Abdul Wali Khan University Mardan
Mardan, Pakistan

Fazlullah Khan 🆔
Department of Computer Science
Abdul Wali Khan University Mardan
Mardan, Pakistan

ISSN 1867-8211   ISSN 1867-822X (electronic)
Lecture Notes of the Institute for Computer Sciences, Social Informatics
and Telecommunications Engineering
ISBN 978-3-031-23943-4   ISBN 978-3-031-23944-1 (eBook)
https://doi.org/10.1007/978-3-031-23944-1

This Springer imprint is published by the registered company Springer Nature Switzerland AG
The registered company address is: Gewerbestrasse 11, 6330 Cham, Switzerland

Preface

We are delighted to introduce the proceedings of the second edition of the European Alliance for Innovation (EAI) International Conference on Application of Big Data, Blockchain, and Internet of Things for Education Informatization (BigIoT-EDU 2022). BigIoT-EDU aims to provide a platform for international cooperation and exchange, enabling big data and information education experts, scholars, and enterprise developers to share research results, discuss existing problems and challenges, and explore cutting-edge science and technology. The conference focuses on research fields such as big data and information education. The use of artificial intelligence (AI), blockchain, and network security lies at the heart of this conference as we focus on these emerging technologies to excel the progress of Big Data and information education.

BigIoT-EDU has three tracks: the Main Track, the Late Track, and a Workshop Track. BigIoT-EDU 2022 attracted over 700 submissions, and Each submission was reviewed by at least Three Program Committee members in a double blind process, resulting in the acceptance of only 205 papers across all three tracks. The workshop was titled "International Workshop on IoT-enabled Big Data Analytics using Machine Learning for Smart Societies" and co-chaired by Muhammad Babar and Mian Muhammad Aimal from Allama Iqbal Open University Islamabad, Pakistan, and the Virtual University Lahore, Pakistan, respectively. The workshop aimed to focus on advanced techniques and algorithms to excel big data analytics and machine learning for advancement of smart societies.

Coordination with the steering chair, Imrich Chlamtac, was essential for the success of the conference. We sincerely appreciate his constant support and guidance. It was also a great pleasure to work with such an excellent organizing committee team for their hard work in organizing and supporting the conference. In particular, we are grateful to the Technical Program Committee, who completed the peer-review process for the technical papers and helped to put together a high-quality technical program. We are also grateful to Conference Manager Martin Vojtek for his constant support along with the whole of the EAI team involved in the conference. We must say that they have been wonderful and it is always a pleasant experience to work with them. Also, we would like to thank all the authors who submitted their papers to the BigIoT-EDU 2022 conference.

We strongly believe that the BigIoT-EDU conference provides a good forum for all researchers, developers, and practitioners to discuss all science and technology aspects that are relevant to big data and information education. We also expect that the future

BigIoT-EDU conferences will be as successful and stimulating as this year's, as indicated by the contributions presented in this volume.

Mian Ahmad Jan
Fazlullah Khan
Mengji Chen
Walayat Hussain
Shah Nazir

Organization

Steering Committee

Imrich Chlamtac   University of Trento, Italy
Mian Ahmad Jan   Abdul Wali Khan University Mardan, Pakistan
Fazlullah Khan   RoZetta Institute, Australia

Organizing Committee

General Chairs

Mian Ahmad Jan   Abdul Wali Khan University Mardan, Pakistan
Fazlullah Khan   RoZetta Institute, Australia
Mengji Chen   Guangxi Science and Technology Normal University, China

Technical Program Committee Chairs

Fazlullah Khan   RoZetta Institute, Australia
Mian Ahmad Jan   Abdul Wali Khan University Mardan, Pakistan
Walayat Hussain   Victoria University, Australia
Shah Nazir   University of Swabi, Pakistan

Sponsorship and Exhibit Chairs

Sahil Verma   Chandigarh University, India
Lan Zimian   Harbin Institute of Technology, China
Izaz Ur Rehman   Abdul Wali Khan University Mardan, Pakistan
Sara Karim   Abdul Wali Khan University Mardan, Pakistan

Local Chairs

Huang Yufei   Hechi Normal University, China
Wan Haoran   Shanghai University, China

Workshops Chairs

Zhang Yinjun   Guangxi Science and Technology Normal University, China
Rahim Khan   Abdul Wali Khan University Mardan, Pakistan

| Abid Yahya | Botswana International University of Science and Technology, Botswana |
| Syed Roohullah Jan | Abdul Wali Khan University Mardan, Pakistan |

Publicity and Social Media Chairs

| Varun G. Menon | SCMS Group of Educational Institutions, India |
| Aamir Akbar | Abdul Wali Khan University Mardan, Pakistan |

Publications Chairs

| Mian Ahmad Jan | Abdul Wali Khan University Mardan, Pakistan |
| Fazlullah Khan | RoZetta Institute, Australia |

Web Chairs

| Mohammad Imran | Abdul Wali Khan University Mardan, Pakistan |
| Yar Muhammad | Abdul Wali Khan University Mardan, Pakistan |

Posters and PhD Track Chairs

| Mengji Chen | Guangxi Science and Technology Normal University, China |
| Ateeq ur Rehman | University of Haripur, Pakistan |

Panels Chairs

| Kong Linxiang | Hefei University of Technology, China |
| Muhammad Usman | Federation University, Australia |

Demos Chairs

| Ryan Alturki | Umm Al-Qura University, Saudi Arabia |
| Rahim Khan | Abdul Wali Khan University Mardan, Pakistan |

Tutorials Chairs

Wei Rongchang	Guangxi Science and Technology Normal University, China
Muhammad Zakarya	Abdul Wali Khan University Mardan, Pakistan
Mukhtaj Khan	University of Haripur, Pakistan

Session Chairs

Ryan Alturki	Umm Al-Qura University, Saudi Arabia
Aamir Akbar	Abdul Wali Khan University Mardan, Pakistan
Mengji Chen	Hechi University, China

Vinh Troung Hoang	Ho Chi Minh City Open University, Vietnam
Muhammad Zakarya	Abdul Wali Khan University Mardan, Pakistan
Yu Uunshi	Shanxi Normal University, China
Ateeq ur Rehman	University of Haripur, Pakistan
Su Linna	Guangxi University, China
Shah Nazir	University of Swabi, Pakistan
Mohammad Dahman Alshehri	Taif University, Saudi Arabia
Chen Zhi	Shanghai University, China
Syed Roohullah Jan	Abdul Wali Khan University Mardan, Pakistan
Qin Shitian	Guangxi Normal University, China
Sara	Abdul Wali Khan University Mardan, Pakistan
Mohammad Wedyan	Al-Balqa Applied University, Jordan
Lin Hang	Beijin Linye University, China
Arjumand Yar Khan	Abdul Wali Khan University Mardan, Pakistan
Liu Cheng	Wuxi Technology University, China
Rahim Khan	Abdul Wali Khan University Mardan, Pakistan
Muhammad Tahir	Saudi Electronics University, Saudi Arabia
Tan Zhide	Anhui University, China

Technical Program Committee

Mian Yasir Jan	CECOS University, Pakistan
Abid Yahya	Botswana International University of Science and Technology, Botswana
Noor Zaman Jhanjhi	Taylor's University, Malaysia
Mian Muhammad Aimal	Virtual University, Pakistan
Muhammad Babar	Iqra University, Pakistan
Mamoun Alazab	Charles Darwin University, Australia
Tao Liao	Anhui University of Science and Technology, China
Ryan Alturki	Umm Al-Qura University, Saudi Arabia
Dinh-Thuan Do	Asia University, Taiwan
Huan Du	Shanghai University, China
Sahil Verma	Chandigarh University, India
Abusufyan Sher	Abdul Wali Khan University Mardan, Pakistan
Mohammad S. Khan	East Tennessee State University, USA
Ali Kashif Bashir	Manchester Metropolitan University, UK
Nadir Shah	COMSATS University Islamabad, Pakistan
Aamir Akbar	Abdul Wali Khan University Mardan, Pakistan
Vinh Troung Hoang	Ho Chi Minh City Open University, Vietnam
Shunxiang Zhang	Anhui University of Science and Technology, China

Guangli Zhu	Anhui University of Science and Technology, China
Kuien Liu	Pivotal Inc., USA
Kinan Sher	Abdul Wali Khan University Mardan, Pakistan
Feng Lu	Chinese Academy of Sciences, China
Ateeq ur Rehman	University of Haripur, Pakistan
Wei Xu	Renmin University of China, China
Ming Hu	Shanghai University, China
Abbas K. Zaidi	George Mason University, USA
Amine Chohra	Paris-East Créteil University (UPEC), France
Davood Izadi	Deakin University, Australia
Sara	Abdul Wali Khan University Mardan, Pakistan
Xiaobo Yin	Anhui University of Science and Technology, China
Mohammad Dahman Alshehri	Taif University, Saudi Arabia
Filip Zavoral	Charles University in Prague, Czech Republic
Zhiguo Yan	Fudan University, China
Florin Pop	Politehnica University of Bucharest, Romania
Gustavo Rossi	Universidad Nacional de La Plata, Argentina
Habib Shah	Islamic University of Medina, Saudi Arabia
Hocine Cherifi	University of Burgundy, France
Yinjun Zhang	Guangxi Science and Technology Normal University, China
Irina Mocanu	University Politehnica of Bucharest, Romania
Jakub Yaghob	Charles University in Prague, Czech Republic
Ke Gong	Chongqing Jiaotong University, China
Roohullah Jan	Abdul Wali Khan University Mardan, Pakistan
Kun-Ming Yu	Chung Hua University, China
Laxmisha Rai	Shandong University of Science and Technology, China
Lena Wiese	University of Göttingen, Germany
Ma Xiuqin	Northwest Normal University, China
Oguz Kaynar	Sivas Cumhuriyet University, Turkey
Qin Hongwu	Northwest Normal University, China
Pit Pichappan	Al-Imam University, Saudi Arabia
Prima Vitasari	National Institute of Technology, Indonesia
Simon Fong	University of Macau, China
Shah Rukh	Abdul Wali Khan University Mardan, Pakistan
Somjit Arch-int	Khon Kaen University, Thailand
Sud Sudirman	Liverpool John Moores University, UK
Tuncay Ercan	Yasar University, Turkey
Wang Bo	Hechi University, China

Contents – Part III

Highway Engineering Cost Evaluation Algorithm Based on Improved Particle Swarm Optimization Evolutionary Computation

Li Zhao[✉]

Chengdu Technological University, Chengdu 611730, Sichuan, China
919873574@qq.com

Abstract. In order to solve the problems of calculation speed and accuracy in highway engineering cost evaluation algorithm, a highway engineering cost evaluation algorithm based on improved particle swarm optimization evolutionary computation is proposed. Firstly, the optimal evaluation scheme of highway project cost is transformed into a dynamic optimization problem of candidate project cost scheme under multi-objective parameter constraints; Then, the improved particle swarm optimization algorithm is used to map the candidate scheme of highway engineering cost, the particle weight is modified according to the particle distance clustering degree and particle information entropy, and then the particle fitness value is calculated to update the local optimal solution and global optimal solution of the particle; Finally, the particle velocity and position update strategy are used to optimize the dynamic iteratively. Simulation results show that the algorithm has better convergence speed and better convergence value, and the calculation accuracy of the evaluation scheme is significantly improved.

Keywords: Project cost · Particle swarm optimization · Multi-objective optimization · Assessment

1 Introduction

With the formation of market economic system and the rapid development of transportation infrastructure construction, the management mode of highway project cost evaluation needs to be deeply studied. In order to more reasonably determine the project cost and effectively control the investment, we need to focus on improving the management ability and innovative thinking. Highway project cost management should be in line with international practice as soon as possible, that is, from the government control of implementing mandatory quota in the past to formulating pricing rules to meet market demand, and carry out micro management and macro control of project cost. It is an important task for highway cost managers to formulate a set of reasonable, standard and effective pricing indicators and indexes, and analyze the existing highway cost data to form a decision-making basis.

M. A. Jan and F. Khan (Eds.): BigIoT-EDU 2022, LNICST 467, pp. 1–6, 2023.
https://doi.org/10.1007/978-3-031-23944-1_1

Over the years, local design units, construction units and highway engineering cost management departments have accumulated a large number of highway engineering cost data, but less electronic storage, sorting, analysis and application. How to use the engineering economic information contained in the data has become an important issue of top priority[1]. Mastering the past, looking forward to the future and strengthening industry informatization is the only way for traffic builders. Therefore, the information construction of highway project cost management is helpful to strengthen the interaction between design and construction, project and cost, improve work efficiency and social and economic benefits. In this paper, a highway engineering cost evaluation algorithm based on improved particle swarm optimization evolutionary computation is proposed. By constructing the fitness function of its evaluation index system, the particle mapping candidate engineering project set is used to dynamically search the optimal evaluation scheme under the premise of dimensional direction and multi-objective constraints. Experimental simulation shows that the algorithm has good evaluation accuracy and execution efficiency.

2 Particle Swarm Optimization

As a kind of intelligent optimization algorithm, particle swarm optimization is proposed by simulating the foraging process of birds or fish. It has been widely used because of its simple calculation process and fast convergence speed, such as pattern recognition, dynamic environment optimization, fuzzy system control and so on. Of course, the more common one is to apply it to the optimization of objective function. It has achieved good results in both single objective function optimization and multi-objective function optimization.

2.1 Principle of Basic Particle Swarm Optimization Algorithm

Through the cooperation and competition among individuals in the population, particle swarm optimization algorithm can find the optimal solution in the search space. Firstly, the algorithm initializes a group of particles randomly in the search space, and each particle represents a feasible solution in the space. Corresponding to the objective function, it has the corresponding fitness value. In the process of optimization, the direction and distance of particles are determined by the speed. In addition to the best position that the particle itself has reached, We also need to learn from the best position that the population has reached; Here, individual extremum and global extremum are used to represent the best position they have reached. We can describe the whole process in mathematical form. There are m particles in a search space[2]. The dimension of the search space is n, that is, the dimension of the particles is also n.

The particle continuously updates the velocity vector and position vector in the search space, and the population records the individual extreme value and global extreme value found according to the updated position vector. It is hoped that the final global extreme value is the global best. The adjustment method is as follows:

$$\begin{aligned} E(t)\dot{x}_{d+1}(t) - E(t)\dot{x}_{k+1}(t) &= E(t)\Delta\dot{x}_{k+1}(t) = f(t, x_d(t)) + B(t)u_d(t) \\ -f(t, x_k(t)) - B(t)u_k(t) &= f(t, x_d(t)) - f(t, x_{k+1}(t)) + B(t)\Delta u_{k+1}(t) \end{aligned} \tag{1}$$

2.2 Improvement of Particle Optimization Algorithm

(1) Adjust inertia weight

When the particle velocity is large, the global search ability of the algorithm is strong. On the contrary, when the particle velocity becomes small, the local search ability of the algorithm is strengthened. In order to make the algorithm search for a wider area as much as possible in the early stage of evolution and improve the convergence of the algorithm in the later stage of evolution, Shi y et al. Used the linear decreasing method to dynamically adjust the inertia weight ω Value, and ω Used to control the influence of previous speed on current speed. In the early stage of evolution, the algorithm pays attention to the global search ability ω Value can avoid the population always searching in a local region and falling into the local optimum; In the later stage of evolution, the algorithm focuses on the ability to further search for more accurate solutions ω The value has become very small with the linear decline, so the local search ability of the algorithm is strengthened.

(2) Introducing domain operator

In the basic particle swarm optimization algorithm introduced earlier, the speed change of particles should not only learn from the best position they have reached, but also learn from the best position reached by all population particles. However, Kennedy et al. Found in their later research that particles often do not need to learn from the experience of all particles, but only from the experience of adjacent particles, so they introduced a neighborhood operator.

(3) Discretization processing

In the traditional particle swarm optimization algorithm, particles search randomly in a continuous space, and their position vector is any state in the continuous space, which is not one of the preset state sets. On the contrary, the discrete particle swarm optimization algorithm team preset a series of discrete states. In the search process, a reaching method is used to transform the state of particles in continuous space into the reaching degree to the predetermined state.

3 Improve the Highway Engineering Cost Evaluation Algorithm Based on Particle Swarm Optimization Evolutionary Computation

3.1 Highway Engineering Cost Estimation Model

The highway cost estimation model needs to adjust the regional and time coefficient differences in the built highway engineering projects, and dynamically select the most similar project a from the perspective of project cost according to the change of target project coefficient. The cost evaluation of engineering projects is based on the consistency of engineering projects. The characteristics of engineering projects can be used to find out the candidate projects most similar to the target project from the completed engineering projects according to the membership degree of fuzzy mathematics principle [3]. On the premise of meeting the constraints, a large number of candidate highway engineering projects can be regarded as population individuals, The population evolution search is carried out for the optimal evaluation scheme according to the evolutionary algorithm, and the predicted cost of the project to be evaluated is output

By analyzing the influencing factors of highway engineering cost evaluation, the characteristic factors of the project, including terrain, highway cross-section type, highway grade, highway cross-section height and width, pavement structure quality, pavement protection type and pavement thickness, are determined as the characteristic factors of highway engineering project, and a multi-objective evaluation system to measure the similarity of population particles is established.

$$
\begin{cases}
E(t)\dot{x}_k(t) = f(t, x_k(t)) + B(t)u_k(t) \\
\quad\quad y_k(t) = C(t)x_k(t)
\end{cases}
\tag{2}
$$

3.2 Improved PSO Evolutionary Algorithm for Highway Engineering Cost Evaluation

Input: Candidate items and parameter values of highway engineering projects

Output: the closest evaluation scheme of the highway engineering project to be evaluated

Step 1: Initialize particles map the candidate scheme of the highway engineering project to the particles of the particle swarm, and initialize the speed and position of the particles within the constraints of the target parameters. The position is the candidate scheme number, and the speed is mapped to the change rate of each parameter in the dimension direction.

Step 2: Particle weight coefficient assignment: cluster the particles according to the speed change, and calculate the particle weight coefficient according to the particle weight mapping function.

Step 3: Particle weight coefficient correction calculates the particle information entropy and particle spacing aggregation degree, and modifies the particle weight.

Step4: Particle fitness value use Eq. (3) to calculate the particle fitness value f (x).

Step 5: Update the individual extreme value of the particle. If f (x) < PWU, pbmle = f (x). Assign the fitness value of the particle to the individual extreme value.

Step 6: Update the global extreme value of the particle. If P = sphwe, then p = PLMI, assign the optimal extreme value of the current particle to the global extreme value.

4 Experimental Simulation

The experimental environment is a PC with Intel corei3-5301g memory Windows XP system, and the algorithm running platform is MyEclipse 8.5 of Java 6.0. During the experimental simulation, based on the historical data of completed projects, through the analysis of the influencing parameters of the cost evaluation of typical highway projects, the main index parameters affecting the cost evaluation of highway projects are finally determined [4], Taking it as the feature vector set of the model, the particle population is set to 100, the solution space is 9-dimensional, the number of iterations is 500, and the weight value range is [0.4,0.9]. Both algorithms run 20 times, and the mean value is taken as the diversity measure. The change of the fitness of the engineering cost evaluation algorithm with the number of iterations using the improved particle swarm optimization is shown in Fig. 1.

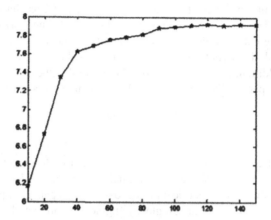

Fig. 1. Fitness value with the iteration times change schematic diagram

It can be seen from Fig. 1 that after 90 iterative optimization, the fitness value of the candidate evaluation scheme of highway engineering changes obviously, and its fitness function converges gradually. In the first 40 iterations, the increase of the curve is large, and the increase slows down after 40 iterations. This is mainly due to the inertia weight mapping of the particle weight, which gives a larger weight at the beginning of the iteration to enhance the global search ability of the algorithm. When the particle fitness value is close to the convergence value, the particle weight is reduced to make

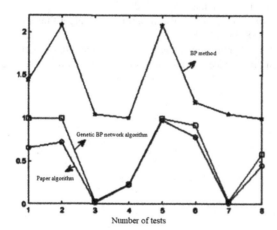

Fig. 2. Three algorithm error area chart

the algorithm have strong local search ability. When the iterative computation is stable, the algorithm converges to the optimal fitness value.

The evaluation accuracy of the algorithm is tested, and the three algorithms are tested for 8 times respectively. The calculation result error is shown in Fig. 2.

It can be seen from Fig. 2 that although BP network estimation algorithm can obtain ideal evaluation results, the error of single point is large, and the oscillation of evaluation results is serious. The variation range of optimized genetic BP network evaluation algorithm between different test points is reduced, but its global search ability is relatively poor compared with the particle swarm optimization evolutionary algorithm improved in this paper. In addition, it can be seen from the figure that the error of the evaluation algorithm in this paper is small, and the calculation accuracy is significantly improved.

5 Conclusion

In essence, project cost evaluation can be regarded as a multi-objective optimization problem. It is a problem to estimate the optimal approximate value of the project to be evaluated according to the historical project data. In this paper, by particle mapping the historical index parameter data of highway engineering project, the multi parameter constraint problem is transformed into a dynamic optimization process of fitness value function. Taking the main evaluation parameters of highway engineering project as the feature vector set, simulation verification is carried out, which proves the effectiveness and accuracy of the algorithm in highway engineering cost evaluation.

References

1. Yuhua, Q., Meichao, Y.: Fuzzy neural network determination of construction cost. Computer Simulation **6**, 184–187 (2012)
2. Hu, W.: Research and application of project cost estimation model. J. Central South University of Forestry Science and Technol. **8**, 163–166 (2011)
3. Yang, C., Gu, L., Gui, W.: Particle swarm optimization algorithm with adaptive mutation. Computer Eng. 16, 188–190 (2008)
4. Huadong, W., Wei, L.: Application of chaotic particle swarm optimization algorithm in WSN coverage optimization. Science and Technol. Bulletin **28**(8), 114–116 (2012)

Implementation of Intelligent Algorithm in Mathematical Modeling Teaching

Zhen Li[✉]

Jiangxi Technical College of Manufacturing Nanchang, Nanchang 330095, Jiangxi, China
lz1215250120@163.com

Abstract. Mathematical modeling is to refine the actual problems in the real world, abstract them into a mathematical model, find the solution of the model, verify the rationality of the model, and use the solution provided by the mathematical model to explain the real problems. This paper first introduces the common intelligent algorithms and expounds the classification of solving categories, and then explores the implementation of intelligent algorithms in mathematical modeling teaching from four aspects: the existing situation, the proposal of mathematical modeling teaching mode, the implementation methods and implementation results of intelligent algorithms in mathematical modeling teaching.

Keywords: Intelligent algorithm · Mathematical modeling teaching · Modeling Competition

1 Introduction

In the 1960s and 1970s, the mathematical modeling competition entered universities in western countries and appeared in the United States in 1985. In the early 1980s, China introduced mathematical modeling into university classrooms. The National College Students' mathematical modeling competition (CMCM) began in 1994 and is co sponsored by the Higher Education Department of the Ministry of education and the Chinese society of industrial and applied mathematics, Over the past decade, the scale of this competition has developed at an average annual growth rate of more than 25%. After more than 20 years of development, most colleges and universities in China have opened various forms of mathematical modeling courses to cultivate students' ability to analyze and solve practical problems by using mathematical methods.

Mathematical model is mainly used to describe practical problems by using mathematical symbols, formulas, programs, graphics, etc., so as to provide new methods and ideas for solving practical problems. This process of abstracting and refining mathematical model from practical topics is called mathematical modeling. Mathematical modeling is an applied mathematics, which returns mathematical theory to reality, It can improve your logical thinking and open thinking ability. Mathematical modeling! Mathematical modeling involves various disciplines and fields. In recent years, with the

M. A. Jan and F. Khan (Eds.): BigIoT-EDU 2022, LNICST 467, pp. 7–13, 2023.
https://doi.org/10.1007/978-3-031-23944-1_2

rapid development of computer technology and artificial intelligence technology, computer methods have been widely used in mathematical modeling, Intelligent algorithms play an important role in promoting the development of mathematical modeling[1]. Intelligent algorithms are widely used in mathematical modeling, such as artificial neural network method, simulated annealing algorithm, genetic algorithm, grey system, etc. these methods have common characteristics: self-learning, self-organization, self adaptation, simplicity, generality, strong robustness and adaptability to parallel processing Associative memory, pattern recognition and automatic knowledge acquisition are widely used.

2 Application of Neural Network Method in Mathematical Modeling

2.1 Intelligent Algorithm Classification

Swarm intelligence algorithms, such as ant colony algorithm (ACA), fish swarm algorithm (AFSA), chicken swarm algorithm (CSO), particle swarm optimization (PS0), longicorn whisker search algorithm (Basa), firefly algorithm, cuckoo search algorithm (CSA), frog leaping algorithm (SFLA), etc. Evolutionary algorithms, such as genetic algorithm (GA), differential evolution algorithm (DE) and immune algorithm, are invented based on physical laws. Such as simulated annealing algorithm (SA), algorithms that simulate human specific thinking activities, such as neural network (ANN), fuzzy logic control, tabu search (TS). Hybrid heuristic algorithms, such as genetic neural network, fuzzy neural network, neural network optimized based on simulated annealing algorithm, adaptive simulated annealing genetic algorithm (SAGA), etc. The neural network is used for the prediction problem in mathematical modeling, as shown in Fig. 1.

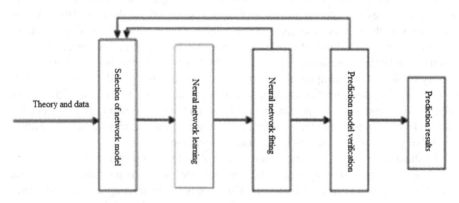

Fig. 1. Struts frame structure

Application of neural network to prediction problems in mathematical modeling

2.2 Classification and Clustering of Artificial Neural Networks

There are two kinds of neural networks commonly used in mathematical modeling: BP neural network and self-organizing neural network. BP neural network is a feedforward neural network based on error back propagation algorithm, which is mainly used to realize nonlinear mapping; Self organizing neural network is mainly used for clustering and pattern recognition. Typical topics include: DNA sequence classification (question a in 2000), cancer judgment (question 2001), breast cancer diagnosis (question C in 2001). Clustering: clustering refers to clustering according to "birds of a feather flock together". According to the principle, the samples without category are clustered into different groups, and the category corresponding to each sample is unknown in advance. For example, set a given sample set K, and then give the requirements for classification; it is hoped that the network can automatically divide the samples in the set into several categories according to the requirements[2]. The network with this ability is called a network with clustering ability. Classification is slightly different from clustering. Classification is to give objects according to a certain standard First define the category, and then classify according to the category. The category corresponding to each sample is known in advance. If there is a sample set K, it is divided into m disjoint classes: R_1, R_2,..., R_m. If it is agreed that when x belongs to R, the ith component of its output y is 1, and the other components are 0, expressed as

$$y_i(x) = \begin{cases} 1, x \in R_i \\ 0, other \end{cases} \tag{1}$$

3 Category Classification and Case Analysis of Mathematical Modeling Problem Solving

3.1 Problem Solving Category Classification

In the modeling competition over the years, it can be found that intelligent algorithms are used very frequently, but the intelligent algorithms used for different types of problems are different. First, for optimization problems, the intelligent algorithms commonly used by students include genetic algorithm, particle swarm optimization algorithm and ant colony algorithm. Simulated annealing algorithm. Tabu search algorithm, hybrid neural network, etc. In this aspect, students can solve the multivariable optimization model by using the intelligent algorithm, which can effectively reduce the situation of falling into the local optimal solution similar to the traditional optimization algorithm in the optimization process, and can find the global optimal solution more effectively than the traditional algorithm. Second, for the problem of regression prediction, students can use BP neural network to carry out regression prediction after training, which can achieve better results. Using neural network can realize automatic modeling and reduce the trouble that students can't model because they don't understand the mechanism of the model. Third, for clustering related problems, students can use self-organizing mapping neural networks (SOM / SOMs) for clustering analysis. Both this method and K-means are unsupervised learning clustering algorithms, but compared with K-means and other clustering algorithms, they are better in visualization and can form a better topological graph. Fourth, for the problem of comprehensive evaluation, students can use fuzzy neural network to solve it, input the processed fuzzy data into the neural network, and extract fuzzy rules by using the learning ability of neural network, so the fuzzy system has the generalization ability. It does not need students to construct the evaluation model, so that the model can deal with accurate information and fuzzy information, which enriches the application of neural network and fuzzy system.

To sum up, intelligent algorithms are widely used. They can get results for most of the models in the modeling competition, which is convenient for students to understand and use. For some troublesome problems in modeling, neural network can provide another idea of automatic modeling and give students more solutions to problems[3]. Therefore, teachers should pay enough attention to these two parts in teaching, and provide better methods for systematic learning of intelligent algorithms.

3.2 Case Analysis

In question a of 2018 mathematical modeling competition, the second and third are optimization problems, which can be solved by intelligent algorithm; In 2017, the platform pricing scheme of question B involves clustering, and self-organizing mapping neural network can be used for relevant operations: in 2016, question 3 needs to be optimized in the mooring system design of question A. at this time, swarm intelligence algorithm can be considered for optimization, such as PSO; In question B of 2015, the third one also involves optimization. At this time, intelligent optimization algorithm can be used for optimization. Through the statistics of mathematical modeling competitions in recent 5 years, the proportion of optimization problems in the competition is as high as 61.43%, among which the application of intelligent algorithms is numerous. The importance of intelligent algorithms to mathematical modeling can be seen.

4 Implementation of Intelligent Algorithm in Mathematical Modeling Teaching

4.1 Current Situation

First, the phenomenon of traditional "cramming" teaching is serious. When conducting intelligent learning teaching, teachers take themselves as the leading to explain the relevant contents, not combined with practice, but simply explain the knowledge and cases in textbooks. Students can not participate in it autonomously, have poor understanding of intelligent algorithms, and can not get a good understanding of intelligent algorithms. Second, only pay attention to theoretical explanation and assessment, ignoring practical teaching. At this stage, the assessment is basically based on theory. Teachers overemphasize the learning status of theory and pay insufficient attention to algorithm practice assessment. Third, the emerging flipped classroom. The micro class teaching model overemphasizes students' individual autonomous learning. For students with weak foundation and students in a passive state in learning, it is difficult for students to better absorb modeling related knowledge. Moreover, relevant research shows that

34.10% of the reasons affecting the reform of teaching methods are caused by the lack of teaching facilities. Flip classroom micro class teaching can be well implemented in universities with better equipment, but in some schools, it may not get good results due to the lack of equipment. Fourth, when teachers are not prepared for relevant courses, there may be scattered and unsystematic teaching courses.

Through the above analysis, it can be seen that the most serious problem in current teaching is that teachers can not effectively mobilize students' interest in mathematical model and mathematical modeling, and teachers do not give full play to students' subjective initiative, which makes the need to reform mathematical modeling course extremely urgent.

4.2 Implementation Method of Intelligent Algorithm in Mathematical Modeling Teaching

Intelligent algorithm teaching is divided into the following modules: genetic algorithm (CA), particle swarm optimization (PSO), simulated annealing algorithm (SA), ant colony algorithm (ACA) and neural network (cann). These are the intelligent algorithms commonly used in modeling. The teaching modules are divided in turn. When introducing ANN, teachers can explain BP neural network (BP), Hopfield neural network (HNN) and convolutional neural network in turn (CNN) and generative countermeasure network (can) Based on theory and focusing on assessment practice, teachers need to teach students the mathematical knowledge and computer methods required by the intelligent algorithm before teaching. In the process of giving case practice, teachers can let capable students try different methods, such as MATLAB software package and self programming, python or mathemat ICA carries out practice and urges students to compare the implementation effects of the same problems, so that students who have spare power can give full play to the space, and can better understand the algorithm and improve the level of modeling and programming. When teaching intelligent algorithm, teachers should first analyze the theory and restore the essence and process of the algorithm in combination with appropriate expression. For example, in group optimization algorithm, teachers can use ratio More classic "rabbit climbing" Vivid explanation can help students master the objectives and essence of the algorithm, and can effectively reduce the fear of some students for learning intelligent algorithms. In practice, teachers can divide groups in the form of three people in groups, subdivide the knowledge points needed for teaching in weekly and monthly units, and carry out mathematical modeling of intelligent algorithms in both in class and after class In class, teachers cooperate with students to install the required teaching modeling software, such as MATLAB and Anaconda (Python), Mathematica, lingo, etc. then teachers subdivide the knowledge points and teach in parallel from both theory and practice[4]. In theory, students need to master the corresponding mathematical knowledge, model application and essence. In practice, teachers are required to give corresponding cases and problems for students to think about. After class, teachers give tasks in different periods of time, so that students can organize group learning after class every week Preview results and problems are fed back in class. Every month, when teachers complete the teaching of specific knowledge points, they guide students to use matlab or Python for mathematical modeling practice by setting cases and problems of knowledge points related to intelligent algorithms. Finally, they carry out corresponding teaching and discussion in class in a teacher-student discussion teaching mode.

4.3 Implementation Effectiveness

After Yulin Normal University used this model for mathematical modeling teaching, the situation that the modeling competition won more than the third prize at the provincial level in recent three years is shown in Table 1.

Table 1. Awards after using this mode

Competition year	Number of participating teams	Award rate (%)
2016	50	24
2017	50	40
2018	50	42

It can be seen that the expected effect of the teaching mode based on teacher-student discussion teaching mode and supplemented by intelligent algorithm modeling practice and flipped classroom teaching mode after class is very ideal, which is worthy of learning and advocating this mode of teaching.

5 Conclusion

This paper discusses the classification of intelligent algorithms and lists common intelligent algorithms. In mathematical modeling teaching, teachers should pay attention to intelligent algorithms because they have the characteristics of strong robustness, simplicity and efficiency that traditional algorithms are difficult to compare. Therefore, this paper proposes to use the mixed teaching mode for teaching, that is, the teaching mode based on teacher-student discussion in class and supplemented by intelligent algorithm modeling practice and flipped classroom teaching mode after class. Compared with the existing teaching mode of mathematical modeling course, the mixed teaching mode has certain reference significance in mobilizing students' enthusiasm, improving students' programming writing and improving teachers' teaching quality. This mode better considers the combination of theory and practice, but it takes a long time for teachers to use this method to teach Intelligent Algorithms, It also puts forward certain requirements for its ability to master intelligent algorithms.

References

1. Zhang, L.: Feasibility and principles of implementing flipped classroom in mathematical modeling teaching. Education and Teaching Forum (12), 237–238 (2017)
2. Ma, Z.: Discussion on teaching mode of mathematical modeling course. College Mathematics **4**, 5661 (2018)
3. Dongyu, S.: On the basic construction of research teaching model in Colleges and universities. Heilongjiang Higher Education Res. **10**, 155–157 (2018)
4. Huaping, J.: Application of intelligent algorithm in mathematical modeling competition. Computer System Appl. **25**(8), 149–154 (2016)

Research on English Chinese Translation System for Tourism Based on Globish

Liu Yan[✉]

Jingchu University of Technology, Jingmen 448000, Hubei, China
dingdong83@163.com

Abstract. This paper studies the English-Chinese translation system for tourism based on Globish. With the rapid development of social economy and tourism, people's living standards and cultural literacy are constantly improving, and geological tourism has been paid more and more attention and favored by people. Machine translation can help realize the auxiliary language communication between people. As a branch of the field of natural language processing, it involves knowledge in many other fields. Due to the limitation of human understanding of language knowledge and the limitation of computer processing natural language, machine translation has become a difficult problem for researchers all over the world. The subset translation system based on Globish specification is an implementable system with much simpler complexity than the complete translation system of natural language. It can be applied or embedded in practical application systems such as electronic dictionary, mobile phone, MP3, MP4 and so on in the future.

Keywords: English Chinese translation system · MT cultural difference

1 Introduction

The so-called complexity means that the grammatical markers are complex, and they can work when the social life is narrow and the vocabulary is small. Once there is more social communication, it will be troublesome. The former means that it can be observed on the surface; From the perspective of economic principle, with the development of human society and the increase of vocabulary, it is also possible for human beings to abandon some external form redundancy to reduce a certain cognitive burden.

In my personal opinion, this may be related to the relationship between language and thinking. The subject thinks that "simplification" is the simplification of language form (Language surface), which is actually a kind of pseudo brevity, or a kind of solid complexity hidden in the depths of thinking. From the perspective of economic principle, yes, every language develops in a certain direction under the action of this principle [1]. However, from the perspective of cognition, the burden of human cognition has not been fundamentally reduced.

In other words, language processing is an information processing process, which will not make rapid progress with the simplification of language form, and the operation

M. A. Jan and F. Khan (Eds.): BigIoT-EDU 2022, LNICST 467, pp. 14–25, 2023.
https://doi.org/10.1007/978-3-031-23944-1_3

should be carried out. If it is not appropriate, for example, when using DOS system in the past, you need to enter the corresponding command for an operation; Now when using the graphical interface system, you only need to click the mouse to carry out an operation - from the perspective of the operation process, the work is simplified and there is no need to type character commands, but from the perspective of the actual operation of the computer, the work also needs to occupy resources; Or think again, double clicking to open a minesweeping game is the same as double clicking to open a large 3D online game, but the subsequent resource occupation is different. In a sense, the simplification of language form may be like this.

Take English as an example. English beginners don't have to learn many morphological changes and feel very relaxed, but soon they will realize that this is an illusion. Due to the lack of clear formal markers in English structure, he will fall into some difficulties. For example, some words can be used as verbs or nouns, saying "having cut the meat" or "a cut of".

"Meat"; You can say "kick a person" or "give him a"

"Kick"; You can say "horse", or "horse"

The so-called simplification brought about by this phenomenon is very debatable. First, when can verbs be used as nouns? In "taking a ride" or "give him a kick", nouns clearly reflect the action itself; In the examples of "having a cut on the head" and "eating a cut of meat", nouns also do not directly express the action, but the result of the action, and their actions are different. In the former example, "cut" refers to the wound caused by cutting, while the latter refers to the amount of meat cut. So I began to find that this apparent simplicity actually masks the strangeness and arbitrariness of a lot of usage. This is not a problem for people who started speaking English as children, but it will be difficult for people whose native language is completely different from the structure of English.

Secondly, in many cases, verbs cannot be used as nouns directly. The nouns related to them either have different forms or do not exist. As mentioned earlier, "this formal brevity is actually a kind of pseudo brevity, or a kind of solid complexity hidden in the depths of thinking."—— The simplicity of many languages in form makes people think that they are also very concise in structure.

Let's take another look at French. The reflexive verbs in French seem simple, but they actually confuse four verbs with different logic (reflexive verbs worthy of the name, simple intransitive verbs, mutual verbs and active words without case) at a high price. This usage is certainly not confused for the French, but it is quite confusing for a second language learner.

Modern people's minds are becoming more and more critical and analytical. Theoretically, the development of language should be more and more logical and regular - in fact, people who speak a language always feel that the language structure they say is very logical, but they are likely to ignore the difference between habit and logic.

The problem mentioned by the subject lies in this contradiction: under the restriction of the principle of economy, people's language form tends to be concise; Under the requirements of logic, people's thinking cannot be concise with the simplicity of form. With the progress of society and the development of language, human beings can only recognize more and more things [2]. We have to admit that human cognitive ability is not unlimited, it must bear more and more burdens.

In order to achieve the balance between cognitive ability and cognitive tasks to be completed, how to deal with relatively "redundant" information has become an important task. Therefore, in a relatively stable state for a long time, with the increase of cognitive things, people's thinking may begin to rely on the regular and logical traces left by habit, and make it concise in form, so as to reduce a certain cognitive burden.

Perhaps it can be explained as follows: when "social life is narrow and vocabulary is small", the logic and regularity of a language make it have a relatively complex grammatical system, which can express what it needs to express as accurately as possible; With the increase of cognitive burden, maintaining this relatively complex grammar system can not meet the needs of the principle of language economy, so we began to simplify the form accordingly. In such simplification, habit leads to native speakers still understand the simplified language, but second language learners will fall into confusion due to lack of logic and regularity [3].

The same input sentence from English gets different translation results. Different translation platforms have different translation results. The rules of word order from English to Chinese and the superlative expression of English adjectives all determine the different results of translation. The reason for this different result is that each translation software is based on its own knowledge base and corpus, and there is no unified rules and algorithms.

At present, several countries all over the world are committed to the research of machine translation. However, the computer is not the human brain. Machine translation needs to be realized: strong real-time, multilingual, whole sentence translation, multi field and so on. So far, these powerful functions can not be fully realized. Therefore, in this context, this paper puts forward such an idea, which adopts a simple and standardized language. In the restricted sub domain environment (such as tourism), through a platform such as machine translation system, it can obtain simple output with the simplest input, that is, the translation between subsets of different languages, Finally, it can enable people of different languages to communicate successfully.

2   Related work

2.1   Machine Translation

The development of machine translation roughly goes through three stages: syntactic analysis, phrase based, and nervous system. When I was at school, I read Feng Zhi-wei's "machine translation" and talked about the use of machine translation based on syntactic analysis. Last week, I found that I was in a group with Mr. Feng: to make a long story short, now machine translation has reached the stage of nervous system, and the translation is natural and smooth, which has a great potential to replace artificial translation. Since MT is so powerful, capital is also optimistic about the future of Mt. In 2020, with the outbreak of machine translation, a hundred flowers bloom in English, Chinese and English, and domestic Internet companies have entered the market, such as Baidu, Alibaba, Jinshan, Tencent and Youdao. Tencent even pulled out three teams of transmart, translation Jun and Tencent civil translation to do machine translation. University based machine translation teams have also launched their own machine translation, such as calf translation of Northeast University, cloud translation of Xiamen University, machine translation of Tsinghua University, etc. In addition, there are some small companies developed independently, such as Caiyun translation, Oumi translation, Daniel machine translation, etc. In addition to Google, Amazon, South Korea's naver papgo and Japan's rozetta are foreign machine translators. Of course, they will not lack Chinese [4]. Finally, English Chinese and English become the most competitive language for machine translation.

At present, attention mechanism is very popular and widely used in many fields such as machine translation, speech recognition and machine vision. The reason why it is so popular is that attention gives the model the ability to distinguish.

The main problem to be solved is how to map the variable length input x to a variable length output y in machine translation. The sequence model can better learn the grammatical knowledge of sentences. However, there are still two obvious problems when applying sequence to learn machine translation:

Compress all the information of input x to a fixed length implicit vector Z. When the input sentence length is very long, especially longer than the initial sentence length in the training set, the performance of the model decreases sharply;

$$\Delta w(i, y) = -\eta \frac{\partial e}{\partial w(i, y)} \tag{1}$$

Encode the input x into a fixed length Z and give the same weight to each word in the sentence. However, the translation between words generally has a corresponding relationship. If each word is given the same weight, there is no discrimination of corresponding translation, which often degrades the performance of the model.

$$D(x_i, x_j) = \sum_{l=1}^{m} d(x_{il}, x_{jl}) \tag{2}$$

In the traditional neural network machine translation task, the neural network model mainly applies an encoder to learn the knowledge in the source sense, and outputs a fixed length implicit vector Z. Then, the knowledge in the hidden vector is learned and translated into the target sentence by using decoder (cyclic network). Because the implicit variable Z is a fixed dimension and there is no corresponding word alignment translation in the whole translation task, the translation performance is limited [5].

The decoder is allowed to use the feature knowledge of different parts of the implicit variable Z in each output step. In addition, the attention mechanism allows the model to strengthen the learning of different features in Z according to the implicit variable Z and the generated words. Figure 1 shows the usage diagram of attention in the article. Its main usage is to calculate a weight factor first α, Then according to α The implicit variable Z (represented by H in the figure) is weighted and summed. Among them, α The larger the value, the greater the contribution of the corresponding H hidden variable to the information of decoding and translation.

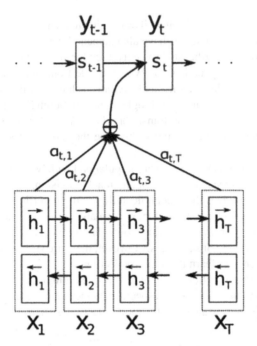

Fig. 1. Usage diagram of attention

The mid-1980s to the early 1990s is the second important period since the recovery of machine translation research in China. Two practical systems of great significance in the history of machine translation came into being in this period. One is the "ky-1" English Chinese machine translation system developed by the Academy of Military Sciences, which is the translation system later developed as "Yixing". It is the first commercialized machine translation system in China. The other is the "863-imt" English Chinese machine translation system developed by the Institute of computing of the Chinese Academy of Sciences, which won the first prize of the national science and technology progress award [6]. With the continuous progress of translation technology, the research of machine translation in new fields has also begun, such as voice translation system and so on.

Machine translation has gone through ups and downs for decades. Although translation technology has made great achievements, from the perspective of the practical machine translation system, its translation quality is not satisfactory. Hutchins, a famous machine translation critic, said in his speech at the machine translation summit that the quality of machine translation has not made substantive progress so far, and many unsolved problems 50 years ago still exist today.

2.2 Corpus

There are differences in the accuracy between machine segmentation and manual segmentation. In the later stage, the correction of manual segmentation is needed to improve the accuracy of machine segmentation. In short, corpus is a data warehouse used to store language materials [7]. Corpus is divided into many types:

Oral corpora, monolingual corpora, bilingual corpora or corpora comparing English and other languages may also come from different sources, some from news materials, some from online chat and forum comments. Different types and different sources will lead to different characteristics of corpora.

For example, if it comes from a press release, the vocabulary may be more written. If it comes from a forum or post bar, the words may be relatively colloquial, and there may be some new words in all aspects. In short, the source of the corpus will affect the vocabulary of the corpus. More deeply, corpus is the carrier of corpus. When studying corpus, there is a knowledge called corpus linguistics. It is a knowledge of linguistic research based on corpus. Specifically, we study the methods of natural language machine-readable text collection, storage, annotation, brief description, statistics and so on.

The accuracy of a word splitter may not be high enough. Make multiple word splitters into a bidding machine. The Jieba word segmentation algorithm of Python has not been updated for a long time, but the accuracy is relatively high. There is also a word segmentation of the shortest path that I try. The shortest path itself is the result of initial segmentation. A more rigorous word segmentation device is to use the language model to judge which result is good after the word segmentation result of the shortest path is obtained.

First of all, you should make it clear whether you need to establish a monolingual corpus or a bilingual corpus.

1. The establishment of monolingual corpus is relatively simple. You only need to prepare relevant corpus (ancient Chinese / modern Chinese / English / other languages) and import the corpus into antconc software for retrieval. I know that there is a specific method written in the post of the great God: establish your own exclusive English corpus, and mom won't worry about your writing any more.
2. To establish a bilingual corpus, you need to first prepare the original text and translation of bilingual control (such as Chinese-English control), enter the tmxmall online alignment page, import the corpus for sentence level alignment, and then export it to TMX format, which is your own bilingual corpus, which can be used for subsequent learning and research [8].

Before the introduction of attention mechanism, the decoder extracts knowledge and learns according to the fixed implicit variable Z during decoding and translation. However, after the introduction of attention, the implicit variable Z changes at different times, as shown in Fig. 2 below.

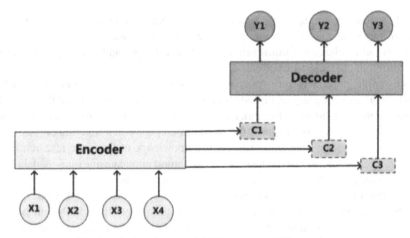

Fig. 2. The implicit variable Z changes at different times

Therefore, alignment can be said to be a further processing of the original corpus. By introducing the structural decomposition of bilingual sentence pairs, they are decomposed into word or phrase structures, and then the corresponding parts of each pair are aligned respectively, so as to create a processed instance database with sufficient translation knowledge.

3 Research on English Chinese Translation System for Tourism Based on Globish

English and Chinese are two different languages. Each language has its own independent and distinct system, and there are great differences in morphology and syntax. However, there are some similarities between the two languages. For example, the subject predicate word order and verb object word order are consistent. It is precisely because English and Chinese have both similarities and differences, so in translation practice, we can not use one method for translation. Literal translation and free translation are two important translation methods [9].

Literal translation is a translation method or translated text that maintains both the content and form of the original text. Free translation, also known as free translation, is a translation method or translated text that only maintains the content of the original text and does not maintain the form of the original text. Literal translation and free translation are interrelated and complementary, and at the same time; They coordinate with each other, permeate each other and are inseparable. Through a correct understanding of the relationship between literal translation and free translation, we can know more about when to use literal translation and free translation, as well as the skills, principles and problems that should be paid attention to when using literal translation and free translation, so as to finally achieve the purpose of improving translation ability and level.

The reason for the ambiguity of phrase structure is that the attachment relationship of nouns and prepositions is not easy to analyze clearly, so that different attachment methods may produce reasonable semantics. For example, the two divisions of the whole verb object structure of "bite / Hunter's dog" and "bite / Hunter's dog" are meaningful, but the different division methods lead to ambiguity. The identification of structural ambiguity is a difficult problem in machine translation, which involves deep analysis and understanding of natural language. Since it is impossible for us to make machine translation on the basis of understanding natural language, we can only study machine translation as an application technology, so it is difficult to achieve structural disambiguation only at the grammatical and even semantic levels.

The freedom and breadth of language make it impossible for us to completely solve the formal expression of knowledge and knowledge-based operational reasoning, and there is no consistent method to solve ambiguity in machine translation, resulting in inaccurate translation selection and unsatisfactory translation quality.

The predicate dominant word is usually the key to determine the sentence structure. In compound sentences with clauses and participle phrases, the accuracy of machine translation system in identifying predicate leading words is not high, and the structural analysis of some sentences with long and complex structure is not accurate, which makes the semantics of the translation and the original text very different.

Since there are active and passive voices in both English and Chinese, when translating from Chinese to English, people often simply think that it is OK to deal with the voice of the original sentence. In fact, this is not the case. In English, the passive voice is used much more frequently than in Chinese. If you translate blindly according to the voice of the original sentence, it will often make the translation very awkward [10]. Therefore, we need to flexibly use the conversion between voice in Chinese-English translation.

The composition of Chinese passive sentences can be roughly divided into two categories: one with obvious passive markers (i.e. "Bei" and "Rang") and the other without such markers. People usually use the latter type of passive sentences. But no matter which type, the passive voice can still be used when translating into English.

Part of speech tagging can be seen as a mapping process from one symbol string (word string) to another symbol string (part of speech string). Such a process can usually be realized by establishing a language model.

At present, the commonly used linguistic models can be summarized into three categories: rule-based model, distribution theory model and hidden Markov model.

This model is based on the hypothesis of word distribution, which indicates that the semantic and grammatical functions of a word determine its combination with other words. Mutual information (MI) is usually used to characterize the connection strength between two words. For mutual information, the formula is defined as follows:

$$MI(x, y) = \log_2 \frac{p(x, y)}{p(x)p(y)} \tag{3}$$

The production indicates that a noun phrase (NP) can be composed of a determiner and a nominal, or a proper noun (pronoun); A nominal component can be a noun, pronoun or a collection of adjectives and nouns. Context free rules can be nested hierarchically [11].

The symbol string a flight can be derived from the non ultimate symbol NP. Generally, the analysis number is shown in Fig. 3 to represent such a derivation based on these rules.

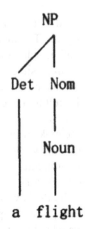

Fig. 3. Derivation of analytic number rule

The formal language of context free grammar is a set of symbol strings derived from the specified initial symbols, so it can also be used to define a sentence. In simplified English grammar, the set of symbol strings derived from the initial symbol s is the set of sentences. In short, the problem of language differences is a problem that needs to be studied continuously. Only with an in-depth understanding of language can we formalize and standardize language through computer, and break through the difficulties brought by language problems to machine translation.

4   Simulation Analysis

If the attention mechanism is separated from the encoder decoder framework in the above example and further abstracted, it is easier to understand the essence of the attention mechanism.

Conceptually, attention can be understood as selectively screening out a small amount of important information from a large amount of information and focusing on these important information, ignoring most unimportant information. The main focusing process is reflected in the calculation of the weight coefficient °. The larger the weight, the more focused it is on its corresponding eigenvalue, that is, the weight represents the importance of information, and the corresponding feature is the knowledge it needs to focus on [12].

Based on this, we can see that the application steps of attention mechanism can be divided into three steps:

1. Establish the correlation between the existing decoding results and the information of the hidden variable Z. this step can be understood as the process corresponding to the formula eij = a (SI-1, HJ) in Fig. 2;
2. Normalize the original score of the relationship obtained in step 1, that is, the calculation formula of CIJ in Fig. 2;
3. Weighted sum the values in the hidden variable Z according to the normalized weight coefficient, as shown in the calculation formula of Ci in Fig. 2.

We usually regard the process of machine translation as a process of reasoning with knowledge. The representation of knowledge base is the basis of the whole translation process. How to summarize, organize and express the knowledge used in machine translation has become an important task in the process of machine translation. The calculation code is shown in Fig. 4 below.

```
numEntries = len(dataSet)
labelCounts ={}
for featVec in dataSet:
    currentLabel = featVec[-1]
    if currentLabel not in labelCounts.keys():
        labelCounts[currentLabel] =0
    labelCounts[currentLabel] += 1
shannonEnt = 0.0
for label in labelCounts.keys():
    prob = float(labelCounts[label])/numEntries
    shannonEnt -= prob*log(prob,2)
return shannonEnt
```

Fig. 4. Syntax rule code

According to the limited number of words and simple grammar rules of Globish global language, we put forward the idea of standardizing this language to the subset of knowledge base required by machine translation, and obtaining the transformation from one language meaning to another language meaning through machine translation technology, It should be feasible to use it as an auxiliary language translator to realize the communication between people of different languages.

Generally speaking, the more information a dictionary contains, the more favorable it is for translation [13]. Here, we use 1500 Globish English words as the basic dictionary. First, in order to avoid the complexity of machine translation caused by the openness of language knowledge. Second, the dictionary under such a limited scope is suitable for the research of translation in limited sub fields. For the commonly used tourism words that do not appear in 1500 words entered in the source language sentences, we have specially established another small tourism dictionary. The two dictionaries are independent of each other, but they are interdependent. If we continue to expand this system in the future, we can continue to add professional dictionaries, such as science and technology professional dictionaries, weather professional dictionaries and so on [14].

Based on the particularity of Globish language, it can use certain gestures and images as auxiliary means of communication, which inevitably inspires such an assumption. When the source input language obtains the target language through machine translation, and the target language cannot be understood subjectively, we can again ask whether the machine translation system can re translate, and try to use more vivid pictures to show the original intention of the source language in combination with the search of the picture library in the translation process. Because the meaning of pictures is the same for people in different languages.

5 Conclusion

The restricted translation system established in this paper needs to do a lot of work. Due to the limited working time in this paper, only a few knowledge bases, the research of translation algorithms and the framework model of the system can be given. For further work, the following aspects should be considered: for the automatic alignment of bilingual instance pairs, because the instance sentence pair capacity of the system is small, the means of manual alignment is adopted. In order to accurately find the corresponding target language sentences from the source language sentences in the instance database, we need not only a relatively large instance database, but also automatic alignment at the sentence level, phrase level and vocabulary level. When the granularity of language units becomes smaller, the difficulty of analysis will be greatly strengthened This paper uses the case-based machine translation algorithm to analyze the word level of language fragments when the source input sentences cannot be matched in the case database. This analysis is only based on the shallow analysis, and does not involve the problem of grammar and semantics.

References

1. Akui, T., Fujiwara, K., Takinoue, M., et al.: System concentration shift as a regulator of transcription-translation system within liposomes. SSRN Electronic J. **24**(8), 102859 (2021)
2. Palumbo, G.: "Visible" at last? some notes on english as a target language and translated books in the US. ELOPE English Language Overseas Perspectives and Enquiries **18**(1), 55–69 (2021)
3. Ri, R., Nakazawa, T., Tsuruoka, Y.: Modeling Target-Side Inflection in Placeholder Translation (2021)
4. Ahm, A., Ss, B.: Application of the MTSVD method in the experimental x-ray spectrum unfolding in the diagnostic energy range using CR film and Plexiglas wedge. Radiation Physics and Chemistry **183**, 109393 (2021)
5. Shahab, M.T., Miller, D.E.: Asymptotic tracking and linear-like behavior using multi-model adaptive control. IEEE Transactions on Automatic Control **67**(1), 203219 (2021)
6. Corrente, G.: Translation of Quantum Circuits into Quantum Turing Machines for Deutsch and Deutsch-Jozsa Problems (2021)
7. Hussien, A.A.: Cyber Security Crimes, Ethics and a Suggested Algorithm to Overcome Cyber-Physical Systems Problems (CybSec1). **12**(1), 23 (2021)
8. Luo, Y., Lin, M.: Flash translation layer: a review and bibliometric analysis. International Journal of Intelligent Computing and Cybernetics, ahead-of-print(ahead-of-print) (2021)
9. Aghasafari, P., Yang, P.C., Kernik, D.C., et al.: A deep learning algorithm to translate and classify cardiac electrophysiology. eLife Sciences **10**, e68335 (2021)
10. Wang, Y.: On the Chinese-english translation of current political culture-loaded words in news from the perspective of intercultural communication. In: 2021 5th International Seminar on Education, Management and Social Sciences (ISEMSS 2021), pp. 353356 (2021)

11. Zheng, S.: A study of the Chinese-english translation of culture-specific items in publicity texts of Guangzhou's intangible cultural heritage. Theory and Practice in Language Studies **11**(6), 749–755 (2021)
12. Li, T., Hu, K.: Reappraising Self and Others: A Corpus-Based Study of Chinese Political Discourse in English Translation (2021)
13. Tan, Z., Ke, X.: On EST sentence translation based on english and chinese structures: natural linear expansion vs. reversed linear expansion. Theory and Practice in Language Studies **11**(4), 396–402 (2021)
14. Zhang, R., Wang, X., Zhang, C., et al.: BSTC: A Large-Scale Chinese-English Speech Translation Dataset (2021)

Research on English Language Learning Algorithm Based on Speech Recognition Confidence

Jing Sheng[✉]

Wuchang University of Technology, Hubei 430070, China
wclgxyxf@sina.com

Abstract. Speech recognition technology is the key to the realization of a language learning system. The research of large-scale continuous speech recognition has been carried out for more than 20 years. Although significant progress has been made, it is still far from wide application. Because the current English learning software can not fully meet the requirements of users, this paper proposes a method to introduce the confidence of speech recognition into language learning. After discussing the basic principle of confidence and its role in language blind learning, a new algorithm is proposed, and based on this algorithm, an English language learning system based on confidence technology is finally established.

Keywords: Confidence · Language learning · Speech recognition

1 Introduction

In real life, language (including voice and text) is one of the main tools for people to exchange ideas and emotions. It is also one of the main tools for human history and cultural inheritance, which contains rich information. With the continuous development of society, various machines have gradually participated in human production and social life. In particular, the emergence of computers and the development of computer technology have completely changed human living conditions and living standards. With the rapid development and increasing popularity of computer and Internet technology, the main application of computer has developed from simple numerical operation to complex data and information processing. It is necessary to manage rich digital media information such as audio and video. At the same time, the need to improve the efficiency of human-computer interaction has become increasingly prominent. People hope that in the future, computers can really "understand" human language and communicate with users through "listening" and "speaking". As the most direct and effective means of interpersonal communication, speech technology has attracted the attention of many researchers.

More and more people hope to use computers as a tool for foreign language learning/teaching. At present, some software have combined speech recognition technology in English language learning system to train and improve learners' pronunciation and oral

M. A. Jan and F. Khan (Eds.): BigIoT-EDU 2022, LNICST 467, pp. 26–35, 2023.
https://doi.org/10.1007/978-3-031-23944-1_4

ability These software include Caroline in the city/CNN Interactive English Traci talk of CPI and Encarta Interactive English learning of Microsoft. Although these software are successfully embedded into the speech recognition engine, they still can not provide users with accurate feedback results to help them correct their wrong pronunciation [1]. Eskenazi once proposed five standards to determine the quality of computer-aided pronunciation training software, one of which is that learners can get the necessary corrective feedback. Without this timely feedback, learners will be confused in the learning process and gradually lose interest in the learning process. In order to solve this problem, this paper proposes a new English language learning method based on speech recognition confidence technology. The speech recognition is shown in Fig. 1.

Speech recognition is an interdisciplinary subject. In the past two decades, speech recognition technology has made significant progress and began to move from the laboratory to the market. It is expected that in the next 10 years, speech recognition technology will enter industries, home appliances, communications, automotive electronics, medical care, home services, consumer electronics and other fields. The application of speech recognition dictator in some fields was rated as one of the ten major events of computer development in 1997 by the American press. Many experts believe that speech recognition technology is one of the ten important scientific and technological development technologies in the field of information technology from 2000 to 2010. The fields of speech recognition technology include: signal processing, pattern recognition, probability theory and information theory, phonation mechanism and auditory mechanism, artificial intelligence and so on.

It has long been a dream for people to communicate with the machine by voice and let the machine understand what you say. The image of China Internet of things school enterprise alliance compares speech recognition to "the auditory system of a machine". Speech recognition technology is a high technology that enables the machine to convert the speech signal into the corresponding text or command through the process of recognition and understanding. Speech recognition technology mainly includes three aspects: feature extraction technology, pattern matching criteria and model training technology. The voice recognition technology of the Internet of vehicles has also been fully cited. For example, in the Internet of wing trucks, you can set the direct navigation of the destination by pressing one button to communicate with the customer service staff orally, which is safe and convenient.

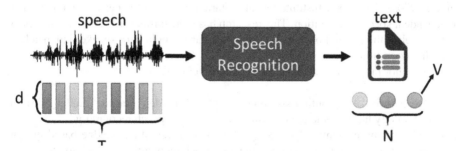

Fig. 1. Speech recognition

2 Speech Recognition Technology

2.1 Overview of Speech Recognition Technology

As the most important and natural communication tool, language is one of the important sources of human information. Using speech to realize the interaction between human and computer mainly includes three technologies: speech recognition, natural language understanding and speech synthesis. The main task of automatic speech recognition is to complete the transformation from speech to text; Natural language understanding is to complete the transformation from text to semantics; Speech synthesis is to output the information users want by voice, that is, text is transformed into speech.

As the key technology of human-computer interaction, speech recognition technology involves linguistics, acoustics, physiology, psychology, informatics, digital signal processing theory, pattern recognition theory, computer and other disciplines. Speech recognition technology has a very broad application prospect and has been successfully applied in the fields of industry, communication, finance, confidentiality, transportation and medical treatment.

During the research and development of speech recognition, relevant researchers have designed and produced speech databases in Chinese (including different dialects), English and other languages according to the pronunciation characteristics of different languages. These speech databases can provide sufficient and scientific training speech samples for relevant research institutions and universities at home and abroad to carry out Chinese continuous speech recognition algorithm research, system design and industrialization. For example: MIT Media Lab speech dataset, pitch and voicing estimates for Aurora 2, congress speech data, Mandarin speech frame data, speech data for testing blind source separation algorithm, etc.

In speech recognition, the simplest is the speech recognition of specific person, small vocabulary and isolated words [2]. The most complex and difficult to solve is the non-specific person, large vocabulary and continuous speech recognition. Speech recognition system is essentially a pattern recognition system. Its basic block diagram is shown in Fig. 2. Complex systems are further refined by introducing more knowledge on this basis.

At present, the IBM speech research group, which is in the leading position in large vocabulary speech recognition, began its research on large vocabulary speech recognition in the 1970s. At&t's bell Institute has also started a series of experiments on speaker independent speech recognition. This research has gone through 10 years, and its result is to establish the method of how to make a standard template for speaker independent speech recognition.

The major progress made during this period includes:

(1) the maturity and continuous improvement of hidden Markov model (HMM) technology has become the mainstream method of speech recognition.
(2) more and more attention has been paid to the research of knowledge-based speech recognition. In the process of continuous speech recognition, in addition to recognizing acoustic information, more linguistic knowledge, such as word formation,

syntax, semantics, dialogue background, is used to help further recognize and understand speech. At the same time, in the field of speech recognition, a language model based on statistical probability is also produced.

(3) the rise of the application of artificial neural network in speech recognition. In these studies, most of them use multilayer perceptual networks based on back propagation algorithm (BP algorithm). Artificial neural network has the ability to distinguish complex classification boundaries. Obviously, it is very helpful for pattern division. Especially in the field of telephone speech recognition, it has become a hot spot in the current application of speech recognition because of its wide application prospects.

In addition, the technology of continuous voice dictator for personal use is becoming more and more perfect. In this regard, the most representative are ViaVoice of IBM and dragon dictate system of dragon company. These systems have the ability of speaker adaptation. New users do not need to train all the words, so they can continuously improve the recognition rate in use.

The development of speech recognition technology in China: (1) there are scientific research institutions and institutions of higher learning in Beijing, such as the Institute of acoustics, the Institute of automation, Tsinghua University, Northern Jiaotong University, etc. In addition, Harbin Institute of technology, China University of science and technology and Sichuan University have also taken action.

(2) at present, many speech recognition systems have been successfully developed in China. These systems have their own characteristics.

In the aspect of isolated word large vocabulary speech recognition, the most representative is the ted-919 real-time speaker specific speech recognition and understanding system successfully developed by the Department of electronic engineering of Tsinghua University in cooperation with China Electronics Corporation in 1992.

In the aspect of continuous speech recognition, the computer center of Sichuan University implemented a subject limited continuous English Chinese speech translation demonstration system on a microcomputer in December, 1991.

In the aspect of speaker independent speech recognition, a voice controlled telephone number checking system developed by the Department of computer science and technology of Tsinghua University in 1987 has been put into practical use.

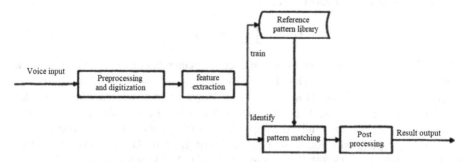

Fig. 2. Basic principle block diagram of speech recognition system

2.2 Acoustic Model

At present, the acoustic models of speech recognition systems are measured on HDM. HMM is a probabilistic model that describes the statistical characteristics of random processes with parameters. It has strong modeling ability for dynamic time series. It consists of two parts: an implicit Markov chain with a certain number of States and an explicit set of random functions. Each random function is associated with a state in the chain. The information of the implicit process can be obtained through the observation sequence generated by the explicit process. Figure 3 shows the HMM with five jump states from left to right, and the middle three states are real output states.

Acoustic model is one of the most important parts of speech recognition system. Most mainstream systems use hidden Markov model to model. The concept of hidden Markov model is a discrete time domain finite state automaton. Hidden Markov model HMM means that the internal state of the Markov model is invisible to the outside world, and the outside world can only see the output value at each time.

For speech recognition system, the output value is usually the acoustic feature calculated from each frame. Using HMM to describe speech signals requires two assumptions. One is that the internal state transition is only related to the previous state, and the other is that the output value is only related to the current state (or the current state transition). These two assumptions greatly reduce the complexity of the model. The corresponding algorithms of HMM scoring, decoding and training are forward algorithm, Viterbi algorithm and forward backward algorithm.

The input of the acoustic model is the feature extracted by the feature extraction module. Generally speaking, these features are multidimensional vectors, and their values can be discrete or continuous. In the early acoustic models, vector quantification is often used to map the signal directly to a codebook K, and then calculate the probability BJ (k) that a model J outputs the codebook. However, this method is rough, and its performance is greatly affected by VQ algorithm. If VQ itself has poor performance, the estimation of acoustic model will be very inaccurate. Therefore, the continuous probability distribution should be adopted for the characteristics with continuous values. Because the distribution of speech signal features can not be directly described by simple probability distribution, such as Gaussian distribution, etc., Gaussian mixture model or Laplace mixture model are commonly used to fit the distribution of speech signal. Here, the mixed Gaussian distribution can be expressed as a weighted combination of several Gaussian components GI. Namely:

$$G(x) = \prod_{i=1}^{n} w_i \cdot G_i(x) \tag{1}$$

where $G_i(x)$ is the mean value of μ_i variance is σ Gaussian distribution of i. From a mathematical point of view, when I tends to infinity, any continuous distribution can be approximated by Gaussian mixture model. However, the Gaussian mixture model also has a problem, that is, its computation is too large. Suppose that for a Gaussian mixture model containing n mixed components, its dimension is m dimension, then at least times of operation is required to get the result. If i models need to be calculated, the time complexity is O (MNK). In contrast, discrete HMM is relatively simple. Only one VQ and I table lookup operations are required to calculate the probability values of all models. Therefore, a semi continuous hidden horse model combining the two has emerged. The idea is that the output probability is not only determined by BJ (k), but also multiplied by the probability of VQ, that is, the probability that the signal belongs to the sub codebook.

In terms of accuracy, the continuous hidden horse model is better than the semi continuous hidden horse model, and the semi continuous hidden horse model is better than the discrete hidden horse model. From the perspective of algorithm complexity, it is just the opposite.

Gaussian mixture model (GMM) is a commonly used statistical model in speech signal processing. A basic theoretical premise of the model is that as long as the number of Gaussian mixtures is enough, an arbitrary distribution can be approximated by the weighted average of these Gaussian mixtures with arbitrary accuracy. The probability density function of a Gaussian mixture distribution containing m components is a weighted combination of M Gaussian probability density distribution functions, which is defined as:

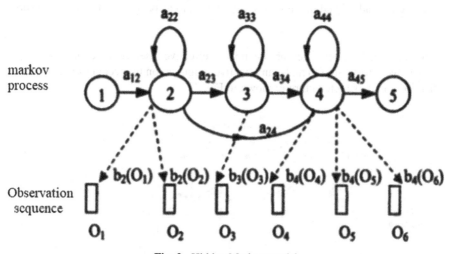

Fig. 3. Hidden Markov model

3   Confidence in Speech Recognition

In speech recognition, confidence is used to evaluate the reliability of speech recognition results. The value of confidence is usually between 0 and 1, which is used to indicate whether a word in the speech recognition result is correct or not, or whether the whole sentence recognition result is reasonable. A good confidence score will expand the application range of speech recognition to a great extent.

In essence, the problem of confidence is a two kinds of classification problem to judge whether the recognition results are correct or not. Therefore, the key and focus of confidence research is how to find effective features and find a method to calculate confidence from these features, so as to achieve better discrimination ability. If the method of manual judgment is adopted, in the case of no reference answer, we often need to rely on the semantic level information and combine our own experience and knowledge to obtain a better judgment effect, which is difficult to use in the computer [3]. At present, the information used for confidence calculation mainly includes the following three categories:

(1) The information of the recognition result itself, such as acoustic score, language score, state residence time, word length and so on, can be obtained directly from the recognition result.
(2) The information in the search process, such as the number of competitive paths, word graph density and other information, can not be directly obtained in the recognition results, but is reflected in the dynamic process of search. It can be calculated by the confusion network generated by the lattice obtained from the recognition result.
(3) The information provided by the auxiliary model, such as acoustic likelihood ratio, not only needs to identify the result itself, but also needs to be calculated with the help of additional models (usually referred to as background model or inverse model).

The focus of confidence research is how to effectively select and comprehensively use the above information to make an effective judgment on the recognition results.

The audio DNN architecture is shown in Fig. 4.

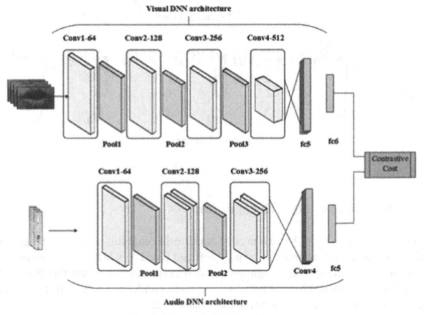

Fig. 4. The audio DNN architecture

4 English Language Learning System Based on Confidence

4.1 Algorithm Overview

The system consists of two independent subsystems: speech recognition and confidence measures evaluation The reason for adopting this structure is that we can reduce the cost of the whole system without changing the structure of the existing identification system.

There are three problems worth noting in the design of English language learning system: first, it is necessary to establish an alternative hypothesis model base that can reject out of vocabulary words and misidentified words; Secondly, an effective step should be selected to adjust the rejection threshold to minimize the false alarm rate and false rejection rate False alarm rate refers to that non vocabulary words are misjudged as in - vocabulary words, and false alarm rate refers to that vocabulary words are misjudged as non vocabulary words; Thirdly, the decoded information is effectively accumulated and synthesized to calculate the confidence of the whole sentence, and on this basis, the accuracy of the whole sentence is evaluated.

As shown in Fig. 5, in the first stage (speech recognition), all HMM models are trained by using the speech database, and then the likelihood and dwell information are obtained by veterbi beam search. In the second stage (confidence evaluation), the likelihood ratio is calculated from the decoded information in the first stage, and then combined with the subjective test of the trainer's pronunciation, a large number of statistics are made on the likelihood ratio to determine an objective distortion policy standard, and on this basis, the correctness of the learner's pronunciation is evaluated [4].

4.2 Alternative Hypothetical Model

We choose the context independent anti phoneme model and the anti thesaurus word model corresponding to thesaurus words as alternative hypothesis models. The former can be trained according to the confusing phoneme set, and its function is to reject non thesaurus words. In this system, the easily confused phoneme set of consonants is composed of all other consonants, and the easily confused phoneme set of vowels is composed of all other vowels. The latter can be trained according to the easily confused word set, and its function is to refuse misunderstanding. In this system, the confusing word set of a thesaurus word is composed of all other thesaurus words. The anti phoneme model adopts the left to right 7-state non jump continuous hidden Markov model, and each state contains 16 mixing degrees The model forms of thesaurus words and anti thesaurus words adopt the left to right 7-state non jump continuous hidden Markov model, and each state contains 5 mixing degrees Finally, all thesaurus models and alternative hypothesis models are obtained by using Baum Welch re estimation algorithm.

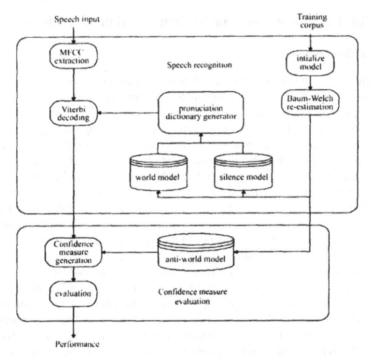

Fig. 5. English language learning system based on confidence

5   Conclusion

With the development of speech recognition technology, speech recognition system has been more and more widely used, but at present, the performance of speech recognition is far from perfect, and there are still many incorrectly recognized words in the recognition results. In order to correctly evaluate the reliability of the recognition results, the speech recognition system introduces the speech confidence into the speech recognition post-processing after obtaining the preliminary recognition results. Speech confidence can be regarded as a pattern classification problem. Generally, the primitives marked with confidence in the recognition results are marked as correct and wrong based on different confidence features or feature combinations, so as to evaluate the reliability of the recognition results. The primitives of confidence markers often use words. At the same time, they can also use speech frames, phonemes and sentences.

References

1. Zhang, Y.: Research and development of Chinese speech recognition technology. J. Guangxi Radio and Television University **14**(4), 18–22 (2003)
2. He, X.: Research and development of speech recognition. Computer and Modernization. **79**(3), 3–6 (2002)
3. Eskenazi, M.:Using automatic speech processing for fureign language pronunciation tutoring: some issues and a prototype. language Learning & Technol. **2**(2), 6276 (1999)
4. Liu, J., Liu, J.: Principle of confidence and its application in speech recognition. Computer Research and Dev. **37**(7), 882–890 (2000)

Research on English Teaching Ability Evaluation Algorithm Based on Big Data Fuzzy k-means Clustering

Xiaomei Li[(✉)]

College of Foreign Languages, Jingchu University of Technology, Jingmen 448000, China
kxsd05@126.com

Abstract. This paper studies the evaluation algorithm of English teaching ability based on big data fuzzy k-means clustering, which is that the improvement of the evaluation method of students' learning effect of English teaching ability evaluation can stimulate more students to improve their learning interest and motivation, promote students to consciously use scientific learning strategies for English learning and cultivate good learning habits. Moreover, the improvement of evaluation methods can enable more students to learn to evaluate themselves positively and optimistically, enjoy the learning process and develop good character. This paper presents an evaluation algorithm of the English educational capacity based on large data fuzzy k-means clustering. K means the most basic and most used method in classical analysis. Method to find classification centres and classification centres from classification data. His main advantage is simple and fast. When the results of the group are dense, the difference between groups is important, and the effect is the best. The algorithm has a relative scalability and an effect on a large scale of data. Using this method to evaluate English instructions, it has better information and analysis capabilities and improves the precision of teaching and application of instructions.

Keywords: Big data · Evaluation of English teaching ability · K-means clustering algorithm

1 Introduction

Language ability refers to the ability to understand and express meaning, intention and emotion by listening, speaking, reading, reading and writing in social events. Cultural character refers to the understanding of Chinese and foreign cultures and the knowledge of good cultures. It is the knowledge quality, humanistic cultivation and behavior orientation of students under the background of globalization. Thinking quality refers to the individual characteristics of people's thinking, which is reflected in the level and characteristics of logic, criticism and innovation of their thinking [1].

Teaching is a complex project, involving many links, which can not be measured by a fixed amount, but can be guided by scientific and effective methodology, and assist

© ICST Institute for Computer Sciences, Social Informatics and Telecommunications Engineering 2023
Published by Springer Nature Switzerland AG 2023. All Rights Reserved
M. A. Jan and F. Khan (Eds.): BigIoT-EDU 2022, LNICST 467, pp. 36–46, 2023.
https://doi.org/10.1007/978-3-031-23944-1_5

teachers' teaching practice experience, constantly adjust strategies and constantly evaluate, so as to achieve a better teaching effect. Similar to the teaching of any other subject, English teaching should also meet some basic elements. Teaching should refer to textbooks, teaching materials, teachers, teaching means, teaching methodology, teaching process, teaching purpose, teaching detection and evaluation and phased teaching reflection. But different from other subjects, we should think about a question, what is English teaching? Or what are the contents of "teaching" and "learning" in English teaching?

Since the introduction of English learning and various English grading tests into China, an endless stream of grading guidance, teaching materials and teaching forms have emerged one after another, and there have been various categories, according to the age of children, teenagers and College English; According to the grade test English and professional vocabulary of the industry, business English; And interpretation, translation and graded reading according to the ability objectives. How to choose suitable tutoring learning for yourself and your family from so many categories has become a seemingly difficult but actually easy thing to operate. We will analyze the existing forms of English education and how to effectively carry out English learning from different dimensions. However, in different dimensions, we should always remember to distinguish the two different levels of "teaching" and "learning", but we can't completely oppose each other. Because teaching and learning are often carried out at the same time.

Therefore, this document applies to information technology and large data analysis technology to teach evaluation and resource information that have a positive and important meaning to improve the quantitative management and planning capacity of the instruction. The application to the evaluation and resource information teacher has a high practical value and is consulted with the quantity of the management of the instruction process and improvement of the plan capacity. In the process of post-value English education, many advances are effective and there are many limits to evaluating English-educated capacity. Therefore, quantitative text and analysis are conducted at the English-taught level, and the parametric model and large data analysis are designed to limit the English-taught level. It is necessary to assess the ability to learn English by using large data formats and classic methods. On this basis, it can improve the predictability of an English educated capacity assessment by building the parameters of strict competence and the objective function and the statistical analysis model of the educated capacity assessment.

2   Related Work

2.1   Big Data Technology

With the continuous evolution and development of communication technology, communication equipment is also replaced from generation to generation. Data applications constantly put forward higher requirements for the granularity, scope and type of original data. For example, after using nfv (network function virtualization) technology, new virtual network elements, Internet of things devices, 5g (the 5th generation) new devices, etc.; The upgrading of communication standards also brings new communication function technology points, such as voice over LTE (voice over LTE) technology, minimum road test technology, son (self-organizing network) technology, etc.; The upper data application also puts forward new requirements for the original data, such as the positioning requirements for MR (measurement report) and the reduction of data acquisition cycle. Telecom operators need to conduct in-depth research and propose original data acquisition requirements to equipment manufacturers, promote equipment manufacturers to carry out original data development, and provide original data from equipment timely and accurately.

Big data has the characteristics of "large volume, diverse structure and strong timeliness". To make good use of all kinds of big data, data preparation and processing of data sources is a necessary pre link. Telecom operators' big data is facing a complex production environment: many equipment manufacturers, complex types of network elements, complex data types and fields, and intertwined field definitions and telecom technology. The pre-processing of ETL (extraction, conversion and loading) in the traditional data processing system is not enough to meet the requirements of data analysis, correlation, standardization and accuracy in the complex environment of telecom operators [2]. Therefore, in terms of the research on the key technologies of data acquisition and analysis, it is necessary to fully study the data acquisition and analysis technologies such as the original data providing capacity of network element equipment, data interface mode, original data analysis and standardization, cross industry data fusion, multi-level data association, etc. on the basis of traditional ETL pre-processing data, according to the characteristics of large data coverage, large volume and dynamic complexity of telecom operators, Sort out and analyze the original network data, and preliminarily process it into usable regular and meaningful metadata. This work is the foundation of big data technology architecture. In addition, actively looking for and exploring other related data sources other than network data and introducing them into the big data system after pre-processing related to collection and analysis is also a research direction that needs to be paid attention to in the research of collection and analysis technology [3].

With the development of IT technology, data interface technology is also evolving, such as the simplification of CORBA (Common Object Request Broker Architecture) interface, efficient encryption of FTP (File Transfer Protocol), streaming message processing and other technologies, which provide technical conditions for the upgrading of data acquisition interface. Telecom operators need to specifically study various data requirements, study the interface mode to obtain the data required by the application from the manufacturer's network element equipment, OMC (operation and maintenance center), link interface and other channels, and put forward the technical scheme to transform the existing interfaces that do not meet the application requirements.

2.2 K-means Clustering Algorithm

Firstly, K objects are randomly selected as the initial clustering center. Then calculate the distance between each object and each seed cluster center, and assign each object to the cluster center closest to it. The termination condition can be any of the following:

$$J(\prod, W) = \sum_{k=1}^{K} \sum_{x \in \pi} \sum_{d=1}^{D} (x_{id} - v_{kd})^2 \tag{1}$$

Add objects to a specific sculpture can lead to an error. So you can give all objects and all family permissions to indicate how many objects belong to the family. Probabilities based on methods may also be such a burden, so it's better to use fuzzy c methods with natural and non-probable characters.

$$\min f(x_1, x_2, ..., x_n) = \frac{1}{m} \sum_{i=1}^{m} \left[Y_i^0 - Y_i \right]^2 \tag{2}$$

In the application, it is found that when measuring clustering, the best clustering result corresponds to the extreme point of the objective function. Because there are many local minimum points in the objective function, the implementation of the algorithm is in the direction of reducing the objective function [4]. If the initially selected point falls near a local minimum point, It will cause the algorithm to converge at the local minimum. Therefore, the random selection of the initial clustering center may make the result fall into local optimization, and it is difficult to obtain the global optimal solution. From the execution process of K-means algorithm. Figure 1 below shows the objective function of the image in the clustering process.

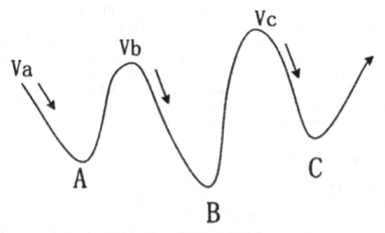

Fig. 1. Objective function of image

K-means algorithm may converge to the suboptimal solution prematurely due to the influence of the initially selected clustering center. In view of this, many scholars have proposed improved algorithms based on genetic algorithm and neural network algorithm. Different from traditional algorithms such as genetic algorithm and neural network algorithm, fish swarm optimization algorithm is a new swarm intelligent computing technology, Compared with the traditional methods, its advantage is that the improved algorithm does not need the prior distribution knowledge of the data to be classified, is less affected by the selection of the initial solution, needs less parameters to be set and adjusted, and the implementation is simple. Now fish swarm optimization algorithm has been applied in the fields of function optimization, neural network training, system recognition and so on. Experiments show that fish swarm algorithm is more efficient and faster than genetic algorithm and neural network algorithm in solving global optimization problems.

Unsupervised neural network clustering algorithm simulates the characteristics of lateral inhibition and self-organization of neurons. It clusters data through repeated learning, and also through several units competing for the current object. The unit whose weight vector is closest to the current object is called active or winning unit. It adjusts the weight of the acquisition unit and its nearest neighbor [5]. The neurons in the output layer are a node matrix arranged in two-dimensional form. Each neuron in them is the representative of the input sample. The input node is below. If the input vector has n elements, there are n nodes at the input end. Each neuron in the input layer is connected with each neuron in the output layer through weight. The learning process of neural network can be divided into two steps: one is the neuron competitive learning process. For each input vector, competition is generated between neurons through the comparison between the input vector value and the weight value. The second is the side feedback process of the neuron layer of the competitive layer. For each input vector, side feedback will be generated between the adjacent neurons of the competitive layer. For the winning neuron, it will be the center of the circle, the excitation side feedback to the adjacent neurons and the suppression side feedback to the distant neurons [6]. The result of learning is to keep the weight vector of neurons in the clustering region close to the input vector, so as to gather the input vectors with similar characteristics.

In line with the traditional post-value evaluation of the English teacher, the classification precision of the evaluation algorithm is lower. This document is therefore the first time an English post-competence evaluation system is established in higher professional colleges. To assess precisely the implementation of English trained post-competence, first you need to complete the design of its restricted parameters, this is the information sample model of post-competence restricted parameters.

2.3   Evaluation of English Teaching Ability

English teaching methods and ideas are not formed enough, and there is always only one and single idea of English teaching. Knowledge points are a systematic and interrelated process. The explanation of a certain knowledge point inevitably involves other knowledge points. As a supplement, if there is no framework for the knowledge point, it will lead to confusion in English teaching ideas, and there is no coherence, systematicness and systematicness in the explanation. There are often situations such as not knowing how to start for different age groups, unclear key points of explanation, ahead of English teaching, and the way of English teaching can not be adjusted in time. The children's classroom should be lively and interesting to encourage children to speak and express more and correct basic mistakes. The classroom in middle school should have a certain amount of knowledge and be modular, involving the basic thinking of English phenomena. We should listen to students raise questions and give solutions. The knowledge in high school should be systematic, highly relevant and in-depth, Express complex things in simple language. How different are adults and grade examination. Therefore, if there are no appropriate ideas for English Teaching of different age groups, English teaching is bound to be laborious for teachers to explain, but students can't grasp the key points, and the effect of English teaching is not satisfactory.

The purpose and pertinence of single and long-term classes are not clear, and the emphasis of English classes for different age groups is different. The class types should be carefully distinguished, such as word class, grammar class, explanation class, consolidation class, problem solving class, oral expression class, etc. The setting of classroom purpose is to set effective classroom links, English teaching resources and English teaching control. If it is a word class, we should have skills such as word reading, pronunciation and intonation adjustment, continuous reading and different aspects of word expansion, and maintain the interest of the class at the same time. If it is an oral class, there should be a topic - Discussion - expression - correction - expansion - in the process of expression. Without clear classroom goals, there will be no differences in classroom English teaching processes, methods and materials.

Finally, the learning after the beginning of the teacher's career is not enough. English teaching is a dynamic process of continuous learning, continuous progress and keeping up with the characteristics of the new era. One method can not run through the whole career of English teaching [7]. Therefore, as the main body of teachers, we should take the initiative to study, constantly study the methods of English teaching and the appropriate ways of English teaching, as well as the characteristics and common problems of students.

I don't understand the learning process and stage. English learning for different purposes will have some basic ideas and different characteristics. For most students and adults, learning English has no direction at all. I don't know where to start and how to learn it well. There is no evaluation standard. Should we remember words or learn grammar, should we recite articles, should we write compositions, etc. For English learning with different goals, there are still great differences in methods, including teachers' teaching ideas, and teachers' ideas will directly affect whether students can learn well and find appropriate ideas, and whether there is any effect. For how to arrange the teaching process and teaching evaluation, we will talk about it in a separate chapter later, so we won't repeat it here.

It is the influence of teachers' teaching level. Teachers' teaching ideas and methods, including the arrangement of teaching contents, will affect students' learning cycle and understanding of knowledge point framework. Teachers have no rules and methods to teach, and students have no methods to learn. It is easy to be laborious and boring, so they lose interest in English; Once you lose interest and enthusiasm for this, you don't have to think about other promotion tests. And for students who participate in the examination and grade examination, the loss of interest in English will affect the learning of other disciplines, so in fact, any discipline should have a scientific method as a guide.

3   Research on English Teaching Ability Evaluation Algorithm Based on Big Data Fuzzy k-means Clustering

The level of university teachers is directly related to the level of talent training. Therefore, how to scientifically and reasonably evaluate the teaching ability of university teachers is an urgent problem for colleges and universities [8]. The information sampling model of English teaching ability constraint parameters is established. The existing evaluation methods of teachers' teaching level have a good effect on the processing of decentralized evaluation data, but the processing effect of distributed and centralized evaluation data is not satisfactory [9]. Although the distributed and centralized data can be discretized in some ways, it is often easy to cause the loss of evaluation data information and affect the evaluation results in this process.

1. Textbook analysis. Correctly explain the position, function, key points and difficulties of the teaching materials, and analyze and think about the teaching materials with reference to the textbooks and syllabus.
2. Purpose analysis. Explain the thinking and analysis of how to properly determine the teaching purpose and requirements based on the analysis of teaching materials and students' cognitive characteristics.
3. Process analysis. Explain the idea of how to organically combine teaching activities and learning activities to arrange the design process.
4. Analysis of teaching methods. Explain how the choice of teaching methods (including the use of necessary teaching means) can maximize students' learning enthusiasm and initiative, so as to optimize the thinking and analysis of teaching purposes.
5. Evaluation and analysis. Explain the conception of teaching evaluation, feedback and adjustment measures and the design of teaching measures. 6. Lecture time: no more than 20 min. Note: in general, lecture is to analyze a class. Teaching means such as videotape and projection can be used as auxiliary tools for lecture.

The processing results of distributed and centralized data are good, but the results of this kind of methods in teacher evaluation are rare. On the basis of previous studies, this paper puts forward an application model of analytic hierarchy process based on Rough Set Theory in teacher evaluation. Using the rough set theory and the original evaluation data, the attribute space of the evaluation index is reduced to obtain a new evaluation index system [10]. Combined with the range mapping theory, the multi-scale principle is formulated to construct the evaluation matrix, and the multi-scale analytic hierarchy process model is established to evaluate the teaching quality of teachers, as shown in Fig. 2. The model organically integrates the subjective and objective factors in the evaluation process, improves the subjectivity of the traditional analytic hierarchy process and the low calculation accuracy of the model, and makes the evaluation results more fair and scientific. English teaching ability constraint index parameters are a set of nonlinear time series.

Evaluation indicators are the basis of evaluation work and the core link of evaluation activities. The design of evaluation indicators of College Teachers' teaching level should not only reflect the teaching level as comprehensively as possible, but also be as simple and easy to operate. According to the guiding principles, scientific principles, key principles and feasibility principles of teachers' teaching evaluation, We choose the teaching evaluation index currently used in our school as the evaluation index of the student evaluation index system. Build an information flow model of differential equation to express the constraint parameters of English teaching ability as follows:

$$SSE = \sum_{l=1}^{K} \sum_{x \in L_l} Dist(x, Z_l)^2 \tag{3}$$

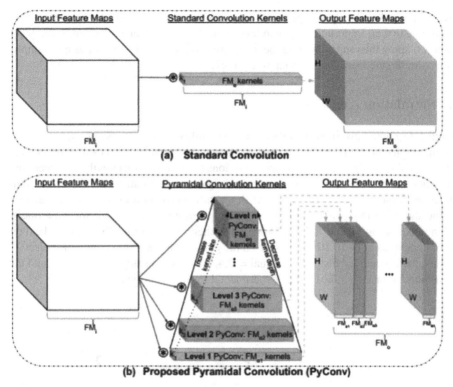

Fig. 2. Multi scale analytic hierarchy process model

Consider a large data feature with a classic K symbol algorithm to consider the classification and integrity of the English educated capacity index parameters, form the corresponding educated resource allocation plan and consider the evaluation of the English educated capacity [11]. Evalui la kapablon de granda datumo- modelo kaj ekstrahi la kapablon- limigitan informon.

$$AVF(x_i) = \frac{1}{m} \sum_{f=1}^{m} f(x_{ij}) \tag{4}$$

The complete K-meaningful classification algorithm is used to classify and synthesize the post-competence indicators, to form the educational resource allocation plan, and to implement the scientific evaluation of the post-competence of the English teacher. The process of post-competence evaluation and has a high practical value [12].

Judgment matrix, but in the actual teacher evaluation, the data obtained are generally close to or even the same data. In this case, if the scaling method is still adopted, the evaluation results will have the same teacher scores. Therefore, we refine the scale to improve the accuracy of the model. In order to facilitate the quantification of comparative judgment, it is specified to use 1 to 18 respectively to represent the judgment according to experience. Compared with element J, element I is equally important to absolutely important, and the middle number represents the progressive value between the above two judgment levels. By comparing the indexes at the same level of the index system according to their importance in the indexes at the upper level, due to the large amount of data, we apply the range mapping theory to process the data. Taking B1 as an example, other similar, we use the range mapping theory.

4   Simulation Analysis

English teachers have improved their teaching ability in the process of exploring new evaluation methods. Therefore, the exploration and Research on the evaluation method of students' learning effect has created conditions for the common growth of teachers and students, which is a subject of great practical significance. Firstly, the experiment combines the k-means algorithm with English teaching evaluation to show the advantages of the algorithm in global optimization. In the following matlab simulation experiment, the number of individuals is 10. In order to test their optimization efficiency, make their initial positions at $(-10, 10)$ farthest from the global extreme value, randomly select 10 points, their perceived distance is visual $= 2.4$, each moving step is step $= 0.4$, and the crowding factor is $8 = 0.618$. The experimental results are shown in Fig. 3.

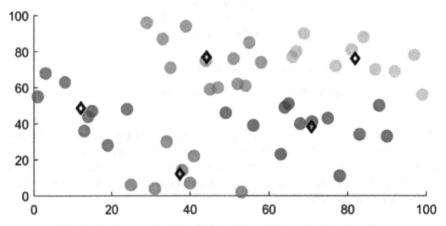

Fig. 3. Iterative results of English teaching ability evaluation algorithm

Randomly select 100 points, and the initial setting of the individual is the same as above. This experiment mainly compares the clustering effects of K-means clustering algorithm and clustering algorithm based on fish swarm behavior improvement [13]. In practical application, it is found that the k-means algorithm may converge to the suboptimal solution prematurely due to the influence of the initially selected cluster center. Therefore, this paper mainly puts forward an improvement scheme for the disadvantage that k-means algorithm is easy to fall into local extremum due to its dependence on initial value and can not reach global optimization.

Through simulation experiments, it is found that English teaching ability evaluation and K-means algorithm are easier to converge globally under the same number of iterations, and the more individuals, the stronger the ability to jump out of local extremum. The simulation curve also shows that the hybrid algorithm is more efficient in convergence speed than the basic algorithm.

The performance of several clustering methods is evaluated through the comparison of several table methods. It can be seen from the experimental results that the K-means clustering problem based on fish swarm has higher space-time cost than the k-means algorithm. This is because the complexity of the two algorithms must be greater than that of the basic algorithm [14]. However, in theory, this space-time cost is inevitable. However, on the whole The search speed and accuracy are slightly improved. From two aspects, the overall performance of the improved clustering problem is improved, which is obtained at the expense of some space-time overhead. Therefore, the improved English teaching ability evaluation algorithm scheme based on K-means clustering problem is effective.

5 Conclusion

This paper studied the evaluation algorithm of the English educated capacity based on large data fuzzy k-means clustering, establishing the evaluation method of the English educated level based on large data fuzzy k-means clustering and information fusion, establishing the restricted parameters index model of the English educated level of evaluation and analysis, And using the quantitative recursive analysis method The goal of zero is to analyse the large data model of the Chinese instructive evaluation. It understands the direct extract of the English teacher's ability to limit function information. The basis for the construction of the limited parameter analysis model, evaluate the English syllable by the ability of a large data-information model (using a quantum binding method), extract the limiting functions according to the direct functions of the information, and integrate the K-signal classical algorithm It classifies and integrates the competent index parameters of the English teachers' mail; Completes the preparation of trained file allocations and understands the scientific evaluation of the competition of English teachers' mail. Combine a large database of K characters with a classic algorithm to consider the classification and integrity of the English-trained capability index parameters, and this base will form a corresponding file allocation plan to achieve the evaluation of the English-trained level. The study shows that this method has a good precision in evaluating the ability of an English teacher to improve the effectiveness of the use of an English educated resource.

Acknowledgements. This thesis is acknowledged by *A Study on the Reform of Advanced English Classroom Teaching from the Perspective of Students* (KC2020069) ,*A Study on Standardization of English Signs in Public Places in Jingmen* (KC2020070) , *A Study on the Principles of Chinese Culture Lessons Guided by Gurriculum Design (2021GA061).*

References

1. Shalaby, M., Mohammed, A., Kassem, S.: Supervised fuzzy C-means techniques to solve the capacitated vehicle routing problem. International Arab J. Information Technology **18**(3A), 452–463 (2021)

2. Philipo, G.H., Jande, Y., Kivevele, T.: Clustering and fuzzy logic-based demand-side management for solar microgrid operation: case study of Ngurudoto Microgrid, Arusha, Tanzania. Adv. Fuzzy Syst. **2021**(2), 1–13 (2021)

3. Islam, M.K., Ali, M.S., Miah, M.S., et al.: Brain tumor detection in MR image using superpixels, principal component analysis and template based K-means clustering algorithm. Machine Learning with Applications **5**, 100044 (2021)

4. Parlina, A., Ramli, K., Murfi, H.: Exposing emerging trends in smart sustainable city research using deep autoencoders-based Fuzzy C-means. Sustainability **13**(5), 2876 (2021)

5. Zhang, S., Huang, W., Wang, Z.: Combing modified Grabcut, K-means clustering and sparse representation classification for weed recognition in wheat field - ScienceDirect. Neurocomputing **452**, 665674 (2021)

6. Jasim, W., Mohammed, R.: A survey on segmentation techniques for image processing. Iraqi J. Electrical Electronic Eng. **17**(2), 73–93 (2021)

7. Mbf, A.: Fuzzy k-Means: History and Applications - ScienceDirect (2021)

8. Chen, Z.: Using big data fuzzy K-means clustering and information fusion algorithm in english teaching ability evaluation. Complexity **2021**(5), 1–9 (2021)

9. Zhang, C., Guo, Y.: Mountain rainfall estimation and online English teaching evaluation based on RBF neural network. Arabian Journal of Geosciences **14**(17) (2021)

10. Lu, C., He, B., Zhang, R.: Evaluation of English interpretation teaching quality based on GA optimized RBF neural network. J. Intelligent and Fuzzy Syst. **40**(2), 3185–3192 (2021)

11. Zhang, Y.: The development of an evaluation model to assess the effect of online English teaching based on fuzzy mathematics. Int. J. Emerging Technologies in Learning (iJET) **16**(12), 186 (2021)

12. Zhuo, X.X., Yao, G.Z.: Analysis of teacher's classroom discourse in senior high school english reading teaching from language ability development perspective. DEStech Transactions on Economics Business and Management (eeim) (2021)

13. Meng, Z., Wang, X., Zhou, J.: Ways to improve the teaching ability of college teachers in the New Era **5**(6), 5 (2021)

14. Johnston, J.P., Andrews, L.B., Adams, C.D., et al.: Implementation and evaluation of a virtual learning advanced pharmacy practice experience. Currents in Pharmacy Teaching and Learning **13**(7), 862–867 (2021)

Research on English Teaching in Higher Vocational Colleges Based on Big Data Analysis

Xiao Yang[(⊠)] and Liu Zhen

Hubei Preschool Normal Junior College, Wuhan 430000, Hubei, China
myzone_23@163.com

Abstract. Big data analysis is an important part of English Teaching in higher vocational colleges. Because of its huge database, complex theoretical knowledge and wide simulation range, it is difficult to carry out and implement English Teaching in Higher Vocational Colleges Based on big data analysis. The teaching research and scientific research of Higher Vocational and technical education have always been weak, and the English teaching methods are still relatively lagging behind. English multimedia teaching is basically the broadcasting of voice lessons and PPT electronic manuscripts, ignoring the valuable resource of network data analysis. Carry out the teaching and learning interaction of the course on this network data platform, gradually optimize the interactive environment through multiple rounds of action reflection in the teaching process, learn the methods of theoretical analysis, and master the ability to use professional knowledge, so as to cultivate students' scientific research ability and comprehensive quality.

Keywords: Big data analysis · Higher vocational English · Teaching research

1 Introduction

The term big data is proposed with the explosive growth of global data. It is mainly used to describe huge databases. Compared with traditional databases, big data usually includes a lot of unstructured data and needs more real-time analysis. At the same time, big data also brings us new challenges. How to effectively organize and manage data has become an urgent problem to be solved. Big data is large, diverse, fast and valuable, which has brought great help to our learning and scientific research [1].

Higher vocational education is an important type structure of higher education in China. It is a high-level vocational education under the new social and economic conditions. The proposal and implementation of higher vocational education meets the needs of scientific and Technological Development and industrial structure adjustment, and is the product of deepening educational reform. Comparatively speaking, although English Teaching in higher vocational colleges has been constantly groping for improvement in recent years, for example, the English textbooks adopted by many higher vocational colleges have made great adjustments and improvements in content, adding a large number of practical and practical contents. Most higher vocational colleges are equipped with

M. A. Jan and F. Khan (Eds.): BigIoT-EDU 2022, LNICST 467, pp. 47–52, 2023.
https://doi.org/10.1007/978-3-031-23944-1_6

multimedia classrooms, changing the monotonous teaching mode dominated by teachers in the past, It emphasizes the participation of students, but fundamentally speaking, higher vocational English teaching still does not get rid of the basic format of teacher-centered and classroom centered. Students' participation is mostly limited in the classroom and carried out around the teacher's baton. The contents of class discussion, homework after class and examination are stipulated and arranged by the teacher [2], The initiative of learning is not really in the hands of students, so the current teaching methods of Higher Vocational English teaching are inconsistent with the emphasis of Higher Vocational Colleges on cultivating students' innovative ability and learning ability. Compared with the investment and achievements of many higher vocational colleges in professional teaching and practical reform, higher vocational English Teaching reform lags behind. Most students do not understand the importance of English learning methods to English learning success. They simply believe that they can learn English well as long as they work hard. Most of them will not take the initiative to use all kinds of resources to help themselves learn. In addition to English teachers, they rarely think of using or asking for help from senior students, parents, relatives, friends and other social resources around them to help them learn English. Higher vocational students have the requirements of learning English. They need to master the methods of learning English. Their requirements of learning English are potential and strong.

2 Big Data Analysis Technology

Big data analysis technology is a technical means to explore the essential characteristics of things by deeply mining data laws 2. Based on big data analysis technology, we can fully collect and deeply mine the English teaching data of online enrollment expansion students, study and implement targeted teaching strategies according to the data analysis results, so that teachers can more accurately grasp the blind spots and difficulties in students' learning, and improve the English learning ability of online enrollment expansion students in higher vocational colleges; At the same time, it is also a beneficial attempt for the online English teaching model.

Data analysis, also known as knowledge discovery, is a technology to find its laws from a large amount of data by analyzing each data. The process of knowledge discovery usually consists of three stages: data preparation, law search and law representation. Data preparation is to select the required data from the data stored in the data center and integrate them into a data set for data analysis; Law finding is to find out the law contained in the data set by some method; Rule representation is to express the found rules in a user understandable way (such as visualization) as far as possible. If we can analyze these data, explore their data patterns and characteristics, and then find the interest and behavior law of a group or organization, professionals can predict the possible change trend in the future. Such a data analysis process will be of great help to the work.

Victor Mayer Schoenberg cited various examples in the big data age to illustrate a truth: when the big data age has arrived, we should use big data thinking to explore the potential value of big data. In the book, the author mentioned most about how Google uses people's search records to mine the secondary utilization value of data, such as predicting the trend of influenza outbreak in a place; How does amaon use the user's purchase and browsing history data to make targeted book purchase recommendations, so as to effectively improve the sales volume; How does forecast use the discount data of all airline ticket prices in the past decade to predict whether the time for users to buy tickets is appropriate.

3 Research on Big Data Analysis in English Teaching in Higher Vocational Colleges

At present, the forums on the websites of many colleges and universities in China have specially opened up the column of English learning, but the students' enthusiasm for participation is not very high. The above three well-known forums with the theme of English learning are all set up by the websites with the theme of English learning. Although they have their own different characteristics, they also have a lot in common, For example, with strong technical support and the participation and management of a large number of full-time staff, it has rich information and fast knowledge updating. It attaches importance to adopting certain means to encourage learners' participation, and can maintain learners' learning interest and enthusiasm in various ways. Figure 1 below shows the research path of English teaching.

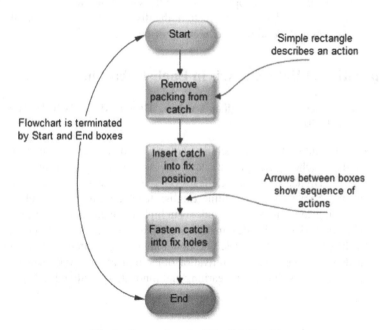

Fig. 1. Research path of English Teaching

Big data analysis technology teaching can break through the one-to-one limitations of traditional classroom teaching and be flexible. Because the information on the Internet can be stored, queried and reused, the learning based on big data analysis technology breaks through the traditional time and space constraints to a great extent, so that students have more control. Students can choose their own learning time and learning content according to their needs, which can not only give more development space to excellent students, but also allow students with weak foundation to adjust their pace, It will not lose confidence and interest in learning because it can't keep up with the teaching progress [3].

Big data analysis technology allows users to set their own nicknames. In this form, big data analysis technology can encourage every student to participate in the discussion. It changes the situation that only a few students with quick thinking have the opportunity to express their views in the classroom, and greatly expands the participation of the discussion. Most higher vocational students have the problems of limited vocabulary and poor oral foundation. Many students are silent because they are worried about making mistakes. They have no enthusiasm in class and are unwilling to communicate with teachers. In the teaching of big data analysis technology, students who are relatively introverted and lack self-confidence can log in to the big data analysis technology forum anonymously, boldly express their views and improve their views in continuous feedback. Because online discussion is not a direct face between people, it can help students overcome stage fright in classroom discussion and increase individual speaking opportunities. The form of online discussion is more open and free than classroom discussion, which can allow many people to speak at the same time, and can fully mobilize the enthusiasm of each student to participate in the discussion, so as to avoid the "free riding" phenomenon in the traditional classroom discussion.

4   Application of Data Analysis in English Teaching

4.1   Explore Efficient Online English Teaching Design Methods in Higher Vocational Colleges

Higher vocational online English teaching platform needs to match efficient teaching design methods. Teachers can optimize and innovate unique online English teaching design methods in Higher Vocational Colleges Based on the analysis results of teaching big data and the characteristics of online English teaching platform. Combined with the English learning characteristics of students in higher vocational colleges, we should adopt the online English teaching design method and actively explore the teaching effects produced by different teaching modes. We should not only pay attention to the mastery of skills, but also pay attention to the cultivation of learning ability; At the same time, we should stimulate students' interest in learning and innovate the online English teaching mode.

4.2   Data Analysis Method

Use the online teaching platform to carry out higher vocational English teaching, make an overall analysis of the learning data of all online students, and master the learning characteristics of the overall students [4]. At the same time, analyze the continuous learning data of each student to understand the learning situation of each student. Deeply excavate the analysis results of teaching data, feed back to subsequent teaching links, dynamically adjust teaching strategies, focus on strengthening the teaching proportion of students' weak links in English learning, enrich online teaching methods, and improve the effect of Online Higher Vocational English learning.

4.3 Adhere to the Teaching Concept of "Student-Centered"

Online English Teaching Research Based on big data analysis should adhere to the teaching concept of "student-centered". Whether online teaching or offline teaching, as long as it is the teaching process, students must be the main body of teaching activities. Students can achieve teaching objectives by giving full play to their subjective initiative, consciously building subject knowledge and skills, and forming thinking and values corresponding to what they have learned.

"Student centered" in online English Teaching, teachers can analyze and mine the overall students' teaching data, and then adjust the teaching strategies according to the results. Sometimes it is difficult to achieve the teaching objectives. It is not necessarily the students' intelligence factor. To a large extent, the teachers' teaching methods do not respect the students' cognitive development rules and can not arouse the students' inner resonance. Teachers can through the analysis of a single student's continuous learning data Analyze and excavate, and carry out targeted teaching according to the results. Online teaching increases the possibility and scientificity of single guidance, which can well make up for students' weakness. Developing students' advantages and both are the concrete embodiment of the "student-centered" teaching concept, which should also be implemented in other online teaching designs [5].

In online English teaching design, teachers can use advanced big data analysis technology. However, they can not blindly rely on this technology. Although data analysis is objective, it will also abandon many subtle factors. When using data analysis results to adjust teaching strategies, teachers should combine their own teaching experience, use data analysis results scientifically and reasonably, and compare the objective data analysis results with teachers And form a more scientific teaching strategy.

5 Conclusion

Through the case study of Higher Vocational English teaching based on big data analysis, the data analysis technology is used to test the phased teaching effect, abandon the subjectivity of teachers' judgment, strengthen the accuracy of the teaching model, meet the students' personalized learning needs while meeting the students' general learning needs, respect the objective law of the coexistence of communism and personality in students' learning, and combine the teachers' teaching The targeted and dynamic adjustment of teaching strategies based on learning experience can form a more accurate judgment on the application of teaching strategies.

References

1. Tan, Y.: Research status of big data analysis. Problems and countermeasures. Inf. Comput. (Theor. Ed.) **19**, 143–144 (2017)
2. Gu, J.: Big data and big data analysis. Softw. Indus. Eng. **4**, 17–21 (2013)
3. Chen, S.: Big data analysis and high-speed data update. Comput. Res. Dev. **52**(2), 7333–7342 (2015)
4. Zhao, X.: Internet plus primary school English video teaching research. China's Off Campus Educ. **2**, 161–162 (2017)
5. Lei, B.: Internet plus era based on WeChat's pol interactive teaching mode of. Educ. Teach. Forum **2**, 3–4 (2017)

Research on Enterprise Marketing Education Strategy Based on Data Mining Technology

Xiao Na[✉]

Inner Mongolia Honder College of Arts and Sciences, Inner Mongolia Autonomous Region, Hohhot 010070, China
xiaona20062021@163.com

Abstract. This paper studies the enterprise marketing strategy based on data mining technology. With the rapid development of China's social economy, the enterprise competition under the market economy is becoming increasingly fierce. How to win the leading position in the fierce environment has become an important issue concerned by managers. Customer is the foundation of enterprise survival, and customer value is the core strength of enterprise profitability. When formulating marketing strategies, enterprises should fully tap customer value and implement targeted marketing strategies for different types of customers based on customer value theory. Through the in-depth analysis of the value of customers in the enterprise marketing strategy, this paper divides customers into different types based on customer value, and then puts forward corresponding marketing strategies according to different types of customers, so as to promote the enterprise to improve the marketing effect in the highly competitive environment and realize the long-term development of the enterprise.

Keywords: Data mining technology · Enterprise market · Marketing strategy

1 Introduction

The research on enterprise marketing education strategy based on data mining technology is the research on the strategies used by enterprises to implement their marketing strategies. The research involves collecting information from various sources and then analyzing it, which helps to make decisions on the company's future course of action. It also helps identify new trends and patterns that other companies can take advantage of. With the increasingly fierce market competition, the new economy represented by the Internet, knowledge economy and high and new technology and centered on creating consumer demand has developed rapidly, forcing enterprises to constantly explore and innovate in marketing, and marketing came into being. Marketing is a marketing method for enterprises to promote products suitable for market groups by adopting marketing means for the market. Marketing is the inevitable trend of enterprise marketing from traditional marketing to personalized development in the new market environment. It is the organic combination of enterprise marketing innovation and marketing potential

M. A. Jan and F. Khan (Eds.): BigIoT-EDU 2022, LNICST 467, pp. 53–63, 2023.
https://doi.org/10.1007/978-3-031-23944-1_7

rules. When carrying out marketing activities, enterprises should grasp the particularity and novelty of marketing, formulate a set of targeted marketing plans, do a good job in the details of each plan, and strive to obtain good marketing results [1].

Big data mining refers to mining valuable information for users from massive data with multiple data types, rapid changes and low data value density, so as to provide and serve users. Compared with traditional data mining, big data mining relies on the vigorous development of cloud computing, Internet of things, mobile Internet, mobile intelligent terminal and other technologies in terms of technical development background, data environment and breadth and depth of mining. Focusing on the characteristics of big data, this paper analyzes the problems of existing data mining systems with the help of advanced technology, The scope of real-time processing and multidimensional analysis of complex data is broader, and the mining and analysis is deeper and more comprehensive.

Intelligent knowledge management discusses how to use possible technical means to build a systematic scheme, so that a large number of complex data can provide intelligent and personalized services of knowledge, improve the ability of enterprises to use information, and finally improve the decision-making level of decision-makers. The traditional knowledge management focuses on the "knowledge management system" from the aspects of algorithm, structure and process. It does not pay attention to the intelligent management of knowledge itself, does not conduct systematic research on knowledge management, and does not design the method of knowledge integration and utilization, so that when the amount of knowledge is too large, the traditional knowledge management platform is difficult to complete the task. Therefore, knowledge itself should also have a certain intelligence and be able to manage itself.

2 Related Technologies

2.1 Data Mining Technology

Data mining tools can predict future trends and behaviors, so as to well support people's decision-making. For example, through the analysis of the company's entire database system, data mining tools can answer similar questions such as "which customer is most likely to respond to our company's e-mail promotion activities and why". Some data mining tools can also solve some traditional problems that consume labor time, because they can quickly browse the whole database and find some very useful information that experts are not easy to detect.

The records in the database can be divided into a series of meaningful subsets, namely clustering. Clustering enhances people's understanding of objective reality and is a prerequisite for concept description and deviation analysis. Clustering technology mainly includes traditional pattern recognition methods and mathematical taxonomy. Figure 1 below shows the technical process of data mining.

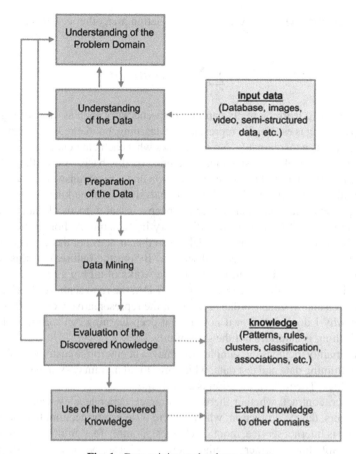

Fig. 1. Data mining technology process

Data association is an important kind of discoverable knowledge in database. If there is some regularity between the values of two or more variables, it is called correlation. Association can be divided into simple association, temporal association and causal association. The purpose of association analysis is to find out the hidden association network in the database. Sometimes the association function of the data in the database is unknown, even if it is known, it is uncertain, so the rules generated by association analysis have credibility.

Support of association rules

The support of association rules is the ratio of the number of X and Y transactions contained in the transaction set to the number of all transactions, which is recorded as

$$support(X => Y), \ support(X => Y) = supportXUY = P(XY) \qquad (1)$$

Support reflects the probability that the items contained in X and Y appear simultaneously in the transaction set.

$$support(X => Y)min\_sup, \ confidence(X => Y)min\_conf \qquad (2)$$

Call association rule x = > y as strong association rule, otherwise it is if association rule.

$$SSE = \sum_{l=1}^{K} \sum_{x \in L_l} Dist(x, Z_l)^2 \tag{3}$$

At present, deep learning really can't do high-end work such as discovering knowledge. Deep learning is essentially representation learning, but the representation learned by deep learning is unexplainable. No one knows what each element means. Therefore, it is meaningless to make any statistical inference on this basis. As for the ML model that emphasizes prediction rather than explanation under many answers, it seems to me that it is fruitless. The so-called "Risk factor analysis is to mine knowledge from data [2]. Mining knowledge from data has always been a research focus of data analysis, or ml, for example, KDD has knowledge discovery in its name. Although medicine and economics basically only use linear models to do this, it does not mean that only linear models can be used to do knowledge discovery. Before the outbreak of this round of deep learning, the most important representative works of all big guys were related to knowledge discovery It is now relevant, such as LDA, the representative work of David BLEI, Wu Enda and Michael Jordan, and SCM, the representative work of Pearl Judea. The reason why I don't mention it now is that deep learning can't do this at all, not because this thing is naturally not the goal of ml.

The data mainly includes the sample information of enterprise customers. The data is divided into training data and test data, which are stored in train CSV and test_ noLabel. CSV in two files. The field description is as follows:

Id: number, contract: whether there is a contract, dependencies: whether there are family members, device protection: whether there is device protection, Internet service: whether there is Internet service, monthly charges: monthly fees, multiple lines: whether there are multiple lines, partner: whether there is a spouse, payment method: payment method, phone service: whether there is telephone service, senior citizen: whether it is the elderly, tv program: whether there is a TV Festival Total charges: total cost, gender: user gender, tenure: number of years of tenure, chun: whether the user is lost.

2.2 Enterprise Marketing

The company implements procurement management strategy and makes cost-effective purchase decisions for a group of efficient suppliers. The company can decide to adopt a single source procurement strategy, which involves obtaining high-quality services from a single supplier. Establish supplier optimization and relationship establishment.

SRM technology can help implement the above purchase strategy in order to implement the above purchase strategy. 8msassrm one-stop e-procurement platform is based on cloud computing and provides enterprises with e-procurement management based on big data. Data support decision-making and promote the implementation of the above purchase strategy. It can not only manage the purchase projects of independent institutions through the unified platform data center, but also share the information resources including suppliers (such as experts and product markets), so as to make the price more favorable, the purchase time faster, and realize the efficient cooperation of the supply chain [3]. Due to the complexity and diversity of procurement activities, e-procurement technology needs to establish e-procurement business and technical standards, provide flexible and convenient procurement tools, and improve the workflow customization of procurement projects. Enterprises must strengthen the decision-making of supplier management and integrate external resources to develop the ability to comply with the company's own procurement management decisions. The following Fig. 2 shows the process of enterprise marketing strategy.

Fig. 2. Enterprise marketing strategy process

The imperfect purchase management system will lead to the increase of enterprise costs and huge financial pressure. As an important means for companies to promote cost savings, how to effectively implement the E-bidding strategy has become a key issue [4]. Therefore, in order to achieve the purpose of reducing costs and increasing efficiency, enterprises urgently need to implement e-procurement strategy. The promotion method is to ensure that the organization purchases approved products from approved suppliers according to the negotiated contract pricing, and to ensure that the company obtains the highest service and value at the lowest possible price. In terms of managing indirect expenditure, the most important recruitment challenges include: gaining customer trust at the procurement and mining levels; Negotiate the best savings potential; Collect user recruitment needs in the channel; Ensure compliance with negotiation suppliers and pricing terms; Manage supplier performance; Implement continuous process improvement plan to ensure sustainable success. The implementation of the company's E-bidding procurement strategy requires a reliable e-recruitment and mining platform. You can choose to standardize the management of the bidding process through 8msaas SPT electronic bidding and procurement system, so that enterprise suppliers, consumers and other stakeholders in the supply chain can maintain real-time cooperation and realize the whole process of automated bidding and procurement.

Online management of the whole process from purchase plan, approval, bidding, supplier selection, bidding to order/contract management makes the procurement process standardized and transparent, and maximizes the procurement efficiency. This is also a good way for the company to seize short-term video dividends and obtain users, and the best time to increase brand exposure. How to accurately and quickly enter the game market, establish barriers, and achieve product effect stickiness with users [5].

Understand the ecological composition of short video, the relationship between development rules and basic logic: understand the ecosystem of short video, the rules of development and basic logic. Mingdao: grasp the path planning and core obstacles for enterprises to enter the field of short-term video, and grasp the core barriers of the road plan in the field of short-term video. More and more companies begin to pay attention to the full range of enterprise new media operations and develop sophisticated new media operating systems to better capture traffic, obtain customers and strengthen brands.

Use method+tool+practice form, introduce theoretical thinking, teach strategies, implement tools in practice, and realize the methods that can be mastered and the goals of tools that can be used. Operation awareness – the laws and underlying logic of new media operation, and the combination of new media operation rules and basic logic.

The development law of new media and product logic. The relationship between the development rules of new media and product logic. Operational thinking – build the business ideas and working methods of new media. Practical work: build a new media operation matrix model of the enterprise and establish a new media operation matrix model of the company. New media content is targeted at content IP construction.

New media content selection and planning principles, four new media content topic selection planning principles [6]. Build community positioning planning and process design, and establish social group positioning plan and process design. Evolution of hypertools in the mobile Internet era 1 In the era of mobile Internet, the development of SuperMap has changed. Barriers – establish core barriers and create the construction of enterprise content IP.

2.3   Marketing Risk Warning

The data generated in enterprise operation can directly reflect the quality and efficiency of enterprise development, while the traditional analysis of indicators is basically a summary analysis after the event, which can find the point of problem, but the problem has appeared at this time. Risk early warning is to give early warning to possible risk points before problems occur, and change the "make up for the lost" analysis into pre-warning, so as to effectively avoid potential problems and losses to the enterprise. The project uses big data mining technology to build the index network architecture of strong correlation indicators [7].

When an indicator changes, its strong correlation indicators will also change due to its influence. For example, indicators such as power sales revenue, power sales and market share obviously have obvious correlation in the logical relationship. Therefore, when power sales change, its positive correlation indicators will change significantly. Therefore, when the power sales of enterprises are improved, their strong correlation indicators will change accordingly, or when analyzing the change indicators, such obvious correlation can help us quickly locate the causes of data anomalies. In fact, in addition to these known and obvious associations, there may be some unknown associations between different indicators of different businesses, waiting for us to explore.

Data analysis in the big data environment can not only be used to analyze the currently known risks, but also predict the unknown risks according to the correlation between the data. For example, an enterprise successfully constructed the prediction and analysis model, financing decision-making model and early warning model of cash flow gap by using high beam software consulting and strong information strength; Using mstr analysis framework and data mining technology, integrate the data pool of the company's finance and other business departments into a standard, centralized and comparable database; Based on this database, a fund decision support system is built [8]. Combined with different means such as enterprise cash flow prediction, financing decision-making, management cockpit and early warning model, decision-makers can successfully build a multi-dimensional comprehensive analysis service platform for dynamic fund management.

3   Research on Enterprise Marketing Strategy Based on Data Mining Technology

Cluster analysis is a computer algorithm, which can automatically cluster a group of objects to form a class of objects with similar characteristics. Each object (hereinafter referred to as customer) contains certain variables to determine the position of the customer in the customer space [9]. The role of data mining technology in marketing strategy is shown in Fig. 3 below.

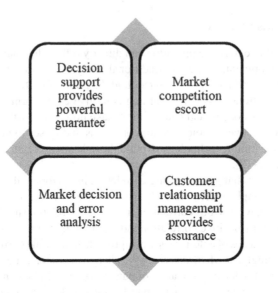

Fig. 3. The role of data mining technology in marketing strategy

For the above different customer types, the marketing strategy adopted by the enterprise should aim at the different customer groups, maintain the relationship between the enterprise and customers, maximize the value of customers in the enterprise's profit objectives, promote the transformation of customer types, and form long-term customer resources [10]. When marketing based on customer value, enterprises should pay attention to providing high-quality products and services and providing personalized services for customers. Because gold customers have high requirements for the product and service quality of the enterprise. For this kind of customers, enterprises should strengthen personalized and high-quality marketing management, optimize and upgrade the service management system, and provide convenience for customer service experience. At the same time, we should increase scientific research investment in products and services, strengthen the optimization and upgrading of products and services, and improve customers' loyalty to enterprises through the construction of a win-win system for enterprises and customers. Enterprises should actively maintain customer relations and improve the level of customer relationship management.

Compared with gold customers, silver customers have strong liquidity and low loyalty. They pay more attention to the cost of cooperation with enterprises. Therefore, for such customers, enterprises should strengthen customer relationship management and reduce customer loss. Through the investigation of customers' needs and market conditions, we can deeply understand the development of the industry, so as to provide reference basis for negotiation with customers and provide customers with better products and services [11]. At the same time, enterprises should establish experienced marketing teams, create a good marketing atmosphere and attract more customers for cooperation. Enterprises should strengthen communication with customers, make full use of brand marketing strategy and enhance customer loyalty. For copper customers, the brand effect of the enterprise itself is more attractive than the products and services provided, which can attract customers' attention and improve the possibility of cooperation between customers and enterprises. At the same time, for such customers, enterprises should strengthen communication, truly understand the real needs of customers, and then provide customers with personalized services. Enterprises should also pay attention to tap the value potential of copper customers and enhance customer stickiness and loyalty.

4   Establish Prediction Model

It can be seen that when enterprises apply the prediction model in practice, there may be many explanatory variables related to the target behavior in customer behavior and value data, but it is difficult to determine which variables have the greatest impact on the target behavior only through simple and isolated analysis. In addition, when the selected variables are applied to all customers and "similarity" scores are given to customers to find customers with high tendency (i.e. high "similarity" score), due to the large amount of data, ordinary analysis methods are difficult to support. Therefore, after establishing the theoretical basis of prediction analysis, it also needs the support of strong prediction model [12].

The process of establishing prediction model, that is, by establishing basic data set and applying prediction tools. These software load customer data, generate customer clustering (clustering) and prediction models, and provide descriptive reports and models to evaluate customer database) and identify the most meaningful explanatory variables for a certain target behavior. Use these explanatory variables to score customers, judge the similarity between each customer and customers with target behavior, and finally determine the tendency of customers to have target behavior. As shown in Fig. 4 below, a marketing prediction model is established.

There are five main stages in the process of establishing the prediction model:

(1) Define modeling parameters;
(2) Generate model;
(3) Verify the performance of the model;
(4) Analyze and understand the built model;
(5) Use and update models.

With the rapid development of the Internet, e-commerce is also undergoing earth shaking changes. The future development trends are as follows:

1. From online to offline. The trend in the future must be the integration of online and offline. Offline search for online channels will be expanded, and online search will blossom. The combination of online first and offline will be closer! JD.COM. Alibaba 9. Tencent and others have seized the new retail market is a good example [13].
2. E-commerce is increasingly infiltrating into our lives. In the future, e-commerce is definitely not as simple as online shopping. E-commerce is bound to be more closely integrated in all aspects of life, such as medical treatment, travel, transportation and so on! The penetration of e-commerce into the service industry will be carried out to the end!

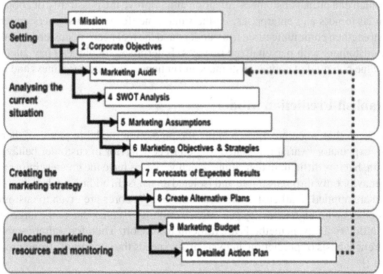

Fig. 4. Establish marketing prediction model

3. The rise of mobile e-commerce. In the past, I used to surf the Internet with my computer in my arms. Now I surf the Internet with my mobile phone in my arms before I go to bed. All the things that can be done on the PC end can be operated on the wireless end. All shopping activities can also be completed on mobile phones. Consumers are increasingly concentrated on the wireless end, and e-commerce is bound to shift to the wireless end [14].

4. The rise of overseas e-commerce. With the improvement of national living standards, more and more people tend to go shopping online to improve their quality of life. Cross border e-commerce has sprung up against this background. Jd.com, tmall and other large e-commerce platforms have launched their own overseas purchase channels. Chinese overseas purchase will become more and more convenient and faster!

5   Conclusion

The research on enterprise marketing education strategy based on data mining technology is a research paper on enterprise marketing education strategy. The authors of this paper used data mining technology to analyze their survey results, and they concluded that there are four main factors that affect students' learning experience in University. These factors include: 1) student characteristics, 2) teacher characteristics, 3) course content and 4) teacher-student interaction. They also found that according to the importance of these four factors to students' learning experience, they can be divided into two categories: 1) curriculum content factor (CCF), including curriculum outline.This paper studies the enterprise marketing strategy based on data mining technology. Combined with data mining theory, starting from the actual needs of the enterprise market, this paper puts forward the marketing process of enterprise application data mining, subdivides customers through customers' business consumption, and improves the response rate of targeted marketing scheme through data mining prediction model.

References

1. Wang, X.H.: Research on the marketing strategy of tourist attractions based on E-commerce—a case study of Wuyi mountain. J. Dezhou Univ. (2018)
2. Belova, T., Dunin, M.: Taking into account the importance of marketing trends when forming an enterprise strategy. Herald UNU Int. Econ. Relat. World Econ. (36) (2021)
3. Purwihartuti, K., Karnawati, H., Kristianingsih, K., et al.: Marketing strategy planning based on customers expected services: evidence from Sharia Cooperatives in Bandung. In Proceedings of the 4th International Conference on Arts Language and Culture (ICALC 2019) (2020)
4. Khmiadashvili, L.: Digital marketing strategy based on hotel industry study in Tbilisi. IJASOS Int. E-J. Adv. Soc. Sci. 5(14), 922–927 (2019)
5. Zhang, R., Pei, M., School, B., et al.: Influence of online and offline marketing strategy conformity on customer trust: based on product type to regulate. J. Hubei Univ. Arts Sci. (2019)
6. Wang, Y.: ITMC marketing sandbox business strategy analysis based on the analysis of market environment. J. Hunan Indus. Polytech. (2019)
7. Di-Yao, W.U., Zhang, X.Y.: System design and application of data mining in Chinese materia medica based on strategy pattern. China J. Tradit. Chin. Med. Pharm. (2019)
8. Xue, J.: Research on books information management of university based on data mining technology. Inf. Technol. (2019)
9. Zhou, Q.: On strategy for cultivation of vocational consciousness in Higher Vocational College students based on information technology. Vocat. Tech. Educ. (2018)
10. Zhang, M., Li, L.: Marketing strategy of "Yiping" pharmaceutical industry in Guizhou Province based on SWOT analysis. Shandong Chem. Ind. (2018)
11. da Costa Júnior, J.F., de Rezende, J.F.D., dos Santos Cabral, E.L., de Medeiros Florentino, D.R., Soares, A.R.: The impact of big data on SME's strategic management: a study on a small british enterprise specialized in business intelligence. J. Manage. Strategy 9(4) (2018)
12. Yang, S., Ding, J., Chen, L.: Research on the administration rules of Chinese patent medicine in treating impediment syndrome based on data mining. J. New Chin. Med. (2019)
13. Huang, L.: Research on mobile marketing strategy based on SICAS model—a case study of Yili Group. Am. J. Ind. Bus. Manag. 09(4), 1059–1075 (2019)
14. Gao, S.: A research on the marketing strategy of artificial intelligent robot: based on the perspective of customer delivered value theory. In: Proceedings of the 8th International Conference on Social Network, Communication and Education (SNCE 2018) (2018)

Research on Evaluation of Physical Education Teaching Quality Based on Comprehensive Integrated Evaluation Method and SVM

Liang Liang[✉]

Guangdong Business and Technology University, Guangzhou 526060, Guangdong, China
935748819@qq.com

Abstract. The construction of college physical education teaching quality evaluation index system should fully reflect the characteristics of modern college physical education teaching, pay attention to the evaluation of teachers' teaching personality and teaching style, and adopt diversified evaluation methods. While strengthening college students' teaching evaluation, we should choose diversified evaluation subjects to reflect the objective reality of teaching fairly, objectively and accurately. Combining the analytic hierarchy process with the improved open grade method, this paper puts forward the comprehensive integrated assignment method to solve the disadvantage that the weight is difficult to determine accurately, and applies it to the evaluation of physical education teaching quality combined with SVM.

Keywords: SVM · Integrated valuation method · Evaluation of physical education teaching quality

1 Introduction

However, the current physical education teaching quality evaluation system also has many problems. Among them, how to formulate a comprehensive and accurate evaluation model and index system is a complex problem, and how to measure the proportion of each index is also a problem of great research value. At present, what needs to be done is to make the evaluation model into a system and publish it on the campus network, calling on teachers and students to participate in the evaluation, so as to supervise the quality of physical education teaching in the school [1].

With China's comprehensive promotion of educational modernization and the further development of fair and quality education, physical education curriculum teaching reform also pays more and more attention to fair and quality physical education. The reform of "integration of physical education curriculum" is a sharp weapon to promote fair and quality physical education [2].

From the student-oriented orientation of physical education curriculum concept, the hierarchical setting of physical education curriculum objectives, the structured arrangement of physical education curriculum content, to the diversified presentation of physical

M. A. Jan and F. Khan (Eds.): BigIoT-EDU 2022, LNICST 467, pp. 64–75, 2023.
https://doi.org/10.1007/978-3-031-23944-1_8

education curriculum implementation and the diversified application of physical education curriculum evaluation, we can jointly play a role in promoting the all-round development of students and highlight the value of physical education curriculum integration. Figure 1 below shows the hierarchical flow chart of educational courses.

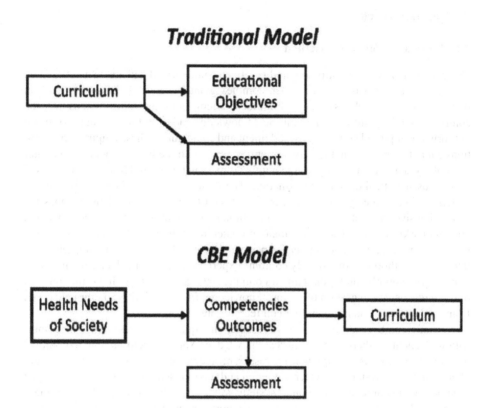

Fig. 1. Flow chart of educational curriculum stratification

Based on the long-term and unsolved difficult problems such as low-level repetition and skimming of physical education curriculum, the continuous decline of students' physique, the failure to develop exercise habits and the lack of outstanding skill mastery, through the sharp weapon of physical education curriculum integration, carry out the integrated reform from the trinity of national curriculum, local curriculum and school-based curriculum, It is not only a strong call for school physical education in the new era, but also an inevitable demand to deepen the teaching reform of physical education and better promote the all-round development of students.

The basic education curriculum and textbook development center of the Ministry of education proposed to conduct curriculum integration research in four disciplines: moral education, physical education, music and art, and defined the requirements of scientific and systematic construction of curriculum integration. This is of great significance to promote and guide the teaching reform of physical education. The integration of physical education curriculum and teaching reform ushered in new development opportunities, changed understanding, grasped good opportunities, improved system, and the improvement of physical education quality is expected to reach a new level.

2 Related Work

2.1 Integrated Valuation Method

The comprehensive integration method is refined, summarized and abstracted based on the research and practice of four open complex giant systems: social system, human body system, geographic system and military system. In these studies, it is usually the combination of scientific theory, empirical knowledge and expert judgment to form and put forward empirical assumptions (judgment and conjecture). These empirical assumptions cannot be proved in a rigorous scientific way. With the help of modern computer technology, a model including a large number of parameters should be established based on various statistical data and information, These models are based on experience and understanding of the system, and have been tested for authenticity. This includes the comprehensive integration of emotional, rational, empirical, scientific, qualitative and quantitative knowledge. Through human-computer interaction, repeated comparison and gradual approximation, and finally form a conclusion. The essence of comprehensive integration method is to organically combine expert groups, statistical data and information to form a highly intelligent human-computer interaction system. It has the function of comprehensive integration of various knowledge, from sensibility to rationality, and from qualitative to quantitative. Its main features are as follows:

Organic combination of qualitative research and quantitative research; The combination of scientific theory and empirical knowledge; Apply system thought to combine multiple disciplines for comprehensive research; According to the hierarchical structure of complex giant system, the macro research and micro research are unified [3]; It must be supported by large-scale computer system, which not only has the functions of management information system and decision support system, but also has the function of comprehensive integration; Emphasize the combination of man and machine, but focus on people. The application of comprehensive integration method to the exploration and research of open complex giant systems has opened up a new scientific field, which is of great strategic significance in theory and practice.

Data processing is as follows:

$$E(t)\dot{x}_k(t) = f(t, x_k(t)) + B(t)u_k(t) \tag{1}$$

It minimizes the design of the algorithm. For the loss function in function approximation, the empirical risk is the error rate of training samples, while for the loss function in regression problem, the empirical risk is the square training error, and the ERM criterion of loss function in probability density problem is equivalent to the maximum likelihood method. Some classical methods, such as least square method and maximum likelihood method in regression problem, are the application of empirical risk minimization principle under special loss function [4]. The traditional neural network learning method also applies the principle of empirical risk minimization.

Bagging: sub sampling from the training set to form the sub training set required by each base model, and synthesizing the prediction results of all base models to produce the final prediction results [5];

$$y_k(t) = C(t)x_k(t) \tag{2}$$

Boosting: the training process is stepped. The base model is trained in order - one (parallel in Implementation). The training set of the base model is transformed every time according to a certain strategy. Linear synthesis of the prediction results of all base models to produce the final prediction results;

$$u_{k+1}(t) = \Gamma_{p1}\Delta\dot{e}_k(t) + \Gamma_{p2}\Delta\dot{e}_{k+1}(t) \tag{3}$$

The generalized bias describes the difference between the predicted value and the real value, and the variance describes the dispersion of the predicted value as a random variable. The relationship between deviation and variance is shown in Fig. 2 below.

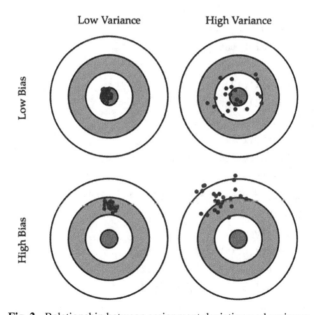

Fig. 2. Relationship between assignment deviation and variance

Defining the difference between the values of random variables is the prerequisite for calculating variance. Generally speaking, we encounter numerical random variables, and the difference between values can not be more obvious (subtraction). But what about the differences of the models? We can understand that the differences of models are the structural differences of models, such as the differences of weight vectors in linear models, the structural differences of trees in tree models, etc. In the study of model variance, we do not need to quantitatively calculate the square difference, but only need to know its concept.

2.2 SVM Technology

The key of SVM is to solve a (linear or nonlinear) constrained quadratic optimization problem. Successfully solving the optimization problem of SVM is the key to realize SVM. Among them, the inner product kernel of support vector and sample vector is the key to construct learning algorithm [6]. The learning machines constructed by the existing inner product kernel learning algorithms include polynomial machine, radial basis function network and two-layer perceptron. The improvement ways of training algorithm are divided into decomposition method, modified optimization problem method, geometric method, incremental learning method, and learning algorithm based on principal component analysis method. In recent years, Osuna aiming at the problems of slow training speed and large time and space complexity of SVM, a decomposition algorithm is proposed and applied to face detection [7]. Mitra and Syed proposed an incremental training algorithm, which realizes incremental SVM learning directly through support vectors. Most of the open source implementations of SVM are based on Platt's SMO algorithm, as shown in Fig. 3 below.

```
target = desired output vector
point = training point matrix


procedure takeStep(i1,i2)
        if (i1 == i2) return 0
        alph1 = Lagrange multiplier for i1
        y1 = target[i1]
        E1 = SVM output on point[i1] - y1 (check in error cache)
        s = y1*y2
        Compute L, H via equations (13) and (14)
        if (L == H)
                return 0
        k11 = kernel(point[i1],point[i1])
        k12 = kernel(point[i1],point[i2])
        k22 = kernel(point[i2],point[i2])
        eta = k11+k22-2*k12
```

Fig. 3. SVM part code

SVM method is proposed from the case of linear separability. Considering the two-dimensional two types of linear separability as shown in Fig. 3, If the classification line separates the two types of data without error and the distance between the nearest point and the classification line is the largest, such a classification line is called the optimal classification line (becoming the optimal hyperplane in the multi-dimensional space). The second condition is to maximize the classification spacing, even if the confidence interval of the bound of generalization ability is the smallest, so as to minimize the real risk. Figure 4 below shows the optimal classification line under the condition of linear separability.

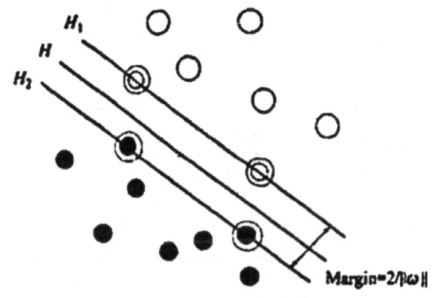

Fig. 4. Optimal classification line under the condition of linear separability

2.3 Physical Education Teaching Evaluation

However, in terms of the positioning of physical education, it has been positioned at the level of "physical education" for a long time. Undoubtedly, it dwarfs the due value of physical education.

(1) Sports can make people's life more secure, such as mastering swimming, safe self-help, etc. by strengthening the education of survival skills, people's life will be more secure;

(2) Sports can make people's life more quality. Scientific exercise can enhance physique and health. A healthy life is a more quality life. Strengthen health education and improve the quality of life;

(3) Sports can make people's life more meaningful. Physical education can cultivate students' sports spirit such as hard-working, tenacious struggle and courage to take responsibility. It can make contributions to the country with energy, courage and sense of responsibility, and fully feel a more meaningful and valuable life. The evaluation customization strategy is shown in Fig. 5 below.

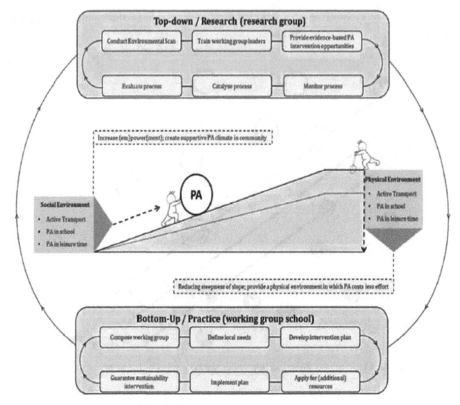

Fig. 5. Evaluate customization strategy

The logic of physical education promoting health is mostly understood as that school physical education lays the foundation for lifelong physical education, lifelong participation in exercise promotes health, has health, and naturally has the basic guarantee of happiness. This logical chain looks accurate, but the value orientation of school physical education is not far enough.

In other words, the real value of school sports is not only "lifelong sports", but also has higher value. It is a sports that serves a healthy and happy life, namely "Life Sports".

The reason for repositioning the real value of school sports as "Life Sports" is that sports can change life, not just let people participate in physical exercise for life. Sports more point to the shaping of perfect and sound personality, especially the shaping of students' sports spirit through school sports.

"Physical education curriculum integration" advocates the organic combination of learning, practice and competition. It pursues not only learning and practice to master skills, but also the sports spirit of tenacious struggle, teamwork and never say die through competition [8]. These spirits can be extended to help students' development in their future life. Figure 6 below shows the flow chart of student development strategies.

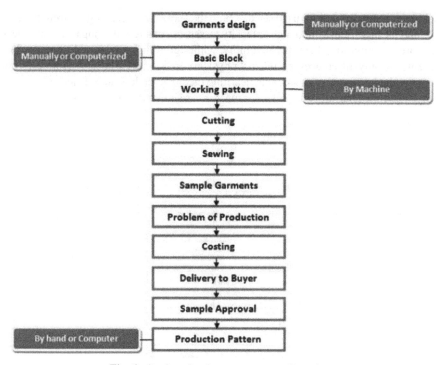

Fig. 6. Student development strategy flow chart

In a certain sense, the understanding of the value of school physical education can not only stay in laying the foundation for "lifelong physical education", but in laying the foundation for people's happy and healthy life, that is, re grasp the value and significance of school physical education from the height of "life physical education". Based on the actual "Life Sports" value of school sports, the focus of physical education curriculum teaching reform should also change accordingly, strengthen the school sports value of "Life Sports" and better serve the students' higher and more meaningful life development needs in the future.

3   Research on the Evaluation of Physical Education Teaching Quality Based on Comprehensive Integration Valuation Method and SVM

Physical education classroom is the main position for the implementation of physical education curriculum. No matter what aspects we emphasized in the past to improve the quality of physical education teaching and study the factors affecting the quality of physical education teaching, we can not avoid the problem of "everyone benefits" in physical education teaching. However, looking at the analysis of physical education teaching, it is not difficult for us to see that both the sports skill teaching of strengthening skills and the high-density and high-intensity classroom of strengthening physical fitness pay more attention to collectivity and unity, while ignoring individual differences [9]. There are not only differences in students' physical condition, skill basis and interests, but also individual differences in students' learning methods, understanding and acceptance ability. The flow chart of support vector machine is shown in Fig. 7 below.

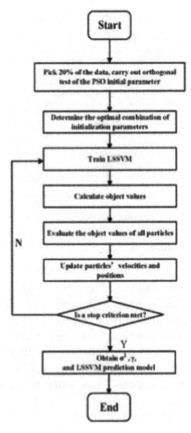

Fig. 7. Support vector machine process

Therefore, the future physical education curriculum teaching reform should attach great importance to the "everyone benefits" ignored in the past. "Everyone benefits" is to pay attention to every student's right and opportunity to receive physical education, and to reflect a fairer and higher quality physical education. The key is to pay attention to individual differences, be able to treat differently and teach at different levels. The implementation of physical education curriculum benefits every student, pays attention to "everyone benefits", and also considers the adaptability of objective conditions.

$$E(t) = f(t, x_d(t)) - f(t, x_{k+1}(t)) + B\Delta u_k(t) \tag{4}$$

Modern physical education teaching evaluation absorbs the viewpoint of system theory and holds that all the elements involved in physical education teaching evaluation are interrelated to form a physical education teaching evaluation system [10]. In this system, the combination of each part determines the overall function. Whether physical education teaching evaluation can play its role well depends on whether the overall function of the system is optimized [11]. Therefore, in the process of formulating the evaluation scheme, modern physical education teaching evaluation attaches great importance to the organic combination between each link and the internal requirements of each link, and opposes the local concept of traditional physical education teaching evaluation.

4 Data Processing

Kernel function cache consumes a lot of memory, so libsvm has no choice in mathematics, but there is still much room for improvement in engineering, such as its kernel cache implementation [12, 13].

Since the standard SVM kernel function uses the inner product of two high-dimensional vectors, according to several conditions of the inner product, the SVM kernel function is a positive definite kernel, that is, $K(Xi, XJ) = K(XJ, Xi)$, then we can store twice as many kernel functions in the same memory, and the performance can be improved.

There are many optimization methods for the calculation and storage of kernel functions. For example, someone samples the kernel function matrix of $N \times N$, calculates only a limited number of kernel functions, and then solves the intermediate value by interpolation. Others use float to store kernel function values, which reduces the space requirement by twice.

According to the evaluation results of the three two-class classifiers, the more times the data belongs to which category, that is, which category the data belongs to, and evaluate a group of data [14]. The evaluation results of the three classifiers are as follows: the evaluation results obtained by excellent and good classifiers are good; The evaluation result obtained by the excellent and poor classifier is excellent; The evaluation result obtained by the good poor classifier is a good level, and the program automatically judges that this category is defined as a good level by two classifiers, then this kind of data belongs to a good level. The training code is shown in Fig. 8.

```
minValue = 320.9;
maxValue = 8338;
[rowLen, colLen] = size(data);
train_num = rowLen;
hidden_unit_num = 9;
in_dim = colLen - 1;
out_dim = 1;
p = data(:, 1:in_dim)';
t = data(:, colLen)';

[SamIn, PSp] = mapminmax(p, -1, 1);
[tn, PSt] = mapminmax(t, -1, 1);
SamOut = tn;
MaxEpochs = 50000;
lr = 0.05;
E0 = 1e-3;
rng('default');

W1 = rand(hidden_unit_num, in_dim);
B1 = rand(hidden_unit_num, 1);
W2 = rand(out_dim, hidden_unit_num);
B2 = rand(out_dim, 1);
ErrHistory = zeros(MaxEpochs, 1);
```

Fig. 8. Training code

5 Conclusion

The internal evaluation of physical education teaching quality in Colleges and universities is an evaluation method based on reality, facing the future and pursuing development. It pays attention to the diversity and developmental function of evaluation. In order to promote and improve the improvement of physical education teaching quality and narrow the gap between China's physical education teaching activities and western developed countries, the research on physical education teaching quality evaluation is of great significance, An evaluation method aimed at improving the quality of physical education teaching from within the school through evaluation. Under the existing conditions, internal evaluation is a feasible system. However, this evaluation method has some limitations if it wants to be applied on a large scale. This paper puts forward an evaluation model of physical education teaching quality based on comprehensive integration evaluation method and SVM. The results show that the algorithm proposed in this paper can accurately reflect the situation of physical education teaching quality and accurately determine the weight of physical education teaching quality evaluation index.

Acknowledgements. 2021 Young Innovative Talents Project in Guangdong Universities: An Empirical Study on "Flipping Classroom" Teaching Mode of Basketball Major in Universities under the Backround of Information Technology (WQNCX125).

References

1. Pu, Y., et al.: The impact of climate risk valuation on the regional mitigation strategies. J. Cleaner Prod. **313**, 127786 (2021)
2. Han, H., Zhao, L., et al.: Estimating ecological value of small hydropower using contingent valuation method: an application to Tongjiqiao Reservoir in Zhejiang Province, China. Chin. J. Popul. Resour. Environ. **10**(1), 87–95 (2012)
3. Moya, E.C.: Active methodologies in physical education: perception and opinion of students on the pedagogical model used by their teachers. Int. J. Environ. Res. Public Health **18**, 1438 (2021)
4. Liu, S.: Research on the teaching quality evaluation of physical education with intuitionistic fuzzy TOPSIS method. J. Intell. Fuzzy Syst. **40**(5), 1–10 (2021)
5. Wang, Y., Sun, C., Guo, Y.: A Multi-attribute fuzzy evaluation model for the teaching quality of physical education in colleges and its implementation strategies. Int. J. Emerg. Technol. Learn. (iJET) **16**(2), 159 (2021)
6. Damanik, F.J., Setyohadi, D.B.: Analysis of public sentiment about Covid-19 in Indonesia on twitter using multinomial Naive Bayes and support vector machine. IOP Conf. Ser. Earth Environ. Sci. **704**(1), 012027 (2021). (11pp)
7. Dinh, T.V., Nguyen, H., Tran, X.L., et al.: Predicting rainfall-induced soil erosion based on a hybridization of adaptive differential evolution and support vector machine classification. Math. Probl. Eng. **2021** (2021)
8. Azis, T., Kasim, K.F.: Gender identification of Sitophilus Oryzae using discriminant analysis and support vector machine: a comparison study. IOP Conf. Ser. Earth Environ. Sci. **765**(1), 012018 (2021). (8pp)
9. González-Castao, C., Marulanda, J., Restrepo, C., et al.: Hardware-in-the-loop to test an MPPT technique of solar photovoltaic system: a support vector machine approach. Sustainability **13**, 3000 (2021)
10. Hamzah, M.A., Othman, S.H.: A review of support vector machine-based intrusion detection system for wireless sensor network with different kernel functions. Int. J. Innovative Comput. **11**(1), 59–67 (2021)
11. Khun-Inkeeree, H., Tulyakul, S.: Teacher motivation, preventive strategies toward lesson implementation in physical education teachers. Technium Soc. Sci. J. **19**, 144 (2021)
12. Engelhardt, S., Hapke, J., Tpfer, C..: Implementation and effectiveness of cognitive-reflexive activating physical education: a scoping review. In: Proceedings of the AIESEP-Conference (2021)
13. Wang, L., Deng, W.: A research-oriented teaching model for public physical education in colleges based on extenics theory. Int. J. Emerg. Technol. Learn. (iJET) **16**(1), 247 (2021)
14. Pérez-Pueyo, N., Hortigüela-Alcalá, D., Hernando-Garijo, A., et al.: The attitudinal style as pedagogical model in physical education. Int. J. Environ. Res. Public Health **18**(2), 374 (2021)

Research on Film Visual Concept and Creative Method in the Era of Virtual Production

Ziwei Xu[✉]

Wuchang University of Technology, Wuhan 430223, Hubei, China
xzw8466488@163.com

Abstract. In the era of virtual production, digital film special effects are not only functional tools, but also essential means of expression. Film stunts have become a common means in films and a new film language. With the omnipotent virtual image, digital stunt provides unprecedented expression possibility and creative space for the film. It not only realizes the epoch-making change in film creation, changes the audience's viewing thinking and consumption concept, but also endows the film theory with a new topic of the times.

Keywords: Film · Virtual production · D effect

1 Introduction

Film art satisfies people's visual freshness and develops people's imagination. At the beginning of the birth of film, it is regarded as a kind of magic and known as the "seventh art". Film art is different from the independent creation of painting, music, dance, sculpture and other art forms. From the beginning of its birth, film must rely on science and technology to develop.

Before studying the visual concepts and creative methods of movies in the era of virtual production, please allow me to share with you a thinking proposition put forward by American filmmaker Oakley Anderson Moore on the current development status of digital technology and the possible development trend of movies in the future: "What kind of films would you make if your tools matched the speed of thought?" Obviously, the presupposition of Oakley Anderson Moore's question is closely related to the development of contemporary film virtual production technology and real-time rendering technology [1]. Moreover, the answer to this question actually involves how to understand the world, how to understand the world and how to construct the story on the basis of the possibilities provided by realizable technology The problems of the world.

2 Virtual Production Technology that Subverts the Traditional Concept of Film Production

In the context of classical film theory, whether Andre Bazin discusses the realistic function of film photographic documentary through "photographic image ontology",

M. A. Jan and F. Khan (Eds.): BigIoT-EDU 2022, LNICST 467, pp. 76–81, 2023.
https://doi.org/10.1007/978-3-031-23944-1_9

or Siegfried Kracauer explains "material reality restoration" People often think that the story world is a mirror representation or reflection of the real world and exists as an asymptote of reality or another scene. This traditional concept of film production constitutes "photographic realism" However, in the era of full penetration of contemporary digital technology into film production, the film virtualization production, which began with virtual design and digital assets, continues to override the "photographic realism" based on the index concept Aesthetic principles form a relatively independent digital world that is different from the real world and has a juxtaposition relationship with the real world, which means that the real world and the digital world are not just "mapping or projection" between subject and object in the current film world In fact, it is a juxtaposed coexistence relationship. In this process, the digital world has established a set of operation logic and operation rules around its own discourse order; at the same time, it has also formed its own value system and aesthetic standards. With the comprehensive integration of digital technology and film culture, people's cognition of self and others is constantly constructed Concept further shapes the multiple expression of emotional demands and values in human culture, and extends to a new understanding of the universe, the world and life.

In recent 10 years, with the rapid development of digital technology, especially around "visualization" The gradual development of virtual production technology as the core has imperceptibly subverted people's inherent film concept, greatly blurred the clear boundary between virtual and reality in traditional cognition, and formed a new visual concept and aesthetic paradigm of contemporary film. Then, how to define film virtual production? Compared with traditional film production and its process, virtual production is superior What is the potential? Why should we pay attention to virtual production? How will virtual production affect the visual concept, narrative expression and audience aesthetic experience of future films, as well as the level of production management and creative methods, and even the overall construction of future film industry? Such problems are just a series of important propositions that current film research institutes should face and seriously consider [2].

Based on the characteristics of virtual production, David Morin, chairman of the Joint Technical Committee of film virtual production, expressed virtual production (VP) at a more specific level as "a new film production method that can mix real shots and computer-generated images at the same time to obtain real-time feedback and make decisions on visual effects and animation in real-time scenes" What David Morin said is just in response to the famous saying of the international excellent visual effect team weta Digital: "virtual production is the field where the physical and digital worlds meet." This statement is incisive, and also explains the core proposition of virtual production to a certain extent, that is, between the real physical world and the virtual digital world, virtual production technology is constantly expanding the territory of the film story world, constantly forming a new film viewing experience mode, and constantly creating more imagination and more possibilities.

3   The Influence of Virtual Production Era on Film Visual Concept

3.1   Impact of Virtual Production on Film Aesthetics and Film Theory

At present, the debate on digital stunts in domestic theoretical circles mainly focuses on the relationship between digital image and reality. Most scholars believe that the emergence of digital film stunts has subverted Bazin's cornerstone of film image ontology to a great extent, such as Zhang Gedong "The images created by these computers show that the film can no longer be a simple copy of material reality. The 'visual lies' it creates also subvert the traditional concept of 'truth'." This argument is also recognized by Ni Zhen, Chen Xihe and others. But at the same time, most people also believe that the image produced by this computer can also give people a realistic feeling, which is both a virtual reality and a real reality. Its relationship with reality is no longer a simple "copy and recovery", but "imagination and presentation" "Therefore, we all choose the word "virtual realism" to define digital images.

The argument that "virtual realism" replaces "photography" is undoubtedly an exploration of the characteristics of film wonders and an expansion of the concept of film aesthetics. The author believes that the theory that digital images "subvert" Bazin's film photography ontology is untenable. "The involvement of digital technology in film production has surpassed the traditional film form with photographic images as the main body, and the characteristics of film noumenon have changed. It is no doubt that the material basis on which Bazin relies has changed, and the aesthetic interpretation of film must be adjusted accordingly. However, Bazin's aesthetic core, that is, the worship of truth, is still the highest criterion for film art creation Although film digital technology makes the relationship between image and reality more obvious, the pursuit of reality in digital film is still consistent with the core of Bazin's theory." In fact, whether it is "virtual reality" or "digital reality", the emergence of digital stunts has indeed put forward new propositions for traditional film theory and brought new development to film creation. A recognized fact is that digital stunts have formed a new "film language" and created a richer film time and space for films [3].

3.2   Impact of Digital Stunts on Film Production

Although digital stunt is also a comprehensive technology formed by early shooting, modeling design and later optical synthesis, the application of these technologies is completed by computer. It no longer has a distance between imagination and reality by means of high-tech digital synthesis, digital image processing and three-dimensional animation, and truly realizes the perfect integration of narration and modeling. It starts from the sub lens script The shadow of digital stunts is always there. During script planning and narrative arrangement, digital stunts let the creator jump out of the traditional linear thinking mode and completely break the concept of time and space, as shown in Fig. 1. The pictures originally limited to shooting technology can be realized. The creator has let go of his hands and feet and can give full play to his imagination. It is stunts embodied in the production process In the early stage of shooting, in addition to on-site shooting, there are more and more scenes such as scene setting, blue screen, model and digital skylight painting, and the requirements for lighting and props are also very different from the traditional shooting requirements. The requirements for scene setting and props personnel are not just to make some physical models, but to draw the required scenes and props in the computer for later stage In this way, in the post synthesis processing, computer technology began to show its skills, and the original special effects methods of traditional methods such as masking and overlapping were replaced by the powerful functions of various computer software.

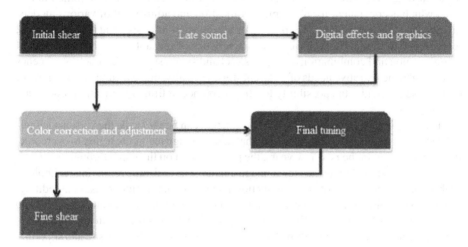

Fig. 1. Virtual film and television production process

4 Visualization, Real-Time and Digital Assets

As a development trend of film production in the future, virtual production technology integrates different types of new technologies and processes in the game and interactive entertainment industry. Based on virtual design and digital assets, it uses visual conceptual design, virtual shooting, visual dynamic preview, digital performance and real-time rendering engine as technical support, Create a different production process from the past.

Among them, "visualization" can be said to be the core issue of film virtualization. And the so-called "visualization" That is, based on the overall visual concept of a film, real-time character design, scene space design, dynamic preview, etc. these character modeling, spatial scene and dynamic preview can be not only the existing part of the film digital assets, but also the new creation based on virtual design by film creators and artists. In addition, the newly created characters and To a certain extent, the space scene itself may be transformed into the constituent elements of film digital assets. At the same time, because these digital assets carry different functions and values, Wei company also includes a series of role types such as Hulk, the lion king of Disney Company, and even Gemini man directed by Ang Lee In fact, Will Smith and so on have become an important part of film digital assets. In the future era of film virtual production, digital assets will constitute an important productivity of the film industry.

The definition of film digital assets can be roughly divided into two categories: 3D assets and image assets. Among them, 3D assets include model assets, material assets, special effects assets, animation assets, etc.; image assets include ordinary picture assets, traditional video assets, high-tech video assets, etc. the basic characteristics of film digital assets determine its important role in the future film virtualization production Value. Firstly, film digital assets have the characteristics of reusable, which can be reused in different films and games; secondly, digital assets can be changed and modified in real time, which is convenient for real-time modification and adjustment of various models, images and other asset types in the process of film conceptual design and film production; moreover, film digital assets have the characteristics of reusable The characteristics of reconstruction and combination can reconstruct and synthesize new characters or scenes according to the narrative needs of different stories. Finally, the real-time visualization of digital assets provides the possibility for the emergence of film virtualization production technology [4].

The real-time performance of virtual production can be said to be the current technology hotspot and the technology direction that many foreign teams are trying to overcome. It is expected that in the next few years, the pictures seen on the scene through the monitor will reach the final broadcast level image quality. The real-time rendering technology enables all the processes of film production from shooting, script adjustment, editing, sound mixing and visual effect production, can be carried out at the same time. It is no longer necessary to follow the linear mode of traditional film production and strictly follow the technical steps step by step. As Ben Grossman said: "While on-site and shooting, the creator can make some creative decisions. For example, 'do you want this digital tree to be a little left in the background?' we can 'finish' by clicking on the tablet."

This means that in the creation process based on film virtual production, all operations are actually based on nonlinearity and real-time. Among them, visual effects (VFX) is no longer fully covered in the final stage of production as before, but has been started when the film is still shooting. In the process of virtual shooting, the final visual effect has been presented in real time, and in this process, editing and adjustment can be carried out in real time, and the results of editing and adjustment can also be presented in real time, which is exactly a production method that can not be imagined and realized by traditional film production technology.

5 Conclusion

In the current era of virtual film production, it can be said that it has begun to establish a new film production concept and production process form of "story vision". As a production scheme of a set of real-time computer graphics system, it can provide more information for filmmakers' decision-making. As the American filmmaker Scott Clark Higgins said: The concept of "Preview" refers to the visual expression and presentation of some scenes and even the whole film before the film really starts shooting, so as to help the creative team tap creativity, explore narration and plan the technical scheme during actual shooting in a digital virtual environment without bearing the actual production cost. It forms a technical scheme that can be used to guide real shooting and post production and can be used throughout the whole production process The shared vision of the film between the two teams can save the final production time and cost.

References

1. Xu, X.: Digital stunts make gun hunt more exciting. Film Telev. Technol., 9 (2002)
2. Zhang, G.: Film technology and art in the digital age. Contemp. Film, 3 (2003)
3. Hao, B.: Digital stunts and visual authenticity. Film Telev. Technol., 1 (2002)
4. Ma, P., Guo, G.: Challenges and reflections in difficulties. Contemp. Film, 3 (2003)

Research on Intelligent Analysis and Processing Technology of Financial Big Data Education Based on DM Algorithm

Ting Zhao[✉]

Shandong Vocational College, Jinan 250000, Shandong, China
tingting0909@163.com

Abstract. Aiming at the problem of account risk discrimination and prediction in financial system, an intelligent analysis and processing technology based on K-means clustering algorithm study the analysis and processing technology of financial data in detail, this paper fully analyzes various management requirements of the financial system, and completes the automatic execution of a large number of standardized financial work and the identification, prediction and analysis of account risk by using process automation technology and neural network algorithm. In addition, by introducing k-means algorithm, this paper studies and classifies, so as to realize the comprehensive analysis and evaluation of various abilities such as debt repayment, development, operation and profitability of financial accounts, so as to avoid the one sidedness and subjectivity of artificial risk evaluation to a great extent.

Keywords: Data mining · Big data · Financial management · Intelligent analysis · Data processing

1 Introduction

With the continuous emergence of cloud computing, mobile Internet, Internet of things, new technologies and applications, the processing of big data becomes more and more important. According to statistics, more than 50% of enterprises currently generate more than 1 TB of data every day, and 10% of enterprises exceed 10 TB. What's more surprising is that 5% of enterprises have generated more than 50 TB of data every day. Especially in the financial, Internet, telecommunications and other industries, it has almost reached the point that "data is the business itself". Data itself becomes more and more valuable for an enterprise [1]. If an enterprise can not effectively use the commercial value of data mining, it will not be able to achieve an industry-leading position in modern business.

In the daily operation of the financial system, traditional accountants need to complete a variety of work, such as accounting, report review and analysis [2]. However, these works usually have the disadvantage of less functions, which is difficult to meet the growing management needs. In order to avoid this shortcoming of the system and fully tap the diversified value of the financial system, many technology companies at home. From

M. A. Jan and F. Khan (Eds.): BigIoT-EDU 2022, LNICST 467, pp. 82–91, 2023.
https://doi.org/10.1007/978-3-031-23944-1_10

2000 to 2010, Huawei, ZTE and other domestic technology companies tried to establish a Global Financial Shared Service Center for the first time, so as to reduce the financial management cost and business efficiency [3]. With the rapid rise of human resource costs and the emergence, a variety of financial and accounting work such as project funds and labor fees occupy, which directly leads to the continuous rise of financial management costs, by introducing the process automation technology and artificial neural network algorithm, this paper realizes the automatic execution of a large number of mechanical repetitive work, and completes the scientific identification and prediction of account risk. This paper uses data mining algorithm to learn and classify a large number of financial data samples, further optimize the work execution strategy of the financial system, and try to avoid the subjectivity and one sidedness of manual risk evaluation [4].

"Big data" is different from the traditional model. Financial big data refers to the use of big data management through all links of application, approval, transaction, reimbursement, payment, accounting and reporting; Fast archiving, storage, accounting, consulting and other services of financial information, paperless management, standardized, unified and automated information management; Comprehensively analyze financial and tax related indicators to help enterprises make business, investment decisions, risk early warning, cost control and tax self inspection. Use big data management to run through all links of application, approval, transaction, reimbursement, payment, accounting and reporting; Fast archiving, storage, accounting, consulting and other services of financial information, paperless management, standardized, unified and automated information management [5]. Comprehensively analyze financial and tax related indicators to help enterprises make business, investment decisions, risk early warning, cost control and tax self inspection. The market-oriented economic form and the advent of the big data era have brought more financial crises. Traditional manual accounting and manual calculation can not meet the demand. In the face of various data from outside and inside the enterprise, financial personnel have a higher sensitivity to the data, and carry out purposeful data mining on various big economic and social data, so as to realize the value of financial management, compared with the original small data era, enterprises need to deal with massive, non structural business data. The financial department needs to quickly collect, sort out, analyze and utilize the data, and integrate the effective information to realize the optimal allocation of resources, which makes the data mining and management become a hot issue for enterprises [6]. However, it is difficult to deal with such huge data by relying on traditional accounting methods, which has also become a difficult problem for every enterprise. As shown in Fig. 1. The large size of big data not only means a large number, but also, more importantly, it contains great value. Therefore, within a certain period of time, big data can be captured, analyzed, sorted out by enterprises, and used by enterprises, investors or other users. The difference between the big data era and the small data era lies in: first, the sudden increase of data, which are mostly non structural business data; Second, in the face of these massive data, accounting practitioners are required to have short response time and fast response speed. Therefore, how to collect data, sort out data, analyze data, use data, and integrate these effective data and allocate resources is one of the difficulties that enterprises need to face at present.

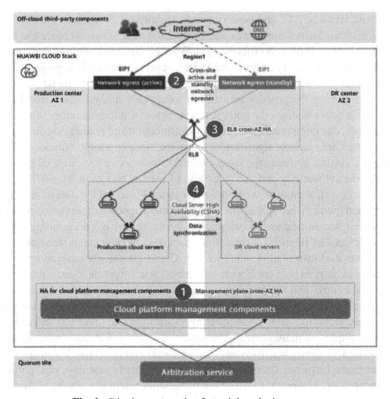

Fig. 1. Big data enterprise financial analysis process

2 Research on Data Mining

2.1 Definition of Data Mining

It is the deepening of the concept of "knowledge discovery". Knowledge discovery and data mining are the product of the combination of artificial intelligence, machine learning and database technology. Data mining is to extract people's interesting knowledge from the data in a large database, as shown in Fig. 2. These knowledge are hidden.

2.2 Classification of Data Mining System

According to different standards, data mining systems can be classified as follows:

(1) Classify according to the type of knowledge obtained. Based on the data extraction function of feature, separation, association, classification and set, develop independent value analysis, deviation analysis, similarity analysis, etc. In addition, data mining systems may differ in the size or abstraction level of mining knowledge. This includes the extensive knowledge of the upper abstraction layer, the original or multi-level knowledge of the original data layer and different levels of abstraction.

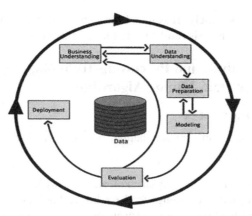

Fig. 2. Data mining process

High tech data retrieval system must support multidimensional abstract knowledge retrieval [7]. Data extraction system can be divided into data query rules and irregular data extraction models, such as exceptions and group values.

(2) These technologies (such as automation systems, interactive search systems, query drivers) or data analysis methods used (such as: database or data warehouse technology, machine learning, statistics, visual perception, pattern recognition, neural network, etc. explain the meaning of relevant parameters. Complex data mining systems generally use different data extraction methods or apply them to efficient integration technology. Maybe so, maybe.

(3) From result analysis to process analysis
Take the sales business as an example. In the past, financial analysis mainly focused on the sales results of terminals, so as to realize the analysis of product channels, organizations, quantities, amounts and other contents. However, this analysis method can not trace the source of product sales. It can only make qualitative judgments based on the results, and it can not provide accurate reference, background personnel can collect and process special information, and can also collect and analyze intermediate data and information such as consumer evaluation and promotional activities, which is of great significance for enterprises to timely adjust their business strategies and improve their business efficiency [8].

(4) From single analysis to diversity analysis
In order to judge a customer's operating conditions, it is not comprehensive to analyze its financial statements according to the traditional financial analysis idea. It must be supported by financial data and non-financial data to get a more accurate conclusion. Financial analysis should change from the previous single analysis to multi-channel information analysis, expand the data content, and help enterprises understand their own business more comprehensively [9].

(5) Change from periodic analysis to real-time analysis. In the past, the collection of terminal information and the issuance of financial analysis reports are mostly regular, which is not comprehensive enough for sudden projects, and is not conducive, personalized strategies and refined financial analysis can achieve real-time query,

information can be timely transmitted through the network, and enterprises can timely refer to the analysis results for business adjustment.

3 Intelligent Analysis and Processing Technology of Financial Big Data Based on Data Mining Algorithm

3.1 Technical Characteristics

Process automation is a software automation, which is suitable for financial sharing system.

1) Process automation technology is an automation software running on the computer desktop. This technology belongs to the robot technology in the software field, which can complete the automatic software operation of mechanical repetition and clear rules. Students majoring in big data and financial management mainly study the basic theories and knowledge of financial management, accounting and financial management, and receive basic training in financial and financial management methods and skills [10]. They not only have solid professional knowledge of financial management, know the accounting practices at home and abroad, but also can adapt to the new accounting business characteristics such as artificial intelligence, intelligent financial decision-making and big data accounting, and understand both finance and data technology, It is an interdisciplinary financial management professional with strong professional ability, high comprehensive quality and innovative spirit, integrating professional knowledge and technical skills. As shown in Fig. 3.

Fig. 3. Enterprise financial sharing system

The main destination of graduates is to further study in first-class universities, become a reserve of high-level teachers, and become financial accounting, financial intelligent analysis and decision-making in large accounting firms, Internet companies, securities companies, fund companies, institutions, government agencies and other data intensive enterprises and institutions An industry elite in complex big data accounting business processing and system logic design.

2) Process automation technology has far more accuracy and efficiency than manual work. On the premise of maintaining data processing speed and accuracy, process automation technology has all-weather and uninterrupted working ability, especially suitable for large-scale enterprise financial operation.

3) Process automation technology is based on non-invasive plug-in software. By simulating the user's basic operation, it does not affect the user's operation software architecture at all. Its implementation cycle is short and easy for non professionals to understand.

4) Process automation technology has the characteristics of low cost and low risk. It does not need manual intervention. As long as the execution rules are reasonably set, there will be no errors in the corresponding execution process, and provides highly reliable process inspection.

This paper uses process automation technology to realize a variety of highly repetitive process execution, including invoicing process execution, automatic reconciliation, collection write off and credit management. Taking Invoicing business as an example, the detailed workflow is shown in Fig. 4.

3.2 Feasibility Analysis

In the implementation stage of neural network algorithm, the financial system risk evaluation needs to use mathematical statistical model and neural network algorithm for more accurate discrimination and classification, so as to measure the financial risk of multiple enterprises and realize the liquidity of accounts receivable. As shown in Fig. 5. During the implementation of the algorithm, there are still a certain number of noise samples in the data set, which increases the difficulty of the implementation of the neural network algorithm and reduces the quality of the final result of the algorithm [4].

Through multiple rounds of training of noisy data samples, the system can extract a variety of weight matrices between input layer, hidden layer and output layer. Using these weight matrices, the system can automatically judge the financial status of multiple customers, and obtain the nonlinear relationship between their financial status and multiple indicators. Through detailed analysis and verification, it can be seen that the neural network algorithm is feasible in enterprise financial risk assessment which is shown in Fig. 6.

Big data financial analysis is a set of specialized technologies and methods to collect, prepare, analyze and act on the large-scale financial related data inside and outside the organization (including a large number of non-financial data and unstructured data in addition to financial data and structured data). It is the product of cross-border integration of accounting and information disciplines.

What does big data financial analysis learn?

[primary]: preliminarily master big data thinking, have the ability to use basic data skills to engage in initial data preparation, data collection and collation, data tool

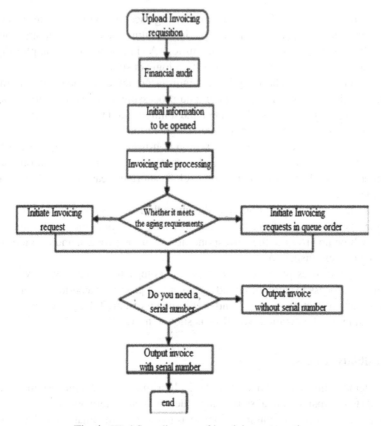

Fig. 4. Workflow diagram of invoicing automation

selection, financial and business application scenario identification, and have the basic professional ethics of big data.

[intermediate]: Master big data thinking, have the ability to find financial and business data needs in work, and use relevant professional tools for data preparation and cleaning, modeling and analysis, visual presentation, and have the ability to use database tools to generate financial statements.

[advanced]: skillfully use big data thinking, have the ability to use data analysis tools and methods to integrate financial professional skills for financial statement analysis, performance management analysis, audit analysis and internal control system analysis, provide professional advice to the management and make good decisions.

What does big data financial analysis do which is shown in Fig. 7.

For enterprises, various economic organizations and professional service institutions, the training of professional abilities across the whole financial field is as follows:

Basic fiscal and tax business processing: account table generation, information collection, and data collation.

Daily business analysis: demand analysis, report analysis and business analysis.

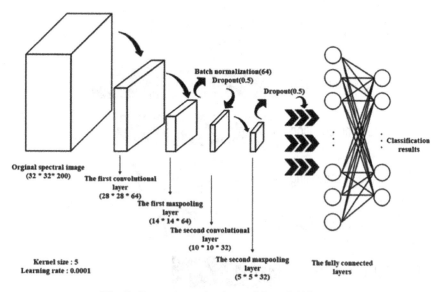

Fig. 5. Processing technology of financial big data

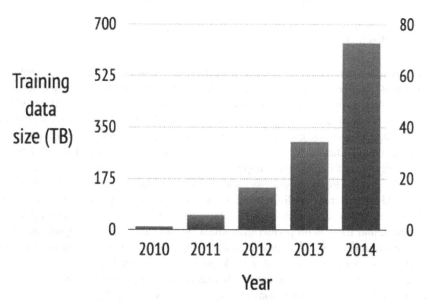

Fig. 6. Processing technology of financial big data

Operation strategy management: business finance, budget performance, audit compliance, financial planning, decision support, strategic analysis, risk management and data strategy.

Fig. 7. The application of financial big data

4   Conclusion

Data mining is a new technology rising in recent years. It has been successfully applied in many fields. As an emerging field, data mining still faces many challenges and unsolved problems, such as the research on mining algorithms to obtain multi class knowledge at a high abstract level, the research on data mining algorithms in object-oriented database, multimedia database and Interne information system, and the research on the security of private data in data mining. In addition, due to the complexity of the real world, the diversity of data and different application objectives, a general data mining system can not be formed to adapt to all situations. Different data mining systems should be established for different applications. For the same application, different data mining systems may produce different results. Their evaluation mostly depends on practical experience, and there is no perfect theoretical system. By making comprehensive use of process automation technology, neural network algorithm and K-means clustering algorithm, this paper puts forward the risk management technology of enterprise financial account, which realizes the automatic execution of high repetitive process and the accurate evaluation, discrimination and prediction of account risk.

References

1. Dan, J., Zheng, Y., Hu, J.: Research on sports training model based on intelligent data aggregation processing in internet of things. Cluster Comput. **25**, 727–734 (2022). https://doi.org/ 10.1007/s10586-021-03469-z

2. Ye, M., Huang, G.J., Gao, P., et al.: Research on intelligent operation and maintenance technology of pumped storage power plant based on 5G. In: IoT and Big Data Technologies for Health Care. Springer, Cham (2022). https://doi.org/10.1007/978-3-030-94185-7_2

3. Zhao, G., Liu, Y., Zhai, K., et al.: Research on intelligent launching control of dual clutch transmissions based on adaptive neural fuzzy inference system. J. Mech. Sci. Technol. **36**(7), 3227–3237 (2022)

4. Qiao, L., Lin, C.W.: Research on standardized feature positioning technology of motion amplitude based on intelligent vision. Mobile Netw. Appl., 1–9 (2022). https://doi.org/10. 1007/s11036-021-01883-6

5. Yang, Z., Zeng, J., Huang, X., et al.: Research on man-machine interface design based on intelligent vehicle (2022). https://doi.org/10.1007/978-3-031-06053-3_19

6. Hu, L., Yue, F.: Research on intelligent peak-cutting and valley-filling charging and swapping mode based on potential game theory. J. Phys. Conf. Ser. **2189**, 012013 (2022)

7. She, J.K., Shi, T.Z., Tang, Y.Q., et al.: Research on intelligent accident warning and simulation for loss of coolant accident in nuclear power plants (2022). https://doi.org/10.1007/978-981-19-1181-1_43

8. Fu, B., Wang, W., Wang, Y., et al.: Research on intelligent testing method of automobiles fuel consumption based on ultrasonic technology (2022). https://doi.org/10.1007/978-3-030-81007-8_11

9. Tao, F., Teng, Y.M., Li, X.H.: Exploration and research on intelligent maritime safety management for offshore oil in new circumstances. Springer, Singapore (2022). https://doi.org/10.1007/978-981-16-9427-1_63

10. Lin, M., Wu, H., Zhang, H.: Research on intelligent management of engineering construction safety oriented to Internet of Things+BIM (2022). https://doi.org/10.1007/978-3-031-04245-4_51

Research on Intelligent Evaluation of College Students' Mental Health Based on Decision Tree Algorithm

Jinling Qi and Zhenzhen Cai[✉]

Mental Health School of Qiqihar Medical College, Qiqihar 161006, China
zhen0425@163.com

Abstract. Students' mental health evaluation is an important part of mental health research. In recent 10 years, domestic colleges and universities have conducted a lot of research on students' mental health evaluation, but there is generally no mature model from theory to practice. In order to solve the problems of high error rate and low efficiency in mental health evaluation, an intelligent mental health evaluation system based on decision tree algorithm is proposed. This paper first analyzes the research status of mental health intelligent evaluation, constructs a mental health intelligent evaluation system, and then uses decision tree algorithm to collect mental health intelligent evaluation data. Analyze and classify the mental health intelligence evaluation data, get the mental health intelligence analysis results, and finally analyze the feasibility and benefits of the mental health intelligence evaluation system through specific simulation experiments. The results show that the system can overcome the shortcomings of the existing mental health evaluation system, improve the accuracy of mental health evaluation, improve the effectiveness and stability of mental health evaluation, and meet the actual needs of modern mental health.

Keywords: Decision tree algorithm · Mental health of college students · Evaluation research

1 Introduction

Mental health is also called mental health or mental health. The former refers to a state, and the latter includes not only the former, but also a kind of service work or a discipline. Paying attention to mental health is to take various measures according to the general law of people's psychological activities, cultivate healthy individual psychological activities, form a sound personality, improve social adaptability, prevent physical and mental diseases and promote mental health.

At present, China's development has entered a new normal. People are facing great competition and pressure in all aspects of life and work, and psychological problems are increasing day by day. The China national mental health development report (2017–2018) shows that 11%–15% of the people are in poor mental health, 44.9% are in mental

M. A. Jan and F. Khan (Eds.): BigIoT-EDU 2022, LNICST 467, pp. 92–103, 2023.
https://doi.org/10.1007/978-3-031-23944-1_11

sub-health, many people have prominent mental health problems, and the data show an increasing trend. According to statistics, suicide has become the main cause of death among teenagers aged 15–34, and many surveys show that the suicide rate of college students is 2–4 times that of their peers. As shown in Fig. 1. College Students' suicide will not only bring great trauma and loss to the family, but also cause a strong psychological impact on the surrounding students and friends, and bring serious adverse effects to the school and society [1]. In the four level work network system of mental health education. Timely and accurate crisis intervention is likely to save more lives. How to accurately identify the crisis, receive early warning in time and take effective measures is the key to realize psychological crisis intervention [2].

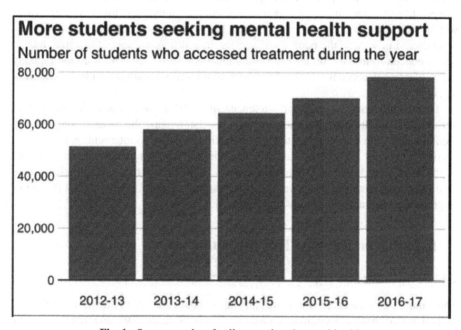

Fig. 1. Survey results of college students' mental health

As we deepen our understanding of this interdependence, it becomes more and more obvious that mental health is for individuals The vital overall welfare of society and the state. Unfortunately, in most colleges and universities in China, mental health and mental illness have not received the same attention as physical health. On the contrary, they have been largely ignored or ignored [3].

Universities and colleges basically achieve student management information [4]. However, most of the current information technology only stays in the use of basic information technology to collect, store and manage student information. In terms of psychological crisis screening and early warning, the research and application of deep mining the hidden correlation by using the accurate.

The development concept of College Students' mental health education in developed countries is more advanced than that in China, and the degree of development is also more mature than that in our country. First of all, it is mainly reflected in the expansion of the scope of mental health education. Mental health education not only focuses on students' inner spiritual world and consciousness, but also involves students' mental state, belief orientation, life attitude, physical health, and the relevant environment. Secondly, mental health education should not only adjust the treatment and counseling after the formation of mental health problems, but also pay more attention to the prevention of mental problems and guide the development of psychology in the direction of health and positive energy. Third, the output forms of mental health education should be diversified. It is not only limited to the process of mental health teachers' imparting knowledge in the course, but also carry out activities such as mental health talk bar, mental health coffee corner, mental workshop, mentoring post station, etc., organize students to go out of campus to participate in psychological drama competitions, participate in social public welfare activities, and improve their mental health status and quality in activities and practice and in serving the people and society. In addition, we should integrate mental health education into the process of professional education, improve the moral quality and professional academic level of teachers, and cultivate students with the charm of teachers' morality.

Due to students' suicide and violence, students' mental health problems have attracted the attention of the whole society. In recent years, the research on students' mental health data extraction methods and psychological crisis intervention models has become a hot spot for scientists at home and abroad. The data extraction method based on the survey data reflects the relationship between the factors that lead to students' psychological problems and the main factors that affect students' psychological problems. Improve the level and effect of psychotherapy [5].

2   Research on Decision Tree Algorithm

2.1   Decision Tree Description

The famous decision tree methods are cart and assistant. It is one of the most widely used inductive reasoning algorithms. A method of approximating discrete value objective function has good robustness to noisy data and can learn disjunctive expression. A decision tree is a classifier of instances (represented as eigenvectors). Nodes test features, edges represent each value of features, and leaf nodes are classified accordingly [6].

It can classify or predict unknown data, data preprocessing, data mining and so on. It usually includes two parts: tree generation and tree pruning. This paper will mainly discuss the generation algorithm of decision tree [7]. Continuous variables must be discretized to be learned. In this paper, the C45 decision tree algorithm is systematically applied and the information gain rate is taken as the segmentation index to solve the problem of multi-attribute bias when using information gain to select test attributes. The definition formula of information acquisition rate is:

$$C_j = t\{t_i | f(t_i) = C_j, 1 \leq i \leq n, t_i \in D\} \tag{1}$$

Figure 2 below shows the decision tree algorithm.

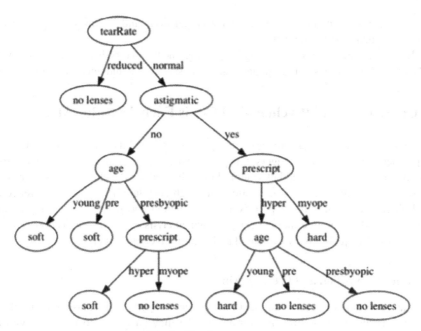

Fig. 2. Simple strategy tree

2.2 Application of Decision Tree in Mental Health Evaluation

Data collection and pretreatment are the basis of evaluation, which directly affects the quality of evaluation. SCL-90 has 90 self-evaluation factors, which are divided into 9 factors, including depression, anxiety, hostility, anxiety, prejudice and mental disease of body, compulsion and interpersonal relationship. Whether nine factors have been identified. These factors mainly reflect the patients' diet and sleep status. These points are defined as the tenth element of diet and sleep. Various factors reflect part of the patient's pain symptoms. The type of symptom distribution can be understood by factor score.

Physical disorders mainly include cardiovascular, gastrointestinal, respiratory and other physical symptoms, headache, back pain, muscle pain, anxiety and so on.

Compulsive symptoms mainly reflect carelessness. This idea is obviously redundant, but it can't get rid of the behavioral symptoms of impulse, behavior and general perception disorders. This is also reflected in this factor [8].

A person's receptivity is mainly manifested in his dissatisfaction and inferiority complex, especially compared with others. The typical causes of this symptom are inferiority complex, anxiety, obvious discomfort and self-esteem, as well as negative expectations in interpersonal relationships.

The main symptoms of depression are depression, decreased interest in life, lack of motivation, loss of vitality and so on. It also reflects depression, pessimism, cognition and physical feelings related to depression. It also includes thoughts about death and suicide.

Anxiety refers to anger, anxiety, tension, tension, and accompanying physical symptoms, such as shivering [9].

Hostility mainly comes from thoughts, feelings and behaviors that reflect the behavior of the enemy. It includes boredom, unconsciousness, conflict and uncontrollable nature.

3   Construction of Psychological Crisis Early Warning Model

The factors affecting the occurrence of students' psychological crisis are complex. From the perspective of student managers, this paper analyzes and studies the students' information that is often contacted but scattered in daily work as the characteristic attribute, and selects six significant characteristics with high correlation with the occurrence of psychological crisis through expert experience method and binary logistic regression analysis, The decision tree model of psychological crisis early warning is constructed, and the model is qualitatively evaluated and quantitatively tested [10].

3.1   Data Acquisition and Preprocessing

This paper investigates several student management experts and front-line counselors, and collects the types of student information that they have the most contact with in the work process and are scattered. After sorting and classifying these information, 17 related attributes are undergraduates from Beijing Forestry University, Taiyuan University of technology and Shanxi University of traditional Chinese medicine as the research samples, and collects a brand-new research data recognized by the respondents [11]. The data collection is carried out by means of online questionnaire; Through the results of family intimacy scale, we can know the living situation of students' native family, so as to obtain the relevant data of family relationship types.

In order to facilitate the analysis and research of data, it is necessary to standardize the value of attributes. Combined with the actual situation, all 17 attributes are assigned with user-defined values in this paper. In the table, "gender", "age", "major", "grade", "student cadre", "University Award", "University punishment", "achievement", "failure", "personality characteristics", "average number of school leave", "type of leave", "type of family location" are displayed 17 related attributes such as "family composition", "whether it is an only child", "family economy" and "family relationship" are taken as the research objects, and the characteristic attributes with high correlation with psychological crisis are selected through effective methods. The prediction goal is to judge whether a student has a psychological crisis. If so, the early warning result type is positive, represented by 1; otherwise, it is negative, represented by 0. The identification standard of whether there is a psychological crisis in the experimental data adopts the research results of major projects of the National Social Science Fund - individual psychological crisis warning tool. Through the score, it is judged that there is a psychological crisis if the score is greater than or equal to 14, and it is not if the score is less than 14.

3.2 Modeling Attribute Filtering

The psychological health problems of contemporary college students must be highly valued by the whole society. As the main position of cultivating talents, universities should also do a good job in education and guidance. We must attach great importance to mental health education in Colleges and universities. It has targeted special compulsory courses such as interpersonal relationship, emotion regulation, love psychology, life education and consumption spirit, so as to improve the ability of college students to resist mental diseases and the ability of communication between people, so that each student can consciously be responsible for their own behavior and body, and the health in daily study and life, and improve their mental health level. Establish a "home school medical school" linkage education mode, and build a "home school medical association" combined with education. At present, the vocational college has established a four level work network model of "school college class dormitory" and a mental health education model of "the progress of activity leaders and teaching consultation in the fourth quarter". Colleges and universities should further establish the linkage mechanism of mental health education departments, establish the concept of "educating all staff, cultivating people in the whole process and cultivating all aspects", mobilize all resources, and build a "home school medical association". Guided by the psychological counseling center of the college, the activities are carried out in cooperation with all departments and for all teachers and students of the school.

(1) Data whitening processing Since attribute data are assigned by category and belong to discrete numerical type, there is a great correlation between the data. The premise of binary logistic regression analysis must ensure that the samples are second-order independent and uncorrelated, so we choose to whiten the data first. Whitening, also known as bleaching or spheroidization, its main function is to reduce the correlation between features and make the covariance matrix of features calculated as 1. Using principal component analysis, the feature vector is obtained without data dimensionality reduction, and then the data matrix X is mapped to the new feature space through linear transformation to obtain a new data matrix, which can achieve the purpose of reducing feature correlation. Then, the square difference normalization of the new data matrix is carried out, and finally the whitened data matrix is obtained [12]. The whitening operation is implemented in Python language, and some key code statements are as follows:

```
X_ _ c = X- np. mean(X, 0)
sigma = np. cov(X, rowvar = False)
l,u = np. linalg. eigh(sigma)
X_ rot = np. dot(X_ _c, u)
p.allclose(np.cov(X_ rot.T), np. diag(np.diag(np.cov(X_ Tot.))))
X_ white = X_ rot / np. sqrt(1)
```

(2) Logistic regression analysis. The research goal of this paper is to build an early warning model of College Students' psychological crisis, and there are many attributes with weak correlation among the 17 attributes collected at present. Therefore,

according to the basic knowledge, relevant work experience and the suggestions of student management experts, first screen out eight attributes with high degree of routine or individualization and low research value, such as gender, age, major, grade, whether student cadre, whether awarded during university, whether punished and the average number of leave in the semester, Then, binary logistic regression analysis is carried out between the independent variable data and the predicted value of the remaining 9 attributes after whitening, excluding the redundant attributes with low correlation that do not enter the regression model, and determining the significant characteristic attributes that are finally used to construct the college students' psychological crisis early warning model. As shown in Fig. 3.

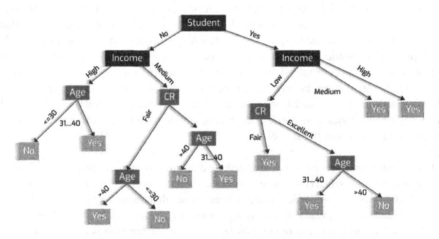

Fig. 3. Early warning model of college students' psychological crisis

3.3 Algorithm Evaluation

As one of the most widely used data mining technologies, decision tree algorithm includes many kinds of algorithms. The earliest decision tree algorithm was the CSL algorithm based on concept learning proposed by hunt et al. In the 1960s (Porter et al., 1989), which was based on Quinlan of the University of Sydney_ ID3 algorithm is proposed, and then C4 5 algorithm and cart algorithm, which have gradually become the two most commonly used classical decision tree algorithms.

$$I(s_1, s_2, .., s_n) = -\sum_{i=1}^{m} p_i \log_2(p_i) \tag{2}$$

C4. 5 algorithm (Matei et al., 2012) is an improved algorithm for the shortcomings of ID3 algorithm. It uses the information gain rate as the attribute selection standard. The larger the information gain rate, the more useful data in the attribute branch, which solves the problem of multi value bias in ID3 algorithm to a certain extent. In addition, it has processing ability for continuous attribute and attribute value vacancy samples, which can enhance the adaptability of data. C4. According to the generated decision tree, the algorithm can extract an if-then classification rule set, and each rule represents a path from the root node to the leaf node. Its disadvantage is that each attribute needs multiple logarithmic operations when calculating the information gain rate, and the data set needs multiple sequential scanning and sorting in the process of tree building. For large-scale data sets, the generation time of decision tree will be affected to a certain extent, resulting in low operation efficiency of the algorithm [13].

Cart algorithm, also known as classified regression tree algorithm, is a non parametric statistical method of binary tree. It uses iterative method to repeatedly establish binary tree from tree root. It selects the attribute with the minimum Gini partition index as the current node on each node of the decision tree, and recursively constructs the decision tree. The algorithm is suitable for the classification of discrete variables and continuous variables. The smaller the Gini coefficient, the smaller the heterogeneity of samples, and the better the segmentation effect The main advantage of cart algorithm is that logarithm operation is not involved in the tree building process, so it has fast calculation speed and high operation efficiency.

In addition to using the Ministry of education, it also established the "work plan for exploring special services for depression prevention and treatment" published on the official website of the National Health Commission last year, and mentioned that every ordinary high school and university will include the screening of depression into the content of students' physical examination. For example, Shihezi University has attached great importance to mental health education for many years. With the advancement of the subject, college students' concept of mental health has been significantly improved, and the concept of seeking help has also been greatly improved. Establishing mental health courses is only one of the relevant measures. Colleges and universities need to do a lot of things to carry out mental health education for college students faster. In promoting the in-depth development of College Students' mental health education during the period of prevention and control, the theme of "5.25" is "concentric war epidemic, healthy growth".

By organizing college teachers to participate in the backbone training class of College Students' mental health education, the professional level of mental health education between teachers and students of Hebei communications vocational and technical college has been further improved. Through the investigation of students' mental health status, we can understand the psychological state of students in the class and grasp the psychological state of each student in time; Through carrying out caring and heart to heart assistance activities, students with family diseases or family diseases during the epidemic were rehearsed comprehensively. Organize counselors and professional teachers to continue to provide psychological support network counseling services to provide students with psychological support and self-help resources. In combination with the actual situation, the "branches" of all departments also used various new media platforms to push articles on the popularization of College Students' mental health knowledge and publicity and education through flexible and diverse forms, and held various online interactive activities. Strengthening the promotion and popularization of mental health knowledge has created a strong mental health atmosphere and improved students' mental awareness and self-help level of mental health.

4 Research on Mental Health Intelligence Evaluation of College Students Based on Decision Tree Algorithm

4.1 Mental Health Intelligence Evaluation of College Students

Improve the curriculum system of mental health education, integrate the mental health education curriculum into the overall teaching plan of the school in combination with the actual situation, standardize the subject setting, and provide public compulsory courses for freshmen. We should fully advocate all students to carry out elective and auxiliary training courses of mental health education, so as to achieve full coverage of mental health education for college students. "Second, carry out publicity activities. Third, strengthen advisory services. Third, strengthen consultation and services. The outline requires optimizing the psychological counseling service platform, strengthening the construction of hardware facilities, establishing psychological development consulting rooms, psychological evaluation offices, positive psychological experience centers, group activity rooms and comprehensive quality training rooms. Actively build a mental health education and counseling service system that combines education guidance, counseling and self-help, as well as self-help and others. Fourth, strengthen crisis prevention. Fourth, strengthen crisis prevention measures. The outline requires improving the psychological crisis prevention and rapid response mechanism, establishing a four-level early warning and prevention system for schools, hospital departments, classes and dormitories, and unblocking the access from school mental health education consulting institutions to school hospitals. And the psychological crisis transfer green channel of mental health professional organizations. The comparison of mental health education between China and the United States, both China and the United States, regard mental health education as an important part of student affairs "student affairs". In China, universities strive to achieve comprehensive coverage of mental health education by setting up compulsory or elective courses, conducting Freshmen's mental health publicity and psychological tests, carrying out mass mental health education activities, and establishing a class spiritual committee system.

College students are an active and healthy group in the social population structure. Chinese and foreign scholars have always regarded college students as the main sample of mental health research. In recent ten years, the research results of College Students' mental health in China have shown a gradual upward trend, and the research methods are empirical research and speculative research. Guo Yongyu once commented on the advantages and disadvantages of these two research models, and pointed out pointedly: "the research of psychology lacks humanistic spirit, and the research of pedagogy lacks scientific spirit".

In the process of mining, it is found that somatization and hostility play an important decisive role in college students' mental health problems. When students have healthy somatization, the probability of mental health diseases is small. Only when hostility and psychosis are at the mild level, students may have obvious mental diseases and need timely intervention. When students' somatization factors are mild hostility and psychotic factors, they play a decisive role in students' mental health. In this case, when students have mild hostility, there will be obvious mental diseases; When hostility is moderate, the value of psychotic factor plays a decisive role in the final result. When psychotic factor is healthy, it means that the psychological problem is not obvious. When psychotic factor is moderate, it means that there is serious psychological disease; When hostility is severe, it indicates serious mental illness. Therefore, it is suggested that psychological educators in universities should focus on the scores of somatization, hostility and psychoticism when analyzing each factor score.

4.2 Intelligent Evaluation Experiment

China pays more and more attention to the research of data mining, and the development of data mining technology is also changing with each passing day. China encourages scholars in major universities to carry out research in the field of data mining. Since the 20th century, many researchers have used the data accumulated in the psychological evaluation system of colleges and universities to carry out data mining, and made a lot of relevant research. For example, Qi Wenjuan and others applied association rule mining to college students' mental health evaluation data in the article "Research on the application of association rule mining in college students' mental health evaluation system". First, preprocess the original data, and then use Clementine 12.0 as the mining platform to establish a multidimensional association rule mining model for college students' psychology; Then, taking the 2011 students' psychological test data of a university in Fujian Province as the source data of the mining model, this paper analyzes the correlation between the psychological symptoms of six student information attributes and nine attribute dimensions, such as gender and only child. Through the analysis of the mining results, we can have a deeper understanding of students' mental health problems, and provide a basis for the planning and decision-making of College Students' mental health education. In the article "application and research of psychological data mining system for higher vocational students", Zhao Xiaoyan used ID3 decision tree algorithm and Apriori association rule algorithm to mine and process the data of students' psychological problems, and explored the hidden relationship between psychological symptoms and attributes, and then analyzed the results, based on which he proposed new methods and ways of thinking to solve and prevent higher vocational students' psychological problems.

Looking at the views of scholars at home and abroad and the current situation of College Students' mental health research in China in the past decade, we can see that college students' mental health still needs in-depth research from theory to practice. From the perspective of social development and people's needs in real life, it is an indisputable fact that mental health research has penetrated into all fields of basic psychology and applied psychology. Mental health research involves all human psychological phenomena, including psychological process, psychological state and personality.

The data processing time results are shown in Fig. 4.

The data processing time of this system is always lower than that of the other two systems. With the increasing amount of data, the data processing time of the three systems changes. The data processing time increases sharply with the increase of information,

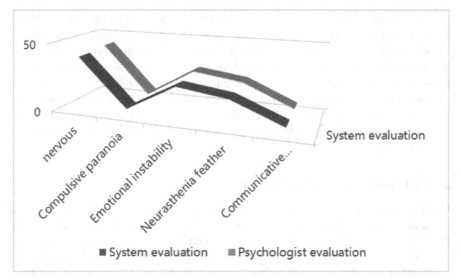

Fig. 4. Data processing time results

and fluctuates greatly The stability is poor, the increase of data processing time of the system in this paper is small, the curve is smooth, the stability is good, and the amount of data reaches 5 × After 103 Gb, the data processing time gradually tends to be stable, which proves that the system in this paper has high data processing efficiency and strong stability.

5 Conclusion

For the selected students with psychological confusion, individual psychological counseling is carried out in the psychological counseling room, with the goal of overcoming psychological symptoms and promoting self maturity. In terms of consultation methods, the visitor centered strategy is used to give psychological support, pay attention to changing cognition, and adopt a variety of special psychotherapy technologies according to different situations, such as reasonable emotional therapy, systematic desensitization and interpersonal training, make detailed consultation case records, and evaluate the consultation effect in combination with the actual performance of life and learning and smhrs score.

Acknowledgements. Heilongjiang Province Philosophy and Social Science research planning project (Grant No. 21EDB078).

References

1. Sun, D.: Construction of evaluation-index system of college teachers' intelligent teaching ability under the background of educational informationization 2.0 (2021). https://doi.org/10. 1007/978-3-030-51556-0_77

2. Guo, S.X., Lin, L.: Research on voluntary intelligent reporting system of college entrance examination based on big data technology (2021). https://doi.org/10.1007/978-3-030-67871-5_10
3. Su, S., Qu, W., Wu, Y., et al.: Intelligent evaluation scheme of ideological and political education quality of college english course based on AHP under the background of big data. In: 2021 6th International Conference on Smart Grid and Electrical Automation (ICSGEA) (2021)
4. Min, J.: Research on the application of computer intelligent proofreading system in college English teaching. J. Phys: Conf. Ser. **1915**(3), 032078 (2021)
5. Wu, Q.: College English learning and evaluation management system based on intelligent classroom. In: 2021 6th International Conference on Smart Grid and Electrical Automation (ICSGEA) (2021)
6. Song, B., Li, X.M.: Research on intelligent question answering system based on college enrollment. J. Phys: Conf. Ser. **1948**(1), 012062 (2021)
7. Wa, N.J.: The application of intelligent speech recognition technology in the tone correction of college piano teaching. J. Phys: Conf. Ser. **1852**(2), 022086 (2021)
8. Li, K., Yu, W.: A mental health assessment model of college students using intelligent technology. Wirel. Commun. Mob. Comput. **2021**(1), 1–10 (2021)
9. Zhang, X., Wang, C., Chen, X., et al.: Research on holographic image and hierarchical classification evaluation of power suppliers based on intelligent system. J. Phys: Conf. Ser. **1802**(3), 032025 (2021)
10. Zhang, X., Yang, L., Zhang, L., et al.: Research on intelligent evaluation and monitoring method for cost of transmission and transformation project. IOP Conf. Ser. Earth Environ. Sci. **645**(1), 012062 (2021)
11. Qin, L.: Research on the construction of evaluation system of intelligent classroom teaching quality in colleges and universities under the information technology environment. J. Phys: Conf. Ser. **1744**(3), 032164 (2021)
12. Research on intelligent subcontracting strategy based on the value evaluation model of waste copper cable. Manage. Sci. Eng. **10**(1), 77–82 (2021)
13. Jia, Y.: Research on the practice of college English classroom teaching based on Internet and artificial intelligence. J. Intell. Fuzzy Syst. **1**, 1–10 (2021)

Research on Interactive Mode of Drama Performance Based on VR Technology

Yan Zhang[✉]

Wuchang University of Technology, Wuhan 430223, Hubei, China
6612358@qq.com

Abstract. With the continuous development of China's social economy, drama performance has gradually appeared in people's life. The emergence of drama performance not only brings a lot of fun to people's life, but also has been widely favored by people in the continuous promotion. In the drama performance, the audience's interaction when watching the works and the grasp of the actors' performance rhythm have an important and decisive effect on the drama performance. In the process of drama performance, drama performers need to grasp the rhythm of interaction with the audience. Therefore, the research on the interactive mode of drama performance based on VR technology is expected to help drama actors better master the interactive rhythm with the audience.

Keywords: Virtual technology · Theatrical performance · Interactive mode

1 Introduction

As a stage performing art that achieves the purpose of narration in various forms such as language, action, dance and music, drama performance has been more and more popular in recent years. For drama performance, whether the final effect of drama performance can achieve the expected effect mainly depends on whether the accurate interaction rhythm of both parties is grasped. In addition, for drama performance, if there is no audience, dramatic art will lose meaningful creation and performance. Alkach Nikolayevich once said that in drama performance, rhythm not only controls the actions of actors, but also enables actors to control the emotions of the audience through rhythm. Drama performance is like a magician, which can put the audience into a hypnotic state to some extent. It can be seen that the interaction and rhythm of both sides in drama performance are very important, and relevant personnel must pay attention to it. This paper will also study the interactive mode of drama performance based on Virtual Reality (VR).

With the development of contemporary science and technology and in order to meet the needs of the future information society, people must improve the interface ability between people and the information society and improve people's ability to understand information. People not only need to be able to observe the results of information processing externally through the window of print output or display screen, but also need to

M. A. Jan and F. Khan (Eds.): BigIoT-EDU 2022, LNICST 467, pp. 104–109, 2023.
https://doi.org/10.1007/978-3-031-23944-1_12

be able to participate in the information processing environment through human vision, hearing, touch, body, gesture or password, so as to obtain the personal experience [1]. This information processing system is no longer based on a single-dimensional digital information space, but on a multi-dimensional information space, and in a comprehensive and integrated environment with the combination of qualitative and quantitative, perceptual knowledge and rational knowledge. Virtual reality technology will be the key technology to support this multi-dimensional information space. In the final analysis, virtual reality technology is to change the computer from good at dealing with digital single-dimensional information to good at dealing with multi-dimensional information that people can feel and contact in the process of thinking, in addition to digital information.

2   VR Technology

2.1   Basic Principles of Virtual Technology

At the bottom of the virtualization scheme is the physical host server. To virtualize these physical host servers, a virtualization layer needs to be run on them. The virtualization layer runs directly on the hardware. The virtualization layer virtualizes the processor, memory, memory and resources into multiple virtual machines. Each virtual machine installs its own operating system, which is isolated from each other, and regards the underlying hardware platform as its own resources. But in fact, it is the virtualization layer that creates this illusion for them. Therefore, the virtualization layer is the support of the virtual architecture.

Virtual technology is a method to allocate resources from a logical point of view rather than a physical point of view. For users, virtualization technology realizes the separation between hardware and software. Users do not need to consider the specific hardware implementation, but just need to run their own systems and software on the environment provided by the virtualization layer. And when these systems and software run, they have nothing to do with the actual physical platform (processor, memory, memory and resources). After the virtualization software is installed on a physical host server, several operating systems can be installed on it. Each operating system is independent of each other at the same time and runs independently without affecting each other. This is different from the traditional method of installing several operating systems on a separate server and running only one operating system at the same time. In this way, the investment cost of hardware is greatly saved, the purchased hardware equipment is reduced, the floor space of the computer room is reduced, and the capital is greatly saved.

The problem with current virtualization solutions is that not all hardware can support virtualization well. Older x86 processors produce different results for specific instructions depending on the execution range [2]. This creates a problem because hypervisors should only be executed in one of the most protected areas. For this reason, virtualization solutions such as Vware scan the code to be executed in advance, so as to replace these instructions with some trap instructions, so that the hypervisor can handle them correctly. Xen can support a collaborative virtualization method, which does not require any modification, because the client knows that it is virtualizing and has modified it.

Virtual reality technology is a system composed of a series of hardware systems and software systems, as shown in Fig. 1.

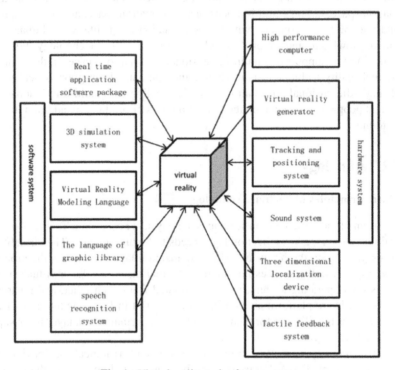

Fig. 1. Virtual reality technology system

2.2 Characteristics of Virtual Reality Technology

Virtual reality, also known as spiritual environment technology, uses three-dimensional graphics generation technology, multi-sensor interaction technology and high-resolution display technology to generate a three-dimensional realistic virtual environment. Users can enter the virtual space and become a member of the virtual environment for real-time interaction by wearing special helmets, data gloves and other sensing devices, or by using keyboard, mouse and other input devices, Perceive and operate various objects in the virtual world, so as to obtain immersive feeling and experience.

Virtual reality technology has the following three main characteristics:

(1) The virtual environment created by immersion can make students feel "immersive" and make them believe that people do exist in the virtual environment, and it can play a role from beginning to end in the operation process, just like the real objective world.

(2) Interactivity is that in the virtual environment, students interact with tasks and things in the virtual environment as in the real environment, in which students

are the subject of interaction, virtual objects are the object of interaction, and the interaction between subjects and objects is all-round.

(3) Imagination is virtual reality. It is an activity that can inspire people's creativity. It should not only enable students immersed in this environment to obtain new instructions and improve their perceptual and rational understanding, but also enable students to produce new ideas.

These three reflect the key characteristics of the virtual reality system, that is, the full interaction between the system and people, as shown in Fig. 2.

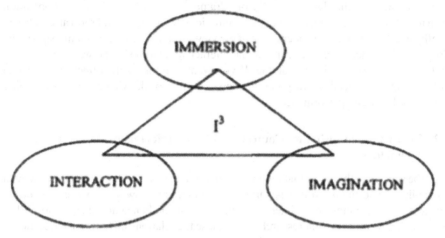

Fig. 2. Virtual technology features

3   Research on Interactive Mode of Drama Performance

3.1   Interaction of Viewing and Acting Relationship in Drama Performance

The interaction of watching and Acting Relationship in drama performance mainly refers to the transformation of the audience from a single information receiver to a person who actively receives and sends information. The transformation of the interaction between the two sides will also have a great impact on the drama to a great extent. In the process of viewing and performance interaction, the audience will change from the previous single viewing to the main body in the whole process. As a collective behavior in drama performance, watching is the main factor that can attract people to interact in drama [3]. Therefore, there is an inseparable relationship between the two in the whole process of interaction. The famous dramatist Ma aislin once said: "in drama performance, the triangular response in drama has a very important impact on the effect of drama presentation". This function can be mainly reflected in a common feeling formed between the audience during the performance. In the past frame stage drama performance, the triangular response relationship can be mainly reflected in the following aspects: first, the response of the audience to the actors. The feedback relationship between audience and drama actor is studied through theory and practice. When the audience reacts to the actors, such as clapping, crying, etc., the reflected information will have an impact on the actors, and finally affect the actors' performance. Second, the audience's response to space. The response of the audience to the space will also have an impact on the performance effect of the actors, which can be mainly reflected in that when the space is large and there are few people, this situation will seriously affect the mood and performance of the actors. Third, the audience's response to the audience. In the drama performance, the characteristics of the audience are mostly unconscious. In this process, the audience's emotions seem to be hypnotized. Most of the audience will follow the steps of the actors, and even devote themselves to the illusory drama performance in the tacit cooperation with the actors, so the collective audience's emotions are rendered and form an emotional confluence. The above is the interaction of the viewing and performing relationship in the drama performance. It can be seen that the interactive relationship between the viewing and performing parties is inseparable. If you want to improve the effect of the drama performance, you need to grasp the interactive rhythm of the viewing and performing parties in the drama performance.

3.2   Interaction and Rhythm Control in Drama Performance Based on VR Technology

It can be seen from the above that for drama performance, the rhythm interaction between the audience and the performer is particularly important. Now how to grasp the effectiveness of the rhythm of the interaction between the audience and the performer has become the focus of relevant researchers. Because the relationship between the audience and the actors is very delicate, we should pay attention to some points in the interaction and rhythm of the two sides of drama performance. First, because the audience's response will eventually be reflected in the actors, in the process of drama performance, the actors need to properly adjust the performance rhythm according to the emotions of the audience, which is a test for the actors and requires sophisticated experience. VR technology can provide a good virtual training environment for the actors [4]. For example, VR technology is used to simulate the depression of the audience in the drama performance, and the actors need to adopt a more enthusiastic performance method to drive the audience and let the audience keep up with their own performance. Second, because dramatic actors have a certain reliance on the audience, so do the audience. Therefore, in terms of the interactive rhythm of drama performance, according to the characteristics of mutual dependence between the two sides, the two sides can resonate and contrast when talking to each other. In this process, what the drama actors need to do is to adjust their emotions and bring the audience's thinking and emotions to the direction of the final requirements of the plot, so that the audience can not only follow the ideas of the performers, And it can improve the effect of drama performance.

4   Conclusion

As a stage performing art that achieves the purpose of narration in various forms such as language, action, dance and music, drama performance has gradually attracted more and more attention with the continuous development of China's economy. For drama performance, the relationship between the audience and drama actors is mutual. Therefore, in the process of drama performance, drama actors need to grasp the effectiveness of the interaction rhythm of both sides. Only in this way can they better attract the interest of the audience and improve the overall effect of drama performance.

References

1. Chunhong, Y.: Rhythm and emotional expression of lines in drama performance. Popular Literature and Art **03**, 168 (2014)
2. Liqiang, S.: Virtualization technology promotes data center revolution. China Education Network, 32–33 (2009)
3. Yang, X.: The significance of subtext to characterization in drama performance. Drama House **03**, 32 (2015)
4. Lanbin, L.: On the characteristics of body language and its role in drama performance. Science and Technology Innovation Guide **19**, 214 (2008)

Research on Language Learning and Cross-Cultural Function Based on Mobile Digital Platform

Qunfang Bai[✉]

Yunnan Land and Resources Vocational College, Kunming 650000, Yunnan, China
baiqunfang@hotmail.com

Abstract. From the perspective of linguistics and cross-cultural communication, this paper analyzes three theoretical problems about confusion and anxiety in cross-cultural communication and language learning, namely pragmatic reasoning, cultural hypothesis, and the degree of confusion and anxiety. With the increasing use of digital mobile platform, more and more teachers begin to pay attention to applying the highly interactive course app based on this platform to the actual teaching process. Therefore, cross-cultural communicators and language learners must constantly expand language and cultural knowledge, enhance signal sensitivity and desire for communication and learning, and improve their intercultural adaptation skills. Language teachers should also pay enough attention to confusion and anxiety, and help students control and reduce confusion and anxiety when necessary.

Keywords: Language learning · Digital platform · Cross-cultural communication

1 Introduction

At present, with the continuous progress of science and technology, language learning and cross-cultural function are facing more opportunities. Digital upgrading is an important basis for language learning and cross-cultural function to move forward in the information age. In the 14th five year plan and the 2035 outline, the Chinese government specifically talked about "accelerating digital development and building a digital China", encouraged the development of high-tech industries, advocated language learning and cross-cultural functions, absorbed new technologies, independent innovation, transformation and upgrading. For language learning and cross-cultural function, digitization has become the core competitiveness [1]. Then, in the face of the characteristics of strong individual, strong link and common ecology in organization and management, how to become more digital, intelligent and humanized has become a research topic of many language learning and cross-cultural functions. The influence of culture on communication is shown in Fig. 1 below.

M. A. Jan and F. Khan (Eds.): BigIoT-EDU 2022, LNICST 467, pp. 110–120, 2023.
https://doi.org/10.1007/978-3-031-23944-1_13

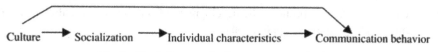

Culture ——▶ Socialization ——▶Individual characteristics ——▶ Communication behavior

Fig. 1. The influence of culture on communication

The mobile digital platform deeply integrates technology and business, and helps language learning and cross-cultural functions to carry out digital transformation through intelligence, customization and mobility. Configuring different application modules according to the business needs of language learning and cross-cultural functions can help language learning and cross-cultural functions break the "information data island" and improve the data processing ability, internal management ability and business collaboration ability, so as to further release the efficiency of language learning and cross-cultural functions. In this process of transformation and upgrading, choosing to cooperate with professional mobile digital platform service providers can enable language learning and cross-cultural functions to obtain high-quality professional services. Workplus, the privatized mobile digital platform of hengtuo high tech, combines instant messaging, mobile office and business collaboration to help language learning and cross-cultural functions achieve high security and strong controllable whole scene cooperation, and provide more efficient, stable and reliable services for language learning and cross-cultural functions.

Workplus free core portal platform, language learning and cross-cultural function level privatization deployment, to meet the needs of different scenarios of language learning and cross-cultural functions. Help language learning and cross-cultural functions upgrade from office platform to ecological collaboration platform, provide a base and four platforms, realize information integration, intelligent collaboration, application integration, customization and personalization, improve communication and collaboration efficiency, and bring "ecology" into the scope of linguistic learning and cross-cultural functions under their own control.

Intelligent collaboration: it supports business collaboration, process collaboration and data collaboration, such as attendance check-in, to-do approval and domain background management, meets the needs of users for cross time and space processing, and realizes data transmission and information synchronization between different terminal devices, cross department channel integration, cross role and cross time and space business process customization and business processing, It has greatly improved users' sense of experience and cooperation efficiency, helped language learning and cross-cultural functions of different scales realize digital lean management and control, and promoted the efficient cooperation between language learning and cross-cultural function organizations [2]. It is also through efficient, comprehensive and complete product advantages and product functions that cloud space can be fully applied to multiple scenarios, including government and enterprise industries, education industries and medical industries. In terms of government and enterprises, with rich application resources and safe data management schemes, it provides large-capacity storage space for the government industry and supports the flow of multi-form documents such as Im, email and tasks; In education, it can deeply combine data security sharing, distance teaching and education industry to improve efficiency; In terms of medical treatment, it can safely store and ensure the improvement of data, and promote the development of intelligent and online hospital management through massive applications.

2   Related Work

2.1   Digital Platform

Under the background of the new era of digitization, the development of platform is accelerating, and the development of mobile Internet makes Internet access everywhere, so that people everywhere can be connected virtually. Wireless interconnection has stimulated the rapid rise, development and use of the platform.

The development and wide popularization of information technology, Internet technology, computer chips and software operating systems have strongly supported the rise of digital platform, making the platform enter a period of rapid development.

The platform is sweeping the world with its rapid development speed and unexpected development scale. Digital technology is a new driving force for future economic development. The digital economy based on bytes and bits will make replication and reorganization easier. In the future, any person or company is likely to establish or transfer their language learning and cross-cultural functions to this digital platform. The proliferating digital platform will be the future economy It is even the core of language learning and cross-cultural function, government and national operation. The development direction of digital platform is shown in Fig. 2 below.

Fig. 2. Development direction of digital platform

With the development of digital economy, we have witnessed the unprecedented spread of technological and social changes all over the world in the past two decades, especially the ubiquity of smart phones and networks [3]. The wind of change is changing our traditional way of life and work, bringing infinite possibilities. From the beginning of the 1990s to the beginning of the 21st century, the revolutionary innovations brought by mobile communication technology and Internet technology, such as catalysts, made the change go deep into every day of people's daily life. 20 years ago, people could not imagine the ways of communication, travel, shopping, social networking, entertainment, consumption and relationship building today. The digital economy platform technology is shown in Fig. 3 below.

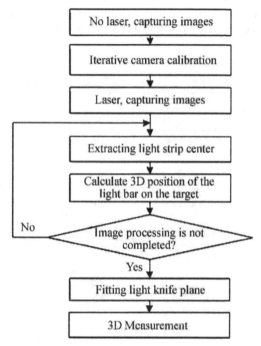

Fig. 3. Digital economy platform technology

Like the technology platform and product platform, the digital platform can improve the reuse rate of the platform through modularization. The biggest difference is that the digital platform is composed of a set of extended code based on information technology and software system [4]. The code forms a code base in the form of modules, and multiple modules become interoperable core functions through appropriate platform operation mode and governance structure, Effectively help the platform organize and coordinate the provision of complementary products and services and technology development. Compared with other platforms, the digital platform generates strong prediction and analysis ability through algorithm driving and data combustion, can provide more personalized services and can predict the general trend. With its technical capability, digital platform can gather a large number of different types of users and services more quickly.

2.2 Language and Culture

Developing the corresponding course teaching application based on the digital mobile platform can introduce students into the learning process by means of strong interactive function and personal experience, and change passive learning into active learning, so as to play a greater role in the teaching field.

Communicators also have different cultural, ethnic and linguistic backgrounds. The term "race" is used here as an inclusive term to refer to the various characteristics of communicators, which are related to their uniqueness as a nation. In many aspects of different ethnic backgrounds, the author would like to refer to language and cultural positions. Running the application is shown in Fig. 4 below.

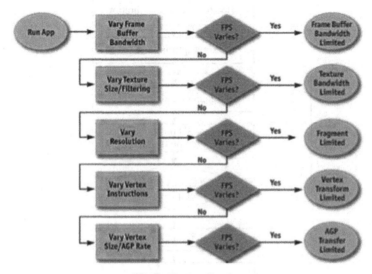

Fig. 4. Run application

Transfer is a psychological term used to describe how a learning event affects subsequent learning events. The transfer can be positive or negative. That is, the previously learned event can promote (positive transfer) or inhibit (negative transfer) the learning of the second event.

Language transfer refers to the transfer of the learning of one language skill to another language. For example, learning Spanish will help Spanish learners learn English reading. Trilingual studies show that the more similar the language structures of the two languages are, the greater the possibility of transfer. Similarly, the more similar the language structures of the two languages are, the lower the degree of uncertainty and anxiety experienced by language users [5]. For example, for a Chinese learner with a low level of English and Japanese, the degree of uncertainty and anxiety in dealing with Japanese transcripts may be lower than when he reads the English version, because there are more similarities between Japanese and Chinese than between English and Chinese.

In a deeper sense, the degree of uncertainty and anxiety is related to the difference between the culture within the group and the culture from which strangers come.

In other words, the greater the cultural differences, the higher the level of anxiety and uncertainty everyone will experience. (ibid.) for example, Canadian tourists traveling in a small town in the United States may find a basically acceptable guest house environment. Due to the similarity of language and culture, uncertainty and anxiety may be at a low level. On the other hand, the same town may be less sensitive to tourists from little-known and culturally different places such as asturki or Kenya. As shown in Fig. 5 below, there are linguistic and cultural differences.

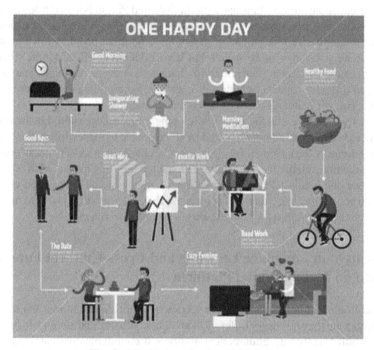

Fig. 5. Linguistic and cultural differences

2.3   Cultural Communication

Alphabetic language is like some process oriented computer programs. Where the requirements change, I directly change the code, while Chinese is more elegant. The grammatical functions are encapsulated into regular Chinese characters. If you need to use it, you can directly "call" a Chinese character and dismantle it when you run out of it. Therefore, from the perspective of use, Chinese naturally has stronger stability, efficiency and natural grammatical standardization.

The reason why we usually don't feel obvious Chinese grammar is that, on the one hand, we are native speakers, on the other hand, Chinese grammar is attached to Chinese characters, and the grammatical rules are naturally hidden in the combination rules of word and sentence making.

However, in any case, it is difficult for us to say that a language is better or worse in an absolute sense, because the advantages and disadvantages of some language features may appear differently in the context of different time scales, and languages will affect each other.

In ancient times, due to the constraints of transportation, science and technology and communication, alphabetic languages were indeed developing according to their own independent paths, with little influence on each other. But now this estrangement has been broken [6]. At present, although there are no natural simple symbols in Chinese for people to use, people are very familiar with English, and Pinyin is also introduced. Some characteristics that Chinese does not have will not affect people's behavior patterns.

I want to emphasize that language cannot directly affect people's intelligence and make someone smarter or more stupid, but it will definitely affect people's behavior patterns, because languages with different characteristics have different learning and use costs in different aspects, which will make people consciously or unconsciously make some behavior choices when using language tools.

Personally, I believe that the future development of Chinese should maintain those excellent characteristics and not be fooled by some people to make alphabetization. Letters are not things at the writing level. The language characteristics of Chinese determine that letters are not suitable for the language characteristics of Chinese. However, in our daily life, we can boldly use the letters in other languages, and make good use of the letters to express some logical relations (because they are simple and easy to mark), but we can't rub the letters into the Chinese kernel as a plug-in function.

3   Research on Language Learning and Cross-Cultural Function Based on Mobile Digital Platform

This paper holds that language ability, expectations of different cultures and languages and group gap are the reasons for different degrees of confusion and anxiety. In particular, language ability (including grammatical ability and communicative language ability) seriously affects the pragmatic reasoning ability and cultural understanding ability of communicators and language learners, which has become the key factor of confusion and anxiety.

Mobile Internet technology has the advantages of openness, sharing and interaction. This advantage is the best way to connect users in the eyes of language learning and cross-cultural functions. Language learning and cross-cultural functions can build communication channels for users, cooperate with b-end users at the first level, connect the upstream and downstream of the supply chain, and listen to the voice of C-end users through Internet data at the second level, so as to establish a stable user pool and drive the improvement of business operation. The smart digital mobile platform is built on the mobile Internet technology, which brings the advantages of mobile Internet technology into the bag. Through digital operation, it supports language learning and cross-cultural multi-functional system service governance, integrated management [7]. With the help of data visualization, it can catch all the traffic calls, server storage, interface debugging time and integrated system through operation visualization, Organize and present the data of access layer, application layer and data layer to realize the digital operation system.

In the engineering field, especially in the manufacturing industry, the importance of sharing design knowledge has been widely recognized, which inevitably requires engineers to share product design knowledge effectively. Like the knowledge of data level and the value of physical quantity in computer-aided design, the sharing of functional knowledge is also very important.

However, in the current application environment, this kind of knowledge is implicit in the data level knowledge. Even the explicit description knowledge is distributed and scattered in the documents written in natural language. The query of knowledge depends on the search of keywords, which makes the technical documents unable to be reused effectively. In addition, a lot of knowledge only exists in the designer's mind. These knowledge are usually unspeakable and highly subjective, and the description of knowledge is highly dependent on the equipment as the design object, so it is difficult to use it flexibly in the design of other equipment.

Therefore, a knowledge description system supporting cross domain sharing of design knowledge is needed. Especially in the systematic description of functional knowledge, we need a viewpoint concept to capture the object concept and a general functional concept to represent the function of artifacts, so that the subjective tacit knowledge can be expressed as conceptual explicit knowledge, so as to achieve the interoperability, sharing and reuse of knowledge. Mizoguchi laboratory designed and developed an ontology framework of functional knowledge. Figure 6 below shows the functional model framework.

In terms of language learning and cross-cultural functions, the application of smart digital mobile platform has really helped the development of language learning and cross-cultural functions, including internal accurate decision-making, better improving work efficiency and improving performance [8]. I believe that the application of Zhishu mobile platform will bring more benefits to more language learning and cross-cultural functions in the future, and always cooperate better with language learning and cross-cultural functions to achieve win-win cooperation!

Intelligent cloud space has become an indispensable part of everyone's life. Almost all data related to life and work are stored in virtual cloud space, and cloud space products with high security, high practicability and high applicability are very important to users. Based on the powerful cloud data management capability of the mobile cloud, the cloud space products of the mobile cloud not only ensure that there is no speed limit for upload and download, but also aggregate a large number of applications by taking the language learning and cross-cultural function collaborative management scene as the entrance, which can help the language learning and cross-cultural function to quickly build an information support system, A language learning and cross-cultural functional application aggregation platform for users in the whole industry.

Moreover, cloud space also has powerful product functions. The first is organization and management. Unified address book presentation, clear organizational structure, support the team to easily reach and efficiently realize interconnection; The second is data management [9]. Provide professional language learning and cross-cultural network disk services, safe storage, global sharing, flexible operation, covering the whole scene

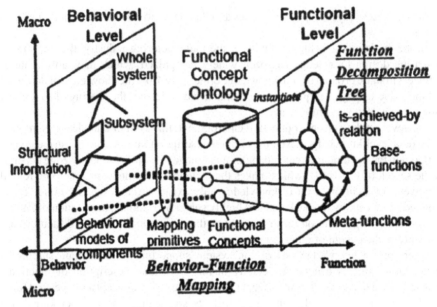

Fig. 6. Functional model framework

of document processing; The third is information collaboration. Integrate IM, schedule, meeting and other functions, connect language learning with cross-cultural functional scenarios, reduce communication costs and comprehensively improve cooperation efficiency; The fourth is mass applications. It can provide a large number of language learning and cross-cultural function application services, covering common application scenarios of language learning and cross-cultural functions, flexible configuration and open access.

4   Cultural Factors

If they are not proficient in the target language, they will not be able to understand each other and express their views; Without a deep understanding of the target culture, all parties are unable to explain and evaluate events in different intercultural situations; Without culturally sensitive knowledge, the parties cannot learn to reveal the implied non central "lens" or assumptions they use for cross-cultural phenomena [10]. Therefore, "knowledge" here refers to the comprehensive acquisition and in-depth understanding of the second language and its cultural and code sensitivity through conscious learning, personal experience and observation. With the improvement of second language ability and cross-cultural sensitivity, communicators are more able to reduce or manage uncertainty anxiety and anxiety (Table 1).

For cross-cultural communicators and second language learners, they should be exposed to the knowledge of new language and new culture. Before entering the target culture, they must understand the target culture as much as possible. At the same time, they must develop sensitivity to diversity. Code sensitivity refers to the use of spoken and

Table 1. Uncertainty and anxiety levels of students with positive and negative expectations

	Students with positive expectation	Students with negative expectation	All subjects
Subject number	58	32	90
Percentage of the whole subjects	64.4%	35.6%	100%
Mean score of uncertainty and anxiety	71.9	85.4	76.7

non-verbal language appropriate to the individual's culture or common cultural norms you communicate. Communicators and second language learners must be sensitive to different cultures and be ready to adapt to different cultural norms.

Motivational factors

"Motivation" in cross-cultural conflict refers to our cognitive and emotional tendencies when communicating with different people. The impact of a person's view of a second language and its culture on cross-cultural uncertainty and anxiety. This is "motivation" "Is a person's expectation of cross-cultural communication. With positive expectations, a person is more willing or inclined to engage in a new language and culture, and more confident in dealing with the upcoming cross-cultural conflicts or setbacks [11]. Therefore, communicators and second language learners must cultivate a strong interest in the new culture and d have positive expectations for cross-cultural communication and learning.

Interactive skills help us communicate effectively and appropriately in specific situations, and help to improve the ability of cross-cultural communication. Low uncertainty avoidance culture pays less attention to ambiguity and uncertainty, and has a higher tolerance for different views. Communicators should learn to observe and tolerate differences. At the same time, participants in cross-cultural situations need to practice supportive communication behavior. Supportive behaviors, such as affinity and the ability to identify with others' positions, can encourage successful cross-cultural communication [12]. Defensive behavior affects effectiveness.

Finally, when students have uncertainty and anxiety, teachers should give feedback and help when necessary. Teachers can allow students to use foreign languages with imperfect performance and give meaningful and sincere praise to students. Teachers can also help students diagnose the specific causes of uncertainty and anxiety and put forward feasible solutions.

5 Conclusion

To sum up, mobile learning has great prospects. Language learners have a real interest in learning interesting, updated and real materials. Rich multimedia learning content creates a comprehensive learning environment for learning, and language learning in context becomes feasible. This helpful learning system can enable learners to obtain the information in the dictionary as soon as possible and improve their understanding and listening level. Text annotation can help learners understand the cultural background and language difficulties in time, and support learners to create and manage their own learning scope, and even achieve seamless learning.

As a research field, mobile learning has promising prospects. There are many different methods, theories and practices in the relevant literature. If these definitions, methods and theories are discussed and related to specific mobile learning practices, mobile learning will penetrate into daily learning more comprehensively.

References

1. Richter, L.M., Naicker, S.N.: A data-free digital platform to reach families with young children during the COVID-19 pandemic: online survey study. JMIR Pediatrics and Parenting **4**(2), e26571 (2021)
2. Pradipta, I.A., Anggraini, R.I.: Journee: digital tourism platform for hidden gems destination. In: Proceedings of the Business Innovation and Engineering Conference 2020 (BIEC 2020) (2021)
3. Rodriguez, D.V., Katharine, L., Son, L., et al.: Development of a computer-aided text message platform for user engagement with a digital diabetes prevention program: a case study. J. Am. Med. Inform. Assoc. **29**(1), 155–162 (2021)
4. Sadykova, D., Pylaeva, E., Zaramenskikh, E.: Value modeling for digital platform. Lecture Notes in Information Systems and Organization (2021)
5. Broekhuizen, T., Emrich, O., Gijsenberg, M.J., et al.: Digital platform openness: drivers, dimensions and outcomes (2021)
6. Zang, S.: Cross-Cultural communication of language learning social software based on FPGA and transfer learning. Microprocess. Microsyst. **81**, 103768 (2021)
7. Rivanti, A.N., Sukmayadi, V.: Cross-cultural teaching construction in textbook for foreign language learning. In: Conference of Applied Linguistics (2021)
8. Lushchyk, Y., Pikulytska, L., Tsyhanok, H.: Authentic social-cultural reading in foreign language learning and teaching. Revista Romaneasca Pentru Educatie Multidimensionala - Journal for Multidimensional Education **13**, 524–542 (2021)
9. Cao, S., Zhou, C., Wang, Q., et al.: Cross-cultural adaptation and validation of the simplified Chinese version of the copenhagen neck function disability scale. Spine, publish ahead of print (2021)
10. Ji, J.: Research on German translation from a cross-cultural perspective (1), 130–134 (2021)
11. Alnak, A., Akmak, E., Okan, Z.: Cross-cultural adaptation of the Nijmegen cochlear implant questionnaire into Turkish language: validity, reliability and effects of demographic variables (2021)
12. Nasser, A.S., Mandhar, A.M., Sangeetha, M., et al.: Psychiatric, cognitive functioning and socio-cultural views of menstrual psychosis in Oman: an idiographic approach. BMC Women's Health **20**, 1–9 (2021)

Research on Mining Algorithm and Its Application in Mine Safety Management Education

Yuqi He[✉]

Lanzhou Resources and Environment Voc-Tech University, Lanzhou 730021, Gansu, China
enter_159@163.com

Abstract. The progress of social times has promoted the development of all walks of life in China. With the continuous development of modern industry, the demand for mineral resources is increasing. However, while mining mineral resources, people also pay attention to environmental pollution and safe production. As a new search and optimization technology, data mining algorithm plays an important role in optimizing the technical decision-making of mine engineering structure. Research on mining algorithm and its application in mine safety management education is the work of Dr. James a.bovard, published by CRC Press in 2013. This book is divided into two parts; The first part discusses the mining algorithm that can be used in mine safety management education. The second part discusses the application of the algorithm in mine safety management education. Taking mining as the background, this paper analyzes the application of big data in mine safety inspection management. The main purpose is to study how to use mining algorithms as an effective tool for mine safety management teaching, and how to effectively apply these algorithms to mine safety management education projects, which provides a reference for future mine work.

Keywords: Data mining · Mine safety · Monitoring management

1 Introduction

China is the first country in the world to recognize, mine and utilize coal. According to historical records, China began coal mining and utilization as early as 2000 years ago, which was popularized in the Tang Dynasty. Coal mining spread all over the country in the song and Yuan Dynasties, and began to enter commercial circulation. In the tide of economic globalization, energy is still the main material basis of economic and social progress. From the composition data of world disposable energy consumption (oil 40%, coal 27%, natural gas 23%, nuclear power 7.2%, hydropower 2.5%), it can be seen that fossil energy consumed (coal, oil, natural gas) accounts for more than 90% of disposable energy consumption. Compared with the world energy structure, coal plays a particularly important role in China's energy structure, accounting for 73.4% of the total energy consumption. Every year, the total amount of coal mined by large, medium and

© ICST Institute for Computer Sciences, Social Informatics and Telecommunications Engineering 2023
Published by Springer Nature Switzerland AG 2023. All Rights Reserved
M. A. Jan and F. Khan (Eds.): BigIoT-EDU 2022, LNICST 467, pp. 121–131, 2023.
https://doi.org/10.1007/978-3-031-23944-1_14

small coal mines in China exceeds 1 billion tons [1]. China's energy structure determines that in a fairly long historical period, Coal is still the most important energy and fuel in China ". Since the founding of new China, especially in recent years, China's coal industry has developed rapidly, made great achievements, and built a number of modern mines and mining areas. It has basically reversed the long-term shortage of China's coal supply and met the needs of national economic development. China's coal output has ranked first in the world for many years, with raw coal output of 1.38 billion tons in 2002, 1.67 billion tons in 2003, and 1.95 billion tons in 2004.

However, behind the rapid growth of coal production, there are a series of coal mine safety accidents. Since 2000, due to the acceleration of economic operation, the demand for energy and raw materials has increased abnormally [2]. Market demand has prompted coal production enterprises to operate at full capacity, and the phenomenon of over capacity production is very serious, which has brought great pressure to coal safety production. Every year, the number of major accidents in coal mines across the country is about 300, especially the frequency of a particularly serious accident that kills more than 100 people is accelerating, as shown in Fig. 1. In 2009, two mines with high modernization level, Shanxi Tunlan Mine and Heilongjiang Longmei group Xinxing mine, also had major safety production accidents one after another, causing 78 and 108 deaths respectively. With the high modernization level of these two mines, such huge casualties can not help but be shocking.

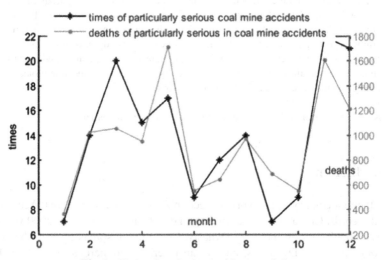

Fig. 1. National coal mine accident trend chart

Since the reform and opening up, China's economic level has been continuously improved. No matter the construction of urbanization or the continuous improvement of science and technology, there is a continuous supply of energy. China's mineral resources are very important for the development of various industries. Due to the particularity of mine engineering itself, it often encounters various large and complex projects, so it is often limited and constrained by external factors in technical decision-making [3].

The characteristics of mine engineering itself determine that it needs multi-objective dynamic optimization to obtain the best technical decision, but many variable factors can not be quantitatively calculated and expressed, which brings great difficulty to the technical decision of mine engineering. In recent years, with the continuous development of mining enterprises, safety accidents still occur one after another. People began to carry out modern mine safety management and monitoring in order to ensure the safety, scientificity and stability of mineral mining. Only relying on manpower and equipment for mine safety monitoring and management can not meet the development needs of the current society and the times. It is necessary to introduce big data processing technology, so as to improve the efficiency of mine safety management and reduce safety accidents caused by various unstable factors [4]. As a global optimization search algorithm, data mining algorithm is simple to operate and can meet the requirements of mine technical decision-making. Therefore, the application of data mining algorithm to mine engineering plays a very important role.

2 Related Work

2.1 Present Situation and Existing Problems of Mine Safety Accidents in China

Coal mine safety production is a major event related to national property and miners' life safety, which has always been highly valued by the party and the government. It is also the top priority for the coal industry from the management department to the production department. The core of coal mine production is to realize high yield and high efficiency of coal production on the basis of safety. Coal mine safety is the top priority of national safety production work. Effective coal mine safety production management theory and method is the fundamental guarantee of coal mine safety production. In recent years, with the increase of coal mining depth and the development of high-yield and high-efficiency mines, safety has become a major topic of general concern. Safety is the fundamental guarantee for the stable, sustainable and high-speed development of the coal industry, and it is the top priority related to the life safety and physical and mental health of coal mine workers, and the protection of national and collective property [5]. As coal mining is an underground operation, the production environment is bad and the production process is complex, which makes the safety problem of coal mine production more important, more complex and more difficult to solve than other industries. Although the state attaches great importance to coal mine safety production and makes great efforts to curb the occurrence of coal mine safety accidents, mining accidents still occur frequently, and the particularly shocking major accidents leave us permanent pain. Li Yizhong, director of the State Administration of work safety, pointed out in his speech at the National Symposium on basic work of safety in key state-owned coal mines in 2006 that coal mine safety production has the following characteristics: first, the risk of major accidents is very high; Second, some key coal mines did not draw lessons, and similar accidents reoccurred; Third, accidents often occur in newly-built, reconstructed and expanded mines. There are obvious loopholes in some newly-built large mines from project approval, geological survey, to design, construction, trial production and other links. Facing the increasingly severe situation of coal mine safety production, management theorists and practitioners have carried out research on coal mine safety production management from the perspectives of technology, management, economy and so on, and have also achieved some research results, but so far a set of feasible theory and method system has not been formed.

In recent years, the total mining volume of China's mineral enterprises has become larger and larger, increasing the difficulty and quantity of work, which has contributed a great deal to China's socialist modernization and people's living needs. However, with the continuous excavation of various mineral enterprises, the current mining work began to gradually turn into underground operation. Only by excavating the corresponding sections and taking various ore bodies in the area can we ensure the smooth progress of the work. However, underground mining has certain difficulties. Due to the poor underground environment, it has brought great obstacles to people's work. The problems of lighting, air circulation and mining section need to be paid attention to. In the process of actual underground mining, due to the large mobility of personnel, it is easy to cross work in various links and types of work, so it is difficult to carry out scientific and orderly management, which is very easy to lead to safety accidents. In serious cases, mine collapse, fire and flood will also occur, resulting in large casualties and property losses [6]. Therefore, the current mine safety supervision is urgent and needs to be solved urgently. According to incomplete statistics, there are more than 1000 mine safety accidents every year. Large and small accidents have not only brought serious trauma to families, but also made many mine staff have psychological shadow, which has a certain impact on enterprises. At present, many mining enterprises have not updated big data technology in time, and have not understood the role of big data technology in the development of mineral enterprises.

2.2 Complexity of Mine Safety Supervision Object

As we all know, the mine working environment and mining area have very complex geological environment and working status, which also increases the difficulty of daily safety supervision. The complexity of mine safety monitoring is embodied in the following aspects. First, the mineral mining work has a certain complexity. Due to the complex production conditions, the underground mining method is generally used in the work, and the roadway is narrow in the daily work process. The environment is bad, the visibility is too low when working underground, and there is a lot of dust. Therefore, various safety accidents occur one after another, which is difficult to be effectively restrained. Second, the production system of mining enterprises has a certain complexity [7]. The work includes mining system, transportation system, lighting system, drainage system, ventilation system and monitoring system. The complexity is high, which also brings great difficulty to the work coordination between various links and is easy to cause relevant safety accidents. Third, the mining working environment is extremely difficult, the underground mining environment is lack, and there is a lack of sunshine in the working process. With the continuous extension of working time underground, the physical fitness of the staff will continue to decline. Therefore, it is easy to be slow in the face of accidents, and it is extremely easy to produce anxiety under the long-term working state, which has brought certain potential safety hazards to the underground mining work. Fourth, the mining work is extremely vulnerable to natural disasters. If the underground mining work is unscientific, it is extremely easy to damage the geological structure of the mineral location and prone to roadway collapse. Fifth, at present, the knowledge level and skill level of the staff of many mineral enterprises are not high, and the recruited mining staff have low educational level and low psychological quality. Therefore, they lack the awareness of self-protection and relevant safety knowledge. Even with simple training, the staff still lack response and self rescue ability in the face of relevant accidents.

Safety education is a major measure to ensure safe production, which plays an important role in doing a good job in coal mine safety. We must do a good job in the key work of people-oriented and addressing both the symptoms and root causes. Many domestic scholars have conducted extensive analysis and demonstration on the causes of frequent coal mine accidents. Although the research ideas are different, they inevitably take human factors as the main cause of frequent coal mine accidents in China. However, there are relatively few domestic studies on the safety education of small and medium-sized coal mine workers [8]. Even in the existing literature, such as the safety production

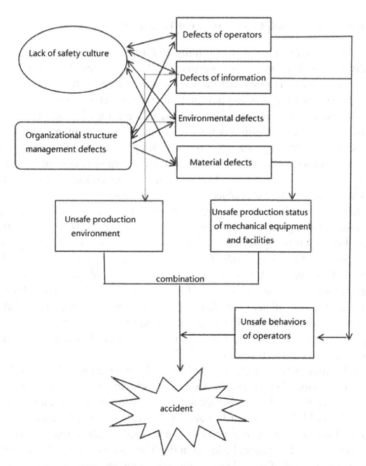

Fig. 2. General flow chart of data mining

publicity materials and safety education training regulations of coal mine enterprises, they only describe the coal mine safety education in a shallow sense, and there is no monograph dedicated to the safety education of small and medium-sized coal mine workers in China. At present, the existing domestic research mainly focuses on coal mine safety management and investment, coal mine safety ideological and political education and so on. Although the topic of coal mine safety production has been concerned by many people, there is relatively little research on the safety education of workers, and the special research on this special group of small and medium-sized coal mines will be even poorer. It can be said that the research on this issue is still immature, and the theory and practice in all aspects are not sufficient. The intrinsic safety culture system of coal mining enterprises in this paper is shown in Fig. 2.

3 Mine Safety Management Education Based on Data Mining Technology

3.1 Data Mining and Safety Management Education

The definition of data mining is data mining in English and data mining in Chinese. A generally accepted definition is proposed by W. J. Frawley, G. piatetsky Shapiro and others: data mining is to extract the knowledge of interest from the data of large databases. These knowledge is implicit and unknown potential useful information in advance. The extracted knowledge is expressed in the form of concepts, rules, rules, patterns and so on. This definition defines the object of data mining as a database. In a broader sense, data mining means the decision support process of finding patterns in the set of actual observation data. The object of data mining is not only the database, but also the file system, or any other data collection organized together, such as WWW information resources. The latest object is the data warehouse.

Education is the cultivation of enlightenment, which is to teach others the most objective understanding, and then form their own values and behaviors in their life experience. Education is a process of preparing a new generation to engage in social life. In this process, the social production experience accumulated by mankind can be carried forward and inherited. In a narrow sense, education only refers to the process of knowledge transmission of school-age children, adolescents and youth. In a broad sense, education is extended to all activities that can increase human knowledge and skills and affect human morality and even behavior. Such education should be an all-round and multi angle education, which is not only provided by special educational institutions such as schools, but also involves all people.

Safety education is an important part of life and life education. However, for a long time, most of our education has emphasized the development of "morality, intelligence, physique and beauty", while ignoring the safety education for the development of individual life. It should be noted that life and life education is the essence and value of education, which is also the fundamental reason why safety education must be included in school education and vocational education [9]. The current safety education in China mainly exists in the field of school safety education and occupational safety education. Occupational safety education is different from school safety education. It has strong practicality and operability, mainly for the purpose of practical application. Through the safety training and re education of enterprise employees, safety management training, three-level safety education into the factory and other forms, the body and mind of the safety education audience are affected in an organized and planned way, with a view to making great progress in safety cognition, safety behavior, safety skills and other aspects. The teaching contents of occupational safety education mainly include safety laws and regulations, post safety responsibilities, safety operation standards, emergency safety measures, etc.

3.2 Positioning of Data Mining Technology in Mine Safety Management Education

Enterprises fail in safety and accidents. Enterprises' active investment in production safety can improve the overall safety of enterprises, reduce or avoid the probability of safety accidents, so as to reduce the economic losses caused by safety accidents caused by safety problems, which is undoubtedly beneficial to enterprises themselves. However, as far as the actual situation is concerned, many enterprises do not have a clear understanding of safety benefits and a strong sense of safety, so they neglect enterprise safety management. One of the very important results is that many enterprise managers are reluctant to invest in enterprise safety. They believe that safety investment increases the operation cost of enterprises, thereby reducing income and profits, or that the probability of enterprise safety accidents is small, and the safety investment should be reduced, This shortsighted behavior is incorrect. The safety investment of enterprises should not be a burden on the income of enterprises. It brings more than the increase of production costs to enterprises. Fundamentally speaking, safety investment itself aims at increasing the economic benefits of enterprises, and its activities also focus on improving the economic benefits of enterprises. Therefore, as a special investment content, the characteristics of enterprise safety investment are of great significance to the enterprise safety management strategy, and the safety benefits it produces have the following characteristics:

First, uncertainty. To be exact, safety investment is not omnipotent, and it is unrealistic to hope that safety investment can completely eliminate the occurrence of safety accidents. Safety investment is a special investment method, which can reduce the probability of safety accidents and accident losses to a certain extent, and try to reduce or even avoid the benefit reduction caused by safety accidents. Even if the scale of security investment is certain, the output it brings is also uncertain. The output of safety investment is affected by market, production environment, human behavior, machinery, time and space and other factors [10]. The theoretical safety benefit describes only our expectations, and the final positioning of safety benefit needs to be determined according to the actual situation of the specific enterprise. Enterprises should not neglect safety management because of the uncertainty of safety benefits, and should not hope that each safety investment can maximize the return benefits.

Second, preventive. Safety investment is generally the safety construction done before or after the safety accident. Its purpose is to ensure the safety of enterprises in the production process, reduce the probability of accidents, and take preventive measures to reduce property losses and worker casualties. The implementation of safety education activities for employees, such as safety knowledge lectures and safety skill training, can reduce the probability of safety accidents in enterprises to a certain extent, prevent losses caused by safety accidents in enterprises, place enterprise safety under the protective net of safety system, and lay a foundation for realizing enterprise safety benefits.

Third, pleiotropy. Safety benefits have many forms of expression. Enterprise safety investment lays the foundation for the normal play of production technology, ensures the smooth progress of enterprise production, and plays a direct or indirect role in promoting enterprise production and economic development. Safety production in enterprises can not only add a protective net to the health and property safety of producers, but also reduce or even eliminate casualties and property losses caused by safety accidents, so as to achieve the purpose of pursuing economic benefits. A safe production environment can meet the dual needs of human psychology and physiology. A comfortable and safe environment can improve the labor productivity of producers and bring more economic benefits to enterprises and society. Personal safety and property safety can improve individual well-being, so that people love work, life and society more, which is conducive to the construction of a harmonious humanistic society.

From the definition of data mining, we can see that as an academic city, data mining and database knowledge discovery KDD (knowledge discovery in databases) have a great degree of coincidence. Most scholars believe that data mining and knowledge discovery are equivalent concepts. The field of artificial intelligence (A1) is used to call KDD, while the field of database is used to call data mining. Some scholars regard KDD as a complete process of discovering knowledge, and data mining is only a part of this process. We tend to follow the former view, which holds that data mining not only inherits the achievements of knowledge discovery in theory and technology, but also has a unique connotation. Data mining focuses on designing efficient algorithms to find knowledge from huge amounts of data. Data mining makes full use of the theories and methods of machine learning, engineering intelligence, fuzzy logic, artificial neural network and fractal geometry.

Research fields closely related to data mining include inductive learning, machine learning and statistical analysis. In particular, machine learning is considered to be most closely related to data mining. The main difference between the two is that the task of data mining is to find understandable knowledge, while machine learning is concerned with improving the performance of the system. Therefore, training neural network to control an inverted rod is a machine learning process, but it is not data mining. The object of data mining is a large database. Generally speaking, the data set processed by machine learning is much smaller, Because of the problem of efficiency, it is very important for data mining. Let's look at the position of data mining in decision support space. K. Parsaye divides the decision support space into four subspaces from the application level: data space, aggregation space, influence space and variation space.

In recent years, with the popularization of computer technology, the Internet has become the largest information network in the world, and its data can not be calculated. How to find useful information from these massive data and turn it into knowledge has become one of the main bottlenecks in the application of computer technology in the 21st century. Data mining technology is produced and developed rapidly to solve this problem. It is one of the most cutting-edge research directions in the field of database, data warehouse and information decision-making in the world, and has attracted extensive attention in various fields at home and abroad. The problem of data mining is to find out hidden and valuable events in the huge database, analyze and deal with these events, so as to obtain meaningful information and summarize useful knowledge as the basis of decision-making. It is widely used. As long as there is a database with analysis value and demand, data mining technology can be used for purposeful mining and analysis. The general flow of data mining is shown in Fig. 3.

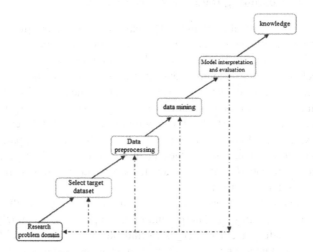

Fig. 3. General flow chart of data mining

4 Application of Data Mining in Mine Safety Monitoring Management

4.1 Continuously Promote the Level of Mine Safety Monitoring and Management

The emergence of data mining technology has brought great convenience and innovation to the current mine safety monitoring and management. Compared with the traditional management methods, big data has various advantages such as high efficiency, modernization, diversification and integration, avoids accidents under the human working environment, and gradually realizes the concentration and storage of mine environmental data. In recent years, China's mine information technology has been continuously improved, and a large number of hierarchical data networks have been formed in all walks of life. Especially for the mining industry, it not only timely collects and processes the data in the daily mineral mining management process and business process, but also summarizes the laws of mineral production and industry development. The early technologies involved many types and could not meet the actual needs in the face of the huge demand for information processing, which limited the utilization of mine information. The continuous innovation of big data technology has made a certain contribution to the current data processing efficiency and use efficiency, and the industry development law that was not found manually has begun to be clearly presented. Using the current data model technology, the actual simulation drill can be carried out through the electronic sand table to truly monitor and online monitor the possible safety accidents in the mining process, so as to continuously improve the level of mine safety monitoring and management.

4.2 Mine Safety Monitoring Data Sharing is Realized

In recent years, China's regulatory authorities have attached great importance to mine safety production, but the data information sharing between regulatory authorities and mining enterprises is still not in place. With the continuous innovation and promotion of big data technology, the resolution and utilization of information data have been significantly improved, which also promotes the establishment of information resource database of mining enterprises and realizes the information sharing between different departments and links. Big data technology continuously integrates the current information technology, lays an effective foundation for the analysis and comparison of safety management of mineral enterprises, judges the most appropriate mining plan, can accurately judge the underground mining state and the safety state of construction personnel, and improves the safety of mine production.

The application and development of data mining technology can effectively avoid the unknown and uncertainty of underground mining operation, accurately predict the occurrence law of safety accidents, so as to find out the source of safety accidents, analyze specific problems, and facilitate daily management and decision-making of mining enterprises.

5 Conclusion

The application of data mining algorithm in mine engineering can solve complex system problems and bring more data support to the development of mine engineering. In order to expand the application of data mining algorithm in mine engineering. Through the above analysis, it can be seen that data mining algorithm is a highly practical optimization method, which can be applied to various complex system structures and obtain the corresponding optimal data according to the calculation requirements. For mine engineering, it is complex, and the application of data mining algorithm can effectively make up for the defects of traditional mathematical models, expert systems and other methods, so as to solve the problems encountered in mine system more quickly and accurately.

References

1. Li, H.: Research on the application of computer statistics technology in the educational information management system of colleges and universities (2021)
2. Huang, Y., Fan, J., Yan, Z., et al.: Research on early warning for gas risks at a working face based on association rule mining. Energies **14**, 6889 (2021)

3. Smith, T.D., Balogun, A.O., Dillman, A.L.: Management perspectives on musculoskeletal disorder risk factors and protective safety resources within the stone, sand, and gravel mining industry. Workplace Health & Safety **70**(5), 242–250 (2022)
4. Zhang, J.: Application of intelligent and efficient fully mechanized mining technology in coal mine. Mechanical Management and Development (2020)
5. Ding, L., Zeng, X.: Application of decision tree model based on C4.5 algorithm in nursing quality management evaluation. J. Med. Imaging and Health Inform. **11**, 2359–2366 (2021)
6. Baumann, L., Arlinghaus, J.: Algorithm-use in the field of lean management principles: state of the art and need for research - ScienceDirect (2021)
7. Zhihua, D., Jialin, W.: Potential customer mining application of smart home products based on LightGBM PU learning and Spark ML algorithm practice (2020)
8. Qiu, H.: Research and application of apriori improved algorithm based on mapreduce (2020)
9. Li, M., Feng, X.: Research on adaptive comprehensive learning artificial bee colony algorithm and its application in constant pressure water supply. J. Phys. Conf. Ser. **1650**(3), 032150 (2020)
10. Qin, G., Li, S., Xu, G.: Research progress on multiscale entropy algorithm and its application in neural signal analysis. Sheng Wu Yi Xue Gong Cheng Xue Za Zhi = Journal of Biomedical Engineering = Shengwu Yixue Gongchengxue Zazhi **37**(3), 541–548 (2020)

Research on National Dance Culture Education and Teaching Based on Data Mining Algorithm

Bing Zhao[⊠]

Hechi College, Yizhou District, Guangxi Zhuang Autonomous Region, Hechi 546300, China
572571603@qq.com

Abstract. National dance is closely related to national traditional culture. As an important part of national culture and education, the teaching of national dance plays an important role in promoting the development of national culture and education because of its unique cultural, artistic and educational value, as well as the inseparable factors with overseas Chinese social folk life and their own career development. Through the national culture education to the national dance teaching, in order to promote the students' understanding of the national culture, to deepen the students' learning enthusiasm of the national dance. Therefore, this article through the data mining algorithm to the national traditional culture and the national dance introduction as well as the national traditional culture and the national dance relations manifests the national traditional culture education to the national dance teaching influence.

Keywords: Folk dance · Cultural education · Teaching research · Data mining

1 Introduction

As a multi-ethnic country, each nation has its own development process and unique culture. National dance is a form of national culture, which contains its own customs and cultural history. It has its own unique style, strong entertainment and mass. It is also a way of expressing people's emotions, Some ethnic groups express their emotions with different dances in different festivals, which has unique charm. Because ethnic dances are closely related to their national life, they are also influenced by ethnic customs, languages and costumes, making them more distinctive.

National dance is formed through the long-term historical development of the people of our nation. It can reflect the changes of a nation, including religious beliefs and production skills. It is the most valuable spiritual wealth. Each nation has its own unique cultural system, and national dance is a form of national culture, is an indispensable part of cultural accumulation. In addition, folk dance can also be used as an important way of communication among nations, regions and even countries. Therefore, based on the data mining algorithm, it is particularly important to comprehensively and deeply consider and study the substantive problems of national dance teaching in China's national culture education (such as teaching form, teacher selection, teaching material content, etc.) [1].

© ICST Institute for Computer Sciences, Social Informatics and Telecommunications Engineering 2023
Published by Springer Nature Switzerland AG 2023. All Rights Reserved
M. A. Jan and F. Khan (Eds.): BigIoT-EDU 2022, LNICST 467, pp. 132–137, 2023.
https://doi.org/10.1007/978-3-031-23944-1_15

2 Data Mining Technology

2.1 Definition of Data Mining

Data mining originated from KDD (knowledge discovery in database), which can be traced back to the end of 1980s. The term KDD was formally formed at the first International Conference on KDD held in Detroit, USA in 1989, while the first International Conference on knowledge discovery and data mining (DM) was held in Canada in 1995. The conference vividly compared the data stored in the database to mineral deposits, thus "counting".

The term "excavation" soon spread. In fact, to be exact, data mining is only one step in the whole KDD process. But because it is the most core and important step in the process of KDD, and in the media, industry and database research circles, "data mining" is more recognized and accepted than "knowledge discovery in database", so data mining has been more widely defined and become synonymous with KDD.

Data mining has a variety of definitions, including "a process of extracting or mining useful patterns or knowledge from massive and mixed data", "extracting hidden and unknown valuable potential information from data" and so on. A widely accepted definition is that data mining is a process of extracting potentially useful knowledge or patterns from incomplete, uncertain, massive and noisy data with great randomness. This definition includes several meanings: (1) data sources must be massive, real and noisy. (2) The new knowledge must be needed and interested by users. (3) The knowledge mined is easy to understand, acceptable, effective and applicable. (4) The knowledge mined is not required to be applicable to all fields, and can only support a specific application to find problems.

In fact, it does accurately show its role, that is, to process and analyze the massive and disordered data, and find the useful knowledge hidden in the data, so as to provide support for decision-making. From the perspective of technology, data mining is to use a series of related algorithms and technologies to extract the information and knowledge that people need from a large number of data. They are hidden in the data and unknown before, but they are valuable potential knowledge that people really need. The extracted knowledge can be expressed in the form of concepts, patterns, rules and so on; Through the analysis of historical data and current data, it can help decision-makers to extract the potential relationships and patterns hidden in the data, and then help them to predict the possible future situation and the upcoming results [2].

2.2 Basic Process of Data Mining

Before data mining, the first thing to do is to define the problem, clearly define the problem and target task, and determine the purpose of data mining. On the basis of clear mining purpose, knowledge discovery is carried out according to the basic steps of data mining. The whole process of data mining has many processing stages, which can be summarized into three stages: data preparation stage, data mining stage, result interpretation and evaluation. The data preparation stage includes data source, data integration, data selection, data preprocessing, data mining, data expression and interpretation. A complete basic process of data mining involves each specific step as shown in Fig. 1.

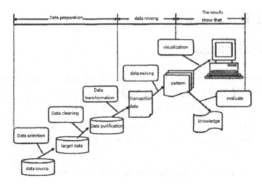

Fig. 1. Data mining process

3   The Problems of National Dance Teaching

Although the prospect of national dance teaching is good, it still faces many difficulties and problems, which restrict the further development of national dance teaching in different forms and degrees.

3.1   The Importance of Teaching is not Enough

The language of a nation is not only the carrier of the national culture, but also an important part of the national culture; The history, society, folk customs, art and other cultures of the Chinese nation, as knowledge, can also be acquired by translating works of art without understanding Chinese, especially those works of art that can convey feelings directly without language communication. However, the characteristics of Chinese culture shown by Chinese language itself are difficult to understand and master without understanding Chinese. But there are still some professional ethnic schools that "in recent years, due to changes in form and changes in the concept of ethnic minorities, ethnic culture education has undergone profound changes. The mode and nature of national culture education are quite different from before. The dominant position of traditional culture and education has given way to Chinese language teaching". It is believed that only by learning the language well can we master the tools for interpreting other cultures. Therefore, some schools focus on the nature of ethnic dance teaching as interest class or second class, with few class hours. Some of them have one class a week, some have two classes a week, and some even don't offer any other art courses at all, The idea of neglecting art teaching should be corrected in time.

3.2   The Teaching System is not Perfect

The cause of national dance in China is just "flourishing", but "national culture education" is rarely known among colleagues in the dance industry, and some schools do not have professional national dance teachers, so the results of dance teaching can be imagined. In addition, it is not difficult to see from the purpose of ethnic culture education that ethnic dance teaching belongs to universal teaching, while the current ethnic dance teaching system has no clear norms. Therefore, the arrangement of actual teaching links can not meet the actual needs of professional seedlings who love ethnic dance and are willing to take ethnic dance as a career, These students can only sigh for the coming of luck in the future and the sound teaching system [3].

3.3 The Teaching Content is not Rich

The curriculum of dance teaching in China can be divided into choreographer, dance appreciation, dance culture, dance performance and dance history. Now the appreciation level of students is gradually improving. For the sake of their own career development and serving the society, some school teachers and students with potential who are willing to regard national dance education as a lifelong career, their learning requirements are no longer simply learning dance, but gradually changing into professional dance performance, dance appreciation, dance arrangement, dance theory, etc., But now the teaching content of folk dance can not meet their learning requirements. The teaching materials of contemporary Chinese national dance are constantly updated and changing, excellent performance plays emerge in endlessly, and the related theoretical research of national dance is gradually deepening, which provides favorable conditions for the development of national dance teaching. However, how to combine the national dance teaching, a new subject, with the domestic dance education perfectly, and how to enrich the teaching content of national dance need more practical experience and time.

4 Improvement Strategies of National Dance Teaching Based on Data Mining

4.1 Strengthen the Teaching Concept of National Culture Education

Some colleagues in the domestic dance industry do not know enough about the importance of carrying out ethnic cultural education. Most of them think that ethnic education "has nothing to do with themselves". They think that ethnic dance teaching is just to teach ethnic minority students at the amateur level to dance one or two ethnic dances and deal with things casually. These biases have greatly affected the further development of national dance teaching. Therefore, in order to carry out national culture education, we must change our teaching concept, put an end to the idea of "attaching importance to language and belittling art", strengthen the contact with domestic academic circles, art circles, business circles, media circles and other units, let more people understand the current difficulties of national culture education and national dance teaching, mobilize the public, offer suggestions and suggestions, and build a cultural, cultural and cultural city together The artistic, loving and friendly "Great Wall of national culture" extends to every corner of the motherland.

We should strengthen publicity, improve the whole society's awareness of the importance of national culture and education, actively carry out national dance teaching and other art education work, and vigorously carry forward the Chinese national culture. This is not only conducive to the development of their own career, is conducive to the inheritance and development of national dance career, but also conducive to the ethnic minorities to maintain national identity, enhance ties and feelings with the motherland: conducive to China to the world, the world to understand China. We should also increase social propaganda, raise the awareness of the whole people, mobilize all sectors of the arts to support the cause of national culture and education, and make due contributions to promoting the prosperity and development of the motherland [4].

4.2   Establish a Teaching System Integrating Popularization and Specialty

National dance teaching should be clear about the nature of the discipline, in line with the principles of discipline construction and the purpose of national culture education, we should learn from domestic dance education, and give consideration to non professional mass education and professional education, which not only meets the needs of professionals who want to take dance as a lifelong career, but also meets the needs of other different levels. The author thinks that at present, our top priority is to make the system clear, the subjects detailed, fulfill their duties, complement and promote each other, so as to promote the maturity of the discipline construction and the improvement of the teaching system.

4.3   Optimize the Content of Teaching Materials

Due to the fact that all ethnic schools in China still pay attention to the "instrumental" nature of language and characters, while teaching focuses on Chinese teaching, art teaching such as ethnic dance only appears as an interest course, and some even do not open it, there are many problems in the selection and compilation of dance teaching materials in ethnic schools. The teaching materials of dance can't just be written in words. Written records don't have the characteristics of dance art. The written teaching materials that have taken a lot of effort to write, even with illustrations, are very difficult to read. Nowadays, there are many modern means, we should make full use of them. If "the teaching materials of technology course are mainly dynamic images, and the language and words are used as instructions and AIDS", it has the characteristics of dance teaching materials and is more practical. Dance is a trinity of visual, listening and kinesthetic art, so the teaching materials should be complementary with images, pictures and words.

Form, to assist teaching. In the face of different ethnic groups, different levels of characteristics of minority students' strong demand for knowledge, the existing domestic dance teaching materials in many ways can not adapt. Therefore, it is urgent to select and compile practical teaching materials scientifically. The types of dance teaching materials mainly include: outline type, text type, dance notation type, image type, etc. different types of teaching materials should be used together.

4.4   Expanding Teaching Methods

National dance classroom teaching is different from other cultural classroom teaching, because of its lively form, teaching in fun, the combination of theory and practice, avoid the boring from books to books, and strong national culture, so it is deeply loved by students. Accurate and scientific application of teaching methods is an important embodiment of dance teachers' ability and an important guarantee to improve teaching efficiency and quality ""Oral and personal teaching" is the most basic and practical teaching method in democratic dance classroom teaching" '"Oral transmission" refers to the way of oral transmission, including narration, explanation, language penetration and so on' "Teaching by example" is the way of demonstration. Demonstration is an image created by teachers themselves and imitated by students In addition, teachers should also pay attention to the use of reasonable and effective methods, means and measures to optimize the organization of teaching according to the teaching content and students' characteristics, so as to improve the teaching efficiency to the maximum possible. Therefore, teachers must make efforts in these aspects in the classroom teaching of national dance.

5   Conclusion

In the excellent culture of the Chinese nation, national dance occupies a place. Inheriting national dance is the unshirkable responsibility of those engaged in dance enlightenment education. Based on data mining algorithm, research on national dance culture education and teaching can contribute to the development and inheritance of national dance in China and the development of national dance.

Acknowledgements. 1. Guangxi Higher Education Undergraduate Teaching Reform Project in 2020: Construction and practice of practical teaching system of dance major in local application-oriented undergraduate colleges, Serial number: 2020JGB332.

2. The Research Basic Ability Enhancement Project of Young and Middle-aged Teachers in Guangxi Universities in 2021: Research on the Inheritance and Development of Maonan Nationality Nuo Dance Culture in the Context of Intangible Cultural Heritage, Serial number: 2021KY0596.

References

1. List poems. On the cultural function of ethnic dance in China. Yihai two thousand and eleven
2. Li, J.: Survey of data mining technology. China Sci. Technol. Expo **4**(33), 9–10 (2010)
3. Fang, H.: Implementation strategy of kindergarten national dance teaching i. take the group dance "Peacock Flies" as an example. Science and education Wenhui (8) (2014)
4. Jing, G.: Research on the theory and practice of minority dance education and teaching in current comprehensive universities. Journal of Hubei University of Economics (7) (2014)

Research on Online English Speech Interactive Recognition System Based on Nose Algorithm

Yanyan Deng[✉]

Ganzhou Teachers College, Jiangxi 341000, China
yan2002412@163.com

Abstract. Speech database evaluation algorithm and recognition function are the key factors affecting speech recognition rate and recognition time. In this paper, an online English speech interactive recognition system is designed by using nose algorithm and Mel frequency cepstrum coefficient windowing function. The system can recognize English speech information accurately and quickly, and use the reference database for evaluation and expert knowledge database for speech error correction, which greatly improves the recognition efficiency. Compared with similar mainstream English speech recognition systems, this system has certain advantages in recognition rate and recognition time. This design provides a reference for the development of English speech recognition technology.

Keywords: NCSE algorithm · Speech recognition · Interactive recognition

1 Introduction

English is an international language. With the deepening of economic, cultural, scientific and technological information exchange among countries, English speech intelligent recognition has gradually become a key research object in the field of information technology. Its goal is to use machines to achieve voice interaction between equipment and humans, make equipment more intelligent, increase entertainment ability, and provide convenience for people who are inconvenient to record people with keyboard and mouse. The goal of English speech intelligent recognition is in line with the pace of modern development. English speech intelligent recognition systems emerge one after another. The first recognition system is called Audry system. Its performance is relatively perfect and has been greatly developed. Recently, the new Audry system uses database computing to recognize vowels and independent words from the basic English grammar. It has high recognition rate, but the recognition time is long, which is only suitable for short sentence recognition. In 1963, the endpoint detection system designed by the former Soviet Union used dynamic programming to realize English speech recognition. The real-time performance of the system is not good, and the ability of online and continuous English speech recognition is not strong. Since then, the famous Bell Labs "has changed the research direction of speech recognition, designed a speech printer, translated English speech on the device display screen, and then conducted human-computer

M. A. Jan and F. Khan (Eds.): BigIoT-EDU 2022, LNICST 467, pp. 138–146, 2023.
https://doi.org/10.1007/978-3-031-23944-1_16

interaction [1]. It is widely used in smart phones with few functions but accurate recognition. Since 1980, HMM (hidden Markov model) has been used Network system has entered people's life. It combines the computing means of Audry system and the human-computer interaction ability of voice printer and improves it. It transforms from detailed speech recognition to overall speech recognition, and improves the stability of online and continuous English speech signals. It is an important milestone in the history of speech intelligent recognition.

Obviously, the development direction of English speech intelligent recognition system is online and continuous human-computer interaction, which requires high recognition efficiency. If we can correct speech errors in the shortest time, it can also greatly improve the system recognition rate, which is a research hotspot in the design of English speech intelligent recognition system.

At present, many technology companies have established rich English recognition databases, such as American English reading and dialogue database, British English database, Chinese adult speaking English database, Chinese Youth English data, children's English database, etc. the pronunciation methods include Chinese, English and American, and cover all ages of children, teenagers and adults.

2 Related Work

[5] present an automatic system to address the assessment of spontaneous spoken language. [6] present an overview of the evaluation and analysis of system performance over all primary evaluation conditions. [7] propose an innovative encoder-decoder structure, called ECTC-DOCD, for online speech recognition which directly predicts the linguistic sequence without blank labels. [8] propose a multi-model i-vector system for short speech lengths. With the development of virtual scenes, the degree of simulation and functions of virtual reality have been very complete, providing a new platform and perspective for teaching design [9]. To solve the problem, the linear predictive coding coefficients extraction method is used to sum up the data related to the English digits pronunciation [10]. In order to improve the efficiency of multimedia English teaching, aiming at the lack of emotion in multimedia English education [11] propose an intelligent network teaching system model based on deep learning speech enhancement and facial expression recognition. [12] introduce an automatic proficiency evaluation system that combines various kinds of non-native acoustic models and native ones, such as Gaussian mixture model (GMM)-hidden Markov model (HMM) and deep neural network (DNN)-HMM. Thus, there is the need to further improve the classification performance of deployed SER systems. [13] propose an SER system based on a novel robust multi-window spectrogram augmentation (RMWSaug) scheme and, transfer learning to handle these aforementioned issues simultaneously. The basic principle of speech recognition is described in detail from the aspects of speech signal preprocessing, feature parameter extraction and HMM model matching [14].

3   Design of English Speech Interactive Recognition System

3.1   System Process Design

As shown in Figs. 1 and 2, it is the workflow of the online English speech interactive recognition system designed in this paper. It can be seen that the system introduces two databases, namely expert knowledge database and reference database. The expert knowledge database is established on common English speech pronunciation errors, which can recognize common speech errors and correct them for users; the reference database passes English standard pronunciation It is established on the basis of feature training and can evaluate the user's voice. The database uses nose algorithm for evaluation. This algorithm is an oral evaluation technology, which can effectively evaluate the pronunciation of non-native speech. The expert database collects the error data of common English voice. The system extracts the voice features through the input of international standard English voice data Reference database. After receiving the user's English voice input, the system extracts the user's voice features, evaluates the user's voice by using nose algorithm combined with the standard English voice data in the reference database, and checks the error according to the evaluation results [2]. Then, it corrects the user's voice by comparing the common English voice errors in the expert database.

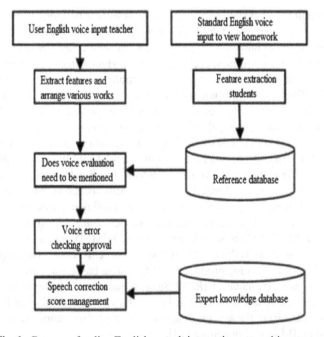

Fig. 1. Process of online English speech interactive recognition system

The system can extract users' oral English features, decode them using the trained reference database features, and score the decoding results according to nose algorithm.

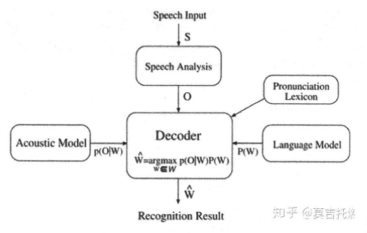

Fig. 2. Reconition system

The scoring results will show the user's oral English speech quality in the form of evaluation items, check the error of the evaluation items, and finally compare the data in the expert knowledge database to correct the user's pronunciation. For the online English speech interactive recognition system, users mainly use hardware devices with limited processing capacity, such as tablet computers and mobile phones. Therefore, the perfect presentation of the system process must be fully considered in the design process of the system, and more alternative voices must be selected in the operation process of nose algorithm to formulate the standard phonetic order, so as to reduce the recognition time and calculation of the system, which is shown in Fig. 3.

3.2 Module Design

(1) Voice training module

The speech training module is the resource base of expert knowledge database and reference database, including English standard phonetics, speech corpus and so on. According to the previous research on speech recognition system, database resources, especially corpus resources, are important resources affecting the function of recognition system. Good corpus resources can significantly improve the recognition rate and effectiveness of the system. Therefore, in the design process, the corpus resources should have the characteristics of consistency, representativeness and universality in order to provide a good foundation for the speech training module. corpus.

The consistency of resources requires that the corpus can correspond to the user's English pronunciation, and the marking points should be detailed and specific; Representativeness requires that the corpus resources should include information such as dialect, speech speed, user age and gender; Universality requires that the corpus resources can cover most of the rules of English pronunciation, and the structure has strong compatibility.

Therefore, the system is designed to organize 100 domestic foreign language school professors and professional teachers (from different regions) to record corpus

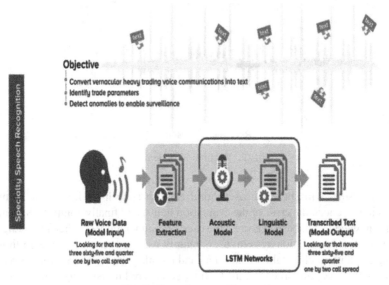

Fig. 3. Speech recognition system

resources. Using the standard sampling mode, each person recorded 50 min of English pronunciation, a total of 18,500 words, a total of 2500 sentences, rated and marked the words, and generated corpus resources [3]. The sampling method is as follows: sensor, blue Yeti Pro; Acquisition element, Maya 66; Coding mode, pulse code modulation; Bit rate, 282 B / S; Channel, stereo.

The phonetic resources in the speech training module include 28 auxiliary phonetics and 20 vowels (8 diphthongs and 12 vowels). In the expert knowledge database and reference database, the probability calculation formula of three words at the same time when parsing phonetic resources is shown in formula (1):

$$\Delta \dot{x}_{k+1}(t) = Q^{-1}f(t, x_d(t)) - Q^{-1}f(t, x_{k+1}(t)) + Q^{-1}B\Delta u_k(t) - Q^{-1}Z\dot{x}_d(t) \tag{1}$$

(2) Identification module design

The system can realize voice correction, database evaluation and other functions. A large number of operations will be carried out during the operation of the recognition module. Therefore, the computing power of the processing chip should be matched. DSP signal processing chip has strong digital signal processing ability, low cost and small volume. It is more suitable for tablet computer and mobile phone users. In addition, the chip also has fast processing function and online interaction function. Therefore, the identification module of the system selects the DSP chip equipped with OMAP 5912zzg platform. The chip has built-in chain bridge technology, DSP operating system, multimedia database and start-up tools. The chip structure is shown in Fig. 4. The chip has a communication interface, a display module and two audio interfaces. The communication interface is externally connected with USB and Ethernet, which can realize the transmission of external data input; The display module is connected with the external display device to realize the display of English speech recognition results; The audio interface can accept microphone and sequence data for data processing. In addition, the interface can also provide headset output and provide users with voice reply and other functions; The other audio interface is connected with 250 kb voice storage processor and interactive vector graph to realize audio data caching with memory card.

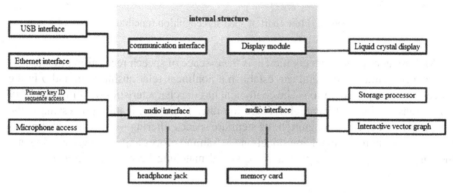

Fig. 4. Chip structure

The chip adopts a 250 kb memory processor, which can realize the functions of memory on demand and fetch on demand. This function can buffer LCD data and voice data. The memory space of the system is expanded through the memory card, and the audio frame buffer can be realized through interactive vector graph. Voice interaction can be realized through 250 kb storage processor and supports multiprocessing mode. The powerful memory management function of the chip can realize the allocation of English speech recognition tasks, and transplant the recognition functions through the Ethernet interface. In order to realize powerful processing function, the system takes the processor on the external tablet computer or mobile phone as the main processor and OMAP 5912zzg chip as the cooperative auxiliary processor, which can effectively improve the efficiency of speech recognition.

4   Design of Speech Recognition Function Based on Nose Algorithm

Recognition function is the basis of realizing English speech recognition function, and its flow chart is shown in Fig. 5. Firstly, the English speech input by the user is processed with the help of Mel frequency cepstrum coefficient. The results of feature processing are unit matched, English part of speech decoded, and finally output after syntax and semantic analysis.

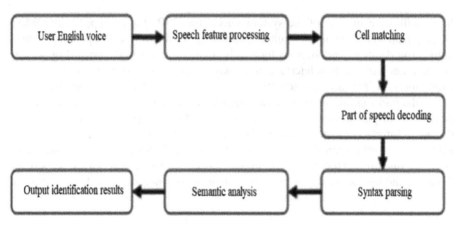

Fig. 5. Flow chart of speech recognition function

Mel frequency cepstrum coefficient is the essence of speech recognition function. It has energy characteristics and can establish a nonlinear relationship with audio in the process of speech recognition. The coefficient has the characteristics of human auditory nerve transmission and has high recognition rate. Therefore, feature processing is the key problem of speech recognition. Its steps are speech filtering $\rightarrow$ speech sampling $\rightarrow$ format conversion $\rightarrow$ signal amplification $\rightarrow$ framing processing. Through windowing, the English speech is smoother and the signal matching between adjacent frames is completed[4].

$$\sup_{0 \le t \le T} \|I - L(t)C(t)P^{-1}(t)B(t)\| \le \rho_1 < 1 \tag{2}$$

The system can automatically select three forms of rectangle, Hamming and Hanning according to the user's English voice characteristics.

In speech recognition, grammar analysis and part of speech decoding are completed through Fourier change, so as to obtain the spectrum line of speech signal. If the frame sequence after Fourier change is k, the expression is as follows:

$$\begin{cases} E(t)\dot{x}_d(t) = f(t, x_d(t)) + B(t)u_d(t) + d_d(t) \\ y_d(t) = C(t)x_d(t) \end{cases} \tag{3}$$

with the continuous progress of artificial intelligence technology and the acceleration of social digital transformation, the tentacles of AI gradually penetrate into various scenes. As the core technology of human-computer interaction, speech recognition has been widely used in life and production. Among them, English, as one of the most influential global communication languages, is highly used all over the world. However, due to the complexity of Chinese English mixing and the differences of languages, it brings great challenges to the accuracy of English speech recognition.

Recently, based on years of technical precipitation in the field of intelligent speech, standard Bay Technology launched English speech recognition function, so that customers can enjoy faster and more accurate English speech recognition services in different scenarios.

1. Accurate identification

   The biggest highlight of this time's speech recognition is that the recognition model is continuously optimized and trained through a large number of English corpus data (Chinese, British and American; children, teenagers and adults; reading and dialogue), so as to greatly improve the accuracy of speech recognition, and the accuracy of English speech recognition is as high as 95%.

2. Instant transfer

   The online real-time transcribing speed is fast. As the user speaks, the voice content can be presented in real time and accurately. The recognition result response time is less than 300 milliseconds. The fast system response makes the information communication extremely smooth and improves the user interaction experience.

3. Reading sentences

   It can carry out intelligent error correction, context judgment and intelligent punctuation insertion according to the user's input context. It is suitable for American English and Chinglish recognition in different scenes, and helps users to transfer and input at will.

   The person in charge of standard Bei speech technology said that due to the influence of complex external factors, such as noise, multi person dialogue and ambiguous accent, speech recognition is affected. Once the recognition error is made, the meaning of the whole sentence may be changed. Based on the accumulation of AI technology and language in-depth research, standard Bay technology adopts a product service-side recognition system based on the integration of wordview modeling end-to-end system and dynamic decoder technology, which can realize large vocabulary continuous English speech recognition and instruction word recognition. The overall recognition speed and accuracy can meet the personalized needs of a variety of speech interaction scenes.

5   Conclusion

Aiming at the defects of the current mainstream English speech recognition system, this paper designs an online English speech interactive recognition system combined with nose algorithm. The system uses the reference database for scoring, carries out error correction through the expert knowledge database, extracts the user's speech features and recognizes them, which greatly improves the recognition rate of English speech and shortens the recognition time. Compared with HMM system, endpoint detection system and Audry system, the system has certain advantages in recognition rate and recognition time, and has strong effectiveness.

Combined with the Chinese recognition ability, standard shell Chinese and English speech recognition will bring more applications to the ground. For example, in the scenario of intelligent customer service, a large number of recorded files of the seats will be converted into words to help improve quality inspection and service; In the live video scene, the voice of the speaker is converted into text in real time, and the corresponding subtitles are automatically output on the screen; In AI online education, students' oral English pronunciation and expression ability are accurately identified and analyzed to quickly improve their oral English ability.

From "Chinese and dialect recognition" to "Chinese and English mix and match free speech", from "real-time online recognition" to "recording offline recognition", standard Bay technology has been committed to bringing more intelligent speech recognition technology and services to users. In the future, when intelligent voice interaction becomes the daily mainstream and the application scenarios are more extensive, standard Bay technology will continue to increase the R & D investment, drive the voice recognition technology to continue to upgrade and iterate, and create a more intelligent voice interaction experience.

References

1. Hu, D., Zeng, Q., Long, C.: Modulation domain spectral subtraction for robust speech recognition. Sci. Technol. Eng. **16**(4), 216–220 (2016)
2. Liu, R., Peng, S., Liu, G.: Embedded speech recognition system based on smart home control. J. Guangdong Univ. Technol. **31**(2), 49–53 (2014)
3. Ma, Y., Chen, C., Jia, G.: Detection and analysis of Tibetan speech pitch cycle based on LPC. Modern Electron. Technol. **38**(16), 13–15 (2015)
4. Liu, Z., Shi, S., Wang, J.: Research on interaction based software model. Modern Electron. Technol. **39**(15), 119–122 (2016)
5. Yu, W., et al.: Towards automatic assessment of spontaneous spoken English. Speech Commun. (2018)
6. Sadjadi, S.O., Greenberg, C.S., Singer, E., Reynolds, D.A., Mason, L.P., Hernandez-Cordero, J.: The 2018 NIST Speaker Recognition Evaluation (2019)
7. Yi, C., Wang, F., Xu, B.: Ectc-Docd: an end-to-end structure with CTC encoder and OCD decoder for speech recognition (2019)
8. Tiwari, V., Hashmi, M.F., Keskar, A., Shivaprakash, N.C.: Speaker identification using multimodal I-vector approach for varying length speech in voice interactive systems. Cogn. Syst. Res. **57**, 66–77 (2019)
9. Li, D.: Emotional interactive simulation system of English speech recognition in virtual context. Complex (2020)
10. Khajehasani, S., Dehyadegari, L.: Speech recognition using Elman artificial neural network and linear predictive coding (2020)
11. Hao, K.: Multimedia English teaching analysis based on deep learning speech enhancement algorithm and robust expression positioning. J. Intell. Fuzzy Syst. **39**, 1779–1791 (2020)
12. Fu, J., Chiba, Y., Nose, T., Ito, A.: Automatic assessment of English proficiency for Japanese learners without reference sentences based on deep neural network acoustic models. Speech Commun. **116**, 86–97 (2020)
13. Yusuf, S.M., Adedokun, E.A., Muazu, M.B., Umoh, I.J., Ibrahim, A.A.: RMWSaug: robust multi-window spectrogram augmentation approach for deep learning based speech emotion recognition. In: 2021 Innovations in Intelligent Systems and Applications Conference (ASYU) (2021)
14. Yang, L.: A novel teaching video speech recognition method based on HMM model. In: 2021 International Conference of Social Computing and Digital Economy (ICSCDE) (2021)

Research on Public Opinion Risk Management and Control Under Network Media Big Data

Xue-qin Zhang[1]([✉]), Zhuang-zhaung He[1], Rui Zhao[1], Xiang-chuan Xiong[2],
and Ya-jun Zhang[2]

[1] StateGridShanxi Electric Power Company Information and Communication Branch,
TaiYuan 030001, ShanXi, China
`fulin36966@163.com`
[2] FuJianXiRong Information Technology Co. Ltd., FuJian, FuZhou 350003, China

Abstract. Big data technology also has unique advantages in public opinion prediction, and has the potential for higher quality public opinion prediction. Basic research methods, mathematical analysis model and application of network public opinion. Starting from the actual needs of network public opinion workers, this paper probes into the process of network public opinion monitoring and early warning, the monitoring method and scope of network public opinion, and starts to design the monitoring and early warning system of network public opinion to guide workers to conduct real-time monitoring and analysis of various network public opinion channels, so as to grasp the overall situation of network public opinion, screen, determine and verify the alarm degree, Effective early warning. Finally, it analyzes from three aspects: the prevention of network public opinion crisis, the treatment of network public opinion crisis and the problems that should be paid attention to in the treatment of network public opinion crisis.

Keywords: Big data · Public opinion and customs · Network media

1 Introduction

Public opinion refers to the subjective reflection of social groups in different historical stages on some social realities and phenomena. It is a comprehensive expression of group consciousness, ideas, opinions and requirements. The stability and development of a society are inseparable from the ideological unity of social members. To achieve this unity, we must first understand and master the ideological dynamics of social members. Therefore, strengthening public opinion information and early warning, mastering the dynamics of public opinion in time and actively guiding public opinion are important measures to maintain social stability and national security.

After the prosperity of the network, the people are directly exposed to a large amount of information, and in the process of disseminating information, the network media breaks the boundary between the sender and the receiver, so that the roles of the two can be easily changed. Therefore, the traditional audience may become the producer and

M. A. Jan and F. Khan (Eds.): BigIoT-EDU 2022, LNICST 467, pp. 147–152, 2023.
https://doi.org/10.1007/978-3-031-23944-1_17

distributor of information. As long as anyone is online, he can become a free disseminator. Information can spread freely across time and space. Netizens can freely choose and interpret information and act accordingly. The freedom of users is unprecedented, the right of network information exchange is equal and popular, the transparency of network communication is improved, and the operability of communicators' control and blockade of information is becoming lower and lower. In such a reality of social informatization, diversified communicators and diversified communication channels, the dissemination speed of gossip is accelerated, the speed of social public opinion from germination to formation is accelerated, and the impact on national affairs and public affairs is significantly increased [1].

The most prominent feature of the network age is the tighter network structure. Users' self generated content makes the number of network content producers grow at a geometric level. There are two-way interactions between users and websites, and multi-channel and multi-level three-dimensional interactions between users. Network content is no longer discrete and has a strong "relationship" attribute. This network structure based on various strong and weak relationships also directly enables the rapid formation and fermentation of network public opinion, which can be turned many times in a short time. Public opinion monitoring in the network era pays more attention to "relationship" and can track the changes of public opinion more quickly and accurately, which is the defect of early network public opinion monitoring.

2 Relevant Theories

2.1 Definition of Public Opinion

The concept of public opinion can be divided into narrow sense and broad sense. The narrow sense of public opinion holds that public opinion is the social and political attitude of the people as the subject to the state managers as the object around the occurrence, development and change of intermediary social matters in a certain social space. 'according to this definition, public opinion is the social and political attitude of the people. The extension is relatively narrow, However, the basic meaning of the interest relationship between the people and state managers is very prominent.

The concept of public opinion in a narrow sense is defined in the social and political attitude of the public subject towards the object of state managers, and holds that "intermediary social matters" are the stimuli of public opinion. However, does the object of public opinion include "intermediary social matters" ? social events and social phenomena that cause public opinion are not all the direct results of the power operation of state managers. On this issue, the broad definition of public opinion pays attention to the problem of too narrow extension of the narrow definition, and extends public opinion to social objective conditions and people's subjective will, that is, social public opinion. Public opinion is emotion, opinion and attitude. This is the most basic understanding of public opinion [2].

From the perspective of systematic analysis, "public opinion", as the emotion, attitude and opinion of the people, is the result of a series of cognitive processes and psychological activities. It belongs to ideology and is the generating element of the public opinion system. Its generation is the result of the interaction of a series of initial elements, including the main body of public opinion "the people": the decision-making intention of state managers as the main object of public opinion, that is, the so-called "political situation"; the intermediary social matters generated by the social unit as another object of public opinion, that is, the so-called "social situation" The three elements of the public opinion system, namely, the public, the political situation and the social situation, are the three initial elements of the public opinion system. The interaction among the three elements: first, the political situation and the social situation act on the people's brain, and generate the public opinion, that is, the social and political attitude, through the processing of the characteristics of the people's elements such as cognition, values, knowledge level, mode of thinking, cultural tradition and other intellectual factors. In addition, the initial elements should also include a special category Information is "public opinion control information", which has a certain impact on public opinion. After receiving public opinion information, the national management system and social unit system generate "public opinion control information" according to the specific situation of public opinion to affect the generation of public opinion. Publicity media, education and culture can be used as means to transmit control information.

2.2 Possibility of Big Data Monitoring Public Opinion

Big data usually refers to large and complex data sets that are difficult to analyze and process with traditional software tools. The processing of big data involves a series of problems from data capture, sorting, analysis, sharing, visualization to storage and transmission. Big data sets often come from daily life, have certain isomorphism with people's actions and communication, and some items are directly attached Time, geography and other information. It can be said that the data set of big data naturally contains various relationships. Therefore, the big data set can provide new information that cannot be brought by several small data sets with the same amount of data. People can find the relationship between data through data mining, establish the law of correlation between data, and then provide various predictions.

Mobile Internet brings "comprehensive microphone" Times. According to the data of the Ministry of industry and information technology, as of January 2014, the total number of mobile Internet users in China had reached 838 million, and the average household mobile Internet access flow had reached 165.1 m. The era of mobile Internet in which everyone can access the Internet from time to time, everywhere and everywhere has brought great challenges to public opinion supervision. In the mobile Internet, every netizen is an information release node, and everyone can access it through wechat and wechat Bloggers and social networks publish their own views, and the original regulatory means are difficult to continue to apply.

Big data technology raises the risk of "metadata". In the era of big data, many seemingly unrelated data may become important confidential data after sorting and analysis. These information may involve macroeconomic data, government dynamics, personal privacy, etc. once leaked, it will have a significant impact. The prism gate incident shows that the national Security Agency (NSA) and the Federal Bureau of investigation (FBI) of the United States It can directly use the huge data resources of Google, Microsoft and other companies to obtain the required intelligence through data mining, association analysis and other means.

3 Public Opinion Risk Control Under Network Media Big Data

The key to dispelling doubts about online public opinion is to have scientific analysis tools, models and criteria. In recent years, some scholars and research institutions have carried out some important research and made some progress. At the same time, there are also some deficiencies [3]. These studies often ignore the nature and characteristics of Internet content and public opinion itself, and ignore the internal deep structure and relationship of content and public opinion, ignoring the content and the laws and conditions of the evolution of public opinion. It is mainly reflected in: first, more mathematical statistical software is used to replace the scientific criterion of public opinion analysis; second, automatic clustering is emphasized, and the improved clustering engine based on suffix tree, or the probability analysis method based on Bayesian probability theory and the traditional K-means eigenvector space analysis method are used. Although there is a breakthrough in presentation, However, there is no in-depth study on public opinion itself. This kind of research simply graphically illustrates the classical probability theory to replace the complexity of public opinion analysis criteria; third, it replaces the deep nature of public opinion analysis with the analysis of hot spots and key levels.

$$J_c = \sum_{i=1}^{k} \sum_{p \in C_1} \|p - M_i\|^2 \tag{1}$$

$$J(\textstyle\prod, W) = \sum_{k=1}^{K} \sum_{x \in \pi} \sum_{d=1}^{D} (x_{id} - v_{kd})^2 \tag{2}$$

For example, although we emphasize the topic detection and tracking TDT technology and try to automatically find and track social hot spots and focus content and public opinion, the analysis mode only stays in the hot spots and focus, and most of the research is not in-depth. It is worth mentioning that Xie haiguang, a doctoral student at Antai School of management, Shanghai Jiaotong University, and Chen Zhongrun, a master's student at the school of international and public affairs, Shanghai Jiaotong University, have worked together to build hot spots (heat), key points (severity), focus (focus), sensitivity (sensitivity), frequency (frequency), inflection points (inflection), difficulties (difficulty), doubts (doubt) and stickiness (viscosity) of Internet content and public opinion And scatter (divergence) and other ten analysis modes and criteria (the first batch). It has established the basic position of public opinion research methods and has been approved and recognized by the majority of public opinion researchers.

The horizontal axis of the coordinate system is used to represent the time t, and the vertical axis is used to represent the relevant information points of an information point (keyword group), so the change of the relevant information points of an information point (keyword group) a with time can be represented by the function fa (t). From a certain time period T1 to T2 in the past, the number of relevant information points RA (T12) = fa (T2) − FA (T1). Since RA (T12) is the data obtained at time point T2, it is called the heat of information point a at time point T2, expressed in RA (T2). Rank r (T2) of all information points (keyword groups) a, B, C. from large to small, that is, generate the network public opinion hot spot ranking list within the time period T1 to T2. As shown in Fig. 1:

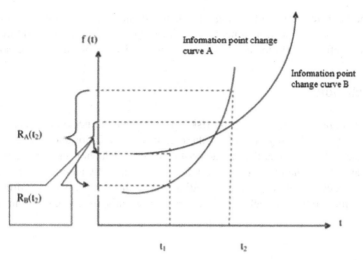

Fig. 1. Schematic diagram of network public opinion hot spots (heat)

4   Analysis of Early Warning System

(1) Importance of indicators

Network public opinion is an extremely complex system, which can cause a variety of factors to change public opinion. Therefore, it is necessary to select important and influential indicators closely related to the operation of public opinion, which is conducive to identify the essential characteristics of public opinion from the macro level, explore the basic laws of public opinion change, and find the boundary between the safety of public opinion [4].

(2) Comprehensiveness of index system

The comprehensiveness of the index system means that for any kind of public opinion, one or a group of indicators can be found from the index system to measure, and there can be no situation that a certain public opinion information can not find the measurement indicators, let alone the omission of important influencing factors and the problem of giving consideration to one and losing the other.

(3) Simplicity of index system

The simplicity of the index system means that while meeting the overall integrity of the index system, the established index system should be as simple as possible, do not use less representative indicators, and delete overlapping indicators with similar meanings. In this way, the index system not only covers the index quantity required for early warning and prediction, and achieves the purpose of early warning and prediction, but also eliminates the non main variables that make little contribution to the subject and may even lead to the emergence of fuzzy judgment results.

(4) Timeliness of index data

Network public opinion early warning and forecasting system is mainly used for timely analysis and effective early warning of medium and short-term public opinion.

Therefore, the timeliness of obtaining current statistical data has become an important requirement for data collection of network public opinion early warning and forecasting indicators. Useful information can be obtained in time by establishing stable channels.

5 Conclusion

This paper studies the public opinion risk control under the network media big data, uses the big data technology to collect the data of user behavior and device behavior, analyzes these data, obtains the characteristics of user behavior and device behavior, and then determines the identity and realizes authentication by identifying the operator behavior and device behavior. Authentication based on big data makes it difficult for attackers to imitate the user behavior Features to pass authentication, so it can be more secure.

References

1. Jiang, S.: Group events caused by enterprise labor disputes from the perspective of public opinion. Theoretical circles (2007)
2. Wang, L.: Handling public opinion in mass emergencies. Leadership (2007)
3. Xu, X.: Research on emergency handling of network public opinion events. J. North China Electr. Power Univ. (2007)
4. Guo, L.: Control of false information on the Internet and guidance of network public opinion. Network news circle (2005)

Research on Quality Evaluation of College Students' Innovation and Entrepreneurship Education Based on Grey Correlation Algorithm

Wei Wei[✉]

Guilin University, Guangxi 451005, China
Wiwen090326@163.com

Abstract. This paper studies the quality evaluation of students' innovative education by using grey correlation algorithm. The qualitative evaluation of students' innovation and entrepreneurship ability is very important. Grey correlation analysis is actually to express the distance between two vectors, and then use mathematical methods to measure the relationship between the two vectors. Therefore, the content to be evaluated must be determined through data analysis. In the process of curriculum reform and innovative education, based on the gray algorithm, we should deepen the evaluation system of students' entrepreneurial basic learning, and build a teaching evaluation index system based on the gray algorithm. At the same time, we should improve the teaching ability of innovation and entrepreneurship, strengthen the construction of innovation and entrepreneurship teaching ability of college teachers, and reform teaching methods and evaluation methods. In summary, the following factors may affect the ranking or objectives of the project. Colleges and universities should create the brand of innovation and entrepreneurship education activities, innovate the education mode, cultivate students' high-quality and targeted innovation and entrepreneurship skills, and improve students' innovation and entrepreneurship skills.

Keywords: Grey correlation degree algorithm · College student · Innovation and entrepreneurship education · Quality evaluation

1 Introduction

Optimize the environment for students' innovation and entrepreneurship. Lower the threshold for students' innovation and entrepreneurship, and encourage various incubators to open a certain proportion of free incubation space to students' innovation and entrepreneurship groups, including the evaluation of the national science and Technology Incubation Center. This reduces the opportunities for students to join the innovation and entrepreneurship team. Create conditions for providing measures to promote students' innovation and entrepreneurship, and studying the mechanism to reduce students' entrepreneurial risk [1].

© ICST Institute for Computer Sciences, Social Informatics and Telecommunications Engineering 2023
Published by Springer Nature Switzerland AG 2023. All Rights Reserved
M. A. Jan and F. Khan (Eds.): BigIoT-EDU 2022, LNICST 467, pp. 153–164, 2023.
https://doi.org/10.1007/978-3-031-23944-1_18

When building service platforms, we should fully consider the role of innovative business platforms such as university science and technology parks, student entrepreneurship parks, and school student spaces, open them to students free of charge, and develop professional service incubators. Deepen the entrepreneurship and employment initiative "schulbank", promote the construction of business demonstration bases and University demonstration bases, and establish stable cooperative relations [2].

In terms of tax and fiscal policies, we should increase the financial support of the central lottery fund of the Ministry of education for the development of students' innovation and entrepreneurship on the existing basis. Strengthen targeted financial support for the education and teaching reform of Central University, take innovative student education and entrepreneurship as an important part of capital allocation, and implement specific tax reduction measures.

Financial institutions are encouraged to provide financial services for student entrepreneurship projects and solve the problem of student entrepreneurship financing in accordance with the principles of market and enterprise sustainability. Guide social capital to support students' innovation and entrepreneurship, promote social resources through market mechanisms, more effectively respond to students' innovation and entrepreneurship needs, and help students' innovation and entrepreneurship projects grow healthily.

Improve the successful transformation mechanism, strengthen the cooperation between local, enterprise and student innovation and entrepreneurship teams, expand the channels of successful transformation, and promote the implementation of innovation achievements and entrepreneurship projects.

In 1989, the United Nations Educational, scientific and Cultural Organization (UNESCO) first reviewed and analyzed the concept of innovation and entrepreneurship education and defined it as an educational method to promote students' professionalism and innovative ability. Many Chinese scientists have examined the content of innovation and entrepreneurship education mainly from two aspects. Some people believe that innovation and entrepreneurship is a new educational concept formed in the process of entrepreneurship basic education and education. Scientists believe that innovation education is one of the contents of entrepreneurship education, and innovation education is a necessary prerequisite for entrepreneurship education [3]. This paper believes that the concept of innovation and entrepreneurship education is not only the combination of innovation education and entrepreneurship education, but also reflects the integration and interaction of the two.

First of all, innovation education is the foundation of entrepreneurship education, which provides additional theoretical support for entrepreneurship education and improves the level of entrepreneurship education. On the other hand, entrepreneurship education can also become a means and form of innovation education. All educational innovations are based on the availability and availability of entrepreneurship education. Compared with other forms of teaching, innovation and entrepreneurship course pays more attention to teaching quality and correct talent training. Innovation and entrepreneurship education is the combination of talents with national economic development and social needs.

2   Related Work

2.1   Grey Correlation Degree Algorithm

A method for determining the degree of correlation between elements by inferring from the geometric shape of the change curve of each element. Based on the quantitative analysis of dynamic trend, this method makes a geometric comparison of the statistical data of time series in the system, and establishes a grey relationship between the basic series and the comparable series. The greater the correlation with the original sequence, the closer the correlation between the change trend and the original sequence, and the closer the correlation with the original sequence. The quantitative comparison method of system design is based on the mathematical basis of space theory to determine the correlation coefficient and correlation coefficient between the original sequence and multiple comparison sequences. The convergence is calculated by calculating the convergence of each sequence. As shown in Fig. 1. Compared with the previous multi factor method, the demand of grey correlation analysis is low. The grey correlation analysis method is also applicable to irregular data. The number of samples should be reduced to 4 to avoid quantitative and qualitative differences in the analysis results. Its basic idea is to measure

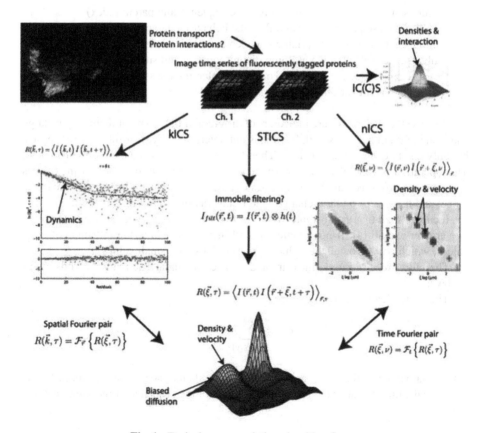

Fig. 1. Typical grey correlation algorithm flow

without considering the original observation data of the rating index, calculate the correlation coefficient and correlation coefficient, and classify the rating index according to its importance. The application of grey correlation involves various fields of social and natural sciences, especially social and economic sectors, such as investment income of different economic sectors, analysis of regional economic advantages, adaptability of industrial structure, etc.

2.2 Analysis Principle

Grey correlation analysis is based on the geometric similarity of sequence curves to determine the affinity. The higher the correlation degree, the smaller the correlation degree between sequences.

Generally speaking, abstract systems, such as social, economic, agricultural, ecological and educational systems, are composed of different types of systems. The driving force of system development is determined by the comprehensive action of various factors. Grey association rules are used to determine the influence of elements on the system.

(1) Parent sequence (also known as reference sequence and parent index)
    The data sequence that can reflect the behavior characteristics of the system is similar to the dependent variable y, which is recorded here as x_0.
(2) Subsequence (also known as comparison sequence and sub index)
    The data sequence composed of factors affecting the system behavior is similar to the dependent variable x, which is recorded here as $x_0, x_1, \ldots, x_m$.

Because these elements are indicators of different things, some of them may be large and some of them may be small, but this is not determined by their intrinsic properties, but only due to different dimensions. Therefore, we need to make them dimensionless. This operation is generally called normalization in the field of data processing, that is to reduce the difference of absolute values of data, integrate them into the approximate range, and then focus on their changes and trends (as shown in Fig. 2 below).

It can be seen that the absolute values of two curves are very large, while the other two are very small [4]. If not handled, it will inevitably lead to the influence of large values, which will "drown" the influence of variables with small values.

Therefore, we need to de measure and toughen the data. The main methods are as follows:

The basic idea is: define sequence:

$$O_v = \sum_{u \in N[v]} w_{u,v} x_u \tag{1}$$

(1) Initial value: as the name suggests, it is to divide the data of this sequence by the initial value. Because the order of magnitude of the sequence of the same factor is

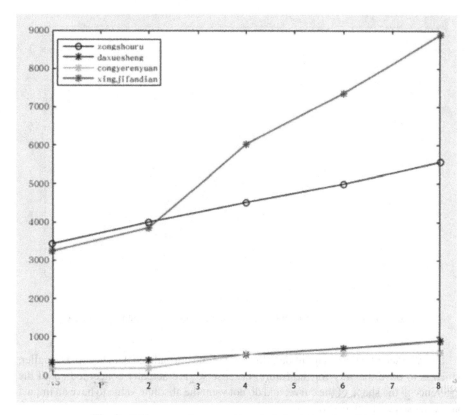

Fig. 2. Difference, change and trend of absolute value of data

not different, these values can be sorted to the order of magnitude of 1 by dividing by the initial value. Formula:

$$O_{v,j} = h\left(\sum_{i=1}^{f_{k-1}} \sum_{u \in N[v]} w_{i,j,u,v} x_{u,i}\right), (j = 1, \ldots, f_k) \tag{2}$$

(2) Mean value: as the name suggests, it is to divide the data of this series by the mean value. Because the mean value of the series with a large order of magnitude is relatively large, it can be reduced to the order of 1 after being removed. Formula:

$$\max \sum_{I} \left[U^I(X^I) - C^I(X^I)\right] \tag{3}$$

In fact, this method is widely used in data processing [5].

In GRA, it seems that average or initial value is often used. Use the above figure to get the initial value, as shown in Fig. 3:

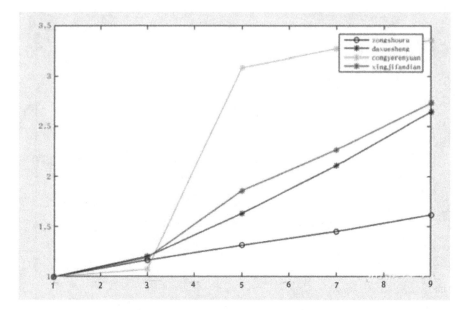

Fig. 3. It seems that average or initial value processing is often used in RA

It can be seen that the magnitude difference of the normalized data becomes smaller, which is to pave the way for the future, because we are actually concerned about the difference in the shape of the curve, and do not want the absolute value to have an impact on the subsequent calculation.

2.3   Innovation and Entrepreneurship Education for College Students

In view of the problems and deficiencies in the research process, further refine measures, clarify responsibilities, and improve the innovation and entrepreneurship ability and level of our school. By analyzing the new situation and new tasks faced by innovation and entrepreneurship students, this paper puts forward the ideas and requirements to promote innovation and Entrepreneurship of students in our school.

First of all, we should seriously follow and unify our thinking, and deeply understand the importance of carrying out students' innovative work. At the national level, innovation is the most important embodiment of national strength. Developing innovation and entrepreneurship education is an urgent need for the country to implement the innovation driven development strategy, develop structural changes and dynamic economic transformation [6]. The development and formation of students' innovative entrepreneurship is one of the needs of national development. From the perspective of schools, deepening innovation and entrepreneurship education is an inevitable choice to actively cooperate with the national innovation development strategy and cultivate students to become innovative and innovative talents in the new era. In view of the important stage of school development, we should speed up the training of innovative and entrepreneurial talents, constantly improve students' creativity, entrepreneurial and innovative ability and entrepreneurial ability, and further improve the adaptability of talent training to economic and social development. So that schools can make more contributions and support for the social and economic development of the service industry.

The second is to improve the system and vigorously promote and study the innovation and entrepreneurship education model adapted to local conditions. Innovation and entrepreneurship basic education is a systematic project of interdisciplinary cooperation, interdisciplinary integration and interdisciplinary participation. We should attach importance to institutional innovation, further improve the working mechanism, deepen the reform of innovation and entrepreneurship education, promote innovation and entrepreneurship education, and ensure the implementation of policies as soon as possible [7]. To find a good connection point, colleges and universities should give full play to their leading role, integrate resources, integrate learning with enterprises, teachers and students, and guide and stimulate students' motivation for innovation and entrepreneurship. Strengthen the construction of practice platform and broaden students' experimental channels. In particular, we should participate in the practice of innovation and entrepreneurship, build information platforms, learning platforms and exercise platforms, expand investment, optimize services, and lay the foundation for innovation and entrepreneurship.

Third, seize opportunities, overcome challenges, and create a working environment in which all members participate. We should recognize the weak links, take students' innovation and entrepreneurship as the key to improve students' comprehensive practical skills and competitiveness, and combine classroom teaching, strengthening practice, guidance and support. We should continue to implement targeted actions, eliminate obstacles and challenges faced by students in the process of innovation and entrepreneurship, and strengthen policy support. Adhere to overall planning and linkage, establish a long-term linkage mechanism, form a cross departmental linkage, Cross School linkage and innovative education coordination mechanism for entrepreneurship education, integrate resources and promote overall planning. Fully support students' innovation and entrepreneurship. Taking the "145" construction characteristic high-level university planning as an opportunity, combined with the medical characteristics of colleges and universities, highlight the characteristics, innovate and entrepreneurship ideas, go deep into the hearts of every teacher and student, and carry out daily conscious activities. In order to create a new situation of innovation and entrepreneurship education for students in our school, we must improve innovative talents, promote the high-quality development of school disciplines, and make positive contributions to the development of school disciplines.

3 Research on the Quality Evaluation of College Students' Innovation and Entrepreneurship Education Based on Grey Correlation Algorithm

As a participant and assistant, the government plays an important role in the development of innovation and entrepreneurship ecosystem in Colleges and universities. It can create a good external environment for innovation and entrepreneurship education in Colleges and universities from many aspects, such as policy formulation, financial support, public opinion formation, service system, department coordination and so on.

All kinds of enterprises, especially well-known enterprises, play an important role in innovation and entrepreneurship education in Colleges and universities. This is the most obvious feeling and goal of students' innovation and entrepreneurship. Therefore, enterprises bear irreplaceable social responsibility in innovation and entrepreneurship education in Colleges and universities.

The ultimate goal of innovation and entrepreneurship education lies in students. Only when students accept the concept of innovation and entrepreneurship and boldly practice innovation and entrepreneurship, can innovation education achieve excellent results. Every student has a family behind him. Family promotion is a powerful guarantee for students' practice, innovation and entrepreneurship. Most "big" data is not the appearance of "large capacity", but the "great value" of data analysis. In addition to descriptive statistical reports, one of the key factors reflecting the value of data is the use of data in various ways. Through data collection, analysis and result extraction, evaluate the teaching quality, so that school leaders and parents can make more scientific and accurate decisions. Compared with the traditional "brainstorming" education policy, big data has further deepened, expanded and deepened the evaluation and analysis of the quality of higher education. As shown in Fig. 4.

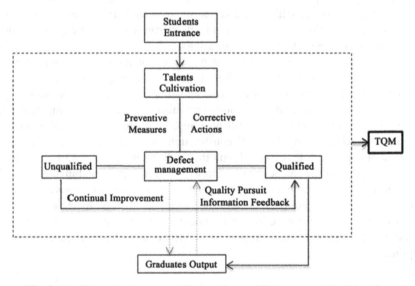

Fig. 4. Quality analysis process of innovation and Entrepreneurship Education

This paper puts forward five levels and 21 sub index systems, and defines the conditions of innovation and entrepreneurship education, the plans and activities of innovation and entrepreneurship education, the methods of innovation and entrepreneurship education, independent innovation and entrepreneurship, etc. Evaluate. Innovate the effectiveness of school education. Eight universities in a city were selected as the respondents. A survey was conducted on students' satisfaction with innovation and entrepreneurship education. Sociological statistical methods showed that a total of 34 A, 52 B, 76 C, 297 D, 37 e, 52 g and 190 h students listed "satisfied", "satisfied", "general", "dissatisfied" and "extremely dissatisfied" in the questionnaire, with values of 100, 80 and 60 respectively. From 40 and 20, we finally reached a satisfactory level.

By observing the above formula, we can find that:

1). The numerator value is the same for all subsequences (the numerator number is actually the distance in all dimensions of all factors from the nearest dimension to the parent sequence (reference sequence, that is, the sequence we want to compare).

2). If the previous data preprocessing is not the initial value, but the mean value or other methods, there may still be a distance between the curves, that is, between the parent sequence and each sub sequence, then dividing the minimum distance with the distance of each dimension below can actually be regarded as a means of canceling the dimension.

For all subsequences, this molecule is the same, so in fact, this coefficient:

$$k < \sum_{i=0}^{n} C(_i^n 1) \tag{4}$$

For two fractions: 1/5 and 1/4, their numerators are the same, and the difference between denominators is 1. At this time, their values differ by 1/20, that is, 0.05. This is the case without + ro max. the numerators are the same, and the difference between denominators represents the distance from the reference sequence. If we add 20 to their numerator and denominator at the same time, they are 21/25 and 21/24. The difference between them is 0.035 [8]. It can be seen that adding this item will lead to the coefficient difference of points with the same distance, which will be reduced due to calculation. Obviously, the larger rho, the smaller the difference between different zeta coefficients.

To sum up, RO is a coefficient that controls the differentiation of the coefficient. The value of RO is 0 to 1. The smaller ro is, the greater the degree of discrimination is. Generally, the value of 0.5 is more appropriate. The value of correlation coefficient falls between 0 and 1.

4 Evaluation of Influencing Factors by Grey Correlation Method

Therefore, the degree of grey correlation is a method to measure the degree of correlation between different factors, that is, the degree of grey correlation. Grey correlation analysis has strict requirements on data format. Please carry out it according to the example. The parent sequence or characteristic sequence is a column respectively. If the parent sequence is not placed, spssau will take the maximum value of the feature sequence as the parent sequence value by default [9].

In grey correlation analysis, the data must be greater than 0. The reason is that if it is less than o, there will be "offset" phenomenon in calculation, which does not conform to the calculation principle of grey correlation analysis. If there is data less than 0, it is recommended to treat it as a null value or fill it (spssau outlier function). The dimensionless methods of data are mean value and initial value respectively. There is no fixed use standard for them. Initial value has more strict requirements on data format. Spssau recommends using mean value method.

The advantage of College Students' Entrepreneurship lies in science and technology. Successful entrepreneurship requires scientific and technological achievements with independent intellectual property rights. The inspiration of scientific and technological creation comes from the accumulation of knowledge. Without the accumulation of knowledge, there will be no discovery, invention and creation. Entrepreneurship has also lost its foundation for success. Entrepreneurs should not only become inventors and scientists, but also entrepreneurs and entrepreneurs. Enterprises need entrepreneurs to operate and manage. Therefore, entrepreneurs also need to have certain operation and management ability. The formation of operation and management ability requires the learning and accumulation of business, marketing, enterprise management, law and other knowledge. Therefore, contemporary college students should form the habit of studying hard, take the initiative to understand the development trend of high and new technology, understand the cutting-edge knowledge of science and technology in the new century, constantly draw nutrition from seeking knowledge, obtain motivation from learning, and realize the transformation from learning to discovery.

Independence refers to independent thinking and action without relying on others. Independent personality is the basic quality of innovation and creation. Without independent personality, you can only seek common ground and obey. Without independent thinking, you can't have originality. Through the ages, all creative people have strong independence. Entrepreneurship is a creative activity, which requires students to have innovative spirit and entrepreneurial ability. Therefore, we should cultivate college students' entrepreneurial ability; We must pay attention to the cultivation of their independent personality and creative thinking ability; Otherwise, people will follow suit and be submissive. If they are only satisfied with the current situation, they cannot create and surpass, let alone face fierce competition.

Entrepreneurship is a kind of creative work. It can't be plain sailing. We will always encounter such problems, setbacks and failures. At present, the success rate of college students starting enterprises is very low. The success rate of undergraduate entrepreneurship is less than 1%, and the success rate of graduate students is only 5% [10]. That is to say, among all entrepreneurs, there is rarely a successful entrepreneurship, and each entrepreneur has to experience setbacks and failures. In the face of setbacks and failures, we need to have a correct psychological preparation for dealing with setbacks, an optimistic attitude towards life, but also an indomitable spirit and the courage and confidence to overcome difficulties. At the same time, entrepreneurs should also have the wisdom to learn from setbacks, be good at discovering and absorbing the value of setbacks and failures, and make setbacks and failures become a ladder for entrepreneurs to climb up, rather than a burden in advance.

Correlation analysis is a systematic analysis of innovation and entrepreneurship education, which is used to quantitatively describe the relationship or trend between innovation and entrepreneurship education or parameters. The idea is to infer the close relationship between the sequence data and reflect the correlation of the data sequence by comparing the geometric similarity between the sample data sequence and the data sequence curve. The development and trend evaluation of grey correlation analysis system is very suitable for dynamic process analysis. Grey correlation is a measurement tool of grey correlation analysis [11], which is used to measure the relationship between innovation and entrepreneurship education. The main object of grey correlation analysis is the state variables of discrete data, such as time series data. Different from the traditional correlation analysis, two such discrete data can neither change the time series nor the nature of the original data series.

Grey correlation analysis is essentially. Firstly, sequence and the ideal data sequence composed of the best index is obtained, the correlation degree is calculated from the correlation coefficient, and then the conclusion is obtained by comparing and analyzing according to the correlation degree. This method is superior to the classical accurate mathematical method. By modeling the objectives, ideas and requirements, the grey system to be studied can gradually change from fuzzy to clear in structure and relationship, and the unclear factors can be gradually clear. This method breaks the constraints that traditional mathematics cannot be ambiguous [12]. It is also different from the traditional correlation. It has the characteristics of simple principle, simple calculation, easy to master, clear sorting and no obvious requirements for data distribution characteristics. Therefore, it has great research and application value. Especially with the support of the development of computer technology, the application scope of this analysis method is becoming larger and larger.

5   Conclusion

Due to the limited domestic statistical data and large gray scale, and the data is affected by human beings and has no typical distribution law, the grey correlation analysis method is introduced to adapt to the occasion with small amount of data. The most important thing of grey correlation analysis method is to find the evaluation object, which may be inherent in the title and may be virtual. Then analyze the deviation degree between each index and the evaluation object, unify the index with different methods, and the value will be different. At present, the achievements of College Students' entrepreneurship are not very optimistic. Among all self-employed college students, the success rate of first-time entrepreneurship is very low. Statistics show that China's overall entrepreneurial success rate has basically reached 30%, while in the entrepreneurial army, the entrepreneurial success rate of college students is only about 3%, accounting for only 10% of successful entrepreneurial enterprises. From the perspective of the low success rate, so we should actively find our own problems and strive to correct them to strengthen ourselves and lay a solid foundation for a smooth entrepreneurship.

References

1. Li, T., Xia, X.: Research on initial power flow calculation automatically for dispatcher training based on grey correlation analysis. Smart Grid **11**(2), 140–147 (2021)
2. Teng, H.: Construction and drug evaluation based on convolutional neural network system optimized by grey correlation analysis. Comput. Intell. Neurosci. **2021**, 1–9 (2021)
3. Chen, F., Cao, H., Zhang, B., et al.: A diagnosis method of vibration fault of steam turbine based on information entropy and grey correlation analysis. IOP Conf. Ser. Earth Environ. Sci. **714**(4), 042055 (2021)

4. Dang, Z.: Construction of Jiangxi Province's "dual cycle" logistics economic evaluation system based on entropy weight grey correlation method. In: International Conference on Economics, Law and Education Research (ELER 2021) (2021)
5. Li, L., Liu, Z., Du, X.: Improvement of analytic hierarchy process based on grey correlation model and its engineering application. ASCE-ASME J. Risk Uncertainty Eng. Syst. Part A Civil Eng. 7(2), 04021007 (2021)
6. Huang, X., Sun, J., Zhao, X.: Credit risk assessment of supply chain financing with a Grey correlation model: an empirical study on china's home appliance industry. Complexity 2021(2), 1–12 (2021)
7. Zhang, W.: Human-computer interaction virtual training system for college students' innovation and entrepreneurship education. J. Interconnect. Netw. 22, 2143001 (2021)
8. Zhao, X., Zhang, J.: The analysis of integration of ideological political education with innovation entrepreneurship education for college students. Front. Psychol. 12, 610409 (2021)
9. Su, G.: Exploration of innovation and entrepreneurship education model in higher vocational colleges based on rural revitalization strategy. SHS Web Conf. 96, 03003 (2021)
10. Tang, D., Li, X.: Thoughts on innovation and entrepreneurship mode reform of college students in the context of COVID-19. Int. J. Electr. Eng. Educ. 18, 002072092098431 (2021)
11. Li, M., Wang, T., Wu, Y.: Impact of innovation and entrepreneurship education in a University under personality psychology education concept on talent training and cultural diversity of new entrepreneurs. Front. Psychol. 12, 696987 (2021)
12. Bai, L., Wang, C., Zhang, L.: Microprocessor and real-time task processing system application in university innovation and entrepreneurship education platform. Microprocess. Microsyst. 104092 (2021)

Research on Student Achievement and Employment Flow Based on Apriori Algorithm Under the Background of Big Data

Linbo Wei[1]([✉]) and Linzheng Ren[2]

[1] Wuhan Business University, Wuhan 430056, Hubei, China
20150116@wbu.edu.cn
[2] Xijing University, Xi'an, Shaanxi, China

Abstract. The era of big data is driving profound changes in many industries, and also brings opportunities and challenges to the reform of higher education teaching management. Student achievement data is an important manifestation of college teaching big data. Introducing big data technology to fully tap the potential laws in student achievement big data is a reform direction of current teaching management. In view of this situation, this paper analyzes and studies the Apriori algorithm and its implementation steps, preprocesses and discretizes the student achievement data, combines the Apriori algorithm, fully excavates the association rules between the student achievement big data and the employment flow, realizes the transformation of the sleeping achievement big data into valuable data resources, and provides theoretical guidance for the employment management of colleges and universities, So as to effectively improve the level and quality of teaching management.

Keywords: Big data · Apriori algorithm · Achievements · Employment flow

1 Introduction

With the rapid development of information society, various industries have formed a large number of data. These data are like treasures waiting for us to mine. Since the first batch of college students to expand enrollment entered the talent market in 2003, employment guidance for graduates has been a key issue of the Ministry of education for a long time. With the continuous expansion of enrollment in Colleges and universities and the rapid development of national information education, information technology is more and more widely used in Colleges and universities [1]. Relevant departments of colleges and universities began to use information technology to collect, store and manage students' personal data, school learning data and employment data. As far as the employment sector is concerned, a large amount of information related to students' employment is stored. Although today, with the rapid development of information technology, colleges and universities have also implemented information management and analysis of data, they usually only use relatively simple and backward methods, only make simple statistics

© ICST Institute for Computer Sciences, Social Informatics and Telecommunications Engineering 2023
Published by Springer Nature Switzerland AG 2023. All Rights Reserved
M. A. Jan and F. Khan (Eds.): BigIoT-EDU 2022, LNICST 467, pp. 165–176, 2023.
https://doi.org/10.1007/978-3-031-23944-1_19

and display, and cannot excavate the real value of these information. Not to mention the guidance and early warning for students in school, as well as the prediction of students' future employment [2]. Therefore, how to extract effective information from campus big data, use campus big data to analyze students' school behavior and employment, dig out the mechanism of their interaction and the laws behind them, and then give early warning and guidance to college students has become an important problem to be solved urgently.

As a direct reflection of students' academic level, students' performance has attracted the attention of students, parents, teachers and schools. However, students' grades are different. How to effectively improve the overall performance based on the existing results has always been a matter of concern.

In recent years, data mining technology has been widely used, which can not only be used for the analysis and research of students' grades, but also for the evaluation of students' comprehensive quality. At present, provinces and cities across the country are facing the reform of the college entrance examination. For example, Jiangsu, Zhejiang and other places will adopt the grade scoring system of the college entrance examination, and the mining of association rules in this paper is closely related to the grade of achievement. In real life, the use of students' scores by schools is limited to the most common descriptive statistics, such as average score, maximum score, growth rate and other shallow levels. They do not make good use of score data for deeper analysis and mining, and rarely think about and study problems such as "whether there is a potential correlation between the scores of various subjects".

The level of economic development in different cities is uneven, and college students lack effective guidance in employment, resulting in their employment choices tend to more developed areas, without fully considering the characteristics of the industry and determining more suitable employment areas. In addition, in regions with inferior economic level, new college students usually lose seriously in the short term. These conditions have a serious impact on China's regional economic coordination and sustainable development.

Massive student achievement data is an important manifestation of big teaching data in Colleges and universities. As an important index of teaching quality evaluation, curriculum achievement is not only closely related to the vital interests of many student groups, but also an important reference for talent training in Colleges and universities [3]. It has important guiding significance for deepening teaching evaluation and reforming teaching management in Colleges and universities. How to reasonably introduce big data technology, analyze the hidden law of massive student achievement data, mine the potential value of these data, and apply them more scientifically to the reform of all aspects of teaching management, so as to better serve the whole process of higher teaching and improve the talent training level of colleges and universities is a direction of current higher education practitioners. Using the Apriori algorithm under the background of big data, this paper deeply analyzes the relationship between student achievement and employment flow, which has important guiding significance for the employment management department of colleges and universities to effectively predict the employment flow of students and make more scientific employment decisions, so as to better guide and educate students [4].

2 Related Work

2.1 Big Data Background

With the accelerating pace of digitalization, networking and intellectualization of the global manufacturing industry, industrial big data has gradually become one of the footholds of the deep integration of the manufacturing industry and the new generation of information technology. Traditional Internet big data focuses on mining the correlation between different attributes, while industrial big data is more purposeful, paying more attention to the physical meaning behind data features and the mechanism of correlation between features. Therefore, industrial big data, as a key factor for the manufacturing industry to improve productivity, competitiveness and innovation, has attracted the attention of all parties.

First, the government attaches great importance to it. Whether Germany's "industry 4.0", the United States "industrial Internet" or "made in China 20,259", all take industrial big data as an important basis for promoting the innovation and development of manufacturing industry in their country.

The first is to lay the foundation for enterprises to seize the high point of their production line and storage through the analysis of their own production line and information technology, and the second is to strengthen the analysis of their own production line and storage intention; On the other hand, enterprises with relatively mature information construction launch products for industrial big data, integrate upstream and downstream resources, and strive to improve their competitiveness through data analysis products.

Third, universities and scientific research institutions should speed up the research of core technologies and strengthen personnel deployment and capital investment for the research of common technologies such as machine learning, distributed computing and parallel computing; Some organizations with technology accumulation have become emerging forces in the industry by providing general solutions for industrial enterprises.

In the context of the current era of big data, the issue of workplace integrity has been paid more and more attention by the society. China is the largest human resources market in the world, with the richest human resources and 920 million practitioners, but the problem of workplace integrity in China is very serious. According to the data of China professional credit network, 85% of the resumes on the Internet in China involve fraud.

The root of workplace fraud lies in information asymmetry, which is the essence of deception. The most effective way to eliminate fraud and deception is to conduct workplace background investigation. By using big data mining technology, analyze the credit status of job seekers in terms of basic information, educational background, work experience, work ability, salary and welfare and workplace ethics, so as to provide employers with accurate workplace credit reports, Make the supply and demand sides of the workplace more easily and efficiently gain trust, improve the efficiency of the human resources market, reduce the costs and risks of all parties, and improve the integrity level of the society.

In recent years, in order to improve this situation, the state has a certain policy preference for some regions, which has led to a certain increase in the number of college students in the western region, but there is still a large loss of college students in the northeast region. In addition, in addition to the differences in economic development and policy treatment between different provinces, cities and districts, cultural customs, natural environment and other factors will also affect the regional flow direction of College Students' employment. These problems should be fully taken into account in the analysis of the guidance strategy of the regional flow direction of College Students' employment. This paper studies the student achievement and employment flow based on Apriori algorithm under the background of big data.

2.2 Introduction to Apriori Algorithm

At present, many algorithms can be used to obtain association rules, which can be obtained by mining frequent itemsets. Apriori algorithm is one of the most commonly used algorithms for mining frequent itemsets of association rules.

The basic idea of Apriori algorithm is to input the minimum support min_ Sup, first traverse the transaction database d to obtain the support of 1-item candidate set C and item set; Cut out the itemset with support less than min. sup in C to obtain 1-itemfrequent set L; Self connect the frequent set LK-1 to obtain the k-item candidate set C, scan each transaction item in the database to obtain the support of each item in the frequent set, and cut the support less than min_ The k-term frequent set LK is obtained from the itemset of sup; By repeating the previous step of iteration until no new frequent sets are generated, all frequent itemsets are finally obtained, and the mining of association rules is completed [5].

It can be seen from the above process that the core of apriror algorithm is to get k candidate sets from the candidate set, and then scan the transaction database every time to calculate the support of candidates. The advantage of this is that the resulting frequent itemsets will not be missed or repeated, but a lot of time is spent on I/O access. Therefore, the key problem of improvement is how to reduce the number of candidate sets and reduce the number of scanning transaction databases. The flow of Apriori algorithm is shown in Fig. 1.

From a technical point of view, data mining (DM) is a process of extracting hidden, unknown but potentially useful information and knowledge from a large number of incomplete, noisy, fuzzy and random actual data.

From the perspective of business application, data mining is a new business information processing technology. Its main feature is to extract, transform, analyze and model a large number of business data in business database, so as to extract the key knowledge to assist business decision-making.

Association analysis is used to find such rules: customers will buy another product when they buy another product. In the above example, most people know the association rules: {diapers} → (beer}; that is, customers usually buy beer after buying diapers. Later, through investigation and analysis, it turns out that when the wife asked the husband to buy diapers for their children, the husband usually bought his favorite beer after buying diapers. However, how to measure whether this association rule is reliable? The measurement criteria are given below.

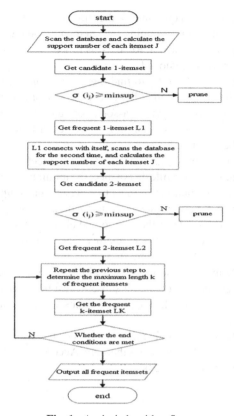

Fig. 1. Apriori algorithm flow

1. Support and confidence

Association rules can be described as: itemset → itemset. The number of transactions in itemset x (also known as support count) is defined as:

$$\sigma(X) = |t_i|X \subseteq t_i, t_i \in T \qquad (1)$$

Support characterizes the occurrence frequency of itemset xuy. Confidence is defined as follows:

$$s(X \rightarrow Y) = \frac{\sigma(X \cup Y)}{|T|} \qquad (2)$$

If the violent method is used to enumerate all association rules and find out the rules that meet the requirements, the time complexity will reach exponential level. Therefore, we need to find a less complex algorithm for correlation analysis.

Apriori algorithm is a method used to find frequent itemsets. The two input parameters of Apriori algorithm are minimum support and data set [6]. Firstly, the algorithm generates the itemset list of all individual items, and then removes the itemsets that do not meet the minimum support requirements after traversal; Next, the remaining sets are combined to generate an itemset containing two elements, and the itemset that does not meet the minimum support is removed; Repeat this process until all itemsets that do not meet the minimum support are removed.

Support (p|h)/support (P). In order to find the association rules, we can form a list of possible rules, and then test the reliability of each rule. Combined with the minimum requirements of reliability, we can get the association rules. Similar to finding frequent itemsets, we can generate many association rules for each frequent itemset, so many association rules will be generated.

Combined with Apriori principle, if a rule does not meet the minimum reliability requirement, then all subsets of the rule do not meet the minimum reliability requirement. Therefore, we can reduce the number of rules to be tested and simplify the problem.

The idea of finding association rules is to start with a frequent itemset and create a rule list. First, limit the right side of the rule to one element, test these rules, and then merge the remaining rules to create a new rule list. The right side of the rule is limited to two elements, which is realized step by step.

According to the definition of support, the following a priori theorem is obtained:

Theorem 1: if an itemset is frequent, all subsets must be frequent.

This is easy to prove, because the support of a subset of an itemset must not be less than that of the itemset.

Theorem 2: if an itemset is infrequent, all its supersets must also be infrequent.

Theorem 2 is the inverse of the previous theorem. According to theorem 2, the itemset tree can be pruned as shown in Fig. 2 below:

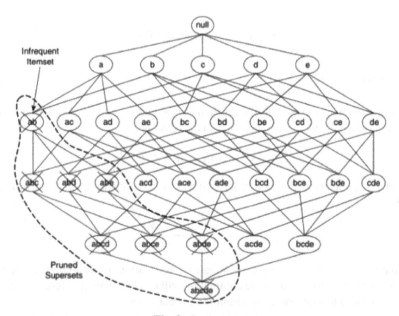

Fig. 2. Itemset tree

2.3 Apriori Implementation Steps

Apriori algorithm is divided into two steps: connection and pruning. The connection process mainly adopts matrix like operation, and the pruning process is to remove the unqualified intermediate results. In order to discover the association rules that users are interested in, we first need to set the minimum support. If an item set a meets the minimum support, then this item set is called frequent item set [6].

In the connection step, assuming that the set of all frequent itemsets is 1 and the set of all frequent k-1 itemsets is 1, L2 is connected with itself to generate the set C of candidate K itemsets. First, perform the first iteration operation, scan all transactions to get all candidate itemsets C, select the frequent itemset L that meets the minimum support in C, then connect the itemset l to get the candidate itemset C, select the frequent itemset L that meets the minimum support in C2 again, and so on, and finally get the frequent itemset l as L.

One feature of Apriori algorithm should be used in the pruning step: all non empty subsets of each frequent itemset must be frequent. Similarly, if the non empty subset of a candidate item set is not frequent, it can be inferred that the candidate item set must not be frequent, so it is necessary to select candidate C. Delete it.

In Apriori algorithm, l is included in C. Therefore, there is a possibility that a project in C is not frequent. According to the statistical results of all transactions, if the number of a candidate item in C is greater than or equal to the minimum support count, it is considered that the candidate item is frequent. If the number of a candidate item in C is less than the minimum support count, the candidate item is infrequent and can be cut from C.

(support = 30%, confidential = 60%); where support = 30% means that in all data records, the probability of a = A and B = B at the same time is 30%; Confidential = 60% means that in all data records, the probability of B = B in the case of a = a is 60%, that is, the conditional probability. Support reveals the probability that a = A and B = B occur at the same time, and confidence reveals the probability that B = B will occur when a = a occurs.

(1) If the closed values of support and confidence are set too high, although the mining time can be reduced, it is easy to cause some infrequent feature items hidden in the data to be ignored and it is difficult to find enough useful rules;

(2) If the closed values of support and confidence are set too low, there may be too many rules, or even a large number of redundant and invalid rules. At the same time, due to the inherent problems of the algorithm, it will lead to high load of calculation and greatly increase the mining time [6].

Apriori algorithm is a method to find frequent itemsets.

The two input parameters of Apriori algorithm are minimum support and data set. The algorithm first generates a itemset list of all individual elements. Then scan the data set to see which item sets meet the minimum support requirements, and those that do not meet the minimum support will be removed. Then, the remaining collections are combined to produce an itemset containing two elements. Next, re scan the transaction records to remove the item set that does not meet the minimum support. This process is repeated until all itemsets are removed.

The algorithm needs to constantly find candidate sets, and then prune, that is, remove the candidate sets of infrequent subsets. The time complexity is determined by the violent enumeration. The exponential level o (N2) of all subsets will be polynomial level, and the specific coefficients of polynomials depend on the underlying implementation.

3 Application of Apriori Algorithm in Analyzing the Relationship Between Student Achievement and Employment Flow

3.1 Data Preprocessing and Discretization

According to the idea and implementation process of Apriori algorithm, this paper takes the achievement data and employment data of 2020 graduates of automation major in a university as the data source to analyze the relationship between student achievement and employment flow. There are a large number of student performance data. Firstly, remove the meaningless redundant data, and select four performance indicators such as CET4 score, computer level II test score, average score of professional courses and the number of failed courses as the screening object. Among them, the average score of professional courses is based on the principle of automatic control The average scores of the three representative professional courses of motor and drag and analog electronic circuit are determined. A total of 156 valid data are sorted out, and the employment flow of students is added as all data mining objects. In order to protect students' privacy, students' names are replaced by numbers [7].

In order to facilitate the processing of Apriori algorithm, the above student data are further discretized. Record the average score of professional courses as item a, lower than 75 points as A0, and reaching or exceeding 75 points as A1; CET4 scores are classified as item B, and scores less than 425 are recorded as Bo, and scores greater than or equal to 425 are recorded as BL; The grade of computer grade II is compiled as item D, and if it fails, it is recorded as do, and if it passes, it is recorded as D1; The number of failed courses is compiled as item e, and greater than 0 is recorded as EO, equal to O It is recorded as E1.

3.2 Analysis of the Relationship Between Student Achievement and Employment Flow

Taking the data of graduate students as an example, this paper analyzes the relationship between student achievement and employment flow. According to the idea of Apriori algorithm, the relationship between student achievement data and employment flow is mined through the following steps [8].

(1) In the first iteration of the algorithm, each item is a member of the set C of candidate items. Scan all student achievement data and count each candidate item to obtain the candidate item set C containing 8 sub items.

(2) Set the minimum support to 10, select the frequent itemset L that meets the minimum support in C, which contains 4 sub items in total, and then the itemset L is self connected to obtain the candidate itemset containing 6 sub items, and then filter the frequent itemset L2 that meets the minimum payment from C, which contains 5 sub items in total, and then connect the 5 sub items to obtain the candidate itemset containing 4 sub items, and then filter according to the minimum support, Get the frequent itemset L [9].

(3) After L is self connected, candidate item set C is generated. C contains only one sub item and does not meet the minimum support, so the cycle is stopped. LS is the final frequent itemset. The generation process of these candidate itemsets and frequent itemsets is shown in Fig. 3.

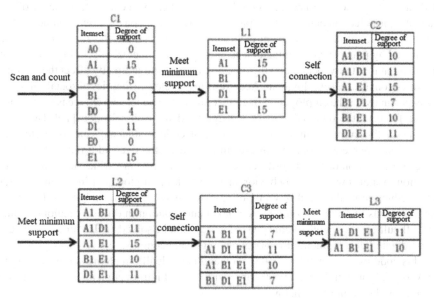

Fig. 3. The generation process of candidate itemsets and frequent itemsets

L is obtained through the generation process of candidate itemsets and frequent itemsets shown in Fig. 2. It is the last frequent itemset. Based on this analysis, there is a correlation between the students who meet the items of (A1 Di EI) or (AI Bi EI) and the employment flow of graduate students. It can be concluded that if a student meets the requirements of automatic control principle, motor and drag and analog electronic circuit, with an average score of 75 points or above, passes the computer level II examination and the number of failed courses is 0, or meets the requirements of automatic control principle, motor and drag and analog electronic circuit, with an average score of 75 points or above The number of courses that pass CET4 and fail is 0, and the student has a high probability of being admitted as a graduate student in the employment flow in the future. For domestic enterprises and foreign enterprises Students who are not employed and other employment flows can also scan all discretized student data to obtain candidate set C according to the above process, and then determine frequent itemset 1 according to the minimum support. Then, through the self connection of frequent itemset and the screening of minimum support, cycle to generate candidate set C and frequent itemset 1 until candidate itemset C; If none of the members meet the minimum support, then 1 is the final association rule [10]. According to the performance characteristics represented by frequent itemset L, the correlation between student performance and corresponding employment flow can be inferred.

4   Simulation Analysis

This paper studies the student achievement and employment flow of Apriori algorithm. In addition to the influence of family factors and social pressure, the formation of College Students' career choice concept mainly depends on their own choice tendency. College Students' job selection behavior is a "rational choice" based on their own characteristics and the analysis of the employment environment. However, this "rational choice" will be affected by many subjective factors, such as college students' psychological quality, employment mentality, personal will, etc. these factors will indirectly affect the regional flow direction of talent employment. According to the relevant theories of social behavior, this paper analyzes the employment of college students, and its own choice is the internal driving force of the regional flow of College Students' job selection [10]. However, in terms of the current employment situation of college students, due to the lack of effective employment guidance, college students lack effective and timely information in the consideration of jobs in different enterprises and regions, which leads to serious deviation in their own choice behavior, and the lack of employment information leads to the reduction of the reliability of College Students' subjective judgment, Blind job selection leads to the polarization of employment situation in different regions. While the "difficult employment" of college students can not be solved, it also hinders the pace of coordinated development of national and regional economy.

This code uses the data set in the book and is gradually implemented according to the Apriori algorithm. It can be compared with the text introduction above. You can see the code as shown in Fig. 4 below.

```
data_ls =[['I1','I2','I5'],
    ['I2','I4'],
    ['I2','I3'],
    ['I1','I2','I4'],
    ['I1','I3'],
    ['I2','I3'],
    ['I1','I3'],
    ['I1','I2','I3','I5'],
    ['I1','I2','I3']]

L, supportData =apriori(data_ls,minSupport = 2)
print('L:',L,'\n')
print("supportData:",supportData)
```

Fig. 4. Apriori algorithm code

5   Conclusion

This paper points out the opportunities and challenges brought by the era of big data to college teaching management, analyzes the characteristics and implementation steps of Apriori algorithm, and takes a college automation major student as an example to fully tap the potential relationship between student achievement data and student employment flow by preprocessing and discretizing student achievement data and introducing Apriori algorithm for analysis and processing, The association rules between student achievement data and student employment flow are obtained. According to the association rules, the school employment management department can easily predict the employment trend of students in school, provide a strong theoretical basis for employment guidance, and timely give early warning and intervention to students who may have employment difficulties, so as to effectively improve the school employment rate. At the same time, it can provide reference for graduates to clarify their positioning in the employment process, reduce detours in the application process and improve employment competitiveness.

Acknowledgements. WHSKL2021128 Project of Wuhan Union of Social Science Research on Talent Cultivation in Local Universities Under the New Employment Situation .

References

1. Pan, D., Wang, S., Jin, C., et al.: Research on Student Achievement Prediction Based on BP Neural Network Method (2021)
2. Zhang, Y., Wang, C.: Research on intelligent management of student achievement data based on improved Apriori algorithm. In: 2021 International Conference on Public Management and Intelligent Society (PMIS) (2021)

3. Maryani, N., Widjajanti, D.B.: Comparison of contextual and scientific approaches to improving student achievement and emotional intelligence. In: 7th International Conference on Research, Implementation, and Education of Mathematics and Sciences (ICRIEMS 2020) (2021)
4. Haug, M.E., Wasonga, T.: Understanding how leadership matters: collective efficacy and student achievement. Athens J. Educ. **8**(2), 197–222 (2021)
5. Jahedizadeh, S., Ghonsooly, B., Ghanizadeh, A.: A model of language students' sustained flow, personal best, buoyancy, evaluation apprehension, and academic achievement. Porta Linguarum **35**, 257–275 (2021)
6. Albert, S.: Employment Effects of COVID-19 across States, Sectors (2021)
7. Kim, J.H., Lee, H.R.: The effect of achievement goal orientation on career decision levels of students majoring in airline service : The dual mediating effect of self-leadership and learning flow. Int. J. Tour. Hosp. Res. **35**(6), 195–207 (2021)
8. Herawati, M., Muhid, A., Hamdani, A.S.: Self-efficacy, social support, academic flow, and math anxiety among islamic senior high school students. Psympathic Jurnal ilmiah Psikologi **7**(2), 315–326 (2021)
9. Manzano, R.D., Ullén, F.: Domain specific traits predict achievement in music and multipotentiality. Intelligence **89**, 101584 (2021)
10. Olagbaju, O.O.: Influence of language anxiety and prior knowledge on ESL students' achievement in expository essay in Ibadan North LGA, Nigeria. Educ. Res. Int. **2021**(2), 1–7 (2021)

Research on System Design of Educational Curriculum Construction Based on Big Data Platform

Jingbin Zhang[(✉)]

Xi'an Fanyi University, Xi'an 710061, Shaanxi, China
`ruibin321@163.com`

Abstract. With the rapid development of online education, the new mode of carrying Internet+ on educational resources breaks through the time and space constraints of the traditional education industry, and solves the unequal distribution of educational resources caused by regional differences and other factors to a certain extent. Therefore, an educational intelligence platform based on big data is designed. Its overall structure includes physical layer, virtual resource layer, logic layer, presentation layer, application layer, network layer and user layer; The big data center module in the platform collects all business data through networks, sensors and other devices, and saves the business data in massive data storage devices; The software design part uses the multi feature fusion acquisition algorithm to collect student data, and completes the early warning of student performance through the performance early warning algorithm based on correlation analysis technology. The basic idea of the website is to provide teaching and learning materials and career planning services based on online video teaching platform. And on this basis, develop multiple plates, guided by interest, combined with Holland's career interest test, so that contemporary college students have a clearer understanding of their future career, so as to carry out targeted learning and planning.

Keywords: Big data platform · System design · Curriculum construction

1 Introduction

Data structure refers to the collection of diversified mathematical elements, which has a certain logical structure and physical structure. The integration of the two can form a complete logical and physical structure. The structure has strong integrity and logic, and meets the standard of physical structure. Based on the rapid development of the Internet industry in the era of big data, the learning methods of users have changed greatly. The learning form of blackboard and books has gradually developed into online learning [1]. Through convenient and intimate online learning, the learning ability has been significantly improved. At the same time, online education has broad prospects for development and has successfully leapt to the forefront of big data applications. However,

© ICST Institute for Computer Sciences, Social Informatics and Telecommunications Engineering 2023
Published by Springer Nature Switzerland AG 2023. All Rights Reserved
M. A. Jan and F. Khan (Eds.): BigIoT-EDU 2022, LNICST 467, pp. 177–185, 2023.
https://doi.org/10.1007/978-3-031-23944-1_20

with the continuous progress of science and technology, the network environment is constantly updated and the needs of users are increasing. It is difficult to obtain public recognition by improving the quality of learning service alone, and it is difficult for users to continuously respond to the teaching tasks specified by the system. Therefore, network online education should actively respond to the learning demands of different users in different time periods through the analysis of big data. Developers analyze users' learning behavior through the data obtained every day, and provide personalized customized services for different users.

The integration of data structure and teaching curriculum can solve the disadvantages of traditional teaching curriculum arrangement, improve the rationality and structure of curriculum arrangement through holistic logical analysis, and form an integrated curriculum structure By setting the semantic retrieval method of data structure and using keywords to search the platform teaching resources, this paper determines the registration and authentication of platform users, so as to strengthen the relationship between students and teachers. Construct a dynamic model of data structure course, in which the teaching resources of data structure course can flow freely and update continuously. The design of online course evaluation function can enable students to conduct self-evaluation through online evaluation and form a diversified evaluation system. Build an after-school online communication community. Teachers can provide guidance for students after class, promote students' after-school learning, and realize online and offline dual teaching.

Organize the cadres and employees of the system to seriously study the "double reduction" work opinions and the requirements of relevant urban meetings, establish special work classes, hold "double reduction" work symposiums, listen to the opinions and suggestions of all parties, formulate the "double reduction" work implementation opinions and "double reduction" work implementation plans of our district, establish the "district level overall planning and school responsibility" work mechanism, improve the regular work meetings and regular scheduling mechanism, establish special work classes, and strengthen departmental coordination, Implement job responsibilities.

Take the implementation of the "double reduction" policy as an opportunity to restart the review and registration of existing discipline training institutions as required. We carried out special rectification of off campus institutions, cooperated with relevant departments to carry out law enforcement inspections for more than 40 times, issued 6 rectification notices, issued 4 letters of closure for rectification, interviewed 9 heads of institutions, banned 2 unlicensed institutions, and suspended off-line training of off campus institutions in the summer. Establish a regular reporting and notification system, strengthen supervision, inspection and exposure, and form a strict and high-pressure situation.

Through various channels, parents are reminded to carefully participate in after-school training, resist illegal training, and carefully choose payment methods. Strengthen family education guidance, provide parents with family education guidance services through parent schools, public welfare training, parent-child activities, etc., guide parents to establish a scientific educational concept, and reduce the heat of off-school training.

2 Relevant Overview

2.1 Big Data Platform

Data collection: data collection is one of the core contents of the education platform. The data generated by students in learning, teachers' teaching data, and some data generated by college entrance examination and usual practice topics can be shared and transmitted. Data acquisition is the premise of data storage and computing platform. For data collection, we select the data collection source and set the collection time, cycle and other parameters. After corresponding processing, the data we collected are stored in the original data warehouse as the basis of the education platform.

This is an era of information explosion. With the explosive growth of information, massive data is born. People usually call this large-scale data set big data. With the rapid development of network and information technology, big data can also be considered to be closely linked in this era, and big data will change some of our lifestyles. If you can make good use of big data, you should first understand big data. What are the characteristics of big data:

(1) volume: the amount of data is large. The amount of data of educational resources includes many students, teachers, classes, etc. the data generated starts with at least p, LP is usually equal to 1000 t, and the amount to be calculated and stored is also large.

The calculation formula is shown in formula 1–3

$$x_k(0) = x_d(0), k = 0, 1, 2, 3, \cdots \tag{1}$$

$$u_{k+1}(t) = u_k(t) + \Gamma_{l1}\dot{e}_k(t) \tag{2}$$

$$\frac{a(i,j)}{1 - a(i)a(j)} < \int \frac{\partial \log(i-1)}{\partial \log(i-1)} di - \frac{1 - \partial \log(i-1)}{\partial \log(i)} di \tag{3}$$

$$\begin{cases} \forall \frac{dx(s,t)}{dsdt} < \frac{x(s,t)}{x(s)x(t)} \\ \exists t - x(t) > 0. \end{cases} \tag{4}$$

(2) Diversity: diversity of types and sources. It can be structured, semi-structured or unstructured. It can be embodied in audio, network log, picture, video, geographical location information, etc. for educational data, it can be video, score, audio, etc.
(3) Value: big data is characterized by a large amount of data. The data value density is relatively low, but in the era of machine learning, we can find valuable data from a large amount of data and make corresponding analysis to obtain greater value [2].
(4) Velocity (timeliness): now most devices are networked. Usually, the data of students and teachers can be recorded in real time.
(5) Veracity: the data collected is usually accurate. We can use these characteristics of big data to improve today's education methods.

Using these five important characteristics of big data, we can promote the progress of education in the field of education, mainly in two aspects.

(1) Purposeful analysis of education data: the generated education data can be used as the data set of machine learning and data mining. Data mining is different from the mining of early web logs. Data mining is a new education model collected more comprehensively and accurately by students' behavior with the support of computer related technology. Educators can find it in the education process of data mining The patterns and laws of these data are used to establish models and predict how students learn.

(2) Improve the teacher's teaching model: collect students' data, from which we can extract and analyze useful data. Then make a data portrait of students' learning methods and class characteristics. The teachers design teaching methods and plans according to the generated analysis.

2.2 Construction Principles of Education System

Building an education management big data platform is not an overnight project. It needs to be gradually promoted from easy to difficult on the basis of the management and control structure. That is, it should be built based on the overall technical route and structure of "large platform, small module, multi-level, personalized and changing as needed", and the specific design should follow the principles of integrity, gradual progress, publicity and pertinence [3].

First, we should adhere to the principle of integrity. Full participation, that is, the government, schools, families, social organizations, students, teachers, parents and other individual citizens should participate in the construction of the big data platform for education management, strengthen the government's macro-control, implement the autonomy of schools, promote broad social participation, and realize the cooperation and sharing of multiple subjects; full caliber promotion should not only pay attention to the openness and transparency of education decision-making It should be clear, scientific and reasonable, pay attention to whether the implementation of policies and systems can be implemented, and strengthen the objective, scientific, open and fair supervision and evaluation of educational governance; fully implement it, realize "key breakthrough" and concentrate on solving bottleneck problems while clarifying various complex relationships and elements related to educational business.

The second is to adhere to the principle of gradualism. No matter how comprehensive consideration and design have been made before, there are some "minor problems" "It is both unpredictable and inevitable. Therefore, the design process should be divided into three stages: initial stage, medium-term and long-term. The initial stage is to sort out the existing business processes and plan the architecture of big data platform. The core is to gather the data flow of various business fields of education and build a big data platform through resource pool; in the medium term, provide big data services inside and outside education, including policy consultation The service ability of education such as business declaration and qualification certification to the society, as well as the internal execution ability such as task implementation at the beginning of the year, project follow-up and fund allocation; in the long term, it is mainly to build the social data sharing ability and realize the integrated development of big data system on the basis of breaking through the barriers to data resources such as Public Security Bureau and Civil Affairs Bureau.

3 System Design of Education Curriculum Construction Based on Big Data Platform

Data acquisition: data acquisition is one of the core contents of the big data education platform. Data generated by students in learning, teachers' teaching data, and some data generated by college entrance examination and usual practice topics can be shared and transmitted. Data acquisition is the premise of data storage and calculation platform. For data acquisition, we choose data acquisition source, set acquisition time, cycle, etc. Parameters. After corresponding processing, the data we collected are stored in the original data warehouse as the basis of the education platform.

Data storage: data storage is one of the important contents of big data education platform. The database used for storage can be relational database mysql, oracle.sqlserver or non relational database, such as redis.hbase. We require that the collected data should be stored in the database according to certain rules (Fig. 1).

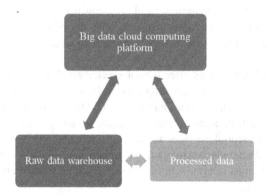

Fig. 1. Big data education platform

Data backup: because there are unsafe factors in data storage, single stored data is easy to be lost due to problems such as power failure and destruction of the server, so we need to do corresponding data backup. Generally, 3–5 copies of data backup will be used in case of emergency [4].

Computing platform: computing platform is one of the core contents of big data education platform, like the role of brain. The computing platform is mainly used to analyze data. Here, it can be a Hadoop big data processing platform. The relevant algorithms and models in data mining will be used in the calculation. The education big data center will effectively integrate data mining and analysis methods, common data mining fields, such as correlation analysis, cluster analysis, classification analysis, anomaly analysis, specific group analysis and evolutionary analysis, and the existing mining algorithms are relatively mature open source tools into the education data center platform. On the one hand, In order to facilitate the data mining program of each business system data, on the other hand, it can be more targeted analysis. On this basis, a variety of models are constructed, such as the prediction model of curriculum learning success, the prediction model of regional education balanced development trend, the diagnosis model of students' learning disabilities, the teaching behavior model, etc.

Improve the level of homework management, strictly control the total amount of homework, and uniformly carry out homework guidance in the first period of after-school delay service in primary and secondary schools in the region, so that students' homework can be completed in school as much as possible. Optimize the operation design and incorporate the operation monitoring into the quality monitoring index system. Improve the quality of education and teaching, optimize classroom teaching measures, innovate classroom teaching methods, establish a high-quality classroom teaching resource sharing mechanism, and promote the balanced development of compulsory education.

Give full play to the main role of the school and focus on improving quality and efficiency. Give play to the leading role of the district teachers' training college, carry out 25 district level theme research and training activities, improve the school's education and teaching ability, and carry out 52 comprehensive visual guidance activities to help the school improve quality and efficiency. The school is required to strengthen the management level, improve the quality of classroom teaching, optimize classroom teaching methods, do a good job in preparation, teaching, approval, assistance and research, let students move and let the classroom live, deal with the relationship between "reducing the burden" and improving the quality, and improve students' learning efficiency in school.

The school has improved its after-school service level and created a position for building virtue and cultivating people after class. 148 schools in the region have carried out after-school delay services, with more than 130,000 students actively participating, realizing full coverage of students with service needs. It has organically combined interest cultivation with after-school services to develop students' interests and hobbies. At present, primary and secondary schools in the region have opened more than 10 kinds of characteristic activities in after-school services, such as science and technology, art and sports, reading, etc.

Strengthen positive publicity, make full use of the financial media platform (more than 20 reports), school led display, parents' letter, parents' meeting and other forms to publicize the relevant policies, experiences and practices of "double reduction" in an all-round way, and actively create a good working atmosphere.

Strengthen risk management and control, cooperate with relevant departments at the district level to strengthen the investigation and remediation of various potential risks, strengthen capital supervision, and protect the rights and interests of labor and employment and the property safety of the people. Guide the transformation of institutions, actively guide the transformation of existing discipline training institutions to non discipline training such as sports, music and dance, and truly become a useful supplement to school education.

Figure 2 shows the system test data. According to Fig. 2, all data are used to test every point. The flipped class room teaching is shown in Fig. 3.

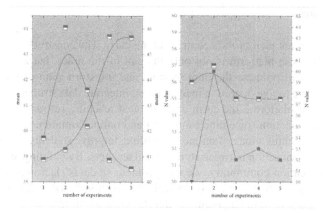

Fig. 2. System multiple intrusion stability test

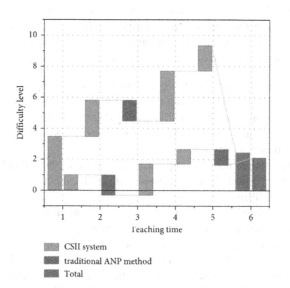

Fig. 3. Compare with the csii sytem and traditional ANP method

Permission management: role and permission management are the basis for the safe operation of the whole system. Different users will enjoy corresponding services according to their permissions only after they are assigned different roles. With authority management, we can ensure that everyone performs their duties and the security of data. The specific functions of role and permission management include: role management, adding roles, deleting roles, modifying roles, user role assignment, role permission Association, group management, etc.

4   Conclusion

Education is the great plan of the country and the party. The construction of education management big data platform is not only the call of the times, but also the need of development. It will promote the improvement and transformation of education system from extensive to fine operation management, integrate data structure courses with teaching resource platform, and form an integrated teaching resource platform. The platform has the functions of online evaluation and online communication, which can realize the dual teaching mode of online and offline, improve students' learning ability and promote the connection between students and teachers. By building an after-school online communication community, we can promote students' learning initiative and stimulate students' interest in learning. Provide information-based overall planning and supervision guarantee for the high-quality development of education.

"Famous schools" attract parents, but what is the real "famous school"? In luyunquan's view, the key to choosing a school is not how famous it is, but the connotation and quality of the school. The future goal of Haidian District is to "urn the school that is still recognized by the people and has developed well, but has not yet become a famous school into a new brand school."

A new school district has been established and a new layout of primary and secondary schools has been laid out. In 2015, Haidian District merged and undertook more than 20 schools, adding more than 10,000 high-quality degrees. When the school in front of the house is listed as a famous school branch, can the people's desire to "go to a famous school" really be realized overnight?

The answer is certainly not that simple. Luyunquan said, "there should be a quota for the output of resources from famous schools. Education cannot improve weak schools by cutting peaks and filling valleys."

Luyunquan calculated an account for the reporter: when a school has a "famous school" brand, from the management team, school running philosophy, backbone teachers, curriculum system construction, all these need the output of high-quality resources of a "famous school", but a "famous school" is always limited even if its own resources are very rich. Even high-quality schools such as the high school attached to the National People's Congress will be unable to continue after unlimited output. Therefore, when combined with the education account book of Haidian District, the concept of "walking on two legs" such as "famous school output" + "connotation development" has become a good method for Haidian District to promote the balance of regional education resources.

Luyunquan introduced that, on the one hand, Haidian District let famous schools, senior schools and high-quality schools help and undertake for schools that are particularly weak and have difficulties in upgrading. On the other hand, Haidian District has made overall improvement through school alliance for schools with good foundation, certain expectations of principals and good teaching team. Through opening and exchange within the school districts, open courses within the region for students to share, and these resources will be shared by the whole district in the future.

Acknowledgements. 1. Xi'an Translation College 2021 University-level Online Curriculum Construction Project (ZK2143) "Introduction to Mao Zedong Thought and the Theory System of Socialism with Chinese Characteristics (Special School)"

2. The first batch of research projects and practical projects of online ideological and political work in Shaanxi universities (2021SPWSXM-Z-8) "Practice Innovation and Exploration of Shaanxi Local Party History Network Education in Colleges and Universities"

References

1. Lu, J.: Construction of teaching resource platform based on WeChat Applet. Comput. Knowl. Technol. **17**(3), 46–47 (2021)
2. Shi, Y.: Construction of classroom teaching model in higher vocational colleges based on big data. West. Qual. Educ. **5**(24), 112–113 (2019)
3. Ling, J.: Thoughts on practical teaching of packaging design course based on big data technology. Light Text. Ind. Technol. **50**(2), 165–166 (2021)
4. Nie, C.: Research on the construction of 3D animation teaching resource database platform under the background of industry education integration. J. Taiyuan City Vocat. Tech. Coll. **3**, 68–70 (2021)

Research on Teaching Design of Network Marketing Practice Based on Big Data Analysis

Chunhui Li[✉]

School of Business Administration,
Guangzhou Huashang Vocational College, Guangzhou 511300, Guangdong, China
lichunhui2020@outlook.com

Abstract. The research focus of this paper is to provide a platform for college students to participate in innovation projects based on the analysis of the characteristics of current college students' innovation and entrepreneurship projects, which can realize the reasonable management and effective reuse of innovation and entrepreneurship project resources, and provide a window for the business transformation of excellent innovation projects. Based on the framework, this paper discusses the design and implementation of a set of College Students' innovation and entrepreneurship resource database system with reliability, ease of use and scalability based on personalized recommendation. At the same time, in order to solve the problems of low resource utilization rate and difficulty in resource search with the increase of resource scale of innovation and entrepreneurship project resource database, the common recommendation algorithm is carried out This paper constructs a personalized recommendation model suitable for college students' innovation and entrepreneurship resource database system, which can help users quickly find the resources they are interested in.

Keywords: College students' innovation and entrepreneurship · Project resource library · Personalized recommendation · Collaborative filtering

1   Related Concepts of Personalized Recommendation System

As the second largest Internet market after the United States, China's huge Internet users have given birth to a huge network consumer group and network marketing space. On the basis of the Internet, network marketing channels emerge as the times require, and make up for the shortcomings of traditional marketing channels. After the development of big data has risen to the national strategic level, the relevant fields will also usher in new development opportunities. Under the background of network marketing, the effective use of information channels in China will also usher in a new stage [1].

2   Research on the Current Situation of Network Marketing Channels in China

On the basis of traditional marketing channel function, network marketing channel refers to providing available products and services through the Internet, using computers or

M. A. Jan and F. Khan (Eds.): BigIoT-EDU 2022, LNICST 467, pp. 186–191, 2023.
https://doi.org/10.1007/978-3-031-23944-1_21

other available information technology means to complete trading activities in the target market.

2.1 Classification of Network Marketing Channels

According to different classification basis, channel types can be subdivided into the following three types.

(1) Direct marketing channel (network direct selling). It is a network channel realized through the Internet, which is directly transmitted from the producer to the final consumer. Traditional middlemen are transformed into service intermediaries, such as professional distribution companies providing goods transportation and distribution services.

(2) Indirect marketing. Through the channel of information communication between buyers and sellers through network middlemen or platforms, middlemen integrate Internet technology, have higher degree of specialization and scale economy, and transaction efficiency is higher than network direct selling. For example, online stores can rapidly expand the scope of the target market at a low cost and find a larger customer group by relying on the Internet [2].

(3) Two channels. It is easier to realize "market penetration" under the buyer's market condition by using the two channels of network direct selling and indirect selling at the same time, which is the best choice of network marketing channel for production enterprises.

2.2 Characteristics of Network Marketing Channel

Network marketing channel is a way for enterprises to communicate with consumers through the Internet, which has obvious characteristics. The development of network marketing channels reduces many unnecessary links in the middle of sales, which is good for both buyers and sellers, and makes the communication between producers and consumers more convenient. In general, the network marketing channel has the following characteristics.

(1) The length of the channel and the complexity of the intermediate links between a product or service from the manufacturer to the consumer are directly proportional to the increase rate and the hidden cost of the product. Internet distribution, instead of the traditional circuitous mode, has the characteristics of short channel, which can shorten the length of the transaction chain, reduce transaction costs and improve efficiency. (2) The relationship is single. The management of network marketing channel can be simplified to a single level of network management. Traditional marketing channels are basically involved in multi-level and all-round management. With the help of Internet, enterprises can skip part of the value chain, mainly by bypassing retailers. Under the background of the Internet, the virtual nature of the network has replaced the advantages of traditional marketing middlemen based on geographical reasons. The high-efficiency information transmission brought by the network optimizes many links in the marketing channel, and finally simplifies to a single relationship. (3) In order to deliver socialized goods to consumers in the shortest time, we must rely on modern logistics distribution

system. With the help of the most widely used logistics distribution mode – "third party logistics", to complete the logistics activities of most enterprises.

3   Realization of System Function Based on Big Data Mining

The centralized signal monitoring system collects and monitors the electrical parameters of various basic signal equipment, including external power grid, switch machine, cable and signal machine. The monitoring diagram of analog quantity is shown in Fig. 1.

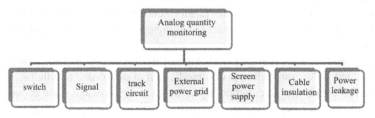

Fig. 1. Analog monitoring chart

3.1   Centralized Monitoring Information Extraction Based on Big Data Mining

From the perspective of function, the definition of data mining is a complex process, which can find effective and meaningful data patterns, and the discovery process is automatic or semi-automatic. The definition makes it clear that data mining is a learning mechanism to discover valuable knowledge patterns in data. At the same time, the definition also emphasizes the engineering characteristics of data mining. There are two views on the understanding of patterns and rules. The first view holds that patterns and rules are the basic forms of objective existence of data features. The work of data mining researchers is to design a program to meet the temporary needs in the absence of models, such as community extraction, association grouping and so on, Data mining provides a tool to extract features. The second understanding is that the pattern is the result of relative motion caused by a non-equilibrium system. In this kind of problem, modeling estimates and refines the inherent relationship through a large number of data. Data mining workers should not only find this existence, but also analyze and explain the generation mechanism of the pattern, so as to become an effective tool that can be used in complex decision-making [3].

From a technical point of view, we are now in the post network era, and data mining will certainly become a hot technology in this era. Taking the e-commerce website as an example, consumer demand analysis has become an important analysis topic, because the subtle action of a user's mouse click determines that the potential user transfers from one supplier to another. In order to early warn the change to loyalty, the analysis clues can naturally start from the order information tracked and recorded in the information database, and then expand to a large number of users who have visited different products. As a result, millions of front desk access to network files, telephone records, sales orders and interviews with business representatives are transformed into customer management information that can be used to predict and identify their future behavior changes, and then the powerful analysis function of its back-end database makes the concept hidden behind the data explicit, The technology and method to realize this process has become the core competitiveness of e-commerce, and this technology is data mining. Data mining is to solve the problem-based data analysis process, including goals and processes.

3.2 Time Series Mining Algorithm

In normal state, the trend of the curve of sampling data with time is the same, that is, the sampling values mentioned above are very close or equal. The normal value is determined based on the traditional simple arithmetic mean value, but the normal value cannot reflect its normal state well. Therefore, only using the traditional simple arithmetic mean method cannot achieve our goal. At this time, we need to use the method of linear density. The definition of linear density: the number of effective points distributed on the line segment per unit length.

According to the definition, the calculation method of distribution density is to first take V consecutive line segments from I to j, and then calculate the distribution density of effective data distributed on them, as shown in formula (1).

$$\rho_{ij} = \frac{\sum_{p=1}^{j} N_p}{\sum_{p=i}^{p=j} 1_{mp}} (i = j - v) \tag{1}$$

It is defined as the sum of the effective sampling values, which are extracted in the corresponding interval of the maximum linear density, then the normal value is estimated. See formula (2)

$$R_0 = \frac{1}{m} (\sum_{i-i_0}^{i_0+v} \sum_i rs) \tag{2}$$

In the formula, m refers to the value of the effective sampling points in the corresponding interval of the maximum linear density. It refers to not only the value of a point, but the value of all the effective sampling points.

4 Network Marketing Channel in Big Data Environment

With the in-depth study of big data, its application scenarios have gradually become diversified. It is still necessary to apply big data information analysis to the research of network marketing channels. The revolution brought by big data is increasingly changing people's work, life and way of thinking. Big data information analysis is bound to have an impact on the research of network marketing channels.

4.1 Steadily Develop Network Marketing Channels

By strengthening the construction of network infrastructure, the coverage ratio of big data increases, the steady development of network marketing channels can be realized, the transmission speed of network marketing information can be effectively improved, so that social groups can understand the main contents of information in the first time, and make appropriate consumption for relevant excellent policies, so as to expand the influence. Whether it is the business in the release of information, or consumers in the process of receiving information, can respond quickly. Therefore, paying attention to the investment in the construction of network infrastructure can effectively promote the normal operation of network marketing channels [4].

4.2   Improve the Utilization Efficiency of Network

The office mode of enterprise network has become an important part of today's enterprises in the process of operation and development. Rich network information resources, as well as the rapid use of the network, can bring a lot of customer resources for enterprises, and promote enterprises in the process of development, increasingly inseparable from network information. Therefore, enterprises should pay attention to the construction of network operation system, according to their own development direction and customer demand and other factors, actively improve the utilization of the network, so as to realize the centralized management of enterprise network, and the innovative development and construction of network information system. Relying on big data, select effective and timely information for accurate application, and comply with the development of the times.

4.3   Develop a Perfect Network Credit System

Building a perfect network integrity system can be said to be an important guarantee for the effective development of network marketing channel business. Because it is different from the traditional marketing channels, does not have a series of security, how to verify the identity to complete a safe and reliable transaction, we need to establish a special network identity information network, develop a perfect network integrity system, and then make an objective and real integrity evaluation of enterprises and consumers through big data. With the continuous development of market economy, the improvement of living standards and the improvement of people's consumption concept, all kinds of businesses and enterprises actively expand their own marketing channels to attract more customers. The development of network marketing channel has become a focus of enterprises. However, how to better establish network marketing channel is inseparable from the analysis and support of big data information, which will also bring economic and social benefits to the industry.

5   Conclusion

As an important part of the whole marketing system, it plays an important role in reducing enterprise costs and improving enterprise competitiveness. It is the key point in marketing channel planning. Effective channel circulation strategy will have a positive impact on price strategy, product strategy and promotion strategy. It is an important means for enterprises to successfully develop the market and achieve sales and business objectives. The purpose of good channel circulation strategy is to build the value of enterprise brand into lasting customer relationship, including the dependence of consumer groups on enterprise products and the strengthening of cooperative relationship. With the support of big data information, enterprises use rich data resources and analysis technology to monitor business activities on the whole marketing channel, so that the whole marketing process of enterprises is under control, so as to realize scientific management of marketing. Data mining combined with modern management system can realize scientific management.

References

1. Ren, Y.: Network marketing channel under the mode of e-commerce. Intell. Mag. (1) (2004)
2. Zhou, H., Ren, Q., Liu, Y.: Research on network marketing channel development of characteristic agricultural products. China Bus. Theory (36) (2018)
3. Ma, X.: Channel conflict and management strategy of o2o network marketing mode under E-commerce. J. Chifeng Univ. (Nat. Sci. Ed.) $32(21)$ (2016)
4. Ni, X.: On the network marketing channel under the mode of e-commerce. Modern Market. (Next Issue) (4) (2018)

Research on Teaching Development and Application of Data Mining Algorithm in Japanese Corpus

Na Qi[✉] and Fei Deng

Xi'an Fanyi University, Xi'an 710105, Shaanxi, China
Qina1528@163.com

Abstract. The application of corpus in teaching will benefit many students and teachers. Teachers can use corpus retrieval tools to count the frequency of vocabulary in teaching materials and use corpus to compile teaching vocabulary according to the progress of learning and teaching and the relevant contents of teaching materials; Based on the research on the teaching development and application of data mining algorithm in Japanese Corpus, this paper attempts to build a small Japanese Corpus to provide a useful reference for Japanese classroom teaching.

Keywords: Data mining · Corpus · Retrieval software

1 Introduction

Corpus refers to a large number of original corpora or processed texts with linguistic information. The texts in the corpus are called corpora, which are usually sorted to form a set of format and logo, especially a set of digital database of huge language materials stored by computer. Since the 1990s, corpus linguistics has developed vigorously. With the ~ rapid development of computer technology and the gradual improvement of multimedia information system, experts and scholars have introduced it into the field of teaching and research [1]. As a collection of naturally occurring languages that can be recognized and processed by computer, corpus itself has the characteristics of reliability and universality, It plays a very important role in the design of syllabus and the evaluation of appropriateness and correctness of language communication. Therefore, the application of corpus in teaching has broad representativeness and very good prospects.

With the development of regional cooperation and the rapid development of international trade cooperation, modern students not only learn the five basic skills of listening, speaking, reading, writing and translation, but also put forward higher requirements for foreign language translation with the development of the times. How to improve the quality of foreign language teaching in limited time? How to train foreign experts more effectively to meet market demand? This poses a challenge to the current foreign language teaching, but it also causes teachers' reflection [2]. The development of information technology and information storage technology provides convenience for foreign language teaching. As shown in Fig. 1 below.

M. A. Jan and F. Khan (Eds.): BigIoT-EDU 2022, LNICST 467, pp. 192–202, 2023.
https://doi.org/10.1007/978-3-031-23944-1_22

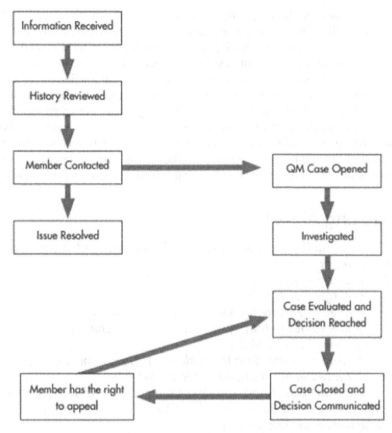

Fig. 1. Development of information technology and information storage technology

Firstly, this paper summarizes the current situation of concentrate construction at home and abroad, and briefly analyzes the properties and functions of concentrate. Secondly, based on the advanced experience of predecessors, this paper studies the development and application of data retrieval algorithms in Japanese documents, and constructs a small Japanese Corpus, aiming to provide a useful reference for Japanese translation teaching in class [3].

2 Related Work

2.1 The Present Situation and Bottleneck of Japanese Teaching

China and Japan are separated by a strip of water and have frequent exchanges since ancient times. Especially with the exchanges in politics, economy and culture, and the number of people learning Japanese is also expanding. In order to keep up with the changes and development of language [4], China's educational circles irregularly introduce the latest Japanese teaching materials and relevant reference books from Japan.

Domestic educators also keep up with the pace of the times and constantly publish newer and more time-effective teaching materials, hoping to achieve the best effect of Japanese teaching. However, the development of language is reflected in all details of social life, and its changes are quite extensive, which cannot be fully described in a few textbooks. At the same time, as a foreign language, the formation of context and language sense is very important. In recent years, with the continuous exploration of Japanese teachers, students' language application ability has been improved, but the effect is not obvious [5]. Therefore, how to ensure that the Japanese learning materials keep pace with the times, form a real context, and strengthen students' sensory understanding and use of Japanese is the focus and difficulty that needs to be strengthened in Japanese teaching. The improvement of teaching method is shown in Fig. 2 below.

Teaching Aims :

1. Improving Reading Skills---- *understanding the feature of a radio report*
2. Enriching Vocabulary
   --- *enlarging vocabulary*
   --- *cultivating students' sense of word   building*
   --- *understanding that synonyms have fine shades*
3. Improving Writing skills
   --- *accurately recording the dialogues with some Japanese to reinforce the authenticity of the report*
   --- *carefully observing and describing details to reinforce the authenticity of the report vivid and humorous description to make the report interesting*

Fig. 2. Improvement of teaching methods

2.2   Application of Corpus in Japanese Teaching

(1)   Vocabulary Teaching

Vocabulary is the most important foundation in all foreign language teaching, not only Japanese. Any Japanese learners feel the difficulty of word memory to varying degrees. This is not that individuals have any lack of memory, but that simple word memory itself is quite boring and chaotic. Therefore, many researchers advocate strengthening word memory through example sentences and articles [6]. According to the traditional teaching materials, example sentences and articles are limited after all, especially the teaching materials are processed learning materials, which have lost the authenticity of the language to a certain extent. Corpus can play a very good role in vocabulary teaching and memory, because the corpus is mainly collected in real life, and its expression is real, comprehensive and intuitive [7]. When learners are exposed to vocabulary, they master a large number of practical use examples, produce language feeling and enter the context. At the same time, the functions of corpus such as self-test and learning progress are added, which is more conducive for students to understand their vocabulary mastery level and the progress of vocabulary memory (Fig. 3).

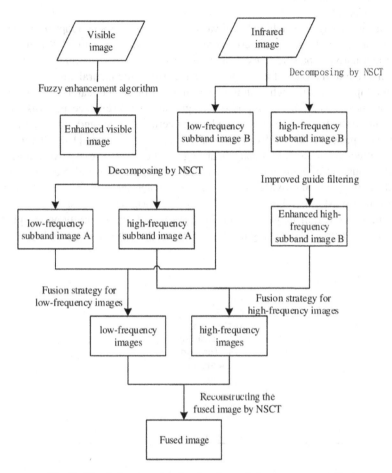

Fig. 3. Vocabulary mastery level and vocabulary memory method

(2) Translation teaching

Chinese Japanese translation is not a simple replacement of two languages, but expresses the meaning of Chinese in Japanese through the understanding of the use of Japanese [8]. Therefore, we should not only master vocabulary, but also master the expression of Japanese. However, the traditional translation teaching simply translates Chinese and Japanese bilinguals through sentence patterns and grammar, which will make the translation too stiff to a certain extent, which is different from the natural expression of the Japanese. Learning based on real corpus is to enable learners to master the most natural and localized Japanese expression [9]. The corpus maintains the consistency with Japanese social and cultural expression psychology by collecting a large number of real corpora and constantly updating them. Corpus learning can improve students' translation level, and corpus is now used as a translation tool The translation function of the tool will effectively cultivate students' translation ability.

(3) Writing Teaching

Japanese writing teaching has always been a difficult point in Japanese teaching. There are generally stiff Japanese expression and "Chinese culture". When students use non-native Japanese to express, most of them seem very unnatural, which is mainly due to the lack of a comprehensive grasp of the natural way of expression of the Japanese. Although with the continuous efforts of educators, the expression of Japanese has been decomposed into grammar and sentence patterns suitable for our study, the language is irregular to a certain extent, and any grammar and sentence pattern cannot fully explain all language phenomena [10]. Therefore, the most effective method of language learning is to be based on extensive contact with real corpus. A large amount of real language information is collected and updated in the corpus, which provides the best learning materials for language learners [11]. Only after mastering a large number of Japanese original expressions can we form a sufficient sense of language, and finally express fully, naturally and in place in Japanese writing. The writing teaching framework is shown in Fig. 4 below.

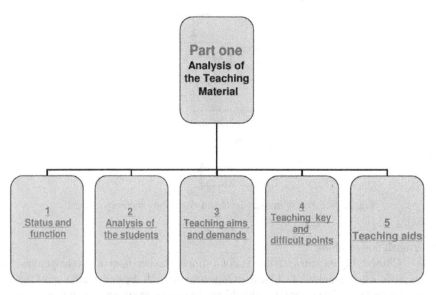

Fig. 4. Writing teaching framework

3 Data Mining Algorithm

3.1 Definition of Data Mining

Data mining is a method of analyzing and extracting useful and interesting knowledge and information from a large number of noisy and incomplete data. The definition can be understood as follows: data should be real and large; What is mined is the useful knowledge of users; The excavated knowledge should be understandable and applied, as shown in Fig. 5:

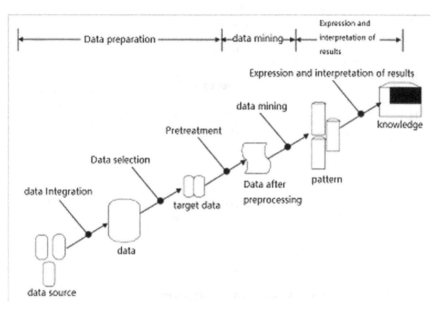

Fig. 5. Data mining process

3.2 Application of Data Mining in Corpus

The theories of linguistics and language teaching provide a solid theoretical foundation for corpus assisted language teaching. Tim Johns and Chris Tribble set a precedent for using corpus technology to assist language teaching. They put forward the concept of data-driven learning (DDL) or classroom indexing (johns2002). The basic concept of data-driven learning advocates "learner centered", allowing students to observe the teaching materials designed by teachers in advance, infer hypotheses according to the observation, and then summarize the answers through mutual discussion. Cognitive psychology believes that the corpus uses a group of identical or similar contextual information to stimulate students through its contextual co-occurrence interface, so that the cognitive schema or the neural network of the brain can be activated [12]; At the same time, students excavate the background of language meaning from the recurring context co-occurrence, summarize the application laws or rules of language, gradually schema knowledge into brain memory, and then transform it into learners' internal language system through processing memory. Modern pedagogy believes that corpus linguistics is an interdisciplinary field that develops synchronously with computer science [13]. The corpus construction framework is shown in Fig. 6 below.

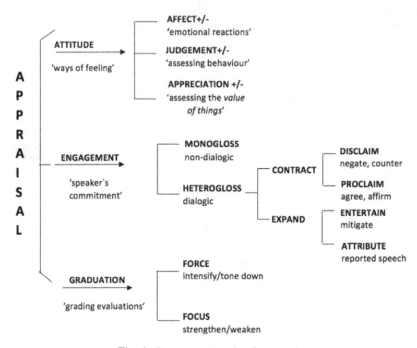

Fig. 6. Corpus construction framework

The corpus is authentic, natural and rich in content, which can reflect the most vivid language use. Learners carry out research on the structure of deep language knowledge by observing the massive amount of language information presented by means of computer retrieval. The context co-occurrence, word frequency table and keyword vocabulary provided by corpus retrieval tools also technically support inductive teaching and inquiry learning [14]. With the help of corpus, students can better understand and apply vocabulary by observing the lexical collocation, grammatical paradigm, semantic and pragmatic functions of phrase chunks jointly constructed by the target word and the surrounding words.

4   Data Based Mining Algorithm

In the past decade, with the rapid development of hardware storage technology and Internet technology, the construction of domestic foreign language database has also shown a good momentum of development. Using the keyword "corpus" to search in

CNKI, we can find that the number of research papers in this field has increased from 481 in 2008 to more than 1000 now [15]. The following Fig. 7 shows the key text data mining.

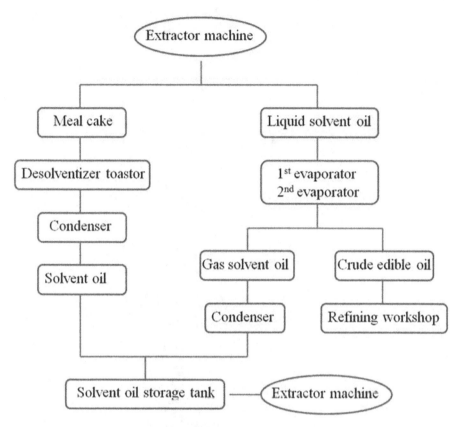

Fig. 7. Key text data mining

However, only 17 references can be retrieved by inputting the three keywords of "Japanese Corpus", and the earliest article on Japanese Corpus was published in 2009. As early as 1982, scholar Yang Huizhong has begun to build JDEST scientific and Technological English computer corpus, which means that the construction and development of tomorrow language corpus is far behind the development of English corpus [16]. Through combing the leading literature, it is found that in terms of domestic research, the Sino Japanese translation corpus built by Professor Xu Yiping of Beijing Foreign Studies University and the Chinese Japanese learner corpus built by Professor Mao Wenwei of Shanghai Foreign Studies University are representative. The corpus construction process is shown in Fig. 8 below.

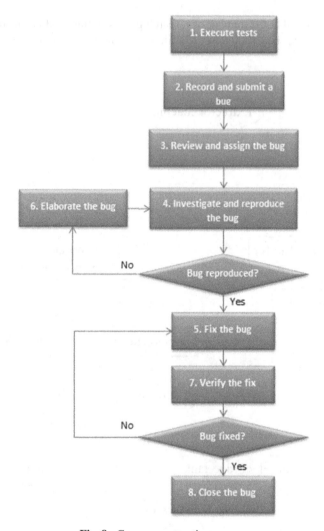

Fig. 8. Corpus construction process

Since its opening in 1997, the Hong Kong Library has a large collection of 10,752 literary works in the past 13 years. Most of the works of some writers are stored in databases. Zenock library deals with short stories, essays, travel notes, book reviews, memoirs and other topics. We can study specific language phenomena from different corpora [17].

It is mainly the famous literary works of famous scholars, such as Su Xinyang, Shen, polarized, Tianshan, etc. In grammar and vocabulary classes, you can directly query the database of famous scholars through synonyms to avoid possible errors in Teachers' own articles. In addition, the database of famous works and articles is highly literary and artistic. In the specific process, language extraction and learning can significantly improve students' Japanese language and literature level [18]. As shown in Fig. 9.

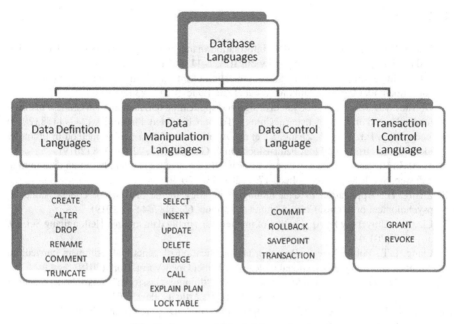

Fig. 9. Language data database structure

5   Conclusion

As an auxiliary tool, corpus can quickly and accurately extract a variety of data from a large number of texts and present them to learners. With the development of computer storage technology and big data retrieval technology, Japanese textbooks are uploaded to the Internet. Learners enrich learning resources by analyzing and summarizing a large number of corpora, making the language information hidden in a large number of texts emerge. In vocabulary teaching, learners can use the context co-occurrence interface provided by the micro text corpus to study collocation, grammatical paradigm, semantic and pragmatic functions by observing the vocabulary of phrase chunks jointly built by the target word and surrounding words, so as to truly realize the vocabulary learning mode of DDL (data-driven learning) under the guidance of teachers. This paper constructs a Japanese dictionary, selects typical novels from Hong Kong Library, makes simple documents, provides Japanese teaching services, improves teaching efficiency, and makes breakthroughs and progress in the future research and development process.

Acknowledgements. First class specialty construction program of Shaanxi Province --Japanese Major Program No. X-YLJS201701

References

1. Yin, X.H.: Construction of student information management system based on data mining and clustering algorithm. Complexity **2021**(2), 1–11 (2021)
2. Yu, H.: Integration, development and application of informatization resources in continuing education under big data thinking. Vocat. Tech. Educ. **51**, 12–23 (2019)
3. Di-Yao, W.U., Zhang, X.Y.: System design and application of data mining in Chinese material medical based on strategy pattern. China J. Tradit. Chin. Med. Pharm. **29**, 1147–1158 (2019)
4. Zhenghong, L.I., Liu, Y., Zhang, L., et al.: Application of data mining method in lithology identification using well log. Fault-Block Oil & Gas Field **47**, 2254–2268 (2019)
5. Tian, Z.: Research on the development of intelligent teaching system based on data mining and web. Sci. Educ. Artic. Collect. **17**, 1128–1139 (2019)
6. Zhang, H.: Application of data mining technology in the analysis of college students' psychological problems. China Comput. Commun. **65**, 4487–4493 (2019)
7. Liu, J.L., University D: Application of mathematics in big data mining. Heilongjiang Sci. **20**, 361–378 (2019)
8. Liang, L.T., Polytechnic S: Research and application of genetic algorithm in curriculum arrangement of higher vocational colleges. J. Hubei Open Vocat. Coll. (2019)
9. Wang, Q.: Development and application of "flipping classroom" smartphone teaching software in higher vocational colleges. Sci. Educ. Artic. Collect. (2018)
10. Zhu, X.M.: The development and application of "3D" microcourse in the teaching of automobile diagnosis. Educ. Teach. Forum (2018)
11. Li, J., Bian, Y., Huang, B., et al.: Design and application of monitoring and warning platform for big data in teaching. Comput. Appl. Softw. (2019)
12. Pu, X., Polytechnic H I: The application of big data thinking in teaching management of higher vocational colleges. China Comput. Commun. (2019)
13. Fang, C.Y., Dong, C.Y., Ze-Yuan, G.U., et al.: Application of data structure diagram in classroom of scientific research——design and development of dynamic display system for brain cognitive process. Heilongjiang Sci. (2019)
14. Badawi, S.: Big data and teaching development in higher education. Int. J. Learn. Teach. (2018)
15. Yang, X.: Teaching reform of "algorithm and data structure" in the view of micro lecture. J. Yichun Univ. (2018)
16. Zheng, X., Polytechnic F M: Application of big data and cloud computing technology in smart campus. China Comput. Commun. (2018)
17. Cao, H.R.: The application of Apriori algorithm in curriculum design of information and computational science. J. Sci. Teach. Coll. Univ. (2018)
18. Zhang, W.: Application and practice of higher vocational teachers management system based on data mining. Comput. Era (2018)

Research on Teaching Innovation of Computer Rendering Course of Environmental Design Specialty Based on PTP Mode

Changming Rao[✉]

Ankang University, Ankang 725000, Shaanxi, China
tang18898490118@163.com

Abstract. Based on the characteristics of computer rendering course of environmental design specialty, using "PTP" The teaching mode tries to innovate the teaching methods to replace the traditional computer renderings teaching mode, and mobilize the students' initiative to participate in the learning content in the way of practice project practice, so as to enhance the students' learning ability and improve the professional skill level through teaching, so as to meet the talent needs of the employer of environmental design specialty.

Keywords: PTP teaching · Environment design · Computer renderings · 3DMAX

1 Introduction

Today's society is an era of rapid development of information technology, and knowledge is changing at an unimaginable speed. Ordinary higher education, which trains senior professionals and professionals, is facing great opportunities and challenges because of the impact of the information society and the rapid growth of social demand for senior professionals.

Teaching reform refers to the reform of teaching contents, methods and systems aimed at promoting educational progress and improving teaching quality. There are many reasons to promote teaching reform, mainly including: (1) the progress of science and technology and the development of social productive forces; (2) Social changes, including changes in political and economic systems and ideological changes; (3) The development of educational science and other marginal disciplines affects the change of educational concepts. Teaching reform can be divided into: (1) individual reform. Reform only on the content of a certain subject, a certain system (such as the examination system), a certain principle and method. (2) Overall reform. It refers to the overall coordinated reform of teaching plans, tasks, contents, methods and systems.

The ways of reform are: (1) reform under the guidance of new theories and policies. After a long period of planning and expert argumentation, a reform plan is formed and carried out in a planned and step-by-step manner. Such reform is often carried out in a

M. A. Jan and F. Khan (Eds.): BigIoT-EDU 2022, LNICST 467, pp. 203–210, 2023.
https://doi.org/10.1007/978-3-031-23944-1_23

country or a large area. (2) Experimental reform. Under the guidance of certain theories, carry out overall or individual reform experiments in a certain area or school to obtain data and accumulate experience and lessons. (3) Extensive reform. After selecting and optimizing the excellent teaching experience or reform experimental results that have been tested by long-term practice, they will be promoted in a planned and step-by-step manner in a large area and scope.

It is an indisputable fact that the reform of classroom teaching has reached the "transmutation period".

Looking back on the curriculum reform in the "foundation period", some weak schools challenged the traditional classroom, created many "method models" characterized by "group cooperation" and "student presentation", and the students' expression and expressiveness have changed qualitatively, "the classroom is full of life vitality", "the students are liberated to the greatest extent", changing the stagnant situation of the traditional classroom.

However, with the development of classroom teaching reform, many problems existing in the early curriculum reform have become increasingly prominent. Many schools seem to return the classroom to the students, but still fail to solve the problem of students' lack of participation in learning - several top students will always participate in the discussion and display, and most students are still bystanders in the classroom.

In addition, many classes pursue "performance" too much, and students sing and dance and present wonderful presentations, but the content of the presentation is superficial, lacking in-depth thinking and in-depth exploration at the thinking level. This kind of class is only prosperous on the surface, and the students don't get much after the excitement.

In order to make the classroom from shallow to deep, we urgently need to break through the existing concepts, find new methods, and create strategies for in-depth classroom teaching reform. Why should the classroom be changed? What should the classroom pay more attention to? This is a question we must think about.

Shenzuyao, President of the Chinese University of Hong Kong, once said, "learn to listen to others' opinions, consider the views of all parties, and work together to realize your dreams", "the purpose of education is to cultivate independent thinking"; Among the educational goals of all countries in the world, the most consistent and important one is to "cultivate students' independent personality and critical thinking ability". It can be seen that the classroom should fully respect students' personality and pay attention to the cultivation of students' thinking ability.

Thinking ability is the core of learning ability. To reform classroom teaching, we must find out the problems in the way of thinking and trace back to the source, so as to choose the correct direction of reform and scientific reform strategies. If we only attribute the problems in the classroom to the educational system, examination oriented needs and teaching methods, it is impossible to solve the fundamental problems.

It is true that performance is the externalization of thinking. We need not doubt the value of performance, nor can we exclude the form innovation of classroom activities, but "performance originates from thinking, and content determines form", the two cannot be biased. Therefore, from focusing on students' expressive power to paying attention to students' thinking power, to realize the organic combination of expression and thinking, and the harmonious unity of form and content is a threshold that must be crossed by the in-depth curriculum reform.

2 Related Work

2.1 Environmental Design

Environmental design is a new subject full of vitality and constantly improving, so there is no comprehensive teaching theory system up to now. At the same time, environmental design is also a design specialty that takes into account art and technology. It needs to master the skills related to it, which is also the necessary professional quality for the occupation of environmental design. It is not perfect in the research object, theoretical system and discipline scope of research, and even does not have an established definition. Moreover, various scholars hold their own opinions and fail to form a large system, which is the state of environmental design at the present stage. Most professional works and relevant experts and scholars in the industry have different definitions, and there is no authoritative statement and standardization [1]. But in a word, it can be determined that environmental design is an emerging specialty, and constantly self-renewal and improvement in the rapid development. At the same time, it also shows the lack of theoretical research of our environmental design education itself. People's life depends on a certain environment, just as there are nomadic civilization, fishing and hunting civilization and agricultural civilization, which shows that people's life and production are closely related to environmental factors. Therefore, environmental design is the design of people's living space. While constantly transforming and adapting to the surrounding environment, human beings also constantly project their own consciousness, realize that in the places created by human beings, they build an artificial environment consistent with their own culture and habits. With the rapid advancement of industrialization, "strong enough to change the natural process that dominates the ecosystem" has become an irresistible today. At the same time, it has also triggered a chain reaction of environmental problems. The emergence of environmental art also conforms to the expectation of the times for urgently solving environmental problems.

As the main body of the artificial environment, the building separates the original space into the internal environment and the external environment of the building. Human beings distinguish the living environment, working environment, business environment, learning environment and other spaces around the interior and exterior of the building through different functions. Therefore, environmental design is a subject to explore how people, buildings and environment coexist harmoniously. The composition of environmental design knowledge structure is shown in Fig. 1. Because of its complex discipline characteristics, the environmental design specialty has rich content and complex discipline structure, which has more complex and multifaceted needs for its teaching [2]. We should consider how to organically combine professional courses with multi-directional professional design courses, and digital media should run through the courses to form a progressive and orderly knowledge link.

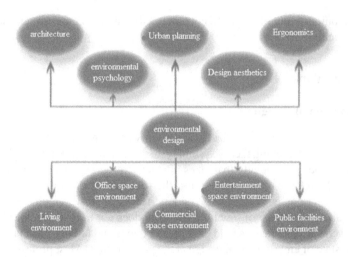

Fig. 1. Knowledge structure of environmental design

2.2   Course and Teaching Characteristics of Computer Renderings

Computer rendering is a very important professional skill course in the curriculum group of environmental design specialty, and it is also one of the necessary skills of environmental design professionals. Through the training of course tasks such as familiar with the operation interface, the use of relevant basic commands, the editing and modification of two-dimensional graphics, the command of two-dimensional to three-dimensional, the parameter setting of camera and material mapping, and the application of Vray dyestuff, it mainly solves the students' basic understanding and post rendering of computer-aided three-dimensional design. Through the study of this course, Be able to master the basic drawing and modification commands and rendering steps of Max, and be able to independently complete the production of indoor and outdoor renderings.

Through the observation of the previous teaching process of computer renderings, it is found that the course is usually arranged for 2–4 weeks of concentrated teaching. As an important practical course, the course has been basically arranged according to project-based teaching, but it has not achieved the expected teaching effect due to various reasons. Especially in the design major admitted by art candidates, the students' theoretical foundation is poor and their logical thinking ability is weak, which makes the teaching of this course difficult. The teaching process is generally teacher-centered and students accept it passively. Except for the practical training course after the teaching of knowledge points, students generally take observation and taking notes as the learning method. In the training course, students mainly copy the homework taught by teachers, and slowly transition from single to copy the whole set of indoor space scheme. Based on such conventional teaching methods, the teaching effect is seriously polarized. Students with strong learning ability may follow the steps independently in the process of teacher demonstration, while students with relatively weak learning ability need to complete the exercises with the help of teachers, and gradually lose their enthusiasm and initiative in learning over time. On the contrary, Students with strong learning ability may find interest in learning and make rapid progress. Such a situation will lead to the widening of the polarization gap, the students with strong learning ability and weak learning ability will not communicate with each other, which is not conducive to the learning of the course, and the teaching objectives are difficult to complete. In the training link, due to the limitations of teaching materials, the practice cases are relatively old, and lag behind in adapting to the discipline development, market demand and technical update. In view of the above situation, it is necessary to adjust the teaching method of computer renderings in time.

3 Information Modernization Teaching in PTP Mode

The teaching of information modernization is reflected in improving the construction of software and hardware facilities, and the construction of software and hardware facilities in Colleges and universities needs to be able to adapt to the general trend of the development of Internet technology in the era of knowledge economy. With the development of Internet technology, the emergence of environmental design online courses, such as micro computing online courses, such as micro courses, Mu courses and flipped classes, has further promoted the changes in the traditional teaching organization, teaching structure, teaching mode, basic teaching content and time allocation. In the traditional environmental design classroom, the organization and arrangement of teaching activities will be limited, The involvement of Internet technology in environmental design makes teaching innovation more ways and possible.

On the one hand, environmental design education needs to share college education software and hardware facilities with other majors, on the other hand, it needs to develop and build software and hardware facilities suitable for environmental design majors. Hardware construction should first vigorously build the campus network and increase the coverage area of the campus network, so that the network can fully cover every place where learning behavior can occur. A comprehensive campus network system can make learning and communication more efficient and convenient. Secondly, we should plan the configuration of various functional classrooms and develop new teaching environments such as smart classrooms. Horizon report 2016 puts forward the concept of "redesigning learning space". The student-centered education concept forces many experts to start thinking about how to redesign learning space to promote students' flexible learning, active learning and collaborative learning. With the development of Internet technology, new teaching forms and learning methods put forward new requirements for classroom form. In the next 3–5 years, profound changes will take place in the form of traditional classrooms. The new classroom environment will support interactive learning of professional disciplines with greater mobility, flexibility and the use of a variety of equipment, so as to promote teacher-student interaction and interdisciplinary problem-solving, as shown in Fig. 2. Based on Internet technology, smart classroom integrates smart teaching, personnel attendance, asset management, environmental smart adjustment, video monitoring and remote control. It solves many problems such as check-in, Q & A, questions, interaction and testing in the process of traditional classroom teaching, and can combine online and offline information to realize remote interaction. The smart classroom encourages interactive inquiry learning. Teachers and students can form a research team together and use technical support for interactive communication and thinking collision, so as to stimulate students' creativity and change the traditional teaching method of classroom knowledge [3]. It also promotes the generation of some new teaching auxiliary spaces, such as the micro class studio where teachers can independently apply for recording and producing "micro classes", and the micro classes produced in the micro class studio are uploaded to relevant platforms for students to learn and share. Teachers majoring in design can make full use of these convenient resources for curriculum design and production. Software construction mainly includes the development and construction of various teaching system platforms, as well as the management, development and application of these platforms, such as multimedia courseware library, digital library, multimedia material library and so on.

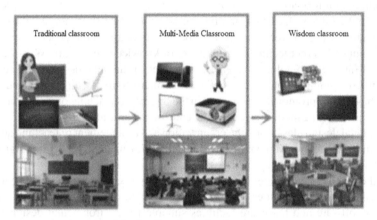

Fig. 2. Classroom development

Let students better enjoy the massive resources provided by the Internet, and the introduction of Internet big data can analyze and judge various use data, so as to help optimize educational resources, comprehensively expand and update the learning content of environmental design education, and enable cutting-edge and excellent design theory and practical skills to enter the classroom timely and effectively for students to learn. We should pay attention to the classification of big data and the design of search engine to facilitate users to quickly screen according to their needs in massive information. Students can use the mobile client to consult and learn the design knowledge at any time after class. The fragmented time can also be fully utilized to improve the learning efficiency of students. At the same time, with the help of the technology learning interactive platform to promote the interaction between teachers and students of design specialty, all kinds of masters and celebrities can also conduct video lectures in real time to interact with design learning.

4   Teaching Innovation of Computer Renderings Based on PTP Mode

PTP mode means that all cognition starts from practice, finds problems through practice, deepens understanding with problems, then condenses problems through independent thinking, and finally carries out practice with problems, that is, "practice cognition practice again" Based on the reality that art majors' learning ability is relatively weak and teaching materials and cases are relatively old, try to take the basic production of computer renderings as the main line and project-based teaching as the guidance. First, encourage students to practice from simple projects and establish a perceptual understanding of the main software involved in this course - Autodesk 3ds Max through initial practice Problems will enter the next round of project practice learning, in order to achieve a learning cycle from practice to theory and then practice. Firstly, each course content is divided into three modules, basic knowledge module (traditional teaching link), application module and development (practice) Module, decomposes the course difficulties into different modules, which are independent and interrelated. Then, starting from the actual needs of design practice, carefully design the contents of each module into comprehensive design tasks, and use project teaching to complete the construction of the course knowledge system and skill system.

4.1   Change the Concept of Curriculum Learning

If you want to integrate the computer effect drawing of Environmental Design Specialty To implement the teaching of this course, we must change the learning concepts of teachers and students. On the one hand, teachers should clarify the training direction and professional characteristics of art students, that is, they need to train students to meet the needs of the development of local market economy, develop in an all-round way morally, intellectually, physically and aesthetically, have a certain theoretical foundation and strong practical ability, and master the basic theoretical knowledge and basic knowledge of architecture, environmental art and so on Skills, have a certain sense of innovation, initially have the basic ability to comprehensively use the learned knowledge to analyze and solve many problems encountered in the practice of indoor and outdoor environmental design engineering, and can be applied senior professionals engaged in environmental design and construction management in enterprises and institutions. Then, in the teaching process of the course, it is necessary to emphasize the application of theory to practice Process, that is, the process of t-p. in the process of learning, it is also necessary to cultivate students' ability to analyze and solve problems from practice and draw conclusions, that is, the process of p-t.

4.2   Reasonably Arrange Teaching Links

1)   Taking tasks as the main line, task-based learning runs through the course teaching from beginning to end. By setting project tasks, learning not only includes large-scale project tasks at the end of the semester, but also includes a series of sub project tasks. Through sub project tasks, piecemeal knowledge points are connected, and

the abstract knowledge separated from social practice is restored to the real situation in time.

2) Support of hybrid learning environment. Project course learning needs the support of network course resources (mu class) and task learning platform to provide learners with functional services such as resource sharing, discussion and posting, exchange and questioning, work display and so on.

3) Integrating multiple disciplines and diversified knowledge acquisition. The setting of tasks integrates multiple disciplines and is closely related to other courses offered by curriculum professional knowledge, which can help learners master more knowledge content and involve various disciplines.

4.3 Optimize Course Assessment Methods

The course of "computer renderings" offered by the "PTP" teaching method should follow the "PTP" teaching concept in the assessment method of the course. The assessment of the original course of "computer renderings" is based on the usual score (accounting for 50% of the total score) + examination score (accounting for 50% of the total score) = the final score. Based on "PTP" The assessment methods of teaching methods are very different from the traditional assessment methods, that is, to improve the assessment results of the practical process (accounting for 60% of the total results). It emphasizes students' process learning, optimizes the measurement of students' usual results, and the proportion of examination results is relatively reduced (accounting for 40% of the total results). This is mainly to change the learning concept of teachers and students on the course of computer renderings and strengthen students' practical ability [4].

5   Conclusion

To sum up, computer effect drawing is the main course for environmental design major to form students' core skills. The embodiment of the production ability of computer effect drawing in the actual project directly affects the competitiveness of students in future design posts. The application of "PTP" teaching method will further improve the computer effect drawing of environmental design major To enhance students' professional quality, so as to effectively improve students' practical application ability.

References

1. Wang, H., Liu, J.: Exploration on PTP teaching mode of social work major in colleges and universities. Educ. Teach. Forum **48**, 126–127 (2018)
2. Wu, D.: Research on teaching reform and practice of computer rendering performance techniques. Popular Lit. Art (24), 192 (2015)
3. Di, R., Zhang, W.: Research on teaching points of computer renderings for environmental art design specialty. Furnit. Inter. Décor. (3), 9–93 (2013)
4. Wang, Y., Wang, J.: On the teaching reform of computer renderings course in colleges and universities. Sci. Technol. Inf. **20**(22), 45

Research on the Application of Cloud Computing College English Teaching Assistant Platform

Yangqu Wang[✉]

Wuhan Technology and Business University, Wuhan 430065, Hubei, China
whskzjw@163.com

Abstract. This paper discusses the application of cloud computing in College English courses. As a tool in the Internet age, cloud provides a broad space for the innovative development of English education and promotes the construction and development of English education at all levels. At present, there are some deficiencies in using rhyme as a tool in English teaching. It is not enough to build, develop and utilize cloud computing platforms that support English learning. Use cloud to define benefits. In the design process, we should fully consider the existing knowledge base, the right to physical and intellectual development, and behavior acquisition. During the implementation of the plan, a complete English curriculum system will be established to adapt group learning and autonomous learning to students' learning habits. In the process of evaluation, the method of combining diversified evaluation and quantitative evaluation is adopted, and scientific and effective teaching feedback is obtained. In this context, we attach importance to the application and construction of English teaching platform, constantly study the different types and aspects of English teaching application, and study English teaching platform. Actively develop discussion platforms and other platforms.

Keywords: Cloud computing · English teaching · Auxiliary teaching

1 Introduction

Cloud computing is a powerful support tool that has a significant impact on all industries, including the education sector. Combine English class with English class. However, there are many problems in the application and platform of cloud based English teaching. This has a significant impact on the development of English teaching applications and platforms Therefore, in addition to English Teaching in many aspects, the application research and development of cloud computing platform also has important practical significance and long-term value. It affects the development of English courses and platform construction, and puts forward optimization suggestions. Using the Internet to improve cloud utilization. English learning plan and platform construction Support. I hope I can now provide reference for learning English in the cloud. The Ministry of education has officially promulgated the College English syllabus as an important guide

M. A. Jan and F. Khan (Eds.): BigIoT-EDU 2022, LNICST 467, pp. 211–222, 2023.
https://doi.org/10.1007/978-3-031-23944-1_24

for College English Teaching in China. Since then, our mainstream College English schools have been carrying out educational reform.

He emphasized the changes in teaching methods and activities, pointed out the short-comings of current college English teaching, and required that scientific English teaching reach an unprecedented level, moving from primary school to teaching evaluation. At present, due to the combination of the principle of educational equity and the principle of educational effectiveness in practice, educational reform has become more complex. From the perspective of teaching evaluation, Multiple Intelligences Evaluation provides us with a practical introduction to cultivate students' abilities in all aspects. According to the new requirements of social development for English teaching, it has become one of the main objectives of teaching. The evaluation of multiple intelligences theory provides a new perspective for English teaching [1].

The reform of evaluation method and system is an important part of the reform of College English teachers. College English teaching should aim at reforming the curriculum system, teaching methods, teaching contents and teaching methods. In particular, English teaching is an important part of College English teaching. It is an important basis for teachers to receive feedback, improve classroom management and ensure classroom quality. It is also an effective means for students to adapt to teaching strategies, improve teaching methods and improve teaching efficiency. Improve the effectiveness of education. Pay attention to students' evaluation, ignoring students' self-evaluation and practical evaluation, students' English class, English class of the subject and classroom management evaluation. The network environment provides very favorable conditions for the development of multi-functional evaluation models.

2   Related Work

2.1   Overview of Cloud Computing

Cloud computing can manage and allocate computing resources on the network, allowing users to use related services on interfaces such as core services. Cloud platform and cloud service are two different concepts in cloud computing. Cloud platform can provide a wider range of network information sources. Unlike cloud platform, cloud service is an abstract infrastructure, but it can also extend related services. Cloud computing can be extended not only to local computers, but also to most computers. Because this is the basic principle, the real cloud computing is parallel computing. Cloud computing allows enterprises to access data online, convert resources into applications needed by enterprises, and access storage systems and computers as needed, which is very beneficial to enterprises [2].

In recent years, cloud computing has developed very rapidly in China. First, in November 2008, the "cloud computing Expert Committee of China Electronics Association", represented by Li Deyi, an academician of the Chinese Academy of engineering, was officially established, with Li Deyi as the chairman. Next, Alibaba software, a subsidiary of Alibaba group, officially signed an agreement with the Nanjing government and established China's first "e-commerce cloud computing center" in Nanjing in 2009. China Mobile, which has hundreds of millions of users, has completed the cloud computing center test and announced that the future development direction will be cloud computing and the mobility of the Internet. With the further development of cloud computing in China, cloud computing has also made many achievements in platform design and educational applications. Represented by Professor Li Jiahou of Shanghai Normal University, he carried out the training of cloud computing assisted instruction throughout the country, which laid a certain foundation for the wide application of cloud computing in the field of education in China, such as the famous Cloud Computing Assisted Instruction Platform: "Anshan No. 1 middle school on the July Bridge", Cloud Computing Assisted Instruction of Shanghai Normal University, etc.

In the CNKI academic literature repository, the literature of recent ten years was searched with the search item "theme", the search term "cloud computing" and "Cloud Computing Assisted Teaching": there were 7278 literatures about "cloud computing"; There are 2250 literatures about "Cloud Computing Assisted Instruction"; At the same time, "cloud computing" and "collaborative learning" were used to search a total of 7 articles, including 4 master's theses and 3 journals; There are 8288 documents about "instructional design", and 2200 in addition to non educational fields. Then search with the search item "title" and the search term "Research on the application of Cloud Computing Assisted Instruction in history teaching". It can be found that there is no relevant literature on the application of Cloud Computing Assisted Instruction in history teaching once. After analyzing the above data, it is not difficult to find that the concept of "cloud computing" is quite novel. Many relevant articles have been published in recent years and started late, The research on "Cloud Computing Assisted Instruction" is also far from enough. There are only a few articles on the exploration of other disciplines other than history, and there is no article in the field of history teaching. Therefore, the author's attempt to combine cloud computing with history teaching in this paper is also of certain significance.

2.2 Object Model Design of Online Teaching Practice Platform

Collaborative learning under cloud computing assisted instruction platform is the development and extension of computer-supported collaborative learning. The research of cloud computing in foreign countries is relatively early, and the literature provided is relatively large. 18,928 articles were retrieved from Elsevier SC with the keyword "cloud computing", among which there are many researches on cloud computing technology, cloud computing application and cloud computing security. According to the analysis of literature, with the maturity of cloud computing technology, many foreign universities have introduced the services brought by cloud computing into the application of campus network. In 2006, American state universities adopted Google's Gmail email service to ensure the email security of 60,000 students; The "general cloud computing service" jointly launched by American SIM tone and Graham primary school brings virtual computer desktops to school teachers and students; In 2010, IBM cooperated with six universities, including Carnegie Mellon University Qatar, Kadar University and Texas A & M University Qatar, to carry out the "Qatar cloud computing program" and other 0. On this basis, the development of cloud computing platform for teaching has also been carried out in succession. China Baihui company, India Baihui company and Google company of the United States have launched Cloud Computing Assisted Teaching Platforms with stable services and friendly interfaces, such as Baihui, Google

Apps, etc. In Elsevier SC, 553 articles were searched with the keywords "cloud computing" and "collaborative learning" as the joint keywords, 46 of which were related, and 11,777 articles were searched with the keywords "collaborative learning" and "instructional design" as the joint keywords, Then search with "cloud computing supported teaching design of collaborative learning" and "teaching design of collaborative learning on the platform of cloud computing assisted instruction" respectively, and there is almost nothing related to it. It can be seen that foreign research in this area is still in its infancy.

The recommended learning resource module first divides the teaching needs and cooperates with the user management module to obtain three important user information, namely, school, major and classroom. Use these three keywords to extract the keyword list of the current user, and redesign the user profile to analyze the professional training needs as text [3]. The keyword list is also used to classify and navigate recommended learning resource pages. Users can click other keywords and filter from the list of recommended items.

Keyword extraction is based on text sorting algorithm. Text sorting algorithm is similar to page sorting algorithm. Sorting algorithm based on image and page order.

PageRank is an algorithm proposed by goge, which is calculated based on the number of links between pages. The voting mechanism determines its meaning by parsing links between pages into sounds between pages. Therefore, the page classification algorithm is implemented as follows:

$$S(V_i) = (1 - d) + d \times \sum_{j \in In(V_i)} \frac{1}{|Out(V_j)|} S(V_j) \tag{1}$$

D is the damping coefficient, generally 0.85. Since the page ranking value of the web page is not zero, it is necessary to introduce the damping coefficient D.

The text sorting algorithm takes words as nodes, establishes the connection by establishing the symbiotic relationship between word nodes, and introduces the concept of edge weight. When using this algorithm to extract keywords, we regard words as nodes, so there is no similarity between the two words. Usually, the weight between words is set to 1 by default, so the algorithm is basically similar to PageRank algorithm. The principle of text sorting algorithm can be explained that the importance of word I is determined by the weight of word I and word J before word I and the sum of the weight between word J and other words. The implementation formula of text ranking algorithm for keyword extraction is as follows:

$$WS(V_i) = (1 - d) + d \times \sum_{V_j \in In(V_i)} \frac{\omega_{ji}}{\sum_{V_k \in Out(V_j)} \omega_{jk}} WS \tag{2}$$

Only when there is a corresponding word with length k in the window, the formula is used to initialize the value of each node, measure the value of the page sequence, and continue the calculation iteration to converge. Define the order of node weight reduction to obtain a maximum of T characters and create an initial keyset. Finally, highlight a word in the original text, connect adjacent words to the keywords of multiple words, and add them to the keyword group [4].

3 Research on the Application of Cloud Computing College English Teaching Assistant Platform

There are many problems in the process of English teaching. In addition to cloud computing, all schools in China should fully capture the laws and benefits of English teaching and supplement English teaching at all levels in cloud computing. We must strive to establish and develop harmonious relations and elements. For example, the formation of English teaching ideas, the innovation of methods and forms, the rich design and integration of content systems, and the improvement of teaching quality are the main work of computing cloud outside the innovation and development of English teaching [5].

As we continue to improve the English teaching concept based on network and information teaching, we must constantly improve the English teaching system, platform and application. The concept of English teaching is the first step to support English teaching and build a platform. Therefore, when popularizing cloud computing English teaching applications and platforms, it is necessary to carefully analyze the development requirements of English teaching concepts, and build and integrate the following ideas. First, adhere to the network and information-based English teaching. Promote all aspects of this work into the track of Cloud Computing Assisted English teaching network and information development; Second, adhere to the educational concept of shared development and promote this work to maintain the development trend of joint development and utilization; Third, adhere to the humanistic education concept, promote this work, maintain the humanized education concept, take students as the center, and strive to innovate all links and aspects of Cloud Computing Assisted English teaching application and platform construction.

Focusing on the network platform and students' autonomous learning, we will continue to integrate and innovate the application and platform construction of Computing Assisted English teaching. English teaching method is an effective means for the application and platform construction of Cloud Computing Assisted English teaching [6]. Therefore, when promoting the application and platform construction of Cloud Computing Assisted English teaching, we must carefully analyze the requirements of this work on the methods and modes of English teaching application and platform construction. On the one hand, we should actively give play to the advantages and convenient role of network platforms and carriers, strive to carry out various English teaching forms and platforms under the network environment, and strive to innovate various ways and channels of Cloud Computing Assisted English teaching; On the other hand, give full play to the subjective role of teachers and students, and strive to carry out English Teaching in the form of cooperation and interaction between teachers and students from all aspects, so as to continuously improve the innovative role of Cloud Computing Assisted English teaching application and platform construction.

3.1 Overall Implementation Scheme of the Platform

Chinese educational technology experts zhaojianhua and Li pointed out that "learning education theory" is the theoretical basis of learner centered and teaching "cooperative learning based" development. In specific teaching practice, the application of coordinated teaching suggestions must be closely related to teaching design. The study found that the current overall concept of composition teaching is more suitable for the harmony of teaching mode.

This paper analyzes the documents about the theme of "teaching design of cooperative learning" in CNKI scientific and Technological Literature Library, studies the teaching and application of cooperative learning in cyberspace, and designs a teaching scheme based on Cooperative Learning under the background of information technology. The concept and research of cloud service collaborative curriculum, the teaching of problem-based collaborative teaching in the context of distance learning and the analysis of relevant literature [7]. The specific cooperative education policy should include seven reference points. Teaching task design, group learning structure design, collaborative learning environment design, collaborative learning activity design, teaching activity design, teaching evaluation.

The overall structure and function distribution of the platform module are introduced in detail. On the basis of the preliminary deployment, this section introduces the general methods to realize the online learning platform. The implementation structure of the platform code is shown in Fig. 1.

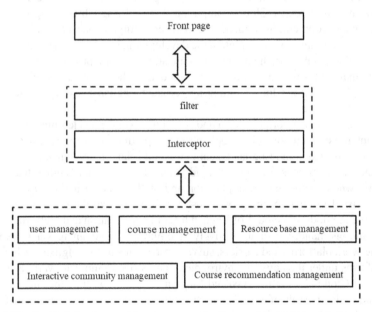

Fig. 1. Code implementation structure of online teaching practice platform

3.2 Cloud Computing Learning Task Design

Cloud computing assisted instruction can save the cost of fixed assets such as funds, manpower and server equipment for schools, and make full use of the convenience of collaboration, resource sharing and unlimited storage space brought by "cloud service" to teaching. Teachers can build a teaching assistance platform suitable for the course according to the needs of the course, which can not only inject new vitality into the course, but also effectively improve the quality of the course [8]. Referring to the use of Cloud Computing Assisted Instruction Platform in various places, the author summarizes its advantages as follows:

(1) A new teaching platform has been created: the creation of cloud computing assisted teaching platform not only breaks the traditional classroom teaching mode, but also makes the construction of network teaching platform easier. At the same time, it extends teaching in time and space, and makes up for the lack of a single classroom teaching method.

(2) Increased communication channels: in the traditional classroom model, the communication between teachers and students is limited to the classroom. The cloud computing teaching platform enables real-time or asynchronous communication and sharing between teachers and students and between students, enriching the means and ways of communication.

(3) Expanded personalized learning space: Cloud Computing Assisted Instruction can not only enrich teachers' teaching ways and methods, but also provide learners with a new platform and space to develop personality. Learners use the cloud computing environment to plan personalized course learning and self-learning management.

(4) Improve collaboration interest: every service is customer-centric, and cloud computing is no exception. Visual resources and tools provide the cloud computing platform with a function to support multiple people to collaborate and modify files at the same time. Online collaboration is convenient and fast, just like face-to-face communication. The humanized design removes all obstacles for collaborative learning, improves collaborative interest, and ensures the effectiveness of collaborative learning.

(5) Take learners as the main body: learners build a personal learning environment, plan and manage personal learning, and freely choose the learning resources and services they need. Learners can store learning resources in personal learning platforms. As long as they can be connected to the Internet, they can use the resources. Cloud computing assisted instruction platform not only provides space for learners' brains to extend and expand, but also provides learners with permission to share resources.

Learning task design is the focus and core of the whole collaborative learning. It can make learners clear their goals and solve problems. In the collaborative learning environment under the cloud computing assisted instruction platform, as shown in Fig. 2, learners' learning and application of relevant knowledge and the cultivation of learners' comprehensive ability are the core of collaborative learning, so we should pay more attention to problem solving and learning task design. When designing learning tasks, the following issues should be fully considered [9].

(1) The designed task should be open, and the standard of exploration results cannot be "correct" or "incorrect". The problem-solving process not only expects learners to master basic theoretical knowledge, but also important is that learners can actively

participate in the collaborative learning process, so as to cultivate learners' ability to apply theoretical knowledge with practical application and solve problems.

(2) The design of tasks should be suitable for the characteristics of learners, and it is best to be within the scope of learners' proximity to the development area, otherwise it is easy to hit learners' learning enthusiasm.

(3) The completion of the task depends on the network and adopts a collaborative way. At the same time, there are also opportunities for autonomous learning.

(4) The design of learning tasks should be close to learners' life and have a certain real situation, so as to stimulate learners' learning motivation.

(5) The results of learning tasks should be easy to generate and submit.

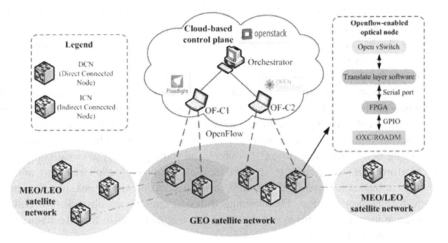

Fig. 2. Design of cloud computing assisted instruction platform

4 Platform Design

Through the cloud computing service platform, teachers can teach at any time and anywhere as long as they have Internet access devices. Similarly, with the application of cloud computing service platform, teachers can also build their own work and life communication circle to enrich their work and life. In addition, the advantages of cloud services, such as communication, convenience and rich information, have a significant impact on Teachers' ability improvement, cooperation and communication, and scientific research progress. The application of cloud computing service platform is conducive to the personal progress of teachers, the improvement of professional quality, and finally the improvement of teaching level. For students, in the process of autonomous learning, autonomy, cooperation and communication are well realized through cloud services, which highlights the subjectivity that students should have in the teaching process. The application of cloud computing service platform is a win–win result for teachers and students.

The structural cluster of NAS file computing system itself is loose, and the distributed characteristics within its architecture are obvious. The advantages of cloud computing architecture are shown in Fig. 3 below:

Fig. 3. Advantages of cloud computing architecture

Because the smallest unit is a file stored in the cluster, computing information can reduce redundancy. The system has a perfect, economical and reliable safety management system. When the client sends a large number of requests, the NAS system capacity is limited, and the cloud NAS service can be used to run the auxiliary computer. The solar cell pack itself is a compact combination [10]. Decompose the file into historical records and save them to the cluster. Compared with group nodes, other records can access each other. The node can use the data group in the file to process the request sent by the client. The increase and decrease of San system nodes can meet the needs of customers. At the same time, self-definition can be further improved. If Sao Paulo wants to start intensive development, it is necessary to improve productivity and effectively reduce costs. However, cost intensive internal data processing and equipment design can effectively increase the price of San services. In order to ensure their cost-effectiveness and high-quality business, their productivity can be reduced accordingly.

(1) It provides great convenience for teachers: ① it provides homework correction and duplicate checking Instant multi-functional annotation and scoring in various forms. When correcting homework, teachers can directly send private letters to students with large problems to tell them where the problems are and how to do them; ② it provides functions such as online attendance, score summary and online test, automatic statistics and data collection; ③ teachers can upload learning related materials, good cases, courseware, video English teaching and other functions inside and outside class Learning resources, and let students download; ④ It provides

favorable conditions for real-time feedback and interactive activities in English Teaching in the classroom, and can realize that most students can participate in classroom interaction.

(2) It is conducive to grasp the overall learning situation of students: in traditional classroom English teaching, teachers mainly rely on observing students' behavior and attention in class to obtain whether students are listening carefully, or judge the learning effect of students through the completion of students' homework. Using this platform, teachers can view students' learning status through some functional modules displayed on various platforms, such as students' attendance, homework, discussion, test and so on; And teachers can record students' participation and interaction, attendance, homework, test scores and so on [11].

(3) It is conducive to the fairness and objectivity of evaluation: by using this platform, the usual homework evaluation can have better timeliness, shorter time and higher efficiency. The data of students' usual performance and homework review can be stored on the server of the platform in real time, It is very conducive to the process assessment of students. When it is necessary to evaluate students at the end of the term, we can make a fair and objective evaluation by checking the students' usual homework results and performance.

One week before class, teachers should upload some materials required for learning to the platform according to the course content, such as courseware, preparatory knowledge that students should know in class, learning objectives, learning content and some case materials. Its forms can also be diverse, including videos, links, articles, courseware, etc. It's best to prepare a learning task list to let students know what requirements they should meet. After data sharing, the teacher first told the students in the wechat group that the new data had been shared on the platform to remind the students to watch, and then issued an announcement. Send a message to wechat group one day before class to further remind students to make corresponding preparations and let students form the habit of checking notices regularly. After the shared materials are completed, it is necessary to prepare for classroom interaction. The interaction module includes courseware interaction and test question interaction. The former can let students participate in the explanation process of class, while the latter can let students participate at the end of a course content explanation, so as to understand the situation of hand-held. There are many types of interactive questions. Teachers can make choices according to the needs of curriculum content. Students need to study the materials before class after the teacher issues the announcement, and prepare for the class. If there are problems, they should mark them in time, or comment on the announcement, or platform, wechat or telephone private letter teachers [12].

Before the formal class, the classroom dispatcher provides three check-in methods: traditional check-in, digital check-in and GPS check-in; In order to prevent students from cheating, it is recommended to use the second and third methods, because you can check the abnormal check-in. Students' attendance will be recorded every time. Teachers can download the overall attendance sheet of the whole class at the end of the term to score students' usual grades, which is also conducive to the process assessment implemented by some colleges and universities. After the formal class, the teacher will be sent to the classroom on the computer web and enter the interactive "courseware interaction" module to start the content explanation. When interaction is needed, click the "interaction" button on the screen, and the platform will display the number of answers, the time of answer and the real-time data feedback of answer. The teacher can adjust his English Teaching in real time according to the answer effect; At the end of a content explanation, teachers can arrange a "test question" interaction to test students' learning results. Similarly, the platform can also obtain students' answer data. For questions with high error rate, teachers can explain in detail again.

5 Conclusion

"Cloud" education platform is a new idea and attempt of cloud computing in the field of education. With the help of cloud computing English teaching platform, cloud computing can be used as a tool for English teaching, which is a real and effective conclusion to improve the efficiency of English teaching. The English learning platform supported by cloud computing promotes the cost savings of infrastructure investment in Colleges and universities. A low technical threshold can help teachers build their own personalized English teaching support network, design personalized English teaching support network, strengthen teacher-student interaction, and improve curriculum design. Improving the quality of English teaching, creating a personalized learning environment for students, improving the quality of English teaching, customizing and planning personalized learning activities, and independently planning learning and learning progress can help students. Develop advanced intelligence and collective wisdom. The advent of the cloud era has brought new opportunities to English teaching and promoted the new development of online English teaching.

References

1. Alnwaiem, A.F., Alazcmi, A.M., Alenezl, A.A.: Kuwaiti instructors' beliefs about English language teaching and their awareness of global English. Engl. Lang. **14**(4), 87 (2021)
2. Walker, T., He-Weatherford, Z., Motha, S.: Christopher Jenks: race and ethnicity in English language teaching: Korea in focus. Appl. Linguist. **42**(1), 192–195 (2021)
3. Jangir, N.K., Bute, A.R., Bansode, A.: digital literacies: a strategy of pedagogy for English language teaching to technical undergraduates. In: WEENTECH Proceedings in Energy, pp. 518–526 (2021)
4. Altameemy, F.A., Alrefaee, Y.: Impact of covid-19 on English language teaching in Yemen: challenges and opportunities (2021)
5. Li, J., Qiao, Z., Zhang, K., et al.: A lattice-based homomorphic proxy re-encryption scheme with strong anti-collusion for cloud computing. Sensors **21**(1), 288 (2021)
6. Zheng, P., Wu, Z., Sun, J., et al.: A parallel unmixing-based content retrieval system for distributed hyperspectral imagery repository on cloud computing platforms. Remote Sens. **13**(2), 176 (2021)
7. Amorim, G.B.: English Language Teaching and Technology in Education: Lessons from Enduring Times (2021)
8. Srivaishnavi, D., Arjun, T., Dhyaneshwaran, K., et al.: Secure ring signature based privacy preserving of public auditing mechanism for outsourced data in cloud computing paradigm. J. Phys.: Conf. Ser. **1916**(1), 012079 (5pp) (2021)

9. Suresha, D., Karibasappa, K.: Enhancing data protection in cloud computing using key derivation based on cryptographic technique. In: 2021 5th International Conference on Computing Methodologies and Communication (ICCMC) (2021)
10. Asrifan, A.: Modul Perkuliahan Research on English Language Teaching (2021)
11. Prithiviraj, S., Chauhan.: English Language Teaching to Rural Students: Challenges and Strategies (2021)
12. Yu, G.: Engl. Lang. Teach. **14**(9), 89 (2021)

Research on the Application of College English Ecological Teaching Model Based on EM Algorithm

Yanwei Jiao[✉]

Xi'an Fanyi University, Xi'an 710105, Shaanxi, China
627346334@qq.com

Abstract. With the progress of modern science and technology and the development of modern life, the concept of ecology is deeply rooted in the hearts of the people, which not only affects many fields such as environment, civilization, ethics and food, but also extends to college English teaching. Therefore, the focus of this paper is to analyze the ecological factors in the current college English teaching system according to the theories and principles of ecological philosophy and classroom ecology, and combine the ecological theory with college English teaching practice to build a new college English ecological teaching model. This paper will investigate the current situation of College English Classroom Ecology and analyze the reasons for the imbalance of College English classroom ecology, and build a new, harmonious, dynamic, balanced and open English ecological teaching model in line with the niche principle, the law of limiting factors, the law of tolerance and the principle of optimum in order to solve the problems existing in College English teaching. The innovation of this study is the effective combination of ecological theory and College English teaching practice, which will help to overcome the shortcomings of non-compliance with ecological requirements, low efficiency and time-consuming in the current college English teaching practice, and promote the continuous reform of College English teaching so as to make new breakthroughs and progress. However, classroom ecology is already a new research direction. Combining it with college English teaching practice and constructing a new college English ecological teaching model is a long-term and continuous improvement process in practice. Therefore, this study has great limitations, but I hope this study can provide new enlightenment for College English teaching practice.

Keywords: EM algorithm · College English · Ecological teaching · Teaching model

1 Introduction

Since the founding of new China, despite the ups and downs of English Teaching in China, some achievements have been made in the compilation of syllabus, teaching materials and language testing, which has effectively promoted the development of

M. A. Jan and F. Khan (Eds.): BigIoT-EDU 2022, LNICST 467, pp. 223–234, 2023.
https://doi.org/10.1007/978-3-031-23944-1_25

English teaching. However, the overall level of theoretical research on English Teaching in China is still very weak, and the theoretical innovation is not enough, which is mainly reflected in: first, the scientific research consciousness, scientific research ability and academic sensitivity of English teaching staff in China are weak [1]. Influenced by the commercialization thought of the times, fewer and fewer English teachers in China devote themselves to scientific research. However, English teaching research "needs to endure loneliness, resist temptation and know longitude and latitude". Fewer and fewer English teachers are willing to settle down to do scientific research, so it is difficult to produce innovative research results. According to a survey by the University Foreign Language Teaching Steering Committee of colleges and universities, among the 14239 foreign language teachers in 311 universities involved in the survey, only 736 academic papers were published in foreign language core journals, only 2.4 in each university, and only 0.02 per teacher on average. The scientific research consciousness and ability of college foreign language teachers are still the same, not to mention the foreign language teachers in primary and secondary schools. The researchers of English teaching theory in China are mainly concentrated in foreign universities or foreign language departments of colleges and universities. The research level of front-line teachers in primary and secondary schools is relatively limited, and there is no authoritative professional research institution of English Teaching in China for unified planning [2]. Therefore, the research topics and results do not pay enough attention to practice, the theoretical improvement is not enough, the research results are not systematic and forward-looking, and the innovation of research results is certainly insufficient. Third, our primary and secondary school English teachers lack of theoretical literacy; However, College English professors and experts lack practical experience, and their theories and views are often not related to the actual situation, which is not helpful to solve practical problems, so it is difficult to form a systematic English teaching theory. Because of this, the research results of English Teaching in China are the same, either the summary of teachers' personal experience, or the empty theory and other word games, which are difficult to produce excellent research results [3]. Fourth, there is no innovation in China's English teaching research as a whole. Whether it is teaching theory, teaching practice or research model, it follows the trend of International English teaching. Not only does it not have its own theoretical innovation, but even the introduction of foreign English teaching theory is blind, and it is basically not connected with China's English teaching practice [4].

Since the reform and opening up, the number of foreign language learners in China has increased sharply, and the shortage of foreign language teachers has become an inevitable fact. Due to the shortage of teachers, the problem that English teachers only speak quantity but not quality in some areas, especially in rural areas, is particularly prominent [5]. According to the sample survey, in some areas of China, especially in the western rural areas, a considerable number of English teachers can't speak and write fluent and standard English. How can such teachers cultivate high-quality English talents? When interviewing teachers and researchers in rural areas, they always think about how to teach and study English. Some teachers have never thought about how to teach and study English. Some teachers have never thought about how to teach and study English in rural areas. Since the enrollment expansion of colleges and universities in 1998, College English teachers have become popular again. Many teachers have several jobs and are tired of coping all day. It is difficult to have time and energy to sit down and prepare lessons, attend classes and reflect [6]. Therefore, how can the trained students become English teachers who will undertake the training of English Teaching in the future? According to relevant research, the ratio of the number of College English teachers to the number of students taught was 1:130 in 2001. More seriously, in some local colleges and universities in China, the academic structure of College English teachers and the requirements of teaching tasks are seriously maladjusted. 73.2% of teachers have only bachelor's degree or below.

The optimization of teaching mode has always been the goal of College English teaching. Teaching reforms aiming at this goal emerge one after another, but it has not fundamentally changed the passive situation of high investment and low output in College English teaching [7]. The main reasons are the unclear definition of College English objectives, the lack of overall concept and the neglect of the dynamic balance between the elements in the teaching system. This paper attempts to construct a stable teaching activity structure and activity program based on EM algorithm In order to change the passive situation of time-consuming and inefficient College English teaching.

2   Related Work

2.1 EM Algorithm

(1) Meaning of EM algorithm

EM algorithm is an iterative algorithm. It is a method for maximum likelihood estimation of parameters proposed by Dempster, laind and Rubin in 1977. It can estimate the maximum likelihood of parameters from incomplete data sets A very simple and practical learning algorithm. This method can be widely used to deal with so-called incomplete data, such as defective data, truncated data, annoying data and so on [8].

Bayesian computing methods can be divided into two categories. Class is an estimate directly applied to a posteriori distribution to obtain a posteriori mean or a posteriori mode, as well as the asymptotic variance or its approximation of this estimate. The other can be collectively referred to as data addition algorithm, which is a rapidly developing and widely used algorithm in recent years. It does not directly maximize or simulate the complex posterior distribution, but adds some "potential data" on the basis of observed data, so as to simplify the calculation and complete a series of simple maximization or simulation. EM algorithm is a general method to solve the maximum likelihood estimation of model parameters from "incomplete data". The so-called "incomplete data" can be divided into two situations: one is that the observation data becomes incomplete data due to the limitation or error of the observation itself, and the other is that it is very difficult to directly optimize the likelihood function of parameters, and it is easier to optimize after introducing additional parameters (implicit or missing), Therefore, define the original observation data plus additional data to form "complete data", and the original observation data will naturally become "incomplete data".

Each iteration of EM algorithm includes an E-step expectation step and an M-step maximum likelihood step. The advantage of the algorithm is that it reliably converges to the local maximum in the - definite sense, that is, under general conditions, each iteration increases the likelihood function value. When the likelihood function value is bounded, the iterative sequence converges to the supremum of a stable value. The disadvantage of EM algorithm is that when the proportion of missing data is large, its convergence rate is relatively slow.

(2) Principle of EM algorithm

The basic principle can be expressed as follows: the data we can observe is y, complete data x = (y, z), Z is missing data, θ Are model parameters. θ On the posterior distribution P of Y (θ| Y) It is very complex and difficult to carry out various statistical calculations. If the missing data Z is known, it is possible to get a θ Simply add a posteriori distribution P (θ| y. Z), using P (θ| y. Z) we can carry out various statistical calculations. Then, looking back, we can check and improve the assumption of Z. In this way, we transform a complex maximization sampling problem into a series of simple maximization or sampling problems.

EM algorithm is essentially similar to local mountain climbing in multivariate space. E and M steps implicitly (and automatically) determine the direction and distance of each step. Therefore, like mountain climbing algorithm, EM algorithm is sensitive to initial conditions, so different local maxima can be obtained by selecting different initial conditions [9]. The EM algorithm may converge to the final parameter value quite slowly, so it can be combined with the traditional optimization technology to accelerate the convergence. Nevertheless, the standard EM algorithm is widely used because it has a wide range of applications and can be easily transplanted to a variety of different problems.

2.2 Definition of Foreign Language Teaching Model

Foreign language teaching mode is a relatively stable teaching activity structure and activity procedure established under the guidance of certain foreign language teaching ideas and theories. The development of foreign language teaching model is closely related to the development of linguistics and psychology. The behaviorist teaching mode prevailing in the 1950s absorbed the research results of behaviorist psychology and structuralist language education at that time, and combined the research results of modern linguistics and psychology with foreign language teaching for the first time. This is a great innovation in the history of foreign language teaching, but this mode is fundamental It ignores people's subjective initiative and creativity. Cognitive teaching model is a foreign language teaching method proposed in the United States in the mid-1960s to address the defects of behaviorism teaching model. This model discusses and studies foreign language teaching from the perspective of psychology, emphasizing meaningful learning and meaningful training. Although the cognitive teaching model attaches importance to human cognitive structure, it ignores the influence of human emotion, value and attitude on learning. Produced in the early 1970s, the communicative teaching model absorbs the research results of sociolinguistics. Language is regarded as a tool of communication. Foreign language teaching content promotes the use of language to a new level from the purpose of communication rather than the structure of language. However, the communicative teaching model ignores the language teaching environment and has the problem of disharmony between teaching objectives and methods.

In the process of developing and discarding the existing foreign language teaching model, the foreign language teaching concept mainly shows the following development trends: from paying attention to grammar rules to cultivating communicative ability and comprehensive language ability; From teacher centered to student-centered, from relying too much on mother tongue to completely excluding mother tongue to consciously using mother tongue; From learning theory based solely on behaviorism or cognitivism to organic combination of the two; From single teaching skills to three-dimensional teaching by using modern media technology to create real context; Listen from the Speaking, reading, writing and translation, as separate skills training, have changed to the concept of overall language teaching; From paying attention to learning to learning, and then to the organic combination of the two. After a series of evolution, although there are still some differences in the definition of foreign language teaching model, a consensus has been reached that foreign language teaching model is a structure and procedure of teaching activities.

2.3 Combing the Relationship Between English Teaching and Adjacent Disciplines

Through the brief review and introduction of the above related disciplines, we can clearly see that this paper defines applied linguistics as the most superior discipline. Applied linguistics includes all aspects of language application, and the scope is open, but the main research object of Applied Linguistics still includes language teaching, mainly studying second language teaching or foreign language teaching; However, language teaching is not the only field of Applied Linguistics. In addition, applied linguistics research also includes language planning, which mainly studies the status of language, the standardization and standardization of language and characters, and even the related problems of national standard language; Secondly, applied linguistics also broadens the broad sense of sociolinguistics to study the relationship between language and society and the social application of language, such as language and ecology, language and gender differences, and the role of language in professions such as international trade, mass media, politics and law. In addition, ontology linguistics and the relationship between language ontology and modern science and technology are also the perspective of applied linguistics research, For example, computational linguistics and language information processing.

Language teaching is a subordinate branch of Applied Linguistics, which mainly includes second language acquisition, mother tongue teaching and even first language acquisition divided by some linguists (this concept is often used in bilingual or more countries such as Singapore and Canada). The second language teaching and learning can be defined as the second language teaching. However, some domestic students and even parents often default the foreign language to English, because most of China's foreign language courses are English: but in fact, foreign language teaching includes Japanese teaching and Russian teaching in addition to English teaching.

The logical relationship of relevant disciplines is shown in Fig. 1

From this relationship, it can be seen that applied linguistics, language teaching, second language acquisition and foreign language teaching are closely related. The original intention of Applied Linguistics and second language acquisition is to promote second language (mainly English) teaching through the study of language and even

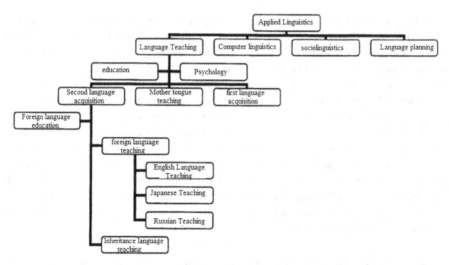

Fig. 1. Logical relationship between adjacent disciplines in English teaching

relevant factors of language acquisition. However, the development of English teaching makes us see that traditional disciplines such as linguistics, psychology and pedagogy are also inseparable.

3 Connotation of English Teaching Ecological Model

When Hogan talked about "the relationship between any language and its environment" in a report, he compared this relationship to the ecological relationship between specific animals and plants and their living environment; Since then, the metaphorical usage of language ecology has been widely used; In recent years, western scholars have added the concept of ecology to Vygotsky's social and cultural theory and Bakhtin's dialogue theory and participation theory. As a systematic, integrated, coordinated and dynamic language teaching and research model, eco language teaching theory examines the inter-action between students, teachers, language and language learning environment and its impact on language acquisition from multiple perspectives; Therefore, we creatively use the emergence theory to have an overall understanding of language and generation, integrate the relationship between language learners and learning environment through symbolism, and interpret the language learning process into the rheology of multi-dimensional space-time scale, so as to interpret language teaching and research more comprehensively and ecologically, and guide foreign language teaching and research more scientifically. Such an ecological model of English teaching includes the process view of teaching, the difference view of teaching, the interaction view of teaching, the importance of teaching situation, the integrity and harmony of teaching content, the democracy and equality of both sides of teaching and so on.

3.1 Ecological Language Generation View

In recent years, "emergence" has gradually become a frontier and hot topic in complexity science and linguistics; The Santa Fe Institute of the United States is famous for studying complexity. In their research program, they have clearly put forward: "complexity is essentially a science about emergence… That is, how to find the basic law of emergence". They even take emergence as "Santa Fe theme" and "Santa Fe concept" for comprehensive investigation and research; In recent years, Chinese philosophical researchers have also focused on the emergence theory.

Language is a multi-agent, complex, dynamic and adaptive system. Language learning is the process of feature emergence. Language, a complex system, is composed of ecology in the interaction between people with desire to communicate and the world being discussed, and it is at different levels (from bottom to top: body, brain, voice and nerve, morphology, vocabulary, construction, interaction and conversation) A complex system in which different sets (individuals, social groups, networks, cultures) and different time categories (evolution, development, rebirth, interaction, neural lateral interaction, neural vertical interaction) constantly adapt. How does the specific language emerge? Macwhinney believes that "there is no complete description of language emergence, but emergence theory has described many language phenomena." Human pronunciation process mainly includes the coordinated movement of tongue, throat and other pronunciation organs [10]. Adult pronunciation has a great impact on children's pronunciation. Therefore, the phonological structure is the physiological restriction of the vocal tract. The experiments conducted by Plaut and Kello with the help of the network structure of connectivity theory show that many early childhood pronunciation characteristics emerge from the process of processing materials through these networks. Smith's research confirmed that children learn new words "using special learning mechanisms in the general learning process".

3.2 Ecological Language Learning Process View

Space has three dimensions: length, width and height; Time also has three dimensions, namely "present", "past" and "future". The three-dimensional dimension of space is well known and familiar to everyone, but the three-dimensional understanding of time has not attracted enough attention, because we often use natural time to cover the light of humanistic time and psychological time. In fact, we can observe and experience "now", "past" and "future" from the perspective of Humanities and psychology, and confirm the difference and connection between the concept of "time". Without the three dimensions of time, there is no time process and time concept; As far as the historical time in humanistic time is concerned, it can be divided into ancient times (including ancient times, middle ages and modern times), modern times, modern times and contemporary time intervals (although the academic circles are keen on "postmodernism", the author believes that postmodernism is not a concept of time, but a problem of value orientation). Humanities and Social Sciences not only involve in the "past" and "present", but also talk about the "future". For example, history, anthropology, sociology and other disciplines all predict or predict the future of history, culture and society. The emerging discipline "futurology" takes predicting the "future" of time coordinates as its own responsibility.

In terms of psychological time, "now" is often associated with the observation and perception activities and generated images of the present, the present, the present and the present; "Past" is often associated with the intentional objects of psychological states or psychological activities such as recall, recall, recall, nostalgia or remembrance; "Future" is closely related to the intentional objects of psychological activities such as prediction, expectation, expectation, expectation, expectation, and even prediction and prophet.

General linguistics research has always taken time and space as an important starting point for language research. However, since Saussure's diachronic and synchronic linguistics to Geographical Linguistics, linguistics has deviated from the understanding of time and space of language. Therefore, some scholars have introduced the concept of time and space to study linguistics as a whole. The concept of time and space takes time and space as the necessary components of the overall existence of the language system. In the horizon of the concept of time and space, time and space must be understood as the existence of concepts. The concepts between them can only be obtained and embodied from the holistic ecological existence of the language system. To understand language from this point of view, we can trace the relationship between language and language rheology from the continuous blending process of time and space, and then reveal the unique rheology of language under the control of language space-time structure, and analyze the process state of language rheology with the space-time characteristics of language rheology, It emphasizes that we should better explore and understand the evolution and law of the overall state of language from the individual state and realistic state of language evolution. The so-called "rheology" refers to the deformation and fluidity of objects under the action of external forces, while the rheology of language refers to the development of three different process states of language existence: constant state, which is the equilibrium state and stable state in the process of language rheology in a relatively fixed time; Divergent change state, which is the absolute movement change state and imbalance state in the process of human language rheology; The state of periodic change, that is, the track of language evolution with rules to follow.

3.3 Characteristics of English Teaching Ecological Model

Under the traditional way of thinking, English teaching research has gone to several extremes: either from the perspective of human subject, biased towards extreme subjectivity, and overemphasized human autonomy, consciousness and initiative; Or from the perspective of language object, limited by pure objectivity, treat people's subjectivity and passivity negatively; Or start from the external factors of the environment, focus on the determination of external factors, and ignore the generativity of language and the rheology of learners. On the basis of criticizing and inheriting the social and cultural theory developed from the traditional teaching theory, the gradually formed ecological language teaching model examines the interaction and influence of language learning students, language and language learning environment on language acquisition from multiple perspectives; It creatively introduces the emergence theory to make a new interpretation of the view of language and generation, integrates the view of language learners and learning environment by means of symbolism, and understands the view of language learning process as the rheology of multi-dimensional space-time scale, so as to make an all-round and ecological interpretation of language teaching and research. Therefore, in terms of layout, this model comprehensively and comprehensively considers various factors and their mutual relations of language, students, teachers and environment of language teaching. Based on the specific national conditions of language teaching in China, it dialectically examines the relationship between language teaching and language teaching policies in China. It has the characteristics of inclusiveness and focusing on students' own development.

4   College English Ecological Teaching Model Based on EM Algorithm

4.1   College English Ecological Teaching Model

The theoretical basis of College English ecological teaching model is educational ecology. Educational ecology studies the law and mechanism of the interaction between education and its surrounding ecological environment. Its core content is the ecological balance of education. The basic principles of educational ecology include the law of limiting factor, the law of tolerance and the principle of optimum, flowerpot effect, niche principle, ecological chain law, educational rhythm, social clustering, group dynamic relationship, overall benefit, edge effect and evolution. Applying the basic principles of educational ecology to construct the ecological teaching model of College English is conducive to discovering and solving the macro and micro mistakes in foreign language teaching, and actively taking measures to regulate the external and internal ecological balance of foreign language teaching; It is conducive to the rational planning and layout of the natural and humanistic ecological environment of the school, and promote the harmonious construction and coordinated development of the inner environment of the educated; It is beneficial to integrate ecological awareness into the whole process of foreign language teaching and promote the transformation of the relationship between the classroom and society and within the classroom.

College English ecological teaching mode is a stable teaching activity structure and activity procedure established under the guidance of the basic theory of educational ecology, as shown in Fig. 2. The model regards students as the ecological subject, and teachers, curriculum teaching objectives, curriculum system, teaching model, teaching resources and monitoring and evaluation system are environmental factors.

Due to the vast territory of China, students from different regions have great differences in language ability, and there are obvious differences in learning interest, learning motivation, learning strategies, learning style, self-efficacy and autonomous learning ability among students. Therefore, after freshmen enter the school, they are divided into L1 and L1 according to the grade examination results and college entrance examination results, combined with students' volunteers L2 and L3 are three different teaching levels, in which L1 represents the general ability level, L2 represents the higher ability level and L3 represents the higher ability level. The teaching objectives are set according to the characteristics of each level; The teaching goal of L1 is the cultivation of language ability, the teaching goal of L2 is the cultivation of cultural ability, and the teaching goal of L3 is the cultivation of professional English ability.

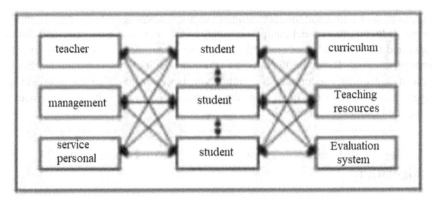

Fig. 2. College English ecological teaching model

The teaching content is set according to the teaching objectives at all levels. The teaching content of L1 is basic language courses such as listening, speaking, reading, writing and translation. The teaching content of L2 is general courses, including humanities and Social Sciences and natural sciences, such as British and American literature, European and American culture, overview of natural sciences, etc. The teaching content of L3 is professional English. Professional English is divided into two stages: primary and advanced. The primary stage is mainly academic English, which mainly helps students get familiar with professional vocabulary, syntactic structure and discourse characteristics, and prepare language and content for the learning of professional English courses. The advanced stage is a professional course in English, that is, professional English in general concept. The courses at this stage are set according to the discipline characteristics of different majors. English is no longer a learning goal, but a tool for professional learning.

According to the principle of educational ecology, only by constantly exchanging material, energy and information with the surrounding environment can the ecological subject maintain its own survival and development. The ecological teaching mode of College English is essentially an interactive teaching mode. Students interact in the input and lose in the interaction; Interaction in output, output in interaction, and interaction runs through the whole learning process.

To sum up, the ecological teaching model of College English has the following characteristics:

(1) Every factor in the teaching ecological environment is interrelated. This model takes students as the ecological subject and constitutes a complex educational ecological chain. These crisscross educational ecological chains represent the complex relationships between teachers and students, students, man-machine, students and resources, students and teaching objectives, and closely connect all factors in the foreign language teaching ecosystem.
(2) The relationship between factors in the teaching ecological environment is dynamic. The ecological teaching mode of College English implements the flexible management system of graded teaching. Students' language ability, cultural ability and

professional English ability are comprehensively evaluated every semester, and then the teaching level of students is adjusted according to the evaluation results. If the teaching level of students changes, the relationship between students and other ecological factors will also change, so as to close the relationship between students and environmental factors.

(3) The relationship between various factors in the teaching ecological environment is balanced. If an L1 student enters L2 through his own efforts, his relationship with various environmental factors and teaching objectives will be adjusted to L2. On the contrary, if a L3 student drops to L2, the relationship between the student and various environmental factors and teaching objectives will be adjusted to L2, so as to maintain the balanced relationship between various elements of the system.

4.2 The Function of College English Ecological Teaching Model

Professor Chen Jianlin pointed out that the ecological teaching of College English should follow two basic principles: first, stabilize the teaching structure and be compatible with the teaching elements; Second, restrict the operation of teaching and promote individual development. These two principles highly summarize the function of College English ecological teaching model.

(1) Stable teaching structure and compatible with teaching elements.

First of all, the teaching structure is stable, as described above. Only when the structure is stable can it have guidance and operability. The ecological teaching mode implements the flexible management system of hierarchical teaching. The teaching elements such as curriculum, resources, teachers and evaluation fully consider the characteristics and needs of all levels, so as to form a stable foreign language teaching ecological structure and compatible with various teaching elements of the foreign language teaching ecosystem.

(2) Restrict the operation of teaching and promote individual development.

The teaching mode is also a teaching activity program. The effective implementation of this program largely depends on the mutual adaptation of students' physiological rhythm and educational rhythm (physiological rhythm describes the imaginary cycle of human body, emotion and intelligence, and educational rhythm describes the operation mechanism of Education). When the two rhythms adapt to each other, it is conducive to the smooth development of teaching activities; If the two conflict with each other, it will lead to the imbalance of foreign language teaching ecosystem and affect the normal operation of the whole foreign language teaching ecosystem and the development of individual students. The ecological teaching mode respects the students' physiological rhythm, reasonably regulates the educational rhythm, and makes them highly harmonious and unified, so as to promote the development of students.

5 Conclusion

The construction of College English ecological teaching model is a subject that keeps pace with the times, and there is an exploration process from theory to practice. At present, the implementation of College English ecological teaching model still faces many problems, such as teachers' teaching ideas, teachers, teaching resources and so on. However, we are in an era of ecological civilization. Ecological teaching is an important part of ecological civilization. I believe that twists and turns are only temporary, and moving forward in twists and turns is the correct development direction of ecological teaching.

Acknowledgements. 1. 2020 project of the 13th Five-Year Plan For Educational Science in Shaanxi Province: Internet Plus Research on the Ecological Teaching Mode of College English (Grant NO. SGH20Q261);

2. Major Theoretical and Practical Issues Research Project of Shaanxi Social Science Sector in 2021: "A Study on the Publicity Translation of Shaanxi's Red Tourism Culture along Yellow River from the Perspective of Eco-translatology" (Grant NO. 2021ND0157);

3. Xi'an Fanyi University Project: Chinese Culture (Bilingual) (ZK2040).

4. Xi'an Fanyi University Project: Chinese Culture Translation (ZK2150).

References

1. Mei, Q.: The research on the application of situational teaching in college English teaching (2021)
2. Guo, X.: Research on the application of data mining in the analysis of college English teaching quality. J. Phys: Conf. Ser. **1744**(4), 042024 (2021)
3. Min, J.: Research on the application of computer intelligent proofreading system in college English teaching. J. Phys: Conf. Ser. **1915**(3), 032078 (2021)
4. Cui, X., Wang, X.: Research on the online college English teaching mode from the perspective of autonomous learning. **5**(11), 4 (2021)
5. Li, J.: Research on the improvement of college English learning by artificial intelligence (2021)
6. Zhai, C.: Practical research on college English vocabulary teaching with mobile technology. Int. J. Electr. Eng. Educ. (2021). 002072092098505
7. Wang, Q.: Research on teaching quality evaluation of college English based on the CODAS method under interval-valued intuitionistic fuzzy information. J. Intell. Fuzzy Syst. 1–10 (2021)
8. Liu, Y., Bai, H.: Teaching research on college English translation in the era of big data. Int. J. Electr. Eng. Educ. (2021). 002072092098431
9. Niu, Y.: Application of task-based language teaching to business English negotiation teaching in higher vocational college. In: 2020 3rd International Seminar on Education Research and Social Science (ISERSS 2020) (2021)
10. Ding, L.: Research on the application of micro class in college business oral English teaching. In: CIPAE 2021: 2021 2nd International Conference on Computers, Information Processing and Advanced Education (2021)

Research on the Application of Decision Tree Algorithm in Practical Teaching of Public Physical Education in Colleges and Universities

Wanbin Su[✉]

Guangdong University of Business and Technology, Guangzhou 526060, Guangdong, China
s15677389680@163.com

Abstract. This paper discusses the application of "decision tree" reasoning in the practical teaching of Public Physical Education in Colleges and universities. Decision tree algorithm is widely used in education, which has strong functionality and expression ability. However, it is less applied in public physical education curriculum, and the research results are insufficient. The research results are incomplete and one-sided, which is not conducive to the promotion of this method in physical education teaching. This is not conducive to the correct training of college physical education teachers. This paper uses decision tree and related rules to build a practical teaching system of Public Physical Education in Colleges and universities, and examines the relationship between teachers' personal factors, teaching practice factors and teaching effects, which provides a decision-making basis for teaching evaluation methods. The relevant factors are comprehensively analyzed. Improve the quality of physical education in Colleges and universities, enrich the teaching materials of physical education teachers in Colleges and universities, and more effectively promote the healthy development of physical education.

Keywords: Decision tree algorithm · Practical teaching of public physical education · Teaching analysis

1 Introduction

Extracurricular physical exercise with the goal of "reaching the standard first and strengthening the body" has been rapidly launched in Colleges and universities across the country. The main purpose of this activity is to create a good environment for Chinese school students to actively exercise on the basis of extracurricular physical exercise, more publicize the concept of health, let students know to put health first, improve students' health cognition and form relatively correct sports behavior, Correctly guide young students to improve their lifestyle and make physical education a relaxation process for students after learning [1]. In this way, students can go out of the classroom after learning, exercise in the sun, stimulate students' enthusiasm for physical exercise and enhance students' physical quality and health. This paper studies the current situation

© ICST Institute for Computer Sciences, Social Informatics and Telecommunications Engineering 2023
Published by Springer Nature Switzerland AG 2023. All Rights Reserved
M. A. Jan and F. Khan (Eds.): BigIoT-EDU 2022, LNICST 467, pp. 235–245, 2023.
https://doi.org/10.1007/978-3-031-23944-1_26

of extracurricular physical exercise, discusses and analyzes the problems and Counter-measures of extracurricular physical exercise in the school, and puts forward effective suggestions and strategies.

Public physical education curriculum and public physical education teaching are the-oretical disciplines differentiated from school public physical education. Public physical education curriculum and public physical education teaching are the lower concepts of curriculum and teaching. Both are unified in the big system of pedagogy. Curriculum and teaching are independent of each other, and they belong to different disciplines. At the same time, there is an internal connection between the two. They complement each other and are indispensable. Curriculum is the premise of teaching. Curriculum theory must consider the problems related to teaching methods and teaching contents. Without the guidance of curriculum theory, teaching activities will fall into difficulties; Teaching is the manifestation of curriculum. It transforms curriculum theory into practice through teaching activities, and constantly enriches and develops curriculum theory in practice, so as to lead a new round of curriculum reform. Therefore, it is of great significance not only to clarify the concept of physical education and public education, but also to clarify the relationship between physical education and public practice.

Public sports is a subsystem of the education system. The development of pedagogy has laid the foundation for the development of social sports. Unfortunately, the public sports discipline has not been fully developed. The research of national sports discipline and national sports discipline has only begun in recent years, and started relatively late. There are few monographs and books on public physical education and public physical education. First of all, we want to understand the importance of national sports plans and public physical education. To understand the importance of public sports and public sports, we must understand the basic concepts of curriculum and education.

To confirm what public sports activities are, we must first know what learning is. The Chinese educator believes that curriculum implementation is based on certain social education goals and students' age characteristics to form ideological norms, procedures and specific means. This view is an important theoretical basis for studying the concept of public physical education.

At present, the research on the concept of public physical education has not been unified. For example, the definition of this public physical education refers to the content, structure, process and process of public physical education provided by the public phys-ical education curriculum in order to achieve the goal of public physical education and the independent development of students. These studies provide an important reference for further study of the concept of public physical education. However, these concepts have no basis for defining the concept of national sports plan. For the definition of pub-lic sports, the author tends to think that public sports curriculum is a public and school curriculum aimed at students. To a certain extent, it determines the content structure, schedule, curriculum, learning process or teaching form of public sports. Or students can choose. And the overall planning or design of community sports culture and function, practical function and physical health that students should adhere to in different learning stages. This concept further discusses the content, organizational form and dignity of the teaching concept of public physical education, which essentially determines the scope of public physical education.

Decision tree algorithm is widely used in electrical, chemistry, tourism management and other disciplines, with high efficiency of operation and demonstration, but it is not widely used in ordinary schools. In universities, the purpose of physical education and physical education elective courses is to improve students' learning motivation and interest, so that they can choose courses independently. However, in the actual training, it should be noted that students have great resistance to the learning process of the selected sports, and their mastery and participation in the project are low. Community sports elective courses provide students with a platform for autonomous learning, but practical teaching shows that in the projects selected by students, technical action teaching only stays on the surface and is not used in the teaching process. This is in contradiction with the purpose of offering elective courses in community sports. Therefore, teachers of Public Physical Education Elective Courses in Colleges and universities should innovate the decision-making algorithm according to their consciousness, interest and their own situation, and finally improve students' interest and applicability to public physical education elective courses. Improve physical fitness, improve communication, and achieve the ultimate goal of lifelong sports.

2 Related Work

2.1 Decision Tree Algorithm

If the segmented subset has been correctly classified, the leaf node is constructed [2]. If some subsets cannot be classified correctly, continue to select the best features from the remaining features, continue to segment the data set and build the corresponding nodes. The generated tree needs to be pruned from bottom to top to make the model simple and have better generalization ability. Specifically, the over subdivided leaf node is removed and its parent node or higher node is used as the leaf node, as shown in Fig. 1 below.

No matter how the decision tree model is optimized, the essence of branching is still to pursue the optimization of some impurity related index.

For the impurity mentioned above, sklearn provides the criterion parameter in the official document to determine the calculation method of impurity. Sklearn provides two options:

1) "Entropy", using entropy;
2) "Gini", using Gini lmpurity. However, when we use the following code to build a decision tree, we will find that if we reproduce this line of code with the same data set, the resulting tree will be different;

splitter
In the description of random_ Before using the state parameter, we will first explain the splitter parameter. Splitter is used to control random options in the decision tree [3]. It has two values, Enter "best", although the decision tree is random when branching, it will give priority to the more important characteristics (Gini coefficient set according to impure or the value of information line) for branching, and enter "random".
random_ state

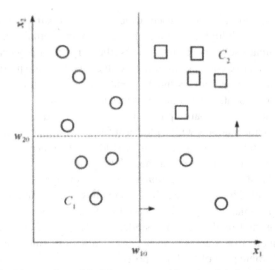

Fig. 1. The pruning of decision tree considers the global optimization

As we mentioned earlier, the decision tree model builds an optimized tree by optimizing nodes, but the optimal node may not necessarily get the optimal tree. Therefore, sklearn chooses to build different trees, and then selects the best one. In each branch, it does not use all features, randomly selects some features, and selects the node with the best impurity related index as the node for branching, In this way, the tree generated each time will be different. When sklearn randomly selects features, especially when the impurity related indicators of multiple features are the same when the splitter is branching, it will randomly select one as the branching point, so random is officially designed_ The state parameter determines the randomness of feature selection, similar to

random. Seed(), ensure the same random_ The decision tree model obtained by state parameter is the same, and the experimental results can be reproduced to facilitate the optimization of model parameters.

random_ State is a parameter used to set the random pattern in the branch, and the randomness will hardly appear in the low dimension data (such as iris data set). We set random for high-dimensional data_ State and splitter parameters can stabilize the model and ensure that there is a decision tree under the same data set, and the results can be repeated for many times, which is convenient for model parameter optimization.

2.2   Decision Tree Generation

The cost of training and testing is small, but it may lead to under fitting.

Post pruning: after training a complete tree, consider the non leaf node from bottom to top. The training cost is large, the risk of under fitting is small, and the generalization ability is strong.

ID3 algorithm (information gain criterion): select the optimal partition feature according to the maximum information gain [4].

ID3 often selects features with more classification levels as division features; Continuous variables cannot be processed and need to be discretized; Sensitive to missing values; Without pruning setting, it is easy to over fit.

C4. 5 algorithm (information gain rate criterion): first find out the features with higher information gain than the average level from the candidate partition features, and then select the one with the highest information gain rate as the optimal partition feature. As shown in Fig. 2.

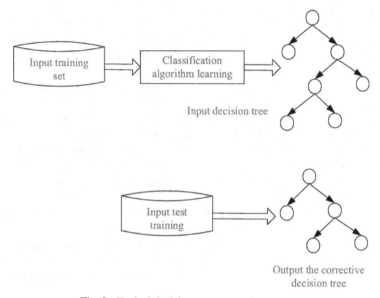

Fig. 2. Typical decision tree generation process

C4. 5 algorithm, the gain rate criterion has a preference for features with less classification level, which corrects the deficiency of ID3 algorithm. The continuous variable processing method is added to process the continuous variable into n-1 dichotomy schemes to find the cut-off point with the largest gain rate.

Cart algorithm (used by sklearn)

Classification tree: Gini criterion

Regression tree: the average value is used to predict the samples reaching the leaf node, and the least square error is used to select the optimal cutting point and optimal partition variable:

$$\min_{j,8} \left[\min_{c_1} \sum_{x_1 \in R_1(j,s)} (y_1 - c_1)^2 \right] \tag{1}$$

Validation set pruning: calculate the error rate of each leaf node, and then calculate the error rate of the parent node and the weighted error rate of the hanging leaf node. If the weighted error rate of the leaf node is greater than that of the parent node, pruning is performed.

2.3 Data Processing

Neither sports data analysis nor model development can be separated from the preparation of sports data. Some people say that 70% or even 80% of the whole work of sports data science is spent on sports data preparation.

Sports data preparation is divided into four links - Sports data integration, sports data cleaning, sports data conversion and exploratory sports data analysis. This is a closed-loop iterative process. For example, after we finish exploratory sports data analysis, we may have to carry out sports data conversion or sports data cleaning, and then start exploratory sports data analysis [5].

The process of sports data preparation starts from sports data collection, which is usually called ETL process (extract transform load). We may need to operate multiple one-to-one, one to many or many to many relational tables to integrate sports data from different sources, and integrate sports data together through key frames.

Sports data cleaning is the preprocessing of sports data after integrating sports data [6]. In this step, we clean up the dirty sports data into relatively regular sports data. If the sports data is not cleaned, it is likely to be garbage in & garbage out.

Different sports data may have different cleaning methods, but no matter what kind of sports data, there are always some common steps and methods in the whole process of sports data cleaning, such as missing value analysis and processing.

Is there a tool that can complete these general processes of sports data cleaning, reduce the time of sports data cleaning and simplify the cumbersome cleaning process? The answer, of course, is the sports data cleaning module in the R language creditmodel package.

If you master this artifact of sports data cleaning, you can despise those who spend 70% of their time in the preprocessing stage of sports data.

3 Research on the Application of Decision Tree Algorithm in the Practical Teaching of Public Physical Education in Colleges and Universities

Data mining is a process of extracting hidden, unknown but potentially useful information and knowledge from a large number of incomplete, noisy, fuzzy and random data. In order to extract data, it must be more accurately called "extracting knowledge from data". Similar terms include knowledge search, data analysis, data integration, and decision support. The field of artificial intelligence is called knowledge discovery, and the field of database is called data extraction. The information contained in the student questionnaire includes: Students' performance in the national sports plan, class hours in the national sports plan, their preferences for sports, the number of sports competitions, the technical level of school physical education teachers, the content of physical education classes, the content of physical education classes, the number of students in physical education classes, the number of students in physical education classes, the number of physical education students, the number of physical education students, the number of physical education students, the number of physical education students and the number of physical education students. The influence of teaching methods and evaluation of Physical Education Pedagogy on physical education pedagogy [7].

Table 1. Questionnaire on students' cognition of the value of physical exercise

Option	Person time	Sort
Bodybuilding	64	1
Comprehensively promote the development of the body	43	2
Pastime	33	3
Education	18	4
Pursue stimulation	15	5

In the survey on the exercise value of students to physical education (Table 1), it can be seen that the first place is fitness (64 people). Secondly, a total of 30 people believe that improving physical fitness is the most important. Finally, a total of 20 people believe that the significance of sports activities lies in entertainment and relaxation. The data shows that most of these students have a correct understanding of the value of physical exercise, and the pursuit of stimulation is still a minority in the survey data. It is noteworthy that there are 33 people who regard physical exercise as entertainment, which shows that physical education teachers need to correctly guide students to carry out sports, so that the student group can have such a cognition: physical exercise can not only relax and entertainment, but also cultivate students' interest in exercise, but the most important thing is to enhance students' physical quality.

In the survey on the exercise value of students to physical education (Table 1), it can be seen that fitness (64 people) ranks first. Secondly, a total of 30 people believe that improving physical quality is the most important. Finally, a total of 20 people believe that the significance of sports activities lies in entertainment and relaxation. The data shows that most of these students have a correct understanding of the value of physical exercise, and the pursuit of stimulation is still a minority in the survey data [8]. It is noteworthy that there are 33 people who regard physical exercise as entertainment, which shows that physical education teachers need to correctly guide students to carry out sports, so that the student group can have such a cognition: physical exercise can not only relax and entertainment, but also cultivate students' interest in exercise, but the most important thing is to enhance students' physical quality.

The former is used to establish the decision tree model of factors affecting college physical education practice teaching, and the latter is used to evaluate the model. The fitting process of the model is through SPSS Clementine 12 The C5 decision tree node in 0 data mining software is realized. The attribute of branch node is that the gain rate of selection information is the largest and not lower than that of all attribute information. The decision tree can be generated, as shown in Fig. 3 below.

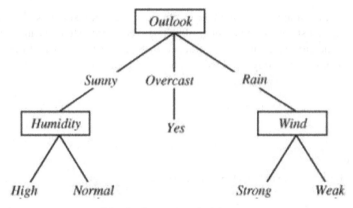

Fig. 3. Sports data decision tree

The table above has 14 pieces of data. If we use the "day" attribute to divide it, there will be 14 branches, and each branch node has only one piece of data, and the information line is 0. Then the information gain obtained by using this attribute is very large. But the consequence is that the generalization ability of the decision tree is very poor, which belongs to serious overfitting. In this way, a problem of ID3 decision tree - the problem of information gain biased selection of features with more values is found [9].

Decision tree algorithm is a teaching method with wide spread and strong operability, which is widely used in practical teaching. Decision tree algorithm can comprehensively improve students' ability, expand students' thinking ability and develop students' innovation ability at the same time. The "decision tree" algorithm of Public Physical Education Elective Courses in Colleges and universities reflects a comprehensive understanding of the basic technology and theory of students' implementation of the selected sports, and improves students' interest and initiative in participating. With the introduction of decision tree "aliism", the relationship between teachers and students is more harmonious, and students have a more comprehensive understanding of the concept and technology of the selected elements, which lays a good foundation for future education and competition.

The quality of physical education teaching is the external expression of the effect of sports activities. Good sports evaluation provides opportunities for guiding, encouraging, promoting and standardizing sports quality. It is an important part of physical education school management and the main means to evaluate the effect of physical education teaching. The school evaluates and inspects sports every semester and collects a large amount of data. Based on the existing qualifications, teachers do not sort out the existing positions, and comprehensively evaluate the accessibility of physical education. The decision tree algorithm is applied to the evaluation system of physical education teaching quality [10]. According to the purpose and characteristics of mining, a mining system is designed. By analyzing the relationship between physical education teaching effect and teachers' age, occupation, education level and workload, it is found that classroom physical education teaching effect is related to teachers' comprehensive quality. Therefore, we should support the decision-making of sports and sports departments, promote the improvement of sports and physical education, and improve the quality of physical education.

4 Simulation Analysis

The original data and data preprocessing method of decision tree algorithm in college public physical education practice teaching is the same as that of decision tree mining algorithm [11]. The original data is processed by data cleaning, data integration, data conversion and other methods, and the square error minimization criterion is used to select features and divide them.

Strengthen the publicity and supervision of extracurricular physical exercise. Schools should actively publicize the importance of extracurricular physical exercise in combination with the requirements of China's education departments and sports institutions, and the education department also needs to strictly supervise the implementation of the school. Only in this way can we ensure that students have enough physical exercise time, and sufficient physical exercise time can bring good help to students in the period of growth and development. Schools can also contact parents to let them understand the importance of sports, and require parents to carry out sports activities with students, cultivate students' interest in sports, and let students experience fun from physical education.

Strengthen the teaching ability and personal quality of physical education teachers. School administrators must recognize the great responsibility of physical education teachers, give sufficient care to physical education teachers, regularly carry out ability training for physical education teachers, emphasize the important role of physical education teachers in extracurricular physical exercise, and have reasonable workload calculation methods and fair professional title evaluation [12].

Only in this way can we ensure the healthy development of school physical education. Specifically, the problem of lack of school equipment and venues can be solved from three angles: first, students can prepare their own sports equipment according to their hobbies of sports; Secondly, the school communicates with other departments to make full use of the sports equipment and venues of these units to alleviate the problem of insufficient school venues and equipment; Finally, schools can apply for education funds, raise funds from all sectors of society, build more sports venues and buy a sufficient number of sports equipment.

The selection and application of teaching methods must be based on the teaching content, suitable for the characteristics of students, treated differently and taught according to their aptitude. Its purpose is to serve the teaching purpose and improve the teaching effect. As several important links of decision tree algorithm, whether it is used alone or comprehensively, or combined with other teaching methods and means, depends on the teaching content, students' characteristics Teaching environment and teachers' own knowledge reserve and other factors.

In the process of popularizing and applying the decision tree algorithm of Public Physical Education Elective Courses in Colleges and universities, we should not only pay attention to the application process of teaching methods and teaching means, but also pay attention to the observation and feedback mechanism in the implementation process of the process, but also establish the evaluation mechanism of teaching effect, which can be tested and evaluated after the end of one teaching, or a one-time evaluation mechanism after the end of the process, In order to ensure the reliability of teaching effect evaluation, we must use a variety of methods to obtain students' feedback on teaching effect [13].

In the implementation of decision tree algorithm in public physical education elective courses in Colleges and universities, we should pay attention to cultivating students' ability to reflect on Problems and academic literacy in different ways in the three stages before, during and after teaching, improve students' comprehensive quality and practical experience, cultivate students' self-study ability and tap students' innovative conscious-ness, Better promote the benign development of physical education teaching in public physical education optional courses.As shown in Fig. 4.

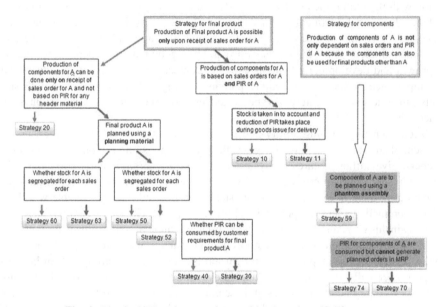

Fig. 4. Physical education practice teaching based on decision tree

5   Conclusion

This paper discusses the application of "decision tree" reasoning in the practical teaching of Public Physical Education in Colleges and universities. Data extraction technology is increasingly used in the field of learning management. In particular, the application of sports discipline rules provides a reliable decision-making basis for university leaders. With the improvement of information management in Colleges and universities, the online evaluation system of physical education teaching quality has collected more and more evaluation information. The evaluation database forms an extensive database together with other university databases and information. Extract knowledge from data, establish prediction model and support decision-making. Data mining technology is different from traditional statistical analysis methods. Its essence is to obtain unknown effective and useful information, rules and knowledge through data mining technology. This paper introduces the methods of extracting college sports data, which provides a new impetus for the development of college sports.

Acknowledgements. 2021 young innovative talents project in Colleges and universities in Guangdong Province: An Empirical Study on the "flipped classroom" teaching mode of basketball specialty course in Colleges and Universities under the background of informatization (wqncx125).

References

1. Zach, S., Rosenblum, H.: The affective domain—a program to foster social-emotional orientation in novice physical education teachers. Int. J. Environ. Res. Public Health **18**(14), 7434 (2021)
2. Danis, A., Zulkifli, A.F.: Exploration of CoachEye application features to improve feedback during physical education. Asian J. Univ. Educ. **17**(2), 132 (2021)
3. Ouellet, C., Verret, C., Roure, C., et al.: Do students with special educational needs have positive experiences in physical education? (2021)
4. Permana, B., Patwari, I.: Komparasi Metode Klasifikasi data mining decision tree dan Nave Bayes untuk prediksi penyakit diabetes. Infotek Jurnal Informatika Dan Teknologi **4**(1), 63–69 (2021)
5. Han, Y., Liu, C., Yan, L., et al.: Design of decision tree structure with improved BPNN nodes for high-accuracy locomotion mode recognition using a single IMU. Sensors **21**(2), 526 (2021)
6. Al, C.: Application of decision tree in classifying secondary school students' tendencies to choose TVET in Malaysia. Turk. J. Comput. Math. Educ. (TURCOMAT) **12**(3), 3002–3012 (2021)
7. Saroj, R.K., Anand, M., Kumari, N.: Environmental factors prediction in preterm birth using comparison between logistic regression and decision tree methods: an exploratory analysis. SSRN Electron. J. **4**(1–3), 100216 (2021)
8. Gu, Z., He, C.: Application of fuzzy decision tree algorithm based on mobile computing in sports fitness member management. Wirel. Commun. Mob. Comput. **2021**(6), 1–10 (2021)
9. Cao, Z., Chen, T., Cao, Y.: Effect of occupational health and safety training for Chinese construction workers based on the CHAID decision tree. Front. Public Health **9**, 623441 (2021)
10. Ham, J.H., Ham, J.S.: A study on the change of teacher recognition of preliminary physical education teachers through teaching practice. J. Korean Soc. Study Phys. Educ. **25**(4), 179–193 (2021)
11. Ren, X.: The practice and thinking of computer virtual reality technology in the teaching mode of physical education in colleges and universities. J. Phys. Conf. Ser. **1744**(4), 042020 (2021)
12. Porsanger, L., Magnussen, L.I.: Risk and safety management in physical education: a study of teachers' practice perspectives. Front. Sports Active Living **3**, 663676 (2021)
13. Vbl, A., Acag, A., Cb, A., et al.: Associations among psychological satisfaction in physical education, sports practice, and health indicators with physical activity: Direct and indirect ways in a structural equation model proposal. Int. J. Pediatr. Adolesc. Med. **8**(4), 246–252 (2021)

Research on the Construction of Business English Education Translation Platform Based on "Internet+"

Zhang Zhang[✉]

Minnan University of Science and Technology, Shishi, Quanzhou 362242, Fujian, China
2065294449@qq.com

Abstract. With the implementation of China's reform and opening up and China's accession to the World Trade Organization (WTO), China's business English translation plays a more and more important role in international trade activities. Business English translation is not something that can be done only by understanding English. Many scholars at home and abroad have devoted themselves to the study of business English translation theory. In this context, it has brought unprecedented opportunities to the construction of business English translation platform. Based on the analysis of the problems existing in the process of business English translation, the research on the construction of business English translation platform based on "Internet" provides reference for translation or related learners, and also wants to attract more scholars to pay attention to business English and its translation.

Keywords: Business English · Internet · English translation

1 Introduction

With the popularization of computer Internet, cloud storage technology and search engine, online auxiliary translation platform based on Internet platform came into being. The translation mode of traditional business English translation software is subject to multiple restrictions of time and space. Translators should not only install CAT software on their own computers, but also complicated software parameter configuration, Translators and translators can't communicate online and can't unify terms during translation, resulting in various problems in the translation process. So how to provide previously turned corpus for continuous translation without installing additional software and changing a computer is a new problem that needs to be solved in the translation industry at present. Based on the above problems and the development of Internet technology, an Internet-based business English translation platform came into being. With the expansion of the demand of the translation industry, the efficiency is low and the cost is high, and different translators also have deviations in the understanding of the same term. Therefore, business English translation tools need to be completely changed,

M. A. Jan and F. Khan (Eds.): BigIoT-EDU 2022, LNICST 467, pp. 246–251, 2023.
https://doi.org/10.1007/978-3-031-23944-1_27

from the previous manual word translation to today's computer-aided translation software client based on C/S architecture to online assisted translation using browser based on B/S architecture. The client that needs to install the translation software needs only one browser. Through the Internet browser, the translator only needs the account and password of one platform to complete all the work of the previous client software on the platform, and the translated data is stored in the server of B/S architecture [1]. Next time, change a place or a computer, It can also continue the work that has not been translated before, breaking the restrictions of time and space. Translators can also save themselves from the pain of purchasing translation software and configuring software parameters. Cat plus the Internet allows translators to carry out business English translation whenever and wherever they have equipment that can connect to the network, which can not be realized by installing a local cat. The combination of the server of B/S architecture with the search engine, big data and high storage technology in the computer makes the text processing and retrieval speed improve rapidly. Compared with the installation of cat client software, translators no longer worry about their computer crash and operating system crash in the translation process.

2 Overview of Business English

2.1 Business English Translation and Its Characteristics

With the gradual growth of international trade and the increasingly frequent international exchanges and communication, business English came into being to provide guarantee for international exchanges and promote the smooth progress of international trade. Compared with ordinary English, business English has great differences in nature and expression forms. Compared with ordinary English, it is more formal and standardized in performance. Therefore, business English personnel should ensure the accuracy of expression in the process of translation. In addition to understanding and mastering the basic characteristics and use methods of business English, they should also deeply understand the geographical environment, customs and religious beliefs of their native country, so as to ensure the accuracy of English translation. In addition, it also has the following characteristics.

(1) Sentence structure formatting. In Business English, when translating contracts, agreements and other documents, because the sentence structure is complex and has the characteristics of formatting, the writing also needs to follow a certain format, so as to ensure the formality and standardization of language expression. For example, the sentence structure of "in accordance with the relevant provisions of this contract", which often appears in business contracts, can be formatted as "as prov ided here". In Business English, the use of specific sentence format will significantly improve the accuracy and standardization of sentences. In addition, when answering the other party's questions, we usually use "we look forward…" The formatted language can not only give people a clear and concise feeling, but also make the other party understand their meaning as clearly as possible.

(2) Language application specialization. Due to the wide range of international trade, the field of communication using business English is also broad, including product

name, goods trade, laws and regulations and so on [2]. These aspects will require that the expression of business English can meet the professional and standardized requirements in a certain field, so as to ensure that both parties can accurately and clearly understand the meaning and content expressed by the other party. For example, "premium is the insurance amount, inquiry is the inquiry" and so on, which can express the characteristics of business English with more nouns and more professional language application.

(3) Vocabulary makes concise. In business activities, the language of expression should be smooth and clear as far as possible. Therefore, the language application of business English should be concise, that is, it can correctly express its own meaning. Therefore, in the process of business communication, some proper nouns or abbreviations are often used. For example, KFC is abbreviated as KFC, Wal Mart is abbreviated as wwmt, FOB is abbreviated as FOB, etc. In addition, when conducting business communication, we should ensure the simplification and application of vocabulary on the basis of objectivity, authenticity and civilization of language expression.

2.2   Cultural Differences in Business English Translation

(1) Way of thinking. The difference in thinking mode is an important embodiment of cultural differences. People in different countries also have great differences in thinking mode due to the influence of cultural education, geographical environment, local customs and other factors. These different characteristics of people's way of thinking in the East and the west not only make the language different in the form of expression, but also bring great obstacles to the normal communication between people. Chinese culture has strong comprehensiveness in the embodiment of thinking mode, but it has strong analysis in western thinking. This difference is reflected in language: in China's comprehensive thinking, the sentence structure is mainly centered on verbs, which will form a "flowing" structure as a whole. However, in Western analytical thinking, it will take the subject or predicate as the center and contain more clauses to form a "tree branch" structure.

(2) Expression. Because Chinese and western people have different language systems and cultural backgrounds, and have fixed application forms in the way of language expression, people in different cultural backgrounds may have differences in the way of expression, even in the face of things with the same concept. There is a big gap between China and foreign countries in speaking habits. Due to the influence of the national pride of "a great country", this national psychology will promote the description in Chinese to become higher, which is very normal for domestic audiences, but in terms of speaking habits in English, it focuses more on simplicity and nature, Simply rely on real emotions for information transmission.

3   Problems in Business English Translation

3.1   Inappropriate Translation Vocabulary

When translating business English, there is vocabulary loss and inaccurate vocabulary application, which is easy to cause misinterpretation and mistranslation, making the language expression inaccurate. Some words may have polysemy, or because of the differences between Chinese and Western cultures, literal translation will misunderstand the meaning of the original text. For example, the same animal has different understanding in different countries. Cat and dog have rich meanings in English, such as "rain cats and dogs", but there is no such expression in Chinese. The difference between eastern and Western cultures is more obvious. In English, fish has a derogatory meaning, such as "a poor fish", while in Chinese, "fish" is the pronunciation of "Yu", which represents an abundant life every year, It is a symbol of auspiciousness and beauty. Therefore, in Business English translation, it is necessary to avoid unnecessary disputes according to the cultural background and social customs of different countries and nationalities.

3.2 The Translation Sentence Pattern is not Rigorous

Due to the different ways of thinking and living habits between China and the west, they are very different in language expression. Western countries pay attention to the abstraction of thinking and logical judgment, strive to complete the sentence structure, and usually describe things and events objectively and more passively. In Western English expressions, long sentences and clauses show complex meanings. Chinese sentences are mostly short sentences and tend to be repeated. They often focus on "people" and "things" and take "meaning" as the axis. In addition to stating some facts directly, they use "words" to convey meaning outside the language and use active techniques [3]. Therefore, when translating, we should take into account the differences brought by different ways of thinking, not only to achieve "shape" similarity, but also to achieve "God" similarity.

3.3 Inaccurate Language Intention

There are differences in language expressions between different nationalities and countries. Whether it is daily language or official statements, it is often necessary to change thinking, translate in a more appropriate language, and make good use of the switch between literal translation and free translation. Such as "don't teach others". Don't display your axe at Lu Ban's door is so straightforward that it's hard for westerners to understand your meaning. Instead, it should be paraphrased as "retain model before an authority", which makes it easier for others to accept and understand. Therefore, we should pay attention to the appropriateness of language in translation. Appropriateness is based on a good understanding of each other's cultural background so that there will be no jokes in translation.

4 Construction Scheme of Business English Translation Platform Based on Internet

4.1 Advantages of the Internet Age

As the core feature of the current information development, the Internet breaks the text expression paradigm of business English pages. The application of short videos can make the pages more lively and vivid. In addition, short videos are time-consuming and creative, so they are the most commonly used media form for overseas tourists. Folk story video is becoming an important cultural supply mode to trigger field business English. This topic explores how to improve the design of foreign business English translation platform, make the convenient mode of the Internet connect with the new sales channels of business English industry, deeply integrate the innovative achievements of the Internet and the entrepreneurial concept of college students into the new service mode, and use the intelligence of the Internet and business English video to comprehensively design the business English video development platform.

The rapid development of the Internet in China is conducive to the connection between online business English videos and local culture, so as to maximize the integration of resources. The Internet is the lubricant for the development of business English short videos. It can not only show the characteristic culture of the scenic spot, eliminate excessive publicity of business English scenic spot, but also broaden the employment channels of college students [4]. As long as tourists have a smartphone, they can get a variety of Internet services. The Internet provides technical support for English Business English translation platform, which makes business English translation present a variety of development modes.

4.2   Setting of Business Translation Courses

The situation and environment of language provide a great foundation for language learning and make the achievement of translation more remarkable. Therefore, from the perspective of innovation and entrepreneurship, the construction of business English translation platform should aim at cultivating innovative talents in the new era and constantly improve the level of translation talents. In order to achieve this effect, educators should pay attention to the unity of theory and practice, make students' skills develop in a practical direction on the premise of strengthening students' professional foundation, and lay a solid foundation for the realization of subsequent innovation and entrepreneurship goals.

Business translation English exists as English for special purposes, especially under the mechanism of innovation and entrepreneurship. The existence of this major has strict requirements for students' good communication ability. Therefore, English translation teachers should pay attention to the systematicness and scientificity of the course content to make the practicality of this course more prominent. In the process of teaching, teachers should actively use multimedia technology to instill ideas and awareness about innovation and entrepreneurship for students, and establish an independent network platform, as shown in Fig. 1, so as to realize the long-term development of students.

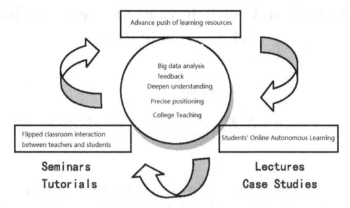

Fig. 1. Internet Business English teaching model

4.3 Business Translation Theory Teaching and Practice

Translators from the perspective of innovation and entrepreneurship emphasize the subject status of translators. As the subject of entrepreneurship, translators change the content in different languages and cultural backgrounds to realize the continuous development of translation process and entrepreneurship process. Translation teachers should be aware of their leadership, guide and supervisor, understand students' needs, make students adapt to this teaching mechanism, constantly improve students' translation foundation and entrepreneurial awareness, and lay a solid foundation for subsequent development.

5 Conclusion

At present, the development process of economic globalization has been in a critical period, and the degree of foreign exchange of the whole society is constantly improving. For business English online translation platform, whether in the field of life or work, it will play a more and more important role in the future. Therefore, we must actively explore the development direction and design technology application of business English online translation platform under the background of the Internet era, so as to continuously meet the requirements of technology upgrading and social development.

References

1. Chen, S.: Problems and countermeasures in business english translation teaching in higher vocational colleges. Sci. Technol. Inf. (21), 570, 602 (2017)
2. Hu, S.: Cultivation and teaching reform of English practical translation ability of higher vocational students. Chin. J. Educ. (05), 41–42 (2014)
3. Wang, Y.: Problems and reform in business english translation teaching. China Univ. Teach. (09), 71–73 (2017)
4. Chen, Y.: Design of English online translation platform based on Internet and Android platform. China New Commun. **21**(06), 60–61 (2019)

Research on User Behavior of College English Mobile Learning App

Kailing Sun[✉]

Yunnan Engineering Vocational College, Kunming 650300, Yunnan, China
sk18488@163.com

Abstract. With the acceleration of global integration and the deepening of the concept of lifelong education, people's demand for English mobile learning is higher and higher. Due to the inconvenience of time and space and other factors, the traditional learning methods limit people's learning. Therefore, breaking through the time and space constraints and using mobile devices such as mobile phones to learn English anytime and anywhere has attracted more and more attention, and the English mobile learning app has also emerged. At the same time, hundreds of millions of people's time and use of mobile phones are increasingly valuable. Based on the user behavior data of English mobile learning app, this paper mainly studies three aspects: user attributes, behavior and loss, and describes the behavior characteristics of English mobile learning app users, which provides a certain reference value for precision marketing.

Keywords: Mobile learning app · College English · User behavior

1 Introduction

With the rapid development of information technology, mobile learning has gradually become an indispensable means of learning. It takes the wireless network as the media carrier, mainly with the help of mobile terminal equipment, and obtains learning information, resources and services through the wireless mobile network framework. "In essence, it can be regarded as the result of the interaction between modern education and advanced Internet technology. It is an extension of digital learning technology in the context of the era of big data." Under the influence of mobile learning, learners can learn more conveniently, have personalized experience effect, and personally feel the learning content and expanded knowledge. The learning experience brought by new technologies such as mobile devices is an important symbol of educational modernization. The classroom is an important place for learning. In the context of mobile learning, the teaching classroom has also been given an intelligent coat, which has changed the traditional teaching methods and has the advantages and advantages of improving learning efficiency.

There are many apps for spoken English. Especially with the increasing demand for learning spoken English in recent years, apps for learning spoken English are emerging

M. A. Jan and F. Khan (Eds.): BigIoT-EDU 2022, LNICST 467, pp. 252–263, 2023.
https://doi.org/10.1007/978-3-031-23944-1_28

one after another. The connotation of mobile learning can be analyzed from the following aspects:

First of all, mobile learning is developed on the basis of digital learning. It is an extension of digital learning. It is different from general learning. Michael Wenger, an e-learning expert of Sun company, put forward his unique opinion on mobile learning. He believes that mobile learning is not a new thing, because in traditional learning, printing textbooks can also well support learners to learn anytime and anywhere. It can be said that textbooks have become a tool to support mobile learning long ago, Mobile learning has always been around us.

Secondly, in addition to all the characteristics of digital learning, mobile learning also has its unique characteristics, that is, learners are no longer limited to the computer desk, and can learn for different purposes and different ways freely and anytime, anywhere. The learning environment is mobile, and teachers, researchers, technicians and students are all mobile.

Finally, from the perspective of its implementation, the technical basis of mobile learning is mobile computing technology and Internet technology, that is, mobile interconnection technology; The implementation tools are miniaturized mobile computing devices, or ia devices. In the process of discussing the concept of mobile learning, sariola et al. Made such an analysis on the characteristics of the equipment realized by mobile learning: portability, that is, the equipment is small in shape, light in weight and easy to carry; No linearity, that is, the equipment does not need to be connected; Mobility means that users can also use it well in mobile.

Today's mobile learning method, which is more suitable for people's life, is to enjoy the ease of "leaving after use" without taking up mobile phone memory and pressure through wechat applet, H5 and other ways without downloading and waiting.

It has been more than a year since the wechat applet was released in early 2017. During this period, it has also experienced more than 50 version function updates, large and small, including updates of entry, sharing, development, interaction, etc. it presents an increasingly open cnvironment, and its slogan has changed from "run out and go" to "run out and come back".

Applet is a new application form independent of public name. It is essentially a tool. The strong attribute of the tool itself: improve efficiency and go after use. Therefore, the design of small programs is based on the principle of lightness and quickness, and users are encouraged to "use and go" [1].

Wechat uses its own HTML and CSS components, and provides a set of self-defined syntax for wechat. Therefore, the use experience of small and medium-sized programs in wechat is smoother and faster than that of ordinary H5.

For small and medium-sized institutions and individuals, making a shaped app requires a lot of human and financial resources, which will bring great pressure on enterprise finance. However, if the early app development is transformed into small program development, this phenomenon will be greatly changed, and enterprises can put more energy into marketing. Taobao tmall jd.com has been saturated. Now, if you enter these battlefields again, the cost is relatively high (platform usage fee, deposit, smashing traffic and platform bonus), which is not affordable to ordinary businesses. So small programs are a good entry point for them.

Short books, knowledge transfer, The vision of "Let knowledge have no distance". The short book is to meet the needs of education practitioners at each stage. For the field of online education: go deep into each link of teaching, learning, practice and examination, redefine online teaching, and link its functions. For the field of knowledge payment: build a perfect business closed loop, comprehensive content, courses and service forms, and easily realize diversified cash needs.

For the field of community and private domain traffic management: customer service under mobile ecology, exchange community, comprehensive Q & A, point-to-point, point-to-point, automated real-time customer service, and better connect people [2].

SaaS service tools that provide one-stop content realization solutions. Make the revenue system richer and the marketing more diversified, and easily embed the operation of various platforms.

As a young generation exposed to information technology, college students can skillfully apply various mobile software, be active in various mobile platforms, and use communication related social functions, voice and video, viewing official accounts, online payment and other related functions. WeChat mobile phone mobile phone official account, micro-blog mobile phone platform and other mobile phones, APP and so on are common in College English teaching. These mobile platforms can fully meet the needs of college students, promote students' learning and make students' English learning convenient and interesting. Therefore, College English teaching should further improve the application of mobile platform and guide students to actively participate in English teaching.

2   Related Work

2.1   Mobile Learning Development Technology

In recent years, with the development of network technology, more and more mobile learning platforms began to appear in the public's vision, and many enterprises gradually began to use mobile learning platforms for enterprise training. So what is the mobile learning platform? The answer is very simple. Mobile learning platform is the carrier to provide mobile learning methods.

Participated in cordova.com in mobile terminal hybrid development React Native. Weex and flutter are now mainly responsible for the development and maintenance of flutter related projects. From the current popularity of mobile terminal hybrid development technology: flutter is a well deserved upstart in 2019 and an old king of react native, while uni app and weex have sprung up in a small circle.

I started mobile development from Android, and then learned and participated in mixed development projects in the following order:

Cordova -> React Native -> Weex -> Flutter

In fact, this is also the chronological order of their open source and promotion. The oldest Cordova technology is still used by projects such as uni app, so there is no best but the most appropriate for different project scenarios.

In fact, the best resource to learn a framework is the official document, which is the most complete document. First look at the document to understand the implementation principle and use method of the framework, and then search the open source project of high star on the Internet to see how the bosses use it, so as to strengthen their understanding of the framework.

Secondly, the most common routine for individuals to learn a framework is to do development projects. As shown in the figure below, many open-source projects have been done. The most suitable open-source project for personal training is GitHub app, because GitHub's API is very standard, complete documents and rich functions, which can comprehensively take care of all aspects that need to be understood, and it is free.

With the development of mobile development, Internet companies are emerging one after another. Some companies are forced by competition and want to develop faster and more cost-effective, so they no longer meet a set of code on Android and a set of code on IOS. At the same time, other technology fields and major companies also covet this big cake and launch relevant technologies one after another. In this way, cross platform technology came into being and began to take root in the company.

Android and IOS ecosystems are too big. We can compare them to the first level ecosystem. Those who want to subvert these two systems have appeared, but both have failed. Therefore, establishing a secondary ecosystem is the most secure strategy. The Android platform is more open. Therefore, the center of the secondary ecosystem is Android, and the forms of the secondary ecosystem are diverse, For example, magic reform establishes its own ecology on the basis of Android system, or launch various cross platform technologies to establish ecology. There are too many frameworks produced by cross platform technology. Many of them have declined before we learn to understand them, and have become an excessive product of the development of cross platform technology. Whether the product of cross platform technology is unreliable or trend, I think you will have your own understanding after reading this article.

There is no standard answer to the classification of cross platform technologies. Here, they are classified into five types: web app, hybrid app, language compilation and conversion, native rendering and self drawn UI [3].

In addition to using native and web to develop apps, HTML5 + native can also be used for hybrid development, which is hybrid. There is a little story about the birth of hybrid. The app of a second-line Internet company is mainly native. HTML5 develops soy sauce. As the application becomes more and more complex, it is finally found that there is a maximum number of native methods. Some pages need to be embedded with HTML5 pages. So native and HTML5 team made the first hybrid project together, This set of code is compatible with three terminals and highly efficient, so hybrid app has become the mainstream of the company, and other companies in the industry have followed suit. The architecture of native app is shown in Fig. 1 below.

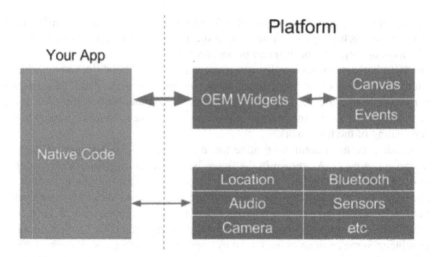

Fig. 1. Architecture diagram of native app

Through the API provided by the native SDK, app can communicate with the underlying system to create UI components or access system services. These components are rendered to the mobile screen, and the corresponding events generated by the screen will be passed back to the components. Because the system components of each platform are different, you need to develop separate apps for each platform, which is not necessary for hybrid app. The native UI components of hybrid app are used to display the interface with complex interaction and high rendering requirements, and others can be presented to HTML5 [4].

Although hybrid app has high development efficiency and can be cross platform, the hybrid experience is not as good as the original. For the team that needs to quickly try and error and quickly occupy the market, hybrid app is a good choice. After the team stabilizes in the later stage, it is better to make the original app with better experience or use other cross platform technologies with better experience.

There are many technologies related to hybrid, such as phonegap, Cordova, Ionic, vassonic and so on. Let's have a look.

2.2 Advantage Analysis of Mobile Learning Combined With Intelligent Classroom Teaching

Mobile learning has three main characteristics: connectivity without geographical restrictions, diversified situations dominated by virtual information, and convenience to break the restrictions of time and space. It can enable learners to greatly improve the occupancy and utilization of resources and realize resource sharing. Mobile learning has influenced the reform of classroom teaching and formed an intelligent classroom. The combination of the two brings great convenience to classroom learning.

Mobile device is an important medium to realize intelligent classroom. It breaks the time and space constraints of traditional classroom teaching and makes the form of distance education more convenient and easy to operate. Mobile devices have the advantages of small volume and portability. Learners can realize real one-to-one classroom teaching through mobile devices. Learners use mobile devices that are not limited by time and space to obtain the learning materials required by each learner [5]. Through the personalization and flexibility of learning material output, mobile devices can expand the scope of intelligent classroom teaching, enable learners to preview classroom teaching contents more efficiently and comprehensively, and also meet the personalized needs of learners' active learning. Learners choose relevant resources suitable for their own learning according to their own foundation and interests, and realize students' personalized learning with the help of teachers' accurate resource library.

The intelligent classroom brought by mobile learning makes learners' learning process independent and scattered, but its learning resources are modular, and the resources obtained online are also massive.

With the help of mobile learning, intelligent classroom teaching can better fit the learners' learning motivation, make the learning content meet the unique segments selected by each learner, make the learning objectives have more flexible self-regulation, more in line with the humanistic learning theory in teaching practice, and stimulate the learners' subjective initiative. Smart classrooms create many informal learning environments. Teaching activities have strong flexibility and operability, which can promote the teaching process to be more suitable for learners' learning habits, give learners more learning space and meet humanized learning needs.

The concept of mobile learning integrates people into modern education and teaching activities, creates the autonomy of intelligent classroom, and realizes a new low intelligent classroom teaching research - teaching process, learning process, learning practice and its interconnection with the Internet. Learners can formulate their own learning plans and goals according to their own learning situation, and improve learners' learning autonomy, which is an educational innovation brought by new technology [6]. Intelligent classroom has changed the traditional teaching form of "one lecture hall". Under the influence of new media, combined with learners' learning habits and characteristics, follow the teaching law of teachers' leading and students' main body. As the organizer and guide of course teaching, teachers need to design accurate learning materials for students in advance, help students build a framework for autonomous learning and promote students' effective learning. Intelligent classroom provides teachers with a platform for effective guidance and students' effective learning, solves the problem that teaching resources are too complex to be used effectively, meets the most basic learning needs of students, and obtains learning resources more effectively and conveniently with the help of intelligent classroom teaching system.

2.3 User Behavior Research

User research is indeed somewhat embarrassing now. Fortunately, current practitioners are trying to intervene in products/business processes more deeply and seek integration with data analysis, experience design and other departments.

However, the product manager 3, who says that user research is unnecessary, is probably just a chore, because the main task of the product manager is to plan and drive the implementation of product functions, which needs to achieve business objectives on the basis of meeting user needs 8; You can't do without understanding the users here.

The change of the design concept/business environment of the past year needs to be replaced by the balance of the product design concept/business environment of the past year. For the product manager, we need to pay attention to the comprehensive influence of the Internet. Therefore, at present, the companies that have set up user research posts are basically large companies or Party B companies such as Tencent/Netease, which pay more attention to in-depth insight user research. This will require the product department to have the ability to master user driven business. For example, Tencent's 10/100/1000 rule will ensure that the product team will always keep an understanding of users.

Moreover, looking at user research alone, we are slowly seeking integration in different directions, such as design or big data; The requirements are becoming higher and higher.

In fact, user research has not really gained a foothold in China. Further, it is professional and well-trained user research, such as formal demand communication and scheme planning, objective and orderly scheme and rigorous analysis. What is popular now is user research based on experience and intuition [7].

Now users and researchers need to be deeply involved in the product business, rather than simply standing on the research position - user research can play a more role only when they clarify the work objectives, truly intervene in the products, operations and other businesses, and truly track the whole research from demand generation to promotion and implementation.

3 Research on User Behavior of College English Mobile Learning App

English mobile learning app is frequently used, and there are many such applications installed. These people should be enthusiastic users of English mobile learning app. They have the highest demand for English mobile learning and will have the highest loyalty to English mobile learning app. These users will become loyal customers of the enterprise. The second group of people have not used English mobile learning app to learn English for a long time, and the use frequency and installation number of app are the lowest. This kind of people are likely to learn English only occasionally or on a whim. This kind of people will be the most unstable customers in the enterprise and have the risk of loss at any time. The third group has recent use records, and the frequency of using English mobile learning app in observation time belongs to the medium level. This kind of people may need to learn English to some extent, but their learning needs are not as large as those of the first group. These customers will become the key development customers of the enterprise. The enterprise should take effective marketing measures to retain these customers and strive to develop into loyal customers. As shown in Fig. 2 below, the analogy histogram of English mobile learning app learning English is shown.

Based on the selection of association rule indicators, there are 13 indicators entering the association rules. Next, the association degree between the user behavior of English mobile learning app will be found through data mining. Here, the user's activity in using English mobile learning app is divided into two levels [8]. In the establishment In the

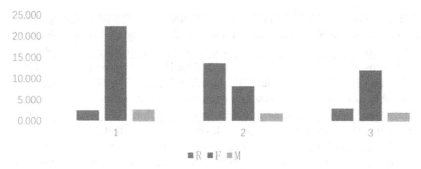

Fig. 2. English mobile learning app learning English analogy histogram

actual operation of Apriori association rule model, we first determine the minimum support and confidence of input parameters through the optimization of model parameters, as shown in Fig. 3:

$$rules < -apriori(data, parameter = list(supp = 0.1,$$
$$conf = 0.4,$$
$$minlen = 2,$$
$$target"rules"))$$

Fig. 3. Minimum support and confidence of parameters

It can expand the scope of College English learning. Compared with English Teaching in other age groups, College English knowledge is more difficult to master, more professional and more practical. Its evaluation is not only based on test results. At the same time, the university course time is relatively loose, and students' time is relatively free. With the help of mobile platform, students can learn English anytime and anywhere, breaking through the limitations of traditional teaching mode.

It can fully meet the personalized learning needs of college students. College English learning is no longer limited to exam oriented education, but emphasizes the rational use of English knowledge on the basis of understanding, which has high requirements for students' understanding ability and language organization ability. At present, the application of English is expanding, which makes the evaluation of oral English ability more important. The application of mobile platform stimulates students' interest in learning English. Students can get English according to their actual needs, such as downloading and watching relevant English videos, so as to exercise their listening, speaking, reading and writing skills [9].

Strengthen the publicity of mobile platform and improve students' awareness of independent application. The application of mobile platform requires students to have a high degree of autonomy. Students need to reasonably allocate their spare time to study college English. Therefore, in order to improve the efficiency of student time use, improve the quality and efficiency of English learning, and fully meet the individual needs of students, universities should increase publicity and education on mobile platforms, such as opening the WeChat official account of College English learning, improving the interactive platform for teachers and students and expanding the content of College English teaching according to the needs of our college English teaching. Improve college students' awareness of using mobile platform and strengthen English learning.

Reasonably allocate network resources to ensure the application scope of mobile platform. In terms of mobile platform hardware construction, colleges and universities should strengthen the construction of network system to ensure that wireless network or 4G, 5G and other mobile networks cover all corners of the university campus and ensure that the mobile network is unblocked, so as to fully meet the mobile learning needs of college students and improve the sex price ratio of mobile platform. In the software construction of mobile platform, colleges and universities can establish official account of WeChat, push English learning information regularly according to students' learning needs, increase the amount of information pushed by WeChat platform, attract students' attention, stimulate students' enthusiasm and exploration, and guide students to better invest in English learning.

Improve the network environment of English mobile learning platform to ensure students' efficient learning. At present, due to the extensive coverage of information network, a large number of advertisements and even bad information appear on various mobile platforms, which seriously affects college students' English learning. As an important field of cultivating talents, education shoulders the important mission of educating people. Therefore, universities should optimize the environment of English mobile learning platform and set up advertising barriers for WeChat official account established by the University. For foreign mobile platforms such as Kingsoft Ciba and Youdao dictionary, colleges and universities should actively communicate with developers to provide a good online learning environment for students' learning and ensure students' efficient learning.

Based on the campus network platform, carry out the learning of College English courses through mobile system. The system consists of students, teachers and administrators.

Students: after learning and registering, students can choose what they want to learn and find out the knowledge related to English classroom teaching content [10]. Before class, students can consult the content related to English texts, such as documents, micro class videos and other video materials, so that students can have frequent and convenient access to relevant learning information and enter the learning situation, So as to effectively preview and lay a foundation for classroom learning. When students encounter difficulties in the preview process, they can also ask questions and wait for and check the answers of the course teachers. After class, students check the assignments and tests assigned by the teacher and complete them within the specified date.

Teachers: after registration, the teacher module can answer questions online and assign students' English mobile learning tasks, and manage and supervise students' learning. For example, monitor students' recitation of words and listening practice every day, detect the effect of students' after-school test and autonomous mobile learning, and give feedback in class in time.

Administrator: the administrator module is mainly used to maintain, add, modify and other related operations on user information, learning materials and teaching resources.

4   Simulation Analysis

App mainly has three development modes: native development mode, web development mode and mixed development mode, as shown in Fig. 1. The application developed in the native development mode is called nativeapp. Nativeapp is developed in different development languages according to different operating systems, so this type of application has stable performance and good user experience. However, due to the need to develop separately for different operating systems, the development cycle is long, the maintenance cost is high, the update speed is slow, and the update process is complex. The application developed through web development mode is called web application. Compared with native apps, web apps have shorter development cycle and lower cost, and can support a variety of platforms [11]. However, the application performance under this development mode is poor, especially in the case of poor network, it is difficult to use, the ability to call the local file system is weak, the message push is not timely, and the user experience is poor. According to the advantages and disadvantages of the above two applications, the third application, namely hybrid application, is derived. This application was developed in mixed mode. The essence of its development is to use WebView as a container in nativeapp to directly load HTML5 pages, and then realize the two-way communication between the underlying hardware and application pages through jsbridge middleware. Hybridapp not only has the advantages of strong local application stability and good user experience, but also has the advantages of low development cost and cross platform. It will become the main trend of application development in the future.

Vocabulary. Com has made great efforts to help you remember words faster and more effectively, including picture memory, synonym memory, context memory of relevant articles, word spelling practice and so on Www. 68mn. And vocabulary The all English learning environment allows you to learn English like your mother tongue when you remember words. Www. 68 mn. Because of vocabulary Com has a large amount of English corpus. Children's shoes with poor English foundation will certainly be a little difficult to use [12]. It is recommended to use vocabulary When reciting words, reduce the number of words recited every day. Www. 68mn.

Online English English dictionary is definitely vocabulary com. Basic and complete definitions of words, types and examples of words in different meanings, word family, use examples, and everything you want to know about the word Almost all can be found. Com. Word family can also help you find words with the same root, so that you can remember a group of words by remembering a word. It's great to think about it (Fig. 4).

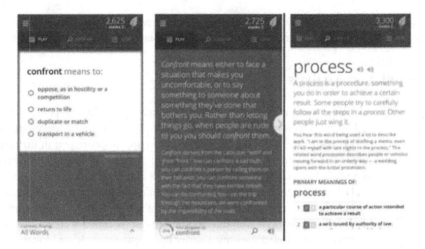

Fig. 4. Vocabulary. Com learning end

5   Conclusion

In short, in the context of globalization, exchanges between countries are becoming more and more frequent, information technology is changing with each passing day, and English is becoming more and more important. In College English teaching, the effective application of mobile platform can effectively stimulate students' enthusiasm in learning English, cultivate students' autonomous learning ability and improve students' English application ability. Therefore, College English teachers should actively promote the advantages of mobile platforms, and recommend mobile platforms with better application effects, such as WeChat official account, App "memoryless words" and "Jinshan word tyrant". This will tap the value of cyber source, enrich English learning information, enhance the application value of mobile platforms, improve students' English learning ability and promote the long-term development of English teaching.

References

1. Kalhoro, A.A.: Smart agriculture on computers and handheld devices. Int. J. Adv. Trends Comput. Sci. Eng. **10**(2),1177–1182 (2021)
2. Farzana, A.: A Comparative Study between English and Bangla: The Perspective of Phonemics, Morphology and Syntax (2021)
3. Yoon, T., Yang, J.: A case study of primary English learners. STEM J. **22**(1), 155–177 (2021)
4. Erarslan, A.: The role of job satisfaction in predicting teacher emotions: a study on english language teachers. Int. J. Contemp. Educ. Res. (2021)
5. Seok, J.: A Study on Effective English Teaching Using Movies (2021)
6. Guan, A.: Research on blended teaching model in college english based on mobile learning APP. J. Contemp. Educ. Res. **5**(1) (2021)
7. Nkhoma, D.E., Soko, C.J., Banda, K.J., et al.: Impact of DSMES app interventions on medication adherence in type 2 diabetes mellitus: Systematic review and meta-analysis. BMJ Health Care Inform. **28**(1), e100291 (2021)

8. Lee, J., Schnall, R.: Validity and Reliability of the Korean Version of the Health-ITUES Scale for Usability Assessments of Mobile Health Technology (Preprint) (2021)

9. Magomedov, S., Lebedev, A.: Protected network architecture for ensuring consistency of medical data through validation of user behavior and DICOM archive integrity. Appl. Sci. **11**(5), 2072 (2021)

10. Rusek, R., Frigola, J.M., Llinas, J.C.: Influence of User Behavior on Energy Consumption and Its Relation With Comfort. A Case Study Based on Sensor and Crowd-Sensed Data (2021)

11. Bendayan, R., Zhu, Y., Federman, A.D., et al.: Multimorbidity patterns and memory trajectories in older adults: evidence from the english longitudinal study of aging. J. Gerontol. Ser. A Biol. Sci. Med. Sci. (3) (2021)

12. Chaoyi, W.U., Gao, W.: A comparative study on english child metaphor "gift" and chinese child metaphor "Baobei". 中美英语教学: 英文版 **18**(2), 8 (2021)

Simulation and Nonlinear Observer of Multi Scroll Chaotic System

Hang Zhu(✉)

Sanda University, Shanghai 200135, China
zhuh@sandau.edu.cn

Abstract. At present, the generation of multi scroll chaotic system mainly lies in constructing appropriate nonlinear function to generate multi scroll chaotic system, but the chaotic characteristics of multi scroll chaotic system are not fully analyzed. Because the analysis of multi scroll chaotic system is difficult to use the traditional dynamic theory, and the traditional control theory is difficult to study the control of multi scroll chaotic system, there are few literatures on the analysis and research of multi scroll chaotic system at home and abroad. However, the research on the control and synchronization of multi scroll chaotic system has important theoretical significance and application value for engineering application. The application of multi scroll chaotic system to engineering field has great development prospects.

Keywords: Chaotic system · Multi scroll · Nonlinear observer

1 Introduction

Chaos is an interdisciplinary subject, which is widely used in physics, mathematics, control and other fields. Because the attractor of multi scroll chaotic system has complex structure and dynamic characteristics, it has a wide application value in the fields of communication security and information science. At the end of the 19th century, the famous French scientist Henri Poincare discovered an unpredictable complex phenomenon when studying celestial mechanics. This phenomenon is called "chaotic phenomenon". Henri Poincare proposed the famous Poincare cross section analysis nonlinear dynamic system. Poincare is considered to be the first scientist to discover chaotic phenomenon. Lyapunov function method proposed by Lyapunov, a famous Russian mechanics scientist in 1892, is used to solve ordinary differential equations. It is an important basis for the theoretical analysis of the stability of ordinary differential equations. Lyapunov exponent is an important index to judge chaotic and hyperchaotic phenomena. In the 1960s, American scientist Lorenz found chaotic phenomena in atmospheric motion, This is the first time to find chaos in deterministic equations. Since then, the prelude of chaos research has been opened [1]. Since then, complex chaotic phenomena have been found in many fields such as mathematics, biology, economics and so on.

M. A. Jan and F. Khan (Eds.): BigIoT-EDU 2022, LNICST 467, pp. 264–273, 2023.
https://doi.org/10.1007/978-3-031-23944-1_29

Using nonlinear circuits to generate various types of chaotic attractors has gradually become a research hotspot in the field of information science and physics. How to keep the system as simple as possible and regularly improve the complexity of system behavior is an unsolved problem. In order to solve this problem, people focus on multi wing chaotic system and multi scroll chaotic system. Compared with the traditional double scroll and single scroll chaotic system, the dynamic behavior and topology of multi scroll chaotic system are more complex. When the number of scroll is more, the greater its randomness is, the more conducive to information encryption. When we study the circuit of multi scroll chaos, we can encrypt the information into different scrolls or bond waves at different times. In order to increase the number of unidirectional or multidirectional vortices in the system, Suykens and others first proposed the concept of generating multi scroll chaotic attractors in Chua's circuit in 1991. After Suykens proposed the concept of multi scroll chaotic attractors, scientists at home and abroad conducted in-depth research on how to generate multi scroll chaotic attractors. Wang Faqiang et al. Generate transversely even multiple vortices in the four-dimensional system through the constructed piecewise linear function; The grid multi scroll chaotic system constructed by Chen Shibi et al. Is realized by polynomial and step function; Chen Long et al. Generated multi scroll chaotic attractors in Chua by translation transformation; Yu Simin, a famous scientist in China, has produced a series of multi scroll chaotic systems through various nonlinear functions. Due to the characteristics of multi scroll chaotic system, it has a wide application prospect in the field of nonlinear science and secure communication.

The dynamic characteristics of chaotic systems are highly complex, and they are similar to random systems and noise disturbances, which makes it difficult to model and control chaotic systems. On the one hand, people do not want to see this nature, so they hope to eliminate it; On the other hand, some special application fields can be generated by using the special properties of chaotic systems. The modeling and control of chaotic systems play an important role in both utilization and elimination. For the needs of practical applications, this project studies the modeling and control of chaotic systems with unknown models. In the aspect of modeling, we explore the structural modeling of chaotic system, not only describe the output characteristics of chaotic system, but also try to express the structural characteristics of chaotic system to a certain extent. In the aspect of control, we try to establish a simpler controller structure to facilitate the realization of the controller, and apply the idea of robust control to reduce the dependence of the controller on the model. Finally, we try to combine the modeling and control of chaotic systems, and establish the general steps of modeling and control of chaotic systems with unknown models. This will provide effective tools for the modeling and control of a series of actual chaotic systems. Therefore, the research of this paper will have high theoretical significance and practical application value.

Chaotic system is a deterministic nonlinear system. Its dynamic behavior is very complex, and its trajectory covers the entire attractor of the chaotic system. The trajectory of the system is very sensitive to the disturbance and the initial position. The two similar trajectories will be separated by the exponential law, so it is difficult to predict the system behavior. Because all kinds of nonlinearity exist in the real world, chaotic systems can be said to be everywhere. The research on chaotic systems has important theoretical significance and practical application prospects. This project mainly focuses on the modeling of chaotic systems and the design of controllers. In the research of chaos modeling, the dynamic characteristics and generation mechanism of chaotic system are studied. A switched fractional order chaotic system for generating multi scroll chaotic attractors is constructed, and a switching strategy for generating multi scroll chaotic attractors is designed; A new fractional order system is designed and its control is realized; The application of extended fractional Kalman filter in fractional order chaotic system is studied. The chaotic synchronization is realized and the system parameters are identified at the same time. The limitations of this method are analyzed; The evolution process from period to chaos of dynamic system motion state is studied, and its practical application is extended. A chaotic weak signal detection method based on Melnikov function is designed to detect the amplitude and phase of weak signal at the same time. In the design of the controller, the robustness and adaptability of the control strategy are mainly studied. Through the robustness and adaptability of the controller, it can adapt to different working environments. An adaptive synchronization method for a class of fractional order chaotic systems with unknown parameters is designed, and the adaptability of the controller is improved by using the method of parameter identification; A compound adaptive control method is designed, which combines feedback and adaptive feedforward control to solve the problem of unknown or slow time-varying system parameters; A simple fractional order controller with adjustable parameters is designed. By adjusting the parameters, the dynamic performance of the controlled system can be controlled, and the fractional order chaotic system can be controlled; A variable structure controller with adaptive idea is proposed, which combines robustness and adaptability well, and can track the amplitude of disturbance to adaptively change the robustness of the controller. The above-mentioned methods have played a certain role in promoting chaos modeling, control and application. Some of the control methods are relatively novel, which can play a positive reference role for similar problems in other related fields.

2   Overview of Chaos

2.1   Definition of Chaos

With the development of nonlinear science, people have a better understanding and mastery of complex phenomena in neural network, economics, fluid mechanics and other sciences. Chaos is a special existence in nonlinear science. It is a seemingly random and uncertain phenomenon naturally occurring in deterministic systems. Chaotic systems have complex dynamic behavior. The famous scholar Devaney defined chaos as follows in the 1990s, which is generally recognized by most scientists.

Let (a, P) be a metric space, F: $a \to A$ is a continuous mapping, and confirm the three necessary and sufficient conditions of chaotic system as follows:

(1) F the set of periodic points is dense in a;
(2) F is topologically transitive on a;
(3) F is sensitive to initial conditions;

Internal regularity is an essential feature of chaotic system, which can be presented by dense periodic points. Chaotic system has topological transitivity. It is a complete whole and can not be divided into several subsystems. Small changes in the initial value will cause great changes in the iteration of chaotic system, resulting in the unpredictability of chaotic sequence. Only when a system has these three typical characteristics at the same time can it be considered as a chaotic system.

Chaotic system means that in a deterministic system, there is a seemingly random irregular movement, and its behavior is uncertain, unrepeatable and unpredictable, which is called chaos. Chaos is an inherent characteristic of nonlinear dynamic systems and a common phenomenon in nonlinear systems. According to the properties of dynamic systems, chaos can be divided into four types: temporal chaos, spatial chaos, spatiotemporal chaos and functional chaos.

Chaos is a deterministic, quasi random process in nonlinear dynamic systems. This process is neither periodic nor convergent, and it is sensitive to the initial value. Chaos theory is a theory that nonlinear systems exhibit bifurcations under certain parameter conditions, and periodic motion and aperiodic motion are intertwined, leading to some aperiodic ordered motion.

Chaos theory has been widely used in many scientific disciplines, including mathematics, biology, information technology, economics, engineering, finance, philosophy, physics, politics, demography, psychology and robotics.

2.2 Basic Characteristics of Chaos

Although there is no clear definition of chaotic system at present, researchers have mastered many characteristics of chaotic system, which are roughly as follows:

(1) Certainty. Although chaotic system can show strong randomness, the system itself is a real deterministic system. The randomness of chaotic system can be reproduced again. Compared with the real random system, it is not a one-time behavior.
(2) Initial value sensitivity. The initial value sensitivity of chaotic system is one of the essential characteristics of chaotic system, which can be used as a judgment condition to distinguish it from other systems.
(3) Boundedness. Chaotic systems are bounded. No matter how chaotic the chaotic system is, its trajectory will not go out of this bounded region. This bounded region is called the chaotic domain of attraction [2].
(4) Fractal dimension. This unique property of chaotic system makes the local structure of amplified chaotic motion still get the structure and characteristics similar to the whole, and this special self similarity or symmetry can only be accurately characterized by the concept of fractional dimension.

3 Simulation and Nonlinear Observer of Multi Scroll Chaotic System

Based on the jerk system, a new multi scroll chaotic system is constructed by using the nonlinear function composed of piecewise linear function. The basic dynamics of the new multi scroll chaotic system is analyzed by means of theoretical analysis, numerical simulation and circuit experiment. Compared with the jerk system, the multi scroll chaotic system increases the number of multi scroll in one direction on the basis of the same parameters, Thus, the system has more complex dynamic characteristics and key parameters.

3.1 Multi Scroll Chaotic System

Based on the jerk system, a unidirectional multi scroll chaotic system is constructed by a nonlinear function composed of piecewise linear functions

$$\tau(x_{k+1}) = \cos\left(n\left(\cos^{-1}x_k\right)\right) \tag{1}$$

$$\rho(x) = \begin{cases} \frac{1}{\pi\sqrt{x(1-x)}} & 0 < x < 1 \\ 0 & \text{else} \end{cases} \tag{2}$$

When $x = 0.7$, $k = 1$, $n = 2$, the image of nonlinear function f (x) is shown in Fig. 1.

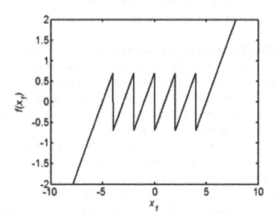

Fig. 1. Nonlinear function f (x) image

It can be seen from the figure that the nonlinear function is a sawtooth wave function, that is, there is a saddle focal equilibrium point, and the nonlinear function is composed of six piecewise linear functions separated by the bond wave with slope ∞, and the corresponding linear function area is the scroll area. Therefore, the six scroll motion associated with the bond wave can be generated under the action of the nonlinear function [3].

$$\begin{cases} x_{n+1} = f_1(x_n, y_n) \\ y_{n+1} = f_2(x_n, y_n) \end{cases} \tag{3}$$

where $\begin{cases} f_1(x_n, y_n) = a_1 + a_2 x_n + a_3 x_n^2 + a_4 y_n + a_5 y_n^2 + a_6 x_n y_n \\ f_2(x_n, y_n) = a_7 + a_8 x_n + a_9 x_n^2 + a_{10} y_n + a_{11} y_n^2 + a_{12} x_n y_n \end{cases}$.

Where a_i ($i = 1, 2, \ldots 12$) is a constant coefficient to be determined.

The system is numerically simulated in Matlab environment, and the results are shown in Fig. 2 (Fig. 3).

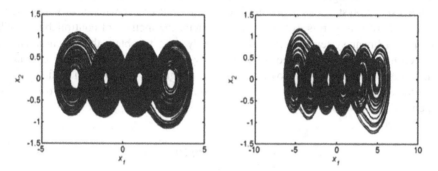

Fig. 2. Chaotic attractor of multi scroll chaotic system

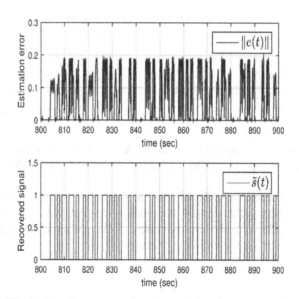

Fig. 3. Chaotic attractor of multi scroll chaotic system testing

The numerical simulation results show that changing the nonlinearity in the jerk system into piecewise linear function increases the number of vortices in one direction, increases the complexity of the jerk system, and widens its application in secure communication. The following takes the six scroll chaotic system as an example to analyze its basic dynamic characteristics, control and synchronization.

3.2 Nonlinear Observer

For two control systems, in order to determine the synchronization, the general methods need to be proved by constructing Lyapunov function or calculating Lyapunov exponent. However, we know that the construction of Lyapunov function is very complex, and sometimes there is no way to construct it, and the calculation of Lyapunov exponent is quite time-consuming, so we need to propose a new observer design method.

If a response system can be constructed so that its difference with the driving system, that is, the error system is exactly a linear system, the method of controllability rank criterion in linear system theory can be directly used to obtain the synchronization between the driving system and the response system without constructing Lyapunov function or calculating Lyapunov exponent, which greatly improves the efficiency. In order to better analyze the observer design method, we consider the general case of the system [4].

The leader

$$\dot{s}(t) = As(t) + Bf(s(t))$$

The follower agents

$$\dot{x}_i(t) = Ax_i(t) + Bf(x_i(t)) + u_i(t)$$

The controller

$$u_i(t) = \sum_{k=1}^{\infty} \left[-c \sum_{j=1}^{N} L_{ij}x_j(t_0 + kh) - cd_i(x_i(t_0 + kh) - s(t_0 + kh)) \right] \delta(t - t_k)$$

where $t_k = t_0 + kh + \tau_k$.

The circuit design of sinusoidal signal tracking control using nonlinear feedback method is shown in Fig. 4. LM741 operational amplifier and + 15V power supply voltage are adopted.

The experimental results are shown in Fig. 5. The circuit experimental results, numerical simulation results and theoretical derivation results can illustrate the effectiveness of the nonlinear feedback method for the control of the new multi scroll chaotic system. The simulation results are shown in Fig. 6 and Fig. 7.

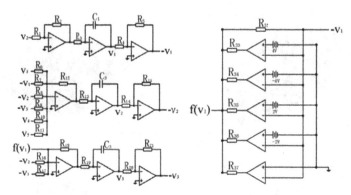

Fig. 4. Bounded tracking control system circuit

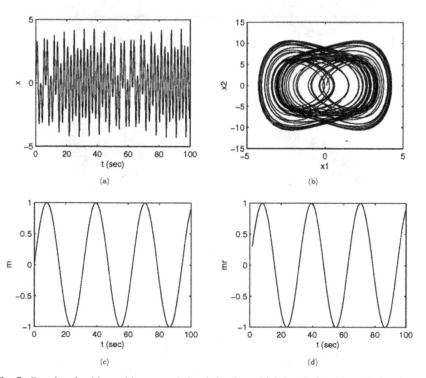

Fig. 5. Results of stable tracking control circuit for sinusoidal signal of multi scroll chaotic system

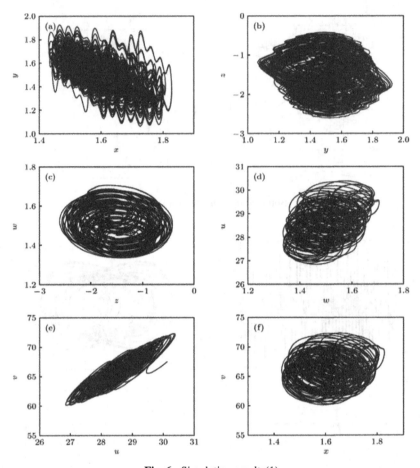

Fig. 6. Simulation results(1)

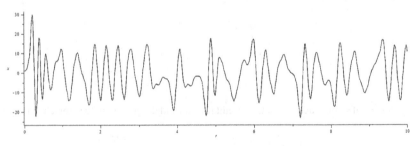

Fig. 7. The simulation results(2)

4   Conclusion

In this paper, the synchronization of multi scroll jerk circuit chaotic system is studied by using nonlinear observer, and a response system is constructed so that the error system is a linear system. Therefore, the synchronization of driving system and response system can be obtained directly by using the controllability rank criterion in linear system theory, without constructing Lyapunov function or calculating Lyapunov exponent, The efficiency is greatly improved. In the numerical simulation, the effectiveness of the proposed method is guaranteed.

References

1. Tang, L., Li, J., Fan, B.: New three-dimensional chaotic system and its circuit simulation. J. Phys. **58**(2), 785–793 (2009)
2. Wang, F., Liu, C., Lu, J.: Simulation of multi scroll chaotic attractor in four-dimensional system. J. Phys. 553289. - 3294 (2006)
3. Chen, L., Peng, H., Wang, D.: Study on the construction method of a class of multi scroll chaotic systems. J. Phys. **57**, 3337–3341 (2008)
4. Liu, Z.: Basis and Application of Chaotic Dynamics. Higher Education Press (2006)

Research on the Training of Outstanding Engineers in Architectural Education Based on Ant Colony Algorithm

Pengcheng Yin[1]([⊠]) and Si Li[2]

[1] Changchun University of Architecture, Changchun 130000, Jilin, China
mgaisai163@163.com, mgaisai@yahoo.com
[2] Changchun Rudder Real Estate Development Co., Ltd., Changchun 130000, Jilin, China

Abstract. By analyzing the current situation of higher education and the advantages and disadvantages of traditional student training methods, focusing on the training methods of students' engineering application ability and innovation ability, this paper explores a new training mode of engineering and technical talents in line with the specialty of civil engineering. Combined with the quality of teachers, teaching contents and teaching methods of civil engineering specialty, this paper puts forward some reform suggestions to deal with the current situation of education, and defines the training requirements of the excellent engineer program in the construction industry. The suggestions also have important reference for promoting the actual talent training mode of local and national higher education and improving the quality of engineering and technical talent training.

Keywords: Ant colony outstanding engineer · Higher education · Personnel training

1 Introduction

With the acceleration of China's modernization process and the development of modern scientific research and industry, the dependence on new functional materials is increasing day by day. To solve the current industrial reform problem in China is also inseparable from the support of new functional materials. Therefore, we urgently need new excellent composite engineering talents with extensive knowledge and practical ability. The goal of new engineering construction is to cultivate diversified and innovative excellent engineering talents in the future through new ways of inheritance and innovation, intersection and integration, coordination and sharing. New engineering focuses on the combination of new technology and traditional industrial technology, and emphasizes the practicability, intersection and comprehensiveness of disciplines. However, for the functional materials specialty, the existing experience in its curriculum is old and outdated, so it is difficult to form an integrated teaching model of the integration of school, enterprise and research [1]. Therefore, under the background of new engineering, only by doing a good job in the series reform of discipline basic curriculum knowledge system and

M. A. Jan and F. Khan (Eds.): BigIoT-EDU 2022, LNICST 467, pp. 274–280, 2023.
https://doi.org/10.1007/978-3-031-23944-1_30

teaching mode and scientific research engineering practice, can we drive the connotative development of multi-disciplinary integration and innovative engineering project talent training.

Due to the industrial characteristics of civil engineering, there are many reasonable places in higher engineering education, including the lack of connection between teaching and practice and the difficulty of passive teaching to stimulate students' innovative consciousness. The reform needs to focus on the key points. Higher engineering education should formulate effective reform plans according to the above two points, so as to revitalize the higher engineering education system, alleviate the urgent needs of society and enterprises for talents, and enable tens of millions of engineering and technical talents who are about to engage and are already engaged to be competent for work and realize life value and social value. Therefore, the implementation of the "excellent engineer training plan" of the talent training mode of architecture specialty is imminent, which is a powerful weapon to alleviate the contradiction between construction enterprises and engineering technical talents.

2 Ant Colony Algorithm

2.1 Artificial Ant Colony System

The ant colony algorithm is inspired by the real ant colony behavior. The behavior of artificial ants is also a mechanism simulation of the real ant behavior in nature. Then this system simulating the real ant colony behavior can be called artificial ant colony system. Its operation principle is shown in Fig. 1. It is assumed that the distance from position h to position B and position D is 1, and the distance from position C to B and D is BH and B Half of D, that is, the distance from B through C to D is 1. Suppose that 30 ants start from a to B, and another 30 ants start from e to D. the walking speed of each ant is 1 per time unit, and the pheromone concentration of each ant on its path at time t is 1. In order to make the discussion simple and easy to understand, the pheromone residence time on the path is 1 and At continuous time intervals (T + 1, t + 2) Complete volatilization in an instant. At t = 0, 60 ants arrive at position B and position D respectively. Since there is no pheromone on the paths BH, BC, DH and DC, which path the ants choose to take is completely random, that is, the ants at D and B choose to go to DC or DH and BC or BH with equal probability. Therefore, it can be considered that there are 15 ants at t = 0 respectively Ants take DC, DH, BC and BH.

2.2 Basic Ant Colony Algorithm Model

Ant colony algorithm is a simulation of the foraging behavior of real ants in nature. It is an application of mechanism, so the real ants must be abstracted first. The purpose of abstraction is to more effectively describe the mechanism that the real ant colony can be used for reference by the algorithm, and abandon the factors irrelevant to the establishment of the algorithm. In this way, the abstract artificial ant can be regarded as a simple agent, which can complete the construction process of the simple solution of the problem, and can also influence each other through a communication means [2].

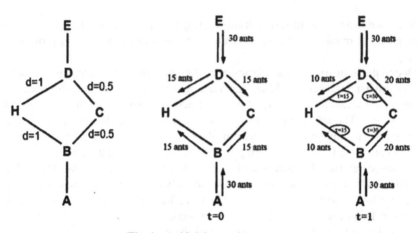

Fig. 1. Artificial ant colony system

The abstraction of real ants is divided into three points: the first point is the description of the problem space. The real ants in nature exist in a three-dimensional environment, and the solution of the problem space is usually carried out in a two-dimensional plane. Therefore, it is necessary to abstract the three-dimensional space of ant foraging behavior into a plane. This abstraction is feasible because real ants walk in a continuous two-dimensional plane, but their search behavior is discrete, which does not conflict with the computer processing of discrete events. Therefore, the problem space solved by ant colony algorithm can be described by graph. The second point is the abstraction of the search path. In the process of foraging, the real ant mainly determines its forward direction according to the amount of information in the environment, while the artificial ant moves on the plane node. Therefore, the foraging process can be abstracted into the construction process of the solution in the algorithm, and the pheromone can be abstracted into the trajectory existing on the edge of the graph. At each - node, the artificial ant perceives the pheromone trajectory concentration on the edge connecting the node and adjacent nodes, and determines the probability of moving to the next node according to the concentration.

Here we combine the famous classical TSP problem to illustrate the ant colony algorithm. The simple image description of TSP problem is: given n cities, a traveler starts from a certain city, visits each city once and only once, and then returns to the original departure city to find out the shortest itinerant path. Its mathematical description is as follows:

$$\begin{cases} E(t)\dot{x}_d(t) = f(t, x_d(t)) + B(t)u_d(t) \\ \qquad y_d(t) = C(t)x_d(t) \end{cases} \tag{1}$$

3 Analysis of the Current Situation of Higher Education

With China's economic development and the rapid improvement of science and technology, all kinds of new industries and enterprises have sprung up, and all kinds of daily necessities are changing with each passing day, resulting in the impetuous phenomenon of today's college students. All kinds of new technologies have also impacted this group, which also shows that college students have high eyes and low hands, This makes college students have empty views and shallow understanding of professional knowledge, which is also the biggest opinion of employers on college students and the biggest doubt on Chinese education. At the same time, with the continuous enrollment expansion of colleges and universities in recent years, there are more and more Chinese college students. However, the quality of students trained is uneven, which is difficult to ensure that enterprises obtain professionals with corresponding quality and skills. Taking civil engineering as an example, combined with the excellent engineer training plan, this paper expounds the problems existing in undergraduate education and teaching as follows:

3.1 The Connection Between School Education and Social Practice is Insufficient

Under the current higher education system, teachers majoring in civil engineering graduate from Chinese traditional university education. It can be said that these teachers have very solid basic knowledge and theoretical knowledge, but they lack engineering practical experience in real construction projects. Some even work as teachers in educational institutions or colleges and universities just after graduation. Therefore, they teach the students according to their own learning methods and contents at that time. The advantage is that the students have solid theoretical knowledge, but to a certain extent, it weakens the close combination of school education and social practice. Even some conservative teachers have great prejudice against social practice, Therefore, the students brought out by such teachers have varying degrees of confusion and confusion after work. They feel that many theoretical knowledge they have learned in the university classroom is useless. The employer will also feel that he only knows the theoretical knowledge in books, but he doesn't know how to apply it in the face of practical engineering projects.

3.2 The Theoretical Knowledge of Undergraduate Education is Not Closely Related to Engineering Application

What higher education conveys to the society should be professional engineering and technical talents with solid theoretical knowledge and familiar with engineering application. However, the latter has actually been criticized by employers. They believe that educational institutions do not know what they are teaching. It is a highly practical engineering major, but they teach college students who can't do it. At the same time, they also feel sleepy about what these universities teach. In fact, the current undergraduate education does pay attention to solving and verifying problems, but there is less design guidance for engineering application. For example, for a mechanical knowledge point, students only know how to solve it in book examples, but they are at a loss when changing to actual engineering projects, resulting in insufficient ability of students to solve practical problems, insufficient Association of knowledge and insufficient innovation ability [3]. In fact, the examples in the textbook are only the simplification, abstraction or extension of practical engineering problems. Breaking this layer of "window paper" is also the responsibility of professional teachers to some extent.

4 Research on the Talent Training of Excellent Engineers in Architecture Specialty Based on Ant Colony Algorithm

4.1 Reform Suggestions for Teaching Content

(1) Simplify theoretical derivation and pay attention to practical application

For the civil engineering major, due to the large number of courses and the arduous tasks of students and teachers, it is necessary to summarize all courses as a whole. Interdisciplinary is necessary and important, but if some knowledge points of multiple disciplines are similar, or even the knowledge points are listed and repeated, it will be meaningless, which will not only increase the burden on students, but also make teachers feel overwhelmed. For civil engineering, the course contains a large number of calculation formulas. For example, a large number of formulas are involved in mechanical formulas, structural calculations, engineering and economic calculations, etc. How to avoid students' headache? These formulas are a big problem. Many students lose interest in this course because of the complexity and dryness of the formulas. If there are more such courses, he will feel that learning is boring, so his grades will decline and eventually disappear from the public [4]. Therefore, it can reduce the derivation of the formula and increase the application of the formula. It is not necessary for students to know how to deduce the formula. Even some complicated formulas do not need to be remembered, but only require students to use them, which greatly increases the learning interest of college students.

(2) Pay equal attention to the quantity and quality of courses, and clarify the logic and function of courses

Due to the large number of courses, the mixing of various courses will give students a headache, and teachers will not know what knowledge they have taught students and what they have not learned. Therefore, a scientific and reasonable curriculum arrangement plan is very necessary. Only when the curriculum arrangement is clear and students know what to do in the first step and what to do in the second step, can they arrange their own time, effectively strengthen training for their weak links, and take the initiative to walk on the road of learning step by step. For teachers, this arrangement can also let teachers know what step their students have learned, so as to know what they should teach and how to teach next. Teachers and students need interactive communication in class and after class. After all, a class only lasts for a few minutes, so it is impossible to impart all knowledge to students. Students should communicate with teachers in time and effectively when they encounter problems in self-study after class. Through tools such as telephone or network, Bijing teachers go further than most students. If a teacher gives directions and leads the way, students may suddenly be enlightened.

4.2 Training Requirements for Excellent Engineers

Since the reform and opening up, the construction industry has always been a major pillar of the national economy. With the convening of the 18th National Congress, various policies and ideas have made the current development trend of the construction industry the focus of national attention. How to comply with the call of the state and promote the positive development of the construction industry is the leading direction of training excellent engineers in the future. Then, first of all, we should understand the industrial upgrading objectives determined by Zhejiang Province and the state for the construction industry and the key directions and main tasks of the development of strategic emerging industries, such as the use safety function of buildings, the green environmental protection function of building structures and the full or repeated utilization of materials, so as to comply with the national concept of sustainable development and ecological civilization. Then, starting from education, reform the education mode of specific target industries of construction. Since the construction industry includes not only civil engineering, but also electrical, environmental, planning, etc., in the formulation of education programs, it is necessary to expand students' horizons and thinking in addition to ensuring that students have a solid grasp of basic professional knowledge, To Cultivate National Applied Engineering and technical talents and compound talents with engineering ability and innovation ability.

The specific implementation process of the "excellence plan" should adhere to the principle of "industry guidance, school enterprise cooperation, classified implementation and various forms", be guided by the national demand for engineering and technical personnel, be divided into geotechnical, structural and municipal specialties, and be trained through the curriculum system of "knowledge ability quality" integration, as well as the contact and practice of extracurricular construction companies, supervision companies and construction units. On the one hand, systematically train students to master important basic theories such as architectural structure, architectural drawing, laws and regulations, and even computer technology, and carry out students' engineering skill training and project comprehensive training from the professional knowledge of architecture. On the other hand, students can make continuous progress in the whole process through the research of various experiments in the school and the contact with engineering practice, It not only improves students' practical ability, teamwork ability and comprehensive practical ability in engineering practice, but also cultivates students' comprehensive application ability and creativity of professional knowledge. Under a series of teaching programs, we should greatly improve students' ability to collect information, self-learning, communication and coordination, language expression and teamwork, so as to cultivate outstanding engineers with sustainable development potential of knowledge, ability and quality for the society in the new century.

5 Conclusion

The combination of social construction engineering industry and universities is also the top priority. Only by combining with the industry can we really know what the industry needs. With this goal, in addition, enterprises and universities jointly formulate scientific student education and training plans, so that students can truly master the basic knowledge of their major and receive professional training in enterprises. Enterprises and universities jointly build a common education center in the new era, In engineering examples, we should educate talents, improve education methods, reform education examination system, and effectively improve students' professional quality and professional quality. Implementing the "excellence plan" is an effective measure for architectural professionals in China in the new era. It requires the joint efforts of the state, colleges and universities and architectural students to ensure the quantity and quality of architectural professionals, so as to further improve China's construction engineering quality and finally promote China's progress towards a powerful country with engineering quality.

Acknowledgements. The 13th Five-Year Social Science Project of Education Department of Jilin Province; Contract No.: JJKH20201290SK; Research and practice on training mode of creative engineering talents under the background of "New Engineering".

References

1. Li, R.: Research on practical teaching of new engineering to cultivate the ability to solve complex engineering problems. Educ. Teach. Forum **13**, 84–85 (2020)
2. Li, W., Song, Z., Chen, G.: Exploration and practice of talent education and training of "excellent engineers". A case study of civil engineering major of Qiqihar Institute of engineering. J. Hubei Correspondence Univ. **26**(11), 34–37 (2013)
3. Li, S., Li, W., Guo, X.: Research and exploration on the joint training of applied "excellent civil engineers" by schools and enterprises – taking the training of civil engineering professionals of Changzhou Institute of technology as an example. J. Jiangsu Second Normal Univ. (Nat. Sci.) **31**(6), 116–118 (2015)
4. Li, F., Zhao, Y., Meng, F.: Teaching reform of civil engineering specialty based on excellent engineer education plan. High. Archit. Educ. **21**(6), 40–42 (2012)

Safety Management and Control Measures of Expressway Bridge Construction Under the Background of Big Data

Chao Jiang[1]($\boxtimes$), Jing Huang[2], Youhua Xing[3], and Xiaodan Wang[2]

[1] Shandong High Speed Green Technology Development Co., Ltd., Jinan 250000, Shandong, China
sdjtjiangchao@163.com

[2] Jinan Water Conservancy Project Service Center, Jinan 250000, Shandong, China

[3] Jinan Water Services Center, Jinan 250000, Shandong, China

Abstract. With the rapid development of economy, the development speed of transportation industry is also accelerating day by day. China has a wide land and many people. In some areas, due to the particularity of terrain, highway bridges must be built when building roads. Highway bridges are an important link of highway construction. Highway bridges are easy to appear in the process of construction or after completion, It directly affects the construction quality and progress of the whole highway. Therefore, based on the background of big data, this paper mainly analyzes the quality problems and causes in highway bridge construction, and puts forward quality control measures in highway bridge construction.

Keywords: Highway bridge construction · Big data · Safety management · Control measures

1 Introduction

The development of national economy has promoted the prosperity of highway transportation in China. At this stage, the construction scope and scale of Expressway in China are gradually expanding, which is highly concerned and valued by all fields of society. The expressway not only deepens the economic and cultural exchanges between regions, but also provides more convenient travel conditions for the broad masses of the people, and promotes the social and economic development to a certain extent. The construction level of the expressway can reflect the comprehensive strength of a country to a certain extent. As an indispensable part of expressway, the construction of expressway bridge contains many requirements, and its construction is a comprehensive and systematic task. It is easy to be affected by various external environmental factors [1]. Therefore, it is necessary to strengthen the construction quality control of expressway bridge engineering to avoid quality problems in construction. At the same time, strengthening the construction quality control of expressway bridges can improve the quality and service performance of the whole expressway project, and its importance can be seen.

M. A. Jan and F. Khan (Eds.): BigIoT-EDU 2022, LNICST 467, pp. 281–287, 2023.
https://doi.org/10.1007/978-3-031-23944-1_31

Highway bridge construction projects have the characteristics of great difference, complex construction technology and great unpredictability. In order to control the safety risk of the bridge construction site and prevent the occurrence of construction accidents, combined with the actual situation of the bridge project of the second bid section of Beijing Baotou expressway, this paper puts forward the safety management and control measures of Expressway Bridge Construction under the background of big data.

2 Related Work

2.1 Definition of Safety Accident

The occupational safety and health management system specification (occupational safety and health evaluation series OHSAS18001) defines an accident as an unexpected event that leads to death, occupational related diseases, injury, property loss or other losses. Most literatures describe that accidents are accidents that stop or interfere with the process of production or activities contrary to people's wishes and will. Accidents always stop or interfere with the process, and may be accompanied by human injury and material damage. From the perspective of system dynamics, accident can be regarded as a process, which is a process in which the disturbance of some elements of the system finally leads to unwanted harmful results after a series of intermediate events.

The bridge construction process is mainly to organize personnel, materials, equipment and tools to complete the bridge construction through a series of organization and management means according to the work plan, objective laws and conditions, operation standards, etc. There are many types of accidents that stop or interfere with the process during bridge construction. The root causes of these accidents also involve the design unit, construction unit, supervision unit and other participants of the project, as well as the factors of natural forces. The main factors causing accidents during construction are shown in Fig. 1.

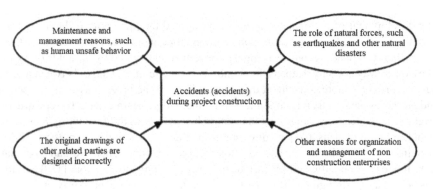

Fig. 1. Causes of accidents during construction

2.2   Characteristics of Bridge Construction Safety Accidents

Compared with general safety accidents, bridge construction has its own characteristics. Before studying the specific causes of bridge construction safety accidents, clarifying these characteristics plays a vital role in better analyzing the causes of accidents.

(1) Severity. Safety accidents during bridge construction often have a great impact, which will directly lead to casualties or property losses, and bring huge losses to the lives and property of constructors. Major safety accidents often lead to mass casualties or huge property losses.

(2) Complexity. The complexity of bridge construction process determines that there are many factors affecting the safety production of bridge engineering, and the causes of safety accidents are complex. Even if it is the same kind of safety accidents, the causes may be diverse. For example, it is also a bridge collapse accident. For different bridge types, different geological conditions and different construction processes, the accident causes obtained after accident analysis may be very different. In this way, when analyzing safety accidents, it increases the complexity of judging their nature and causes (direct causes, indirect causes, main causes), etc. [2].

(3) Variability. Many potential safety accidents in bridge construction are not static, but may develop and deteriorate over time. If they are not rectified and handled in time, they may often develop into serious or major safety accidents. Therefore, when analyzing and dealing with the hidden dangers of engineering safety accidents, we should pay attention to the variability of hidden dangers of safety accidents, and timely take effective measures to correct and eliminate them, so as to prevent their development from deteriorating into safety accidents.

3   Common Quality Problems in Expressway Bridge Construction

(1)   Bridge crack

In the construction of expressway bridges, bridge cracks are one of the common problems. If the bridge cracks cannot be treated in time, or the treatment technology is not in place, it may lead to serious situations such as bridge crack extension or crack fracture. In serious cases, it will also lead to bridge collapse and cause a large number of casualties. In the process of expressway bridge construction, if the temperature control of concrete pouring is wrong, it will lead to a large amount of hydration heat, which will continue to accumulate in the concrete, resulting in thermal expansion and cold contraction after formwork removal, and then bridge cracks. In addition, due to the concentration of prestress in the web, the concrete vibration may not be in place during concrete pouring, which will lead to holes in the concrete, reduce the strength of the concrete, weaken the bearing effect of the web, and lead to bridge cracks.

(2)   The expansion joints of expressway bridges are seriously damaged

In addition to the above diseases of expressway bridges, another disease is the problem of expansion joints of bridges. Bridge expansion joints are usually set between two beam ends, between beam ends and abutment or at the hinged position of the bridge in order to meet the requirements of bridge deck deformation. It is required that the expansion joint can expand freely in two directions parallel and perpendicular to the bridge axis, be firm and reliable, and the vehicle shall travel smoothly without sudden jump and noise; It shall be able to prevent rainwater, garbage and soil from seeping and blocking; Installation, inspection, maintenance and elimination of dirt shall be simple and convenient. After the bridge passes through, due to the rolling impact of overloaded vehicles, and due to the impact of the natural environment, the rubber plates between the bridge expansion joints age too quickly, which affects the connection between the expansion joints, while the embedded steel plates between highway bridges will loosen under the repeated impact of the weight of overloaded vehicles, Thus, there are problems in the concrete and rubber plates on both sides between the expansion joints of expressway bridges.

(3) Uneven pavement

China's expressway pavement and expressway bridge pavement usually adopt the paving method of asphalt concrete. The paving method of asphalt concrete has the advantages of simple construction, easy maintenance and low noise. However, it is also easy to produce the problem of uneven pavement in the construction process, resulting in the inconvenience to the normal driving of vehicles in the use of the bridge. Generally speaking, if there are problems in subgrade materials and waterproof and drainage system, it is bound to affect the quality of subgrade and lead to subgrade subsidence, which will lead to the problem of uneven pavement of expressway bridge. In addition, if the asphalt aggregate ratio is unscientific, it will also cause the unevenness of the pavement[3].

(4) Bridge head depression of Expressway Bridge

Due to improper construction at the bridge head of expressway, there are depressions on the ground. When vehicles drive to these depressions, they will cause severe bumps. The reasons for these phenomena are as follows: during the subgrade construction at the bridge head, the subgrade construction is not carried out in accordance with the relevant national regulations, resulting in the compactness behind the abutment unable to meet the strength requirements, After rolling under continuous heavy load, foundation settlement occurs, resulting in depression.

4 Safety Management and Control Measures for Expressway Bridge Construction Under the Background of Big Data

4.1 Construction Safety Management

(1) Strengthen on-site safety inspection

In the process of highway bridge construction, potential safety hazards can be found in time through safety inspection, which is helpful to avoid safety accidents. Therefore, the safety inspection on the construction site should be strengthened, and a relatively complete safety inspection system on the construction site can be established by combining regular, irregular and special inspection, and based on the experience of similar projects.

① During the regular safety inspection, each team shall carry out self inspection, mutual inspection and handover inspection during the daily construction process, and the safety management department, quality management department, engineering management department and material and equipment department shall jointly carry out a comprehensive and detailed safety inspection on the construction site on a weekly basis, and order the parties concerned to rectify the problems found in the inspection in time. ② The on-site safety officer can be responsible for the irregular safety inspection. During the implementation, the safety officer shall carry out the corresponding patrol inspection according to the environmental changes of the construction site, especially under some severe weather conditions, focus on whether the construction site has taken measures such as wind, flood, collapse and electric shock. ③ In the special safety inspection, the safety management department shall assign a person in charge to lead the person in charge of other departments to conduct professional safety inspection on the key construction projects in the bridge project, reasonably determine the relevant safety inspection contents, issue the safety inspection report, and put forward effective safety management and control suggestions.

(2) Strengthen site safety management

① Set isolation enclosure to isolate the construction site from the outside, and mark the information at the eye-catching position of the enclosure structure: construction overview, site plan, safety management regulations, etc., so that the construction personnel can understand and master the safety operation requirements of the construction site. ② The roads used for transportation shall be reasonably arranged to connect the main roads with temporary buildings, reduce bends and avoid inconvenience to road transportation due to too many bends. ③ Reasonably arrange the stacking of construction materials, stack the construction materials, construction facility components and prefabricated components in order according to the principle of classification, and control the stacking height of materials in strict accordance with the requirements of specifications and standards. ④ In the operation area of the construction site, complete and perfect safety protection facilities, such as safety guardrail, safety net, protective cover, etc., shall be set. No person shall dismantle the safety facilities without authorization for any reason. If it is necessary to change the setting scheme of safety facilities, it must be reported to the safety management department for approval before moving or dismantling the facilities. ⑤ Safety warning signs shall be set up in dangerous parts of the construction, especially for holes in the construction area, protective fences or red light warning signs shall be set up to prevent construction personnel from mistakenly entering them. ⑥Strictly inspect the mechanical equipment entering the construction site to ensure that the service performance of the mechanical equipment meets the requirements of safe construction. During the use of mechanical equipment, it is necessary to follow the principle of "three determinations", strengthen management, establish mechanical equipment account, and do a good job in maintenance, repair and repair, so as to ensure that the mechanical equipment is always in the best operation state and eliminate potential faults in time.

4.2 Safety Control Measures for Bridge Construction

In the construction of Expressway Bridge Engineering, drilling construction, pier and abutment construction and hanging basket construction are more important subdivisional works and links prone to safety accidents. Effective safety control measures should be taken for these links to reduce and eliminate safety accidents, so as to ensure the smooth progress of bridge construction.

(1) Safety control measures for drilling construction

During the drilling construction, the frame shall be stable before construction to avoid frame displacement during construction. The top of the drill frame can be tensioned symmetrically with cable. If the percussion drill is used for drilling during construction, non operators shall not enter the operation site. After construction, the drill bit shall be placed in a safe position and the drilling shall be inspected to prevent safety accidents caused by hole collapse 。

(2) Safety control measures for Pier and abutment construction

During the construction of the pier and abutment at the lower part of the bridge, the following safety control measures can be taken: the construction personnel shall not walk on the installed reinforcement; before the formwork is hoisted, the hoisting point shall be firm and reliable, and the hoisting shall be carried out according to the dispatching of the on-site command, and the overloaded formwork shall not be hoisted; after the formwork is installed in place, the position of the formwork shall be fixed with connectors and stirrups to prevent the formwork from falling and smashing Injury to construction personnel [4].

(3) Safety control measures for hanging basket construction

During the installation of the hanging basket, the anchorage and auxiliary limit devices must be installed; during the welding of the truss system, the unformed truss members should be stabilized to avoid falling and hurting people; when using the hanging basket, the rear anchor and the safety rope of the tensioning platform should be checked frequently; before pouring concrete, the sling and anchorage of the hanging basket should be comprehensively checked.

5 Conclusion

In short, there are many common quality problems in the process of expressway bridge construction. These problems not only threaten the safety of people's lives and property, but also affect social stability to a certain extent. Based on this, the expressway construction department and supervision department need to pay enough attention to the construction of Expressway Bridge Engineering and strengthen the construction quality Control and avoid various quality problems in its construction, so as to improve the overall quality and service performance of expressway, and finally promote the long-term development and prosperity of highway construction in China.

References

1. Zhiqiang, W.: Common quality problems and control strategies in expressway bridge construction. Shanxi Archit. **06**, 187–188 (2012)

2. Qiang, Z.: Some thoughts on quality management and control of expressway bridge construction. Heilongjiang Transp. Sci. Technol. **06**, 135–136 (2012)
3. Yuying, L.: Discussion on technical quality problems in expressway bridge construction. Sci. Technol. Innov. Appl. **02**, 204 (2014)
4. Minghui, W., Kailan, L., Yongbo, Z.: Construction safety management of mountain high-speed railway bridge over Expressway. Railway Archit. **2**, 41–43 (2015)

The Design of English Teaching Resource Management System Based on Genetic Algorithm

Zhikun Hu[✉]

School of Humanities, Tianjin University of Finance and Economics Pearl River College, Tianjin 301811, China
swanky2021@126.com

Abstract. In the process of educational informatization construction, the computerization of educational resources is one of the core contents of educational informatization development. With the rapid development of information technology, computer technology and general recommendation technology and the reform of modern teaching mode, the traditional graduation creation teaching tools can no longer meet the needs of modern teaching. Especially in recent years, the number and type of educational resources are increasing, which is becoming more and more important to teachers and students. Due to the increase in the number and diversity of online education resources, network resource management is more common and important. Network resource management has become a new form. We should establish an educational resource management system that meets the needs of education. This paper introduces the creation and development of educational resources at home and abroad, and determines the content of educational resources according to their own needs. This paper designs and implements an English teaching resource management system based on collaborative algorithm and database management system. The purpose is to provide effective and comprehensive management of English teaching resources and give full play to the functions of teachers and students. The research and development system can effectively manage and use English teaching resources, better meet the needs of students and teachers, and better serve teaching.

Keywords: Teaching resources · Collaborative recommendation · English teaching · Resource management

1 Introduction

Modern society is an information society. With the rapid development of information technology, information construction is being carried out in all fields. Information has a far-reaching impact on all areas of national economic and social life. Governments around the world have clearly recognized that it plays an important role in improving management, reform and innovation. Chinese governments at all levels have also clearly pointed out that we should pay attention to information construction, seize opportunities, and achieve rapid social and economic development [1].

With the development of social informatization, educational informatization is also developing. Most Chinese universities have their own networks. In the internal network of the University, the library has teaching materials, teaching materials, audio-visual teaching materials, multimedia courses, e-books and so on. However, the resources used in school English curriculum are isolated and distributed in different systems. These systems are developed by different companies at different times, so it is difficult to share the resources of different systems to teach English. In order to realize the sharing of English teaching resources and facilitate the use of students and teachers, colleges and universities have invested a lot of human and material resources in the management of English teaching resources[2]. However, this method of managing English learning resources will bring huge costs. With the increase of English teaching resources and the change of students' and teachers' needs, schools have encountered difficulties in building a comprehensive teaching system that meets the requirements of the development of educational informatization. Lack of integration between different application systems, insufficient resource utilization and insufficient coordination. Schools need a lot of human and financial resources to maintain and update their systems, and the resources for English teaching also involve huge costs. This is mainly reflected in the following points.

(1) Massive English teaching resource data is difficult to manage

 The existing English teaching resource management system still focuses on the storage of massive data. The operation and calculation processing capacity after storage is insufficient, which can not meet the requirements of high availability and consistency, and the immediacy of data.

(2) Lack of sharing mechanism of teaching information resources

 Various English teaching resource management systems are built by different manufacturers at different times. English teaching resources have a wide variety of data and different data formats. If we realize the sharing of these multi-source and heterogeneous English teaching resources, we need to standardize these English teaching resources and solve the problem of unified management of these different English teaching resources.

(3) There are many English teaching resource management systems, and the development and maintenance costs are high

 There are many English teaching resource management systems. The data formats of English teaching resources are different, and the data of different information systems can not be shared. It is more difficult for information systems to realize the interoperability at the functional level. The construction of educational informatization is a long-term and arduous project, which needs to invest a lot of human and financial resources. It is impossible to complete it quickly in a short time. It needs to build the teaching information system in stages and steps, generally starting from the basic system and important system [3].

At present, the mode of relying on the network to manage educational knowledge and using these contents to learn has become more and more popular. Its advantage is to implement centralized and open management of a large number of educational knowledge. Teachers and students can choose more personalized and unrestricted outside the classroom. In addition, teachers and students can fully communicate and discuss. At present, higher vocational colleges have built more advanced network equipment and more complete campus network.

In this paper, not only makes the teaching content of our school more centralized and better managed, but also presents it digitally in front of teachers and students, which plays an important role in stimulating their interest, enhancing autonomous learning, promoting learning efficiency and education quality, as well as the cultivation of innovative consciousness [4]. Because the network architecture and basic database interconnection of each higher vocational college are different, and the specialty setting and learning situation of each school also have their own characteristics.

2 Related Work

2.1 Teaching Resource Management

Modern society is an information society. Information technology has had a far-reaching impact on the education sector and brought major changes to education. With the rapid development of educational informatization, educational resource management is developing in two directions. That is the centralized management of educational resources. At present, many schools face many challenges in dealing with educational resources. It is basically a closed control system. They treated the school at the prescribed level. Only some users can access educational resources, which is different from sharing educational resources. The current educational resource management system does not make full use of educational resources, which means that it cannot make full use of educational resources.

At present, when building educational resources that share educational resources across platforms, unified educational resource management and construction standards should be established so that users can use educational resources to work and study in an open environment. In recent years, experts and scholars who conduct information research in the education industry have deeply realized the significance of the unified construction standard of teaching resources, and put forward some unified construction standards in the management of teaching resources. Under the leadership of the Ministry of education, China's relevant technical personnel have formulated the construction standards and norms of China's teaching resource informatization with reference to the construction experience of foreign teaching resource informatization [5]. At present, the informatization construction of teaching resources in Colleges and universities in China is planned and constructed according to these standards.

We have accumulated a lot of theoretical and practical experience in the informatization construction of educational resources in Colleges and universities, which can provide a certain reference for the construction of educational information resources. However, how to effectively manage educational resources, how to better use educational resources in an unplanned environment, and how to manage and create educational resources are still pending.

At present, the textbook management of colleges and universities in China mainly includes three aspects: centralized management of textbooks, open management of textbooks and mixed management of textbooks. The purpose of information construction of educational resources is to realize the exchange of educational resources, so that users can work and learn educational resources under open conditions [6]. At present, there is no unified standard for the management and construction of educational resources, so it is difficult to realize the sharing of educational resources. In order to ensure the sharing of educational resources, the following two problems must be solved:

(1) Dynamic availability. In order to make educational resources easy to use in different educational resource management systems, we must achieve good compatibility of educational resources. This requires the application of unified construction standards and norms in the construction of educational information resources.
(2) Joint mechanism. Educational resource sharing refers to the centralized management of educational resources across different systems, so that users can easily use educational resources, maximize the use of educational resources, and make full use of their respective application capabilities.

2.2 Collaborative Filtering Technology

Collaborative filtering technology is an information filtering technology, which first appeared in tapestry system. The input data of this technology mostly adopts the evaluation of resources given by users. When running the collaborative filtering algorithm, you only need to enter the user item matrix without considering the specific attributes of the recommended products. As shown in Fig. 1. In view of this characteristic of collaborative filtering algorithm, this algorithm is widely used in recommendation systems where the attributes of most recommendation objects are inconvenient to be processed numerically [7]. Advantages of collaborative filtering technology:

(1) The algorithm only depends on the user's historical data (generally explicit data) and has nothing to do with the specific attributes of the recommended products. Therefore, it can be used to recommend products whose attributes are difficult to be quantified, such as books, RBTS, movies, etc.
(2) The essence of the algorithm is that similar user groups share product information, so they can recommend new products and enable users to discover their new points of interest.

Although technology at present, there are still some deficiencies;

(1) Matrix sparsity problem. This algorithm relies on users' evaluation of products to form a matrix. In most cases, users only enjoy the recommendation service and will not cooperate with the recommendation system to score products, resulting in the sparsity of the scoring matrix.
(2) Cold start problem: new users entering the system do not have any historical data, and the products newly added to the system will not have any evaluation. At this time, the system is invalid for new users and new products.

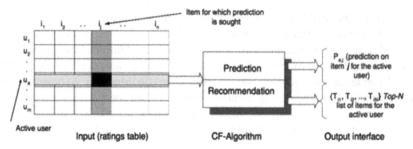

Fig. 1. Principle of collaborative filtering technology

(3) Efficiency problem, this algorithm needs to compare all users or products. With the increase of the number of users or products, the operation efficiency must be lower and lower.

(4) For the problem of recommendation accuracy, the collaborative filtering algorithm alone generally only analyzes the user's explicit data, and does not consider the implicit data with more implicit interest information. Sometimes, the explicit data can not truly reflect the user's interest, so there is the problem of recommendation accuracy.

2.3   Content Based Collaborative Filtering

In 1992. Collaborative filtering technology assumes that users' interests can be obtained by analyzing users' behaviors, and users with similar behaviors have the same interests. Many researchers recommend the earliest versions of personalized filtering technology. Recommendation technology mainly considers two factors: users and recommended objects. In view of the differences between these two factors, collaborative filtering technology can be subdivided into user based and content-based recommendation technology [8]. Another is to model the user scoring matrix, which is called model-based collaborative filtering for short.

The efficiency of user based collaborative filtering is low, and the products recommended by the system are far less than the number of users, then we turn to analyze the similarity between products, the recommendation efficiency will be higher, which is content-based collaborative filtering. This recommendation method is an improvement on the basis of user based recommendation, and has been applied to Amazon system for the first time. The algorithm principle is to obtain the similarity between products by analyzing the evaluation records of all users, and then recommend similar products according to the historical data of current users. Users' interests will change, and the similarity between users is easy to change, but the similarity between products - generally will not change. This recommendation technology is more suitable for the system in which the attributes of the recommended object are easy to be digitized [9].

As shown in Fig. 2, there are three users a, B and C, and three items a, B and C. from the user's history, we can know that user a likes items a and C, user B likes items a, B and C, user C likes items a, and items a and C are similar. Therefore, we guess that user C will also like item C, so we recommend item C to C.

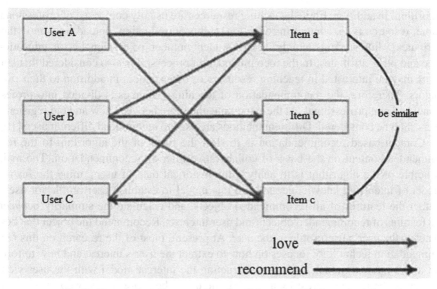

Fig. 2. Description of content-based collaborative filtering principle

The steps of content-based collaborative filtering algorithm are as follows:

(1) Collect data. This step is the same as user based collaborative filtering.
(2) Generate content nearest neighbor set

Calculate the similarity of the collected data to obtain the nearest neighbor set. There are also three similarity calculation methods here:

Included angle cosine calculation formula: each user in the matrix has n-dimensional data, which can be regarded as an n-dimensional vector, so as to evolve the user interest similarity into n-dimensional vector similarity calculation. Included angle cosine is a common formula.

$$\|\Delta x_{k+1}(t)\| \le \left(pk_f + m_2 + m_3\right)\int_0^t \Delta x_{k+1}(\tau)d\tau + \int_0^t (m_1\|\Delta u_k(\tau)\| + pd)d\tau \quad (1)$$

3   Analysis of English Teaching Resource Management System

3.1   Recommended Ideas

In the English teaching resource recommendation system constructed in this paper, it mainly includes two important roles: English teachers and students. From the perspective of teaching resources, it contains many types, such as image, audio, video and so on. Therefore, if the traditional association rule algorithm is used to recommend these English teaching contents, it is difficult to make cross domain recommendation. Therefore, the collaborative recommendation model is selected in the recommendation algorithm. In addition, English teaching resources are usually composed of professional name, resource type, content introduction, author introduction, upload time and other attributes, while students mainly include student number, professional code, education type and other attributes. In the recommendation process, it is also considered that students may be interested in teaching resources of other majors in addition to their own majors. Therefore, the recommendation of teaching resources is divided into professional and non professional. At the same time, the score between new and old registered users shall be considered. Different methods are used to recommend different users[10].

Content-based recommendation is to shift the focus of the algorithm to the recommended content on the basis of collaborative filtering recommendation. The main principle of the algorithm is to analyze the historical data of users, mine the feature model of interested knowledge, and use this model to establish user profile for users, extract the features of all recommended objects, and calculate the similarity between the features of recommended objects and user interests, Recommend the object that best matches the user's userprofile to the user. At present, most of the research on this recommendation technology focuses on how to extract the user's interest and how to form the user's interest model, such as constructing the interest model with the user view, extracting the user's interest by analyzing the user's behavior on the web page (copy, paste, print, etc.) and the number of times the user browses the page.

3.2 Design Principles

The teaching resource management system designs the teaching resource management system as a whole according to the design principles of software engineering, the common enjoyment of teaching resources, open system management, computer network operation mode and other design ideas, aiming at building a teaching resource database convenient for teachers and students to work and study, and based on the actual needs of teachers and students. The design principles of the system are as follows:

(1) Practical principle

    The teaching resource management system serves the work and learning of teachers and students. The teaching resource management system must meet the actual needs of teachers and students. The developed teaching resource management system must be convenient for teachers and students to use. From the teaching resource management system, teachers and students can find the teaching resources they want. If the system can not meet the actual needs of teachers and students, even if the system is powerful and beautiful, it is also a failed system.

(2) Expansibility principle

    In the future management of teaching resources, the needs of teachers and students may change. We should consider this problem when designing the teaching resource management system. When the needs of the system change in the future, the system can be easily upgraded and expanded.

(3) Reliability principle

    The teaching resource management system should be able to ensure normal operation, and should not have frequent failures, which will affect the use of teachers and students. When carrying out the teaching resource management system, we should fully consider the reliability of the system, so that the system can operate normally under bad conditions.

(4) Principles of manageability and maintainability

After the actual operation of the teaching resource management system, it needs to be managed and maintained frequently. Therefore, the cost and maintainability of the system should be considered in the design, so as to reduce the cost and maintainability of the system.

(5) Safety principle

The teaching resource management system should ensure the safety of teaching resources and the safety of users. Illegal and unapproved teaching resources cannot be published to the system. Only users with specified permissions can publish, modify and delete teaching resources. The system must have high security to ensure the safe and reliable operation of the system.

4 Design of English Teaching Resource Management System Based on Collaborative Recommendation

4.1 Architecture

The architecture of teaching management system based on collaborative recommendation is a three-tier architecture, including display layer, business layer and data layer. The display layer is responsible for the display of the page, the business layer is responsible for the processing of the system business logic, and the data layer is responsible for the operation of the system data. The three-tier architecture is not a simple physical three-tier architecture, which does not mean that the system is placed on three computers. The three-tier architecture refers to the logical three-tier architecture of the system. It adds another layer of processing between the client and the database, which is responsible for the processing of the system business logic. The application of three-tier architecture usually puts the business rules of the system, the rules of data access and the verification of legitimacy into the middle tier for operation. Generally, the page of the system does not directly connect to the database or exchange data with the database, but establishes a connection with the database through the middle layer and exchanges data with the database through the middle layer.

Features of three-tier architecture:

(1) The three-tier architecture has a very flexible composition of computer hardware system. Different computer hardware can be selected for each layer, because the system processing load and processing capacity of each layer may be different. Therefore, the hardware selection of each layer can be adapted to the system requirements of its corresponding layer. The system structure is handled according to the three-tier structure, which can make the composition of the system very flexible and the structure clear.

(2) The three-tier system structure has very good maintainability. In the three-tier architecture, each layer can be developed and maintained separately, and each layer can use the development language and development environment suitable for each layer. Therefore, the three-tier architecture has good maintainability.

(3) The three-tier architecture has very good system security. Because each layer is responsible for the processing of its corresponding layer, each layer and other layers are independent of each other, the processing logic of each layer becomes simpler, and the security management of each layer becomes easier to implement. A higher security mechanism can be set for key applications. Compared with the system without layering, the system with three-tier architecture has better security performance.

Combined with the design idea of software engineering and through careful study of system requirements analysis, the software architecture of the system is proposed, as shown in Fig. 3.

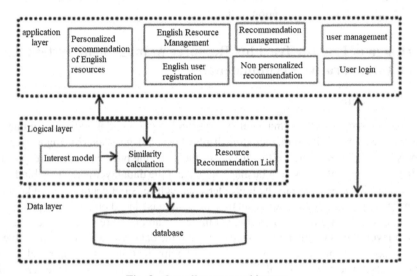

Fig. 3. Overall system architecture

4.2 Functional Module

The teaching resource management system is mainly for all teachers and students to work and study. It can provide teachers and students with the teaching resources they need conveniently and quickly. Therefore, the teaching resource management system designed in this paper has the function of providing students with independent learning anytime and anywhere, providing teachers with daily work and teaching resource management services, and providing other users with the function of accessing and learning teaching resources.

The main function of the teaching resource management system based on collaborative recommendation is teaching resource management, and there are some auxiliary functions in the system. The functional module design of the teaching resource management system is shown in Fig. 4: according to the actual needs of teaching resource management, through careful analysis and research, the main functions of the teaching resource management system include user information management, department information management, teaching information management, curriculum information management, teaching resource information management and statistical information management. Through these functions, the system can easily manage teaching resources and better serve the teachers and students of the whole school. The specific functions of the system are as follows:

User information management: through this module, user information management can be carried out, including user addition, modification and deletion, and different users can be given different permissions.

Department Information Management: through this module, you can manage department information, including adding, modifying and deleting departments.

Teacher information management: through this module, you can manage teacher information, including adding, modifying and deleting teachers.

Course information management: through this module, you can manage course information, including adding, modifying and deleting courses.

Teaching resource management: through this module, you can manage teaching resources, including the addition, modification and deletion of teaching resources, configure teaching resources and open them to designated users.

Statistical information management: through this module, you can manage statistical information, including course access statistics, course content statistics and system access statistics.

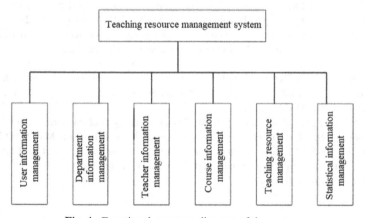

Fig. 4. Functional structure diagram of the system

5   Conclusion

In the process of educational informatization construction, the computerization of educational resources is one of the core contents of educational informatization development. With the rapid development of information technology, computer technology, general recommendation technology and the reform of modern teaching mode, traditional teaching tools can no longer meet the needs of modern teaching. Educational resource management system with general recommendation function is the key to solve the problem of excessive accumulation and low efficiency of existing educational resources. Combined with the recommendation algorithm, an educational resource management system is proposed, and different types of educational resources for managing and managing personal space are proposed. Recommendation module and system management is an educational resource management system, which aims to meet the needs of users representing different functional needs and improve the sharing and use of educational resources.

References

1. Gu Y , Chen J , Liu Z . Course Resources and Teaching Methods of Logistics Management Major Under Emerging Engineering Education[M]. 2021
2. Yan, Q.: Design of teaching video resource management system in colleges and universities based on microtechnology. Secur. Commun. Netw. **2021**(4), 1–11 (2021)
3. Hendy, N.T.: The effectiveness of technology delivered instruction in teaching Human Resource Management. Int. J. Manage. Educ. **19**(2), 100479 (2021)
4. Opatha, H.: Teaching ethics in human resource management education: a study in Sri lanka. Prabandhan Indian J. Manage. **14**(1), 8–24 (2021)
5. Odim, O.O., Adigebi, R.A.: Education and human resources management for effective development of teaching personnel for national development 27-Jul-2021 18–37–41 (2021)
6. Jiansheng, P.: Exploration on the design of immersive teaching method in oral English teaching in higher vocational colleges. Hechi University Xuebao **2**(8), 1150–1162 (2021)
7. Yuan, X.X.: The teaching design of comprehensive english for english majors in higher vocational colleges based on "production oriented method". DEStech Trans. Econ. Bus. Manage. (2021). (eeim)
8. Song, X.: Zhang C . Design of English online teaching assistant system based on deep learning. In: 2021 13th International Conference on Measuring Technology and Mechatronics Automation (ICMTMA) (2021)
9. Albiansyah, A., Minkhatunnakhriyah, M.: The needs analysis of English in bina informatika vocational high school of bintaro as a basis to design English Teaching Materials (2021)
10. Wang, J.: Teaching design of integrated course of reading and writing based on in-depth learning in senior high school- take unit 3 computers as an example. J. High. Educ. Res. **2**(6), 3741–3754 (2021)

The Difference and Forecast Analysis of the Eastern and Western Economic Development Based on Big Data Information

Yan Liu[✉]

Inner Mongolia Honder College of Arts and Sciences Hohhot, Inner Mongolia Autonomous Region, Hohhot 010070, China
wjs060926@163.com

Abstract. China has a vast territory and a large population. Under the comprehensive action of many factors such as natural geography, history and humanities, regional differences and unbalanced development objectively exist, especially the large regional differences between the East and the West. Using the traditional hierarchical clustering method and the qualitative double clustering method with relatively outstanding performance, this paper makes an in-depth research, discussion and bold prediction on the economic regional division scheme and economic growth mode of each province in China. In recent years, the economic development gap between underdeveloped provinces in Western China and coastal provinces in eastern China has been quite prominent, which has attracted extensive attention from all walks of life. Economic development under the planned economic system has played a positive role.

Keywords: Cluster analysis · Economic differences · Forecast analysis

1 Introduction

Economic system refers to the specific economic organization form and economic management system adopted by socio-economic system or production relations, as well as the specific way of resource allocation. It determines how people should engage in economic activities on the basis of a certain social and economic system and under what mutual relationship [1]. It reflects the resource allocation mode adopted by social economy and determines the operation mechanism of the whole national economy. The economic system itself does not have the attribute of independent social system, and the mode is more flexible. The specific economic operation mode will change with the changes of productivity and socio-economic conditions.

As far as China is concerned, there has always been a regional gap, even in the period of implementing the "balanced development strategy" before the reform and opening up. Since the founding of new China, the eastern coastal region has always been the region with the highest level of economic development in China, while the western region has always been the last. In order to meet the needs of the strategy of opening

M. A. Jan and F. Khan (Eds.): BigIoT-EDU 2022, LNICST 467, pp. 299–305, 2023.
https://doi.org/10.1007/978-3-031-23944-1_33

to the outside world and proceed from the overall situation of accelerating national economic development, the state has made major adjustments to the regional economic development strategy and productivity layout, paid attention to macroeconomic benefits, made use of the regional advantages and strong economic development foundation of the eastern region, and implemented the infrastructure construction of the "unbalanced development strategy" and returning farmland (animal husbandry) to forests (grass) and the development of characteristic industries have achieved gratifying results. However, the current economic development gap between the East and the West still exists. In the past two years, the economic development of the East and the West has constituted the main content of this part.

There are many factors affecting economic growth, and the gap in economic development between the East and the west is not the result of a few factors acting alone. It is not only due to the congenital differences between the two regions, but also inseparable from the global economic environment and domestic economic policy changes during this period.

China's "western development" policy has narrowed the development gap between the East and the west to a certain extent, especially in some economic indicators related to GDP. However, paying too much attention to the energy industry and pursuing too much big investment may bring new problems to the western economy, and policymakers need to have a clear understanding of this.

2 Relevant Technical Analysis

2.1 Clustering Algorithm

Clustering is a process of dividing a data set into several groups or classes, and making the data objects in the same group have high similarity; while the data objects in different groups are not similar. The similar or dissimilar description is determined based on the value of the data description attribute. It is usually expressed by the distance between objects. Many fields, including data mining and statistics Both computer science and machine learning have clustering research and application.

Given a dataset containing n objects or data rows, the partition method divides the dataset into k subsets (partition). Each subset represents a cluster (K $\leq$ n). That is, the data is divided into k groups, which meet the following requirements: (a) each group should contain at least one object; and (b) each object must belong to only one group.

$$E_l = \sum_{i=1}^{n} y_{il} \sum_{j=1}^{m} (x_{ij}^r - q_{ij}^r)^2 + \gamma \sum_{i=1}^{n} y_{il} \sum_{j=1}^{m} \delta(x_{ij}^c - q_{ij}^c) \tag{1}$$

$$x_n = x(t_0 + n\Delta t) = h[z(t_0 + n\Delta t)] + \omega_n \tag{2}$$

$$\sum = diag(\delta_1, \delta_2, ..., \delta_i), \delta_i = \sqrt{\lambda_i}, \forall_i \neq j \tag{3}$$

It should be noted that the latter requirement can be relaxed in some fuzzy partition methods.

Given the number k to be divided, a division method creates an initial division, and then uses the circular relocation technology to change the division content by moving the objects in different divisions (groups). A good division measurement standard is usually that the objects in the same group are "close" or related to each other, while the objects in different groups are "far" Or different from each other. Of course, there are many other measures to judge the quality of division.

In order to obtain the global optimal results based on partition clustering analysis, it is necessary to enumerate all possible object partitions. Therefore, most applications use one or two common heuristic methods: (a) k-means algorithm, in which each cluster is represented by the mean of the objects in the corresponding cluster; (b) K-medoids algorithm, each cluster in the algorithm is represented by the object closest to the cluster center in the corresponding cluster. These heuristic clustering methods are effective in analyzing small and medium-sized data sets to find circular or spherical clusters. However, an obvious limitation of the algorithm is that users need to know the K value in advance, but in many cases, the K value is unpredictable. This also limits the application of partition algorithm in analyzing and processing large-scale data sets or complex data types.

2.2 Economic and Reasonable Prediction Technology

The simplest prediction method is to directly explain the trend based on the model. This prediction is the most direct and needs to determine the accuracy of the prediction method according to the ultimate purpose. This prediction assumes that the past trend and past seasonal fluctuations will continue, and also assumes that the trend and seasonal fluctuations are the dominant factors determining the economic indicators in the next few months. Is this assumption correct It really depends on many factors, including the extent to which the time series we consider are affected by cyclical factors and the extent to which the economy changes its cyclical position [2].

In order to reflect the potential overall changes in economic activities, we need to make necessary corrections to the prediction based on the model through leading indicators. These leading indicators refer to certain economic sequences, which always rise or fall before GDP. The National Bureau of economic research has conducted a detailed study on various economic variables and tried to find each variable The variables of whether they decline simultaneously or after the boom of the economic cycle, and whether they rise simultaneously or after the boom of the economic cycle, decline before the boom and rise before the depression are called the leading sequence (the variables that decline at the same time as the boom and rise at the same time as the depression are called the same period sequence, and the variables that decline after the boom and rise after the depression are called the lag sequence). According to the research that has been obtained, important leading sequences include durable consumer goods, stock prices, the number of unemployment insurance applications, etc., these variables tend to rise before the boom and decline before the depression (the same period series includes employment rate, industrial output, company profits, etc., and the typical lag series includes retail sales, personal income, etc.) For example, there is a solid reason why these leading sequences - or leading indicators begin to decline before prosperity and rise before depression: in some cases, the leading sequence indicates the expenditure of strategic sectors in the economy, thus showing the economic expectations of managers and investors. Leading indicators can be used as a sign of the upcoming economic turning point If a large number of leading indicators turn to decline, it can be regarded as a sign of the coming prosperity period. On the contrary, if a large number of leading indicators begin to rise, it may mark the coming depression period.

3 Difference and Prediction Analysis of Economic Development Between the East and the West Based on Clustering Algorithm

Data collection

The macroeconomic data of 31 provinces, cities and autonomous regions in China in recent 9 years were collected and sorted out, focusing on 17 economic indicators in the East and West (Table 1), the selection of indicators is mainly based on the indicators affecting the sustainable development of China's economic regions. The data of each year are from the National Statistical Yearbook, and some indicators are missing in some years, but this does not affect the clustering results as a whole.

Table 1. Query results of system

Serial number	Index	Serial number	Index
1	gross domestic product	1	Employed population of tertiary industry
2	Output value of primary industry	2	Local fiscal revenue
3	Output value of secondary industry	3	Local financial expenditure
4	Industrial output value	4	Living consumption expenditure of urban residents
5	Output value of construction industry	5	Urban per capita disposable income
6	Output value of tertiary industry	6	Living consumption expenditure of rural residents
7	Employed population	7	Rural per capita disposable income
8	Employed population in primary industry	8	Urban registered unemployed
9	Employed population in the secondary industry		

Because the economic analysis data in the East and West have both temporal and spatial characteristics, it is necessary to reduce the dimension of the data to make it suitable for cluster analysis. In this paper, two dimensionality reduction methods are used to generate two groups of new data. The indicators of each year are added with the year ID as new indicators, which reduces the data to the two-dimensional space of new indicators and provinces. This dimensionality reduction method can overcome the lack of information caused by averaging an index in a certain period of time [3].

Firstly, Eisenberg cluster3.0 is used to cluster the data. In this paper, the hierarchical clustering method embedded in the software is used.

The hierarchical clustering method first forms a tree structure according to the similarity of each object. The software provides the cores of four hierarchical clustering algorithms, namely centroid clustering, single Association clustering, full Association clustering and average Association clustering (see Fig. 1 for details).

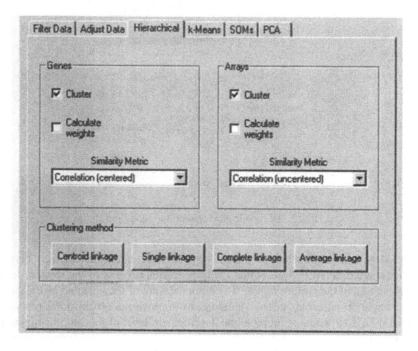

Fig. 1. Eisenberg cluster3.0 operation interface

The centroid of centroid clustering is the mean of all the elements in the cluster. Clustering is generated by maximizing the distance between two clusters. In the single Association clustering algorithm, the distance between two clusters X and Y is the minimum pairwise distance between all elements contained between X and y. The distance of fully correlated clustering is the maximum of the paired element distance between two clusters. The distance between two clusters is the mean of the distance between all paired elements. The clustering results of data3 by cluster3.0 are shown in Fig. 2 below. It can be seen from the pedigree on the left of the figure that some provinces have strong similarities and are clustered into one class, and the distance between classes is relatively large. In the heat map in the middle, the red area represents the area with relatively high economic development level, the green area represents the area with relatively low economic development level, and the black area is the middle area. The economic situation of provinces and cities can be clearly read out from the heat map. Areas with the same or similar colors are mostly clustered into one category, indicating that they belong to similar provinces and cities with a high degree of similarity. The economic gap between the East and the west is shown in Fig. 2 below.

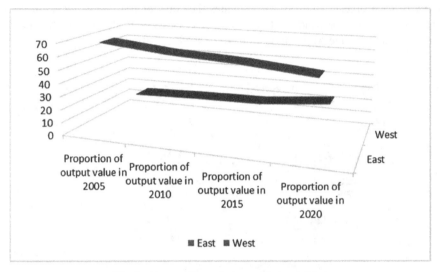

Fig. 2. Economic gap between East and West

One of the main manifestations of the differences in economic development between the eastern and western regions is that the urbanization process of the western region lags behind that of the eastern region. The main measure of urbanization process is the level of regional industrialization. Therefore, to improve the urbanization process of the western region, we must promote the development level of industrialization in the western region [4].

However, in the process of industrialization in China's western region, the western region should absorb the costs paid by the eastern region in the process of industrialization, such as environmental pollution. Therefore, the industrialization process of the western region is different from that of the eastern region. The western region should take the new road of industrialization. Through the new road of industrialization, the western region can obtain rapid development and avoid the cost paid by the eastern region.

4   Conclusion

In this paper, the hierarchical clustering method in the clustering algorithm is used for cluster analysis. This method first clusters the objects with high similarity into small classes, and then gradually reduces the similarity level and expands the cluster scale. The software Eisenberg cluster 3.0 can easily make a heat map for analyzing the results. In terms of economic development speed, there has been a long-term difference between East and West China, and the development of the East has always been ahead of the West. After the founding of the people's Republic of China, in the process of China's two institutional changes, that is, the establishment of the planned economic system and the market economic system, there are differences in China's economic policies between the East and the West. This difference makes the difference in development speed between the eastern and western regions change.

References

1. Ling, S., Xiuli, W.: Overview of China's economic regional division. Xinjiang Finan. Econ. **2**, p. 47-49 (2000)
2. Juan, Y., Changquan, W., Bing, L., Qiquan, L., Weiping, S.: Self organizing competitive neural network and its application in socio-economic zoning. J. Southwest Normal Univ. (Nat. Sci. Edn.) **32**(4), 98–103 (2017)
3. Xuemei, L., Suqin, Z.: Application of cluster analysis technology in data mining. J. Wuhan Univ. (Eng. Edn.) **6**, 396–399 (2009)
4. Yongming, Z.: Study on the division of ecological and economic types in Shandong Province. J. Ningxia Univ. (Nat. Sci. Edn.) **6**, 189–192 (2009)

The Influence of Computer Aided System Teaching on Vocabulary Learning

Jing Liu[✉]

Heilongjiang East University, Harbin 150080, Heilongjiang, China
1366991072@qq.com

Abstract. Computer assisted instruction (CAI) has been widely used in the practice of vocabulary learning in classroom teaching. The methods of vocabulary learning in teaching and the modes of vocabulary learning in teaching have diversified Aiming at the main links of vocabulary learning in college classroom teaching, this paper puts forward the design idea of a practical computer-aided system TCAS for vocabulary learning in college teaching, and uses vfp9 0 to reduce teachers' repeated work and improve the quality of vocabulary learning in teaching. The database design adopts the classic case tool set Sybase PowerDesigner, and gives the main data table structure The experimental results show that when TCAS is used in the actual teaching of operating system and other courses, only a small amount of key information needs to be input or imported into each teaching link of vocabulary learning; At the same time, TCAS has a convenient user interface. In terms of the relationship between vocabulary richness and writing quality, vocabulary variability, vocabulary complexity and vocabulary density are significantly positively correlated with writing quality, and vocabulary errors are significantly negatively correlated with writing quality. TCAS can better meet the needs of College Teaching for vocabulary learning.

Keywords: Computer · College English · Lexical variability · Auxiliary system teaching

1 Introduction

Based on the intelligent adaptive learning engine of artificial intelligence, that is, intelligent adaptive teaching robot, the computer-aided system adjusts the teaching strategy according to the students' state, emotion and ability, and carries out a relaxed classroom teaching rhythm, so as to maintain the students' concentration, improve the learning efficiency, balance the regional differences, and let each child obtain the same high-quality education.

Vocabulary plays an important role in language teaching and learning. In the past three decades, the research on second language writing has attracted more and more foreign scholars' interest. The research fields include the writing process, teachers' and learners' attitudes, practices and beliefs, the social environment inside and outside the classroom, and the most striking is the research on the measurement and analysis of

M. A. Jan and F. Khan (Eds.): BigIoT-EDU 2022, LNICST 467, pp. 306–317, 2023.
https://doi.org/10.1007/978-3-031-23944-1_34

written discourse characteristics, including the accuracy, complexity Fluency, lexical features, overall quality and content of writing. In recent years, China has also carried out relevant research, covering a wide range.

In formal learning, the system will first accurately locate each student's knowledge points through knowledge map and information theory, make a clear picture of each student's learning situation, and use algorithms and technologies to understand the specific learning vulnerabilities, knowledge points, short boards, current advantages of 50% of the students, or 95% of the learning tyrants, and then under the ability shown by the scores, Whether there are still unclear knowledge points and detailed loopholes or expansion space in practical skills, and then continuously and more accurately push the topics and contents consistent with students' knowledge points to students through machine learning and genetic algorithm, so as to distribute them to thousands of people and make personalized recommendations to different students, that is, teach students according to their aptitude, So that students will not waste their time on the knowledge points they have mastered, so as to improve students' learning efficiency.

In order to support the accurate positioning of knowledge points, the knowledge points are divided into nanoscale parts in terms of content. Measured by effectiveness, if a knowledge point is not used, it is not necessary to disassemble it; If you can use it, you can't disassemble it too carefully, so as to achieve the effect of efficient learning.

In formal learning, the system will first accurately locate each student's knowledge points through knowledge map and information theory, make a clear picture of each student's learning situation, and use algorithms and technologies to understand the specific learning vulnerabilities, knowledge points, short boards, current advantages of 50% of the students, or 95% of the learning tyrants, and then under the ability shown by the scores [1], Whether there are still unclear knowledge points and detailed loopholes or expansion space in practical skills, and then continuously and more accurately push the topics and contents consistent with students' knowledge points to students through machine learning and genetic algorithm, so as to distribute them to thousands of people and make personalized recommendations to different students, that is, teach students according to their aptitude, So that students will not waste their time on the knowledge points they have mastered, so as to improve students' learning efficiency.

In order to support the accurate positioning of knowledge points, the knowledge points are divided into nanoscale parts in terms of content. Measured by effectiveness, if a knowledge point is not used, it is not necessary to disassemble it; If you can use it, you can't disassemble it too carefully, so as to achieve the effect of efficient learning.

Through the precise positioning of the computer-aided system, according to the situation of children, the follow-up learning focuses on reading, mainly focusing on the knowledge points focusing on overall reading, and carries out systematic learning. Taking the role of environmental description as an example, the knowledge points are required to point out the role of environmental description based on the scene description and the role of environmental description on the plot based on the article structure, Based on the characterization of the characters, it points out the role of environmental description on the characters, and points out the role of environmental description on the theme based on the content and central idea of the article. It is a compound and high knowledge point. Then before learning this knowledge point, we will first learn the techniques of lyricism by scenery and the methods of depicting the hearts of characters, so as to improve the learning efficiency of comprehensive knowledge points.

With the continuous development and innovation of computer and artificial intelligence, computer-aided system is also rising day by day, and plays an important role in all walks of life. Computer aided system is a general term used to assist in completing various tasks. It involves many industries, such as education, engineering, manufacturing, translation, design, etc. from people's daily life to military activities, it is inseparable from the help of computer aided system [2]. The application of computer-aided system in education is also increasing, and has great effect.

Cai aided instruction is a system used by computer to assist teaching and vocabulary learning. Its main way is to provide convenient teaching for students and teachers. The way of vocabulary learning has changed from the traditional education mode of using blackboard and books and teaching materials to the current use of high technology, including but not limited to multimedia and artificial intelligence, Database and remote network. Through this kind of education mode relying on computer-aided system, we can increase students' interest, improve teachers' educational level and improve the quality of vocabulary learning in teaching. Now, more and more schools have applied CAI to vocabulary learning, and the effect is remarkable.

2   Related Work

2.1   Computer Data Analysis Technology

Data mining is a process of selecting, exploring and modeling a large amount of data in order to find unknown rules and relationships in advance. The purpose of data mining is to obtain clear and useful results for data owners. Data mining is the core technology of discovering knowledge from database. It is developed from machine learning of artificial intelligence. Taking the database as the research object, combined with the traditional statistical analysis method, fuzzy mathematics method and scientific computing visualization technology, the method and technology of data mining are formed.

Data mining methods include decision tree method, set theory method, neural network method, genetic algorithm and so on. Decision tree method uses the principle of information theory to establish decision tree. This method has good effect and great influence. The knowledge representation obtained by this method is decision tree.

Decision tree is a tree structure with sample attributes as nodes and attribute values as branches. The root node is the attribute with the largest amount of information in all samples, the middle node of the tree is the attribute with the largest amount of information in the sample subset contained in the subtree with the node as the root, and the leaf node is the category value of the sample. Data mining is an indispensable part of knowledge discovery in database (KDD), and KDD is the whole process of converting unprocessed data into useful information. This process includes a series of conversion steps, from data preprocessing to post-processing of data mining results, as shown in Fig. 1 below.

Fig. 1. The whole process of converting data into useful information

ID algorithm is the earliest and most influential decision tree method in the world. Its basic algorithm is greedy algorithm. It constructs a decision tree through top-down recursion. The information gain measure is used to select test attributes on each node of the tree. Select the attribute with the highest information gain as the test attribute of the current node [3].

Let's be a collection of s data samples. Assuming that the category label attribute has m different values, define m different CI (I = 1,2,..., m). If Si is the number of samples in category Ci and PI is the probability that any sample belongs to CI, the expected information of a given sample classification is as follows:

$$I(s_1, s_2, \cdots s_m) = -\sum_{i=1}^{m} P_i \log_2(P_i) \tag{1}$$

Assuming that attribute a has V different values, we can divide s into v subsets {S1, S2,... SV}, where SJ contains some samples in s, which have a on a. If a is selected as the test attribute, these subsets correspond to branches growing from nodes containing set s. Let SIJ be the number of samples of class CI in subset SJ, and then divide the entropy or expected information into subsets according to attribute a, as follows:

$$E(A) = \sum_{i=1}^{v} \frac{S_{ij} + \cdots + S_{mj}}{S} I(S_{ij}, \cdots, S_{mj}) \tag{2}$$

The smaller the entropy, the higher the degree of subset division. Then, the information gain of branch A is as follows:

$$G(A) = I(s_1, s_2, \cdots, s_m) - E(A) \tag{3}$$

This ID3 algorithm tends to choose attributes with more values, because the weighted sum method makes the classification of instance sets tend to abandon data tuples with a small amount of data. However, attributes with more values are not always the best attributes. In other words, according to the principles of entropy minimization and information gain maximization, ID3 algorithm lists the attributes that ID3 algorithm should choose, and testing it will not provide too much information.

Set a as the selection attribute, a has five attribute values, and the corresponding weight is. According to ID3 algorithm, attribute a is extended and the corresponding information entropy is obtained. Then, the weighted entropy is defined as:

$$E(A)^* = \sum_{i=1}^{v} \omega_i \times E(B_i) \tag{4}$$

where (B1, B2, BV) is ν The attribute of node selection refers to the weight of the subset. Calculate the weight according to the proportion of subset Bi in the whole set, then calculate the weighting entropy, and select the attribute value by comparing the weighting entropy [4].

In addition, ID3 algorithm is improved to simplify the complexity of information calculation.

Firstly, the basic properties of logP function are studied. Through research, it can be proved that the calculation formula of information is a convex function, so the calculation formula of information can be improved by using the unique properties of convex function. After the model is completed, the model user (customer) will package and meet the use requirements of the business system according to the current background and target completion, as shown in Fig. 2 below.

Fig. 2. Encapsulate and meet the business system

2.2 Computer Aided Instruction System

Computer aided system originated from the United States. Now the United States is still one of the countries with the most sound development and the most widely used CAI in the world. During the development period of 40 years, CAI has mainly experienced five development stages. The first was in the 1950s, when computers had just begun to develop and Cai had just begun to develop. At this time, books such as computer-assisted instruction on vocabulary learning technology appeared. But at this time, because computers are not widely popular, CAI has not sprung up. The second stage was in the 1970s. With the research on vocabulary learning system by computer-aided instruction, the first computer-aided instruction on vocabulary learning system appeared, that is, ibm1500 teaching on vocabulary learning system. However, due to the limitations of conditions and venues, this system is also applied in Stanford University and is not widely used. By the late 1970s, the scope of CAI was expanded to specific subjects, such as mathematics, physics and so on. In the 1980s, with the rise of microcomputers, computers have become teachers' teaching tools for vocabulary learning. At this time, Cai developed greatly and was gradually valued by people. Finally, in the 1990s, with the emergence of multimedia computers, CAI can have a higher development. It can carry out sound transmission, image processing and so on, which has become the development direction of multimedia computers.

Computer aided system is mainly composed of three parts: computer hardware, system software and course software.

In the computer hardware, the main equipment includes but is not limited to projectors, screens, booths, control computers, active speakers, etc.[5]. Computer hardware is the most important part of computer aided system. It can be said that the main development of CAI system is closely related to the improvement of computer hardware level. Therefore, computer hardware is the basis of the whole CAI.

The system software of CAI mainly includes operating system, language processing system, various tool software and writing system. Among them, the system software is an important part of the whole CAI. It can provide functions such as word processing, animation production, video recording, courseware generation and so on, which provides convenience for classrooms and students. For example, our commonly used PowerPoint software is a typical system software. Through this software, teachers can play various courseware in the form of slides and animation to improve students' understanding ability and facilitate students to understand and master relevant key knowledge. Now, CAI can also have software to automatically generate courseware. Teachers don't have to work hard to make courseware by themselves, insert dynamic diagram and voice, but can directly generate the desired courseware through the system to reduce the burden of teachers.

The course software of CAI system is an application software for teaching vocabulary learning, which is compiled according to the teacher's requirements or learning requirements of each school. For example, English course software is common, including voice reading and after-school exercises, while mathematics course software mainly includes after-school exercises and answers, derivation of basic mathematical process, etc.

3 The Influence of Computer-Aided System Teaching on Vocabulary Learning

Compared with traditional English teaching on vocabulary learning, data-driven learning has the main characteristics of autonomy, cooperation, interaction and inquiry. The application of "Data-Driven Learning" model in vocabulary learning in College English teaching is conducive to students' sustainable personalized learning methods and autonomous learning ability.

Database technology is a core technology of information system. It is a method of computer-aided data management. It studies how to organize and store data, and how to obtain and process data efficiently. It is a technology that studies the basic theories and implementation methods of database structure, storage, design, management and application, and uses these theories to process, analyze and understand the data in the database. Namely: database technology is a software science that studies, manages and applies database [6].

(1) Innovate the vocabulary learning mode of teaching and learning, and improve the quality and efficiency of College English vocabulary teaching and learning
(2) With the help of big data technology, visual teaching can be used for vocabulary learning, and hybrid teaching can be used for vocabulary learning. 2. Promote positive interaction between teachers and students and stimulate students' interest in learning. Big data technology can provide an effective entry point for teaching and vocabulary learning interaction between teachers and students. At the same time, the accurate teaching and learning of College English vocabulary can increase students' scores to a great extent, which not only improves students' ability, but also improves teachers' prestige and position in students' hearts, so as to better reflect teachers' functions of "learning to solve doubts" and "teaching and educating people".
(3) Based on the needs of students. Students can find the weak point in their practice in the "intelligent question bank" of big data technology, and then find the relevant practice of the weak point in the question bank of big data technology for re practice and re test, so as to realize accurate self-study.
(4) With the help of big data technology learning tracking table, teachers can timely understand the learning situation and realize data-driven precision teaching for vocabulary learning. After the students submit their practice answers, the teacher can immediately see the students' answers, such as
(5) One question can be based on the vocabulary learning of the class in one teaching, aiming at the situation of students, etc. Teachers can make mistakes according to the weak points of students in the class
    Carry out personalized and accurate tutoring for questions.
(6) Teaching has a significant effect on vocabulary learning. After two years of vocabulary precise teaching and vocabulary learning practice based on big data technology, the average English score of the class taught by the author is 12 points higher than that of other classes at the same level. Students' vocabulary has been greatly increased, their ability to understand sentences and chapters has been greatly improved, and their comprehensive level of English listening, speaking, reading and writing has been improved.

The object of database technology research and management is data, so the specific contents involved in database technology mainly include: through the unified organization and management of data, establish corresponding database and data warehouse according to the specified structure; Using the database management system and data mining system, a data management and data mining application system which can add, modify, delete, process, analyze, understand, report and print the data in the database is designed; And finally realize the data processing, analysis and understanding by using the application management system. The database management system is the core of the database system. All operations of the database, such as loading, retrieving, updating and reorganizing the original data, are carried out under the command and scheduling of the DBMS. It is the bridge between the user and the physical database, and performs the necessary operations on the database according to the widely used commands.

(7) Promote the co creation and sharing of high-quality resources, and promote the accurate teaching of College English vocabulary to improve the level of vocabulary learning

The "teaching and Research Center" in big data technology provides backbone teachers everywhere with lesson sharing and discussion of various types of courses The live broadcast of vocabulary learning exchange seminars at all levels of teaching provides a lot of resources and platforms for teachers to learn from each other and choose more suitable teaching methods (Personalized English Teaching for vocabulary learning) [7]. The author often observes some lessons, lectures and interviews on vocabulary learning in College English vocabulary precision teaching, so as to improve his teaching and research level of vocabulary learning. For example:

1. Big data technology effectively carried out a series of network training activities such as "one classroom", "backbone training class" and realized the wide sharing of high-quality resources of famous teachers.
2. Online and offline three-dimensional training has innovated a new model of teacher training.
3. Organize experts to go deep into the front line and promote the implementation of application.

The emergence of database system is a significant progress in computer data processing technology. It has the following three characteristics: first, data sharing. Data sharing means that multiple users or applications can access the data in the same database at the same time without affecting each other. Multiple applications do not conflict when accessing, accessing and operating the database at the same time, so as to ensure that the data is not damaged; Second, reduce data redundancy. Data redundancy is the repetition of data. Data redundancy not only wastes storage space, but also easily leads to data inconsistency. In the database system, the data has been structured according to the specific data model. In the database, the user's logical data file and specific physical data file do not have to correspond one by one, which effectively saves storage resources, reduces data redundancy and enhances the consistency of data. Third, good data independence. The so-called data independence means that data and application are independent of each other, and there is no interdependence between them. Applications do not have to change with the change of data storage structure, which is one of the most basic characteristics of database [8].

The influence of computer aided system teaching on College English vocabulary teaching method.

1. Pay attention to spelling. English belongs to Pinyin characters. Spelling and spelling are closely related. Using spelling rules to remember words is a more scientific and practical method for English vocabulary learning, which can help students standardize pronunciation and spelling. Teachers should help students find and master the pronunciation rules of vowels and consonants in words and the spelling rules of common letter combinations through a lot of spelling exercises, so that students can infer the pronunciation of words according to the rules and rules and understand the relationship between sound and form. Develop the ability to read and write words when you see words and hear sounds. This method can be implemented from the first day of junior high school. Write down the phonetic symbols next to the letters, teach the students to spell the phonetic symbols step by step, and the students will gradually master the rules of this spelling.

2. Create situations. Lu Shuxiang, a famous linguist, said: words must be embedded in the context before they have life, easy to remember and know their usage. Without context, any word will become meaningless. Context includes sentence, text and context, as well as understanding in a specific cultural context. In recent years, it has been a trend in the test of word use. Creating situations can be refined and integrated according to the relevant topics involved in the textbook, so that students can use and learn in the situation, and then reorganize the review module. This process is actually to build a vocabulary network under the topic. In this way, the originally isolated words have a meaningful connection with words in the topic presentation, and in this presentation, middle school students also use words to communicate thinking while completing various activities, rather than just memorizing mechanically [9]. Dewey, an American pragmatist educator, once advocated that the curriculum should be consistent with students' life experience, so that students can master the knowledge to solve practical problems, and advocated "learning by doing".

There are two modes of database system, one is desktop system, the other is web-based system website. The former does not need the help of the network. After the system is released, there is a desktop icon. Users can enter the login world by double clicking the icon, so it is called desktop system. It only needs -- one client to run. However, because it is not connected with the outside world, the administrator needs to copy the updated system to all users after maintaining the database, which is the key reason why the system does not adopt the desktop system. The web-based system website can well avoid this disadvantage. The system adopts the web-based B/S mode to publish the designed system to the server. The server will assign a website, and the user can log in to the system website by clicking the generated website. Users log in as administrators and can update the database information. Ordinary users can see the updated information of administrators on their own host, which is in line with the original intention of website resource sharing of the system and allows users to experience convenient and fast information services. However, according to the needs of users, if users need to break through the restrictions of the network, the system can be changed to the mode of desktop system.

4   Simulation Analysis

The process of memorizing English words is the process of information storage and retrieval. Cognitive psychology believes that any memory will improve with the increase of processing times, because multiple processing can provide more retrieval routes for memory. The more fully processed, the better the memory effect, that is, memory is closely proportional to the quality of information processing.

Finishing strategy refers to a strategy to understand the deep meaning of learning materials and promote memory through in-depth and detailed analysis and processing of learning materials. The key of finishing strategy is to connect the existing experience in the learner's mind with the vocabulary to be learned, and make full use of the existing experience to deeply process the words to be learned, so as to make them reasonable and meaningful, so as to achieve the purpose of understanding and memory [10]. The familiar mother tongue knowledge or foreign language knowledge that learners have mastered, the vivid image in their mind and a variety of other relevant knowledge and experience can be used as the existing experience.

The most commonly used finishing strategy is association. Association can be divided into affixation Association, contrast Association, relationship Association, proximity Association, similarity association and so on. According to psychology, association reflects the relationship between objective things. It plays an important role in promoting people's mental activities such as memory, imagination and thinking. When using association to learn vocabulary, we can establish an interdependent knowledge structure in the brain through series classification, vertical and horizontal connection, discrimination and decomposition, so as to overcome forgetting and enhance memory. For example, using the same root word (prefix, suffix) memory is a common associative memory method. Derivation is an important word formation in English. It adds a prefix or suffix, or both prefix and suffix, to the root or stem of a word, resulting in a series of homonyms with different parts of speech or different meanings. These homonyms are usually called a "word family". Therefore, if you can remember the root word and master the basic meaning of the pre suffix, you can remember some words.

Therefore, when learners' vocabulary reaches a certain number, they can refine vocabulary, that is, word pronunciation, spelling, grammatical category, contextual meaning and its vertical and horizontal aggregation relationship. Learners form a knowledge network through autonomous and systematic finishing process and activate deep memory.

Vocabulary learning is a very important part of English language learning and the basis of English language [11]. Learners should fully realize its importance, play their positive role, consciously cultivate vocabulary learning and memory strategies, and change the previous single learning mode. At the same time, learners should consider that there are considerable individual differences due to age, personality, gender and other factors. Therefore, the choice of vocabulary learning strategies should vary from person to person.

According to word formation, English vocabulary can be divided into simple words, derivative words and compound words. Simple words are composed of a single free morpheme, mainly short words, such as hand, foot and so on. Such words account for a small number in English vocabulary, but they appear frequently and have strong derivation ability, so they are the main body of English basic vocabulary. Derivatives are formed by root affixes. Root is the basis of derivative words. The same root plus different affixes can mean different meanings or different parts of speech. Compound words are usually composed of two or more free morphemes, mainly compound nouns, compound adjectives, compound adverbs and so on.

According to its grammatical function, English vocabulary is divided into closed parts of speech and open parts of speech. Closed parts of speech refer to all functional words. This kind of words have no complete lexical meaning, but have grammatical meaning; They are limited in number, relatively stable and rarely proliferated, so the word item sequence can not be extended arbitrarily, so they are called "closed parts of speech". They mainly include prepositions, pronouns, determiners, conjunctions and auxiliary verbs [12]. Open parts of speech refer to various substantive words, which are constantly enriched and developed with the development of society, economy and culture. In this kind of words, new words continue to appear, old words continue to disappear or obtain new meanings, so the word item sequence can continue to extend, so it is called "open parts of speech". They include nouns, adjectives and verbs. In addition, there are cardinal words. Ordinal words and exclamations are parts of speech between "closed" and "open". The following Fig. 3 shows the development of vocabulary learning code by computer-aided system.

```
if (rw == BX_WRITE || rw == BX_RW) {
  taint::mark_init(lin, len);
  return;
} else {
  taint::access_type ac_type = taint::check_access(pcpu, lin, len);
  if (ac_type == taint::ACCESS_VALID) {
    return;
  } else if (ac_type == taint::METADATA_PADDING_MISMATCH) {
    taint::mark_init(lin, len);
    return;
  } else {
    // The last case - taint::ACCESS_INVALID in handled further on in the
    // function.
  }
}
```

Fig. 3. Development part code

5   Conclusion

Vocabulary plays an important role in language acquisition. According to the requirements of College English curriculum standards, the teaching mode adapting to the times should be based on modern information technology, and even connected with the body of network technology. The application of computer-aided system teaching technology driven learning model in College English vocabulary precise teaching has become a trend. Computer aided system teaching technology collects a large number of real language materials, uses advanced retrieval software to quickly analyze the data with large amount of information, and gives answers and analysis in real time, which can play a great auxiliary role in Teachers' teaching and students' learning. In a word, CAI technology is especially suitable for College English vocabulary teaching, such as word meaning and word structure in different contexts Collocation makes college English vocabulary teaching more accurate.

Acknowledgements. Financially supported by Scientific Research Project of Heilongjiang East University: An Empirical Study on the Relationship Between Input Patterns and Output Ability of English Vocabulary (Project No. HDFKY200207).

References

1. Nguyen, P.T., Huynh, V., Vo, K.D., et al.: An optimal deep learning based computer-aided diagnosis system for diabetic retinopathy. Comput. Mater. Continua **66**(3), 2815–2830 (2021)
2. Tan, H., Xu, H., Yu, N., et al.: The value of deep learning-based computer aided diagnostic system in improving diagnostic performance of rib fractures in acute blunt trauma (2021)
3. Weng, Y.: The role and impact of deep learning methods in computer-aided diagnosis using gastrointestinal endoscopy. Diagnostics **11**, 2214–2226 (2021)
4. Cui, X., Zheng, S., Heuvelmans, M., et al.: P42.02 Evaluating the feasibility of a deep learning-based computer-aided detection system for lung nodule detection in a lung cancer screening program. J. Thoracic Oncology **16**(3), S477–S478 (2021)
5. Venkatraman, K., Slama, M., Taupin, V., et al.: Tuning critical resolved shear stress ratios for bcc-titanium Ti21S via an automated data analysis approach. Model. Simul. Mater. Sci. Eng. **29**(5), 055014 (2021)
6. Duan, X., Zhu, X., Wang, L.: A prospective data analysis of targeted therapy combined with concurrent radiation therapy for brain metastasis from NSCLC with driver gene mutation. J. Clin. Oncol. **39**(15_suppl), e14006-e14006 (2021)
7. Pan, S., Qin, B., Bi, L., et al.: An unsupervised learning method for the detection of genetically modified crops based on terahertz spectral data analysis. Secur. Commun. Netw. **2021**(3), 1–7 (2021)
8. Yang, S., Liu, X., Zheng, Z., et al.: Fusing medical image features and clinical features with deep learning for computer-aided diagnosis (2021)
9. Mu, S.L., Yong, S.K., Kim, M., et al.: Evaluation of the feasibility of explainable computer-aided detection of cardiomegaly on chest radiographs using deep learning. Sci. Rep. **11**(1), 125–138 (2021)
10. Andrade, D., Ribeiro, L., Lopes, A., et al.: Machine learning associated with respiratory oscillometry: a computer-aided diagnosis system for the detection of respiratory abnormalities in systemic sclerosis. BioMed. Eng. OnLine **20**(1), 2254–2268 (2021)
11. Xq, A., Fy, B., Lei, Z.A., et al.: Computer-aided diagnosis of breast cancer in ultrasonography images by deep learning (2021)
12. Brown, J., Mansour, N.M., Pu, W., et al.: Deep learning computer-aided polyp detection reduces adenoma miss rate: a united states multi-center randomized tandem colonoscopy study (CADeT-CS Trial) - ScienceDirect (2021)

The Reform of Accounting Education in Colleges and Universities Based on Cloud Computing in the Era of Big Data

Liguang Li[✉]

Shandong College of Traditional Chinese Medicine, Jinan 264199, Shandong, China
jcsjc2732@163.com

Abstract. With the rapid development of China's economy, accounting education in Colleges and universities has also achieved long-term development, with the continuous expansion of education scale, the continuous improvement of teaching system and the increasing improvement of teaching quality. Accounting education has played an important role in promoting national economic construction. However, with the development of economic globalization, accounting education presents many problems that are inappropriate to social development. Accounting education must be reformed. Starting from changing the concept of accounting education in Colleges and universities, this paper makes a preliminary discussion on how to give full play to the advantages of cloud computing, build a cloud accounting education platform and change the accounting education mode in Colleges and Universities under the background of the big data era.

Keywords: Big data · Cloud computing · College accounting education · Accounting education reform

1 Introduction

With the rapid development of science and technology, the development of information technology is changing with each passing day, and the era of big data has come, which will have a far-reaching impact on the development of all walks of life, especially in the accounting field dealing with numbers. In order to adapt to the development of the big data era, the accounting methods, business processes and working principles of accounting work need to keep pace with the times, which undoubtedly intensifies the demand for data analysis accounting talents in all walks of life. In view of the many characteristics of big data, in order to give full play to the role of big data, new computing models need to be adopted, and cloud computing, as a new network infrastructure, provides a basic platform for the collection, storage, call and analysis of big data[1]. As the cradle of professional accounting talents to cultivate and promote cloud accounting, college accounting education, how to comply with the trend of the big data era, use cloud computing, reform the traditional accounting education concept and mode, and cultivate comprehensive accounting talents that meet the requirements of the times, is a major topic.

M. A. Jan and F. Khan (Eds.): BigIoT-EDU 2022, LNICST 467, pp. 318–323, 2023.
https://doi.org/10.1007/978-3-031-23944-1_35

2   Problems in Accounting Education in Colleges and Universities in China

(1) The goal of accounting education is not clear. The current accounting education environment is complex, which makes it difficult to determine the goal of accounting education. Whether to teach theoretical knowledge or cultivate ability, accounting education is facing a dilemma. When determining the objectives of accounting education, the adaptability to the environment is still far from enough, and the objectives of accounting education can not be adjusted in time according to the changes of the environment. If the traditional teaching methods continue to be used, it is obvious that they can not meet the needs of the new educational environment. Therefore, the primary task of accounting education is to establish educational objectives that meet the current development needs and make them develop according to the established educational objectives.

(2) The accounting teaching system is not perfect. Under the influence of traditional forms of education, the education system of accounting discipline in China before the 1990s was set up according to the development needs of the industry, resulting in the repetition of teaching contents, which is not conducive to the improvement of students' ability, and makes students mistakenly think that they can master the essence of accounting as long as they memorize by rote, without knowing the accounting theory and process analysis contained therein. Since the 1990s, colleges and universities have changed the setting of accounting education system guided by industry, and determined the curriculum design of accounting specialty with the basic contents involved in accounting. After the test of time, this curriculum system still exposed many inappropriate problems, mainly focusing on accounting and neglecting analysis, which can not meet the needs of the development of educational objectives, Constructing a perfect accounting education system has become one of the important tasks at present.

(3) Accounting teaching level is fuzzy. China's accounting education covers a wide range, including talents at all levels from junior college to doctor, but it exposes an obvious problem, that is, the educational level is vague, the boundary is not clear, the accounting education content from low education to high education has only superficial differences but no deep-seated differences, and the educational objectives at all levels are not clear enough to reflect the differences of accounting talents at all levels, It can not meet the needs of accounting talents at different levels[2].

(4) The setting of accounting specialty. At present, the setting of Accounting Specialty in China is characterized by too detailed division of specialty and too emphasis on the practicability of specialty. Talent training shows the defect of single knowledge structure, which is contrary to the high quality and high ability required in the educational goal. In addition to accounting computerization and audit accounting, many colleges and universities also set up many non-standard majors, which will only occupy students' time to obtain accounting knowledge and is a huge waste of material and human resources.

(5) The effectiveness of accounting teaching practice. At present, there is a lack of unified practice units for accounting majors in Colleges and universities in China,

and enterprises have not established long-term cooperative relations with schools, so that students' practice can not be guaranteed; On the other hand, due to the constraints of practice environment and practice funds, the effectiveness of practice is limited. At the same time, due to the unreasonable setting of the curriculum system, the practical time is replaced by theoretical teaching or the teaching practice is implemented, but the effect is not obvious, and the effect of practical teaching can not be effectively improved.

3 Establish a Cloud Accounting Education Platform and Reform the Accounting Education Model

In order to meet the challenges of big data and cloud accounting to accounting education in Colleges and universities, the author believes that accounting education in Colleges and universities must make changes in order to cultivate comprehensive accounting talents who can adapt to accounting jobs when they step out of school.

3.1 Clarify Talent Training Objectives and Improve Data Literacy

Based on the background of big data, accounting education in Colleges and universities must change the concept and clarify the goal of cultivating students: Based on the cultivation of accounting ability, supplemented by the cultivation of interpersonal relationship and the application of modern scientific and technological means, and centered on the cultivation of accounting management ability, cultivate comprehensive accounting talents suitable for the development needs of the times. That is, increase the students' ability to use data mining software for data analysis and processing in the face of massive data, improve the practical operation ability of cloud accounting system, and improve the students' management ability to use accounting knowledge to serve enterprises and institutions.

Strengthen the construction of teaching staff and improve data literacy. Firstly, we can strengthen technical training by means of practical exercise, exchange training and multi-party cooperation to improve teachers' data analysis and processing ability. Secondly, on the basis of improving data literacy, vigorously carry out scientific research activities of accounting teachers in Colleges and universities to improve their scientific research ability [3]. Encourage accounting teachers to use modern technology to conduct interdisciplinary and inter institutional cooperative research on topics and make contributions to social development. Thirdly, introduce and reserve excellent comprehensive talents to realize mutual assistance and mutual learning among accounting teachers, so as to cultivate a team of accounting education teachers to adapt to the data age. Finally, the corresponding evaluation mechanism should be established to assess the mastery of teachers in all aspects. Only in this way can college accounting teachers introduce cloud accounting resources and new technologies and knowledge systems into teaching, combine accounting theory with the requirements of big data, innovate teaching methods and methods, achieve teaching objectives and promote discipline innovation and development.

3.2   Give Full Play to the Advantages of Cloud Computing and Build a Cloud Accounting Education Platform

Based on SPI framework, under three deployment modes of public cloud, private cloud and hybrid cloud, cloud computing provides users with three service payment modes in the fields of high-performance computing, finance and network, namely infrastructure as a service, platform as a service and software as a service. In the actual situation that the cost of completely building a private cloud is high and most colleges and universities are short of funds for accounting education, colleges and universities can use hybrid cloud to apply cloud computing to the field of accounting education in Colleges and universities, just like enterprises build cloud accounting. Although some software companies have developed accounting cloud learning platforms, most of them have moved the traditional accounting application to the cloud platform. The systems are independent of each other, mainly aiming at the accounting analysis of structured data. The cases can not be updated in time, which is essentially different from the cloud education platform built by cloud computing in this paper.

Constructing cloud accounting education platform is the inevitable trend of the development of accounting education in Colleges and universities. Accounting Majors in Colleges and universities can purchase online cloud computing services from cloud computing suppliers, use the infrastructure (servers, etc.) provided by suppliers to develop network applications for accounting education, rent data analysis and other software required in the cloud, and connect with enterprise cloud accounting system on the basis of information security to realize real-time data sharing. According to the actual teaching needs, modules including accounting data system, accounting teaching system, cloud accounting simulation operating system, mobile terminal system and so on can be established on the accounting education platform. As shown in Fig. 1.

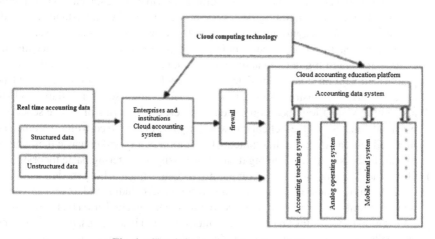

Fig. 1. Cloud accounting education platform

The cloud accounting education platform connects the modules through the accounting data system, and the modules are extensible. Each module can design several sub modules according to actual needs. The data of the accounting data system comes from both the data generated in teaching and the sharable data generated by cloud accounting of enterprises and institutions. On the premise of ensuring the security of business secrets of enterprises and institutions, the data of actual enterprises and institutions are updated to the database in time, and the structured and unstructured data are stored, analyzed and processed through data analysis software.

Accounting teaching system, which can be divided into classroom teaching system, effect control system and so on. In accounting classroom teaching, you can call the data in the data system at any time, and understand the learning effect of students in real time through the teaching effect control system. At the same time, the data generated in the accounting teaching system is stored in the accounting data system.

Cloud accounting simulation operating system allows students to learn to simulate the actual operation of cloud accounting system in practical work. The system can use the data of the platform, such as calling the teaching system to generate the data stored in the data system for targeted practical operation, so as to realize the training of accounting comprehensive talents who are seamlessly connected with the needs of social accounting posts.

The mobile terminal system enables teachers and students to log in to the cloud accounting education platform at any time through mobile phones, iPads and other mobile terminal devices according to permission settings.

3.3   Use the Cloud Accounting Education Platform to Reform the Accounting Education Model

(1) Use the cloud accounting education platform to design and restructure the curriculum system

Because the cloud accounting education platform can use the data on the public cloud, through the accounting data system, we can timely understand the needs of enterprises for accounting posts, so as to design the curriculum system and reorganization. In terms of curriculum, in response to the needs of accounting posts in the era of big data, in addition to setting up general data retrieval courses, practical operation courses of data analysis and processing software should be added, especially unstructured data mining technology software courses, cloud accounting simulation operation system courses, etc. In terms of course schedule, practical courses and theoretical courses should be interspersed with each other, so that students can improve their practical operation ability and enhance their ability to edit, process and calculate big data on the basis of mastering basic theories.

(2) Using the advantages of cloud computing to change the teaching mode

In terms of teaching design, teaching resources, including video, text and other non structural data, are stored in the accounting data system. Based on the introduction of cloud accounting shared data of enterprises and institutions, data monitoring and collection are carried out in real time, electronic teaching materials are produced and used at any time during classroom teaching, so as to apply the latest data and cases to theoretical teaching, In terms of improving students' learning and teaching organization, the use of cloud accounting education platform can, on the one hand, assign students to mine effective resources in network data, and exercise students' ability of data search and screening [4]. On the other hand, on the basis of students' mastering the basic theory, give full play to their initiative, let students voluntarily form a project team in the form of project layout, use all aspects of accounting knowledge, cooperate in different posts to complete the work, and cultivate students' communication and cooperation ability.

For the detection of teaching effect, the learning effect of each student's theoretical courses and practical courses is monitored in real time through the teaching monitoring system and mobile terminal system on the cloud accounting education platform. Teachers can know the teaching effect at any time by viewing students' homework and test results, and students can also know their own knowledge through teachers' comments and suggestions at any time, so as to improve the quality of teaching.

4 Conclusion

With the development of information globalization, modern educational technology has become a necessary means of teaching. It can not only make the knowledge more intuitive and visual, but also enable students to understand the current development status of the accounting industry in time. Through summary, the integration of modern educational technology into accounting teaching has the following advantages: first, it can form the accounting knowledge in books into an objective fact, which is more convenient for students to understand and master. Second, it can effectively improve teaching efficiency. The integration of modern teaching technology has greatly enriched the content of accounting teaching, strengthened the information input to students, and improved the teaching efficiency. It makes the static classroom become a dynamic classroom with sound, turning abstraction into concrete, and students can understand it more easily. Third, it is conducive to students' memory and consolidation. If we only teach according to simple books, students' memory will not last long, but after using modern educational technology and stimulating by sound and pictures, students' memory will be greatly improved.

References

1. Zhenqin, C.: The impact of big data. People's Posts and Telecommunications Press, China (2013)
2. Yongze, L., Guangguo, S.: Current situation and countermeasures of accounting education and accounting education research in China. Account. Res. **15**, 446–458 (2004)
3. Ling, Z.: The impact of cloud computing on enterprise accounting Informatization in the era of big data. Netw. Inf. Eng. **33**, 3341–3352 (2013)
4. Wenwei, Z.: Research on teaching innovation of accounting specialty from the perspective of big data. Vocat. Educ. (2015)

Construction of Quality Evaluation System for Innovative and Entrepreneurial Talent Training Under Artificial Intelligence System

Jinfeng Zhang[1(✉)] and Dongdong Zhang[2]

[1] The Tourism College of Changchun University, Changchun 130607, Jilin, China
zhangjinfengqq@163.com
[2] Changchun University of Architecture and Civil Engineering, Changchun 130607, Jilin, China

Abstract. Building an innovative country and promoting employment through entrepreneurship is China's major development strategy for the future. Building an innovative country needs to vigorously cultivate Bi-innovation talents. Based on the analysis of the quality structure of Bi-innovation talents, this paper puts forward reasonable ideas on the quality evaluation system of Bi-innovation talents from four aspects: evaluation principles, evaluation objectives, evaluation indicators and evaluation methods.

Keywords: Innovation and entrepreneurship · Quality of personnel training · Evaluation system

1 Introduction

At present, the operation mechanism of knowledge capitalization is becoming more and more mature. According to the trend of world scientific and Technological Development and China's unique national conditions, building an innovative country is a major strategic decision facing the future. Facing the new situation, the 17th National.

The actively respond to the needs of national skilled talents and cultivate Bi-innovation talents for the great rejuvenation of the Chinese nation. Education evaluation is an activity to judge the extent to which educational activities satisfy individuals, and a process to judge the actual or potential value of educational activities in order to achieve the appreciation of educational value [1]. The construction of the evaluation system should be implemented as soon as possible. The evaluation system should take the cultivation of innovative and entrepreneurial skilled talents suitable for national development as the ultimate goal, and carry out assessment and evaluation in Colleges and universities. The assessment and evaluation should mainly be comprehensively, dynamically and three-dimensional from the development mode, development adjustment, achievements and experience of innovative and entrepreneurial activities, And actively promote the summarized educational experience and educational laws, so as to cultivate more technical and skilled talents to manufacturing. The operation mechanism is shown in Fig. 1 below.

M. A. Jan and F. Khan (Eds.): BigIoT-EDU 2022, LNICST 467, pp. 324–335, 2023.
https://doi.org/10.1007/978-3-031-23944-1_36

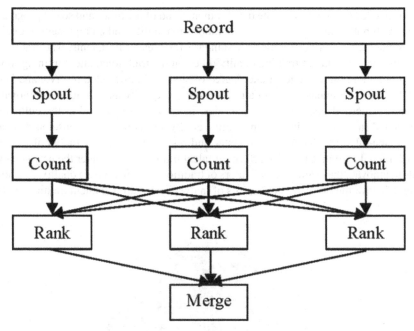

Fig. 1. Operating mechanism.

2 The Traditional Evaluation Mode of Talent Training Quality is not Conducive to the Cultivation of Bi-innovation Talents

2.1 The Evaluation Subject of Traditional Talent Training Quality is Too Single

In the traditional evaluation model of talent training quality in higher education, the government is often a single evaluation subject, and its evaluation activities inevitably have the characteristics of administrative simplification, which leads to the characteristics of non diversification and non specialization in the evaluation of talent training quality, and can not guarantee the professionalism and impartiality of the evaluation results. Talent Training, teachers and students are not only involved in the teaching link, but may be extended to society and enterprises; The teaching place may no longer be limited to the school, but will be extended to all kinds of practical activities and occasions; The complexity and diversification of market economy also inevitably requires the teaching activities of innovation and entrepreneurship education to be complex, diverse [2]. Therefore, the training quality of Bi-innovation talents should adopt diversified evaluation subjects and form a strict and scientific evaluation subject structure of talent training quality.

2.2 The Traditional Evaluation Index of Talent Training Quality Ignores the Characteristics of Bi-innovation Talents

At present, the sceience is raising, including the technology and social economy, there are mandy people think that only the accumulation and reserve of knowledge is not enough.

What is needed to comply with the development trend of the times and social progress is talents with both knowledge reserve and innovation ability and entrepreneurial quality. Ability has become a very important standard for measuring talents. The traditional evaluation index of talent training quality relies on the traditional talent training mode, pays more attention to the level and degree of students' knowledge reserve, and is too weak for the assessment and evaluation of students' quality and ability. For innovative and entrepreneurial talent training activities, more attention is paid to the cultivation of students' innovative thinking, innovative ability, entrepreneurial consciousness and entrepreneurial skills. Knowledge transfer and reserve is no longer the whole content of educational activities [3]. The reform of talent training mode under the new situation needs to innovate the evaluation indicators of traditional talent training quality. As shown in Fig. 2 below, the evaluation indicators of innovative traditional talent training quality.

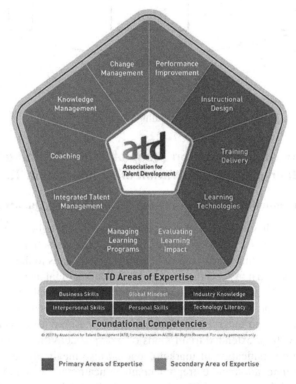

Fig. 2. Innovating the evaluation index of traditional talent training quality

2.3 The Traditional Evaluation Method of Talent Training Quality is not Suitable for the Growth of Bi-innovation Talents

The traditional talent training activities in Colleges and universities still retain the residual procedural color in the era of planned economy from content to form. The curriculum structure is rigid, the content of teaching materials is old, the teaching form is relatively single, and classroom teaching focuses on knowledge teaching and theory indoctrination [4]. Therefore, the traditional evaluation methods of talent training quality are mostly examination papers, papers, graduation designs, etc. to assess knowledge reserves. The innovative and entrepreneurial talent training mode pays more attention to ability training and quality improvement, the teaching forms are more diverse and complex, the teaching contents are more up to date and diversified, and pay more attention to the cultivation of students' practical ability. Which is difficult to evaluate with the traditional talent training quality evaluation method. As shown in Fig. 3 below.

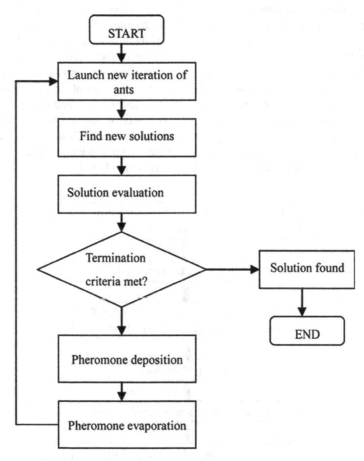

Fig. 3. Traditional evaluation method of talent training quality

3 Construction of Innovation and Entrepreneurship Talent Training Quality Evaluation System Based on Artificial Intelligence System

3.1 Evaluation Principles

(1) Scientific principle. The construction of the quality evaluation system for the culti-vation of Bi-innovation talents in Colleges and Universities under the school enter-prise cooperation mode should adhere to the scientific principle, can scientifically, objectively and reasonably reflect the characteristics and laws of the cultivation of Bi-innovation talents in Colleges and Universities under the school enterprise cooperation mode, and can accurately reveal the internal essence of the cultivation of Bi-innovation talents in Colleges and Universities under the school enterprise cooperation mode. Well [5], in the construction of the quality evaluation system for the cultivation of Bi-innovation talents in Colleges and universities, we should also combine the actual situation, characteristics and laws of the cultivation of Bi-innovation talents in Colleges and universities, scientifically and reasonably select the evaluation indicators, minimize the blindness of the selection of indicators, truly and objectively reflect the quality of the cultivation of Bi-innovation talents in Colleges and universities, and fully reflect the scientific principle. Each evaluation index is an integral whole of the system, as shown in Fig. 4.

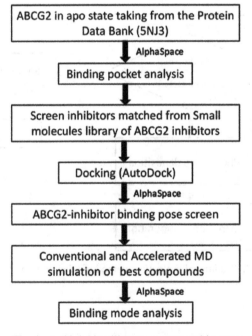

Fig. 4. Artificial intelligence system architecture

(2) Systematic principle. Because the quality evaluation system of College innovative and entrepreneurial talent training under the artificial intelligence system mode is a complete and systematic evaluation system, the construction of College innovative and entrepreneurial talent training quality evaluation system under the artificial intelligence system should adhere to the systematic principle. Although each evaluation index constitutes the quality evaluation system of innovative and entrepreneurial talent training in Colleges and Universities under the school enterprise cooperation mode from different levels and different angles, and each evaluation index is independent of each other, in the whole evaluation index system, there is an internal connection between different indexes, which together constitute a systematic talent training quality evaluation system, Evaluation objectives.

Innovation and entrepreneurship education is a kind of quality education. The orientation of quality education requires us to carry out extensive cultivation of innovative spirit and practical ability for all students, develop students' creative thinking ability, opportunity discrimination ability, foresight ability, risk awareness and psychological quality. The connotation of innovation and entrepreneurship education is not limited to enabling talents to use their innovative ability to start and operate an enterprise [6], It mainly refers to the cultivation and promotion of students' knowledge, skills, comprehensive quality and even personality. From the connotation of innovation and entrepreneurship education, in the final analysis, the evaluation of the training quality of innovation and entrepreneurship talents should be implemented in the aspects of students' innovation ability, practical ability, creativity, employability and entrepreneurship ability, reflect the improvement and change of students' quality, and guide the direction of talent training in Colleges and universities. At the same time, the quality evaluation of Bi-innovation talents should have good guidance and incentive functions, and the evaluated persons can consciously use the recognized evaluation indicators and contents to adjust their personal behavior, so as to achieve the purpose of encouraging students to develop freely in the fields of interest and tap their potential.

3.2 Evaluation Subject

To scientifically and reasonably evaluate the training quality of Bi-innovation talents, we need to establish a diversified evaluation subject under the guidance of the education administrative department, so as to ensure the objectivity and fairness of the training quality evaluation of Bi-innovation talents and the coordinated and balanced development of talent training activities. At the same time, the wide participation of diversified evaluation subjects in talent training quality evaluation can also mobilize their enthusiasm in the process of talent training and ensure their subjectivity in talent training activities [7].

Determination of guiding evaluation subject. The guiding evaluation subject refers to the subject that plays a guiding role and occupies a leading position in the evaluation of talent training quality. According to the higher education law of the people's Republic of China, the administrative department of education has the right to supervise the quality of school education, grasp the direction of the development of national higher education, examine the rationality and unity of higher education talent training activities from the perspective of the overall situation, and play an important guiding role in innovative and entrepreneurial talent training activities.

Determination of process evaluation subject. The process evaluation subject refers to the subject participating in the process of innovative and entrepreneurial talent training activities. Teachers and students are the direct participants in innovative and entrepreneurial talent training activities [8]. The main algorithm of process evaluation is shown in Fig. 5 below.

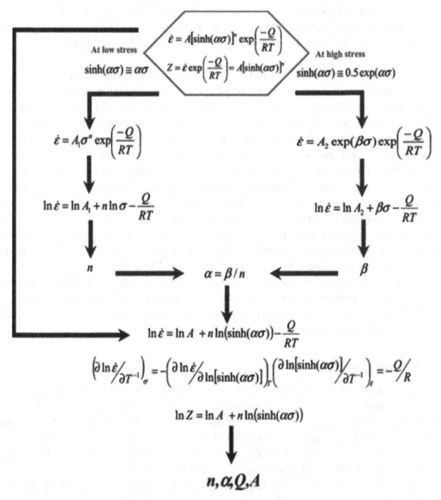

Fig. 5. Process evaluation agent algorithm

The process evaluation subject mainly refers to teachers and students. Teachers are the leaders of teaching activities. They participate in the training of Bi-innovation talents in their daily work, and have the most real and specific understanding of the overall talent training activities. Taking them as the evaluation subject can ensure the professionalism, specificity and authenticity of talent training quality evaluation. At the same time, students, as the object of innovative and entrepreneurial talent training, are the direct experience and experience of teachers' teaching activities, and the carrier of the quality of innovative and entrepreneurial talent training. Therefore, students should also be one of the subjects of innovative and entrepreneurial talent training quality evaluation [9]. By taking the teachers and students involved in the talent training process as the main body to evaluate the training quality of Bi-innovation talents, the school can get more real and effective evaluation and feedback of talent training from them, so as to better promote the development of innovation and entrepreneurship education in Colleges and universities.

Determination of the subject of outcome evaluation. The result evaluation subject refers to the subject that undertakes the results of innovative and entrepreneurial talent training activities, mainly including social evaluation, employers, parents and so on [10]. As the evaluation subject, the undertaker of the training quality of Bi-innovation talents can ensure the diversification and impartiality of the evaluation, objectively and timely reflect the consistency between the talent training objectives and social needs, which is conducive to the timely adjustment of talent training objectives according to social needs and further improve the quality of talent training.

3.3 Evaluation Indicators

The cultivation of Bi-innovation talents requires not only innovative talent training objectives and systems, but also scientific and reasonable talent training quality evaluation index system. The traditional evaluation mode of evaluating students' quality only by examination results has seriously hindered the cultivation of Bi-innovation talents in Colleges and universities. Therefore, It is an urgent problem for colleges and universities to build - a set of assessment and evaluation index system to stimulate students' innovation ability and entrepreneurial enthusiasm.

The quality evaluation index system of bi innovation talents should include "knowledge, ability and quality" The setting of indicators should be combined with the quality structure of bi-innovation talents and around the curriculum system of innovative and entrepreneurial education, which can not only test the level of students' professional education and cultural quality, but also effectively evaluate students' innovation ability, entrepreneurial ability, practical ability and creative ability [11]. Knowledge, one of the quality indicators of Bi-innovation talents training, includes not only individuals, but also people The acquired natural science knowledge, social science knowledge and thinking science knowledge should also include the reasonable degree of innovation and entrepreneurship knowledge and personal knowledge structure. Ability is a necessary condition for completing tasks and achieving goals. Ability is always associated with activities. Only through activities can one understand one's ability. For Bi-innovation talents, we should focus on examining students' innovation ability Entrepreneurial ability and practical ability, optional indicators, such as published papers, participated projects, invention patents, participated social practice, entrepreneurial practice, internship, etc. quality is a relatively stable, internal and basic quality that people have when engaging in activities. The formation and development of quality is a long-term internalization process [12]. For Bi-innovation talents, talent quality evaluation examining the basic ideological and moral quality and cognitive level, indicators should also be set to evaluate students' innovative quality and entrepreneurial quality. Innovative quality and entrepreneurial quality are not separated, but blend with each other. Innovative quality can be carried out in three aspects: innovative imagination ability, logical thinking ability and critical thinking ability [13]. Entrepreneurial quality includes innovative personality and innovative consciousness It should include psychological character, legal consciousness, etc. The entrepreneurial quality evaluation indicators are shown in Fig. 6 below.

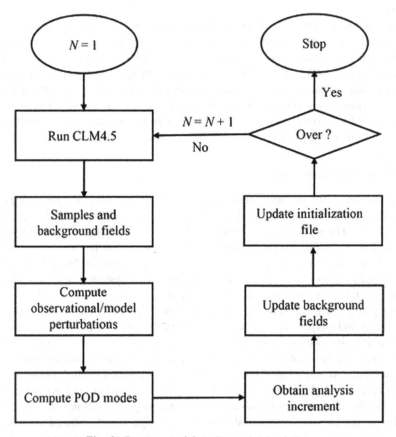

Fig. 6. Entrepreneurial quality evaluation index

3.4   Evaluation Method

Bi-innovation talents often have divergent and divergent thinking quality. In order to cultivate students with this thinking quality, we need to innovate and reform the existing examination system, that is to say, the cultivation of Bi-innovation talents needs flexible and diverse evaluation and assessment methods. We adopt open methods in the academic evaluation stage and try our best Reduce standardized examination evaluation, or try to reduce standardized test questions in examination evaluation, and increase open evaluation methods or assessment contents, so as to fully stimulate students' open thinking [14]. The evaluation method is shown in Fig. 7 below.

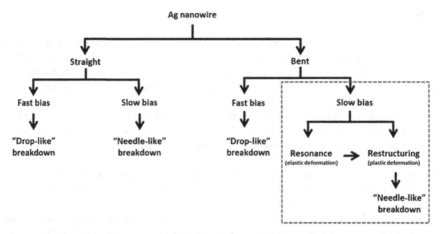

Fig. 7. Evaluation method

At present, many famous universities in China have made bold attempts in assessment methods and methods, such as the test of the reform of the examination system of Tsinghua University: the way of open book assessment, 40% of the test questions have standard answers, 60% have no standard answers, and the test questions without standard answers mainly test the students' ability, there is no right or wrong, only good or bad In the evaluation of innovation and entrepreneurship ability, special credits should be set, and all kinds of innovative science and technology competitions or activities and entrepreneurial activities should be strictly regulated to meet the relevant requirements before effective credits can be obtained. Students' social practice, subject research, designed enterprise plan, completed papers, etc. can be recognized as the performance in a certain way [15].

4 Conclusion

The evaluation method of the training quality of talent for creativity and business creation should change the way of focusing on the "baton" of the Ministry of education and taking the syllabus as the proposition basis, be more informal in the form and content of evaluation, and encourage students to "question, think and innovate" Develop in the direction of seeking differences, expand non logical thinking, dare to design independently and answer creatively. In the evaluation process, we should fully respect students' individual differences, change the past practice of using one model and one way to evaluate each student's situation, focus on advocating students' individual development, and cultivate students' sense and courage of innovation and risk-taking.

Acknowledgements. 2021 Jilin higher education scientific research project "Research on the Quality Evaluation System of Entrepreneurial Talent Training in Private University Based on Improved Fuzzy Comprehensive Evaluation Method" (JGJX2021D657).

References

1. Men, Y., Cai, H.: Design of online training system for innovative and entrepreneurial talents based on interdisciplinary integration. In: Fu, W., Liu, S., Dai, J. (eds.) eLEOT 2021. LNICST, vol. 390, pp. 39–49. Springer, Cham (2021). https://doi.org/10.1007/978-3-030-84386-1_4
2. Xu, C., Zhang, Z.: The effect of law students in entrepreneurial psychology under the artificial intelligence technology. Front. Psychol. **12**, 731713 (2021)
3. Jin, C., Luo, Y., Cao, R., et al.: Research and practice on the training mode of innovative and entrepreneurial talents in colleges and universities: a case study of academic association of "federation of life science research and innovation." Asian Agric. Res. **013**(002), 55–57 (2021)
4. Cetindamar, D., Lammers, T., Zhang, Y.: Exploring the knowledge spillovers of a technology in an entrepreneurial ecosystem—the case of artificial intelligence in Sydney. Thunderbird Int. Bus. Rev. **62**(5), 457–474 (2020)
5. Hu, W., Hu, Y., Lyu, Y., et al.: Research on integrated innovation design education for cultivating the innovative and entrepreneurial ability of industrial design professionals. Front. Psychol. **12**, 693216 (2021)
6. Jiao, G., Li, L., Deng, H., et al.: Exploration on cultivation of practical ability of artificial intelligence talents in universities in the context of innovation and entrepreneurship education. In: 2020 IEEE 2nd International Conference on Computer Science and Educational Informatization (CSEI). IEEE (2020)
7. Wang, S.: Innovative thinking and practice of mobile interaction design teaching in artificial intelligence era. In: IC4E 2021: 2021 12th International Conference on E-Education, E-Business, E-Management, and E-Learning (2021)
8. Khadse, C., Chaudhari, B.S., Patharkar, A.A.: Electromagnetic field and artificial intelligence based fault detection and classification system for the transmission lines in smart grid. Energy Sources Part A Recovery Utilization Environ. Eff. **24**, 1–16 (2021)
9. Gao, Y., Suo, X., Zheng, F.: The teacher evaluation and management system innovation based on the artificial intelligence algorithms. In: Abawajy, J.H., Choo, K.-K., Islam, R., Xu, Z., Atiquzzaman, M. (eds.) ATCI 2019. AISC, vol. 1017, pp. 1144–1149. Springer, Cham (2020). https://doi.org/10.1007/978-3-030-25128-4_144
10. Barik, L., Barukab, O., Ahmed, A.A.: Employing artificial intelligence techniques for student performance evaluation and teaching strategy enrichment: an innovative approach. Int. J. Adv. Appl. Sci. **7**(11), 10–24 (2020)
11. Eliiyi, U.: Artificial intelligence for smart cities: locational planning and dynamic routing of emergency vehicles. In: Bozkuş Kahyaoğlu, S. (ed.) The Impact of Artificial Intelligence on Governance Economics and Finance, Volume 2. AFSGFTA. Springer, Singapore (2022). https://doi.org/10.1007/978-981-16-8997-0_3
12. Chiang, L.H., Wang, Z., Braun, B., et al.: Towards artificial intelligence at scale in the chemical industry. AIChE J. **68**(6), 1145–1157 (2022)
13. Vilone, G., Longo, L.: A novel human-centred evaluation approach and an argument-based method for explainable artificial intelligence. In: Maglogiannis, I., Iliadis, L., Macintyre, J., Cortez, P. (eds.) AIAI 2022. IFIPAICT, vol. 646, pp. 447–460. Springer, Cham (2022). https://doi.org/10.1007/978-3-031-08333-4_36

14. Khan, S.U., Eusufzai, F., Azharuddin Redwan, M., Ahmed, M., Sabuj, S.R.: Artificial intelligence for cyber security: performance analysis of network intrusion detection. In: Ahmed, M., Islam, S.R., Anwar, A., Moustafa, N., Pathan, A.S.K. (eds.) Explainable Artificial Intelligence for Cyber Security. SCI, vol. 1025, pp. 113–139. Springer, Cham (2022). https://doi.org/10.1007/978-3-030-96630-0_6

15. Weigang, L., et al.: New directions for artificial intelligence: human, machine, biological, and quantum intelligence. Front. Inform. Technol. Electron. Eng. 23(6), 984–990 (2022). https://doi.org/10.1631/FITEE.2100227

Construction of Multidimensional and Dynamic College Students' Innovation and Entrepreneurship Platform Based on School-Enterprise Cooperation

Tianyi Sun[✉] and Lei Sun

The First Hospital Affiliated with the Chinese Medical University, Shenyang 110001, Liaoning, China
sunty@cmu1h.com

Abstract. The development of higher education in China is gradually adapting to the development of market and society. On this basis, a new talent training mode of school enterprise cooperation is proposed, which is also consistent with the demand for innovative and entrepreneurial talents in the new era. This study aims to explore the relationship between academic achievement, self-concept, motivation and entrepreneurial intention. The research question is: what is the relationship between high school students' academic achievement (academic achievement), self-concept (self-esteem), motivation (entrepreneurial intention) and entrepreneurial intention? Are there significant differences between these variables among high school students with different academic levels? This paper mainly discusses the construction.

Keywords: College students' innovation and entrepreneurship · School enterprise cooperation · Multidimensional dynamics · Platform construction

1 Introduction

The number of Japanese graduates, and the competition is becoming increasingly fierce. In this case, innovation plays a continuous role in cultivating students and reducing job seekers. In China's social environment, innovation economy has become the mainstream of social and economic development. Encourage students to innovate, establish a public innovation information platform, and provide students with more comprehensive information and more reliable security through the creation of students [1].

The traditional higher education innovation data platform adopts the centralized operation mode, which brings the challenge of trust crisis. Attackers can use their rights. For example, a dishonest administrator lends money to a project to create a business, or replaces another user with a transaction, thereby causing damage to the users of the platform. There are also efficiency problems in the central operation mode. When downloading information, the user must pass the consent form to the administrator, and then upload it to the platform. This does not guarantee timeliness.

© ICST Institute for Computer Sciences, Social Informatics and Telecommunications Engineering 2023
Published by Springer Nature Switzerland AG 2023. All Rights Reserved
M. A. Jan and F. Khan (Eds.): BigIoT-EDU 2022, LNICST 467, pp. 336–344, 2023.
https://doi.org/10.1007/978-3-031-23944-1_37

To solve this problem, we must actively support and support students with creativity and entrepreneurial potential to start their own businesses and collective businesses. This helps to establish innovation, outreach and support mechanisms for students. The school enterprise cooperation mode can guide, enrich their social experience. Due to the lack of policy consistency and financial support, it is necessary to design a student innovation on the basis of systematic analysis.

School enterprise cooperation such as education, secondary school and secondary education. Take advantage of its own development advantages, take measures to cooperate with enterprises, improve enterprise talents, and effectiveness of human resources. The cooperation between schools and enterprises is a "everyone benefits" model, which emphasizes the importance of education quality, school learning and business practice, as well as the sharing of resources and information and enterprises promotes the development of the education sector through market cooperation, enterprise cooperation, and the combination of practice and theory. We should implement the party's basic education policy, fulfill the fundamental mission of developing quality education, promote fair education with builders and successors, and develop German American socialism in an all-round way. The school-enterprise cooperation model is shown in Fig. 1.

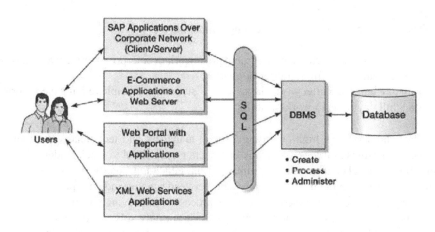

Fig. 1. The school-enterprise cooperation model

2 School-Enterprise Cooperation Under the Background of Innovation and Entrepreneurship Development in China

2.1 Importance of School Enterprise Cooperation Under the Background of Innovation and Entrepreneurship Development in China

(1) Giving full play to the service of colleges and Universities: talent support for regional and urban economic development
Enterprises are an important driving force for the economic development of the district. The development of modern enterprises needs strong human support. At

present, many enterprises will choose excellent college graduates with innovative ability when recruiting talents. Therefore, if schools and enterprises cooperate, colleges and universities can more targeted deliver the talents needed for enterprise development, At the same time, the talents transported can also meet the needs of enterprises to a greater extent in terms of practical ability. After obtaining high-quality talents, enterprises will inevitably play a great role in promoting the economic development of the district and the city by contributing to innovation.

(2) Promoting the reform of talent training in Colleges and universities with the demand Colleges and universities are an important position for talent training. Since the development of modern higher education, China has always paid attention to the cultivation of theoretical knowledge and ability, which also makes the theoretical research work develop to a new height [2]. However, more college students entering the market economy want to go to the market for employment. Therefore, the level of practical ability not only affects the employability and employment prospect of college students, but also poses a challenge to colleges and universities. As college students, whether they start their own businesses or work in enterprises, they need innovation ability. As a guide, the talent training mode of colleges and universities also needs to be reformed.

The implementation methods are roughly as follows:

A. half of them are in school, half of them go to work in enterprises or receive practical training, and rotate by semester or quarter;
B. Full day labor and after work class system - students are employed in the enterprise on a full day basis to work on shifts.

The school teaches high-quality enterprise managers and technicians to promote school and business surveys. Company engineers go to school to teach students At the same time, a teacher in the school improved the education quality of the company's employees. Through the mutual employment between schools and enterprises, students get the right to education, which is not only a process of improving vocational skills, but also a process of creating value for enterprises. It not only solves the contradiction of the shortage of teaching materials, but also improves students' academic performance, so that they can get real income from education.

Through the cooperation between schools and enterprises, enterprises can obtain talents, students can acquire skills and develop schools; School enterprises have achieved a win-win stage.

Partnership mode 4: contract cooperation mode.

Students work at the entrance and then work after graduation Implement student recruitment, recruitment, training, production and internship Students are selected by the school and composed of students and employees employed by the company. As shown in Fig. 2. The training is jointly conducted by the company and the school. Provide training and internship courses for the company. The company plays a more important role in specific training [3].

Short term skill training shall be conducted according to the needs of the enterprise. After the training is completed, the employee can be employed according to the contract

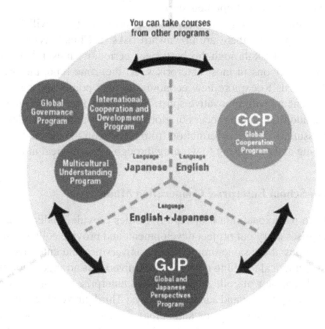

Fig. 2. Practice mode of school enterprise cooperation

after passing the examination organized by the company. This kind of cooperation has strong pertinence. The disadvantage of this cooperation model is that the school is very passive. How many people to train and when to train are completely based on the needs of the enterprise. The school has no initiative. This is a primary cooperation mode, which is generally used more in technical secondary schools.

2.2 Necessity of School Enterprise Cooperation Under the Background of Innovation and Entrepreneurship Development in China

(1) Lack of innovation and entrepreneurship in talent training in Colleges and Universities
From the feedback of college students after graduation, many college students, including some famous college students, have the problem of insufficient practical ability at the initial stage of entering the enterprise, and lack of innovation ability in their long-term work. From the perspective of the proportion of independent entrepreneurship and success rate of college students after graduation, they are also very few. These problems reflect the lack ability in talent training in China. The talents trained under the traditional education mode can no longer meet the development needs of the current era of innovation and entrepreneurship. Therefore, it is very necessary to start school enterprise cooperation and build platform based on this cooperation to truly cultivate high-quality talents.

(2) The solution of problems in China's economic and social development needs the help of innovation and entrepreneurship

At a certain stage of economic and social development, we will face new contradictions. At present, there are downward risks in China's economic development. In order to break through this bottleneck period, we must rely on innovation, which is most obvious in most enterprises. At the same time, the overall social growth also needs to explore new economic growth points and be promoted by more entrepreneurs with innovative spirit, These should rely on Colleges and universities. In addition, in the process of globalization, we are also under great competitive pressure. In the transformation from relying on the development mode of manufacturing and processing to winning through technological innovation.

2.3   Analysis of School Enterprise Cooperation Mode

Both sides plan to participate in a project, universities provide academic and research resources, enterprises carry out project development, and provide college students with practice opportunities at the same time; Second, universities and enterprises cooperate in theoretical and practical teaching respectively. Universities arrange theoretical teaching in the normal semester of college students, and enterprises arrange internships for college students during winter and summer holidays; Third, universities and enterprises cooperate in the form of talent training and output. This mode is also known as "order" cooperation, which is more common in some higher vocational colleges in China.

3   Research on College Students' Innovation and Entrepreneurship Mechanism Based on Multi-dimensional Dynamic Innovation Model

3.1   Research on Multidimensional Dynamic Innovation Model

The multi-dimensional dynamic system analysis method has no modification to the three laws of philosophy, but appropriately modifies the category representing the cognitive stage. Here, the finite and infinite pairs are taken as examples to illustrate that other categories can be treated in the same way. Limited refers to things that are opposite to other things and thus are affected or regulated by other things, that is, things with conditions; Infinity refers to something that is not opposite to, and therefore not affected or regulated by, anything else. As far as complex system analysis is concerned, the existing theories limit its content to the finite, but it is biased because the infinite cannot be specifically defined. It cannot be said that the division between finite and infinite is incorrect, but it is a little too simple [4]. In the past, mechanical analysis occupied the main position, and analysts were difficult to realize (or deliberately ignore) the distortion of time and space, and naturally it was difficult to realize the distortion between finite and infinite. In fact, when space-time is distorted (dimensional distortion), infinity is transformed into finiteness, and finiteness is also transformed into infinity. The multidimensional, as shown in Fig. 3.

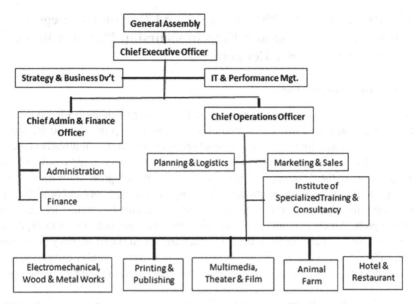

Fig. 3. Research framework of College Students' innovation and entrepreneurship mechanism based on multi-dimensional dynamic innovation model

3.2 Research on the Importance of Influencing Factors of College Students' Innovation and Entrepreneurship Based on Multivariate Support Vector Machine

Also has good generalization and generalization. Because the algorithm of support vector machine (SVM) based on SLT theory has made outstanding progress in solving the problem of "small samples", SLT theory is considered to be the best theory for "small samples" statistics, estimation and predictive learning. Generally, under the premise of controlling the upper bound of fitting ability, SLT theory seeks to obtain higher fitting accuracy. There are three general methods to control ve dimension:

(1) Try to reduce the number of dimensions of feature space;
(2) In the feature space, the distance between the two kinds of sample point sets should be enlarged as much as possible;
(3) In the feature space, try to reduce the distribution range of the two types of sample points

This paper establishes the importance model the soft edge objective function is as follows.

$$u_{k+1}(t) = u_k(t) + \Gamma_{l1}\dot{e}_k(t) + \Gamma_{l2}\dot{e}_{k+1}(t) + \Gamma_{p1}\Delta\dot{e}_k(t) + \Gamma_{p2}\Delta\dot{e}_{k+1}(t) \qquad (1)$$

4 Construction of Multidimensional and Dynamic College Students' Innovation and Entrepreneurship Platform Based on School Enterprise Cooperation

4.1 Platform Demand Analysis

The platform system is of great significance for the transformation of achievements of individuals and universities, the promotion of emerging products, the information exchange among participants, and the incubation and cultivation of innovative products. As shown in Fig. 4. The Internet-based innovation and entrepreneurship platform system carrier to promote the development of scientific and technological innovation oriented technology industry, encourage innovation to promote achievements and products in the market, and is the cradle to promote the exchange of emerging industries and innovation. It can comprehensively promote the innovative economy and become an indispensable part of the innovation economic system. In order users, composed of many parts, which contain different functional requirements, but all require users to be able to easily manage, use, maintain and so on. The overall comprehensive functions of each part of the system:

(1) Project module: the project module is the user's operation process of creating, publishing and browsing products, as well as collecting favorite projects. In the background management, the administrator can add, modify, approve items, and add labels such as classification.
(2) Roadshow module: the roadshow module includes users publishing roadshow videos, and other users participating in the roadshow. The participants of the road-show can have intentions about the project, and then enter the agreement function for negotiation. In the background management, the administrator can perform information maintenance, audit and other operations on the roadshow.
(3) Agreement module: the agreement module is mainly the process of negotiation and game between the two parties. After three handshakes and negotiation, the project can be completed and the credit of both parties can be evaluated.
(4) Resource sharing module: the resource sharing module is mainly composed of upload, download and browse. Users upload different kinds of resources to the platform system and can share them through links. In background management, administrator users can lock, unlock, delete and other operations on resources.

4.2 Overall Design of Platform

The platform function module is shown in Fig. 5. Focusing on the design of the data layer.

4.3 Platform Implementation

The system environment of the platform uses the Windows Server 2008 operating system platform, which is equipped with Intel Core i5 hardware, and the main frequency is 3.0 GHz. The operating memory is 16 GB, the storage space is 8 W, and the network width is

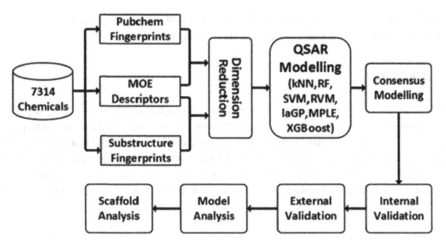

Fig. 4. Multivariate support vector machine model

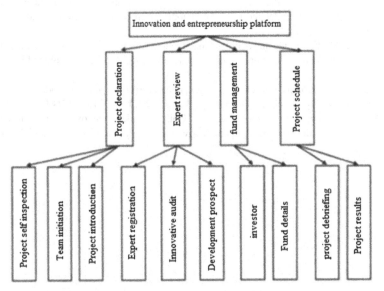

Fig. 5. Overall functional block diagram of student innovation and entrepreneurship experience platform

20 m. MSSQL server 2015 system data storage software. Hadoop platform is composed of three servers connected through LAN. One server is the master node and the other two servers are nodes. Each Hadoop host (server) must first create a user and set the corresponding password. You need to change the "feet" file of the host. Next, you need to configure SSH to obtain control from the master node. Finally, you need to install Java at runtime Hadoop; If you install Hadoop, you need to configure Hadoop. First, you

need to configure environment variables and Java paths. The next step is to configure files, such as the primary site. XML and HDFS websites. XML.

5 Conclusion

This paper analyzes the multiple of student innovation activities (mdm1) in many aspects. As a university, we cannot rely entirely on the role of Companies in the school enterprise cooperation model to cultivate innovative entrepreneurs. They should also make efforts to improve their own teaching activities and teachers. Since we have proposed school enterprise cooperation, not only students can be improved, but teachers can also take advantage of the opportunity. In this way, we can not only get the experience close to students, but also promote the improvement of their teaching activities.

References

1. Zhang, H.: Discussion on the optimization of College Students' innovation and entrepreneurship education system under the mode of school enterprise cooperation. J. Xuchang Univ. **34**(4), 144–146 (2015)
2. Luo, Y., Chen, M.: Thinking and exploration of College Students' innovation and entrepreneurship practice based on school enterprise cooperation mode. Sci. Educ. Guide (15), 178–179 (2016)
3. Wang, H.: Research on the construction of school enterprise cooperation model for innovation and entrepreneurship of college students in Tibet. J. Tibet Univ. **31**(4), 134–139 (2016)
4. Wu, Y., Ni, J., Dong, Y.: Promotion strategy of College Students' innovation and entrepreneurship based on multidimensional dynamic innovation model. Lab. Res. Explor. **35**(2), 205–210 (2016)

The Cultivation Path and Construction Exploration of College Students' Cultural Confidence Based on the Information Platform

Xiaojun Cao[1,2(✉)]

[1] Xi'an Traffic Engineering Institute, Xi'an 710300, Shaanxi, China
1044564178@qq.com
[2] Universiti Teknologi MARA (UiTM), 40450 Shah Alam, Selangor Darul Ehsan, Malaysia

Abstract. College students are the builders and successors of the socialist cause with Chinese characteristics, and they are the practitioners of cultural self-awareness, self-confidence and self-improvement. Their high degree of cultural self-confidence is of great practical significance to the inheritance and innovation of the excellent Chinese traditional culture and the enhancement of the national cultural soft power. Based on the technology of computer platform, this paper elaborates the scientific connotation and essence of cultural confidence, analyzes the current situation of college students' cultural confidence and its influencing factors, and explores the path of cultivating college students' cultural confidence.

Keywords: Computer · College students · Cultural confidence · Cultivation path

1 Introduction

Culture is the enduring pillar of the soul of a people and a nation. Culture is also a representative element of soft power and the source of national creativity, cohesion and vitality. Culture is the crystallisation of wisdom in the development of a nation and a country, and to insist on cultural confidence is to highly affirm outstanding cultural achievements. Adhering to cultural confidence is an important way for the nation to prosper and develop socialist culture with Chinese characteristics, and it is also a strategic condition for practising a strong cultural nation, representing the ultimate purpose of cultural revival of the Chinese nation and the realisation of the Chinese dream.

This is the crystallization of the Party's wisdom in governance, and reflects the Party's firm confidence in leading the nation, the whole nation and the entire people to unite in their struggle. General Secretary Xi Jinping proposed: "To insist on not forgetting the original intention and continuing to move forward, we must adhere to the road, theory, system and cultural confidence of socialism with Chinese characteristics, adhere to the Party's basic line without wavering, and continuously push forward the great cause of socialism with Chinese characteristics." From "three self-confidence" to "our self-confidence", cultural self-confidence is listed alongside road self-confidence, theoretical

M. A. Jan and F. Khan (Eds.): BigIoT-EDU 2022, LNICST 467, pp. 345–353, 2023.
https://doi.org/10.1007/978-3-031-23944-1_38

self-confidence and institutional self-confidence, and it is emphasized that "cultural self-confidence" is a more basic, deeper and longer lasting power. The "Four Confidences" have been changed to "Four Assertivenesses". Cultural self-confidence is a key step in strategic development, which is rooted in the vast and profound Chinese excellent traditional culture system, as well as revolutionary culture and advanced socialist culture, and is the basis for promoting the cultural development of society in the present era. From the perspective of contemporary university students establishing cultural self-confidence, this paper reveals the dialectical and logical relationship between cultural self-confidence, cultural self-awareness and cultural identity, and reveals that contemporary university students establish a high degree of cultural self-confidence, as well as the sense of responsibility to inherit and carry forward the excellent Chinese traditional culture [1]. In the face of the competitive domestic and international cultural environment, contemporary university students should establish cultural confidence, fully understand the connotation of cultural confidence, and shoulder the historical mission of inheriting China's excellent traditional culture. Information platform structure is shown in Fig. 1.

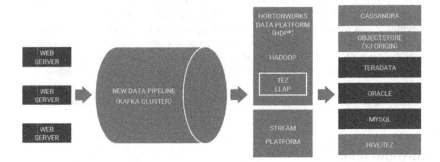

Fig. 1. Information platform structure

2   Related Work

2.1   The Connotation of Cultural Confidence Among University Students

From a broad perspective, cultural confidence refers to the full affirmation of the concept and value of a country, nation and political party of their own culture, their firm belief and confidence in the development of their own culture, as well as the inheritance, promotion and innovation of the essence of their own culture, on the basis of a clear understanding of their own culture.

The degree of cultural confidence is influenced by cultural cognition, cultural emotion, cultural will and cultural behaviour. The article combines these four elements to put forward the following requirements for the cultural self-confidence of university students. Firstly, in terms of cultural cognition, university students should actively study and research the essence and value of Chinese traditional culture, correctly grasp the connotation and meaning of socialist core values, and have a profound knowledge of

Chinese culture; secondly, in terms of cultural emotion, university students should fully affirm the essence and value of Chinese traditional culture, and highly identify with the connotation and meaning of our socialist core values. Thirdly, in terms of cultural will, under the wave of globalization and the collision of multiple cultures, university students should treat multiple cultures dialectically, always maintain the general direction of Chinese cultural development, critically absorb foreign cultures with an open and tolerant attitude, and show a firm cultural will; finally, in terms of cultural behaviour, under the background of the collision of multiple cultures, university students should choose to inherit, carry forward and innovate excellent traditional culture, practice socialist core values, actively participate in cultural exchange activities, and promote the innovative development of culture against the background of multi-cultural impact [2].

2.2 The Current Situation of Cultural Self-confidence Among University Students

(1) Lack of awareness of cultural self-confidence

In current colleges and universities, especially higher vocational colleges, from the top design of the school, a clear talent cultivation goal is determined, that is, to cultivate high-quality technical skill talents, and a clear talent cultivation program is formulated, which puts forward high requirements for students' professional knowledge and professional and technical skills. From the students' studies to graduation, the students are trained according to the set objectives, which plays a direct role in guiding the students' learning and the professional teachers' teaching, but at the same time, it also leads to the phenomenon of "emphasizing skills cultivation but not humanities education". "Humanities education is in a marginal position in most higher education institutions. Guided by the school's talent cultivation objectives, students' psychology and behaviour are more inclined to the learning of professional theories and technical skills, while they care less about humanities subjects such as ideological and political education and general education. At the same time, university students and their parents have a prejudiced understanding of humanities education, believing that having professional knowledge and skills will enable them to find a good job to their liking, and neglecting the positive effect of humanities education on students' humanistic qualities, resulting in students' utilitarianism in their studies and only attaching importance to the learning of professional knowledge and technical skills." This disregard for humanities education has led to the phenomenon of low humanities literacy among university students, which is worrying. This is not conducive to the improvement of humanistic literacy among university students, and it is difficult to mobilize students to participate in cultural construction with a high degree of self-awareness and a strong sense of responsibility, not to mention the enhancement of cultural self-awareness and cultural self-confidence.

(2) Low sense of traditional cultural identity

In the context of economic globalisation and the coexistence of multiple cultures, the exchange of ideas, cultures and values between different regions and countries can be carried out more quickly and conveniently, which is conducive to the mutual benefit of the regions and countries, but it also brings a strong impact on the local culture, and the phenomenon of blindly promoting Western culture and fawning over foreigners has emerged. With the rapid expansion of multicultural ideologies, more and more university students are gradually forgetting and unfamiliar with the excellent Chinese traditional culture and lack a clear understanding of it. Compared with traditional culture, they are more receptive to foreign culture, more enthusiastic about western festivals (such as Valentine's Day and Halloween) and food (such as KFC and McDonald's), and psychologically and behaviourally accept and promote western cultural symbols. Hu Yi has conducted a survey on the attitudes held by university students towards China's traditional culture, showing that students who expressed disinterest in traditional culture accounted for more than 70% of the total number of students surveyed, and only 20% of the students surveyed said they identified with the culture. (This shows that college students do not attach enough importance to traditional culture and have a low sense of identification with the country and the nation's own culture, which is obviously not conducive to the inheritance and innovation of traditional culture and the construction of a strong socialist cultural state [3].

(3) Lack of adherence to mainstream cultural values

At different times, different countries have a main influence and dominant culture, namely the mainstream culture. At present, the mainstream culture in China is the socialist culture with Chinese characteristics, which is the advanced culture of Marxism into China, the wisdom crystallization of inheriting the excellent Chinese traditional culture and the achievements of human civilization, and the culture with the core value system of socialism as the core with the brand of Chinese nation. Then, as an active force in cultural communication, university students should not only adhere to the confidence of the road, theory and system, but also adhere to cultural confidence, arm themselves with advanced socialist culture and enhance their sense of identity and pride in culture. Most university students can identify with the cultural values of their country and nation, actively practice the core socialist values, and inherit and promote the excellent Chinese traditional culture. However, at the same time, we should also see that some university students, due to the fierce impact and greater negative influence of diversified cultures, have developed wrong outlooks on life, values and worldviews, believe in the creed of cynical and timely life, do not have firm ideals and beliefs, insist on self-centredness and personal interests, lack identification with the core socialist value system and lack self-confidence in socialist culture with Chinese characteristics. If these phenomena are not addressed in a timely manner, they will have a negative impact on the formation of the correct outlook on life, values and worldview of university students, and may even lead to the negation of their own culture, value concepts and ideology.

3   Analysis of the Reasons for the Lack of Cultural Self-confidence Among University Students

The phenomenon of lack of cultural self-confidence among university students is influenced by a variety of factors, both their personal factors and the factors of school, family and society, which together restrict the establishment of cultural self-confidence among university students.

3.1 Personal Factors

At present, the main body of college students is mainly the "post-90s", and they have obvious differences from the "post-80s" in terms of ideological awareness, value pursuit, learning tendency and cultural identity. Most of the "post-90s" college students are outgoing, optimistic, cheerful, positive and open-minded, but their psychological quality is not mature enough, they are in a period of easy emotional fluctuation, their anti-stress ability is weak, they have a strong sense of dependence on their parents, lack the spirit of hard work and hardship, they are self-centred and have a weak collective concept. Compared with the "post-80s", the "post-90s" college students have better living and learning conditions, they can use the Internet for shopping, chatting and browsing news, and they can also use the Internet to enhance their studies and learn more about the humanities, history, geography and technology of different countries. They can also make use of the Internet to learn more about the culture, history, geography, technology and so on of different countries, and easily accept new things and become interested in new things. Under the background of multicultural impact, university students will unconsciously absorb western culture and be influenced by western cultural ideas and ways of thinking, leading to blind obedience to western culture. Although most university students hold a positive attitude towards Chinese national culture and adhere to and identify with their own cultural values, it should also be seen that with the accelerated penetration of Western culture, some university students worship Western values, cultural concepts and lifestyles more, while they do not have enough cultural determination and cultural self-confidence in their country and nation itself.

3.2 School Factors

Colleges and universities are the places to cultivate talents and the main place for students to grow and become successful, and they are responsible for building campus culture and cultivating students' humanistic qualities. Some colleges and universities do not pay enough attention to humanities education and do not offer courses in humanities, neglecting the cultural quality education for college students, or although they do offer courses such as Chinese traditional culture, national education and general education, they invest less in human resources and material resources. Due to the nature of elective courses, students psychologically marginalize humanities subjects and do not care whether they really learn humanities knowledge, just to take credits; due to the time limit of elective courses, teachers of humanities subjects are also unable to teach the course knowledge systematically and completely, and can only select relevant chapters to explain, what students learn is only skin deep knowledge, lack of systematic and deep understanding of traditional culture, and it is difficult to enhance the pride of the nation and the country's traditional culture. The lack of systematic and in-depth understanding of traditional culture makes it difficult for students to enhance their pride in the traditional culture of the nation and the country, and seriously affects the formation of a high level of cultural confidence [4].

3.3 Family Factors

The family is a warm harbour for children to grow up in, and parents are their children's initiation teachers. The family cultural atmosphere has a subtle effect on the ideology, cultural literacy and moral quality of university students. In a good family culture atmosphere, parents tend to have a harmonious relationship and can respect and care for each other, and their parents have high cultural quality and good moral quality, which invariably have a profound influence on the growth and success of university students. College students who grow up in a good family atmosphere know more about caring for others, respecting their teachers and teachers, being positive, also taking the initiative to learn cultural knowledge, consciously caring for the development of the country and the nation, easily identifying with and affirming the value ideas of the traditional Chinese culture, and holding firm beliefs in the country and the nation's own culture. Conversely, a bad family culture is one in which parents have a poor relationship, do not respect each other and do not understand the psychological feelings of their children. Then, university students growing up in such a family environment, because they lack the moral culture of mutual respect and care for each other, will not only easily lack a sense of security, but also have a suspicious attitude towards the good moral behaviour of society and others, and their high cultural self-confidence will be difficult to be enhanced.

3.4 Social Factors

With the development of science and technology and the advancement of economic globalisation, exchanges between different cultures, ethnic groups and countries have become frequent, and the fierce impact and mutual collision of multiple cultures, as well as the mutual benefit and promotion of each other's strengths and weaknesses, have become a social development trend. However, we should also see that some Western countries, under the guise of cultural exchange, are infusing the ideology, ideology and values of Western countries into China, and slowly infiltrating the ideology and values of university students. This not only has a fierce impact on the mainstream ideology and cultural confidence of university students, but also makes them confused about their ideology and appear to have an unstable ideological stance. In addition, Western countries also use the Internet media to infiltrate the cultural values of our university students, making them gradually accept Western culture, which in turn reduces some of them to identify with the country and the nation's own culture and weakens their confidence in cultural development and prosperity. These phenomena are not conducive to the cultivation of firm cultural confidence among university students and their healthy growth and success.

4 The Cultivation Path of College Students' Cultural Self-confidence Based on Computer Platform

4.1 Build a "Micro-System" to Create an Atmosphere for Cultivating Students' Cultural Self-confidence

Although the computer platform has unique advantages, the mixed new media environment tends to mislead college students' cultural cognition and reduce the effectiveness of cultivating cultural self-confidence. In order to provide a good cultural environment for college students, different responsible bodies should do something about it and form a potential "micro system" to guarantee the orderly operation of microblogs and other self-media platforms.

First, the government should build a reasonable cultural orientation for society. On the basis of improving existing internet laws and regulations, the government should focus on the control of frequently occurring uncivilized phenomena on the internet, further define the "dilemma" of moral culture, clarify the standards of right and wrong, and provide rational value standards and institutional safeguards from a macro perspective to create a good social environment on the internet.

Secondly, new computer media operators should purify the cultural atmosphere of the virtual environment of the Internet. Firstly, new media operators such as microbloggers should strengthen the real-name authentication of users and enhance their awareness of the rules when using them; secondly, they should strengthen the technical supervision of network operation and management departments to make up for technical loopholes in a timely manner, so as to prevent hackers and vulgar culture from taking advantage of them. Finally, new media platforms such as microblogs should take the initiative to provide a new field for cultivating cultural confidence.

Thirdly, universities need to do a good job in supervising the online cultural environment. Firstly, universities can use "green" filtering software or network security warning system to shield the bad information in the school intranet, so as to reduce the negative impact of malicious network incidents; secondly, the safe use of network and "green use" of network of college students can be combined with the evaluation of merit, To punish the serious college students' network moral misconduct, strengthen the college students' awareness of the norms in the network virtual society, and clear the obstacles for creating a good network cultural environment.

4.2 Broaden the Channels of Cultivating College Students' Cultural Self-confidence Through the Computer Platform

Traditionally, the cultivation of college students' cultural self-confidence is mostly done through traditional media, such as newspapers, radio and television, etc. However, as the new generation of the Internet, college students have long been accustomed to using electronic devices to obtain information, so the traditional channels for cultivating cultural self-confidence can hardly play their original effectiveness.

First of all, in the era of new media, a linkage mechanism between computer platforms and traditional media should be built, based on the professionalism and credibility of traditional authoritative media and the intelligent communication means of new media such as microblogs and WeChat, to realize the complementary advantages and mutual appreciation of social cultural resources, so as to consolidate and enhance the status of Chinese excellent traditional culture in the minds of college students and improve the depth and breadth of Chinese cultural self-confidence. Secondly, as the main place to cultivate students' cultural confidence, universities should take the initiative to present the long-standing Chinese history and civilization to students, so as to enhance their sense of cultural identity and pride. In this way, we can enhance the self-education of students' cultural self-confidence, and on the basis of this, we can absorb multiple cultures, and at the same time tolerate the coexistence of excellent heterogeneous cultures without losing the orthodox cultural roots.

Finally, colleges and universities can make use of the unique user attention mechanism under "micro communication" and use the new media platform as a carrier to expand the channels of cultural self-confidence education for college students in multi-directional interaction. On the one hand, universities can infiltrate the cultivation of cultural self-confidence of college students into the blog posts and exert a subtle influence on students; on the other hand, universities can understand the students' status in school from their microblogs in time, which is more conducive to strengthening the attention to the personalized development of college students and conducting more targeted education on cultural values. Secondly, teachers or counsellors of universities can forward the hot news from microblogs to class groups, so that students can think about, analyze and discuss the hot events and guide them to cultivate correct cultural and moral cognition. In addition, the two-way interaction under the mutual concern mechanism can enhance the emotional communication between teachers and students, as both teachers and friends, as shown in Fig. 2, so that both sides can reach a consensus on cultural cognition and values, further broadening the channel of cultivating cultural self-confidence among college students.

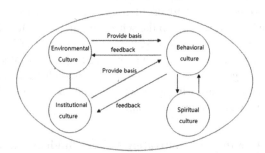

Fig. 2. Computer-based platforms for cultural interactions

5   Conclusion

In conclusion, the new computer media platform represented by microblogging will definitely become an important position for cultivating the cultural confidence of college students. Universities should recognize the shortcomings of the new media in the process of information dissemination based on the advantages of cultivating traditional cultural confidence, and make good use of the advantages provided by the computer platform to turn the impact into opportunities, so as to provide an effective path for cultivating the cultural confidence of college students.

Acknowledgements. Planning subject for the 13th five year plan of Shaanxi education sciences (SGH20Y1376); the Program Supported by Youth Foundation of Xi'an Traffic Engineering Institute (21KY-63).

References

1. Liu, S.: The consideration and interpretation of the main body of Chinese cultural confidence. J. Jianghai Stud. (1), 40–45 (2009)
2. Huang, Q., Xue, Y.: The lack of cultural self-confidence among contemporary Chinese university students and its countermeasures. J. Chengdu Univ. Technol. (Soc. Sci. Ed.) **2013**(2), 110–113 (2013)
3. Lin, X.: Cultivating cultural self-confidence among college students in the new media. China Adult Educ. (11), 72–74 (2017)
4. Exploring ways to cultivate cultural self-awareness and cultural self-confidence among college students in Lei Bin. Chin. Foreign Enterp. Cult. (12), 13 (2014)
5. Yang, X.S.: A new metaheuristic bat-inspired algorithm. In: González, J.R., Pelta, D.A., Cruz, C., Terrazas, G., Krasnogor, N. (eds.) NICSO 2010. SCI, vol. 284, pp. 65–74. Springer, Heidelberg (2010). https://doi.org/10.1007/978-3-642-12538-6_6
6. Liu, L., Liu, X., Zhou, X.: Decoupling method of multivariable system based on fuzzy neural network. J. Ocean Univ. China **43**(2), 99–104 (2013)
7. Cai, W., Han, H.: Research on port logistics demand forecast based on BP and RBF neural network combination model. J. Zhengzhou Univ. (Eng. Ed. Zhengzhou) **40**(05), 1–7 (2020)
8. Yan, W., Zhang, X.: Speech recognition system based on TMS320C5409. J. Taiyuan Univ. Technol. **6**, 524–527 (2007)
9. Li, J., Liu, D., Zhu, Y.: Decoupling control of VAV air conditioner based on neural network. J. Shenyang Jianzhu Univ. (Nat. Sci. Ed.) **29**(1), 187–192 (2013)
10. Zheng, L., Li, G., An, J., Lou, F.: Mathematical modeling and optimal control of underground ventilation and air conditioning in station. Math. Probl. Eng. **2022**, 1–16 (2022). Article ID: 5032564

Based on Big Data Analysis of the Phased Development of China's Marketing

Mei Zhao[(⊠)], Peng Li, Chenglong Li, Shengzong Han, and Wenyu Shao

Shandong College of Information Vocational and Technology, Weifang 261061, China
649217846@qq.com

Abstract. The marketing of China is based on the phased development of the market. The first phase, from 1985 to 1993, was mainly focused on product promotion and brand-building. The second phase, from 1994 to 2003, was about developing a comprehensive national strategy for marketing. In 2004, China's government launched a third phase which focuses on building an integrated national strategy for marketing with the aim of achieving sustainable development in all aspects of marketing. The phased development analysis of Chinese marketing based on big data is a research paper describing the analysis and discussion of the phased development of Chinese marketing. The author analyzes the evolution of Chinese marketing from the initial stage to today, and discusses how this evolution is affected by factors such as economic growth, political change, technological innovation, social change and cultural differences. This article provides readers with an understanding of what the Chinese market is like today and how it has developed over time. This paper analyzes many changes brought by big data analysis to marketing from the aspects of saving time and cost, changes in the nature of marketing, market segmentation, etc., and finally puts forward some strategies for the application of big data analysis in marketing. It also explains why the current situation of China is different from that of other countries in terms of culture, politics, etc., so as to provide readers with insights.

Keywords: Marketing management · Big data analysis · Characteristic · Strategy

1 Introduction

Marketing theory was born in the United States at the beginning of the 20th century. The emergence of marketing ideas has had a significant impact on American society and economy. It gives guidance to thousands of enterprises, provides a basis for the formulation of enterprise marketing plans, and also vigorously promotes the improvement of the social status of middlemen. Marketing thoughts have also changed people's views on society, market and consumption, and formed new values and codes of conduct.

In the 1950s, Professor Bolton first proposed 12 basic elements for guiding marketing practice activities, and the relevant definition of marketing mix was introduced and rapidly developed in this stage [1]. This combination of elements enables relatively clear analysis in this field in the marketing operation link, and at the same time carries

M. A. Jan and F. Khan (Eds.): BigIoT-EDU 2022, LNICST 467, pp. 354–364, 2023.
https://doi.org/10.1007/978-3-031-23944-1_39

out supporting definition work for the specific research scope of marketing. In the 1960s, McCarthy carried out a new integration of the theory and designed a new 4P combination theory. The formal production of this combination enables the industry to explore and grasp the key nodes of the market context from the various negative factors existing in the extremely special market changes, and further effectively fit the evolving marketing atmosphere.

In the 1980s, with the continuous deterioration of the competition in the contemporary market environment and the rapid growth of the current international trade system, the theoretical analysis of marketing gradually developed [2]. The initial 4P combination ignored the government and social forces that had a significant impact on the operation. In order to solve the various defects of this combination, Kotler made a supplementary analysis in 1986, adding two new P's of political power and public relations. The new combination is called the 6p combination of "big marketing", which highlights the focus on political and social factors.

At the 2017 "world telecommunication and information society day" Theme Conference, Jiang Zhengxin, deputy general manager of China Unicom, made it clear that as an important strategic business of the group, China Unicom attaches great importance to the development of big data [3]. First, accelerate the layout, take the lead in establishing big data companies, introduce first-class talents and technology, and implement the strategy of national concentration of big data; Second, apply the management and decision-making methods based on big data analysis to their own business management decisions; Third, carry out big data services externally to realize the realization of data assets; Fourth, establish a perfect big data security management system to ensure data security and information security. China Unicom has also repeatedly stressed the need to "create a new Unicom" with big data. In order to achieve this goal, China Unicom needs to adopt appropriate marketing strategies, give full play to its big data advantages, actively expand the market, promote the development of "big data + industry" and increase revenue.

With the continuous emergence of big data applications, market demand has continued to explode, ushering in important development opportunities for China's big data industry. With the promotion of favorable policies, a series of industrial markets around big data have taken shape. The big data industry development plan (2016–2020) points out that it is expected that by 2020, relevant services and products around big data will generate more than 1trillion yuan of revenue. Obviously, there is a huge market space for big data business [4].

2   Related Work

2.1   Characteristics of Big Data Era

First, the data scale is extremely large. Up to now, the total printed information produced by human beings is only 200pb (1PB = 210tb), while the comprehensive scale of all the words once spoken by human beings is about 5eb (1eb = 210Pb). At present, the data scale of many enterprises has reached the scale of EB [5].

Second, the data types are complex. The diversity of such data also leads to the basic classification of structured and unstructured data. Compared with the previous structured data focusing on the convenience of storage, new unstructured elements are constantly increasing, covering various data such as logs, audio and video, and such increasing data puts forward more stringent requirements for related processing capacity.

Third, the value density is relatively low. There is an inverse correlation between the actual value density and the data size. For example, relevant video files, monitoring data totaling one hour, may only have 1–2 s of useful information. How to use powerful algorithms to efficiently realize the value of data and achieve good "purification" operation has gradually evolved into one of the urgent problems to be solved in the contemporary big data environment.

Fourth, the processing speed is extremely fast. It belongs to the most critical feature of big data. According to the "Digital Universe" report released by IDC, it is estimated that the global comprehensive data will increase to 35.2zb by 2020. In the extremely huge data, the efficiency of data processing is the core factor that affects the survival of enterprises.

In the new environment of the 21st century, with globalization, technological growth and the rapid popularization of the network, the marketing atmosphere faced by enterprises is experiencing tremendous changes. One of the key elements in the commercial warfare activities in the new era is the effective development of information resources. For the relevant marketing enterprises, the actual efficiency of information response will have a significant impact on the comprehensive competitiveness and endanger the survival of the enterprise. Today, with the rapid development of information technology, the marketing mechanism has also made remarkable development, bringing a brand-new data revolution, breaking the constraints of the old systems in all aspects, relying on the unique systems in all aspects, building a marketing system that fits the information environment, and the marketing mode with information technology as the core can certainly replace the relevant traditional mode [6]. The specific mode and quality of information acquisition have gradually evolved into one of the core links of contemporary competition. Therefore, introducing networks and supporting tools to optimize traditional marketing is one of the main trends of future development. As shown in Fig. 1.

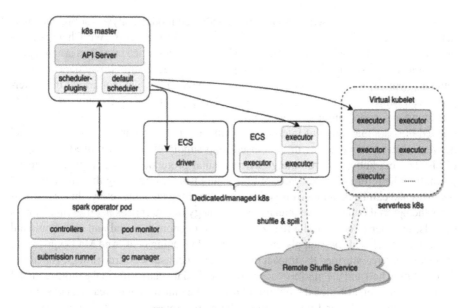

Fig. 1. Big data marketing mode

2.2 Big Data Marketing Analysis

In traditional marketing activities, in order to carry out brand promotion and publicity, enterprises often use TV media or paper media to put brand advertisements on the public, and increase brand exposure through a large number of advertisements to achieve the purpose of expanding sales. Although this way of publicity through mass media has a relatively wide range of radiation, it also has many disadvantages: on the one hand, it is unable to segment the consumer market, which makes the brand promotion cost high and the actual promotion efficiency low; On the other hand, enterprises cannot judge the preferences of the actual audience, nor can they grasp the timely feedback of the promotion audience and the resulting actual consumption conversion rate. Therefore, the marketing reform from mass media oriented to consumer oriented is imperative. Personalized marketing based on consumer customization has gradually replaced the traditional mass media advertising, which is the predecessor of big data marketing. With the popularity of communication equipment, the continuous enrichment of sales channels and the emergence of new digital social media, user data has shown a big explosion trend [7]. At the same time, more and more enterprises begin to realize the value of big data, and rely on multi platform big data collection, cloud computing, text analysis and other big data prediction and analysis technologies to analyze and depict user portraits in real time, analyze consumers' shopping preferences, so as to segment the consumer market, and use big data marketing technology to accurately launch advertisements from various sales channels and social media to improve marketing efficiency, Bring the return on investment of brands and enterprises that subvert the traditional advertising marketing in the past.

In recent years, some scholars have also conducted model analysis for big data marketing, providing a more scientific basis for enterprise managers. Wu Chengxia and others targeted the supply chain system in which big data service providers are independent subjects, and specifically compared and analyzed three enterprise payment methods: retailer payment, joint payment and cooperative payment, which confirmed that enterprises can achieve a win-win situation in the supply chain with the help of big data marketing and cooperation among enterprises. Ma Deqing and others have also incorporated big data marketing of Internet platforms into the collaborative operation model between different enterprises in the closed-loop supply chain, and proved the impact of big data marketing in promoting environmental protection concepts to consumers, promoting the return of more waste products, and further improving the environmental goodwill and call back of enterprises. On the basis of big data marketing, this paper analyzes the optimal collaborative management strategy of enterprises in different business periods, in order to achieve the realization of the economic, social and environmental benefits of the closed-loop supply chain system. Ma Deqing et al. And Ma Deqing et al. Further research confirmed the impact of considering consumers' free riding behavior in the exhibition hall and the platform's adoption of big data marketing in the multi-channel retail environment, affirmed the important role of the platform in increasing consumers' brand stickiness and brand goodwill with the help of big data marketing, and showed that big data marketing, as an important marketing means in the era of multi-channel retail, can effectively enhance the market competitiveness of e-commerce platforms [8]. Xiang et al. Took big data marketing as an important operation tool of the network platform, studied the cooperation strategy between enterprises in the closed-loop supply chain, and found that big data marketing can effectively promote the improvement of product sales and recovery rate. Enterprises should more support the network platform for big data marketing. At the same time, they found that when manufacturers share the cost of the network platform, retailers have free riding behavior. In the closed-loop supply chain system of third-party recycling, Xiang et al. Considered the impact of supply side enterprise technological innovation investment, big data marketing and enterprise overconfidence on enterprise decision-making and performance level in the closed-loop supply chain. At the same time, they found that enterprise overconfidence and recycling cost sharing contract can effectively stimulate enterprise technological innovation and big data marketing investment, And then greatly reduce the manufacturing and recovery costs of the whole closed-loop supply chain system.

3 Marketing Theory

In 1960, McCarthy, an American scholar, put forward the marketing strategy in his book basic marketing, as shown in Fig. 2. That is, product, price, place and promotion. Among them, products are specific products, virtual services, ideology or combinations of the above that are provided by enterprises and can meet the needs of consumers. In order to realize the smooth implementation of the enterprise's strategy, it is necessary to constantly introduce and develop new products; Price strategy is the embodiment of product value, which has certain variables. Consumers generally measure the value of products through the price of products. The price and pricing strategy of products will directly affect consumers' purchase decisions and are inseparable from the profitability of enterprises; Channel strategy is the way of product sales and the process of delivering the products of an enterprise to its target customers [9]. Channel strategies generally include sales location, supply chain, inventory status, communication between enterprises and end users, etc.; Promotion strategy is a process in which enterprises stimulate consumers by changing their sales behavior, usually transmitting product information to potential consumers in a short time, so as to promote sales growth, which has certain risks.

Philip Kotler, the "father of modern marketing", further confirmed the marketing mix method with 4Ps as the core in marketing management: analysis, planning and control (First Edition) in 1967.

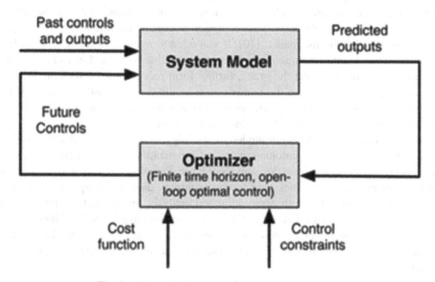

Fig. 2. Schematic diagram of marketing mix model

Big data marketing is a widely used marketing method based on massive data on multiple platforms and with the help of big data analysis technology, focusing on "Internet + industry". By collecting and mining a large amount of data and analyzing big data, Internet enterprises can have a certain prediction ability, explore new business opportunities, better serve customers, innovate business models, and increase the benefits of enterprises.

Big data marketing generally includes four processes: data collection, data mining analysis, prediction analysis and data result feedback. Compared with traditional marketing methods, big data marketing has the advantages of high timeliness, personalized customization, high cost performance and relevance promotion.

The advent of the big data era has brought great changes to social production and life. The innovative technology represented by mobile Internet has brought a large amount of user behavior data, and also provided unprecedented space and potential for industries and enterprises to obtain more profound and comprehensive insight. It has also made big data marketing break through the boundaries of Internet enterprises, so that all industries can really have the opportunity to have a deep understanding of their own market environment, service objects, customer groups or even competitors.

Based on the evolution of marketing ideas, it can be concluded that "marketing" belongs to the basic definition of continuous growth. It is based on the transaction activities between enterprises and consumers in the initial stage, and then evolved into a special existence with complex purposes. At the same time, it links all aspects of the relevant participants. It needs to form a more scientific communication bridge based on the links in all aspects. In order to achieve effective mutual benefit in all aspects, we should explore the regular relevant data in the special data system. Data mining exerts this kind of bridge effect. The marketing based on data mining technology takes relevant relationship marketing as the core, highlights the influence factors in all aspects of the environment, maintains effective communication, effectively adjusts the current marketing policy with reference to specific market conditions, and forms a good and stable relationship with the market [10]. If you want to maintain a stable relationship, you need to bring good continuous service to users, so that users can form a high degree of trust in the enterprise and the brand, further form recognition for the enterprise or specific products, and achieve the improvement of the comprehensive interests of the enterprise. Therefore, accurate positioning marketing and arming traditional marketing mode with modern technology are the inevitable way out.

With the rapid development of modern technology, marketing is gradually evolving towards new trends such as automation and informatization. Among them, the related data is relatively complex: from the analysis of basic operating statements to the relevant information exchange activities, and various complex data in the operation links, it is required to conduct in-depth exploration and analysis, and predict the future trend on this basis. Traditional tools are difficult to solve the unique needs of this kind of information, so more novel technologies are required to process it and find the valuable key information. Data mining is the core technology to accelerate the growth of marketing system.

4   Phased Development Analysis of Chinese Marketing Based on Big Data

With the rapid development of modern information technology, especially the rapid progress of computer technology, data mining has made a significant impact on traditional marketing. Relying on the powerful functions of the database, it brings reliable support for such two-way interaction, good information communication and sharing, and effective integration of various elements, which makes the new marketing system born. In the past, the marketing mainly focused on products, and there was a certain quantitative analysis demand in this link, but it did not cover all the data. At the same time, it failed to promote the digital marketing to the core position of the comprehensive marketing process. The existing impacts are concentrated in the following three aspects:

① Rely on data mining and supporting editing operations to form a complete database. The actual data needs to cover information and records. For example, Nestle has built a large-scale database containing 20 million materials, which comes from various promotional methods.

② Select the corresponding consumer. The new database model makes the personalized marketing have good feasibility, so that the relevant enterprises can effectively serve the general users and provide them with personalized products. It represents that the supply of products is realized with reference to the specific needs of users. Relying on the supporting data mining operation, we can assist relevant marketing subjects to carry out supporting market analysis, judge the interests, habits and needs of specific subjects, further form accurate prediction and vigorously develop the market, and improve the effect of marketing activities. Relevant marketing based on data mining can usually provide targeted marketing data. If the data is relatively complete, it can simulate its activities to build models, draw up efficient marketing plans, and provide users with more targeted products. Therefore, carry out more targeted communication, improve the comprehensive feedback rate, increase the comprehensive sales volume, and achieve effective cost control. As shown in Fig. 3:

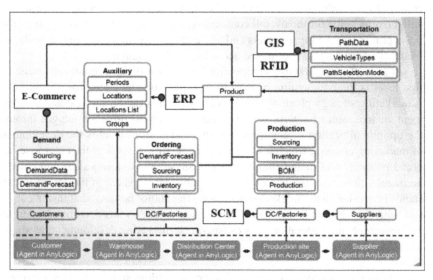

Fig. 3. Accurate marketing based on big data

③ Extend marketing profit. Through the relevant data mining operations, enterprises can realize richer profits. By referring to the relevant data statistics and consumption models, they can expand and maintain the relationship with relevant users, that is, they can detect their current needs, predict their future needs, effectively solve their existing basic needs, and achieve the effect of maximizing profits. At the same time, the basic data obtained through relevant data mining can expand the needs of users for relevant products and services; Referring to the relevant association analysis, the current needs of the user may lead to other association needs. In terms of marketing, to effectively address such needs, we can explore new growth points on the basis of current profits.

④ Reduce marketing costs.

Marketing cost is a difficult problem that all aspects focus on. The comprehensive cost of traditional schemes is relatively high. Even if such schemes can reap corresponding profits, the actual marketing effect is not ideal because the comprehensive cost is too high. Therefore, effective cost control is required. At the same time, marketing can detect the basic needs of users without realizing unrelated services, so as to control relevant costs. At the same time, the marketing department adjusts the channels according to the specific needs and controls the comprehensive communication expenses. Under the new environment, it is necessary to focus on customers and efficiently develop existing data to achieve the ideal effect of "$1 + 1 > 2$" in marketing.

Excluding the above related problems, this mode has other advantages. For example, first of all, provide supporting consumer information for relevant enterprises, and apply it to telephone, service and other aspects. Secondly, provide corresponding counterattack methods. Supporting marketing based on data mining has significant enlightening value for the overall competition, can reflect relevant user characteristics, optimize marketing, products and services, and enhance user trust. Finally, the feedback is efficient and optimized according to the actual effect.

At present, the marketing competition in China is divided into three levels: the first level is the competition of marketing skills, such as price; The second level is marketing strategy planning, which mainly focuses on the survival and development environment of enterprises, and establishes competitive advantages through the optimal allocation of enterprise resources; The third level is the development of marketing concept, which infiltrates the marketing concept of the enterprise into brand publicity and image communication, shapes the unique values and cultural heritage of the enterprise, and ensures the stable development of the enterprise and stands invincible in the market competition. The author believes that this is consistent with the division of the four levels of marketing, so this division is scientific and represents the general process of enterprise marketing development, as shown in Fig. 4.

The division of marketing levels has important guiding significance for enterprise marketing management. The author believes that there are mainly the following points:

(1) In the marketing practice, in order to avoid the trouble of price war and advertising war, enterprises should shape their brands. However, due to the inconsistent understanding of brands and ways to enhance competitiveness, the marketing and brand management of enterprises are lost. The common misunderstanding is that advertising is regarded as an important and even the only choice to shape and maintain the brand, resulting in enterprises just out of the "price war" and falling into the "advertising war".

The division of marketing levels provides theoretical guidance for the marketing practice of enterprises, so that enterprises can clarify their position in the market competition, so as to make decisions that are more in line with the current situation of enterprises, get rid of the perplexity of marketing "strange circle", and make the development of enterprises move towards normalization.

(2) Although marketing is divided into four levels, the four levels of marketing are jumping, and the development of enterprises does not have to follow the four levels in turn. The division of marketing levels can enable enterprises to have an overall and overall strategic planning for the development of enterprises. According to the development goals of enterprises and their own strength, they can choose marketing strategies suitable for the current situation of enterprises, and provide guidance for the marketing development of enterprises.

Brand war is the ultimate goal of enterprise development, but not all enterprises have the strength to carry out brand construction, maintain and innovate the brand. This requires enterprises to size up the situation and determine the strategic steps of enterprise development. Clear strategic planning can make enterprises develop orderly and healthily.

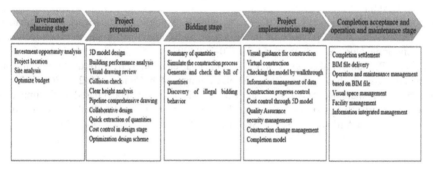

Fig. 4. China marketing stage of big data

5   Conclusion

Big data is the product of the development of IT technology to a certain stage. As an innovative business, it brings a major opportunity for all walks of life to achieve transformation and win competition, and has attracted the attention of many countries and enterprises. The Chinese government attaches great importance to the development of big data industry, and the outline of the 13th five year plan clearly promotes big data as a national strategy. Therefore, 2018 is also known as the year of big data government delivery. At present, there are only a few enterprises with strategic concepts and strategic management functions in Chinese enterprises, and the management of most enterprises is still in the stage of operation and management. "Non strategic operation" has no obvious disadvantages in the initial stage of enterprise development, but once it enters the rapid growth period, it becomes the key to affect the progress of enterprise marketing development.

References

1. Wang, G.: Research on the development of safety education content in the field of physical education based on big data analysis. J. Phys. Conf. Ser. **1744**(3), 032243 (4pp) (2021)

2. Yang, J., Shi, Y.: Development strategy of educational robot industry based on big data analysis. In: Sugumaran, V., Xu, Z., Zhou, H. (eds.) MMIA 2020. AISC, vol. 1234, pp. 62–68. Springer, Cham (2021). https://doi.org/10.1007/978-3-030-51556-0_10
3. Guan, H., Zhao, X.: Study on the prediction system of shrimp field distribution in the east China sea based on big data analysis of fishing trajectories. J. Ocean Univ. China **20**(1), 228–234 (2021). https://doi.org/10.1007/s11802-021-4518-5
4. Liu, Y.: Research on the marketing strategy of rural characteristic tourism based on the analysis of big data. J. Phys. Conf. Ser. **1744**(4), 042081 (2021)
5. Zhang, L.: Optimization of the marketing management system based on cloud computing and big data. Complexity **2021**, 1851–1863 (2021)
6. Yang, Y.: Clustering and prediction analysis of the coordinated development of China's regional economy based on immune genetic algorithm. Complexity **41**, 2231–2242 (2021)
7. Xiao, J., Wang, W., Tsai, S.B.: Coupling of agricultural product marketing and agricultural economic development based on big data analysis and "Internet+." Mob. Inf. Syst. **2021**(8), 1–10 (2021)
8. Ontalba, M.N., Corbacho, J.N., Baeza, A., et al.: Radiological alert network of extremadura (RAREx) at 2021: 30 years of development and current performance of on-real time monitoring. Nucl. Eng. Technol. **54**(2), 770–780 (2021)
9. Zheng, B., Sun, S., Shao, G.: Cooperative antenna selection method for directional antenna ad hoc networks based on ALOHA. Wirel. Commun. Mob. Comput. **16**, 254–267 (2021)
10. Abula, K., Abula, K., Abula, B., et al.: An analysis of gravity model based on the impact of China's agricultural exports – a case study of western and Central Asia along the economic corridor. Acta Agriculturae Scand. Sect. B, Soil Plant Sci. **71**(6), 432–442 (2021)

Exploring the Practical Teaching of a Specialized Interim Course in Electronic Information Engineering Under the Background of Artificial Intelligence

Liu Li[✉], Wang Ying, and Li Qing

Wuchang Shouyi University, Hongshan District, Wuhan 430064, Hubei, China
ll_yu09@163.com

Abstract. Electronic information technology in China is rapidly developing. With the submission of the idea of artificial intelligence, higher education corresponded to the growth rate of the industrial revolution and the new economic environment. Artificial intelligence meets the progress logic of the Department and provides breakthroughs for education facing under the new environment. In this paper, we analyze the needs of human resources in the insertion system, knowledge system, internal core and processor linear. On the other hand, the author explained the selection of the contents content integration experiment platform and the practical program design of the "insertion system" practice education of the electronic information engineering.

Keywords: Electronic information engineering · Artificial intelligence · Embedded courses · Practical teaching

1 Introduction

With the rapid development of information technology, computer science and technology specialization has been developing rapidly in recent years. As an application-oriented university, we must timely grasp and predict the new trends in the development of technology fields". The R&D; "D-application acceleration" of artificial intelligence formally expressed that artificial intelligence has become an important component of the national strategic emerging industry; from 2010 to 2019, artificial intelligence engineering majors have been deeply embedded in the national strategic layout to talent stockpiling, and more than 500 colleges and universities across the country have been opened one after another. The Party's 19th Congress built a net-strong country, digital China and a smart society, promoting the deep integration of the net, big data, artificial intelligence and the real economy, and the deep integration of the digital digital economy. We must develop the economy, share the economy, cultivate new growth points, and form new driving forces. Under such a new situation, how to effectively combine the specialization of electronic information engineering and artificial intelligence, and how

M. A. Jan and F. Khan (Eds.): BigIoT-EDU 2022, LNICST 467, pp. 365–376, 2023.
https://doi.org/10.1007/978-3-031-23944-1_40

to turn on the cultivation of the practical education of embedded courses, is a question that all artificial intelligence engineering education workers should think about [1].

Insertion system practical education is an important professional course in the Department of Electrical Engineering, and an important component of the education system. It is increasingly emphasized as a means of experimentation to verify knowledge, train skills, and cultivate competence. The IEEE's survey of the world's science and engineering education problems shows that the most important skills that science and engineering students should have are the ability to innovate and the ability to solve real problems. Therefore, it is an important goal of education to enhance students' ability to innovate in the field of embedded system applications through practical education. Although the current mosaic education includes some practical operations, it has not yet reached the rich operation and practice level.

For the embedded course education plan, this course list lists the courses according to the certain meaning of "embedded system is a special computer system", that is, the definition of this list is "after learning, you can build a fully functional and special computer system from the chip circuit level", which is similar to the existence of a full stack of engineer course guides. In practice, not everyone needs to realize from IC to product, but it has both deep expertise and wide knowledge, which is popular in the industry. The content of embedded system development is shown in Fig. 1 below.

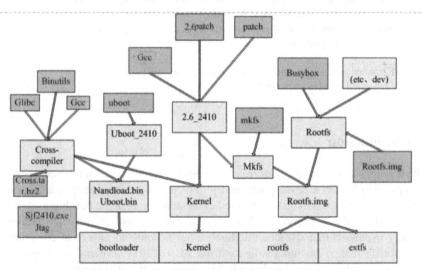

Fig. 1. Content of embedded system development

1. Due to work reasons, high-speed signal processing is required, so at present, FPGA HDL design, electromagnetic compatibility design, and automatic control leading course signal and system are added, of course.. With more signals and systems, basic courses need more big things [2].

2. Supplement C+ + language. It was a necessity. I forgot to add it. Another digression: the use of C++ in MCU design is becoming more and more popular. Whether Arduino or mbed, its library implementation is C++.
3. Remove LabVIEW programming design,
4. Add QT programming.
5. Remove Android development. Originally, Android was mostly used as a mobile terminal for simple user interface interaction. Since wechat applet opened ble's APL, Android applications began to be a little tired in the embedded side. (of course, Android is also mostly used for advertising machines, but if the scheme is not limited, it is more convenient to choose X86 platform for development.)
6. Remove SSH development. Since the change of python, there is no need to worry about the back-end. Build small projects by yourself, and hand over large projects to the professional back-end.
7. Modify Java language to Python language. Without Android and SSH, Java is useless. However, in order to better understand the idea of OO, we still need a language with OO programming as a leading course. Although C++ also needs to be learned, the OO environment is not very pure, so it is changed to python [3].
8. Between comments, remove front-end knowledge. Before, I added the front-end knowledge because I crossed the front-end for some time to write JS vue。 But I still recommend learning. After all, the applet is written in JS. And now in terms of Internet interaction, web interaction has the highest cost performance.

This article focuses on the problems of the current practical education model based on the characteristics of embedded system education and the talent cultivation goals of the local engineering college. Through the optimization of teaching contents and appropriate improvement measures, the teaching level of embedded systems will be enhanced.

2 Related Work

2.1 Artificial Intelligence Concept

What is artificial intelligence "Ai"? The scientific basis and connotation of classical artificial intelligence. The theme of church Turing theory, which was formed and widely accepted in 1936, is that Turing machines can "imitate" any calculation. Based on the above two achievements, we obtain the Godel Turing lemma: using Turing machine can "imitate" some reasoning [4]. "Imitation" in church Turing theme has the same mathematical definition as "imitation" certified by Godel. At the same time, it has accumulated a large number of research results and constantly produced new imitation methods. "Symbolism", "connectionism" and "behaviorism" imitate different functions of intelligence respectively, and belong to classical artificial intelligence. In addition to word expression, the second problem also implicitly involves common sense, emotion and causal reasoning. Turing believes that after about 50 years of research, AI relying on "functional imitation" will be able to make humans think they are "intelligent" through this test. The working principle of training method has not been strictly mathematically defined, so it is not interpretable.

With the rapid development of AI and other new technologies, robots and artificial intelligence can realize the intellectualization of the middle and lower reaches of the manufacturing industry through scene closure, so as to realize the high-end in the whole industrial chain, so as to ensure the basic position of the manufacturing industry. This will subvert road transportation and travel modes, destroy the living and working forms of a considerable number of people, and promote great changes in relevant industries. Disruptive innovations are also taking place in industries such as smart appliances, healthcare and AI accelerated scientific research and R &amp.

In the Internet era, information circulation (acquisition, transmission, analysis and application) has become the mainstream, and the big data market of the whole industry has gradually formed a scale. How to make good use of the big data that has begun to take shape in different fields to seek the development and growth of enterprises and organizations and seek a new economic growth model; How to cultivate professionals with strong comprehensive quality under the market demand for talents in the direction of big data. The above two aspects are not only the test of big data market economy to enterprises, but also an important reason for China's colleges and universities to pay close attention to market development and vigorously build big data related majors. However, at present, the core courses of big data related majors in most colleges and universities are only for data mining and analysis, display and application [5]. And where does the data come from? How to transmit and share? These aspects are often not included in the curriculum system of big data related majors. This means that the talents trained by the existing big data related majors are not enough to fully support the big data industry, and there is still a certain gap in the field of data acquisition, transmission and sharing.

However, the acquisition and transmission of data are just within the scope of the Internet of things. Therefore, the development of the Internet of things and big data can be effectively integrated. The Internet of things engineering specialty can provide hardware support talents for the field of big data, so as to achieve high-precision and rapid acquisition and transmission of data. The big data specialty can provide software talents for the field of Internet of things to realize effective data analysis and processing. The interworking of the two specialties can further promote the improvement and development of the information technology industry chain in today's rapid growth of the Internet of things and big data.

2.2 Analysis of Embedded System Teaching at Present

Embedded system is a special computer system, which is a part of device or equipment. Generally, an embedded system is an embedded processor control board whose control program is stored in ROM. In fact, all devices with digital interfaces, such as watches, microwave ovens, video recorders, automobiles, etc., use embedded systems. Some embedded systems also include operating systems, but most embedded systems realize the whole control logic by a single program.

Alphago, driverless, wearable devices, industry 4.0, smart home and other terms refresh our screen every day. They are all new products of smart electronics and representative works of embedded technology. Embedded technology, a special computer system centered on application, based on computer technology and free cutting of software and hardware, is ubiquitous, and a new era of intelligent Internet of things has come.

The characteristic of embedded technology is to combine hardware and software, integrate artificial intelligence technology, and promote the realization of intelligent environment in animal networking. As the core technology of the Internet of things, embedded technology will open a new era.

Embedded system course is an interdisciplinary course, which covers computer, electronic technology, information science and so on. The design of embedded system includes both hardware and software. With the continuous emergence of embedded new technologies, the complexity of software and hardware is also increasing, which makes the courses that college students find difficult to learn more difficult, more content to learn, and teachers feel heavy teaching tasks and pressure. To sum up, the current embedded system teaching generally has the following three problems. The application example of embedded system is shown in Fig. 2 below.

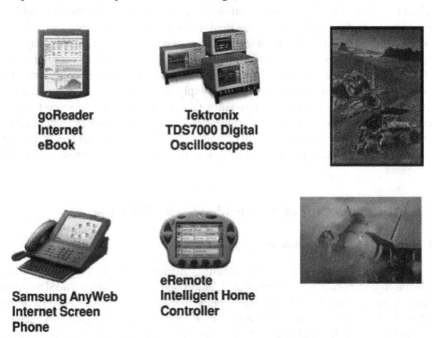

Fig. 2. Embedded system application example

(1) Less class hours. At present, there are about 40 theoretical class hours and about 10 practical class hours in embedded technology courses in Colleges and universities. The knowledge system of this course is relatively complex. In addition, there are many contents and few class hours, especially the practical class hours. For such a highly practical subject, 10 class hours obviously can not meet the requirements of cultivating students' ability [6].

(2) Software and hardware teaching imbalance. Limited by the requirements of professional direction, in terms of content selection, some colleges and universities focus on hardware, while others focus on software. The development of embedded system requires both software and hardware; The development of embedded technology is also a process in which hardware development and software development promote each other. The imbalance of teaching will inevitably lead to the imbalance of students' ability, which restricts the development of students' independent design ability.

(3) Single teaching means and low quality of teachers. Most of the current embedded course teaching is still the traditional ppt mode, students' interest is generally low, and there is always a lack of dynamic teaching methods such as heuristic and project-based. At the same time, most of the teachers have no working experience in enterprises and are unable to provide students with development experience.

The rise of artificial intelligence has prompted most relevant enterprises to enter the track of transformation. The transformation of enterprises means the transformation of the demand for technical talents [7]. The simple embedded teaching system can no longer meet the needs of the times Artificial intelligence technology is a complex of many technologies, including embedded technology, sensor technology, wireless communication technology, mobile computing technology and advanced data processing technology, which requires colleges and universities to comply with the trend of the times, adjust the training plan, improve the teaching quality, take the needs of enterprises as the guidance, and pay attention to the cultivation of students' professional quality. For embedded system designers, they should constantly update their knowledge system and accept the new requirements, challenges and technologies brought by the application of artificial intelligence.

3   Practical Teaching of "Embedded System" Course

3.1   Embedded System Knowledge System

The knowledge system of embedded system is mainly shown in Fig. 3. Embedded hardware engineers need to master module 1, embedded system engineers need to master module 1 and module 2, and embedded application engineers mainly need to master module 3. The course system of electronic information engineering generally includes the contents of module 1 and module 2, but it generally lacks the necessary knowledge of embedded operating system transplantation such as compilation principle, data structure and operating system. This makes it very difficult for students to learn complex operating systems (such as Linux and wince), so they choose small kernel embedded operating systems (such as μ C-os) is more operable.

ARM mainly sells chip design technology and does not directly engage in chip production, semiconductor manufacturers buy ARM microprocessor cores, according to their respective application areas to add peripheral function modules, forming ARM microprocessor chip, Students have the basic knowledge of microcontroller principles and microcomputer interface principles [8], the ARM architecture, instruction system, hardware and software debugging tools, registers and peripheral functions are still quite unfamiliar, such as the choice of the core as the outline, students can not master a specific chip, resulting in slow development; such as the choice of a chip as the outline, and will weaken the ARM design concept, confined to the chip itself, it is difficult to It is difficult to understand the chip itself.

Cortex is the latest generation of ARM cores, including the M series for the price-sensitive embedded field, emphasizing the determinism of operation and the balance of performance, power consumption and price, which is suitable for embedded teaching in electronic information engineering and easy for students to complete the effective transition from microcontroller to ARM.

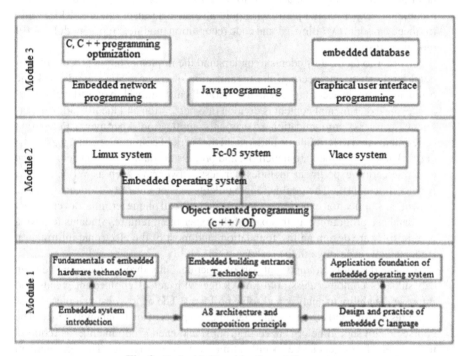

Fig. 3. Embedded teaching knowledge system

3.2 Reform Ideas of Embedded Teaching in the Context of Artificial Intelligence

(1) Theoretical course plan setting

Artificial intelligence technology is a multi-disciplinary technology, it is necessary to add new disciplines for artificial intelligence on the basis of the original embedded curriculum system. Artificial intelligence-oriented disciplines involve not only basic disciplines such as sensor technology, RF technology, communication networking technology, but also application disciplines including network security and system development. Due to the limitation of training program hours, most universities are already saturated with theoretical courses, and adding new courses involves objective resistance to the revision of training program and syllabus [9].

(2) Adjustment of practical teaching system

The purpose of experiments is to make students enhance their understanding and learn basic application. The content of experiments depends on the platform of experiments. Although the traditional embedded experimental platform is much more functional than the microcontroller platform, but. To meet the requirements of AI capability development, it needs to be further extended in terms of functionality. The architecture of artificial intelligence includes the perception layer, network layer and application layer, and the embedded technology is applied to the perception layer and network layer. In addition to the basic processor, display, button, motor module, the experimental platform should also have a sensor module, RFID radio frequency module two-dimensional code recognition module, xigbee module, WIFI module and so on.

In order to facilitate students to understand the implementation process of artificial intelligence engineering, the organization of experiments should break the original system, in accordance with the hierarchical relationship of artificial intelligence, the experimental content is divided into perception and identification experiments, wireless communication experiments, application experiments. Perception experiments aim to let students understand the work of common sensors, master the network node implementation method, and process the data of sensing devices. The communication experiment includes wireless networking such as WIFI, Zighee, Bluetooth, etc. [10]. The goal is to let students master a variety of means to build networks. Application experiments mainly include cell phone terminal development and database programming, this part of the experiment requires students to have a certain software design ability foundation, and most of the electronic information students have a shortage in the reserve of this ability.

Course design is an important part of practice. Only through the course design can students combine classroom knowledge with actual engineering needs and improve the ability to analyze and solve problems. The course design topics should be representative and cover all major technical aspects of artificial intelligence. The course design should be organized in groups, and each group member is required to complete the project in the specified time by working together. The management of the course design process is the key to ensure the effectiveness. The instructor is responsible for the guidance and supervision of the process, and can communicate and share information with students through the form of network platform.

(3) Externship expansion

Off-campus internship is an extension of on-campus teaching. Let students go out of school to the front line of enterprises to directly feel and participate in the implementation of the actual project, which is conducive to understanding the current situation and trends, broaden their horizons, but also make students realize the distance between their own ability and the level of demand of enterprises, is a good exercise for the will [11]. In recent years, the internship education outside the university has been paid more and more attention, and many universities have cooperated with enterprises to set up internship bases in enterprises, and students are willing to learn and work in a new environment, while enterprises can prepare for the training of talents.

4   Embedded Practical Teaching

Nowadays, the Internet has penetrated into all aspects of daily work and life. Making full use of the network environment to organize teaching can carry out targeted teaching activities more conveniently and flexibly. Compared with traditional classroom teaching, network platform teaching has the characteristics of autonomy, interaction and pertinence [12]. Establish a course website, build a communication platform between teachers and students, and integrate classic teaching links such as Q & A, questioning and discussion into the network. Students can ask questions and questions to teachers on the network platform, and teachers can scientifically and conveniently answer students' questions and solve their doubts on the network. At the same time, a discussion area can be established to facilitate teachers and students to discuss professional issues. Making full use of online teaching resources and extending the process of teaching and learning outside the classroom not only stimulate students' interest in learning, but also deepen and expand classroom teaching. The following Fig. 4 shows the code compilation of embedded development classroom.

Fig. 4. Embedded development classroom code compilation

Embedded system development is a highly practical course, and experimental teaching is an important part of course teaching. Through the experiment, it can help students deepen their understanding of theoretical knowledge, strengthen students' practical ability, and comprehensively master the development, design and debugging technology of embedded system.

At present, the practical teaching links of embedded system development include: confirmatory experiment, comprehensive design experiment, curriculum design, college students' innovation experiment, scientific research project and so on.

Confirmatory experiment is the basis of experimental teaching. The experimental content is closely combined with the teaching content of theoretical course. It is the most basic application of basic knowledge and an important part of practical teaching. Comprehensive design experiment is the deepening of confirmatory experiment to further cultivate students to comprehensively use their knowledge and design embedded systems. Embedded course design is a comprehensive application of the course content. Through this practical link, students can fully master the development and design methods of embedded application system. College Students' innovation experiment is an innovative experiment carried out by students in their spare time under the guidance of teachers [13]. Through innovative experiments, students have accumulated project development experience, cultivated their own innovation ability, and laid a solid foundation for further embedded project research and development. Scientific research project is an application project suitable for practical teaching combined with the cutting-edge scientific and technological application of embedded system. It can broaden students' vision, expand students' thinking, and play a good auxiliary role in teaching.

The content of the experimental course starts with a simple routine of port control LED display, and completes the experimental process of building a new project, writing a program, downloading program debugging and viewing the experimental results. Through this simple experiment, students can preliminarily master the use of uview3 IDE for ARM development environment and arm software simulator, as well as the general steps of program download. In the future, the experimental difficulty will be gradually increased. At present, the experimental projects include interrupt experiment, serial communication experiment, a/D conversion experiment, etc. During the experiment, pay attention to stimulating students' learning enthusiasm and interest in hands-on experiment. Actively encourage students to use a variety of different software algorithms to complete the same experiment, improve students' programming ability and broaden students' thinking [14].

Reform the design of experimental teaching links, and gradually change from the previous "verification based" to the experimental curriculum teaching design mode of "verification supplemented by self innovation".

For example, in the experiment of "matrix lesd character display control", the experiment requires to understand the lattice principle and verify the program given in the experimental instruction. These are often completed successfully by students. This verification experiment model does not give better play to students' creativity. This experiment can be positioned as a design experiment, which requires students to display a variety of Chinese characters, characters and graphics on the LED screen, with dynamic display effect. The experiment is conducted in groups. After the experiment is completed, each group shows its own experimental results, and finally the experimental results are scored [15]. This requires students to modify the source program to realize the corresponding functions on the basis of reading the source program. Through the experiment, the students successfully completed the single display of English characters and Chinese characters, designed rich and colorful patterns, such as cartoon animals, character expressions, flowers and trees, and realized the dynamic display of Chinese characters and graphics (left and right scrolling, up and down scrolling, flashing). The experimental effect is good. The experimental results show that the competitive incentive mechanism displayed in groups mobilizes students' enthusiasm and gives full play to students' innovative ability.

5 Conclusion

The course of embedded system itself has complex knowledge structure and strong practicality, so teaching and learning are faced with great difficulties. In the context of artificial intelligence, embedded system courses must focus on multidisciplinary integration, more comprehensive. The difficulty becomes greater. In this paper, an improved teaching model is given to meet the needs of the era of artificial intelligence in terms of theoretical teaching, practical activities and off-campus extension. In practice, it has been shown that the effect of converting more pressure into motivation has been achieved, and both interest and ability have been significantly increased. The development of artificial intelligence still needs a large number of talents, and it needs the unremitting efforts of educators to promote the reform of embedded system teaching and improve the quality foundation of talents.

References

1. Zhu, Z.: Composition of online teaching and academic ability under the background of artificial intelligence and HTML. In: 2021 5th International Conference on Computing Methodologies and Communication (ICCMC) (2021)
2. Wei, H.: Integrated development of rural eco-tourism under the background of artificial intelligence applications and wireless internet of things. J. Ambient Intell. Humanized Comput. **67**, 1–13 (2021)
3. Ekici, B., Kazanasmaz, Z.T., Turrin, M., et al.: Multi-zone optimisation of high-rise buildings using artificial intelligence for sustainable metropolises. Part 1: background, methodology, setup, and machine learning results. Sol. Energy. **224**(2), 373–389 (2021)
4. Lukkien, D., Herman, N H., Buimer, H P., et al.: Towards responsible artificial intelligence in long-term care: a scoping review on practical approaches. Gerontologist (2021)
5. Liu, W., Shen, M., Zhang, A., et al.: Artificial intelligence rehabilitation evaluation and training system for degeneration of joint disease. ZTE Commun. **19**(3), 10 (2021)
6. Andersson, J., Nyholm, T., Ceberg, C., et al.: Artificial intelligence and the medical physics profession - A Swedish perspective. Physica Med. **88**(2), 218–225 (2021)
7. Sanches, A.: An embedded systems remote course. J. Online Eng. Edu. **11**(2), 1 (2021)
8. Evans, S.Z., Evans, J.: Undergraduate research embedded across course levels and types through scaffolded projects. J. Sch. Teach. Learn. **21**(1), 152–170 (2021)
9. Bandyszak, T., Jckel, L., Kls, M., et al.: Handling uncertainty in collaborative embedded systems engineering (2021)
10. Simons, R.L., Man-Kit, L., Eric, K., et al.: Re(Setting) epigenetic clocks: an important avenue whereby social conditions become biologically embedded across the life course. J. Health Soc. Behav. **62**, 436–453 (2021)
11. Xu, X.: Material database management system based on heterogeneous multi-processor and computer embedded system. Microprocess. Microsyst. **82**(2), 103926 (2021)

12. He, N.: Incorporating on-going verification & validation research to a reliable real-time embedded systems course. In: 2013 North Midwest Section Meeting (2021)
13. Hu, H., Jin, S., Wang, Y., et al.: Research on teaching practice of app inventor course with embedded in computational thinking. Int. J. Embedded Syst. 1(1), 1 (2021)
14. Reform and practice of teaching team of embedded system course. Creative Educ. Stud. 09(1), 29–33 (2021)
15. Shi, L., Wang, J.: Research on teaching reforms of embedded system course under new situation for IOT speciality. In: 6th Annual International Conference on Social Science and Contemporary Humanity Development (SSCHD 2020) (2021)

Research on Interactive English Grammar Learning System Based on Android Platform

Jian Gong[1,2(✉)]

[1] Henan University of Animal Husbandry and Economy, Zhengzhou 450000, Henan, China
tongtong88flora@hotmail.com
[2] Philippine Christian University, Manila, Philippines

Abstract. In recent years, with more and more Chinese learning English, there are more and more English learning software, but most of the software are lack of good pronunciation evaluation and feedback correction. However, in English pronunciation learning, especially for non-native English learners, effective feedback motivation is very important. This has become a bottleneck restricting intelligent English learning software. According to the characteristics of Android mobile learning platform, this paper designs an interactive English grammar learning software based on Android platform, which is based on online learning algorithm and interactive system Combined with C-SVC and v-svc data analysis, this paper expounds the main algorithm ideas in the development process based on Android, which is used to improve and promote the learning of English grammar. Finally, the implementation of the interactive system proposed by the algorithm, the results show that the system search accurate, comprehensive content, conducive to English grammar learning, has strong practicability.

Keywords: Interactive system · Android · Mobile learning · Online learning algorithm

1 Introduction

The application of mobile devices is a new field, and its combination with education is more and more close. The traditional digital learning can make the educated get the education resources they want at any time by combining with mobile computing technology, so as to achieve the autonomy of learning. English is the most common language in the world, so it is a hot topic in education. English learning is becoming more and more critical to personal development. Among them, English grammar is a key and difficult point in learning. If you want to really understand English, you must have a certain grammar foundation. Therefore, the English grammar learning system based on Android platform can bring convenience and help to learners, and you can get the desired English grammar knowledge in your spare time (Wang 2013).

There have been some research results on education and learning on mobile devices. ASAF Shabtai et al. Used the knowledge based temporal abstraction algorithm to expand

M. A. Jan and F. Khan (Eds.): BigIoT-EDU 2022, LNICST 467, pp. 377–385, 2023.
https://doi.org/10.1007/978-3-031-23944-1_41

the loading function of smart phones in 2010. Wu Zhizhong and others also proposed the use of DS theory, combined with multiple algorithms, to improve the accuracy of search information data on distributed mobile devices.

In this paper, through the construction of interactive system platform, build a comprehensive, efficient and accurate learning platform, which is conducive to learners and knowledge more closely interact, and provide more diversified education experience for English grammar learning through online learning algorithm. Finally, an example system is formed, grammar learning system interface proves the completeness of the system and the accuracy of the search.

At present, the speed reading training market is dominated by offline classroom training. Individual enterprises have some simple speed reading or memory training software in PC (personal computer) stand-alone version, but those with complete functions have not been seen. For the knowledge and skills training of various disciplines in primary and secondary schools, the traditional school classroom education is mainly used. In terms of software, there are some teaching auxiliary group software for some disciplines, such as English vocabulary memory mobile app and online homework training system, such as "homework together".

However, offline training, relying on human resources, is inefficient, and the training process is difficult to record and monitor. Once you leave the classroom, the training is difficult to carry out, and the function is single, which can not reflect the application of what you have learned. You think you just read the article and have no obvious understanding of improving the subject performance; The operation system of related technology is only for the subject training of individual subject knowledge, and only for the subject training of individual subject knowledge. In addition, teacher training is difficult, which can not solve the problem of large-scale teacher training. The trained teachers are easy to lose. The loss of teachers seriously affects teaching. It is difficult to expand the teaching scale and hire famous teachers to teach all courses on site.

2 Related Work

(Sherman et al. 2018) discuss the experience of usage of the virtual learning environment MOODLE in Maritime English studying while the training of students of marine specialties. A student response system (SRS) is proposed to support teachers in organizing in-class activities in a flipped class (Liu et al. 2019)). (Matveeva 2020) describe the content of the English for Specific Purposes (ESP) electronic learning pack developed by the author for college students majoring in Information systems and programming and published on the interactive platform "Moscow Area Digital College", the system of exercises for language and communicative competence development, and some issues on using the learning pack on the Moscow Area Digital College platform. This research was conducted at one of the MTS in Cimahi who had applied ICT/Padlet in the learning process (Haryudin et al. 2020) . (Jung 2020) attempt to introduce a sample of engaging mobile-assisted learning activities toward the use of multiple mobile apps like TIMeS (Taylor's Integrated Moodle e-Learning System), Naver Blog, and Quizlet. The present research study was conducted in one of the private sector universities of Lahore city in Pakistan (Salahuddin et al. 2020) . Contribution of (Karamcheti et al. 2020) is to create an interactive natural language interface that efficiently and reliably learns from users to complete tasks in simulated robotics settings. (Zhao 2021) propose a search and filter scheme based on the orientation of the training model in English grammar area, elaborates on the details, constructs a whole set of function structure from representation to weight, and gives the experimental results, which prove that the system has a good filtering effect and is fast. Other influential work includes (Tan et al. 2019), (Tan et al. 2022).

3 Android Application Construction Principle

The Android application is written in Java language, and the construction process of the application is shown in Fig. 1. Like ordinary Java se, Android programs need to use sun JDK to compile source java files into bytecode files (. Class files). After that, all bytecode files can be further transformed into DEX files by using special tool software DX (Ruan 2014).

In order to form the final application package, Android comes with a package tool AAPT. Through AAPT software, all the DEX files, layout files (XML files) and various resource files of the program can be packaged together to form a file with APK suffix, that is, application installation package (APK). Apk can be decompressed and installed on the mobile phone to form the final executable program. Dalvik virtual machine reads instructions and data from it to make the application run.

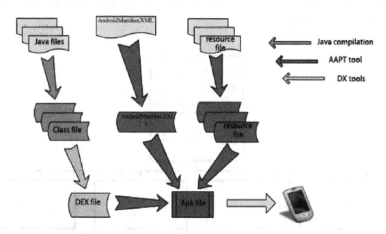

Fig. 1. Android application construction process

After the APK file is successfully installed on the mobile phone, the system will optimize the DEX file in the program and form the dee file before running the application, and the system will place the optimized file in the cache. The virtual machine makes the program run by directly executing the optimized Dee file. The corresponding dey file will remain in the cache until the APK file changes.

Application component is an important cornerstone of an Android application. Each component exists as an independent entity and plays a specific role. An Android can have one or more components at the same time, or it can not have one component. There are four different types of application components in Android: activity, service, broadcast receiver and content provider.

4   Interactive System Platform Modeling

The mobile Android terminal is mainly responsible for data collection. After collecting the education data, it detects the accuracy and repetition rate of the data collected by the system, and then displays the syntax data in the system interface through its own system platform, Therefore, it is mainly divided into the following processes: first, build the simulation platform of Android system; second, collect relevant English resource information through Android mobile terminal combined with data programming, mainly including words, sentences, videos and grammar; finally, integrate the information. However, the Android interactive system platform of smart phones will also be disturbed by other information, which will cause troubles for English grammar learners: first, a large number of useless junk information will appear in a short time when the platform is started, which makes it slow to run; second, many pictures and a large number of files will pop up in a short time, which leads to the loss of learners' online expenses and data traffic; third, it will cause the loss of students' online expenses and data traffic, There may be malicious files on the platform, which will harm the memory. Solving the above problems can make it easier for users to accept English grammar learning effectively. Generally, the learning structure of English grammar based on interactive system platform is shown in Fig. 2.

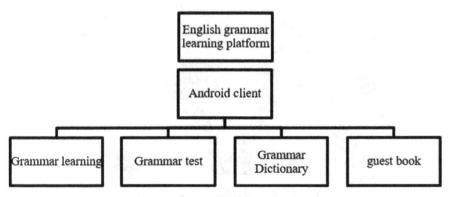

Fig. 2. The structure chart of English grammar learning system

The above three common problems are the core of the platform of the search system, and the key link of the system construction. Therefore, the main part of the interactive system platform is to analyze and study the English grammar data obtained, and build a smooth search and display interface. We set the standard threshold by searching information by users, so as to provide accurate feature profile, that is, information required by customers. In addition, we detect the deviation range between the feature profile and the accurate information of the sample (Banggui 2011). If the deviation value is less than the threshold value, it is correct; if the deviation value is greater than the threshold value, it is considered as error information.

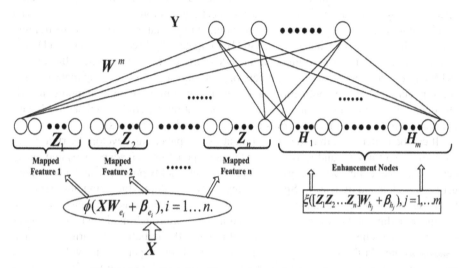

Fig. 3. The artificial intelligence interactive learning system

As shown in Fig. 3, the artificial intelligence interactive learning system 10 includes a student identification module 100, a student acquisition module 200 and a human-computer interaction module 300.

The student identification module 100 is used to identify the student ID of the student. The student acquisition module 200 is used to obtain the student training information of the preset database according to the student ID. The human-computer interaction module 300 is used to display the student training information, receive the student interaction information generated by the student according to the student training information, and obtain the student training data according to the student training information and the student interaction information. The system 10 of the embodiment in this paper trains students anytime and anywhere through the interactive information of students, so as to meet the learning requirements of different students, so as to effectively improve the applicability and practicability of training, high efficiency, simple and easy to implement.

It is understandable that firstly, the system identifies the identity information of students and obtains different student training according to different students, so that the training can be carried out according to the situation of students, improve the applicability of training, make the training more targeted and improve the efficiency of training. Moreover, the time and place of online human-computer interaction training are more flexible. Through mobile terminals (such as tablet computers) and the Internet, you can practice online anytime and anywhere, which is more applicable and practical. The online video teaching of famous teachers directly listens to the lectures and teaching of famous teachers in China, and the practice methods are diversified. For example, it is designed as a breakthrough mode. Through the practice method of computer games, it can enhance the interest of learning, stimulate the learning initiative, combine learning with playing, strengthen the ability of students' speed reading memory, and imperceptibly improve the speed reading performance and ability.

Further, in one embodiment of this paper, the student training information includes visual training data, fast reading data and subject application data, wherein the visual training data includes one or more of one point staring material, yellow card training material, three-color card material, 3-shaped card material, 3D card material and Datura card material, and the fast reading data includes Sirte grid material, instant flash material Memory grid materials, visual perception materials, keyword training materials and speed materials. Subject application data include one or more of mind mapping materials, liberal arts application materials, science application materials, English vocabulary materials, English grammar materials and English reading materials.

It can be understood that the embodiment of this paper can develop the right brain through visual training, and fully develop the great potential of readers to expand visual perception, visual memory ability and coordinate and quickly process visual information between the left and right brain. Speed reading memory training; Including Shure square, flash, memory square, visual perception, keyword training and speed reading of articles. In this embodiment, the training is designed as a breakthrough mode, which enhances the interest and challenge of learning and stimulates the initiative of learning through game learning. At the same time, the embodiment of this paper also provides English vocabulary memory training, grammar training and English reading training, and uses the artificial intelligence speech platform to realize the standard phonetic intelligent reading (such as the comparative reading of English vocabulary and Chinese and English paragraphs).

Set training data sample: $\{z_i = (x_i, y_i)\}$, where the formula of the starting problem of C-SVC is expressed as follows:

$$min\frac{1}{2}\|w\|^2 + c\sum_{i=1}^{n}\xi_i \tag{1}$$

The duality problem with this problem can be expressed as follows:

$$min\frac{1}{2}aQa - ea \tag{2}$$

By formula and sample data, we get q is n × Finally, the decision function of English grammar data information is derived by extending formula (2)

$$sgn(w\phi(x) + b) = sgn\left(\sum_{i=0}^{n} y_i a_i k(x_i, x) + b\right) \tag{3}$$

The training sample data is very large, the data redundancy and repetition rate of processing and analysis are also very high, which causes a great amount of time and time waste for the platform operation. At the same time, the algorithm also improves the difficulty and the accuracy is not optimistic, so it is difficult to achieve the standard and expected effect. According to various problems, the data processing algorithm mentioned above can effectively compress the original training samples, analyze the sample data, and improve the rationality of sample selection, It can reduce the algorithm time, reduce the difficulty of the algorithm, greatly improve the accuracy of the algorithm, provide the users with the effective resources they want, and let the learners learn English grammar efficiently anytime and anywhere.

The Android interactive system platform of smart phone provides learners with more English grammar learning modes, including video and text, which can bring more learning fun and more learning forms for users. This is also a great advantage of interactive system platform which is shown in Fig. 4.

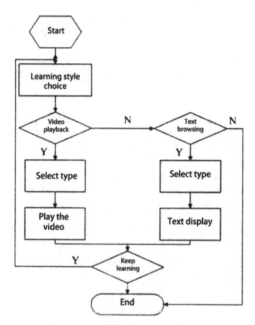

Fig. 4. Grammar learning flow chart

5 System Implementation

In the example, we build the platform using Android 2.3.1 operating system. Through Java programming combined with the interactive system platform and online learning algorithm proposed in this paper, we design the English grammar learning software. The software has a huge database for English words and English grammar, When searching, it can accurately display the information resources learners are looking for, and has memory function for historical data, and the system will automatically pop up the relevant grammatical information when searching (Wenzhao 2015).

After the grammar search, the grammar information obtained by the system platform has many typical examples, as well as related language sources, which has strong integration and rationality, and provides better learning experience for learners. In addition, we have grammar learning videos in the interface, combined with the player, which can increase learners' acceptance.

Compared with the traditional Surendra algorithm and CAMSHIFT algorithm, online learning algorithm has a good advantage in processing data, and has a good improvement in judging the redundancy of huge data. The speed comparison of the three algorithms in processing data shows that the online learning algorithm has shorter processing time, because C-SVC and v-svc can effectively reduce the transmission of error messages (Fig. 5).

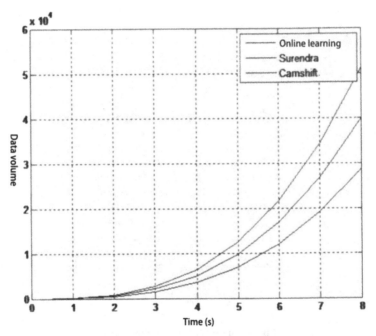

Fig. 5. Efficiency chart of three algorithms for data processing

6   Conclusion

Based on the data collected by Android interactive system platform of smart phone, this paper uses C-SVC and v-svc to train samples effectively, so as to obtain more reasonable samples, reduce data processing time and data complexity. Based on the online learning algorithm, this paper uses the advantages of SVM in less data processing. The online learning algorithm has the ability of self-improvement, which helps to optimize the problem detection function of Android smartphone interactive system platform. In actual operation, data collection will be affected by the type of simulated data, This algorithm can also identify and judge automatically, with less interference of error information. The example analysis algorithm is efficient, accurate and has high practical value, which provides a better English grammar learning platform for learners.

Acknowledgements. 1. Project of Henan humanities and social science in 2020 (2020-ZZJH182):Study on Flipped Class based Wechat in College English Teaching\014278.

2. School level Project of Research and innovation Fund 2020: A case study of Publicity on Chinese culture based on CGTN and Bilibili.

References

Wang, L., Wu, H., Wang, L.: Design and implementation of English grammar mobile learning system based on Android. Comput. Modernization. **8**, 232–235 (2013)

Ruan, Y., Yalei, M.: Design and implementation of English grammar mobile learning system in smartphone environment. Electron. Test. **5**, 13–15 (2014)

Banggui, X.: Mobile learning system based on Android platform. J. Xihua Univ. Nat. Sci. Ed. **30**(5), 81–84 (2011)

Wenzhao, W., Yujiao, X.: Design and implementation of mobile learning system for university computer courses based on Android. Autom. Instrum. **12**, 155–156 (2015)

Sherman, M.I., Popova, H., Yurzhenko, A.: Interactive course "Maritime English" in the professional training of future mariners (2018)

Liu, C., Sands-Meyer, S., Audran, J.: The effectiveness of the student response system (SRS) in English grammar learning in a flipped English as a foreign language (EFL) class, interactive learning environments (2019)

Tan, D.A.L., Lee, B.C., Ganapathy, M., Kasuma, S.A.A.: Language learning in the 21st century: Malaysian ESL students' perceptions of Kahoot! Int. J. Virtual pers. Learn. Environ. (2019)

Matveeva, N.V.: Teaching English for specific purposes to future programmers on the Moscow area digital college platform. In: 2020 International Conference Quality Management, Transport and Information Security, Information Technologies (IT&QM&IS) (2020)

Haryudin, A., Resmana, I.F.: The implementation of ICT (PADLETE) in learning English in writing skills (2020)

Jung, G.W.: Engaging mobile-assisted learning activities using multiple mobile apps for foreign language practice (2020)

Salahuddin, A., Ajmal, F., Saira: Effectiveness of learning management system for teaching English language at higher education level. sjesr, **3**, 1–9 (2020)

Karamcheti, S., Sadigh, D., Liang, P.: Learning adaptive language interfaces through decomposition, arxiv (2020)

Zhao, J.: English grammar discrimination training network model and search filtering, complex (2021)

Tan, D.A.L., Lee, B.C., Ganapathy, M., Kasuma, S.A.A.: Language learning in the 21st century, research anthology on developments in gamification and game-based learning (2022)

Research on the Application of Computer Technology in the Dissemination and Promotion of Folk Art Culture

Ping Wang[✉]

Hexi University, Zhangye 734000, Gansu, China
symbolqqpp@163.com

Abstract. As an indispensable part of China's cultural treasure house, folk art is a special spiritual pursuit and a form of artistic expression. It is extremely important to study the function of folk art in cultural communication. With the rapid development of social economy, the world has entered the era of electronic communication, and the application of computer technology has become an indispensable teaching aid. We should infiltrate the dissemination of culture. From the connotation and essence of folk art, this paper discusses and studies the cultural dissemination and promotion of folk art, and the application of computer technology in cultural dissemination and promotion.

Keywords: Folk art · Cultural communication · Computer technology

1 Introduction

As an indispensable part of our cultural treasure, folk art has been an important field of our traditional culture. Therefore, the development of folk art has important value for the cultural communication of our country. With the trend of globalization becoming more and more strong, it is very important to study the function of folk art in cultural communication. With the advent of information age, computer technology provides more convenience for people's life and learning, and becomes an indispensable helper. At the same time, computer multimedia teaching has begun to walk away from university classroom, which has become an effective means to improve classroom efficiency and teaching effect. The vivid computer plays a more important role in the spread and promotion of the folk art culture. It not only breaks the traditional mode of teaching book knowledge by blackboard, but also vividly displays the rich knowledge and cultural image in front of the public through computer technology [1].

Classification of culture is shown in Fig. 1.

The emergence and development of folk art, to a large extent, stems from the practicality of materials. The perfect combination of artistic aesthetics and practicality is its endless driving force. In other words, practicality makes it naturally have a "fickle" gene that is good at adapting to the times. Therefore, in order to inherit folk art, it is necessary to promote its value and role in contemporary life and make it conform to the life

M. A. Jan and F. Khan (Eds.): BigIoT-EDU 2022, LNICST 467, pp. 386–394, 2023.
https://doi.org/10.1007/978-3-031-23944-1_42

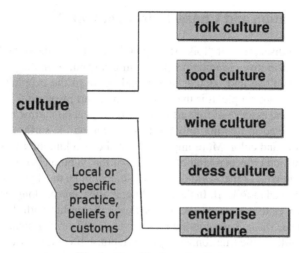

Fig. 1. Classification of culture

aesthetics and cultural demands of modern people. In the specific operation, we should adhere to the concept of "seeing people, seeing things and seeing life", enrich and adjust the content, achieve variability through innovation in form and function, and constantly endow it with reasonable and appropriate modern connotation, so as to rejuvenate its vitality and vigor.

Practice has proved that this idea is feasible. For example, the Miao batik in Danzhai County, Guizhou Province, has promoted inheritance and protection through production and operation. Through the industrial development model of "company + farmer + base", it has built handicraft enterprises and batik professional cooperatives, paid attention to industrial optimization and brand innovation, and made them cultural consumption objects. It has not only cultivated new economic growth points, broadened the channels for people to increase their income, but also effectively inherited batik skills, It has become one of the excellent protection practice cases of 50 national intangible cultural heritage representative projects in 2019.

For another example, woolen embroidery is an intangible cultural heritage project that has been inherited in Shanghai for more than 100 years. Relevant departments of Shanghai Municipality guide and support relevant enterprises to creatively design new woolen embroidery products, develop derivatives and expand new sales markets; We also support craftsmen to build learning centers, integrating production, sales, exhibition and training, and integrating inheritance and protection into contemporary economic, social and cultural construction; Show your skills in major domestic and foreign affairs activities, and make your appearance in special forms and ways, such as carrying out activities to celebrate the 70th anniversary of the founding of new China by embroidering the national flag, inviting Chinese and foreign guests to embroider the Expo mascot at the Expo site, and holding foreign exchange exhibitions. These have become effective ways of inheritance and protection.

2 The Generation and Characteristics of Folk Art

In 1980s, the real discussion of "folk art" began. Folk refers to the basic level from the people, the most primitive common people, from farmland, from the grass-roots level, from the most primitive and popular understanding, from the people's art, is the art created by the working people, it is the root of all other art inspiration.

The meaning and essence of folk art far exceed the general narrow art category. The value of art embodied in it is not only the beauty seen on the surface, but also in the form, composition and color. More importantly, it shows a kind of art expression with deep meaning, which reflects a kind of life state of the common people, It expresses a kind of spiritual pursuit of the working people. For example, the theme of "auspicious" is generally displayed in folk art. In the modeling, it often appears longfengchengxiang, durian kaibaizi, wealth and peace, etc. it has close relationship with the pursuit of the value of the people. Through the continuous innovation and development of the common people, folk art will dig the true connotation of art, praise life, praise life, and constantly tap the essence of life, It is also a yearning for a better life for the common people. Folk art is a special spiritual pursuit, and also the creation of aesthetic. It is also an artistic connotation precipitated with the times, and it is a human aesthetic consciousness. Although as an artistic expression, it has some essential differences with other forms of ordinary art.

Folk art is divided into sacrifice, entertainment, decoration and entertainment. Among them, sacrifice refers to the tribute that the working people have announced in the process of sacrifice to express their memory for the dead - some tribute, and the other is some gods and portraits created by the working people according to some folk legends; Entertainment refers to the items such as shadow, puppet, face spectrum and other props created by the working people in the ordinary entertainment process, and some entertainment devices that appear in the folk at ordinary times, such as facial

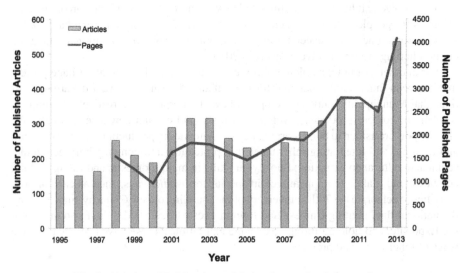

Fig. 2. Number of Publication articles and pages for flok art culture

makeup: the folk art of decoration is the decoration created by the ordinary people in order to express their yearning for a better life and the decoration of ordinary life, and also some embroidered shoes Embroidered pillow, etc.; Folk art of entertainment refers to some performing instruments and props created by ordinary people in ordinary life deduction, such as lion dance, lamp, color and other miscellaneous performances: the folk of wearing refers to the unique dress culture of each region [2].

We can see from Fig. 2 that the spread and promotion of folk art culture is increasing. We can see from the number of articles and pages published from 1995 to 2013, as shown in Fig. 2 The number of articles has increased from less than 200 in 1995 to nearly 500 in 2013, and the number of pages has increased from less than 1000 to more than 4000 today. This also fully shows that the effect of the spread and promotion of folk art culture is still very good.

3 Analysis of the Cultural Communication Function of Folk Art

3.1 The Function of Folk Art Inheritance

In the long history of Chinese culture, folk art occupies a very important position, whether it is its aesthetic value or its practical value, has its unique cultural meaning. Folk art is continued on the basis of traditional culture. Representative ones, such as stone age pottery and stone tools, some back baskets and pottery arts from the folk are valuable. Many of the folk paper-cut and embroidery have left cultural characteristics. For example, some totem paper-cut and embroidery are a kind of cultural transmission, Many patterns on the pottery also have certain moral meaning, and these representative cultural conformity always appear repeatedly in folk art works. From the beginning of the 20th century, Mr. Zhongjingwen began to discuss what is called "folk art" to the concept of people since the 1950s. Only in the 1980s did you really investigate and study the folk art, and then put forward the conclusion that "folk art is the art for the benefit of life". What is the definition of folk art? In the most traditional concept, "folk art" refers to the art created by ordinary people in ordinary life. Inspiration is all from life, relying on life, closely related to life, involving all aspects of life, such as clothing, food and living, etc., which has been extended on this basis, And the people's good expectations for life and their spiritual pursuit are added, and the values of customs and beliefs are integrated. Therefore, "folk art" is a common concept of universal use, which is "folk art" is the common concept of common use through the daily life of the people, the integration of spiritual state and the yearning for a better life, Its development has important value for the overall progress and inheritance of folk art forms.

3.2 The Function of Protecting Traditional Culture

Traditional folk art is developed on the basis of farming culture. However, with the changes of the times, the folk art has changed unprecedented. The largest carrier of folk art, the demand and existing state of national culture have also changed. The internal driving force of folk art culture change is the cultural heritage. With the continuous deduction of mainstream culture, folk art culture has changed a certain degree and has been lost. Culture needs to be constantly protected and inherited. Only in this way can culture be continuously inherited. Therefore, in the treatment of cultural communication, the cultural communication is a key factor in the development of the cultural development, The protection of folk art has already surpassed the art itself, because it touches the development of Chinese culture, especially the development of traditional Chinese culture, which is related to the transmission and regeneration of local culture of a nation and a region. In this sense, the development of folk art is of great significance to the protection of traditional culture in China. In today's society, the trend of globalization is becoming stronger and stronger. Therefore, the international cultural exchange and collision are more and more frequent. In the process of cultural communication, it is necessary to face the impact of global culture, so the function of folk art for the protection of traditional culture cannot be ignored [3].

3.3 The Function of Maintaining the Essence of Art

Folk art is a living culture, its value and significance have already surpassed art. The most common expression of folk art is oral and manual, which is also the most important external form. Oral communication is the main carrier of language, and hand transmission is the carrier of object, The performance of folk culture is carried out through the way of mutual promotion and complementation of oral and hand handed down. In the long cultural journey in China, the cultural connotation and details of folk art are mainly communicated by people-oriented way, and carried out communication through practical practice. Especially in some technical folk art categories, hand transmission is the main basis, which can ensure the more ancient and more real cultural form and cultural details, The culture inherited by this way is more stable, and the cultural value displayed by the folk art preserved by material will be more intuitive and clear. The value of most of the documents of folk art protection is to record and organize the traditional culture through the cognition of traditional culture, and then record and organize according to the characteristics of the nation and region, so folk art is a gene bank of national culture, which plays a good role in bridge for the inheritance of national culture, and folk art retains the most basic spiritual memory, It retains the most essential understanding and pursuit of culture. Art is the pursuit of art, spirit and connotation. In the current society, the spiritual connotation and excellent skills of art have been greatly impacted.

4   The Application Strategy of Computer Network Technology in the Dissemination of Folk Art Culture

The development of computer network technology has not only changed the way we live, study and work, but also laid a solid foundation for us to better spread folk art culture. Different from the traditional way of spreading folk art culture, computer network technology is not only more effective, but also more in line with the lifestyle of contemporary citizens, so the resistance encountered in the dissemination of folk art culture is often smaller. However, in order to better play the role of computer network technology in the spread of folk art culture, we must accurately find the application method, so as to promote the healthy development of folk art culture on the basis of ensuring the effectiveness of computer network technology application [4].

4.1 Correctly Look at the Role of Computer Network Technology in the Dissemination of Folk Art Culture

Computer network technology has both advantages and disadvantages in the process of folk art culture dissemination. Therefore, we should correctly treat the role of computer network technology in folk art culture dissemination, give full play to the value advantages of computer network technology in folk art culture dissemination, broaden the environment and scope of folk art culture dissemination, and expand the audience, Strengthen cultural exchange and interaction, promote the diversification of information, and promote the inheritance and development of folk art culture; It is necessary to clarify the disadvantages of computer network technology in the process of folk art culture communication and avoid it to the greatest extent.

4.2 Develop MOOCS and Micro Courses for Online Teaching of Folk Art Culture

Education is not only an effective means to cultivate talents, but also an important basis for inheriting and developing folk art culture. We are in the era of information explosion. Although young students are more and more capable of accepting new things, they have been dazzled by all kinds of information for a long time. So if educators can integrate these complicated folk art culture into a complete system, So it can not only improve the efficiency and effect of students' learning folk art culture, but also greatly reduce their learning burden. For students majoring in computer network, the popularity of smart phones, tablet computers and other mobile terminal devices enables students to learn online resources with the help of these devices. MOOCS, micro class and other computer network technology have been widely used in English teaching, but as far as the current situation is concerned, MOOCS, micro class and other online teaching resources about folk art culture are very few, so in this case, it is not conducive to the spread of folk art culture" If students want to learn folk art culture better, they must develop online teaching resources of MOOCS and micro courses according to their actual needs. On the one hand, it creates conditions for students to learn folk art culture, so that they can use their spare time to learn folk art culture; On the other hand, it can also lay a foundation for teachers to carry out folk art culture education and teaching. In a word, in order to spread folk art culture in the whole school, we should first form a good learning atmosphere of folk art culture and cultivate students' awareness of autonomous learning of folk art culture, so as to further play the role of computer network technology, as shown in Fig. 1 (Fig. 3).

4.3 Make Use of Computer Network Technology to Do Well in the Propaganda of Folk Art Culture

Although folk art culture is an excellent traditional culture in China, in fact, there are very few people who have a deep study on folk art culture. With the continuous improvement of people's living standards, art culture has become an integral part of many people's lives. But art is a simple appreciation for many people. The reason why they like it is not because of the non colorful folk art culture. It is the responsibility and obligation of every Chinese children to spread folk art culture, but almost everyone, including

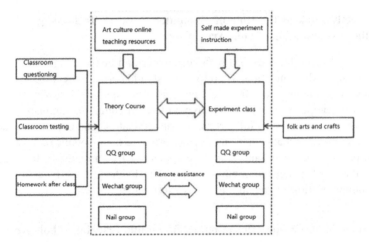

Fig. 3. The teaching mode of MOOCS art culture

young college students, are all working hard for their future, and they do not regard the dissemination of folk art culture as their own responsibility. As we all know, computer network technology is a powerful tool for the dissemination of cultural information. We can make full use of the advantages of computer network technology in the dissemination of cultural information and make good use of computer network technology to do the propaganda work of folk art culture. First, the official website is the platform for spreading the advantages of folk art culture. Whether it is the official platform of the government or the official platform of the school, it can open a special module for the study of folk art culture, which is convenient for the people to learn folk art culture. Secondly, for schools, it can learn from the teaching concept of "curriculum thinking and politics", and require teachers to integrate folk art culture into the teaching content, so that students can receive the baptism of folk art culture constantly and promote the students' all-round development; Finally, the government should strengthen the supervision and management of the publicity of the folk art culture in schools, require the school to implement the publicity of folk art culture in practice, learn to reflect on its own, and ensure the effectiveness and effectiveness of the publicity work of folk art culture, so that schools, including the society, can form a good atmosphere for the study of folk art culture [4].

4.4 Expand the Communication Way of Folk Art Culture by Using Computer Network Technology

In the background of the Internet era, computer network technology has become an integral part of our lives. Just as the sound communication needs media, we need media in the process of spreading folk art culture. We know that different media often have different effects on sound transmission, such as sound in solid faster than in water and air. This means that we should also choose the appropriate media in the process of spreading folk art culture, so as to spread folk art culture faster in the shortest time. Chinese folk art culture is unique in the world, and it is a bright pearl in the history of China and even the whole human development. Therefore, it is of great significance to inherit and develop this precious intangible cultural heritage for the development of all mankind. Computer network technology has been widely used. In the past, "illiteracy" refers to those who are illiterate. In the new era, the meaning of illiteracy has changed greatly, which mainly refers to those who have no ownership of computer network technology. Science and technology is always the first productivity. If a person's ideas and ideas cannot keep pace with the times, he or she will be easily eliminated by the society. Before the advent of the Internet era, the way people spread folk art culture is more traditional and single, not only time-consuming and laborious, but also unsatisfactory effect. In the background of Internet era, we can use the powerful information dissemination function of computer network technology to expand the way of folk art culture communication, and break the traditional folk art culture communication mode thoroughly, and improve the speed of folk art culture communication while facilitating people to learn folk art culture.

5   Conclusion

As one of the most advanced technology means, computer network not only repre- sents the level of science and technology in a country, but also constantly changes our life. The application of computer network technology in the process of folk art culture communication can not only broaden the environment and scope of folk art culture com- munication, but also promote the diversified development of information; Moreover, it can expand the audience, strengthen the cultural exchange and interaction, and promote the inheritance and development of folk art culture. In short, in order to play a better role in the dissemination of folk art culture, we must find the application method accurately, so as to ensure the effectiveness of the application of computer network technology, and promote the healthy development of folk art culture.

Combined with modern design and art design education, it is also one of the important starting points for the innovative "variable" of folk art. Folk art creation is more out of the consideration of use, with strong maternal and practical characteristics, which is similar to the concept of "form obeys function" in modern design, and is essentially the unity of aesthetics and practicality. However, the integration of folk art into modern design activities is not the rote application, patchwork and generalization of patterns of folk art elements, nor the simple extraction of traditional classical patterns, nor the fixed stylization and stereotype, but a systematic design, which obtains new forces through the absorption of the cultural tension of folk art and forms the highlights and innovations in the design.

The construction of "intangible cultural heritage workshop (batik) training and teach- ing center" in my school is to introduce folk art resources into the teaching of students majoring in art design, hire batik intangible cultural heritage inheritors to set up spe- cial courses, so that students can experience the original production process of folk art, derive and promote from the batik art itself, broaden the ideas of teachers and students to obtain art resources, and promote the integration of folk handicrafts and modern design, Explore cross-border integration. This can not only inject folk wisdom into design edu- cation, but also make colleges and universities become one of the main forces for the revitalization and development of folk art.

References

1. Sun, J.: Chinese folk art course. Tianjin People's publishing house, Tianjin (2008)
2. Qiao, X.: Cultural protection principles of folk art. Chinese culture bulletin. (1) (2012)
3. Haiyan, M., Deliang, O.: Application and practice of computer network technology in the split classroom teaching of introduction to western culture. J. Changji Univ. **05**, 98–101 (2017)
4. Minghui, Z., Limin, Z.: Design of computer network platform based on Internet of things mode – taking tea culture promotion as an example. Fujian tea **39**(01), 5–6 (2017)

Research on the Application of Data Mining in the Quality Analysis of College English Teaching

Zhe Li[✉]

Shandong Management University, Jinan 250100, Shandong, China
lizhefz@163.com

Abstract. In order to give full play to the role of data mining technology, do a good job in analyzing the quality of English teaching in colleges and universities, and provide help for the improvement of teaching quality, this paper will carry out relevant research. This paper first introduces the basic concept of data mining and its relationship with English teaching quality analysis, and then proposes a design scheme of data mining teaching quality analysis system. Through the research, the system can give full play to the role of data mining technology and promote the development of college English teaching quality.

Keywords: Data mining · College English · Teaching quality

1 Introduction

Modern education theory believes that the past teaching is too general, there is a problem of insufficient pertinence, leading to part of the students can not get high-quality education, which is the key factor of the past teaching quality is difficult to improve, so the modern education concept advocates to strengthen pertinence of teaching. To do this, the majority of the university interdisciplinary teachers teaching quality analysis, to find out the root cause of poor quality, dealt with in the targeted, but in the analysis of teaching quality, many teachers have encountered difficulties, of which the representative is quality analysis ability is insufficient, the teaching quality analysis involves a lot of, many class teaching quality data, each data have a value in the quality analysis, and related to each other, so to do well in quality analysis, to accurately analyze each data first, after the comprehensive analysis of data combination, so as to get the result of the deep, obtain accurate development direction, and magnitude of huge data and complex relationships between data lead to teachers cannot rely on execution analysis work, the quality of results cannot be guaranteed by conventional technical tools, so how to carry out ideas and do a good job of analysis has become a problem worth thinking about. To solve this problem, data mining technology has been put forward in related fields. This technology can give consideration to both efficiency and quality of results in the

M. A. Jan and F. Khan (Eds.): BigIoT-EDU 2022, LNICST 467, pp. 395–401, 2023.
https://doi.org/10.1007/978-3-031-23944-1_43

analysis of teaching quality, which is one of the few technical tools that can meet the requirements of teaching quality analysis. Therefore, in order to give full play to the role of technology, this paper will take college English teaching as an example to carry out relevant research.

2 Basic Concepts of Data Mining and Its Relationship with English Teaching Quality Analysis

2.1 Basic Concepts

Data mining is a data processing tool, but has the very big difference with the conventional data processing tools, which is characteristic of the general data processing tool data processing efficiency, can handle huge amounts of data in a short period of time, but can't give attention to both data processing results, the results tend to be shallow, can only be used for simple judgment, such as in the English teaching quality analysis, judged only by scores between whether to pass the student performance, and in contrast, the data mining technology, its performance also has efficient data processing, and the degree of efficiency than conventional tools, at the same time also can balance the quality, the result not only can be used to judge whether to pass the exam, students can also judge fail reason, student performance or other aspects of the defect, therefore, data mining tools have advantages over conventional data processing tools [1, 2].

Data mining can ensure quality of the results, because the tool was developed based on artificial neural network, artificial neural network is a kind of according to produce human neural network structure logic model of machine, can let the machine system by a way similar to human intelligence, the most prominent feature of operation process is to establish data relations, the ability to integrate different types of relationships, to tell people why one piece of data, or why one piece of data changes, and how it relates to other pieces of data. In addition, there are many forms of artificial neural network in data mining [3]. Table 1 introduces three common forms, among which feedforward neural network is the most common form, which is suitable for teaching quality analysis. Therefore, this paper will carry out subsequent analysis centering on this form of neural network.

Table 1. Three common forms of artificial neural networks in data mining

In the form of	The characteristics of
Feedforward neural network	Moving forward logically leads to only one result
Feedback type neural network	Logic repetition, can give a variety of feasible results
Convolutional neural network	Logic loop, can constantly optimize the last result

2.2 Relationship

College English teaching quality analysis work is must carry out a work, but the work involves large amount of data, and data type many, data update is very fast at the same time, the reason is that the data base from the students, and students huge population base, the nature will produce a great deal of data, much class, and students learning activity is evolving, so data is being generated all the time [4, 5]. On this basis, to do a good job in teaching quality analysis, all data must be integrated and analyzed efficiently, otherwise there will be data omission, or new data left over for a long time and other problems [6]. But in reality, university teachers as human, its limitations, there must be ability cannot be efficient for processing data, and the conventional technical means and unable to ensure quality of the results, so data mining has become one of the few in the college English teaching quality analysis tools are available, and that data mining is closely relationship with quality analysis work. Table 2 shows the advantages of data mining in college English teaching quality.

Table 2. Advantages of data mining in College English teaching quality

Handling	Indicators	
	Processing efficiency	The results of quality
Data mining processing	1 min/30000	High
Artificial processing	1 min/50	High
Routine technical tool processing	1 min/30000	Low

3 Data Mining Teaching Quality Analysis System Design Scheme

3.1 Algorithm Selection

To use data mining tools to analyze the quality of college English teaching, must through the system can identify the data, to achieve this goal, the need for algorithm selection, namely there are many data recognition algorithm can be implemented in system, but the algorithm performance differences between, if the choice of algorithm performance is insufficient, can lead to data mining results appear quality problem, it is not conducive to its use, indicating that the selection of algorithm is very important [7, 8]. The selection of algorithm in this paper is mainly carried out according to two indexes of convergence and efficiency. The reference algorithms include KNN algorithm and decision tree algorithm. Table 3 shows the specific performance of the two algorithms.

Combined with Table 3, it can be seen that the efficiency of the two algorithms is the same, but the KNN algorithm is higher in convergence [9, 10]. Therefore, KNN algorithm will be selected for system design in this paper. KNN algorithm is a kind of sample set for data, extracting each data within a set of tags (see formula (1), on behalf of the people know each data and the relationship between the category, at this

Table 3. Specific performance of the two algorithms

The algorithm name	Indicators	
	The convergence	Efficiency
KNN algorithm	Good	High
Decision tree algorithm	Medium	High

time when there is no label of new data input after the training sample set, to extract all the characteristics of every new data, the new data characteristics comparing with the existing data label, to know the distance between the new data and each data, select the group of data closest to the data, let the new data in the group of data move to the existing data, so that the new data into the existing data classification, according to the classification can be identified to the new data. In this process, because the new data will only be combined with the most similar existing data, the classification that the new data finally enters is very accurate and there is no generalization representation, which is also the reason for the excellent convergence of this algorithm. In addition, KNN algorithm is not without its disadvantages, such as high complexity, high memory requirements and large storage requirements in practical application. However, these disadvantages can be made up by other technical means, or some of them will not affect the teaching quality analysis, so its disadvantages do not hinder its use.

$$Max = \begin{cases} A = (a1, a2, ...a3)/K \\ B = (b1, b2, ...b3)/K \\ C = (c1, c2, ...c3)/K \end{cases} \tag{1}$$

where, Max is the maximum value of the data sample set, indicating that the sample contains all the existing data, A, B and C are the data classification items in the data sample set, (a1, a2... a3), (b1, b2... b3), (c1,c2... c3) is the existing data of several items in A, B and C respectively, and K is the label value of each item in each category.

3.2 System Design

According to the algorithm, the data mining system can be designed according to the analysis demand of College English teaching quality. Figure 1 is the overall framework of the system.

Combined with Fig. 1, the system firstly takes the modern popular online teaching platform as a data acquisition platform, which can collect all the data generated during students' online learning, and then preprocesses the data to improve the quality of initial data. Secondly, the pre-processed data will enter the transfer layer, which is essentially a communication network with data transmission capability, so the data can be transmitted to the database, which has huge data reserves and meets the application requirements of KNN algorithm. Finally, the algorithm will regard all the data stored in the database as the data sample set, and then operate under the drive of artificial neural network and the basic flow of the algorithm to obtain the results, which will be displayed through the output layer. The implementation method of this system is as follows.

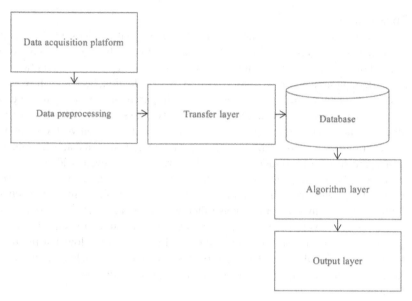

Fig. 1. Overall framework of the system

(1) Data collection platform

Because the ideas such as "Internet +" gradually into the field of education, so a lot of colleges and universities have established the online teaching platform, the platform in a short period of time to get the thorough application, the majority of students are form online learning habits, so will the platform as the data acquisition platform, can students all online data collected, the data can represent the students learning, it also shows that through data analysis, students' learning situation problems can be known, which can expose the problems of teaching quality. For example, the learning situation data of a student shows that the student's practical ability is insufficient for a long time. This phenomenon represents the weakness of practical English education in colleges and universities, and teaching quality can be effectively improved if it can be strengthened.

(2) Data preprocessing

For data collection is through the platform comes to implement the features of the record, so all the data are raw, and there is no specification requirements, it is easy to appear quality problem, common quality problem is data repeat, such as students learning because of the error in the platform, so repeated twice in a row, and even more of the same operation, it will generate a number of the same data, only one of these data items is valuable, and the others can be deleted, otherwise the amount of data will be too large and the mining efficiency will be affected. In order to do this, the data should be preprocessed. In view of common problems, the data preprocessing tool selected in this paper is the deduplication tool, which is now relatively mature and can directly obtain existing resources from the network, without secondary development.

(3) Transfer layer

Transfer layer is a communication network, so that colleges and universities set up network communication environment can directly, but it is important to note that out of respect for data communications security, colleges and universities in the network communication environment for network selection, before i can set up the system data communication for performance requirements of the communication environment is not high, so a lot of kinds of network communication environment all can achieve the purpose, however, the security of some network communication environments is not high, and they are vulnerable to external attacks. Once the attacks are successful, students' personal information and even academic achievements may be leaked. Therefore, it is necessary to choose a secure network communication environment. Target, more conform to the requirements of the network communication environment such as Ethernet and VPN private networks (VPNS), two kinds of network in terms of safety performance, but there is a difference in cost and implementation difficulty, including Ethernet cost is low, but the implementation is difficult, the latter is reversed, so the reasonable selection of colleges and universities should be combined with their own conditions.

(4) Database

Because KNN algorithm needs a large amount of data support, data collection includes all the data, but it also brings huge data storage requirements. If the database capacity is insufficient, the system operation will be affected. Focus on this requirement, this paper select the database for the cloud database, the data storage capacity of the infinite, and able to tinkering with its safety, cost is lower, so different from traditional mass physical database (although the capacity of the database is very big, but there is still a limit, and the expansion operation need to add a physical server, so the cost is very high), Is a virtual database, does not occupy physical space space, very suitable for this system.

(5) Other parts

The KNN algorithm is integrated into the system through program development, and the feedforward neural network is built to obtain the algorithm program module, which can be installed in the system application framework. After completion, the network is extended to the system and the teacher's client, and the data output can be realized.

4 Conclusion

To sum up, blockchain technology has been gradually applied in many fields in modern development, including the promotion of cultural and creative products. However, the application of this technology in the promotion is different from other fields, so targeted analysis should be conducted. In the right way of application, blockchain technology can provide accurate direction, strong security protection and reasonable logic support for the promotion of cultural and creative products, and promote the promotion work more effective, indicating that the technology has high application value in the promotion of cultural and creative products.

References

1. Raut, A.R., Khandait, S.P.: Review on data mining techniques in wireless sensor networks. In: IEEE Sponsored 2nd International Conference on Electronics and Communication System (ICECS 2015). IEEE (2020)

2. Admass, W.S.: Developing knowledge-based system for the diagnosis and treatment of mango pests using data mining techniques. Int. J. Inf. Technol. **14**(3), 1495–1504 (2022)

3. Alsubaie, W.A., Albishi, H.Z., Aljoufi, K.A., Alghamdi, W.S., Alyahyan, E.A.: Predicting customer churn in banking based on data mining techniques. In: Krishnamurthy, Vallidevi, Jaganathan, Suresh, Rajaram, Kanchana, Shunmuganathan, Saraswathi (eds.) ICCIDS 2021. IAICT, vol. 611, pp. 27–39. Springer, Cham (2021). https://doi.org/10.1007/978-3-030-926 00-7_3

4. Widyati, R., Ashari, A., Afiahayati.: A review of using data mining and machine learning for predicting drug loading modeling in solid lipid nanoparticles containing curcumin. J. Phys. Conf. Ser. **1918**(4) 042015 (2021)

5. Shafiabadi, M., Pedram, H., Reshadi, M., et al.: An accurate model to predict the performance of graphical processors using data mining and regression theory. Comput. Electr. Eng. **90**(1), 106965 (2021)

6. Rodr Guezherrera, A., Reyesandrade, J., Rubioescudero, C.: Rationale for timing of follow-up visits to assess gluten-free diet in celiac disease patients based on data mining. Nutrients **13**(2), 357 (2021)

7. Romanov, F.D.: Discoveries of variable stars by amateur astronomers using data mining on the example of eclipsing binary romanov V20 (Abstract). J. Am. Assoc. Variable Star Observer **49**(1), 115 (2021)

8. Zhu, Z.W., Zhu, P.S., Miao, Y.Y., et al.: Characteristics analysis for Chinese patent medicine containing Jujubea Fructus based on data mining. Zhongguo Zhong yao za zhi= Zhongguo zhongyao zazhi= China J. Chin. Mater. Med. **46**(9), 2344–2349 (2021)

9. Linlin, L.I.: The intrusion data mining method for distributed network based on fuzzy kernel clustering algorithm. Int. J. Auton. Adapt. Commun. Syst. **14**(4), 1 (2021)

10. Bahtiar, A.M., Dwilestari, G., et al.: Data mining techniques with machine learning algorithm to predict patients of heart disease. In: IOP Conference Series Materials Science and Engineering, vol. 1088(1), p. 012035 (2021)

Research on the Application of Data Mining Technology in Physical Training

Jiying Wei[✉] and Jun Guo

The Rocket Force University of Engineering, Xian 710025, Shaanxi, China
1348822535@qq.com

Abstract. Data extraction methods have been widely used in different departments and achieved good results. The most typical example is the combination of data extraction technology and economics, which plays an important role in product classification, customer classification and market segmentation. This paper discusses the application of data mining technology in physical training. First, collect a large amount of data from sports training, and then use the data extraction method to extract useful information. On the one hand, in order to improve the performance of athletes, on the other hand, we can organize scientific training on the physical status indicators of athletes to prevent injuries. This paper discusses several common motion data extraction algorithms.

Keywords: Data mining · Physical training · Application countermeasures

1 Introduction

Since the 20th century, information and information technology have developed rapidly, and the information age has officially arrived. People's work and life, food, clothing, housing and transportation, fitness and medical care are inseparable from information and information technology. The traditional mode of information dissemination has developed into a modern mode of information dissemination that integrates computer technology, software technology, network technology, data management technology and communication technology. With the rapid development of network technology, the information content processed, produced and transmitted by the network as the carrier includes: current political news, electronic publications, image text, video and audio, etc. it is the development trend, and compared with the traditional communication mode, the advantages are very obvious. Therefore, digitizing the information resources expected to be transmitted is the premise of realizing the development of communication relying on network technology.

Data development is an important science and technology in China, and this special technology has aroused great interest. It is an interdisciplinary engineering technology, which is widely used in many industries. In this process, technology and effectiveness are enriched. At present, we have a lot in common by combining sports and data acquisition technology, including statistical related knowledge. For example, sports training can

M. A. Jan and F. Khan (Eds.): BigIoT-EDU 2022, LNICST 467, pp. 402–412, 2023.
https://doi.org/10.1007/978-3-031-23944-1_44

overcome the difficulties of sports training and effectively play the dual positive role of sports training and artificial intelligence on the basis of learning sports theory [1]. At present, the combination of mining technology and physical exercise has become an important link in China's related scientific and technological sports industry. At the same time, these two technologies are also important means for further development and in-depth study of Chinese computer and related information technology. The combination of these two factors is reflected in the resource management of the two departments in the future.

The traditional physical training method of teaching by words and deeds is boring, and it can not intuitively show the essentials of complex movements such as gymnastics. This topic adopts virtual reality technology. While athletes wear inertial sensors, it can clearly reproduce, freeze and slow motion images for each athlete's three-dimensional human model scene, and analyze and compare sports data, which is conducive to enhancing the image and vividness of physical education teaching and training.

Collect, integrate and utilize the posture data in the monitoring process, and build a sports training analysis and evaluation system based on the "public cloud platform". Realize the sharing of sports resources, interactive learning and training, improve the efficiency of education and training, break the barriers such as regional restrictions, meet the needs of personalized and differentiated sports training, and lay a foundation for accumulating digital sports resources that are still very scarce at this stage.

At present, sports training and teaching are not closely combined with modern teaching technology, and there are not enough digital sports resources that can be used for training and teaching or as selection criteria. If quantitative training parameter standards can be formulated, it will provide reference basis for the training and selection of athletes, prevent human factors in the process of coach selection, create a good environment for the selection of athletes, and avoid burying any sports talents [2]. Most of the traditional sports training methods are that each coach leads a number of sports teams, and the training plans formulated are all unified standards, which can not develop personalized training courses for each athlete. If we can quantify the training conditions of athletes, we can analyze the strengths and weaknesses of each athlete and formulate personalized training plans. The research of this topic is the application of data mining technology in sports training, which integrates, processes and analyzes the measured posture data, and creates a posture database for sports events.

2   Related Work

2.1   Research Status of Data Mining Sports Training

At present, the research on sports, training and management abroad mostly focuses on the decision support of sports training management for specific projects and professional athletes, while the decision support of sports training management for college students and how to use intelligent agent technology to realize a universal and open system have not been publicly reported. Figure 1 below shows the implementation process of intelligent agent technology.

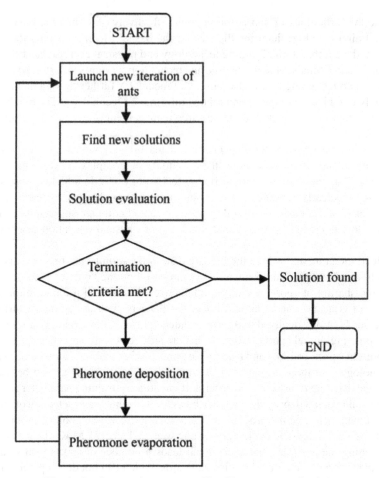

Fig. 1. Implementation process of intelligent agent technology

Although the research and development of DSS in China began as early as 1985, it is still in its infancy. In CNKI cross database search, 12471 papers related to DSS from 1985 to 2008 were retrieved, but only 12 research papers on Decision Support System in sports field were retrieved. Luo Yufeng and others have developed sports psychological counseling and psychological training intelligent decision system (SPCTS) and sports evaluation decision support system (SEDSS) by using literature retrieval, computer methods and other research methods. Sun Qinghua et al. (2000) established a system model for the diagnosis and evaluation of Rowers' competitive ability and a decision support system for the optimization design, simulation and regulation of training process by using literature retrieval, investigation, system analysis and life cycle methods. Chen Peiyou et al. (2002) designed a decision support system for weightlifting training (wst-dss) by using literature retrieval, on-site follow-up investigation, system analysis, software engineering and evaluation methods. Shaoguihua et al. (2004) used literature retrieval and computer methods to build a comprehensive fitness information analysis and decision support system ihia-dss. Wu Weibing et al. (2007) studied and designed a sports training function monitoring decision support system using computer methods [3].

As shown in Fig. 2 below, it is the expansion of sports decision-making.

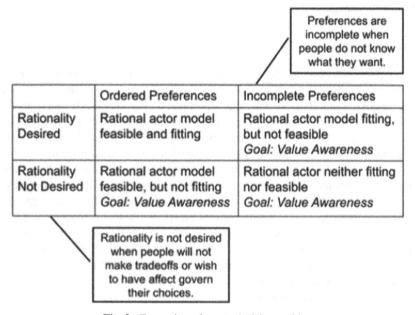

Fig. 2. Expansion of sports decision-making

Sports is a highly comprehensive discipline, which includes sports human science, sports humanities and Social Sciences, etc. before 2000, the research field of sports application decision support system was limited to sports training, sports evaluation, sports management and other fields. Compared with the extensive research fields of sports science, the application of DSS in the field of sports needs to be further expanded.

In the intelligent future, it is very urgent to build a health management system to realize prevention oriented, physical and medical integration and comprehensive and active health management. Wearable devices are the guarantee of health management. Through wearable devices, we can capture massive data in people's daily behaviors. Accurate identification of human behavior based on wearable devices is a necessary condition to promote health management. In daily life, people's behavior types are complex and diverse. Only through data mining technology, mining useful information and using it in real life, can we create great value. However, due to the complexity and diversity of human activities, most of them identify simple human activities through data mining algorithms, such as classification learning algorithms, which are difficult to apply to practical problems; In addition, human behavior recognition is of great significance in many fields such as health management and mobile medicine [4]. Therefore, it is very urgent to recognize complex and diverse human activities based on data mining technology to promote intelligent and personalized health management.

Therefore, by comprehensively analyzing the relationship among data mining, health management and human behavior recognition, we can find that data mining is a tool to realize human behavior recognition and health management, human behavior recognition is a guarantee and means to realize health management, and the ultimate goal is to achieve prevention oriented, physical and medical integration and comprehensive and active health management.

2.2 Development Trend

National fitness has become a long-term national policy in China. However, the general low physical quality of citizens, especially the decline of physical quality of college and middle school students, has become a major problem for the country. Of course, there are many reasons for this. Through the research and analysis of the existing college students' sports, training, management and other aspects, combined with the computer artificial intelligence theory and the existing analysis and research of the decision-making methods of sports and training management, this paper finds out a decision-making support method that conforms to the modern sports training management theory, improves the physical quality of college students, and improves the competitive level of college sports [5]. The purpose of this subject is to construct a sports training management decision support system based on data mining technology. In view of the current problems in the management of College Students' physical training, we should improve it and derive a scientific and reasonable physical training method and plan that truly conforms to the physical quality of college students.

The general flow of data mining technology is shown in Fig. 3.

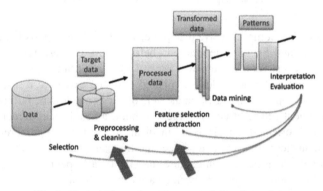

Fig. 3. Technical process of sports training data mining

① Develop data mining system for specific application

Early data mining applications mainly focused on helping enterprises improve their competitiveness. With the increasing popularity of data mining, data mining also increasingly explores other applications. Generally, there are some limitations when using general data mining system to deal with specific application problems.

Therefore, developing data mining system for specific application has become one of the development trends of data mining technology.

② Data collection and integration of database system, data warehouse and network database database system, data warehouse and WWW are the most important information processing system and the core module of data analysis. This paper focuses on the method of data extraction and seamless integration in this information processing environment.

③ Standardization of data mining language

Standardization work such as language standardization usually contributes to the development of data acquisition system. If we want to improve data mining systems in different application industries, we can use standardized data mining system development language to improve the interoperability between different data mining systems.

④ Research and development of visual data retrieval technology

Visual data retrieval technology is an effective method to extract useful knowledge from offshore data. The system research and development of visual data retrieval technology can enable users to create visual models and improve data extraction to the basic function of data analysis tools.

⑤ Privacy protection and information security in data mining

The maintenance of information security and the protection of privacy have always been an important topic in computer science. With the increasingly wide application of data mining technology and the increasing popularity of telecommunications and computer networks, this topic has also become an important problem that data mining needs to face [6]. It has also become one of the research trends of data mining technology to continuously develop methods and tools related to privacy protection and information security, and ensure the security and privacy in the appropriate mining process and information access.

3 Importance of Physical Training

3.1 Improve the Social and School Teaching System

At this time, China has not only strengthened the reform of physical education, but also attached great importance to the research on the rich content of physical education. Sports is a fast and complex systematic process. Many middle schools in China attach great importance to sports and sports statistics. Through professional collection and analysis, these data can reflect that the school plays an active role in improving relevant physical education courses and some physical education courses, classifying its teaching system and other teaching forms [7].

The importance of sports training is partly reflected in the processing and collection of sports related data. It provides guidance for the formulation of physical education curriculum, effectively reduces the improper situation of physical training in schools or social groups, reflects the improvement of data system and curriculum, and improves the data collection of physical training. As shown in Fig. 4 below, the development framework for the processing and collection of sports related data.

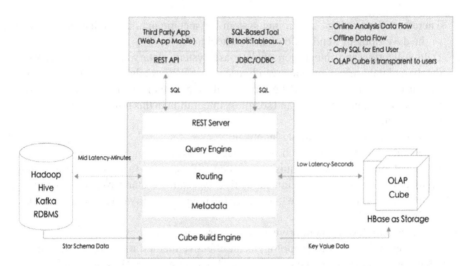

Fig. 4. Development framework for the processing and collection of sports related data

3.2 Improve People's Physical Quality

Physical exercise in China aims to improve people's physical fitness. At present, the physical quality of teenagers in China is low, which is mainly a cultural topic, and physical education is increasingly ignored. This not only makes it difficult to improve vocational education and welfare, but also makes it impossible for some sports to establish a system. This is why we should strengthen physical exercise. Improving the quality of College Physical Education Teaching at this comprehensive level is of great significance to solve many problems in college physical education teaching [8].

To some extent, the education of data mining technology refers to the activity education within the framework of human biology. This kind of activity can not only reasonably treat many existing physiological diseases, but also help the physiological, biological and psychological indicators such as tibial movement, human blood lipids, heartbeat, and significantly improve the physical quality of the human body.

3.3 Enrich the Practical Experience of Human Technology and Activities

Among many projects in China, some difficult training projects currently exist play a guiding role in the development of the sports industry. Generally speaking, many current scientific research achievements in China are closely related to relevant training and sports research projects. China's sports training content is generally diverse, according to different groups to carry out training in line with their actual situation, which is not only conducive to improving the enthusiasm of the audience, but also take into account the differences of different groups [9]. China's sports training projects are generally carried out with the support of many years of technical activities. Such practical experience can not only enrich the activities and technical development of relevant cities, but also fundamentally improve the work enthusiasm of relevant staff.

The significance of sports training fundamentally requires that the relevant sports staff must have certain industry ethics and moral standards, and carry out their own development on this basis. Generally speaking, China's coaches and relevant sports staff have rich practical experience, which can effectively act on other industries. After a long time of exploration and training and Research on sports training itself, many staff will find that many problems are related.

In the human body model, in order to simplify the complex human body structure, the human body is abstracted into several parts, and each part is usually regarded as a rigid body to simplify the complex motion of the human body.

The commonly used rigid body models include 17 rigid body models, 16 rigid body models and 14 rigid body models. It is obvious that the more rigid bodies in the model, the better the motion of the human body can be refined. In order to study the more accurate motion posture of the human body, the 17 rigid body model is adopted in this subject. As shown in Fig. 5 below, the movement landing data measurement diagram.

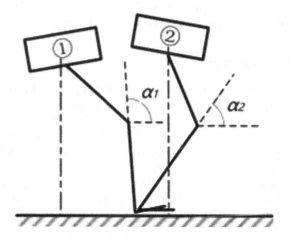

Fig. 5. Motion landing data measurement chart

The rigid body model includes: hip, chest, left shoulder, right shoulder, head, left and right upper arms, left and right forearms, left and right thighs, left and right calves, hands and feet. Each part of the limbs is connected by joints [10].

"Upstream and downstream" limbs: the limbs connected on both sides of the joint are divided into "upstream" and "downstream". The hip of the human body is the upstream limb of all body parts, and the downstream limb is the one that radiates from the hip to the limbs and then to the corresponding distal end of the limbs.

Limb coordinate system: it is required to establish a right-hand rectangular coordinate system for each limb based on the actions of natural drooping of the upper limb, palm forward, toe forward and visual front. The point on the limb is the coordinate origin o, the horizontal forward direction of the vertical body surface is the positive direction of the x-axis, the horizontal left direction of the side of the body is the positive direction of the y-axis, and the positive direction of the z-axis perpendicular to the ground is the positive direction of the z-axis, referred to as Z-system. When analyzing the relative positional relationship of adjacent limbs, the positions of the downstream limbs are determined in turn based on the upstream limbs, and the complete human posture is finally determined by level transmission.

Sensor coordinate system: refers to the measured value output by the sensor. The coordinate system of the sensor itself is taken as the reference system, and its own coordinate system is referred to as s system for short [11].

Ground coordinate system: the positive directions of X, y and Z axes are taken as the reference system of all limbs relative to the ground, which is called G system for short.

For sports training, a good balance can be achieved based on the use of data mining technology. Generally speaking, it can improve human activity experience and meet people's practical technology.

4   Application of Data Mining Technology in Sports Training

According to the different information needed will be different. The applications of common data mining algorithms in sports training include the following.

4.1   Decision Tree Algorithm

The principle of determine how to classify, which category is the first node, and the classified image is similar to a tree, so it is called decision tree. The decision tree can be obtained through the operation of Clementine and SPSS software, and the probability of correct classification will be obtained for the reference of decision makers. Decision tree algorithm is also widely used in sports training. For team games, such as basketball, football, volleyball, etc., by collecting the score and defense data of each player on the court, we can calculate whether the efficiency value of each player is positive or negative, so as to judge how helpful the players are to the team, and then arrange which players play or combine better, It greatly improves the scientificity of the coach's troop arrangement [12].

4.2   Neural Network Algorithm

Neural algorithm is the mathematical structure of network. The weights and thresholds of all neurons are calculated through a series of training algorithms. The application of neural network in nonlinear systems can be used in mathematical expressions that are difficult to explain. Artificial neural network algorithm includes sensor, neural network, self-organizing mapping and so on. Whether the behavior of athletes has changed, and whether the data has collected useful data. As shown in Fig. 6.

It is known that there are many methods for measuring the correlation between features and categories, such as distance measurement, information measurement, dependency degree and so on. However, the mrmr method only measures the correlation between features and categories by mutual information, that is, mutual information measurement [13]. Therefore, this section explores the difference and difference between the relaeff method based on Euclidean distance metric and the mrmr method based on information metric in calculating the correlation between features and categories.

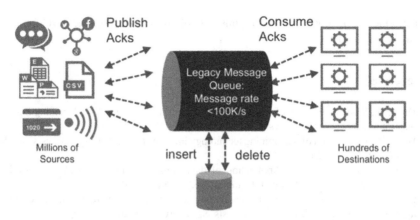

Fig. 6. Big data sports training

First, the correlation between features and categories, i.e. the weight of features, is calculated by ReliefF method and mrmr method.

The ReliefF method calculates the correlation between various features and categories based on the Euclidean distance. The specific steps are as follows: first, randomly select a sample R from the sample data set D, then find k nearest neighbor samples h from the samples with the same category as the sample R from the remaining data sets based on the Euclidean distance, and then find k nearest neighbor samples m from the samples with different categories from the sample R, Calculate and update the correlation between each feature and category based on the weight formula. Since the samples are randomly selected in the iterative process, it is often repeated for m times to obtain the average weight of each feature. When calculating each feature weight, the value of K is taken as 3, that is, three nearest neighbor samples h with the smallest Euclidean distance are selected from the samples with the same class of sample R, and three nearest neighbor samples m are selected from each class of samples with different class of sample R [14]. Due to the large scale of the data in this paper, there are many sample categories, and each person has his own style characteristics during sports, so m is taken as 100, i.e. repeated sampling for 100 times.

5 Conclusion

In many areas of sports training, you can use data mining technology to make decisions. This paper introduces the algorithm used in data mining training. In the era of leading science and technology, data mining technology will continue to play an important role in various fields, including sports training, and lead the scientific and technological revolution. According to the principle and algorithm of data mining, this paper analyzes the most common data mining algorithm in the field of sports training, and believes that data mining will play an important role in various fields in the future, which is very beneficial to improve sports training and athletes' academic performance. Of course, this document has many shortcomings. The author will also improve the method, deeply study the new changes of sports training mining technology, and promote the development of China's sports industry.

References

1. Deng, H., Wang, J.: Design of real-time data analysis system for physical training based on data mining technology. J. Phys: Conf. Ser. **1982**(1), 012206 (2021)
2. Hong, X.: Application of data mining technology in software engineering. J. Phys. Conf. Ser. **2066**(1), 012013 (2021)
3. Zheng, Q., Li, Y., Cao, J.: Application of data mining technology in alarm analysis of communication network. Comput. Commun. **163**(8), 84–90 (2020)
4. Qian, L., Liu, J.: Application of data mining technology and wireless network sensing technology in sports training index analysis. SpringerOpen **2020**(1) (2020)
5. Wang, J., Li, C., Li, J., et al.: Application of data mining technology in risk prediction of metabolic syndrome in oil workers (2020)
6. Zhang, X., Shen, J., Wu, P., et al.: Research on the application of big data mining in the construction of smart campus. Open Access Libr. J. **8**(11), 10 (2021)
7. Guo, X.Y., Wang, J.F., Liu, T.F.: Exploration of professor liu taofeng's experience in the treatment of eczema based on data mining technology. (004), 50–55 (2020)
8. Wang, Z.: The effective application of quality development training in physical education teaching reform. Bull. Sport Sci. Technol. (2020)
9. Hu, G.R., Liu, H.: Application of data mining technology in portfolio optimization. J. Phys: Conf. Ser. **1648**, 042064 (2020)
10. Zeng, Q., Dong, S.: Application of computer data mining technology in internet industry. J. Phys: Conf. Ser. **1648**, 032006 (2020)
11. Zhang, S.: Application of data mining technology in the analysis of e-commerce emotional law. J. Phys: Conf. Ser. **1852**(2), 022044 (2021)
12. Li, M., Li, Q., Li, Y., et al.: Analysis of characteristics of tennis singles matches based on 5G and data mining technology. Secur. Commun. Netw. **2021**, 1–9 (2021)
13. Belov, M., Korenkov, V., Tokareva, N., et al.: Architecture of a compact data grid cluster for teaching modern methods of data mining in the virtual computer lab. Eur. Phys. J. Conf. **226**(4), 03004 (2020)
14. Zhou, Z., Gu, B.: Application of computer data mining technology in E-business. J. Phys. Conf. Ser. **1744**(4), 042107 (2021)

Research on the Transformation of Financial Accountants in Manufacturing Enterprises Under the Background of Cloud Computing

Ning Han[✉]

Business School, Sichuan University, Chengdu 610000, Sichuan, China
2056955435@qq.com

Abstract. With the development of science and technology, big data cloud computing and other related technologies have been widely used. In the development process of processing enterprises, more and more enterprises are aware of the positive impact of data resources on their own development. In order to improve the overall competitiveness of enterprises and adapt to the new environment, some manufacturing enterprises have gradually expanded the use of big data in the process of transformation and development. On this basis, this paper analyzes and discusses the problems of manufacturing financial accounting, and provides effective guidance for the transformation of manufacturing financial accounting.

Keywords: Cloud computing · Manufacturing financial accounting · Transformation

1 Introduction

The traditional accounting method will be replaced by the financial robot, and the accounting function will change accordingly. From the perspective of the ability requirements of enterprises for accountants, enterprises pay more attention to the tax planning, financial analysis, economic prediction and decision-making ability of accountants, and there are few accountants with this ability at present. In order to promote the development of manufacturing enterprises, comprehensively improve their economic and social benefits, make comprehensive use of modern strategic means to realize the informatization of manufacturing enterprise management, and gradually expand the information scale with the help of cloud computing, So that accountants and departments can establish a good interactive relationship. Through effective communication and exchange, clarify the problems and challenges in the actual development of manufacturing enterprises [1].

Since the 1980s, the Financial Sharing Center of Ford Motor Company of the United States has been established and started operation in Europe. At present, a large number of multinational groups and large groups around the world have established and operated financial shared service centers. After an in-depth investigation of more than 30 European multinational enterprise groups implementing the financial sharing mode,

M. A. Jan and F. Khan (Eds.): BigIoT-EDU 2022, LNICST 467, pp. 413–424, 2023.
https://doi.org/10.1007/978-3-031-23944-1_45

Accenture found that the average operating cost of accounting decreased by about 30%. Financial sharing service has been widely recognized and fully used in the world's large multinational enterprises. Practice has proved that financial sharing service is a powerful tool to promote the transformation of enterprise accounting and the continuous optimization and innovation of accounting business. The financial sharing center itself has higher information transparency, faster response to business, and less management and control risks. This mode is praised as a new management mode that improves service level and frees business departments and senior managers from the shackles of daily basic business. Figure 1 below shows the framework of the Financial Sharing Center.

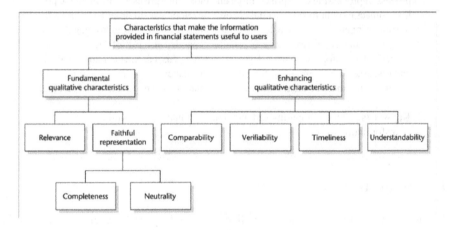

Fig. 1. Financial Sharing Center framework

Under the influence of the international atmosphere of foreign multinational groups building financial shared service centers, some companies in China have also begun to build financial shared service centers. In 2006, China UK Life Insurance Co., Ltd. introduced the financial sharing operation mode to achieve the purpose of expanding the scale and reducing the number of accountants. After the establishment and operation of the National Financial Sharing Service Center, centralized accounting, payment and accounting reimbursement have been realized. In terms of paying wages, drawing various reserves, insurance and re insurance, relevant departments and accounting departments should be connected. Depreciation of assets shall be uniformly accrued by the company headquarters. The financial sharing operation mode makes the group's accounting personnel shift from the past accounting bookkeeping work to decision-making, control and performance evaluation activities, and the accounting organization is gradually transformed. The group has centralized control over limited resources, so that its resource allocation ability and market competitiveness are constantly strengthened.

With the rapid development of information technology industry, accounting data information has shown a trend of changing from simple structure to massive and complex big data. How to quickly and effectively collect, collate and analyze accounting data information is a great challenge for enterprise accounting work; On the other hand, in the face of the constant changes in the economic environment and industrial development, the accounting function of enterprises can not only be satisfied with accounting, but also realize the usefulness of accounting information to business decisions. Therefore, the accounting transformation of enterprises is imperative.

Financial sharing service refers to the enterprise group separating a large number of repetitive and low value-added work related to accounting business from the original company in its internal branches, subsidiaries and business units, and centralizing all the work to the Financial Sharing Center. The practice of financial sharing mode has been widely used by a large number of European and American enterprises. Practice has proved that this mode can indeed bring about cost reduction and efficiency improvement, and help enterprises to carry out accounting transformation.

Therefore, accountants are also facing transformation. Because different accountants have different professional competence, their role in the accounting field is also different after the transformation. Previous scholars focused. However, with the change of national policies and the development of the times, new things such as online services and cloud accounting also provide accountants with many new opportunities. This paper will focus on how accountants in the transition period seize new opportunities and improve their comprehensive quality. Become economic management talents to meet the needs of the times.

2   Related Work

2.1   Cloud Computing Concept

At present, the understanding of cloud computing is constantly changing, and there is no common and consistent definition. A Chinese grid and cloud computing expert said, "cloud computing distributes tasks in a resource pool composed of a large number of computers, so different application systems can access computing power, storage space and various software services as needed." Manufacturers build data centers and supercomputers through distributed computing and virtual technology to provide data storage and analysis services for enterprise technology developers and customers. For example, rent a data warehouse from Amazon. In other words, scientific settlement services should be free or required. In a broader sense, "cloud" means that manufacturers build network server clusters to provide online software services, hardware leasing, data storage, computer analysis and other services to different customers [2]. Quantiyun's calculations include users in the country, software manufacturers such as Google, other suppliers and service types such as online financial software. Google announced its Google package. The cloud computing development framework is shown in Fig. 2 below.

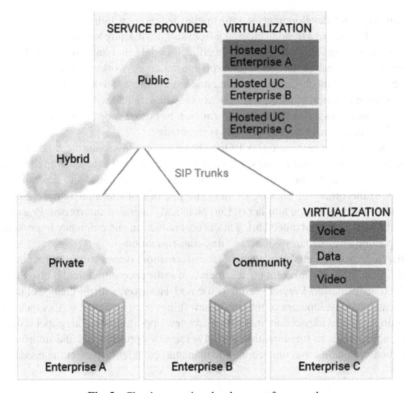

Fig. 2. Cloud computing development framework

The impetus to promote the development of the company's Financial Shared Service Center comes from the reform of enterprise financial management. As the object of financial management, financial data records all kinds of economic matters in the process of enterprise operation, which supports the normal operation of enterprise business. It mainly goes through the following stages: manual processing stage, the disadvantages are low speed, low efficiency and high error rate; In the mechanical treatment stage, the disadvantages are huge system and high cost; In the stage of electronic computer processing, the disadvantage is that the accounting procedures are independent and no system is formed; In the network processing stage, cloud computing is used to solve the above problems, realize the integration of business, information and accounting, and improve the enterprise information sharing.

2.2 Cloud Computing Enterprise Financial Accounting

The late 1970s was the initial stage of accounting informatization in China. Accounting computerization is the primary stage of its development, which has experienced three steps from preliminary research, accounting development to management development. It reflects that accounting combines the most advanced information technology, complies with the tide of informatization, and constantly improves the management of enterprise financial information, which has brought historical changes to accounting methods. However, for small and medium-sized enterprises that have been struggling for a long time, information technology has developed slowly and is in a passive state. Because informatization construction requires a lot of initial investment and continuous follow-up maintenance costs, these factors seriously restrict the improvement of informatization level of small and medium-sized enterprises [3]. Nowadays, the popular cloud computing in the field of information technology is to use web pages to deliver services to users after combining various software resources and hardware resources on the basis of the Internet. This technology has become mature and gradually popularized in large and medium-sized cities. In order to keep up with the trend of the times, many large enterprises have joined the team of cloud computing to seek the rise of enterprise informatization level, and also help enterprises easily and smoothly transfer accounting information system management business to the cloud platform. The construction of accounting informatization mode of small and medium-sized enterprises is deeply affected by the cloud computing industry, and the pace of accounting informatization of small and medium-sized enterprises is accelerated.

The cloud computing architecture is shown in Fig. 3.

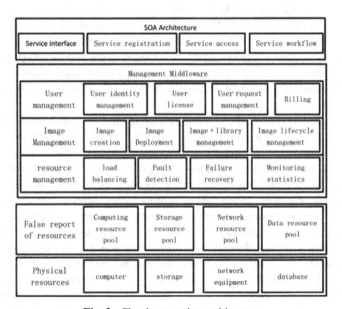

Fig. 3. Cloud computing architecture

3 Transformation Necessity Analysis

3.1 Impact of Big Data Cloud Computing on the Accounting Industry

(1) Source of accounting information. In classical accounting, information mainly comes from structured data that is easy to analyze, process or use directly. The era of big data has not only produced structured data, but also produced a large number of unstructured data. We must integrate these non constructive and structured data through large-scale data processing technology, determine their relevance, and use quantitative methods to reflect, analyze and evaluate the development of the company.

(2) With the popularity of big data, a single key can be made to replace the traditional artificial intelligence accounting information. At the same time, new problems such as accounting information security, frequent hacker attacks, serious leakage of trade secrets, computer viruses and so on also follow.

(3) The number of basic accounting Posts decreased. Science and technology have replaced manpower, and the accounting posts in the accounting industry will gradually disappear. A large number of accountants who are only engaged in accounting are about to lose their jobs. The accounting posts in the traditional sense are no longer important or even needed [2]. The transformation of Accountants is imminent, transforming to managers and senior accounting posts, Now the current situation of the accounting industry is the proliferation of basic posts and the shortage of senior posts. Therefore, under the impact of science and technology, seizing the opportunity and changing the current situation is the primary task of the accounting industry and accountants.

After building the financial sharing platform, the company began to promote the transformation of accounting operation mode by organizational process reengineering, and carried out corresponding management team configuration to ensure the realization of transformation. Among them, the functions of the accounting departments of the provincial headquarters are transformed to formulate price strategies and product planning, while the accounting departments of the county and city branches are transformed to create business performance and channel operation. Among the horizontal businesses within the company, the labor and product transactions are carried out through the virtual settlement system, which enables each branch to make the management objectives of business plan and budget, business model and analysis, development evaluation of specific projects and performance evaluation based on economic benefits. In the vertical business, through the division of small grass-roots accounting units, various resources are sunk into the grass-roots level and given the right to manage and control the resources, realizing the vertical penetration of right control, resource control, task allocation and incentive system, improving the professional ability of the front-line business units and reconstructing the integrated operation system connecting the market. As shown in Fig. 4 below, it is a framework for building a financial sharing platform.

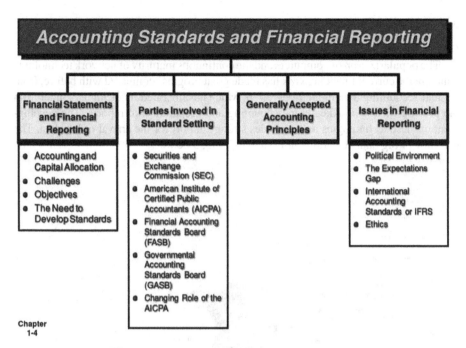

Fig. 4. Build a financial sharing platform framework

Starting from creating precise and refined marketing projects, we have built a technologically leading information service network. Market activities controlled by big data technology with marketing projects as the carrier, and 20 post evaluation indicators of profitability were set, and 47 key points of market control were established. Implement lean cost management to improve the efficiency of enterprise resource allocation. With the goal of value-added, the information system integrates lean production services, lean product design and lean supply chain through the use of big data technology, automatically prompts exceptions and warnings, and then obtains analysis reports to achieve lean cost management [4].

In this stage, the accounting operation focuses on customer experience, risk drivers, operating income growth, resource allocation efficiency, and integrates with the business development objectives. Relying on process optimization, establishment of information system and transformation of accounting personnel, a refined value growth and creation system has been built. According to the overall goal of accounting transformation, the company combines budget alignment with market-oriented allocation of internal resources to realize dynamic budget management, promote the maximization of enterprise benefits, and transform budget management into target oriented.

3.2   Transformation Requirements

(1) The way of thinking should be changed

The popularization of computers and the continuous maturity of network technology, although the current financial work has made great progress compared with before, from manual accounting to computer operation, which has liberated financial personnel from the previous heavy bookkeeping, accounting and preparation of reports. The development of these technologies also provides strong support for the arrival of big data. The text flow of big data development is shown in Fig. 5 below.

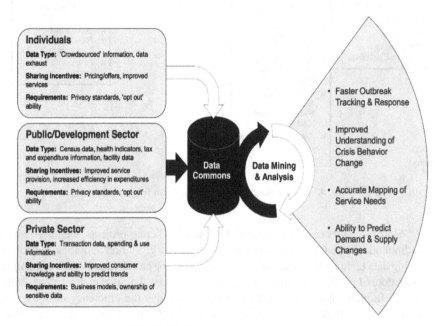

Fig. 5. Big data development text flow

(2) The ability to analyze and process data should be improved

In the context of big data, if financial personnel analyze data in the traditional way, it will inevitably lead to low data utilization and low work efficiency. This requires financial personnel to change the traditional way of financial data analysis and be able to classify, mine, process and analyze huge data groups. It also requires financial personnel to analyze these data from a long-term perspective and provide reliable decision-making basis for enterprise managers. It also puts forward higher requirements for financial personnel to process data [5]. They must keep pace with the times and master new technologies and tools, Improve the efficiency of data analysis and processing.

(3) The management level should be improved

In the past, the traditional financial accountants did some work for the enterprise in bookkeeping, accounting and preparing statements. They thought that they could not participate in the enterprise management and were easy to limit themselves to the primary stage of accounting and data processing. The financial personnel often ignored the importance of the report to the enterprise's future decision-making, and helping the enterprise make decision-making was also a way of management, This awareness must be raised.

3.3 Transformation Path

In a theoretical sense, the arrival of big data cloud computing will lead to the update of accounting theory, and accountants should update their knowledge reserves. In a practical sense, the actual work of Accountants has been greatly affected, so we should find a way to adapt to the current situation as soon as possible. With the change of talent demand, accountants should consider changing to management accounting and compound application accounting. In theory, the transformation from "accounting type" to "management type" mainly involves three aspects: one is to increase the financial evaluation from profit to economy.

The second is the transformation from financial accounting to management accounting, and the third is the transformation from independent accounting to Financial Sharing Center: in fact, it mainly focuses on the requirements for accountants, such as (1) breaking through the limitations of traditional financial accounting, changing the way of thinking, and thinking from the perspective of enterprise development strategy and enterprise management. (2) Strengthen learning, constantly enrich and improve the knowledge structure, and constantly improve the professional level. (3) Further familiar with management control and information analysis, find the connection point between business and finance by understanding the production business process of the enterprise, understanding the flow and transformation of various resources of the enterprise [6].

4   Measures to Strengthen Accounting Transformation of Manufacturing Enterprises Under the Background of Cloud Computing

4.1   Build a Financial Strategy System and Broaden Financial Management Functions

Cloud computing and other related technologies continue to innovate and develop with the development of big data, the function of management accounting has been strengthened, and financial accountants enter into strategic decision-making to provide effective help for enterprise budget and various economic decisions. In the process of transformation and development of enterprise financial accounting, we should combine the all-round development of other departments of manufacturing enterprises and constantly expand their functions. In fact, once the financial accounting management of manufacturing enterprises is separated from other business departments, it will greatly reduce the work efficiency of manufacturing enterprises and seriously affect the development of manufacturing enterprises. This not only requires enterprises to improve the level of financial accounting management, but also to make the construction of financial accounting structure meet the company's strategic objectives, highlight the importance of financial standardized accounting system, highlight the functions of financial value creation, risk prevention and control, decision support and form a unified financial standard system, so as to further promote the construction of financial sharing, Broaden the all-round development of financial management functions, gradually improve the relevant cost management awareness of business departments, and enhance the overall financial concept of enterprises [7]. Figure 6 below shows the financial strategy system.

Objectives and Stakeholders

Mergers and Takeovers

Calculating Valuations

Merger Issues and Exit Strategies

Financial Strategy and Performance

Accounting and Reporting

Dividend Decisions

Sources of Finance

Financial Risk Management

Leases

Capital Markets and Shares

Capital

Fig. 6. Financial strategy system

4.2 Strengthen Information Construction and Promote the Transformation of Financial Intelligence

In the process of transformation and development of manufacturing financial accounting, we need to comprehensively strengthen the information construction in combination with cloud computing, so as to maximize the use of accounting information and give full play to its value. In the process of information construction, considering the actual development of the enterprise, through effective cost budget and industry development, the work requirements for financial accounting of manufacturing enterprises [8]. Therefore, by deeply matching the accounting standards with the enterprise business process, establishing a sound standardized financial control system, gradually realizing the financial information control platform with the in-depth integration of industry and finance, realizing the effective connection of multiple modules of the enterprise, accelerating the transfer of the focus of financial work from accounting to management, and realizing the refined and specialized accounting of front-end business on the basis of focusing on data authenticity and disclosure compliance, Therefore, the information platform relies on the high-speed and fast accounting of the company's business activities, standardizing the accounting of economic activities, systematically collecting bottom data, and effectively improving the accounting quality and efficiency, so as to effectively realize the transformation and innovation of financial accounting [9]. At the same time, it is also necessary to encourage scientific and technological personnel to innovate, so that the staff can further strengthen the analysis and utilization of accounting information and provide guiding suggestions for the development of enterprises by establishing corresponding information interaction platforms.

5   Conclusion

In short, the development of cloud computing provides effective technical support for the transformation of enterprise accounting. The transformation from traditional financial accounting to administrative accounting makes production enterprises better adapt to market demand and realize the sustainable development of production enterprises. Using financial intelligence can not only simplify business processes and achieve efficient and fast accounting, but also promote financiers to get rid of a large number of repetitive businesses and make the company's financial model develop from accounting to management. Provide more reliable support for enterprise decision-making and promote the development of manufacturing enterprises.

References

1. Yan, Y., Chu, D.: Evaluation of enterprise management innovation in manufacturing industry using fuzzy multicriteria decision-making under the background of big data. Math. Probl. Eng. **2021**, 1–10 (2021)
2. Li, Y., Xie, T.: The influence of fiscal subsidy on the innovation behavior of manufacturing enterprises under the background of "The Belt and Road". Proc. Bus. Econ. Stud. **4**(1), 12 (2021)
3. Yu, Y.: Application and optimization of enterprise financial sharing service center based on cloud computing (2021)
4. Ou, L., Zhang, Z.: Research and analysis on cloud accounting of enterprises under the background of new economy. J. Phys. Conf. Ser. **1852**(4), 042077 (2021)
5. Jiang, H.J., Yao, H.L.: Study on the transformation of Foreign trade enterprises in Guangdong Province under the background of cross-border e-commerce. In: 2021 6th International Conference on Social Sciences and Economic Development (ICSSED 2021) (2021)

6. Wei, Y.C.J.: The evolution of managerial cognition of manufacturing enterprises in the context of digital transformation: China experience (2020)
7. Lin, T.C., Sheng, M.L., Wang, K.J.: Dynamic capabilities for smart manufacturing transformation by manufacturing enterprises. Asian J. Technol. Innov. **1**, 1–24 (2020)
8. Erbay, H., Yldrm, N.: Combined technology selection model for digital transformation in manufacturing: a case study from the automotive supplier industry. Int. J. Innov. Technol. Manage. **19**(07), 2250023 (2022)
9. Zhou, L., Wang, F., Wang, N., et al.: Application of industrial robots in automated production lines under the background of intelligent manufacturing. J. Phys. Conf. Ser. **1992**(4), 042050 (2021)

Research on the Teaching Design of Public Management in the Era of "Internet +"

Lu Jiang[1] and Kefei Wang[2(✉)]

[1] Dongpo Academy, Jinjiang College, Sichuan University, Meishan 620860, Sichuan, China
[2] The Information Management Center, Jinjiang College, Sichuan University, Meishan 620860, Sichuan, China
wkf371@sina.com

Abstract. The effectiveness of moral education in Chinese universities is very limited. With the advent of the Internet plus era, flipped classroom can give full play to the information teaching means, reconstruct the teaching process, promote students' autonomous learning, and thoroughly implement the basic task of Li De Shu Ren. In the general transformation period of colleges and universities in China, the discussion on the management mode of colleges and universities is becoming more and more intense. Scientific management is the only way for colleges and universities to survive and develop, and also the key to achieve results and benefits. Based on the Internet plus, the new public management theory represent the general trend of new management in universities.

Keywords: Internet · Public administration · Teaching model

1 Introduction

In 1980s, the teaching and research of public administration was restored in China. After nearly 20 years of development, the public management discipline has gradually grown into an independent research field, which plays an important role in the research of social science and Management Science in China, and has become a popular specialty of undergraduate and graduate education in our country and a major pillar of Party and government cadre training. Especially since the end of 1990s, with the establishment of market economy system and the deepening of administrative system reform, the establishment of the first-class public management discipline and the initiation of the postgraduate education of master of Public Management (MPA) major, and the large number of undergraduate courses in public management in Colleges and universities, The subject of public management has become a subject full of vitality and great prospect in the field of social science and Management Science in contemporary China [1].

Public management is a kind of management concept and management mode which is produced by the defects of government management. On the one hand, it emphasizes the "publicity" of management objectives, that is, public power must perform public functions; On the other hand, it emphasizes the supervision, restriction and standardization of public power, and the scientific method of using public power.

M. A. Jan and F. Khan (Eds.): BigIoT-EDU 2022, LNICST 467, pp. 425–433, 2023.
https://doi.org/10.1007/978-3-031-23944-1_46

The contents of public management in the sense of discipline include government management, administrative management, urban management, public policy, development management, educational economic management and labor and social security. The rise of public management benefited from the new public management movement of globalization. However, after entering the 21st century, the new public management has encountered new challenges in practice, and the research of public management has entered an era of contention. As one of the four branches of modern management science, public management is the discipline with the most development potential and broad prospects in the future world and contemporary China. Since the emergence of public management as an independent discipline in China in the 1990s, the development of Public Management Science in China has shown vigorous vitality. With the development of contemporary Chinese economy, the deepening of reform and the construction of a harmonious society, the role of public management has been paid more and more attention by the society. Chinese public management has become the largest growth point of Chinese social science research. Huangdaqiang, former director of the Institute of administration of Renmin University of China, founded the first Institute of administration in China and trained the first batch of master's degree students in administration in China. In China, the school of public management of Renmin University of China is the most important teaching and research base of public management in China (in the latest discipline evaluation of the Ministry of education, the first level discipline of public management of Renmin University of China ranks first in the country). Professor xiashuzhang of Sun Yat sen University was the first person who proposed to introduce public management education in China, and Sun Yat sen University is also one of the earliest places where public management rose in China. Public management is a public sector with the government as the core, which integrates various social forces, widely uses political, economic, managerial and legal methods, strengthens the governance ability of the government, improves government performance and public service quality, so as to realize public welfare and public interests. As an integral part of public administration and public affairs, public management focuses on regarding public administration as a profession and public managers as practitioners of this profession. It is a branch of public administration, which studies the activities, technologies and methods of various public organizations with government administrative organizations as the core to manage public affairs. Public management is a theoretical school and branch of public administration that pays attention to the technology and methods of public organizations or non-profit organizations, public projects and performance management, and public policy implementation. It is a knowledge framework formed in the middle and late 1980s, driven by the integration trend of contemporary social science and management science and the public sector management practice, especially the "new public management" movement, with the solution of public sector management problems as the core and the integration of related knowledge and methods of multiple disciplines. Public management is still consistent with public administration in some basic principles and management concepts, such as the subject of management, the content and scope of management activities, and management objectives.

2   The Characteristics of Public Management

Public administration or public management is a discipline group system which uses the theories and methods of management and political economics to study the management activities and rules of public organizations, especially government organizations. According to the research and teaching reform practice of public management in recent years, the characteristics of public management can be summarized as follows.

1. Professional management in the field of public policy. This means letting managers manage, or, as hood put it, "having senior people exercise active, significant, and discretionary control over the organization". The most typical reasonable explanation for this is that "the premise of entrusting responsibility is to make a clear distinction between behavioral responsibilities".
2. Clear criteria and measurement of performance. This requires the establishment of objectives and the setting of performance standards. During the demonstration, its supporters put forward that "assigning responsibilities requires a clear description of objectives; improving efficiency requires a firm focus on objectives".
3. Pay special attention to output control. Allocate resources to each area based on measured performance, because "it is the goal rather than the process that needs attention".
4. Within the public sector, there is a trend from aggregation to differentiation. This includes decomposing some large entities into "cooperative units formed around products", whose funds are independent and linked to each other on the basis of maintaining a certain distance. "Inside and outside the public sector", these units can be managed and "gain the efficiency advantage brought about by specific arrangements". Its necessity proves the rationality of this approach.
5. The public sector is moving in a more competitive direction. This includes "subscription contract terms and public bidding procedures", and its rationality lies in that "competition is the key to reducing costs and achieving higher standards".
6. Emphasis on private sector management. This includes "no longer adopting the 'militarized' public service ethics" and being more flexible in terms of personnel employment and remuneration. The rationality of this change is that "it is necessary to transfer the 'proven effective' management means of the private sector to the public sector for use".
7. It is emphasized that resource utilization should be more mandatory and economical. Beacon fire headhunter regards this as "reducing direct costs, strengthening labor discipline, resisting trade union requirements, and reducing the cost of making employees comply with the enterprise." the necessity of checking the resource needs of the public sector and doing more with less money "proves that this approach is reasonable.

On the whole, the new public management is developed on the assumption of self-interest, based on the public choice agent theory and its transaction cost theory, and based on the traditional managerialism and Neo Taylor doctrine. Its core points are: emphasizing the priority of economic value, emphasizing the market function, emphasizing the large-scale use of enterprise management philosophy and technology, and emphasizing the customer-oriented administrative style. After all, the new public management represents a direction for people to continuously improve the government and realize the ideal government governance in the real world. It is too early to draw a conclusion whether it means the arrival of a model era of government governance.

2.1 Characteristics of Public Management Discipline Adapting to Government Demand

With the deepening of the socialist political system reform, in the process of building a clean and efficient government, the demand for talents in public management discipline is increasing by government departments and non-governmental public management institutions. Many government departments lack the talents who have systematic knowledge of public management, and there is a talent gap. By absorbing the professional talents cultivated in Colleges and universities, the government administration will be more scientific, standardized, professional and legal. Therefore, the cultivation of public management professionals in Colleges and universities should also be aimed at different government departments, and different professional directions should be set according to the actual public management situation in China, so as to connect effective college training with government reception. Effective cooperation between government and university is conducive to the optimization of human resources allocation and saving the cost of talent training and talent recruitment between both sides [2].

2.2 The Market Characteristics of the Public Management Subject Employment in Multiple Directions

In modern market economy, although the government's market capacity is weakening gradually in the deepening of marketization, the role of government supervision and management of the market is gradually strengthening. Under the condition of global economic integration, whether it is state-owned enterprises, private enterprises or foreign-funded enterprises, the relationship with the government is becoming increasingly close and cooperation is becoming more and more extensive. Therefore, enterprises need to know the government system and master the specialized talents of administrative laws and regulations. On the one hand, through the communication and contact between the public management professionals and the government, it is conducive to establish good relationship and obtain policy information between enterprises and the government; On the other hand, it is helpful for the enterprise to make correct decision-making by analyzing and predicting the public policy by the public management talents. Therefore, in addition to government agencies, all kinds of enterprises are also important channels for talents transmission. At present, the demand for public management talents is increasing.

2.3 Market Characteristics of the Diversification of Knowledge of Talents in Public Management

The cultivation and discipline construction of public management discipline talents should be closely combined with the national conditions of our country, especially in the light of the actual situation of public management in China, and require special personnel to master the professional knowledge and skills required by public management, have a wider knowledge, and be able to comprehensively use the knowledge of economy, management, foreign languages, computers and other knowledge to solve the problems of public management and public policy, It is suitable for the development of socialist market economy, the need of running the country according to law and administration according to law. The demand for public management talents is mainly government departments. Therefore, the cultivation of public management talents should be based on the characteristics of government functions and professional requirements, reflecting the characteristics of interdisciplinary, compound and practical talents training. The training of public management talents with diversified knowledge is to explore the mode of public management talents training with Chinese characteristics, In order to meet the needs of government management talents in the new situation [3].

"Internet +" represents a new economic form. It refers to the combination of the Internet and traditional industries based on Internet information technology to complete economic transformation and upgrading by optimizing production factors, updating business systems, and reconstructing business models. The purpose of the "Internet +" plan is to give full play to the advantages of the Internet, deeply integrate the Internet with traditional industries, enhance economic productivity through industrial upgrading, and finally realize the increase of social wealth.

The central word of the concept of "Internet +" is the Internet, which is the starting point of the "Internet +" plan. The "Internet +" plan can be expressed in two levels. On the one hand, the word "Internet" and the symbol "+" in the concept of "Internet +" can be understood separately. The symbol "+" means a plus sign, which means addition and association. This shows that the application scope of the "Internet +" plan is the Internet and other traditional industries. It is a new plan for the development of different industries, and the application means is through the combination and in-depth integration of the Internet and traditional industries; On the other hand, "Internet +" as a whole concept, its deep meaning is to complete industrial upgrading through the Internet of traditional industries. Through the application of openness, equality, interaction and other network characteristics in traditional industries, and through the analysis and integration of big data, the Internet tries to clarify the relationship between supply and demand. Through the transformation of the production mode and industrial structure of traditional industries, the Internet can enhance the driving force of economic development and enhance efficiency, so as to promote the healthy and orderly development of the national economy.

3   The Teaching Organization Form of Public Management Subject Under the Internet

Traditional classroom teaching should be managed by teachers at a fixed time and place. Teachers play a leading role in traditional teaching methods. This kind of teaching mode has been inherited for more than 2000 years in China, and its form and concept have been deeply rooted. Although this kind of teaching idea has always been the talent training standard of our country, there are still some problems. For example, it is difficult for students to play their initiative and independence in learning, it is difficult for teachers to take into account the individual differences of students in teaching, and it is difficult to implement the concept of teaching students in accordance with their aptitude. At the same time, the teacher centered classroom teaching mode is solidified, and it is difficult to attract students' attention. Although the traditional teaching method is the mainstream teaching mode, there are still many disadvantages, which should be made up by the network teaching mode supported by Internet technology. Only by adopting network technology and modern education concept and reconstructing teaching organization form can we realize perfect teaching mode. First of all, on the basis of traditional classroom teaching, teachers should actively expand a variety of network communication teaching forms, organize and supplement the teaching content through the internet teaching platform. In the traditional teaching process, teachers pay more attention to imparting the theory in books. Due to the limitation of time, students are unable to discuss and ask questions independently in class. In the network teaching platform established by teachers outside the classroom, students can sort out the problems existing in classroom learning and feed them back to teachers. Teachers can answer the questions on the network platform, or students can discuss them on the platform. The blended teaching mode makes full use of the learning time in class by teachers, and the network teaching platform which is not influenced by time and place after class can be grasped by students, so as to give full play to students' learning initiative and self-management ability. Teachers can also master their own teaching methods and effects through the network platform, so as to continuously improve their teaching methods and improve the teaching level. The internet teaching mode is shown in Fig. 1.

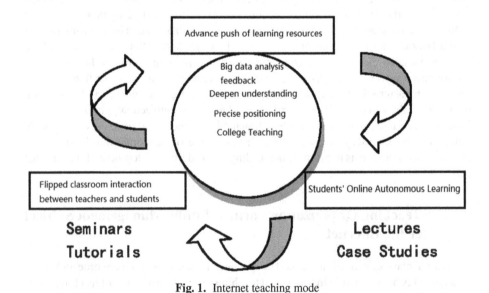

Fig. 1. Internet teaching mode

4   Establish a Modern Relationship Between Teachers and Students

In the traditional teaching mode, teachers play a leading role in classroom teaching. The relationship between teachers and students is relatively single. Teachers are the authority of classroom management and imparting knowledge, students are not allowed to question in all aspects. This unequal relationship leads to the gap between teachers and students, and there is a great sense of distance between students and teachers. In the environment of modern basic education, the idea of exam oriented education is still dominant. Teachers' authoritative teaching under this idea has a great impact on the development of students. In the environment of higher education, this kind of education idea is not very obvious. However, college students are deeply influenced by exam oriented education in junior and senior high schools. Even after entering colleges and universities, facing some young teachers with active ideas, they can not establish modern friendship between teachers and students. In the mixed teaching mode, the traditional classroom and internet teaching platform are combined with each other. Teachers can communicate with students outside of teaching on the network platform and talk about some relaxed and pleasant topics. Through this new form of social networking, students are more familiar with and proficient in operation, and more comfortable in the exchange of ideas. In the mixed teaching mode of colleges and universities, teachers still dominate the relationship between teachers and students. Teachers can't teach with traditional authority, but should teach on the basis of mutual respect. In the teaching work, we should pay attention to our own behavior and keep a sense of closeness with students. In the network platform after class, we should actively interact with students, listen to students' suggestions on teaching, so that students can fully feel the personal charm of teachers and maintain good feelings between teachers and students.

5   Change the Teaching Process

In the traditional classroom teaching mode, the teaching process of "teaching before learning" is generally adopted. Students are totally unfamiliar with the knowledge of textbooks, and they learn by relying on the classroom teaching and guidance of teachers. With dozens of minutes of classroom time, it is difficult for students to really understand the classroom knowledge and content. This teaching mode determines the leading role of teachers in the classroom, and students can only passively accept knowledge. In the blended teaching, the form of "learning before discussing" is adopted, which includes three stages: Students' autonomous learning before class, interaction between teachers and students in class, and students' consolidation and review after class. Teachers' participation in students' learning is not high, so we should design and plan these three stages as a whole, so that students can devote themselves to teaching activities. In the stage of autonomous learning before class, teachers should group the students and push the teaching videos, learning materials and related test questions to the students in advance through the network. Through the preview of these learning materials and teachers' video handouts, students can learn the relevant knowledge of the course in advance, find and summarize the existing problems, and bring them to the next stage of classroom learning. In the second stage of classroom learning, teachers should abandon the idea of full house in traditional teaching, fully mobilize students' learning enthusiasm, improve students' participation in classroom learning, and constantly improve teaching efficiency. Teachers should set up some related problems in classroom teaching, or leave some questions in some key links, so that students can learn to deal with the problems found in learning by themselves.

In the classroom, increase the opportunities for students to discuss in groups, so that students can discuss classroom knowledge within the scope of groups, and increase students' team cooperation ability. The consolidation review after class depends on the enthusiasm and initiative of students. Teachers can use the Internet platform to establish the learning mode after class. Students can ask questions and interact with each other through the network platform, as shown in Fig. 2.

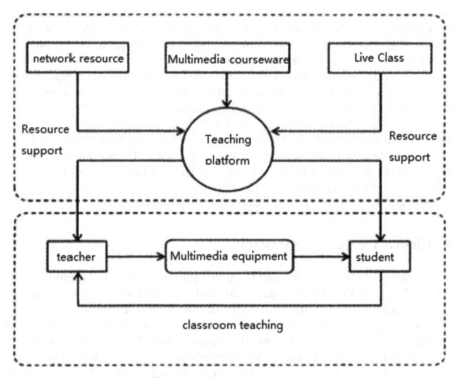

Fig. 2. Classroom teaching mode

6 Conclusion

In the era of "Internet plus", social and economic forms have changed greatly. As a group of young people, college students have changed a lot in their thinking mode, prompting universities to make new teaching reforms in time. The mixed teaching mode is an education mode that meets the requirements of the objective environment under the premise of the development of the new era. At the same time, it is very consistent with the students' way of thinking. Colleges and universities in the establishment and development of mixed teaching mode, adhere to the student-centered teaching concept and consciousness, make full use of teaching resources, orderly combination of online and offline courses, play the maximum effect of mixed teaching mode, cultivate more and more advanced, in line with the development concept of the times comprehensive talents.

References

1. Tao, Y., Tao, Y., Xie, A., et al.: Research on the development of College Students' innovation ability in the blended learning environment. Coal High. Educ. **36**(01), 85–88 (2018)
2. Yang, J.: Teaching mode of universities in the context of Internet plus. Educ. Teach. Forum **41**(23), 216–217 (2019)
3. Qin, J.: The exploration of classroom teaching in Colleges and Universities under the mode of "Internet plus education". Eng. Technol. Res. **34**(03), 238–239 (2018)
4. Lamare, R.: Massive MIMO systems: signal processing challenges and research trends. Ursi Radio Sci. Bull. **86**(4), 8–20 (2017). View at: Google Scholar
5. Butterfield, J.D., Krynkin, A., Collins, R.P., Beck, S.B.M.: Experimental investigation into vibro-acoustic emission signal processing techniques to quantify leak flow rate in plastic water distribution pipes. Appl. Acoust. **119**(APR), 146–155 (2017). View at: Publisher Site | Google Scholar
6. Luo, G., Qi, K., Xiong, X.: A RGB LED driving structure and signal processing based on tone-to-color conversion. Wuhan Univ. J. Nat. Sci. **22**(3), 252–256 (2017). View at: Publisher Site | Google Scholar
7. Sainath, T.N., Weiss, R.J., Wilson, K.W., et al.: Multichannel signal processing with deep neural networks for automatic speech recognition. IEEE/ACM Trans. Audio Speech Lang. Process. **25**(5), 965–979 (2017). View at: Publisher Site | Google Scholar
8. He, K., Stankovic, L., Liao, J., Stankovic, V,: Non-intrusive load disaggregation using graph signal processing. IEEE Trans. Smart Grid **9**(3), 1739–1747 (2018). View at: Publisher Site | Google Scholar
9. Liu, L., Larsson, E.G., Yu, W., Popovski, P., Stefanovic, C., de Carvalho, E.: Sparse signal processing for grant-free massive connectivity: a future Paradigm for random access protocols in the internet of things. IEEE Signal Process. Mag. **35**(5), 88–99 (2018). View at: Publisher Site | Google Scholar
10. Maheswari, R.U., Umamaheswari, R.: Trends in non-stationary signal processing techniques applied to vibration analysis of wind turbine drive train-a contemporary survey. Mech. Syst. Signal Process. **85**, 296–311 (2017). View at: Publisher Site | Google Scholar
11. Chakravorti, T., Patnaik, R.K., Dash, P.K.: Detection and classification of islanding and power quality disturbances in microgrid using hybrid signal processing and data mining techniques. IET Signal Process. **12**(1), 82–94 (2018). View at: Publisher Site | Google Scholar
12. He, M., Nian, Y., Gong, Y.: Novel signal processing method for vital sign monitoring using FMCW radar. Biomed. Signal Process. Control **33**(MAR), 335–345 (2017). View at: Publisher Site | Google Scholar

The Reproduction of Foreign Language Learning Simulation Scene Based on Virtual Reality

Zhang Liqun[✉]

Xi'an Fanyi University, Xi'an 710105, Shaanxi, China
15755857@qq.com

Abstract. With the rapid development of Internet technology and the increasingly fierce competition in the foreign language industry, the traditional foreign language learning methods can not meet the current needs. How to apply technology to innovate learning methods in foreign language learning has become the primary problem of development. The progress of technology has brought new ideas to the development of foreign language learning media. As an immersive, interactive and selective technology, virtual reality technology can enhance user experience, meet user needs, and provide technical support for foreign language learning innovation and reform. The virtual reality technology is used to reproduce the foreign language learning scene and simulate the real foreign language learning events that cannot be recorded in the learning due to technical means and timeliness. It can not only fully display the information contained in foreign language learning, but also enhance the user experience through the characteristics of virtual reality technology, so as to maintain the enthusiasm for foreign language learning and stimulate the interest in learning, Bring a new and explorable way for the development of foreign language learning industry.

Keywords: Virtual reality technology · Foreign language learning · Simulation scene reproduction

1 Introduction

Under the background of globalization, foreign language ability, as a significant feature of human capital, is an important part of human ability. Many countries attach great importance to the cultivation of foreign language ability. Students begin to learn foreign languages from primary school. After entering the University, foreign languages are important compulsory basic courses regardless of their major. Foreign languages have more and more important communication and learning value. Oral communication ability plays a very important role in foreign language listening, speaking, reading and writing ability, It is regarded as the goal of language learning in the 21st century. In order to improve the effectiveness of foreign language learning, develop learners' potential and help countries participate in international competition, information technology has been

M. A. Jan and F. Khan (Eds.): BigIoT-EDU 2022, LNICST 467, pp. 434–445, 2023.
https://doi.org/10.1007/978-3-031-23944-1_47

introduced and integrated into foreign language learning [1]. On the whole, the technical means, teaching mode and teaching content of foreign language learning are constantly updated and changed in the direction of virtualization and contextualization. Taking China as an example, the technical media of foreign language education have evolved from traditional books, blackboards and chalk to projectors, tapes and tape recorders, and then to the later language laboratory, and to the current computer, multimedia and network technology [2].

Over the years, in order to improve the effect of oral foreign language teaching, countries have given strong support to teaching at the levels of technology, policy and capital, but the effect of foreign language learning has been criticized. "Dumb foreign language", "low willingness to communicate" and poor students' autonomy have almost become a distinctive label of learners' oral foreign language level in various countries [3]. Judging from the standard of meeting the needs of national and social scientific, technological and economic development, the foreign language practical education in many countries is ineffective to some extent, resulting in the low oral English ability of students for many reasons, such as the lack of immersion environment of the target language, the neglect of the cultivation of oral English ability in teaching strategies, the lack of autonomous learning environment, the lack of learning tasks Lack of adequate teacher guidance, lack of learning partners, lack of in-depth integration of media technology in teaching, etc. [4]. However, for the cultivation of oral foreign language ability, sufficient comprehensible input and output are the most direct factors affecting foreign language learning level. Therefore, how to effectively improve students' foreign language learning motivation and promote their learning investment is the primary problem to be solved in foreign language learning.

Virtual reality technology is a high-level virtual technology. It is rated as the most important development discipline in the 21st century and one of the important technologies affecting people's quality of life. It is also known as "immersive multimedia" or "computer simulated reality". Its interactivity, immersion and authenticity all refresh the "cold" impression of technology. It can expand the depth and breadth of human-computer interaction, Achieve realistic full sensory interaction - real visual, auditory, tactile, and even olfactory experience. Applying virtual reality technology to foreign language learning can expand other information technology assisted foreign language learning in terms of experience and teaching function [5]. In terms of experience, virtual reality technology can provide participatory, interactive and real experience; In terms of function, cultural factors and nonverbal communication contents in language communication can be incorporated into the interaction design of virtual environment, so as to bring real and situational communication feelings to learners. Virtual reality technology has brought a new dawn to improve the effectiveness of foreign language learning and students' willingness to learn foreign languages. Foreign language education experts and scholars have gradually focused on the integration of virtual reality technology and foreign language learning. In May 2018, the first academic conference with the theme of "VR foreign language learning" - VR foreign language learning and international talent training seminar was held in Hangzhou, This paper discusses how to promote the transfer of industrial achievements of virtual reality technology to foreign language education through the integration of "industry, University and research", which proves that China has started the integration process of virtual reality technology and foreign language education [6].

2 Related Work

2.1 Concept and Characteristics of VR

Virtual reality (VR) is a highly interactive, computer-based multimedia environment. In this environment, users become "participants" in the "virtual reality" world. Broadly speaking, virtual reality refers to a fast and intuitive interactive computer system, in which users often forget that they are in it. Virtual reality technology integrates computer simulation technology, computer graphics technology, multimedia technology, sensor technology, network technology and other high-tech technologies to realize a realistic three-dimensional virtual environment such as viewing, listening and touching similar to the real life environment, and through the Internet of things Sensors enable users to interact and experience objects in the virtual environment in a natural way [7].

2.2 3I Features

In 1993, Professor Burdea of the United States and Professor Coiffet of France pointed out the concept, characteristics and characteristics of virtual reality system in virtual reality technology They have made a detailed analysis and Research on the structure and applications in various fields. They summarized the characteristics of virtual reality system as: immersion, interaction and imagination, which is commonly referred to as "3" I "later The characteristics are shown in Fig. 1, and 3I is also used as the quality measurement standard of VR system. In the educational application research of virtual reality technology, it has been widely used to represent the virtual reality experience with 3I characteristics. 3I characteristics appear in the virtual reality research in the educational fields of medicine, language, mathematics, science, pedagogy, art and so on, and play a significant role in students' learning.

(1) Immersion

Slater defines immersion in the following way: Immersion refers to the objective level of sensory fidelity provided by the VR system. Sherman and others believe that immersion refers to the immersion degree of perception level and the success degree of communication between users and the virtual world. Bowman believes that immersion is objective and measurable. One system can have higher immersion than another system, and immersion can also be adjusted and manipulated. Not every virtual reality environment needs high immersion. The setting of immersion mainly depends on the design purpose of virtual reality system, and immersion should not be regarded as a single structure, It should be regarded as a combination of many components. Any or all components can promote the immersion of VR system. Immersion is not all or nothing. As implied by immersion and non immersion, immersion is a multi-dimensional continuum [8].

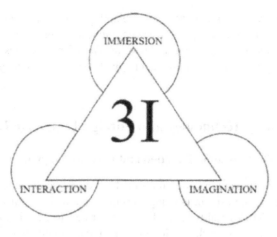

Fig. 1. 3I in virtual reality

(2) Interactivity

Interaction is a way to communicate with the system, but unlike traditional human-computer interaction (using 1-2-dimensional means such as mouse, keyboard or keypad), interaction in VR is usually carried out through 3-dimensional (3D) means, such as space ball and head mounted device (HMD) Burdea believes that the interactive characteristics of VR system are diversity, real-time and stronger sense of human active participation. Virtual reality technology provides a highly interactive environment, allowing users to become real participants in the computer-generated world. In the virtual world, users can interact with various stimuli. VR constitutes a 3D interface, which makes the interactive subject actively exchange with the world recreated by the computer. The possibility of not limiting the one way interaction paradigm represents the strength of the new technology: users are not only external observers of the environment, not passively experiencing the reality created by the computer. On the contrary, users can actively build and adjust the immersive three-dimensional environment. Wang Weiguo and others believe that the interactivity of virtual reality technology is reflected in the interaction between people and the environment. The environment can act on people, and people can also feed back and control the environment with natural behavior. Natural behavior includes their own language and body movements. The virtual simulation system with interactive function can respond to people's behavior in real time.

(3) Imaginative

Virtual reality is obviously both interactive and immersive. However, the third feature of virtual reality is easy to be ignored. Virtual reality is not only a medium or high-end user interface, but also has applications involving practical problem solutions in engineering, medicine, military and other fields. These applications are designed by virtual reality developers. The degree to which an application can solve a specific problem, that is, the degree to which the simulation performs well, largely depends on human imagination, that is, the third "I" of VR. Imagination in virtual reality environment refers to the ability of human brain to perceive non-existent things. The technology used as a cognitive tool can help learners clarify their thoughts and engage in meaningful learning. Therefore, a successful VR environment will stimulate learners' ability to creatively perceive and imagine non-existent things.

3 Virtual Reality Technology and Foreign Language Learning

3.1 Virtual Reality Education Function and Foreign Language Learning

Due to the interactivity and flexibility, multimedia such as video, image, sound, animation or simulation can be used in language teaching in a meaningful way and improve the teaching effect. Virtual reality technology is described as using immersive computer simulation environment, in which people can interact. It integrates these traditional multimedia and significantly improves user immersion, especially in visual perception. Virtual reality is not only a new tool, but also a new concept, a paradigm of human-computer interaction and a new way of using computers. Virtual reality has achieved qualitative changes in the following aspects: from pictures to immersive three-dimensional environment, from observation to experience, from use to participation, and from interface to virtual world. The use of virtual reality (VR) in education can be regarded as the natural development of CAI or CBT.

Foreign language learners should convert visual and auditory cues into information. The information conversion function of immersive VR teaching system can provide a new learning method to motivate students. VR makes the simulation closer to the real life experience, so that students can be more immersed in the 3D environment. They can also improve their skills through more realistic practice. VR system helps to improve students' concentration in language learning, so as to help them understand what they remember. In addition, VR system allows students to study in a "foreign country" in a simulated environment, which is more conducive to let students understand the real culture of the language they are learning. VR immerses or attracts learners into a learner centered and learner controlled computer-generated environment. Compared with traditional classroom learning, VR can bring higher cognitive participation. VR helps to access resources and tools because it makes use of the interface structure used by people in the real world, and its interaction mode is more intuitive and natural. VR also improves the interaction between participants. Its shared environment enables learners to use index language and provide them with complete conversation records as future learning resources. Virtual reality environment for language teaching has the following advantages:

1) VR can enhance learners' self-awareness and virtual avatars reduce emotional filtering;
2) Embedded recording tools can enhance language and cognitive awareness in the learning process;
3) VR supports interaction by locating participants in a shared environment, thus allowing a common language reference point;

4) VR can enhance dialogue management and teamwork by allowing collaboration;
5) Support switching in various rapidly changing scenes;
6) It can support the implementation of NLP tools;
7) VR's spatial metaphor is a more natural way of organizing information resources, which conforms to the operation intuition and supports the multi-mode interface of learning resource access;
8) Resource sharing function to realize real-time cooperation;
9) Encourage learners to actively participate in creating and organizing their learning environment.

3.2 The Advantages of Virtual Reality Experience and Foreign Language Learning

Virtual reality experience is usually represented by telepresence. At present, a series of studies have been produced to support the role of telepresence in improving learning performance. Some studies have shown that learners' perception of social presence will significantly affect learners' investment in online learning. There is a positive correlation between presence and performance, which is regulated by task types. Nash makes a comprehensive analysis of the relationship between telepresence and learning effectiveness, which can affect users' telepresence and affect learners' low-order and high-order cognition and learning effectiveness by adjusting the visual, auditory, tactile and kinesthetic parameters in the virtual environment. Dengel et al. Studied the correlation between telepresence and learning performance in immersive virtual reality learning environment. The research shows that strong telepresence has much impact on learners' learning effectiveness Positive impact on. Some studies have found that compared with non multimodal control, multimodal CVE (collaborative virtual environment) developed with realistic immersive environment framework can stimulate students' higher sense of presence and improve students' academic performance. Some researchers believe that a strong sense of presence will enhance users' attention to the task [9]. Virtual reality is the simulation and Simulation of the real world, which makes the experience of VE or remote operators full of fun and improves their learning motivation. Therefore, they pay more attention to the task itself. The virtual reality environment is easy to cause a commensurate emotional arousal state, just like the state in the real world task, So as to promote the improvement of learning effectiveness.

It can be seen that the experience advantage of virtual reality helps to improve learners' learning motivation and learning performance. Some studies also explain the impact mechanism of virtual reality experience on learners' motivation and performance through flow experience and cognitive absorption. However, most studies only focus on the sense of presence in a single dimension, and do not analyze the sense of presence as a multi-dimensional and complex structure. In addition, in the research on the improvement of the effectiveness of virtual reality experience on language teaching, Most studies do not integrate the experience design of the systematic teaching environment with the motivation theory to provide an in-depth analysis of the effectiveness improvement mechanism of virtual reality teaching, that is, there is a lack of systematic research results on the effectiveness mechanism of virtual reality teaching. This study intends to make an in-depth study on the experience perception and teaching effectiveness mechanism of virtual reality environment from these aspects.

3.3 Application Potential of Virtual Reality Technology in Foreign Language Learning

(1) Enhance cross-cultural understanding

By immersing learners in a variety of visual representations of concepts and providing control over these representations, virtual reality technology has great potential to promote cross-cultural communication. Canto believes that the functions provided by SL - task simulation, real-time collaboration, identity exploration and flexible multi-mode can promote cross-cultural communication ability and meaning negotiation. Students regard technology mediated TBLT as a positive innovation in foreign language learning and cross-cultural understanding. The European Commission's project found that problem-solving and interactive tasks similar to the real world can optimize learners' target language acquisition and enhance their cross-cultural and spontaneous communication skills.

(2) Support task-based and meaningful language learning

The virtual environment is suitable for task-based language teaching (TBLT) methods, such as real task, learning while doing, rich input, inductive learning, collaboration and personalized instructions. Virtual reality environment provides an immersive dynamic space that supports task-based services for language learners. SL's simulation and embedded support function for teaching content provide students with flexibility to carry out real-world tasks that cannot be carried out or are too heavy in the traditional classroom. From the perspective of teaching, it is different from other two-dimensional web1 Compared with 0 or 2.0 tools, simulation tasks in SL make learning more meaningful, realistic and interesting.

(3) Enhance students' interest in learning

Virtual reality environment can enhance students' learning interest through the following functions: Virtual Reality Assisted Foreign Language Teaching Support role-playing and collaborative learning model can effectively improve learners' motivation and learning retention; Adding game elements to the virtual reality learning environment can effectively improve learners' learning interest and concentration. The real situation provided by virtual reality technology can enhance learners' interest in learning; Immersive simulation can enhance the learning experience, enable students to make meaningful connections, improve learners' creativity and promote their learning initiative; The interaction between learners and the virtual world will stimulate learners to find more information and enhance their interest in learning.

4   Reproduction of Foreign Language Learning Simulation Scene Based on Virtual Reality

4.1   An Analysis of the Principles and Strategies of Constructivist Oral Foreign Language Teaching

The research on language development shows that constructivism is an important theoretical basis for the design of foreign language oral communication activities. Constructivist learning theory defines learning as a positive, social and collaborative process through which learners use symbolic systems (such as language) or material tools (such as computers) to build knowledge with others. Some scholars have proposed the principles of Constructivism applied to foreign language teaching, including: (1) in the classroom, learners can choose to be based on action orientation Carry out creative classroom learning, task/project learning and learning by teaching (LBT) in the form of cooperative learning. Based on meaningful and real project/task learning, learners can have a longer memory of skills and knowledge, which is conducive to the transfer of knowledge; (2) Paying more attention to learners' centrality means more individualization of learning and learners' autonomy; (3) Learning awareness, language awareness, cross-cultural awareness; (4) Pay attention to the overall language learning experience. The provision of content-based, real and complex learning environment has a great impact on the improvement of experience. Dai Weidong and others believe that the principles of foreign language learning under the guidance of Constructivism Theory - task/activity teaching, trial/discovery learning, inquiry learning/inquiry learning, cooperative learning/interactive foreign language teaching [10].

To sum up, this study summarizes the constructivist foreign language learning principles as follows:

(1) Personalization

That is, the student-centered principle, which emphasizes the personalized scheme designed around learners in terms of learning environment, learning methods and learning content. Personalized learning environment is conducive to stimulate students' learning enthusiasm, increase learners' learning investment, improve concentration and increase learners' sense of self-efficacy [11].

(2) Mobilize enthusiasm

That is, let students have the will, motivation and interest of autonomous learning. For the development of oral foreign language ability, how to improve students' learning enthusiasm during students' autonomous learning time is the key. Using advanced information technology to create a personalized foreign language learning environment that can mobilize students' enthusiasm is a feasible way to improve students' foreign language practical ability, For example, game based learning and interesting learning experience are introduced into classroom and online learning tools to improve students' learning interest [12].

(3) Meaningful

That is, communication is carried out through learning content, learning activities and learning tasks with clear objectives and close to life. It emphasizes taking problems as the center, taking activities or tasks as the carrier of teaching and practice, stimulating more real oral output, connecting knowledge and skills with life, and realizing the transformation of students' role in teaching from passive receiver to active explorer [13].

(4) Contextualization

The contextualization principle includes: the contextualization of foreign language oral activities, the contextualization of scene and environment, and the contextualization of teaching resources. Let learners participate in real communication events in the "real" cultural scene with the common language of people in the target language country [14]. This principle is conducive to stimulate learners' interest in participation, understand the culture of the target language country, cultivate cross-cultural communicative competence, and absorb and internalize the learned knowledge.

(5) Interactive

That is, learners should communicate, interact and negotiate with teachers, learning partners and native speakers in the language situation, so as to make the language understandable, increase the opportunity of output and promote language acquisition.

At the research level of constructivist oral foreign language teaching strategies, some scholars believe that teaching strategies should include: research and project-based, role-playing, diversified learning environment, situation-based, theme and content-based, critical thinking, oral speech and so on. Dai Weidong further refined the teaching strategies, including task/activity teaching, trial/discovery learning, inquiry learning/inquiry learning, cooperative learning/interactive foreign language teaching. On the basis of absorbing and integrating the previous research results, this study summarizes the constructivist oral foreign language teaching strategies as: situational learning, task-based learning, collaborative learning, exploratory learning, personalized learning and reflective learning.

4.2   Analysis on the Effect and Mechanism of Virtual Reality in Foreign Language Learning

A series of studies have proved that the principle of constructivism is the basis of learning and understanding in virtual reality environment.

Foundation. As Burdea and Coiffet said: constructivist learning involves the exploration and discovery of the pre constructed artificial real world: the constructivist learning process provided by VR technology requires educators to check the learning model and how the technical characteristics support learning. Virtual reality has unique functions, most of which can be used in all aspects of constructivism teaching [15]. This study integrates the functional characteristics of self-determination theory, constructivism teaching theory and virtual reality technology to construct the effect mechanism of virtual reality foreign language learning, as shown in Fig. 2:

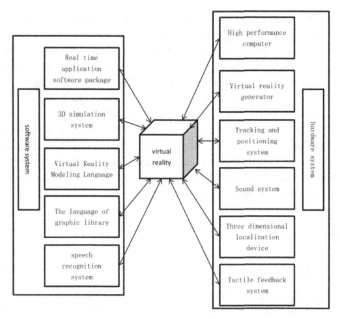

Fig. 2. The effect and mechanism of virtual reality in foreign language learning

Due to its unique technical advantages: immersive experience, realistic experience and interactive experience, virtual reality technology can provide better simulated situations for language practical learning, allowing learners to learn at the time, place, occasion, plot and time preset by the designer Carry out language practice activities in context. The design principles of situational learning function supported by virtual reality technology include: providing real background and environment to reflect the use of knowledge in real life; Provide authentic and authentic language learning resources, including text, audio and video, and guidance materials for native speakers; Provide activities and tasks close to real life as the carrier of foreign language practice to realize the construction of meaning. For example, learners can communicate with waiters and strangers in foreign "real" cafes. Their pronunciation is authentic. The chat content with learners is daily topics such as ordering and greeting. Learners can interact with them. If learners' words or actions are inappropriate, they will give immediate feedback, Learning activities similar to this real situation will make it easier for learners to master oral communication skills, cross-cultural communication skills, and retain knowledge more deeply.

5   Conclusion

The effectiveness of technology is inseparable from people's perception, acceptance and application. With the development of networking, mobility and intelligence of education, students' perception, acceptance and willingness to participate in the educational model have increasingly become the key factors determining the success or failure of education, and the satisfaction of learners' needs and motivation are the internal core driving force to improve teaching effectiveness. On the basis of systematically combing the classical theoretical structure of telepresence, this study internalizes the 3I characteristics of virtual reality technology into the dimensional design of telepresence, and constructs the theoretical framework of virtual reality foreign language learning telepresence combined with the application background of foreign language learning. The theoretical framework of telepresence consists of spatial telepresence, immersion, reality, interaction and social telepresence, Combined with the research literature of the classical sense of presence scale, this paper formulates the effect mechanism of virtual reality foreign language learning simulation scene, modifies the structure of the scale through reliability and validity test, and verifies the correlation between each dimension of sense of presence by empirical analysis.

References

1. Song, Y.: Basketball technology simulation application based on virtual reality. Math. Probl. Eng. **2021** (2021)
2. Zhu, X., Kou, F.: Three-dimensional simulation of swimming training based on android mobile system and virtual reality technology. Microprocess. Microsyst. **82**, 103908 (2021)
3. Taunk, N.K., Shah, N.K., Hubley, E., Anamalayil, S., Trotter, J.W., Li, T.: Virtual reality-based simulation improves gynecologic brachytherapy proficiency, engagement, and trainee self-confidence. Brachytherapy **20**(4), 695–700 (2021)
4. Yu, S., Han, J.: Virtual reality platform-based conceptual design and simulation of a hot cell facility. Int. J. Adv. Manuf. Technol. **116**(1–2), 487–505 (2021). https://doi.org/10.1007/s00 170-021-07139-7
5. Li, D., Yi, C., Gu, Y.: Research on college physical education and sports training based on virtual reality technology. Math. Probl. Eng. **2021** (2021)
6. Kwegyir-Afful, E., Kantola, J.: Simulation-based safety training for plant maintenance in virtual reality. In: Cassenti, D.N., Scataglini, S., Rajulu, S.L., Wright, J.L. (eds.) Advances in Simulation and Digital Human Modeling. AISC, vol. 1206, pp. 167–173. Springer, Cham (2021). https://doi.org/10.1007/978-3-030-51064-0_22
7. Ding, M., Chen, Z., Du, T., Luo, P., Tenenbaum, J., Gan, C.: Dynamic visual reasoning by learning differentiable physics models from video and language. Adv. Neural Inf. Process. Syst. **34**, 887–899 (2021)
8. Almousa, O., et al.: Virtual reality technology and remote digital application for tele-simulation and global medical education: an innovative hybrid system for clinical training. Simul. Gaming **52**(5), 614–634 (2021)
9. Judd, D.L., Kelly, B., Corral, J.: Using virtual reality for movement system examination in a doctor of physical therapy curriculum. J. Phys. Ther. Educ. **35**(4), 324–329 (2021)
10. Chen, R., Sharma, A.: Construction of complex environmental art design system based on 3D virtual simulation technology. Int. J. Syst. Assur. Eng. Manag. 1 (2021)
11. Chen, C., Ren, A.Z., Zhang, X.: A building fire simulation system based on virtual reality. Ziran Zaihai Xuebao/J. Nat. Disaster **16**(1), 55–60 (2007)
12. Chen, G., Gan, Z., Sheng, J., Lu, X.: Equipment simulation training system based on virtual reality. In: 2008 International Conference on Computer and Electrical Engineering, pp. 563–567. IEEE (2008)
13. Liu, C.: Research on virtual reality simulation based on VRML and VRMLScript. Comput. Eng. Appl. (2002)

14. Chang, K., Gao, J.L., Yuan, Y.X., et al.: Simulation system of urban water supply network based on virtual reality. J. South China Univ. Technol. (Nat. Sci.) **36**(12), 43–46 (2008)
15. Yang, D.L., Liu, S.Y., Yang, B., Zhou, B.: Research the training system of the oilfield staff simulation based on virtual reality technology. Adv. Mat. Res. **807**, 2863–2867 (2013)

The Design of the English Teaching Resource Management System Based on Collaborative Recommendation

Hu Hui[1](✉) and Luo Xiao[2]

[1] Sichuan University Jinjiang College, Meishan 620860, Sichuan, China
eskahh@vip.163.com
[2] Chengdu University, Chengdu 610106, Sichuan, China

Abstract. The design of English teaching resource management system based on collaborative recommendation is a book published by Dr. Li in January 2012. The book was first published as a master's thesis at Seoul National University in South Korea in 2006. This book describes the design and implementation of an e-learning system for English teaching based on collaborative recommendation. This article will teach you how to design an effective resource management system so that it can be used as a model for other schools. This book will help you improve your teaching skills and ensure that you can get the best results from your students. The author uses this book to show all the steps involved in designing such a system and explain why it should be done in this way rather than in any other way.

Keywords: Collaborative recommendation · Resource management · English language teaching

1 Introduction

With the growth of modern information in Pb level, it is the focus of current computer research and thinking to strengthen the mining of these information to improve the efficiency of data utilization. In the context of massive data growth, education departments and academic institutions have accumulated a large number of teaching resources. For English education institutions, how to recommend these resources to different learners so that learners can combine their own needs and improve the application value of different teaching resources is the focus of the relevant departments of English education institutions. At the same time, the problems of "resource overload" and "resource lost" are seriously troubling educational institutions. Therefore, it is urgent to introduce modern intelligent recommendation algorithm other actual situations, so as to improve the use efficiency of English teaching resources. In order to enable learners to quickly find resources that meet their own requirements and hobbies, Wang Linlin (2017) built an interest model and selected personalized recommendation algorithm according to English learners' interests to complete the recommendation of teaching resources. Based on the previous research, this paper constructs an intelligent recommended English teaching resource platform from the perspective of software design, and designs it in detail [1].

Most schools have multi system operation, and different platforms and systems come from different developers or suppliers. The data coding and format in their data storage system are not unified, and the data compatibility is poor. Without the help of professional departments or professionals, it is difficult for ordinary foreign language teachers to effectively process and use these data.

The existing online teaching resource platform and teaching management platform basically operate separately, the functions are incompatible with each other, and the data cannot be shared, resulting in the phenomenon of "data island" [2]. The teaching management function of the curriculum resource platform is not ideal. The teaching management system, especially the mobile teaching management software, lacks the support of teaching resources and cannot immediately call teaching resources online, resulting in teachers having to teach across platforms in actual teaching. In addition, the intelligent technology level of most platforms is not high. For example, the capacity of online test question bank is not large enough, and the effectiveness of online writing and correction is not high. A few platforms can provide online oral practice function, and intelligent diagnosis and push services can not meet the needs of students' adaptive learning [3]. Most platforms provide relatively limited data to teachers, mainly statistical data such as attendance, answer and achievement, and lack process data. Even some platforms only provide basic data sharing, and the rest of the data needs to be paid. Teachers simply cannot obtain more process monitoring data, and the data export, analysis and application functions of the platform are very inconvenient to use. Due to the problems of learning experience and knowledge structure, the vast majority of Higher Vocational English teachers do not have the ability to obtain, sort out, clean up, analyze and apply data. In particular, they need to receive professional training in teaching analysis, teaching decision-making mode and operation methods based on big data. From information-based teaching based on platform and software to data-based management and teaching, there is still a long way to go to truly build a new paradigm of data as a service [4].

2   Related Work

Collaborative design technology combines computer technology, multimedia technology and network communication technology with advanced manufacturing technology to support collaborative work of collaborative members who are separated in time, distributed in space and interdependent in work, so that members of the working group can work together, negotiate interactively, divide work and cooperate in the network sharing environment distributed in different places, develop the same product in parallel, and jointly complete the design task, So as to shorten the product development cycle to the greatest extent [5].

At present, there are two main ways of using information technology and Internet technology to carry out product collaborative design in different places: asynchronous collaboration and synchronous collaboration. Asynchronous collaboration refers to the way in which different product designers obtain and exchange product design information with the help of the platform provided by the Internet and communication services such as FTP, email, BBS, etc., design respectively, and then communicate with each other to gradually improve; Synchronous collaboration refers to the way in which different product designers share all kinds of technical resources and design resources to complete product development under the same design platform. Among them, the way of remote synchronous collaborative design is more efficient, but the technical requirements are more complex [6]. In fact, people usually combine the two methods when designing in different places. The more components of synchronous collaboration, the higher the efficiency of collaborative work.

At present, the research on personalized recommendation of online teaching abroad mainly includes: ETEC experimental center of ounl University in the Netherlands comprehensively analyzes the needs of users for recommendation services in the online learning system, and deeply studies the recommendation model and specific recommendation technology. By analyzing the different recommendation technologies suitable for different learning situations, a comprehensive recommendation strategy combining multiple recommendation service technologies is constructed, which makes the system suitable for a wider range of learning situations. Mohamed Koutheair Khribi proposed an online automatic recommendation system based on hybrid filtering recommendation technology. The system combines content-based filtering and collaborative filtering to recommend according to the user's recent navigation history. Tang et al. "Put forward an intelligent e-learning recommendation system, which can evolve itself and realize the adaptability to learners and open network environment [7]. The information resources in the system are not fixed, and the learning resources on the network can be integrated into the system according to the interaction behavior between users and the system."

3   Collaborative Recommendation Technology

3.1   Introduction of Collaborative Recommendation Technology

Its basic idea is to obtain the historical preference information of target users explicitly or implicitly. The information is compared with the preference information of other users, and other users who have similar preferences with the target user are found, and these similar users are called nearest neighbors. The weighted evaluation value of the nearest neighbor is used as the target user's evaluation of the resource, and based on this, the resource is recommended to the target user [8]. Because collaborative recommendation technology does not use the user interest model, nor the weighted feature vector of resources, but from the user's point of view, looking for neighbors with similar preferences, there are no many shortcomings in content-based recommendation technology, which can be used to recommend objects with complex structure [9]. As shown in Fig. 1.

Collaborative recommendation technology has the following advantages.

① Because collaborative recommendation technology is from the user's point of view, it does not need to build complex weighted eigenvectors for resources, which reduces the system's manpower and time costs.

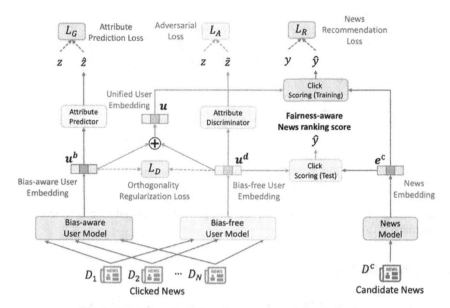

Fig. 1. Principles of collaborative recommendation technology

② Collaborative recommendation technology is based on the preferences of the nearest neighbor to recommend resources for the target user, so it can recommend some new and interesting resources that the target user does not consider. This is different from content-based recommendation, which can only recommend resources in the defined resource types in the user interest model for users.

③ Collaborative recommendation technology can make use of the feedback information of the target user and the feedback information of the nearest neighbor, so it can quickly modify the recommendation content and accelerate the speed of personalized learning [10].

3.2 Implementation Process of Collaborative Recommendation Technology

Because it is difficult to collect user's historical preference information implicitly, most of the existing collaborative recommendation systems use the display method to obtain user's preference information by collecting user's score of items. All users' scores of all items constitute a user item score matrix, and each item in the matrix represents a user's score of a certain item. The recommendation process for target users is to get the nearest neighbor by using the score in this matrix, and then get the recommendation result for target users by using the neighbor's score [11]. Therefore, collaborative recommendation has three main steps: user information representation, nearest neighbor selection and recommendation result generation, as shown in Fig. 2.

According to Pearson similarity, the predicted score of user U_i and teaching resource D_m can be obtained.

$$P(i,j) = \overline{R}_i \frac{\sum_{n \in Ni} sim(i,N) \bullet (R_{n,j} - \overline{R}_N)}{\sum_{n \in Ni} sim(i,N)} \tag{1}$$

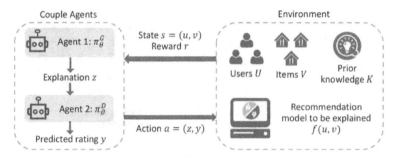

Fig. 2. Model of collaborative recommendation

Thus, through the above prediction, we can get a recommendation set, and finally recommend it to users.

4 System Design

In this paper, the construction of intelligent recommended English teaching resource system is a new way to improve the quality and efficiency of English learning. It is a unique software tool that can be used by teachers, students and parents to create an effective learning environment for children. The construction of intelligent recommendation system uses artificial intelligence technology to automatically recommend the most appropriate materials for each user at any time, which enables users to learn more effectively [12]. The construction of intelligent recommendation English teaching resource system mainly includes three modules: 1) recommendation module; 2) Textbook module. As shown in Fig. 3.

Fig. 3. English teaching resource management system

Overall architecture: using B/S structure mode to build, the overall architecture of the system is divided into three layers: application layer, logic layer and data layer. The overall framework system is shown in Fig. 4.

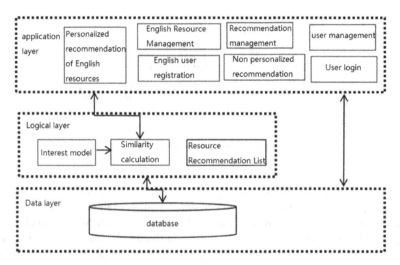

Fig. 4. Overall system architecture

The content-based recommendation is subject to the following assumptions: for a specific target user, the user is likely to remain interested in items similar in content to the information items that the user was interested in in in the past. Its working principle is to establish an interest model file for each user to describe the user's interest preferences. At the same time, extract the content features of each item to get the feature vector of the item [13]. When recommending the target user, compare the user interest model of the target user with the feature vectors of all items to obtain the similarity between them, and recommend the items with high similarity to the user.

5 System Implementation

Based on the data set generated after the system has been used for a period of time, with the accuracy of recommendation as the evaluation standard, 2000 user records visiting the English website during this period are randomly selected, and their score records are exported, a total of 60000.

Thus, the result shown in Fig. 5 is obtained. Which shows the advantages of this algorithm.

The development differences between different colleges and universities are becoming increasingly prominent, which once again leads to the unbalanced development and utilization of English education resources between schools. Therefore, it is of great significance to plan and allocate College English textbooks as a whole and improve the use efficiency of College English textbooks. As part of the comprehensive three-dimensional teaching reform, we should strengthen the sustainable development and

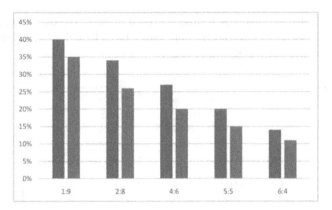

Fig. 5. Accuracy comparison

utilization of College English resources and increase the opportunities for teachers and students to participate. Some universities have not made overall planning and allocation for the development and utilization of College English teaching resources, and face many challenges. Insufficient attention has been paid to the development and use of English textbooks, and the English textbook system in some regions and colleges and universities is underdeveloped and lagging behind. The development and use of College English textbooks in the eastern developed regions are effective, but there are still problems in the development and use of College English textbooks in the central and western regions [14]. The main problems of poor development and utilization of educational resources are reflected in the lack of overall planning and layout, and the lack of strict and effective management planning for the development of College English educational resources, which makes most schools have problems in the utilization and optimization of English teaching resources. In the process of allocating its educational resources, it will also face many complex and cumbersome difficulties. The way of resource development and utilization is relatively single. With the continuous development of social information technology, it not only provides technical and systematic support for the construction of College English teaching platform, but also makes students' learning channels more extensive. At present, many public welfare websites are used to store and put in high-quality English teaching resources. They also enhance the effect of the development of networked English teaching resources by updating and configuring the field of English teaching and optimizing and updating the resources by relevant teachers and experts. However, some colleges and universities have not fully invested in the construction of English shared resource platform in the development of College English teaching resources, and the way of resource development and utilization is relatively single. In terms of the investment and setting of teaching resources, it is not combined with the actual teaching situation of English resources and students' learning situation, nor can it form an English platform for the cultivation of students' learning ability, which makes the effect of resource development and utilization low. Some students and teachers are not enthusiastic enough to participate in the learning of English teaching resource sharing platform, and lack the initiative to search and mine English teaching resources, The effect comparison is shown in Fig. 6.

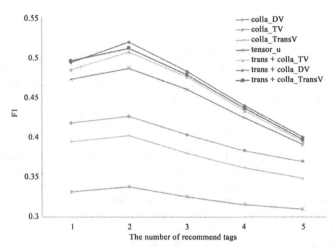

Fig. 6. Effect comparison

6 Conclusion

To sum up, a teaching resource management system with collaborative recommendation function is the key to solve the problem of excessive accumulation and low efficiency of current teaching resources. This paper jointly recommends the introductory algorithm of the textbook management system, which is suitable for different types of textbook users. The educational resource management system includes personalized space management, resource management, recommendation module and system management, which should meet the different functional needs of different users and better use and share educational resources. With the change of the world pattern, traditional English teaching can neither meet the requirements of the development of the times nor meet the intellectual needs of students. In order to improve the development efficiency of English textbooks, we must adhere to the principle of active development and use, avoid "public, University and public" College English textbooks, and better connect them with life. Cultivate students' correct learning ideas and awareness through English materials. At the same time, the introduction of English education materials close to life into the classroom can also ignite students' interest in learning, resonate between students and English teaching content, promote classroom teaching to better conform to the trend of the times and keep pace with the times, prevent simple dogmatism and ideological problems, and improve the level of education. In the development and utilization of living English education resources, the resource materials should be updated regularly. If the resource materials are too old and not close to students' study and life, they will not be accepted by students.

Therefore, in order to improve the effect of the development and application of English education resources, we need to enhance the level of resource development through the principle of life.

References

1. Liu, H., Duan, X., Dai, S.: On intelligent recommendation technology of teaching resources in open education. J. Yancheng Inst. Technol. (Soc. Sci. Ed.) **30**(4), 81–84 (2017)
2. Mishan, F., Strunz, B.: An application of XML to the creation of an interactive resource for authentic language learning tasks. ReCALL **15**(2), 237–250 (2003)
3. Wang, X., Yang, Y., Wen, X.: Study on blended learning approach for English teaching. In: 2009 IEEE International Conference on Systems, Man and Cybernetics, pp. 4641–4644. IEEE (2009)
4. Geng, Y., Mitchell, B., Zhu, Q.: Teaching industrial ecology at Dalian university of technology: toward improving overall eco-efficiency. J. Ind. Ecol. **13**(6), 978–989 (2009)
5. Liang, Y.: Research on the key technology of the personalized English learning system. In: 2015 International Conference on Education Technology, Management and Humanities Science (ETMHS 2015), pp. 1233–1236. Atlantis Press (2015)
6. Golam, A.M., Kusakabe, T.: A qualitative study of English teaching in Bangladesh: a case study of Madrasa education. US-China Educ. Rev. **8**(3), 106–122 (2018)
7. Juan, L., Yahaya, N.B.: Model-view-controller based context visualization method for multimedia English teaching system: a case study of multimedia technology teaching. Int. J. Acad. Res. Progress. Educ. Dev. **9**(2), 14–34 (2020)
8. Chen, G.: Design of college English halving classroom teaching system based on big data. J. Phys. Conf. Ser. **2066**(1), 012082 (2021)
9. Zhu, Y.: Design of integrated management system for English teaching resources based on artificial intelligence. In: 2021 2nd International Conference on Artificial Intelligence and Education (ICAIE), pp. 29–33. IEEE (2021)
10. Zhu, Y.: Research on English teaching of professional skilled talents training based on artificial intelligence. J. Intell. Fuzzy Syst. 1–12 (2021). (Preprint)
11. Song, X., Zhang, C.: Design of English online teaching assistant system based on deep learning. In: 2021 13th International Conference on Measuring Technology and Mechatronics Automation (ICMTMA), pp. 579–582. IEEE (2021)
12. Liu, Z., Li, H., Song, W., Kong, X., Li, H., Zhang, J.: Research on hybrid recommendation method of learning resources based on bipartite graph. Audio Visual Educ. Res. **39**(8), 85–90 (2018)
13. Li, Q., Wei, W., Cai, Z.: Personalized recommendation algorithm for e-commerce based on hybrid user and item collaborative filtering. J. Sun Yat Sen Univ. (Nat. Sci. Ed.) **55**(5), 37–42 (2016)
14. Ma, R., Bian, Y., Chen, C., Wu, H.: Personalized recommendation algorithm for e-commerce based on Hadoop—taking movie recommendation as an example. Comput. Syst. Appl. **24**(5), 111–117 (2015)

The Direction of English Teaching Reform in the Context of Internet Plus

Meizhi Wu[1]([⊠]) and Tong Yao[2]

[1] Jinjiang College of Sichuan University, Meishan 620000, Sichuan, China
wmz66789012@163.com
[2] Sichuan Tourism University, Chengdu 610100, Sichuan, China

Abstract. With the rapid development of science and technology and the popularization of network, the Internet is more and more widely used in English teaching, which brings great challenges to college English teaching. Internet English teaching not only improves students' learning efficiency, but also cultivates students' ability to find and solve problems. At the same time, the Internet also brings a good opportunity to innovate English teaching methods. Therefore, how to seize the opportunity and reform teaching methods under the tide of the rapid development of the Internet has become a real concern of schools. This paper analyzes the challenges faced by College English education in the Internet plus era, and puts forward suggestions for the study of English teaching strategies in the new era, which has positive guiding significance for the realization of the innovative development of English education and the effective training of comprehensive talents with high quality.

Keywords: Internet · College English · Reform in education

1 Introduction

Internet plus is becoming an irresistible trend of the times. It has broad prospects and unlimited potential in its integration with various fields. Multimedia and other network tools have gradually penetrated into all walks of life, which has a great impact on the production and environment of all industries. At the same time, due to the development of information technology, the Internet has also had a great impact on College English teaching. Many teachers use multimedia and other tools in teaching. Internet teaching also brings strong challenges to teachers. Teachers need to know more knowledge than before. Teachers are no longer a single source of knowledge under the traditional teaching mode [1, 2]. Teachers under Internet teaching may only become the guides of students. Students can get more knowledge through the network. Students should also learn how to find information and how to seek resources from the network. For college students, Internet English teaching not only improves students' learning efficiency, but also improves students' interest in self-learning, and improves students' ability to find and solve problems. The application of multimedia tools such as the Internet has greatly

M. A. Jan and F. Khan (Eds.): BigIoT-EDU 2022, LNICST 467, pp. 455–463, 2023.
https://doi.org/10.1007/978-3-031-23944-1_49

enriched the classroom content, increased the interest of the course, expanded students' vision, improved teachers' classroom efficiency and teaching quality to a certain extent, and contributed to the efficiency of students' English learning [3]. However, Internet plus has a negative impact on College English teaching to some extent, which makes the English Teaching in colleges face greater challenges. Therefore, this paper attempts to make a strategic research on the combination of today's advanced Internet technology to assist college English teaching. It is hoped that the strategies to solve the problems can be found on the basis of research, so as to make English teaching meet the needs of social development and cultivate talents to adapt to development [4, 5].

The trend of economic globalization is becoming more and more obvious, and the international application ability of English has been gradually enhanced. As the largest language of global communication, the importance of English is self-evident. If countries want to develop foreign trade and cultural export, they must need more English talents. Therefore, the current English education reform in China is urgent. With the implementation of the new curriculum reform, The focus of English Teaching in junior middle school has changed from improving students' examination ability to cultivating students' core English literacy [6]. Teachers are required to give consideration to students' actual control and application ability of English while teaching theoretical knowledge, cultivate students' good English thinking and help them establish a complete English language system.

Teaching reform is the most important and concerned topic for College English teachers. However, the current content setting of College English teaching is very unreasonable, which directly leads to the failure to improve the quality of English teaching and the lack of targeted training of students' English core literacy. Teachers still haven't got rid of the shackles of traditional teaching ideas. When arranging and designing teaching content, Teachers will still focus on emphasizing the basic knowledge of English and improving students' test taking skills, while ignoring the cultivation of students' English communication and application ability, resulting in students only learning how to do questions, but not effectively mastering English knowledge [7].

Moreover, in the actual classroom teaching, most teachers are still used to following the traditional teaching methods, still focusing on their own explanation and lack of effective interaction with students, which makes students always in a passive learning position and can not mobilize their learning enthusiasm, resulting in the poor quality of English teaching. In the teaching classroom, teachers always spend most of their time explaining basic knowledge, Students can neither give full play to their subjective initiative to learn, nor get the opportunity to practice English, so the English classroom is particularly boring and boring, and students naturally can't cheer up to learn, which is of no help to students' English learning enthusiasm and the effective cultivation of core literacy [8].

Teachers should be deeply aware of the shortcomings of the traditional English teaching model, actively transform their teaching ideas, focus on cultivating students' core English literacy, abandon the teaching methods of traditional exam oriented education, strive to expand their own teaching ideas, innovate teaching methods, carry out diversified teaching activities, pay attention to stimulating students' learning interest and improving students' learning enthusiasm, So as to comprehensively enhance students'

English core literacy. Teachers should also realize the importance of cultivating students' English thinking [9]. When teaching basic knowledge, they should also give consideration to the guidance of students' thinking, so as to promote their English thinking to be continuously enhanced, so as to improve their English level and provide sufficient power for effectively cultivating students' language literacy.

2 Related Work

Therefore (Li, 2019) combine the actual situation of students in independent college, reform the English teaching of accounting, to improve the professional English quality of finance and accounting students in independent college, giving them more competitive advantage in employment. (Kong, 2019) discuss the construction and application of college English online open course in a vocational college in China. The application of the research results can mobilize the enthusiasm of students, improve the efficiency of classroom teaching, and improve students' practical application ability in English (Wang, 2019). The artificial intelligence and big data are introduced into English teaching to propose a new teaching Eco-environment construction method to meet the needs of the social development and international communication in English (Sun et al., 2020). Taking college English teaching as the research direction (Wei, 2020) explore the path and strategy of College English Teaching Reform under the ideological and political theory of curriculum, so as to provide necessary help for improving the quality of College English teaching and enhancing the comprehensive quality of college students. (Ning, 2021) focus on the reform of college English teaching under the modern apprenticeship training mode. The research results show that the model constructed has certain practical effects (Yu et. al., 2021). Other influential work includes (Chen, 2019), (He, 2020), (Zhou, 2020).

3 Advantages of Internet Assisted English Teaching in Colleges and Universities

3.1 Optimizing Classroom Teaching with Internet Application Technology

Under the background of "Internet plus", the concept of classroom teaching design follows the student centered approach, giving full play to students' initiative and initiative, and cultivating students' broadness, flexibility and creativity in thinking. Students are regarded as the masters of learning, and teachers' responsibility is to inspire and guide students and play their role of instructing and dispelling doubts. Firstly, teachers can apply network technology to serve course teaching, make full use of multimedia technology in classroom teaching, present the knowledge to be taught by adding pictures, audio, video or animation effects, present useful and important information on the screen, and transfer the knowledge to students vividly and specifically [10]. At the same time, students can also participate in it, express their views and expand learning information by displaying ppt related to textbook knowledge content. Secondly, teachers can use network resources to train students' listening, speaking, reading and writing ability. For example, listening teaching is an important part of English teaching. Making rational use of network resources can effectively improve the quality of listening teaching. Teachers can download listening materials and supporting exercises related to the course from the Internet and provide them to students for classroom training after necessary modifications [11].

Finally, teachers can adopt the teaching method of "flipped classroom" to make students change from passive learning to active learning. Turn over the traditional learning process (teachers speak and students listen). Teachers make knowledge points into micro courses and upload them to the network platform, so that students can complete independent learning of knowledge points and concepts in extracurricular time [12]. The classroom becomes a place for teachers and students to interact, mainly used to answer doubts and report and discuss in groups, so as to achieve better teaching results.

3.2 The Internet Uses Online Micro Courses to Assist Classroom Teaching

While the traditional form of basic education has been supplemented by the Internet, it has also produced changes in personalized learning and teaching processes, which is also the most important change brought about by the Internet. For the knowledge points of different disciplines, micro courses can better meet the personalized learning of students, and can choose to learn independently, check omissions and fill vacancies, effectively consolidate and strengthen knowledge points. It is an expanding resource and an important supplement to traditional classroom learning. On the one hand, online micro class learning can cultivate students' autonomous learning ability, and students can repeatedly learn a knowledge point through micro class [13]; On the other hand, students can choose weak points to strengthen and consolidate anytime and anywhere according to their needs. Students can watch micro classes freely after class, discuss and solve doubts in class, realize learning before teaching, and meet the needs of students' personalized learning, as shown in Fig. 1.

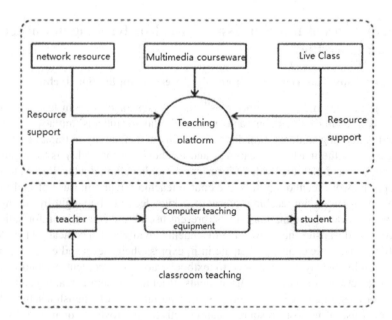

Fig. 1. Internet Teaching

3.3 The Internet Stimulates Students' Interest in Learning English

In the Internet English teaching mode, teachers can use the Internet to show students the English in life through multimedia technology. Especially the students who have just entered middle school, they have a strong learning motivation and curiosity about new things. If this feeling can be maintained for a long time, it will get twice the result with half the effort. However, in traditional English teaching, teachers use command teaching methods. Students may be a little interested in English at first, but in the long run, they will have a psychological resistance, unwilling to learn, or have no interest at all [14]. However, under the teaching mode of the Internet, teachers can connect classes with practice and immerse students through sound, text, pictures and images, which can stimulate their interest in learning English.

4 Challenges Faced by College English Teaching in the Internet Age

4.1 The Internet Challenges Teaching Methods and Teaching Skills

The traditional education is based on teachers and knowledge dissemination. This educational concept does not correspond to the Internet era. In the Internet age, equality in education is required. In this era, students can obtain a large number of learning resources through micro class, Mu class and network. There are also many mobile terminals to provide students with more flexible and diverse learning methods. Students' learning no longer depends on teachers unilaterally. In this case, it is very necessary for teachers and students to establish an equal learning community. The lag of the traditional teacher centered educational concept is particularly prominent [15].

In the traditional English classroom, teachers' teaching and students' learning are the model, and students are passive most of the time. However, in the Internet age, new methods such as micro class, Mu class and flipped class are more and more used in College English teaching, as shown in Fig. 2. Students are required to study independently after class according to the teaching videos and knowledge points prepared by the teacher. In the classroom, we should change the active and passive mode of teachers and students, and realize interactive teaching through student student communication and teacher-student communication. This requires teachers and students to complete the transformation of role and orientation with the help of modern teaching means. In the specific implementation process, it often involves the application of a variety of technologies. For example, flipped classroom requires teachers to make high-level teaching videos. However, at present, most college English teachers have heavy teaching tasks, great work pressure, do not have corresponding teaching skills, and their ability to carry out curriculum reform and innovation is obviously insufficient. This also limits the breadth and depth of the role of the Internet in teaching.

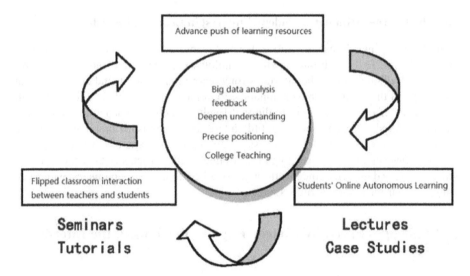

Fig. 2. Internet teaching mode

4.2 Challenges to Students' Learning Ability in the Internet Age

At present, the network is more and more developed, the application of the Internet in English teaching is more and more common, and students gradually accept the application of the Internet in learning. The abundance of network information provides great convenience for students' learning. Students can query on the Internet when they encounter complex problems, solve their doubts in time, facilitate students' daily learning, and make students more dependent on the application of the Internet to a certain extent. However, the application of multimedia in English teaching also reduces students' autonomous learning ability to a great extent. Although the rich information on the Internet can answer students' questions in time, it also leads to students' excessive dependence on the Internet because of its convenience. When students encounter slightly more complex problems, they are often used to searching for answers directly on the Internet instead of getting answers through their own thinking [16]. This behavior will reduce the process of independent thinking when students encounter problems in learning, At the same time, it also reduces the time for students to discuss this issue with other students, and is not conducive to cultivating students' language expression ability and team spirit. In addition, there are serious loopholes in some English software at present. Students are easy to be misled by wrong information on the network because their English level can not be accurately identified, which is not conducive to English learning.

Massive Internet information has both advantages and disadvantages. In the Internet era, students have more ways to obtain knowledge. In this era, if students want to improve the effect of English learning, they must have a strong awareness and ability of autonomous learning. However, if students' learning ability is poor, it is difficult to collect and learn the educational resources they need through the network, but they will be lost in the network. Therefore, the Internet age also has high requirements for students' learning ability.

5   Strategies of College English Teaching Reform Under the Background of Internet

5.1   Optimize Teaching Methods and Apply Technology to Optimize Classroom Teaching

In the traditional teaching method, "blackboard and chalk". On the other hand, in the traditional teaching mode, students' learning is passive acceptance, which is not conducive to active inquiry learning. Therefore, in the Internet era, it is difficult to optimize teachers' teaching methods Slow down.

Multimedia teaching is adopted in Teachers' teaching. The teaching form of combining pictures and text and combining sound and painting will increase classroom fun, enhance students' classroom experience, mobilize students' enthusiasm for classroom participation and increase their desire for independent learning after class. Multimedia teaching through the Internet will enhance classroom fun and students' experience. Compared with the original book teaching, teachers should use computers and take more effective measures In order to enrich and diverse classroom teaching forms, multimedia teaching is carried out.

"Student oriented", change the traditional pure professor teaching into student group autonomous learning, in which teachers participate in inquiry learning with students. Answer students' questions in time and guide students' autonomous learning, so as to enhance students' motivation for autonomous learning and strengthen students' will for autonomous learning; at the same time, use new communication tools to arrange homework after class, such as wechat and QQ Many middle schools have used WeChat group and QQ group to arrange and collect home-work, answer questions about students' questions, share and spread advanced knowledge of disciplines, etc. this experience is worth learning. Internet plus In this context, the concept of classroom teaching design should follow the principle of student-centered, give full play to students' mobility and initiative, and cultivate students' broadness, flexibility and innovation of thinking.

5.2   Improve the Comprehensive Quality of English Teachers

As an advanced teaching method, internet teaching has higher requirements for the comprehensive quality of English teachers compared with the traditional teaching mode. The new teaching methods not only require teachers to have better expression ability and professional quality, but also require English teachers to have good communication and communicative ability, so as to communicate effectively with students in time. Moreover, due to the Internet Network teaching needs to apply computers. Therefore, using the Internet for teaching also requires teachers to have high learning ability and computer application ability. In this way, when using computers for teaching, teachers can operate flexibly, which is conducive to the improvement of classroom efficiency. However, because using the Internet for teaching is a new teaching mode gradually emerging in recent years, it is difficult to guide teachers As a result, some English teachers have poor mastery of computers and can not adapt to the development of modern technology in time. Therefore, schools can organize English teachers to carry out vocational skills training to improve their ability and level of using computers, so as to meet the requirements of the new teaching model. At the same time, teachers should strengthen their amateur learning to improve their professional ability and level To ensure that they can adapt to the development trend of the new era and provide better learning conditions for students.

6 Conclusion

The Internet has opened up a new vision for College English teaching. As teachers and students, they should have full psychological and skills preparation, and constantly improve their cognitive and practical level in teaching and learning skills and teaching means. Network resources are natural English teaching tools, and teachers should improve their ability to collect and integrate various network teaching resources. In College English Teaching The Internet plus teaching method and teaching mode, extracurricular teacher student interaction and so on. The times will bring many changes. With the rapid development of science and technology and the popularization of the Internet, the Internet is more and more widely used in English teaching, which brings great challenges to college English teaching. Internet English teaching not only improves students' learning efficiency, but also cultivates students' ability to find and solve problems.

References

1. Liang, M.: Research on College English teaching strategies in the era of Internet plus. Overseas English (2017)
2. Liao, F.: Internet based English extension teaching explores. Foreign Lang. (3), 160–162 (2013)
3. Liao, S.: "Internet plus education" background of college English flipped classroom teaching mode. J. Career Acad. Jiamusi (7), 360–362 (2016)
4. Sun, T.: English classroom teaching and English learning in the network environment . J. Changchun Norm. Univ. (1) (2016)
5. Sun, C.: Advantages, misunderstandings and countermeasures of multimedia assisted English teaching. Research on foreign language teaching in basic education (2003)
6. Chen, W.-L.: Exploration of the construction of English teaching skills course under the background of "Internet plus". J. Changchun Inst. Educ. (6), 71–73 (2016)
7. Chen, G.: Exploration of reforming integrated English course. In: Proceedings of the 5th International Conference on Arts, Design and Contemporary Education (ICADCE 2019) (2019)
8. Li, Y.: A Practical research on the reform of accounting English course teaching under the transformation of "application" in independent college. In: Proceedings of the 2018 8th International Conference on Education And Management (ICEM 2018) (2019)
9. Kong, S.: Practice of college English teaching reform based on online open course. Engl. Lang. Teach. **12**, 156–160 (2019)
10. Wang, J.: Research on blended teaching mode of college English based on rain classroom. In: Proceedings of the 2018 6th International Education, Economics, Social Science, Arts, Sports and Management Engineering Conference (IEESASM 2018) (2019)
11. Sun, M., Li, Y.: Eco-environment construction of English teaching using artificial intelligence under big data environment. IEEE Access **8**, 193955–193965 (2020)

12. He, B.: The cultivation of cultural competence of non-English majors under the strategy of "culture going out". In: 2020 International Conference on Educational Science (ICES2020) (2020)
13. Wei, F.: On the new path of college English teaching under the background of "curriculum ideology and politics" (2020)
14. Zhou, S.: An analysis of the application of computer-based multimodal discourse analysis in English teaching reform (2020)
15. Ning, K.: Exploration of college English teaching reform under the training mode of modern apprenticeship system (2021). (IF: 3)
16. Yu, L., Peng, N.: Research on English teaching reform based on artificial intelligence matching model. J. Intell. Fuzzy Syst. (2021)

The Path of English Subject Under Genetic Algorithm in the Construction of College Campus Culture

Meizhi Wu[1] and Tong Yao[2(✉)]

[1] Jinjiang College of Sichuan University, Meishan 620000, Sichuan, China
[2] Sichuan Tourism University, Chengdu 610100, Sichuan, China
yaotong2011@gmail.com

Abstract. Culture is the soul of a country and a nation. To build a socialist cultural power, we must adhere to a high degree of cultural consciousness and cultural self-confidence, fully stimulate the cultural creativity of the people in the whole society, and strive to realize the great rejuvenation of the Chinese nation. In terms of cultural construction, campus culture, as a special cultural form, is produced with the emergence of higher education. This paper is a preliminary study on the path of English discipline in the construction of campus culture in Colleges and Universities under the background of big data.

Keywords: Campus culture · Big data · English subject · Construction path

1 Introduction

As a special cultural form, campus culture comes into being with the emergence of higher education. The University was first born in medieval Europe. It is a "rational and systematic specialized scientific pursuit engaged by well-trained professionals" under the common influence of the Christian Church and guild organizations. Since its birth, modern university is a learning center characterized by autonomous education. It is usually built in areas with superior natural conditions and relatively mature urban development. The birth of modern university itself is a far-reaching cultural phenomenon. A considerable part of its self-government tradition, degree system and management model have been used so far, which has laid a foundation for the formation of a systematic and standardized university culture.

On the one hand, under the guidance of the theory and system of socialist culture with Chinese characteristics, the main goal of the construction of campus cultural connotation in Colleges and universities is to help contemporary college students improve their own quality, improve their cultural level and correct their ideas. On the other hand, it is also to educate students to correctly grasp the theoretical connotation of the new socialist system with Chinese characteristics and establish a correct world outlook Outlook on life and values, so as to guide students to correctly deal with the relationship between man and

M. A. Jan and F. Khan (Eds.): BigIoT-EDU 2022, LNICST 467, pp. 464–472, 2023.
https://doi.org/10.1007/978-3-031-23944-1_50

man, man and society, man and nature in life practice. In this sense, the construction of socialist culture with Chinese characteristics is consistent with the construction of campus cultural connotation in Colleges and universities [1]. At the same time, based on the big data background, it is also a practical requirement to improve the quality of talent training in Colleges and universities to promote young students' cultural consciousness and cultural self-confidence through the construction of campus cultural connotation.

Campus culture is a part of the cultural construction of socialist harmonious society. Only by adhering to the correct direction of advanced culture and taking the connotation of socialist harmonious culture as the theoretical basis, can we create a good humanistic environment for the construction of harmonious campus and bring cultural heritage and spiritual support to the fundamental goal of cultivating high-quality talents for higher vocational education. As a higher vocational college, she is facing the direct impact of market economy and knowledge economy. She needs all-round literacy to enrich its cultural heritage and enhance its vitality and competitiveness. Therefore, the construction of campus culture in higher vocational colleges has its particularity, urgency and necessity.

"We must put the development of advanced socialist culture in a very prominent position, focus on improving people's quality and promoting people's all-round development, strengthen ideological and moral construction, develop education, science and culture, and cultivate socialist citizens with ideals, morality, culture and discipline". The socialist cultural construction adheres to the guidance of Deng Xiaoping theory, the important thought of Three Represents and the scientific outlook on development, which determines that the socialist campus cultural construction must take the training of qualified builders and successors of the socialist cause as the fundamental starting point and foothold. The fundamental task of higher vocational education is to cultivate high-quality applied talents to meet the needs of socialist construction. Every link of school work should put the goal of cultivating talents in the first place. Only when the construction of harmonious campus culture is closely combined with the central work of cultivating talents, can it adhere to its correct direction and guidance, and show its influence and cohesion in the construction of harmonious campus.

Under the condition of market economy, in order to ensure the quality of talent training, we must adhere to the idea of education first and moral education first, and put the firm and correct political direction in the first place. This determines that the construction of campus culture must take advanced culture as the fundamental direction and adhere to the socialist core value system as the theoretical basis. The socialist core value system is the foundation of socialist harmonious culture and the ideological foundation and cultural source of building a socialist harmonious society. It comprehensively and systematically expounds the fundamental direction, spiritual essence and profound connotation of the construction of socialist harmonious culture from the aspects of guiding ideology, ideals and beliefs, value orientation, moral norms and behavior. Building a harmonious campus and building a harmonious campus culture, without the guidance and guidance of the socialist core value system, will lose its direction and soul. Only by deeply understanding and grasping the theoretical and practical benefits of the socialist core values in the construction of campus culture can we deeply understand the fundamental goals and tasks of the construction of campus culture.

In the process of building a harmonious campus, adhering to the correct direction of advanced culture and guided by the socialist core value system is to guide teachers and students to establish a correct world outlook, outlook on life, values and outlook on honor and disgrace, and bring intellectual support and spiritual guarantee to teachers' career development, cultivation of teachers' ethics and students' growth and success through the construction of campus culture, It brings a solid cultural and ideological foundation for higher education to achieve the goal of cultivating high-quality talents.

2 Related Work

2.1 Core Literacy of English Discipline

The interpretation of English curriculum standards for senior high schools (2017) mentioned that the development of core literacy of Chinese students is the concretization and refinement of the party's education policy. In order to establish the internal relationship between core literacy and curriculum teaching, and fully tap the unique educational value of curriculum teaching of each discipline for fully implementing the party's educational policy, implementing the fundamental task of Building Morality and cultivating people, and developing quality education, each discipline has condensed the core quality of the discipline based on the essence of the discipline. It is also mentioned that through research, front-line teachers highly agree with the concept of developing discipline core literacy. This defines the correct values, necessary characters and key abilities that students should achieve after learning the course of the subject.

For English subjects, the English curriculum standard for senior high schools (2017 Edition) clearly puts forward the core literacy of English subjects. Discipline core quality is the concentrated embodiment of the value of discipline education. It is the correct value concept, necessary character and key ability gradually formed by students through discipline learning [2]. It is mentioned that the specific goal of ordinary high school English curriculum is to cultivate and develop students' core qualities such as language ability, cultural awareness, thinking quality and learning ability after receiving high school English education. The core qualities of English discipline mainly include language ability, cultural awareness, thinking quality and learning ability, as shown in Fig. 1.

2.2 Connotation of University Campus Culture in the New Era

"Culture" is a concept with complex connotation and extensive extension. Since the 1950s and 1960s, many scholars at home and abroad have taken culture as the research object and carried out a large number of studies, covering many fields such as culturology, anthropology, pedagogy, politics and so on. According to incomplete statistics, since 1963, there have been more than 200 conceptual definitions of the word "culture" in various documents. It can be said that "culture" is one of the most complex, mysterious and difficult concepts in the whole field of Humanities and social sciences. As a sub form of culture, it is always difficult to form a clear and accurate conceptual consensus on the connotation definition of university campus culture. According to the current

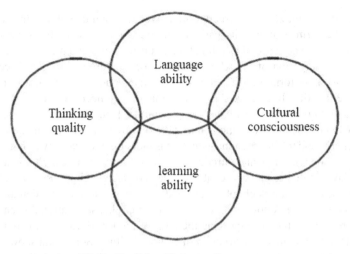

Fig. 1. English subject core literacy map

domestic research, many scholars define university campus culture from the perspective of constituent elements and give various explanations such as "two elements theory", "three elements theory" and "four elements theory".

Although it also objectively makes a theoretical clarification of college campus culture, there are still some problems, such as vague definition, weak academic rationality and so on. From the analysis of the connotation of campus culture by many scholars, its concept composition generally includes three parts: first, clarify the main contents of campus culture, such as material environment construction, spiritual civilization construction and so on; The second is to clarify the extension of campus culture, including making a relatively clear distinction between campus culture and other subculture types in terms of discussion boundary, field scope, carrier approach, etc. [3]; The third is to explain the relationship between the main bodies and internal elements of constructing and participating in the construction of campus culture.

3 Analysis on the Necessity of Campus Cultural Connotation Construction in Colleges and Universities Under the Background of Big Data

3.1 Comply with the Objective Needs of Social Development

Since the 18th National Congress, China has entered a new stage of development in politics, economy, culture and other aspects. Objectively, it also puts forward higher requirements for the construction of campus culture in Colleges and universities. This "high requirement" is mainly reflected in the demand for the construction of campus cultural connotation in Colleges and universities. The so-called "connotation construction" mainly refers to deepening and enriching the content of university campus culture, improving and optimizing the structure of university campus culture, innovating and expanding the form of university campus culture, so as to make the subculture construction which is very special as a function and orientation and plays a leading role in the cultural construction of the whole society more mature and standardized, and get rid of the past mere formality The construction status quo that is a mere formality and a mere superficiality. To achieve this transformation, we need to analyze the necessity of building and optimizing university campus culture from three angles: first, from the reality of China's social development, under the situation that the reform has entered the deep-water area and the international situation is more unpredictable, we should enhance our country's talent training and introduction strength, attract more high-end talents, and give full play to colleges and universities to lead advanced culture, Realizing the social function of scientific and technological breakthrough is our realistic demand to solve the main social contradictions and improve our comprehensive national strength.

From the perspective of improving the level of higher education, it is imperative to strengthen the connotation construction of campus culture. Some data show that China has the largest higher education school running system in the world. Both the number of schools and the number of college students rank first in the world. However, in terms of quality, China's higher education is still in the rising development stage of "big but not strong", and there is still a big gap compared with the world's first-class higher education power [4]. To improve the school running level of colleges and universities in China, in addition to making efforts on hard indicators such as hardware facilities, scientific research ability and teaching staff, we should also pay attention to the cultivation of university spirit and shape a more realistic and pragmatic campus culture. Only by realizing modernization and high-level development in spiritual style, can a university really shoulder the educational task of "being virtuous, friendly to the people and ending in the best", which comes down in one continuous line with the connotation construction of campus culture.

3.2 Inevitable Requirements for Realizing the Fundamental Task of "Building Morality and Cultivating People"

For young students, the university stage is the "jointing and booting stage" in their life. A good campus cultural atmosphere is more helpful for students to buckle the first button of life, precipitate and form a spiritual realm and value orientation in line with the positioning of the school. This is an important way to respond to a series of fundamental problems of "who to cultivate people, who to cultivate, and how to cultivate people". At the same time, the connotation construction of China's college campus culture in the new era must also be led by ideological and political education, pay close attention to the main position and channel of Ideological and political theory course, implement the ideological guidance to all aspects of students' life and learning, and help students strengthen their ideals and beliefs and establish lofty life goals, These should be realized by the perfect development of the connotation construction of campus culture in Colleges and universities. We used the formula (1) and formula (2) to normalizing the data.

$$R = \frac{r - (g + b)}{2}$$

$$G = \frac{g - (r + b)}{2},$$

$$B = \frac{b - (r + g)}{2},$$

$$Y = \frac{(r + g)}{2} - \frac{|r - g|}{2 - b}. \tag{1}$$

$$S = w_1 \times N(\bar{I}) + w_c \times N(\bar{C}) + w_o \times N(\bar{O}) \tag{2}$$

4 The Path of English Discipline in the Construction of Campus Culture in Colleges and Universities Under the Background of Big Data

(1) Adhere to education oriented. In the construction of campus culture, we should always adhere to education, integrate the diversity, interest, ideology and knowledge of activities, so that students can not only increase their knowledge, but also cultivate their sentiment. We should make full use of the advantages of human resources of the University and hire experts and professors with certain attainments in all aspects to set up a series of lectures on English for students. Carry out various forms, high-grade, healthy, vivid and elegant campus cultural activities to implement education from beginning to end. At the same time, we should stand at the height of talent training in the new century, always take the pursuit of knowledge and advocating science as the purpose of campus culture construction, take facing modernization, facing the world, facing the future and cultivating high-quality talents as the direction and goal of campus culture construction, and adhere to the educational direction of combining scientific education with humanistic education.

(2) Give full play to the role of associations and take associations as the leader. Community activities play an important role in the construction of English campus culture. Based on the principle of active support and steady development, we should establish a certain number of community organizations such as art troupe, speech troupe, calligraphy association, chess club, computer club and Youth Volunteer Association, and strengthen the guidance and management of these student community activities. On the one hand, we should encourage and create conditions to carry out healthy and positive community activities, so as to make it a campus cultural activity place to broaden horizons, increase talents, cultivate creativity, expand information circulation channels, improve cultural quality, enhance the spirit of unity and cooperation, and radiate youth and enthusiasm; On the other hand, we should strengthen guidance and management, participate in community activities, guide community work, and timely find and correct unhealthy and problematic communities and their activities. According above analysis, we know the model can be the following

formula to establish.

$$\begin{cases} e(k) = r(k) - y(k) \\ x_1(k) = e(k) - e(k-1) \\ x_2(k) = e(k) \\ x_3(k) = e(k) - 2e(k-1) + e(k-2) \end{cases} \tag{3}$$

$$\begin{cases} w_i(k+1) = w_i(k) + \Delta w_i(k) \\ \Delta w_i(k) = -\lambda \dfrac{\partial J_C}{\partial w_i(k)} \end{cases} \tag{4}$$

where $= 1, 2, 3$; take $0 < \lambda < 1$. Represents the first-order difference, x_2 represents the system error, and x_3 represents the error accumulation.

(3) Vigorously improve the level of English campus culture. As a place for cultivating high-level socialist talents, colleges and universities should make use of campus culture to vigorously cultivate students' ability to distinguish between truth, goodness, beauty and falsehood, evil and ugliness, so as to prevent them from swallowing some cultures without distinguishing good from bad. We should guide them to speak English and absorb the spiritual wealth created by mankind. In fact, young college students have the desire to improve their literary appreciation taste and cultural literacy. Practice has proved that symphonic concerts, concerts of self created and self performed songs, dances, paintings, calligraphy, speeches, recitations, appreciation of literary classics and films in Colleges and universities are very popular with students. We must carry out high-level cultural and art festivals, academic festivals, cultural weeks and other activities in a planned and targeted manner, create a strong campus cultural atmosphere, moisten students' hearts with elegant culture, cultivate students' sentiment, improve students' taste and cultivate their healthy and upward spiritual psychology. We should resolutely oppose and resist vulgar, low, vulgar and even decadent culture and the ideology of hostile forces to occupy the position of campus culture.

(4) Create a new and healthy campus culture network. With the rapid development of computer and communication technology, college students are more and more common and skilled in using the network in their own life. The university campus is becoming the most densely populated area of Internet users in China. It is undeniable that the network environment has a subtle impact on college students. Therefore, we should adhere to the correct guidance of public opinion, establish a campus cultural network with the purpose of cultivating "Four Haves" new people, focusing on actively promoting the all-round development of students and forming a good school spirit. Campus culture network should seek advantages and avoid disadvantages, and give full play to the role of network in the construction of campus culture in Colleges and universities. We should strive to create a healthy, elegant, civilized and upward online culture rich in the characteristics of the times and close to students' life, and earnestly achieve the "Three Combinations", that is, first, combine the construction of network culture with the practical improvement of College Students' Ideological and political quality, and strive to stimulate college students' enthusiasm for patriotism, school and collective love; Second, combine the construction of online culture with the practical improvement of College Students' cultural quality,

and strive to cultivate college students' good spiritual outlook, ideal pursuit, mode of thinking, emotional will and creative potential; Third, combine the construction of online culture with the practical improvement of College Students' physical and mental quality, and strive to cultivate students' good psychological quality.

The college campus culture simulation is shown in Fig. 2.

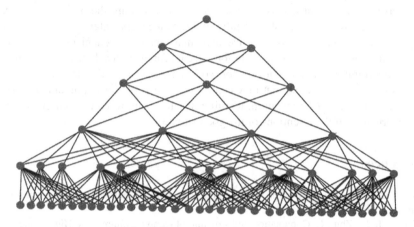

Fig. 2. College campus culture simulation

5   Conclusion

With the continuous development of socialist market economy and the continuous deepening of globalization, in the era of big data, innovation and progress began to become the mainstream of social development, and the connotation construction of College English campus culture also encountered new opportunities and challenges. As the most important and concentrated place of higher education, colleges and universities are an important position for inheriting civilization and innovating culture. They shoulder the important task of cultivating talents for the country in the new era. University campus environment is the internal environment of school education environment, an important carrier of university material culture and spiritual culture inheritance, and a comprehensive educational force that can continuously influence and shape people. In a word, the cultivation of excellent college students is inseparable from the education of colleges and universities and the shaping and edification of a good campus environment.

The situational simulation classroom of the college uses "fixed" and "activity" signs to display the corporate culture concept of the major. Fixed is the general concept, such as the development direction, professional ethics, business philosophy, humanistic concept and other signs; The purpose of the activity is to constantly change various pre prepared objects or signs according to the characteristics of various majors, so that students can get different corporate culture feelings when understanding different knowledge and skills, and create favorable conditions for future employment.

We should increase investment and implement it step by step. Incorporate the campus culture construction plan into the school's 14th five year development plan, decompose the planning objectives into the annual school work plan, implement them step by step, raise funds through multiple channels, increase the investment in school building renovation, campus greening and beautification, environmental layout and festival activities, improve the conditions for school-based teaching and research, and ensure the scientific research funds.

Deepen management and guarantee system. Teachers are the main body of campus culture construction. We should fully mobilize teachers' intentions and creativity, innovate management systems, improve talent management mechanisms, improve evaluation and incentive mechanisms, care for and care for every teacher, so that talents can create opportunities, have a platform for work, have space for development, and have rewards for performance, so that they can have a sweet job, have a dream, and have a run, and form a ratio of dedication, learning, teaching and research, and growth Than the performance of the intentions of the good situation.

References

1. Wei, J.: Connotation, function and approach of cultural construction in Colleges and universities. Educ. Occup. (12) (2015)
2. Shi, J., Ji, L., Zhu, X.: Connotation and structure of campus culture. Res. High. Educ. China (5) (2005)
3. Lu, Y.: Connotation analysis of harmonious campus culture. Res. Ideol. Polit. Educ. (1) (2008)
4. Gao, L.: Problems and countermeasures in the construction of campus culture in colleges and universities. J. Huanggang Norm. Univ. (2) (2008)

Application of Computer Network Technology in Enterprise Information Management

Guangjun Liu(✉)

Wuchang University of Technology, Wuhan 460223, Hubei, China
10873536@qq.com

Abstract. With the rapid development of China's national economy and social informatization, the overall situation of informatization construction is increasingly showing the prominent characteristics of paying more attention to application, effectiveness and coordinated development with economy and society. Taking the rapid development of enterprise informatization as the background data, this paper introduces the definition of enterprise informatization management. According to the actual situation, this paper focuses on the role and application of computer technology in enterprise informatization management, as well as the deficiencies and improvement measures of computer in enterprise informatization management, and analyzes the important significance of computer technology to enterprise informatization efficient management.

Keywords: Information management · Enterprises · Computer · Network technique

1 Introduction

With the development of enterprises, as the core of enterprise network and data storage, the data center carries the key equipment such as core network switching equipment, server and storage, as well as many business systems running on the equipment. With the increasing amount of data generated by network scale and informatization, the management and operation and maintenance of data center have become more and more important and complex [1]. How to safely and quickly carry out network management and create application system in data center, how to manage business safely and efficiently, how to dynamically adjust resources and reduce operation cost according to various needs, how to be flexible, efficient Safely sharing and managing various resources will be difficult problems and challenges encountered in enterprise information construction. The application of computer network technology will provide better solutions to the above problems.

M. A. Jan and F. Khan (Eds.): BigIoT-EDU 2022, LNICST 467, pp. 473–479, 2023.
https://doi.org/10.1007/978-3-031-23944-1_51

2   Related Work

2.1   Introduction to Computer Network Technology and Enterprise Informatization

(1)   Computer network technology

The so-called computer network technology mainly refers to the use of local area network or modern network technology to create a network platform, carry out communication and realize information sharing at a long distance. Computer network has been applied to many aspects of enterprise production, operation, management and so on. Using computer network technology, enterprises can use the network to carry out transactions, quickly obtain and share various information of enterprises, and improve economic benefits. The important feature of computer network is to save money, that is, enterprises can trade on the network management platform, save human and material resources and reduce capital investment. In addition, it is necessary to increase scalability, let users add processors according to their own needs, expand network performance, and avoid problems caused by too much workload as much as possible.

(2)   Enterprise informatization

The so-called enterprise information management mainly uses network technology to manage enterprises scientifically. Enterprise information should be preserved, disseminated and managed electronically, so as to continuously improve the enterprise's information management ability and improve the enterprise's modern management level. Computer technology is the core of information management, which can shorten the space distance in the enterprise and make the cooperation between departments closer [2]. The management and decision-makers can use the network to quickly obtain the key information inside and outside the enterprise and implement rapid and accurate management. At present, enterprise information management mainly includes financial information, procurement information, sales information, quality supervision information and human resources information.

2.2   Necessity and Importance of the Application of Computer Network Technology in Enterprise Informatization

With the development of the times, the level of computer network technology has been continuously improved. The Internet age has been an inevitable feature of the development of the times. Therefore, the application of computer network technology in enterprise informatization is an inevitable product of the development of the times. In addition, the application of computer network technology in enterprise informatization development can not only help enterprises quickly integrate effective resources, It can also effectively improve the office efficiency of enterprises and create a new pattern of development and competition of modern enterprises. Before the development of enterprise informatization, the management of each unit of the enterprise was relatively rough and disorderly, and the enterprise also relied heavily on the staff of the enterprise in office and communication. The emergence of informatization management can effectively improve the modern management level of the enterprise, improve the accuracy of information, and build a platform for information resource sharing, To promote the sustainable and healthy development of enterprises, the hierarchical structure of computer network technology is shown in Fig. 1. The application of Internet in enterprise work brings considerable benefits, which can greatly shorten the gap between multinational enterprises and lay a solid foundation for unified management.

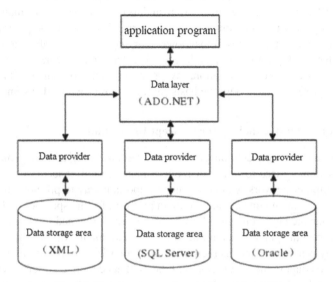

Fig. 1. Computer network technology hierarchy

3 Specific Application of Computer Network Technology in Enterprise Information Management

3.1 Using Computer Technology for Enterprise Management

First of all, the application of computer network technology to enterprise internal communication can realize more compact contact between various departments of the company. For example, the use of communication and other technologies in enterprise management shortens the distance between all employees of the company from the top to the grass-roots level. On the one hand, this "zero distance" management is more conducive to the construction of corporate culture, on the other hand, it is conducive to improving the implementation efficiency of managers' decisions. The use of computer technology to assist enterprise communication ensures the standardized operation of the company, optimizes the management structure of the company, and realizes the "flat" management of the enterprise. The company conference adopts the mode of network conference, which saves costs and improves efficiency. Now, network conference is gradually becoming the main way of enterprise conference [3]. Accelerating the research and development of various communication software suitable for enterprises is of great significance to realize more smooth communication between various departments of enterprises. Secondly, use computer technology to analyze enterprise information. The screening of effective information is of profound significance to enterprise managers who need to make correct decisions. The amount of information collected at all levels of the enterprise is huge. Managers cannot have the time and energy to analyze massive information and make decisions in time. Traditional information analysis is solved by special enterprise departments. Due to work errors and other reasons, the use of human resources can easily lead to the loss or distortion of some information, and its effect is poor. Once managers make wrong judgment, it will bring losses to the enterprise. The use of computer technology can avoid the common mistakes of manpower summarizing and analyzing information. The computer has high efficiency and accurate calculation. It can well complete the analysis and processing of information, save manpower and cost, and most importantly, provide enterprise managers with the basis for making reasonable decisions.

3.2 Use Computer Technology for Concept Innovation

Firstly, computer network technology promotes the innovation of management concept and promotes enterprises to establish modern management concept. The wide application of computer network technology is an important way to promote the reform of enterprise management concept and the main platform for the specific implementation of modern management concept. Many large-scale state-owned enterprises in China have grown up in the planned economic system environment. Although they have gone through many reform and reconstruction, system transformation and other schemes in recent years to adapt to the development of the market economic system, they still have not fundamentally changed the traditional enterprise management concept and lack open ideas and accurate market information, Without a perfect market emergency plan, it can not really comply with the trend of global economic development. Facing this practical problem, Chinese enterprises must pay attention to the innovation of management concept, so as to improve the reform and innovation of enterprise management mode and method.

Secondly, the use of computer network technology to establish the overall management concept of enterprises. The informatization development project of formulating objectives, establishing plans and carrying out enterprise management step by step should, on the one hand, establish the overall concept and scientifically and reasonably combine enterprise informatization management with enterprise business strategy, development objectives, commodity characteristics and management mode. At the same time, we should establish a clear application purpose of computer network technology, truly understand the great role of computer network technology in enterprise information management, so as to create the core technology of the enterprise, improve the comprehensive competitiveness of the enterprise, and formulate a clear implementation plan. On the other hand, the application of computer network technology should be consistent with the reality of enterprise development and master the crux of the problems encountered in enterprise development. Therefore, we should build an overall management concept to promote the overall improvement of enterprise management level, prevent a one-sided management problem, and avoid the lack of information and the waste of funds.

3.3 Using Computer Technology for Financial Management

First, using computer technology to monitor financial data can ensure the accuracy of financial information. With the rapid development of modern enterprises, their scale is expanding rapidly, and all kinds of financial data and information are increasing rapidly. The traditional financial management can not adapt to this situation. Because the computer can store a large amount of data, and can analyze, budget and judge various accounting files, so as to provide accurate information for the financial management of enterprises, the computer is widely used, and the computerization of property is paid more and more attention by many large enterprises. Finance is the lifeline to maintain the development of enterprises and has an important impact on the healthy and sound development of enterprises. The accuracy of its data is directly related to the decision-making direction of enterprises. Using computer technology for financial monitoring can enable managers to obtain correct data at any time, which has great advantages over human monitoring. Secondly, the use of computer technology for financial analysis can ensure the scientificity of financial analysis. Computer network technology has sufficient accounting search ability. The accounting information of each year, quarter and month can be stored in the computer. As long as it meets the financial search requirements, the computer can quickly query all relevant accounting information and data. At the same time, the use of special financial analysis software for financial analysis can avoid manual errors, provide the most scientific analysis results for enterprises, improve the accuracy of managers' decision-making and realize the healthy development of enterprises.

4 Some Suggestions on the Choice of Enterprise Informatization

(1) Improve information recognition. With the change of time, the value of information resources will fluctuate greatly. Therefore, as an enterprise, on the one hand, we should fully improve the information recognition of the enterprise, and the collection of relevant information must be large. In order to improve the recognition of information, information keywords can be determined according to the classification of information resources, especially in the selection of search methods. We know from our understanding that as long as the type positioning of an enterprise's information management is reasonable, the keyword positioning is accurate, and the scientific and reasonable route is selected, the time required to retrieve information will be well shortened, which is also of great help to improve the efficiency of information collection [4]. This requires us to redefine the information collection according to the type and time of information collection, and make reasonable choices for the collection methods, schemes and sorting and summary methods. Only through these efforts can enterprises obtain the information resources they most need.

(2) Dig the value of information and improve the development of information. We call the necessary analysis, classification and sorting of information resources information management. Only through these efforts can we improve the practical value of information and transmit these information to relevant departments through the role of information platform, so as to achieve the purpose of use. Enterprises can

also establish their own information resource database and classify and store information resources in time, which will make the rational development and utilization of information resources. Enterprises can also establish local area networks with relevant units, so as to expand the amount of information, and then adopt online retrieval to realize the sharing of information resources.

(3) Strengthen the information awareness of enterprises. At present, the information construction of enterprises is still unclear for many reasons. One of the main reasons is that enterprises have a vague understanding of informatization. The majority of enterprises must change their traditional ideas and realize the importance and necessity of informatization. The construction of enterprise informatization should not only pay attention to the construction of hardware facilities such as computers, but also pay attention to the organic combination of people, technology and management. Among them, people should be the first element and still be in the dominant position.

(4) Enterprises make rational use of limited funds. As an enterprise, we should reasonably use our limited funds, because an enterprise's investment in information construction is limited, so we must consider how to spend the least money and do more things. According to this goal, the enterprise management goal should not blindly seek the latest technology when carrying out information construction. We must adopt rolling investment methods according to the actual situation of the enterprise, carefully analyze the problems we need to solve urgently, choose a scientific and reasonable route suitable for ourselves, and make scientific and reasonable systematic arrangements for these work. Enterprises must change the blind management mode with hardware as the main investment mode, and pay attention to both hardware and software systems.

(5) Enterprise informatization should focus on the big and start with the small. At present, the characteristics of Chinese enterprises are large quantity, but the scale is generally small. Industries and cities are widely distributed, and the business situation is also mixed. Therefore, Chinese enterprises should adopt the strategy of overall plan and divisional implementation in the process of information transformation. At present, most enterprises have realized the transition from accounting type to management type in financial software, and established a relatively fixed financial system. Therefore, through the establishment of enterprise websites, we can well publicize our enterprise image to the whole society and improve the popularity of our products.

5 Conclusion

To sum up, under the tide of globalization, only by vigorously strengthening the information construction can Chinese enterprises survive and develop in the highly competitive market. The application of computer network technology has promoted the reform of enterprise management mode, made the development of enterprises more healthy and improved economic benefits. How to make computer network technology make more contributions to the macro development and micro operation of enterprises has become an important topic. I believe that with the in-depth research of this topic, computer technology will be deeply integrated into the information management of enterprises.

References

1. Osmanthus fragrans. Enterprise information analysis and decision making (1997)
2. Cao, B.: Application of computer network technology in enterprise information management. Intelligent City (05), 96–96 (2017)
3. Qin, H.: Research on the application of computer network technology in enterprise informatization. Silicon Valley (09), 97–98 (2014)
4. He, Z.: Research on the application of computer network technology in enterprise informatization. Inf. Comput. (14), 139–140 (2016)

Research on Feature Picking of Domestic Waste Sorting Based on Neural Network Training

Yufei Huang[✉], Zhengjie Lu, Jixin Sun, Bo Wang, and Shude Liao

Hechi University Key Laboratory of Artificial Intelligence and Information Processing, Hechi, China
294942615@qq.com

Abstract. Through the analysis of the status quo of domestic waste treatment, three common and recyclable domestic wastes of plastic bottles, cardboard and cans are selected as the classification samples to study the classification of the overall domestic waste. Based on MATLAB, a nerve that can be used for domestic waste sorting is designed. The network model realizes the effective classification of the domestic garbage images after real-time acquisition of the images by the camera, and borrows the MATLAB GUI toolbox to design a GUI that is easy to operate and has strong practicability. The research provides an implementation method for the effective sorting and treatment of domestic waste.

Keywords: MATLAB · Domestic waste · Neural network · GUI

1 Introduction

China is a country with a large population and its waste production is even larger. According to the statistics of the Organization for Economic Cooperation and Development, the amount of urban solid waste generated in China reached 234 million tons in 2016, an increase of 88% compared to 1996. If these rubbish are not treated timely and effectively, it will cause great damage to the living environment of mankind [1]. Effective garbage disposal includes reduction and recycling [2]. Hundreds of millions of tons of domestic waste contains a large number of valuable and recyclable resources. If these recyclable resources can be recycled and reused, then a good solution can be found to the problems of environmental pollution and resource shortage. Therefore, there is an urgent need for a method that can effectively and quickly sort domestic waste.

Behind the rapid development of the city, a series of "urban diseases" have been triggered, especially the continuous increase in the output of urban garbage and the failure to carry out reasonable and effective garbage classification and treatment, which has damaged the overall image of the city, reduced the social evaluation of the public, and brought great trouble to the people's normal life and live and work in peace and contentment. At present, "surrounded by garbage" has gradually become a common problem in the development of some cities in China. It is urgent for the city government and relevant functional departments to reasonably arrange environmental health

M. A. Jan and F. Khan (Eds.): BigIoT-EDU 2022, LNICST 467, pp. 480–490, 2023.
https://doi.org/10.1007/978-3-031-23944-1_52

control, adjust waste classification control measures in real time, and formulate corresponding urban waste classification and treatment plans, so as to better improve the city appearance, maintain the good image of the city, and improve the modern management level of the city and the people's sense of gain and happiness. At present, the dilemma of urban waste classification and treatment mainly exists in the following aspects: the people's awareness of waste classification is weak, waste classification efficiency is low, publicity and promotion efforts are weak Imperfect management system and operation mechanism [3].Therefore, the key to solving the problem of urban waste classification is to continuously strengthen the infrastructure construction of urban waste classification and treatment, strengthen ideological education, strengthen the awareness of waste classification and release and strengthen the treatment process, establish a standardized domestic waste treatment mechanism, improve the efficiency of waste treatment, and constantly popularize the long-term significance of waste classification to the society. The problem of urban waste classification and treatment is a comprehensive systematic project, which must be grasped The key points should be promoted as a whole and should not be rushed. Only by developing the effectiveness and targeted measures of urban waste classification and treatment in depth, can we effectively and reasonably treat urban waste and realize the green and sustainable development of the city.

Wang Yazhuo [4], Yang Yayu [5] and Yu Wei [6] studied and designed the sorting and recycling of recyclable waste and the utilization of the energy produced. Ciprian Cimpan [7] and others reported on the classification of domestic waste in European countries and the United States. The main methods are: through legislation to allow residents to classify household domestic waste, so as to achieve the purpose of classification of domestic waste from the source; establish single-stream material recycling facilities and lightweight packaging waste recycling facilities to separate dry mixed domestic waste, and use machinery Biological treatment(MBT) separates some wet domestic waste. Bo Fan [8] and others discussed the similarities and differences between the determinants of the household waste classification behavior in Shanghai and Singapore, and used the planned behavior theory(TPB) to construct a "motivation-intention-behavior" theoretical model, which provides a good basis for household waste classification. Ideas.

Urban ecological environment governance is a concrete manifestation of practicing the concept of ecological civilization, an important indicator to test the level and ability of urban governance, and an important foundation for urban sustainable development. The modernization drive has pushed the city forward, and at the same time, it has caused continuous pressure on the urban environment. The rapid development of urbanization has resulted in the doubling of the amount of urban domestic waste. In addition, social conflicts such as mass incidents and avoidance conflicts caused by waste site selection, landfill, incineration and environmental impact assessment occur frequently, "And other advanced value orientations, and formulated a large number of laws and regulations through top-level design. However, the limitations of the traditional government led urban domestic waste classification and treatment model restrict the implementation process of domestic waste classification policy, and domestic waste classification is difficult to achieve significant results, affecting the health of the people and the sustainable development of the city. Entering a new stage of development, facing the problem of" surrounded by garbage ", starting from the collaborative governance theory, Solving the dilemma of urban domestic waste classification and treatment through joint action has important practical significance for improving the effectiveness of environmental treatment and promoting the construction of ecological civilization.

At present, the classification and treatment of urban domestic waste is imminent. The public policy practice around the classification and treatment of domestic waste has become a major topic of urban governance, and has also attracted widespread attention in the academic community. At present, the academic research on the classification and treatment of municipal solid waste mainly focuses on four modes. First, the governance mode of the government. This model believes that the government has authoritative and legitimate resource advantages, and can rely on policies and regulations, administrative instructions and other administrative means to promote or hinder the formation and occurrence of the main behavior when dealing with the externalities in the classification and treatment of domestic waste. Some studies believe that the environmental protection work mode under the unified management of the government has cultivated the public environmental protection concept of "government dependence". People will regard the garbage problem as a public problem and a technical problem, and believe that the government and future new technologies can solve the problem of domestic garbage classification. However, more and more studies have paid attention to the "obstruction", "accommodation", "collusion" and other deviations that often occur in the implementation of household waste classification policies by grass-roots governments, and the government has the problem of * failure. The second is the governance mode of market players. The model believes that based on the regulation of the market for economic interests, the market mechanism should play a positive role in resource allocation and classified supervision. Based on the analysis perspective of the whole industry chain, Luo Yuanyuan explored the domestic waste classification and treatment mode, emphasizing the fundamental role of the market mechanism, improving the scale and efficiency of the waste classification industry, and constantly building the domestic waste classification mode of the whole industry chain. However, the competition and cooperation of market players failed to penetrate into the whole chain of domestic waste classification, and the system introduced and operated by enterprises was not standardized, which reduced the efficiency of domestic waste classification and treatment. The third is the main governance mode of the community. The model believes that the community encourages and guides community residents to jointly manage and supervise, gives full play to the democracy, incentive and cost advantages of the community in the classification and treatment of domestic waste, and solves the dilemma of domestic waste classification with community experience. Community is the field of municipal solid waste classification and treatment. The goal of municipal solid waste classification and treatment can be achieved by building a "human relationship" network and forming "face" pressure. However, the problems of community administration, resource investment and supporting laws and policies still face many obstacles L8. Fourth, the collaborative governance model. The model believes that relying on the government, enterprises, communities, the public and other multiple stakeholders, the multiple stakeholders will be included in the domestic waste classification and treatment system. Du Chunlin studied the domestic waste classification model from the perspective of three-dimensional interaction of * government market society * and believed that only by transforming the government from centralized management to diversified interactive governance pattern and exploring the implementation network of multiple subjects, can the general direction of domestic waste classification and governance be grasped and the domestic waste classification work be carried out smoothly.

This article intends to discuss the design of a waste sorting system, using neural networks to establish a model and GUI sorting interface that can quickly, efficiently and accurately identify domestic waste. In this way, the recyclable resources in the household garbage can be quickly identified and recycled, so as to reduce the damage of the household garbage to the environment and reduce the waste of resources.

2   Research Content and Plan

2.1   Collection and Arrangement of Domestic Garbage Image Data Sets

After field visits and investigations and related materials [9], the main composition and approximate proportions of inorganic and organic matter in domestic waste are determined as shown in Table 1 and Table 2, respectively.

Table 1. Main components of domestic waste (inorganic matter)

Element	Grass	Tile	Metal	Cinder and lime soil	Total
Percentage	5	35.98	0.02 –2	35–49	59–90

Table 2. Main components of domestic waste (organic matter)

Element	Animal fur	Plant	Paper	Fiber	Bamboo wood	Plastic	Total
Percentage	1–3	1–18	0.5–5	1–5	1–5	0.5–5	10–40

From the data in the above table, it can be seen that most of the domestic waste is construction waste and animal and plant debris that are not recyclable and will not cause environmental pollution. These wastes can be landfilled or composted. Among them, metals, paper, and plastics are the main ones that have recycling value and high content. Therefore, this paper decided to select three common household wastes: plastic bottles, cardboard, and cans as the samples for this study.

Use matlab tools to collect and process the characteristics of the collected sample images, and classify the image sets, and put them into different folders. After sorting, finally there are 140 photos of each type, and the entire data set has 420 photos. At the same time, image processing methods such as translation, rotation, and flipping images are used to process the data set to expand the data set and meet the data training needs of the neural network. Finally, the size of all images in the calibration data set is unified to 240 × 320, and the original image is replaced.

In order to eliminate the noise information contained in the original image, the image set is preprocessed to improve the image quality, highlight the characteristic information of the target object, and improve the recognition accuracy of the neural network. Through the research and analysis of the data set images in advance, it is found that the noise in the collected image data set is mainly high-frequency components. Therefore, the preprocessing method used in this paper is Gaussian low-pass filter. By reducing high-frequency noise, it can be Reduce the influence of noise in the image on the target features, and preserve the details in the image as much as possible.

2.2 Design

Convolutional Neural Networks (CNN) is one of the groundbreaking research results produced by combining biological neurological knowledge with artificial neural networks. It is an artificial neural network system with deep learning capabilities. Compared with convolutional neural networks Traditional methods have many advantages such as stronger applicability and generalization ability, simultaneous feature extraction and classification, fewer global optimization training parameters, etc. [10, 11].

Comparing the LeNet-5 and AlexNet network models built in matlab (see Table 3 and Fig. 1, the iteration frequency is 100 times), it can be seen that the accuracy of LeNet-5 is only about 30%, which is not suitable for picking research due to the sorting characteristics of domestic waste. While AlexNet performs well with an accuracy rate of over 90%, but the training process is very slow, making the adjustment of the model very difficult, and overfitting occurs during the training process [12]. In response to the above problems, this article combines LeNet-5 and AlexNet models, based on LeNet-5, by introducing activation layer, batch normalization layer and dropout layer, adjusting the learning rate and other adjustments to establish a convolutional neural suitable for household waste sorting Network model [13].

Table 3. Comparison of LeNet-5 and AlexNet network model training results

	The first time	The second time	The third time	The fourth time	The fifth time	Average accuracy
LeNet-5	33.33%	33.33%	33.33%	33.33%	33.33%	33.33%
AlexNet	96.73%	94.37%	93.15%	94.86%	96.43%	95.11%

2.3 Network Structure Adjustment

Commonly used activation functions include Sigmoid function, Tanh function and ReLU activation function. If only the final classification of the model is considered, the Sigmoid function and its combination are better, but the problem of gradient disappearance will occur. Therefore, the ReLU function is more appropriate when building a neural network using matlab, which is consistent with related reports. This research also chooses ReLu function as the activation function of neural network.

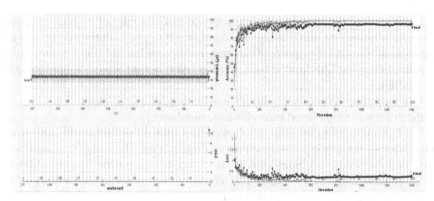

Fig. 1. Network model training results

Refer to the research of S.Ioffe, Hintion, etc., introduce the Batch Normalization (BN) algorithm and the Dropout layer to regularize each element in the output vector to make it have zero mean and unit variance, and reduce Some local feature dependence reduces the occurrence of over-fitting, thereby enhancing the generalization ability of the model, increasing the parameter learning rate, thereby improving the training effect.

Taking into account the superiority of the SGD algorithm and its compatibility with the LeNet model, it was decided to use SGD while introducing momentum to ensure the stability of the neural network, and the given learning rate was 0.01.

At the same time, because the data set used in this article is small and the classification of the results is small, the fully connected layer of LeNet-5 is relatively complicated. Therefore, this article adjusts the fully connected layer of LeNet-5. The specific method is: The sub-fully-connected layer is adjusted from 120 nodes to 36; the second-level fully-connected layer is adjusted from 84 nodes to 25; the third layer corresponds to the output of this article, which is adjusted to 3. And after the first and second fully connected layers, an activation layer, a batch normalization layer, and a dropout layer are added.

2.4   The Determination of Network Structure and Matlab Realization

After all the parameters are determined, the convolutional neural network model is officially built on matlab.

First, load the pre-processed domestic garbage image data set into matlab. Use the fullfile function to import, and the imageDatastore function to construct image data. Then the imported data set is divided into training set and verification set, the ratio of training set, verification set and test set is 6:2:2. The splitEachLabel function divides imds into imds1 and imds2, and the randomize function divides the data set randomly. Finally, the establishment of a formal network structure is carried out. as follows:

Input layer: layers = [imageInputLayer([320 240 m]);

Convolutional layer: convolution2dLaye(5,6,'stride',1,'Padding',2);

In this process, the padding function is applied to fill the edge of the image to ensure that some information about the edge of the image is not ignored during the convolution operation, and the feature map size of the image remains unchanged after the convolution.

Activation layer: This layer is the activation layer, and the activation function is the relu function.

Downsampling layer (pooling layer): maxPooling2dLayer(2,'stride',2);

Batch normalization layer: batchNormalizationLayer;

The batch normalization layer is followed by a similar convolutional layer → activation layer → pooling layer → batch normalization layer. The size of the convolution kernel of the second convolution layer is also 5 × 5, but the number is increased to 16, and the padding function is not used. The remaining parameters are the same as before.

Fully connected layer: fullyConnectedLayer(36);

dropout layer: dropoutLayer;

The second fully connected layer: fullyConnectedLayer(25);

The number of nodes in this layer is 25, followed by the activation layer → batch normalization layer → dropout layer.

The last fully connected layer: fullyConnectedLayer(3);

Assume that the number of household garbage categories to be classified is 3, so the number of nodes is 3.

Finally, Softmax regression is used as the classifier and the classification layer is defined.

Set the training parameters after the structure is built.

At this point, the neural network model is built, HuNet.mat is the neural network model obtained by training, and it can be called directly in subsequent use.

3 Experimental Result

After building the neural network and determining all the parameters, use the processed garbage image data set to train it. The training results are shown in Table 4 and Fig. 2 (the iteration frequency is 100 times).

Table 4. Neural network training results

The first time	The second time	The third time	The fourth time	The fifth time	Average accuracy
95.48%	94.52%	97.62%	95.95%	95.85%	95.90%

It can be seen that the accuracy rate of the 5 training sessions exceeds 90%, the average accuracy rate is as high as 95.66%, and the model does not appear to be over-fitting.

After training the neural network through the training set and the validation set, you need to use the test set to test the model.

Use the test set to test the model in order to evaluate the final performance and classification ability of the model. The test set is a separate pre-divided data set. The

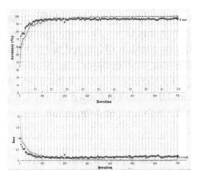

Fig. 2. Neural network training results

pictures in the test set have not appeared in the training set and the validation set, so it can better reflect the final performance of the model. Randomly select 10 images in the test set. The predicted value of the model is shown in Fig. 3. It can be seen that the predicted results are consistent with the true values.

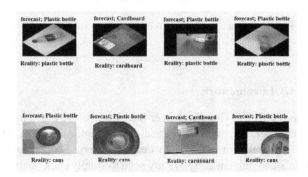

Fig. 3. Test results

4   Build Domestic Waste Identification System and GUI Framework

4.1   Construction of Domestic Waste Identification System

After the neural network model is trained, it is not possible to directly identify and sort domestic waste, and it is necessary to build a domestic waste recognition system to use the model to identify and sort domestic waste. The research content of this article is to sort the domestic garbage, so the image should be obtained through the camera in real time. The imaqhwinfo function can be used in matlab to view the information of the computer-related adapter.

To build a domestic waste recognition system, first import the previously trained neural network model. In order to ensure long-term continuous use after the program is opened, and to make the program more user-friendly, a loop statement is designed to make the program run automatically in a loop to simplify user operations. Note that the image should also be filtered at this time. Then the model is used to predict the image classification, and the prediction result is displayed on the top of the image in the form of text. In order to facilitate the user's observation, the pause function is used to delay the program for 1.5 s. Finally, after the application of the domestic waste sorting system is built, the program is tested and the result is shown in Fig. 4. The system of my hand-held express box is identified as a cardboard, and the result is accurate.

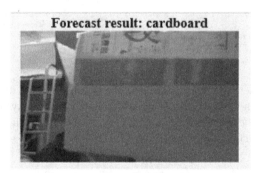

Fig. 4. Operation results of domestic waste sorting system

4.2 Building a GUI Framework

The Chinese name of GUI is Graphical User Interface. As the name implies, GUI is to display the program operation interface to the user in a graphical manner. The appearance of GUI has brought great convenience to ordinary users. People no longer need to memorize complicated commands. They only need to simply click on the corresponding windows, buttons, menus, etc. to achieve operations.

Using the GUI function of MATLAB, a graphical user interface based on the method for sorting domestic waste is designed, which further simplifies the operation of the method for sorting domestic waste and improves the practicality of the method in actual production. Use the command guide to create a GUI in matlab, and select Blank GUI (Default) in the pop-up window to create a blank GUI interface. After the GUI is created successfully, the system will automatically generate a fig file and an m file. The fig file is the vector file that saves the edited GUI user interface, and the m file is the source program file that controls the callback functions and related codes of each control., The editor can be opened and corresponding editing can be carried out, so that the user can realize specific functions when operating the corresponding GUI controls. The designed GUI interface is shown in Fig. 5a.

The interface is very simple and contains only four parts. On the top is the system name. On the left is the display area, which displays the images captured by the camera. On the right, there are two buttons "open camera" and "close camera".

In order to achieve the expected corresponding functions, write the corresponding callback functions for the two function buttons "open camera" and "close camera".

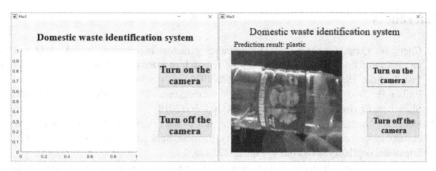

Fig. 5. GUI interface and recognition results

Among them, the "open camera" button is designed with functions: when the user clicks, the program calls the camera, captures a frame at regular intervals, and displays the image captured by the camera in the left display area. Then recognize the image and display the result on the image. "Close the camera" first sets the conditions for jumping out of the loop, then uses the closepreview function to close the camera, and sets the condition for jumping out of the loop to be j == 1, and finally this article uses the imshow(0) function to make the screen black. Figure 5b shows the identification result of the plastic bottle in hand.

When the operation is completed and the program needs to be closed, only the stand-alone "close camera" can stop the program and close the camera. At this time, the screen displays black. When you need to start the system again, the same is to "turn on the camera on a stand-alone machine".

5 Summarize

After many experiments using MATLAB's deep learning toolbox training, a stable neural network model that can be used for domestic waste sorting was obtained, and its feasibility in domestic waste sorting was verified. Based on this model, a neural network model was also designed. A household waste sorting system is set, and a GUI user interface is designed for the system.

Although the neural network built in this paper has a higher recognition accuracy for domestic garbage samples, the actual use environment is complicated and may be affected by various uncertain factors, so the performance of the system in actual use is often unsatisfactory. Suggestion:

(1) Strengthen the quantity and quality of the training set, and pick as many useful features as possible to avoid over-fitting of the model, improve the generalization application ability of the model, and avoid the influence of misinformation such as environmental noise on the model.
(2) Improve equipment performance, and then adopt more advanced algorithms and structures to design more superior models.

References

1. Chen, W., Qing, L., Lixin, L.: The influencing factors of municipal solid waste and the prediction of future trends—based on the research of inter-provincial divisions. J. Beijing Inst. Technol. (Soc. Sci. Ed.) **22**(01), 49–56 (2020)
2. Zhibin, H.: Study on the status quo and countermeasures of waste reduction classification in Shenzhen. Environ. Sanitation Eng. **22**(04), 65–66 (2014)
3. Hang, L., Nong, L.: Analysis on problems and countermeasures of urban domestic waste classification – a case study of nanning city. Environ. Sanitation Eng. **30**(01), 10–16 (2022). https://doi.org/10.19841/j.cnki.hjwsgc.2022.01.002
4. Yazhuo,W.: Research on comprehensive treatment technology of municipal solid waste based on sorting, pp. 32–40. South China University of Technology (2015)
5. Yayu, Y.: Research on municipal solid waste treatment technology and sorting equipment, pp. 17–23. Beijing Technology and Business University (2016)
6. Wei, Y.: Research on node sorting and reduction of domestic waste based on rough source classification, pp. 13–20. Huazhong University of Science and Technology (2019)
7. Cimpan, C., Maul, A., Jansen, M., Pretz, T., Wenzel, H., et al.: Central sorting and recovery of MSW recyclable materials: a review of technological state-of-the-art, cases, practice and implications for materials recycling. J. Environ. Manage. **156**, 183–193 (2015)
8. Fan, B., Yang, W., Shen, X., et al.: A comparison study of 'motivation–intention–behavior' model on household solid waste sorting in China and Singapore. J. Cleaner Prod. **211**, 5–26 (2019)
9. Debao, W., Ying, H.: Analysis of the composition and treatment methods of domestic garbage in my country. Environ. Sanitation Eng. **18**(1), 41–44 (2010)
10. LeCun, Y., Bottou, L., Bengio, Y., Haffner, P., et al.: Gradient-based learning applied to document recognition. Proc. IEEE. **86**, 2278–2324 (1988)
11. Krizhevsky, A., Sutskever, I., Hinton, G.E., et al.: ImageNet classification with deep convolutional neural networks. In: Advances in Neural Information Processing Systems, vol. 25, no. 2 (2012)
12. Hinton, G.E., Srivastava, N., Krizhevsky, A., et al.: Improving neural networks by preventing co-adaptation of feature detectors. Comput. Sci. **3**(4), 212–223 (2012)
13. Kingma Diederik, P., Adam, B.J.: A method for stochastic optimization. arXiv preprint arXiv: 1412.6980 (2014)

Optimization of Extraction Technology of Sophora Tonkinensis Gagnep. by Orthogonal Test Based on Information Entropy Weighting Method

Yanping Wang, Huiying Zhang, Peng Zhang, Jianjing Lan, Hailin Chen, Feiyan Wei, and Zheng Wei[✉]

College of Chemical and Biological Engineering, Hechi University, Hechi 546300, Guangxi, China
292308137@qq.com

Abstract. The L9(34) orthogonal experimental design was carried out with four factors including di-chloromethane-40% ammonia concentration ratio, solid-liquid ratio, extraction time and extraction power. The content of genistein, oxymatrine, matrine, daucostalin and chrysan-thin in the extract was calculated by information entropy weighting method, and the comprehensive score was obtained by weighted treatment. The optimum process was selected by orthogonal analysis with comprehensive score. The optimum extraction process was as follows: dichloromethane-40% ammonia concentration ratiois is 25:1.0, solid-liquid ratio is 1:30, the extraction time is 20 min, and the extraction power is 80 W. The average value of five validation experiments was 0.180. The results showed that the optimized extraction process was stable and feasible, and the extraction rate was high.

Keywords: Sophora tonkinensis · HPLC · Orthogonal test · Extraction technology · Information entropy

1 Introduction

Yam Root is a species of Sophora japonica in legume family (Sophora tonkinensis Gagnep.). Dry rhizome of, Also known as bitter bean root, Broad bean root, Coptis chinensis, Sanxiaoye mountain bean root, Doulian and Robinia pseudoacacia, etc. Recorded in Chinese Pharmacopoeia 2015 Edition, As a traditional Chinese medicine, Kidney bean root has the function of clearing heat and detoxifying, Detumescence and diuresis, Functions of relieving fire and moisturizing [1], Indications: dry mouth and throat, Red tongue and yellow fur, Sore throat, swelling and aching of gum, Lung heat, cough, constipation, yellow urine and many other clinical symptoms [2]. Modern pharmacological research shows that, Flavonoids and alkaloids from the root of kidney bean are antibacterial, It is effective in anti-virus, anti-cancer, anti-inflammatory and improving immunity [3–6]. Yam Root contains alkaloids, flavonoids, polysaccharides, etc.,

M. A. Jan and F. Khan (Eds.): BigIoT-EDU 2022, LNICST 467, pp. 491–501, 2023.
https://doi.org/10.1007/978-3-031-23944-1_53

Among them, alkaloids are the main active components. Pharmacological studies show that the alkaloids of Radix Sophorae have anti-inflammatory properties [7], antiviral [8], Antibacterial [9] And other activities. The root of kidney bean mainly contains alkaloids such as matrine, Oxymatrine, genistein and methylgenistein [10, 11], Flavonoids such as sophoricin, sandalwood glycoside, horsebean root color dihydroflavone, quercetin, rutin, etc. [12], Triterpenoids, small molecular phenols and other chemical components such as lupin alcohol and Sophorae glycol [13]. Alkaloids have many activities, including antitumor, antiviral, antibacterial, anti-inflammatory, analgesic, cardiovascular, insecticidal and so on Yang Fan [14] The extraction and the activity of the crude extract of Sophora japonica were studied, The results showed that the crude extract had good antioxidant activity; Matrine and Oxymatrine can inhibit the proliferation of mdcc-msb (Marek's disease tumor cells) Xu Haitang et al. [15] The research shows that the extracts of mountain bean root extracted with different solvents (chloroform, ethyl acetate, n-butanol, ethanol) have certain antioxidant activities, It also showed a certain inhibitory effect on 7 experimental bacteria (Staphylococcus aureus, Escherichia coli, Proteus vulgaris, Pseudomonas aeruginosa, Klebsiella pneumoniae, Streptococcus haemolyticus B, Candida albicans). At present, although there are some studies on the same genus plants of guan-zunshan Dougen, there are few reports on the extraction methods and activities of alkaloids from guanzhenshan Dougen. As a traditional Chinese medicine, Radix Sophorae has attracted extensive attention because its alkaloids have a variety of pharmacological activities. Traditional extraction techniques, such as percolation [16] (The specific extraction conditions are: The percolation solution is 0.4% hydrochloric acid solution, and the percolation flow rate is 5 ml/min. Collect 10 times the amount of solution Under this technological condition, the extraction rate of extract is 6.8%, and the extraction rate of matrine is 0.331%); Decocting method [17] (In the study, it was found that the contents of matrine and Oxymatrine reached 0.748% and 0.0996% respectively after soaking for 12 h and decocting for 3 times, each time for 1.5 h.); Warm immersion method [18] (The specific extraction conditions are as follows: the extraction temperature is 60 °C, and the extraction is twice For the first time, add 8 times of 0.4% hydrochloric acid aqueous solution and extract for 4 h. for the second time, add 6 times of 0.4% hydrochloric acid aqueous solution and extract for 4 h Under this technological condition, the yield of dry extract is 7.0% The extraction rate of matrine was 0.298%); reflux [19] (The technological conditions were as follows: 10 times of 65% ethanol, reflux extraction time 2 h, extraction twice Under this condition, the average extraction rates of total alkaloids, matrine, Oxymatrine and extract yield were 1.719%, 0.228%, 0.914% and 16.73% respectively). It has the disadvantages of low extraction efficiency and long time-consuming. Microwave method [20] (The technological conditions are: microwave power 500 W, microwave extraction time 20 min, microwave temperature 75 °C, ethanol volume fraction 80%, solid-liquid ratio 1:40 Under these conditions, the extraction rate of matrine from Radix Sophorae was 0.963%). Ultrasonic method (The technological conditions were as follows: ethanol concentration 40%, solid-liquid ratio 1:20, extraction time 1.5 h, extraction twice Under these conditions, the yield of total alkaloids from the root of Sophora is 16.7137 mg/g), Semi bionic method (The process conditions are as follows: add 10 times the amount of aqueous solution each time, soak for 30 min, and then reflux extraction for 3 times. The pH value of each water is 4.5,

7.5, 9.0, and the extraction time is 1.5, 0.75, 0.75 h. Under this process condition, the average yield of oxymatrine is 4.029 g, and the average yield of dry extract is 0.239 g/g.) And other modern extraction technologies, It effectively improves the extraction efficiency of alkaloids from Radix Sophorae, and provides a new idea for its industrial production As the society pays more attention to traditional Chinese medicine, it is of great significance to screen the best extraction process of active components from Radix Sophorae in the field of medicine and industrial production. This experiment uses information entropy to calculate the weight of each index, which provides a theoretical basis for the comprehensive evaluation of traditional Chinese medicine extraction.

2 Materials and Methods

2.1 Materials and Instruments

Yam Root medicinal material, purchased from the medicinal material market in Yizhou District, Hechi City, Guangxi, It was identified as a species of leguminous plant Sophora japonica by Associate Professor Deng Xichao, School of chemistry and Bioengineering, Hechi University (Sophora tonkinensis Gagnep.). Dry rhizome of Matrine reference (Batch number MUST-18040911, mass fraction 98.00%), Oxymatrine reference (Batch number MUST-18041310, mass fraction 98.00%), Genistein reference substance (Batch number MUST-18031516, mass fraction 98.00%), Santalin reference substance of clover bean (Batch number MUST-17060508, mass fraction 98.00%), Sophoricin reference substance (Batch number MUST-17060512, mass fraction 99.99%), All purchased from Chengdu mansite Biotechnology Co., Ltd; Methanol and acetonitrile are chromatographically pure, Produced by Thermo Fisher Scientific (China) Co., Ltd; Ammonium acetate and dichloromethane are analytical pure and produced by Sinopharm Chemical Reagent Co., Ltd; Pure water and ultra pure water are prepared by fusion ultra pure water integration mechanism.

Wkh-1.7-a hot air circulation oven, Qingzhou Jingcheng medical equipment manufacturing Co., Ltd; Shz-d (III) circulating water vacuum pump, Gongyi Yuhua Instrument Co., Ltd; Kq-500de numerical control ultrasonic cleaner, Kunshan Ultrasonic Instrument Co., Ltd; Me204e electronic balance, Mettler Toledo instruments (Shanghai) Co., Ltd; Fusion ultra pure water all in one machine, Ruitai pure water Co., Ltd; De-400g high speed multifunctional powder machine, Zhejiang Hongjingtian industry and Trade Co., Ltd; Lc-20a high performance liquid chromatograph, Configure sil-20ac autosampler, Dgu-20a5r degasser, Lc-20at quaternion pump, Cto-20ac column temperature box, Spd-m20a photodiode array ultraviolet visible light detector, Shimadzu production office of Kyoto Corporation, Japan.

2.2 Test Method

2.2.1 Preparation of Test Article

The kidney bean root is removed from excess sundries and leaves, cut into small pieces, dried in the oven at 60 °C, crushed with a pulverizer, sieved through a 50 target standard screen, and used for standby. Accurately weigh 0.5 g of mountain bean root powder into a conical flask, and add a certain volume and concentration of dichloromethane-40% ammonia water mixture, Dense plug, weigh the mass, test in the ultra-sonic extractor according to the set extraction power and extraction time, and weigh the weight after the test, Fill the weight, shake well, filter by suction, put the filtrate into the evaporating dish, ventilate and volatilize dry, and add an appropriate amount of analytical pure methanol to the residue to dissolve, Dilute to the scale with a 10 ml volumetric flask and shake well. The specification is 0.45 μM microporous filter membrane to obtain the test solution, and the filtrate is placed in the sample bottle for standby.

2.2.2 Preparation of Reference Solution

Accurately weigh the control samples of genistein, Oxymatrine, matrine, santalin and galvisol respectively (dry to constant weight) 2.40 mg, 6.00 mg, 2.30 mg, 2.30 mg and 2.90 mg, Put it into a 25 ml volumetric flask, add pure methanol, dilute to the scale and shake well, A mixed standard solution of genistein (0.096 mg/ml), Oxymatrine (0.240 mg/ml), matrine (0.092 mg/ml), santalin (0.092 mg/ml) and sophoricin (0.116 mg / ml) was prepared.

2.2.3 Liquid Chromatography Conditions

The chromatographic column is aq-c18 (5 μm, 4.6 mm × 250 mm), using acetonitrile (a) −0.01 mol/l ammonium acetate solution (b) as the mobile phase for gradient elution, the elution procedure is: 0–15 min, 10% a; 25 min, 15%A; 35 min, 35%A; 45 min, 50%A; 55 min, 55%A; 70 min, 55% a. the flow rate is 0.8 ml/min, and the injection volume is 10 μ 50. Detection wavelength 225 nm, column temperature 30 °C.

2.2.4 Investigation of Linear Relationship

Accurately measure the mixed reference solution of genistein, santalin, matrine, sophoricin and Oxymatrine prepared under "1.2.2", according to 2 μ L, 5 μ L, 8 μ L, 10 μ L and 15 μ L is injected into the high performance liquid chromatograph, and its peak area is determined under the chromatographic conditions of "1.2.3".

2.2.5 Precision Inspection

Accurately suck the mixed reference solution of "1.2.2", inject the sample for 6 times continuously according to the chromatographic conditions of "1.2.3", measure the peak areas of 5 chromatographic peaks, and calculate the RSD value of peak areas.

2.2.6 Repeatability Inspection

Accurately weigh 6 samples prepared in orthogonal test 1 of "2.7", prepare the test solution according to the method under "1.2.1", inject samples respectively according to the chromatographic conditions of "1.2.3", measure the peak area, and calculate the RSD value of 5 chromatographic peaks.

2.2.7 Stability Investigation

Take the No. 1 test sample solution of the repeatability test in item "1.2.6", place it at room temperature for 0 h, 2 h, 4 h, 6 h, 12 h and 24 h, and conduct sample injection analysis according to the chromatographic conditions in item "1.2.3", determine the peak area of 5 peaks, and calculate the RSD value of 5 chromatographic peaks.

2.2.8 Sample Recovery Test

Accurately measure 5 ml of 6 samples with known concentration, prepare them according to orthogonal test 1 under "2.7", put them into a 25 ml volumetric flask, add 5 ml of mixed reference solution according to 100% of the content of the test solution, dissolve them with methanol, dilute them to the scale, shake them well, and determine them under the chromatographic conditions under "1.2.3".

2.2.9 Content Determination

Prepare the test solution according to "1.2.1", inject and analyze the sample according to the chromatographic conditions of "1.2.3", and analyze the five chromatographic peaks of genistein, Oxymatrine, matrine, santalin and sophoricin.

2.2.10 Orthogonal Experimental Design

Through the single factor investigation results of the pre experiment, four investigation factors, namely dichloromethane-40% ammonia concentration ratio, solid-liquid ratio, extraction power and extraction time, were determined, and three levels were taken for each factor (see Table 1). Taking the extraction rate of genistein, Oxymatrine, matrine, sandal-wood glycoside and sophoricin as the evaluation index, the extraction conditions of the effective active components of Radix Sophorae were optimized by using L9 (34) four factor three level orthogonal experimental design.

Table 1. Orthogonal design factors and levels

Level	Factor			
	A power/W	B Dichloromethane-40% ammonia concentration ratio	C time/min	D Feed liquid ratio/(g:mL)
1	80	25:0.5	20	1:40
2	90	25:1.0	30	1:50
3	100	25:1.5	40	1:60

3 Results and Analysis

3.1 HPLC Fingerprint

According to the sample injection analysis of the test solution of mountain bean root under the condition of "1.2.3", the chromatographic peak resolution of genistein, Oxymatrine, matrine, santalin and homosophorin is good, and the resolution between each peak is greater than 1.5. See Fig. 1 for the chromatogram.

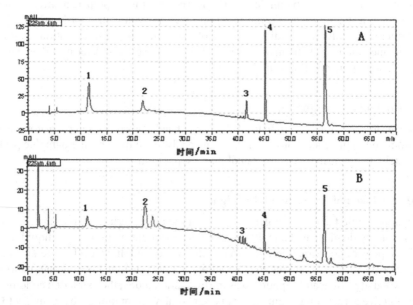

1-genistein; 2-oxymatrine; 3-matrine; 4-sophoricin; 5-santalin from clover bean.

Fig. 1. HPLC diagram of mixed reference solution (a) and test solution (b)

3.2 Investigation of Linear Relationship

The standard working curve is drawn with the concentration of each monomer in the control mixture as the abscissa X and the peak area value a as the ordinate y. The regression equation and correlation coefficient are obtained, as shown in Table 2.

3.3 Precision Inspection

The RSD value of peak area is 1.25%–1.98%, indicating that the precision of the instrument is good.

Table 2. Regression equation and correlation coefficient of each monomer of mixed liquid

Alkaloid	Regression equation	Correlation coefficient	Linear range/μg
Genistein	Y = 112 484X − 7 224.8	0.9995	0.192–1.440
Oxymatrine	Y = 113 802X − 25 564	0.9995	0.480–3.600
Matrine	Y = 96 539X + 8 839.6	0.9976	0.184–1.380
Sandalwood glycoside of clover bean	Y = 337 413X − 271.53	1.0000	0.184–1.380
Sophoricin	Y = 504 994X − 2 370.5	0.9999	0.232–1.740

3.4 Repeatability Inspection

The RSD value of peak area is 1.45%–2.05%, indicating that the method has good repeatability.

3.5 Stability Investigation

The RSD value of the peak area of the stability investigation of the five index components is 1.43%–2.18%, indicating that the stability of the sample is good, and the test solution is stable within 24 h.

3.6 Sample Recovery Test

The average recovery of genistein was 99.82%, and the RSD value was 1.63%; The average recovery of oxymatrine was 98.78% and RSD was 2.15%; The average recovery rate of matrine was 99.56%, and the RSD value was 1.87%; The average recovery of santalin was 99.34% and RSD was 1.93%; The average recovery rate of sophoricin was 99.23%, and the RSD value was 2.18%.

3.7 Orthogonal Test

3.7.1 Orthogonal Test Results

According to the linear regression equation, calculate the content of five index components of the sample obtained from each orthogonal test, and calculate the extraction rate of each index component. See Table 3 for the test results.

3.7.2 Orthogonal Experimental Analysis Based on Information EnTropy Weighting

Calculate the information entropy of each index (Hi): Hi = [0.976 0.977 0.899 0.960 0.991].

Calculate the coefficient of index I(Wi): Wi = [0.122 0.117 0.513 0.203 0.046].

Table 3. Orthogonal experimental scheme and results

Serial number	A	B	C	D	Extraction amount /(mg/g)					Comprehensive evaluation index m
					Matrine	Oxymatrine	Genistein	Sandalwood glycoside of clover bean	Sophoricin	
1	1	1	1	1	0.147	8.714	0.278	0.207	0.456	0.120
2	1	2	2	2	0.167	8.794	0.248	0.454	0.536	0.069
3	1	3	3	3	0.116	7.211	0.264	0.252	0.507	0.098
4	2	1	2	3	0.114	4.526	0.212	0.231	0.457	0.038
5	2	2	3	1	0.039	8.103	0.285	0.158	0.511	0.138
6	2	3	1	2	0.180	8.515	0.339	0.473	0.786	0.183
7	3	1	3	2	0.044	7.842	0.352	0.450	0.721	0.109
8	3	2	1	3	0.021	8.471	0.079	0.152	0.603	0.078
9	3	3	2	1	0.024	7.263	0.243	0.430	0.717	0.168
K_1	0.096	0.089	0.127	0.142						
K_2	0.120	0.095	0.092	0.120						
K_3	0.118	0.150	0.115	0.071						
R	0.024	0.061	0.035	0.071						

Comprehensive evaluation index $Mm = P1m \times W1 + P2m \times W2 + P3m \times W3 + P4m \times W4 + P5m \times W5$, That is, the weight coefficients of genistein, Oxymatrine, matrine, sandalwood rosewood glycoside and gaolihuaisu are as follows: 0.122, 0.117, 0.513, 0.203 and 0.046.

After the calculation of the index content of mountain bean root, according to the formula and steps, the original evaluation index matrix is established, which takes genistein, Oxymatrine, matrine, santalin and gaolihuaisu as the original evaluation index matrix, and the original evaluation matrix (x) is:

$$
X = \begin{bmatrix}
0.278 & 0.248 & 0.264 & 0.212 & 0.285 & 0.339 & 0.352 & 0.079 & 0.243 \\
8.714 & 8.794 & 7.211 & 4.526 & 8.103 & 8.515 & 7.842 & 8.471 & 7.263 \\
0.147 & 0.167 & 0.116 & 0.114 & 0.039 & 0.180 & 0.044 & 0.021 & 0.024 \\
0.207 & 0.454 & 0.252 & 0.231 & 0.158 & 0.473 & 0.450 & 0.152 & 0.430 \\
0.456 & 0.536 & 0.507 & 0.457 & 0.511 & 0.786 & 0.721 & 0.603 & 0.717
\end{bmatrix}
$$

Calculate PIJ and convert the initial matrix into a "probability" matrix (P):

$$
P = \begin{bmatrix}
0.121 & 0.108 & 0.115 & 0.092 & 0.124 & 0.147 & 0.153 & 0.034 & 0.106 \\
0.137 & 0.139 & 0.114 & 0.071 & 0.128 & 0.134 & 0.124 & 0.039 & 0.114 \\
0.173 & 0.196 & 0.136 & 0.134 & 0.045 & 0.211 & 0.051 & 0.025 & 0.028 \\
0.074 & 0.162 & 0.090 & 0.082 & 0.056 & 0.168 & 0.160 & 0.054 & 0.153 \\
0.086 & 0.101 & 0.096 & 0.086 & 0.097 & 0.148 & 0.136 & 0.114 & 0.136
\end{bmatrix}
$$

3.7.3 Analysis of Variance of Orthogonal Test

By introducing the information entropy weighting method to process and analyze the orthogonal test data, it is concluded that the order of factors affecting the yield of effective active components of Radix Sophorae is: d > b > C > A, that is, the material liquid ratio has the greatest influence on the extraction of Radix Sophorae, while the extraction power has the least influence According to the comprehensive analysis, the optimal extraction condition is a2b3c1d1, that is, the concentration of dichloromethane-40% ammonia is 25 : 1.5, the ratio of material to liquid is 1 : 40, the extraction power is 90 W, and the extraction time is 20 min. As shown in Table 4:

Table 4. Analysis of variance

Source of variance	Sum of squared deviations	Freedom	F ratio	F critical value	Significance
A	0.001	2	0.222	4.460	*
B	0.007	2	1.556	4.460	*
C	0.002	2	0.444	4.460	*
D	0.008	2	1.778	4.460	*
Error	0.02	8			

3.8 Validation Experiment

According to the experimental results determined above, the effective active components of Radix Sophorae are extracted according to the best technological conditions, and the validation test is carried out in parallel with 5 samples. The content of each index component in the extract is measured, and the comprehensive score is calculated. The results are basically consistent with the results of orthogonal test, indicating that this process is stable and reliable.

4 Conclusion

There are many chemical components in the root of kidney bean, among which alkaloids, flavonoids and polysaccharides are the main active substances With the development of industrial production, people have done a lot of research on the extraction process. Although much work has been done on the extraction process of alkaloids, especially matrine and Oxymatrine, the best process still needs further study. At present, there is little research on the extraction technology of flavonoids and polysaccharides, which has a certain impact on the development of its resources It is believed that in the future research, the relevant problems will be gradually solved, and the industrialization of Radix Sophorae will be accelerated to meet the needs of the society In this experiment, dichloromethane ammonia water mixture was used as the extraction agent, and the extraction rates of genistein, Oxymatrine, matrine, santalin and sophoricin were used as indicators. The orthogonal experimental design method was used to study the technological conditions of ultrasonic extraction of active components from Radix Sophorae, and the best extraction technological conditions were screened. The primary and secondary factors affecting ultrasonic extraction are Feed liquid ratio > dichloromethane: 40% ammonia water volume ratio > Extraction time > Extract power Considering the content of five indicators and the evaluation of their extraction rate, the optimal extraction process is di-chloromethane-40% ammonia concentration ratio 25:1.5, solid-liquid ratio 1:40, extraction power 90 W, extraction time 20 min Methodological investigation showed that the extraction process parameters were true and reliable, and suitable for the extraction of effective active components from Radix Sophorae.

Mountain bean root is a kind of common traditional Chinese medicine, which belongs to the third grade endangered protected plant in China. It is usually harvested in autumn Yam Root is mainly used to treat sore throat, sore tongue, damp heat jaundice, swelling and heat pain caused by mosquito bites and other diseases In this experiment, the information entropy weighting method is used to calculate the weight coefficients of genistein, Oxymatrine, matrine, santalin and takamorin, and scientifically deal with the weight of each index on the process. A higher extraction rate is obtained from the extraction of the index components of mountain bean root.

References

1. National Pharmacopoeia Committee Pharmacopoeia of the people's Republic of China (Vol. I). China Pharmaceutical Science and Technology Press, Beijing, p. 27 (2015)
2. Gehongqiang. Clinical application and research of Radix Sophorae. Shizhen Nat. Med. (11), 1036 (2000)
3. Tan, C., Fang, H., Hutingjun.: Research progress on bioactive components and pharmacological effects of Radix Sophorae. J. Guangxi Agric. **40**(11), 1494–1497 (2009)
4. Qian, L., Dai, W., Zhouguoqin, et al.: Study on analgesic and anti-inflammatory effects of main alkaloids of Sophora flavescens and Radix Sophorae. Chin. Patent Med. **34**(8), 1593–1596 (2012)
5. Xiao, Z., Song, J., Xu, Z., et al.: Effects of water extract from Radix Sophorae on proliferation and metabolism of human hepatoma cells in vitro. J. Shandong Univ. Tradit. Chin. Med. **24**(1), 63–65 (2000)
6. Xiao, P., Kubo, H., Ohsawa, M., et al.: Kappa-opioid receptor-mediated antinociceptive, effects of stereoisomers and derivatives of(+)-matrinein mice. Planta Med. **65**(3), 230–233 (1999)
7. He, L.J., Liu, J.S., Luo, D., et al.: Quinolizidine alkaloids from Sophora tonkinensis and their anti - inflammatory activities. Fitoterapia **139**, 104391 (2019)
8. Ding, P.L., Huang, H., Zhou, P., et al.: Quinolizidine alkaloids withanti - HBV activity from Sophora tonkinensis. Planta Med. **72**(9), 854–856 (2006)
9. Dai, W., Qian, L., Yang, S., et al.: Study on antibacterial activity of alkaloids and total alkaloids from Sophora flavescens and Vicia faba root. Chin. J. Exp. Formulary **18**(3), 177–180 (2012)
10. Peilan, D.: Comparative Study on Chemical Constituents of Radix Sophorae Flavescentis and Radix Sophorae Flavescentis. Fudan University, Shanghai (2004)
11. Li, X.N., Lu, Z.Q., Qin, S., et al.: Tonkinensines A and B, two novel alkaloids from Sophoratonkinensis. Tetrahed. Lett. **49**(23), 3797–3801 (2008)

12. Li, X., Yan, H., Pang, X., et al.: Study on the chemical constituents of flavonoids in the root of Sophora. Chin. J. Tradit. Chin. Med. **34**(3), 282–285 (2009)
13. Wang, J., Cui, Y.: Research progress on chemical constituents, pharmacological effects and toxicity of Radix Sophorae. Chin. J. Exp. Formulary **17**(4), 229–232 (2011)
14. Yang, F.: Extraction and isolation of alkaloids from sophoraalopecuroides and their antioxidant and anti-tumor activities. Changchun Normal University, Changchun (2012)
15. Xu, H., Lu, J., Zhao, Y., et al.: Antioxidant and antibacterial activity of extracts from Sophoratonkinensis Gagnep. Food Ind. Sci. Technol. **36**(14), 111–114 (2015)
16. Yanming, L., Wei, G.: Comparative study on different extraction methods of matrine from the root of kidney bean. Chem. Technol. Develop. **37**(4), 22–24 (2008)
17. Huangjiwei, Qu., C., Zhuang, H., et al.: Optimization experiment on the decocting technology of Yam root. Tradit. Chin. Med. **28**(4), 339–340 (2005)
18. Yang, X., Bao, Y., Wang, S., et al.: Optimization of extraction process of total alkaloids from Radix Sophorae by central composite design response surface methodology. Shizhen National Med. **30**(8), 1822–1824 (2019)
19. Meng, M., Wang, H., Ren, Y., et al.: Optimization of extraction technology of effective parts of Radix Sophorae by orthogonal test. Chin. J. Exp. Formulary **19**(6), 46–49 (2013)
20. Wang, Y., Wang, Y., Zhu, B.: Microwave assisted extraction of matrine from the root of Sophora. Pesticides **50**(5), 29–31 (2011)

Mechatronics Design of Silkworm Frame Automatic Shelving in Intelligent Silkworm Rearing System

Mengji Chen$^{(\boxtimes)}$, Zhengjie Lu, and Shanye Su

School of Artificial Intelligence and Smart Manufacturing, Hechi University,
Yizhou 546300, China
782723236@qq.com

Abstract. Mulberry and sericulture industry is an important economic sector in Yizhou District of Guangxi and a key industry for the development of Yizhou district. However, at present, the personnel engaged in silkworm breeding in Yizhou are too old, lack of labor force, and the level of mechanization is not high. In particular, most of the silkworm frame handling process is manual operation, resulting in low labor efficiency; At present, most silkworm breeding is ground breeding, and the space utilization rate is low. In view of the above problems, this paper puts forward the mechatronics design of automatic putting on the shelf of silkworm frame under the concept of intelligent silkworm breeding system, in order to improve the mechanization of silkworm breeding, promote the development of silkworm breeding to elevated and improve the utilization rate of breeding space.

Keywords: Silkworm machinery · Silkworm frame on the shelf · Structural design · Control system

1 Introduction

The traditional silkworm breeding process is usually carried out on the ground, which needs to occupy a lot of land area, and the space utilization rate of silkworm breeding area is not high. In recent years, in order to solve this problem, some silkworm breeding workers have gradually developed the silkworm breeding process to the elevated level, which has improved the space utilization rate. Therefore, based on the concept of intelligent sericulture system, the design of a silkworm frame automatic shelving device can promote the development of silkworm breeding industry to the elevated direction, speed up the development process from traditional sericulture to modern sericulture, improve the mechanization level of silkworm production and improve production efficiency [1].

Therefore, based on the concept of intelligent sericulture system, the design of a silkworm frame automatic shelving device can promote the development of silkworm breeding industry to the elevated direction, speed up the development process from traditional sericulture to modern sericulture, improve the mechanization level of silkworm production and improve production efficiency.

© ICST Institute for Computer Sciences, Social Informatics and Telecommunications Engineering 2023
Published by Springer Nature Switzerland AG 2023. All Rights Reserved
M. A. Jan and F. Khan (Eds.): BigIoT-EDU 2022, LNICST 467, pp. 502–512, 2023.
https://doi.org/10.1007/978-3-031-23944-1_54

2   Overall Design Scheme of Silkworm Frame Automatic Shelving System

2.1   System Design Idea

This design is proposed under the concept of intelligent silkworm rearing system, as shown in Fig. 1 below. The intelligent silkworm rearing system mainly realizes the automation of silkworm rearing process and completes the functions of silkworm frame transportation, access, disinfection, leaf feeding and so on. The working process is to take out the silkworm frame from the silkworm rack, transport the silkworm frame to the leaf feeding system and disinfection system through vertical and horizontal transportation, and then transport it back to the silkworm rack for storage. Through the system assembly line work, the efficiency of sericulture is improved and the labor force is reduced. This paper mainly studies the silkworm frame lifting transportation system [2].

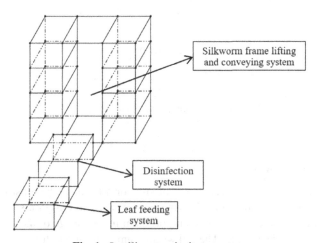

Fig. 1. Intelligent sericulture system

The mechatronics system design of silkworm frame automatic shelving device determines the shape design and size of its mechanical structure by comprehensively considering the working state and process of the device and the actual production application, and then analyzes, calculates and selects each mechanism. The first is to analyze the design of the silkworm frame transported from the previous silkworm raising process into the automatic rack device of the silkworm frame and the lifting and transportation of the silkworm frame in the silkworm raising process of the intelligent silkworm raising system, including the calculation, analysis and design of the combination of key chain and sprocket, as well as the calculation and selection of transmission shaft and hoist. Secondly, the design of the silkworm frame moving horizontally into the elevated floor is analyzed. The design of rodless cylinder linear mechanism can transport the silkworm frame into the elevated floor smoothly. The main parts of the silkworm frame automatic shelving device are designed step by step, and then the combination design of the overall framework is carried out. The designed silkworm frame automatic shelving device should have the characteristics of high work efficiency, simple operation and low maintenance cost in practical application. The overall structure of the system is shown in Fig. 2 below [3]:

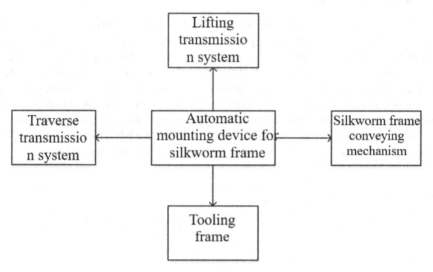

Fig. 2. Overall system structure

2.2 Lifting Mechanism

The vertical reciprocating transportation of silkworm frame is the most important part of the silkworm frame automatic shelving device. How to design a safe and efficient lifting mechanism is the key and difficult problem in the design of the silkworm frame automatic shelving device [4]. The silkworm frame lifting and transportation process is that when the silkworm frame is transported to the lifting mechanism, the elevator lifts and transports the silkworm frame to the corresponding silkworm rack. Based on the structural characteristics of the silkworm frame, there must be a lifting platform to carry the silkworm frame during the lifting and transportation process. The lifting platform often needs counterweight for balance. The schematic diagram of the lifting and transportation process is shown in Fig. 3 [5].

Referring to the design of lifting and transverse three-dimensional garage, there are three commonly used lifting mechanism transmission modes on the market: hydraulic transmission, chain transmission and lifting and steel wire rope transmission and lifting. Although the hydraulic transmission has large power, it is difficult to achieve rapid movement. The silkworm frame has a high, which will greatly reduce the efficiency of silkworm frame lifting and transportation. In addition, the design of such a large stroke hydraulic cylinder is also a difficult problem [6]. The hydraulic transmission is suitable for large and heavy mechanical equipment with low requirements for transmission accuracy. The lifting system of small mechanical equipment should not use the hydraulic transmission system.

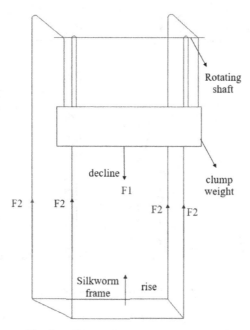

Fig. 3. Lifting and transportation diagram

Steel wire rope lifting has the advantages of large bearing capacity, light weight, small occupied space, etc. However, because the steel wire rope is elastic, long-term lifting of heavy objects may lead to lengthening, and under frequent lifting impact, it may lead to steel wire fracture, difficult maintenance, and greatly affect the safety; The service life of steel wire rope is also low, so it should be replaced frequently, and the cost is high [7].

Chain drive, as can be seen from the mechanical design, chain drive has the advantages of large bearing capacity, low cost and strong adaptability. It can operate normally and stably even under the condition of poor environment such as high temperature, oil stain and dust [8]. The chain drive uses the motor as the power source to drive the transmission shaft to rotate. The upper and lower transmission shafts are driven by the sprocket mounted gear and closed chain. Compared with belt drive, chain drive has accurate transmission ratio and can be used in various harsh environments. Especially in low-speed and heavy load, it has high efficiency and is widely used [9].

Through the analysis of the above three common lifting methods, it is decided to use the chain drive as the lifting mechanism. The motor is used as the power source, the chain and sprocket are meshed to transmit power, drive the transmission shaft to rotate, and drive the device to move up and down. The lifting transmission system designed by the device is shown in Fig. 4 below:

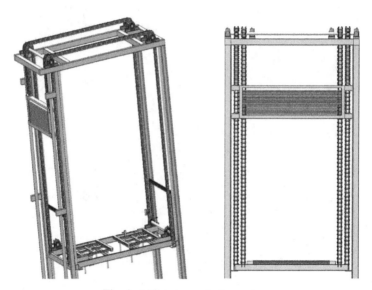

Fig. 4. Lifting transmission system

2.3   Traverse Mechanism

The traverse mechanism is also the main motion mechanism of the silkworm frame automatic shelving device. After the lifting mechanism completes the lifting purpose of the silkworm frame, the traverse mechanism is responsible for pushing the silkworm frame into the silkworm frame for storage. The action to be completed by the traverse mechanism is to push the silkworm frame into the frame and pull the silkworm frame out of the frame. In this process, the guide rail is required to fix and move, and a frame pushing device is required. However, since the silkworm frame is on both left and right sides, the traverse process requires the frame pushing device mechanism to rotate 180° backward. The action function diagram to be realized by the traverse mechanism is shown in Fig. 5.

Among the existing products on the market, the traverse mechanism is widely used in three-dimensional garages. The more common traverse mechanisms include crawler traverse mechanism, chain drive traverse mechanism, fork comb traverse mechanism and sliding fork traverse mechanism. Among them, the crawler type traverse mechanism is mainly transported through the operation of the crawler; The chain driven traverse mechanism is equipped with a carrier plate, which is driven to move through the chain drive; The sliding fork type traverse mechanism is also equipped with a carrier plate, which can drive the carrier plate to access goods by installing a sliding fork on the lifting table; There is no pallet in the fork comb traverse mechanism. As long as the fork comb is set between the lifting table and the storage rack, the goods can be accessed and stored through the staggered movement between the forks and combs.

Based on the structural characteristics of the silkworm frame and the consideration that it is stored on the relatively narrow elevated floor, the above-mentioned transverse structures in different ways are not suitable for the automatic shelf loading device of

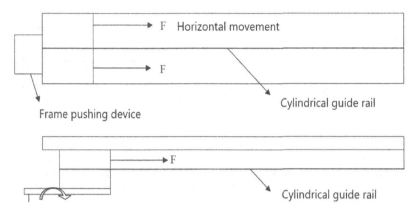

Fig. 5. Diagram of traverse mechanism

the silkworm frame. According to the reliability, durability, construction cost and other characteristics of the design, a transverse push structure that conforms to various characteristic parameters of the silkworm frame is redesigned. The main functions of the designed traverse pushing mechanism and the matters needing attention are as follows: the designed traverse mechanism should be able to complete the access process of the silkworm frame smoothly, efficiently and accurately. While ensuring the completion of the access function, the device should be as light and small as possible, the structure should be as simple as possible, and should be durable, with low installation and manufacturing costs and simple maintenance. The traverse mechanism mainly includes a fixed frame, a rodless cylinder, a rotating cylinder and a silkworm frame grabbing mechanism. When the mechanism works, the slide rail is driven by the air cylinder to move back and forth in a straight line, so as to drive the silkworm frame grabbing mechanism to push the silkworm frame in a straight line, and complete the function of storing and storing the silkworm frame. Considering that the silkworm frame is a wooden flat structure, and the weight is not small when it is filled with silkworm babies and mulberry leaves, the pushing friction will be very large, and there may be jams and deviation of the pushing track during the pushing process, which cannot ensure the accurate feeding of the silkworm frame, affecting the working efficiency of the device. In order to make the silkworm frame accurately access the process, the silkworm frame guide wheel rail is designed at the bottom, as shown in the yellow part of the tooling frame in the following figure.

According to a large number of references and the structural characteristics of the silkworm frame explored on the spot in local enterprises, it is decided to adopt the rodless cylinder linear motion mechanism as the traverse mechanism, which can accurately and smoothly complete the access function of the silkworm frame in the narrow elevated layer. The designed traverse mechanism is shown in Fig. 6:

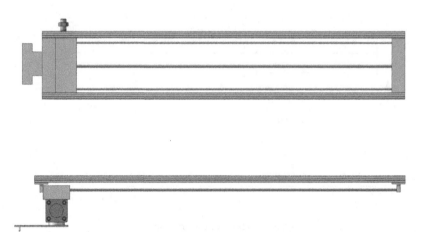

Fig. 6. Design drawing of traverse mechanism

2.4 Tooling Frame

Because the silkworm frame has a height, it is not feasible to access the silkworm frame directly on the plane of the elevated floor, so it is necessary to design a vertically lifting tooling frame device at the lifting frame, which can accurately lift and park at the height of the silkworm frame that needs to be transported or grabbed. When the silkworm frame grabbing mechanism pushes or grabs the silkworm frame horizontally, the tooling frame drops down to the initial plane position, and then the subsequent silkworm frame operation is carried out to ensure the continuity of transmission. The action diagram of the tooling frame mechanism is shown in Fig. 7 below.

The telescopic action of the tooling frame can be realized by using the telescopic cylinder. The silkworm frame guide wheel rail is designed and installed on the two square aluminum that the tooling frame contacts with the silkworm frame to ensure that the silkworm frame can slide into the silkworm frame accurately. The designed tooling frame mechanism is shown in Fig. 8 below.

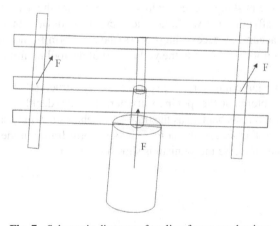

Fig. 7. Schematic diagram of tooling frame mechanism

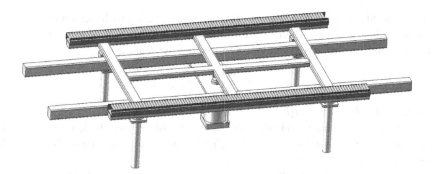

Fig. 8. Design drawing of tooling frame mechanism

3   Design of Transmission Part

3.1   Design and Calculation of Chain Drive

The load of the lifting system is mainly the weight of the lifting table itself and the weight of two silkworm frames transported at a single time. According to the field investigation of similar intelligent sericulture equipment, it is roughly estimated that the mass of the lifting table will not exceed 0.5T, so the mass of the lifting table is taken as m = 500 kg, and the maximum mass of a single silkworm frame is not more than 100kg when it is full of silkworm treasure and mulberry leaves, so the maximum weight of the silkworm frame transported at a single time is taken as m = 200 kg. During the lifting process of the lifting table, there will be an acceleration process between the motor starting and running at a constant speed, but there is a certain gap between the chain drive sprocket and the chain. Due to the effect of inertia, an impact force may be generated. In order to make the lifting process more stable, the acceleration between starting and running at a constant speed should not be too large, and the value generally will not be greater than 1 m/s².

In the movement process, the lifting system experiences three stages: acceleration, uniform speed and deceleration. The external load force in the acceleration process is greater than that in the uniform speed and deceleration movement process. Therefore, this paper takes the acceleration process as the force at the limit to analyze. Stability in the acceleration state can ensure the stability of the whole lifting process[10].

The maximum total lifting force to be provided by the lifting system during the lifting process of the lifting table is:

$$F_m = (M + m)(g + a) \tag{1}$$

where, the gravity acceleration is taken as g = 10 m/s². The lifting platform consists of four lifting points in total, and each lifting point is hung by a two-day chain. In fact, there are 8 chains to distribute the total lifting force. It is calculated that the maximum working tension of each chain during the operation of the chain transmission system is:

$$F_t = \frac{F_m}{8} = \frac{(M + m)(g + a)}{8} = 962.5N \tag{2}$$

For low-speed chain drive, when V < 0.6 m/s, the static strength plays a decisive role because of the large load. Therefore, the chain must be designed according to the static strength. The static strength calculation formula of the chain is:

$$n = \frac{Q}{F_t} \geq [n] \tag{3}$$

From formula 3: $Q \geq [n]F_t = 5.5 \times 962.5 = 5293.75N$

In this design, 8 chains on both sides are used for lifting, and the load on each chain is 926.5n. According to table 13-2-1 of mechanical design manual, 16a double row roller chain is selected as the chain of lifting mechanism.

According to the model of the chain, the basic parameters of the chain are as follows: Pitch $p = 25.4\,mm$, row spacing $p_t = 29.29\,mm$, roller outer diameter $d_{max} = 15.88\,mm$, Inner width of inner link $b_{1min} = 15.75\,mm$ and diameter of pin shaft $b_{2min} = 15.75\,mm$.

3.2 Selection and Checking Calculation of Motor

The lifting motor is the largest driving motor in the device, which is installed on the top of the device and drives the lifting mechanism through chain drive. The speed of the motor is controlled by the frequency converter. During the working process, it is frequently started, accelerated, decelerated, stopped, etc. the stop position should be accurate. The lifting motor drives the total weight of the lifting mechanism and the silkworm frame, and the inertia braking received during the work is large. Therefore, the type selection requirements of the lifting motor are relatively high. By comparing various types of motors, it is proposed to select ype series side magnetic braking three-phase asynchronous motors, which are widely used in automatic production lines and are generally not used for supporting various single machines.

Time required for lifting sprocket to rotate for one circle:

$$t = \frac{\pi D}{v} = \frac{3.14 \times 0.28336}{0.6} = 1.48s \tag{4}$$

Speed of lifting sprocket:

$$n_1 = \frac{1}{t} = \frac{1}{1.48} = 0.68r/s \tag{5}$$

Due to the mechanism designed this time, when the lifting state is stable, it is only necessary to make the rated power of the motor slightly greater than or equal to the actual output power of the motor, that is: $P_{cd} \geq P_d$.

It is known that the total weight of the lift platform and silkworm frame is 700kg, G is 10n/kg, the lifting speed of the lift platform is 0.6m/s, and the efficiency of the working machine is 0.97, which can be brought into the formula:

$$P_w = \frac{Fv}{1000\eta_w} = \frac{700 \times 10 \times 0.6}{1000 \times 0.97} = 4.33KW \tag{6}$$

According to the above calculation, the selected motor model is y160m-6, the speed of the motor is 960r/min, the rated power is 6kW, and the physical drawing of the motor is shown in Fig. 9 below:

Fig. 9. Type series side magnetic braking three-phase asynchronous motor

4   Design of Automatic Control System for Silkworm Frame

The whole control system controls two motors and three cylinders respectively. The main circuit diagram of the system is shown in Fig. 10 below:

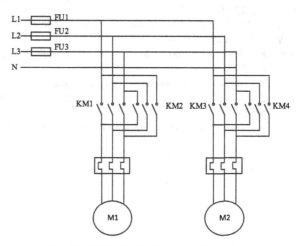

Fig. 10. Main circuit diagram of the system

5   Conclusion

This paper mainly carries out the mechatronics system design for the automatic shelf loading device of silkworm frame, completes the structural design of silkworm frame conveying mechanism, lifting mechanism, traverse mechanism and tooling frame, and carries out the design, calculation and selection of the transmission part, including the calculation and selection of chain, sprocket, lifting motor, transmission shaft and cylinder. The control system is designed, PLC is used as the control chip, and the working process of the system is introduced in detail. A set of three-dimensional models is established by using SolidWorks software. However, there are some deficiencies in this design. When designing the tooling frame and traverse mechanism, the structural design is not very good, and the parameter calculation of some parts is not very accurate. When the silkworm frame automatic shelving device works, various environments and factors are very complex, the analysis of some emergencies is not very in place, and the analysis conclusion is not very accurate.

References

1. Shi set out Intelligent design and application of lifting and transverse three-dimensional garage. Xi'an University of architecture and technology
2. Sun Germany Design of passive comb vertical lifting three-dimensional garage for berth China high tech enterprise, 2017(8), 12–13 + 41 (2017)
3. Huixiang, C., Yanli, D., Pan, L., et al.: Design of intelligent stereo garage control system. China New Commun. **05**(17), 218–221 (2018)
4. Chi, Z., Zhu, F., Xu, W., et al.: Study on chain selection of lifting mechanism of gantry bucket wheel stacker reclaimer. Hoisting Transp. Mach. **2014**(006), 92–95 (2014)
5. Li, Y., Zhou, G.: Problems and countermeasures of elevator counterweight. China New Technol. New Prod. **2013**(10), 8 (2013)
6. Yi, D.: Research on weighing and counterweight construction technology of asymmetric plane swivel bridge. Value Eng. **2020**(12), 186–189 (2020)
7. Ma, Z.: Research on braking technology of three-phase asynchronous motor. Electronic Test. **2019**(18), 40–41+39 (2019)
8. JB / T 10474–2015, roadway stacking mechanical parking equipment
9. Liu, A.: This paper discusses the application of PLC in industrial electrical automation. Digital Commun. World **185**(05), 174–174 (2020)
10. Han, X.: Research and Design of Roadway Stacking Intelligent Three-Dimensional Garage. Zhongbei University

Kinematics Simulation of Mulberry Spraying Plant Protection Robot

Dongyang Wang$^{(\boxtimes)}$, Zhimian Lan, Yufei Huang, Shude Liao, Mengji Chen, and Jixin Sun

School of Artificial Intelligence and Smart Manufacturing, Hechi University, Yizhou, Hechi 546300, China

2906861528@qq.com

Abstract. Aiming at the problems of low efficiency and pollution of artificial plant protection in mulberry garden management, a parallel spraying plant protection robot is studied and designed. Based on the innovative design of spraying plant protection robot, a parallel structure of mulberry spraying plant protection robot is constructed. The kinematics simulation of plant protection robot is analyzed and studied. Based on ADAMS simulation software, the forward kinematics and inverse kinematics simulation of the robot are realized. It provides a valuable reference for the application of mulberry spraying plant protection robot.

Keywords: Mulberry Garden spraying plant protection · Robot · Innovative structural design · Kinematics simulation

1 Introduction

Because mulberry management machinery is affected by geographical environment and scale requirements, mulberry management is still dominated by manual management. The existing agricultural spraying plant protection machinery is mainly semi-automatic plant protection machinery, such as manual knapsack sprayer, manual compression sprayer, knapsack spray duster, stretcher type mobile sprayer and small mobile smoke machine [1]. It is characterized by manual operation, small working space and compact structure. With the continuous expansion of robots in the field of agricultural plant protection, the variety of spraying tasks and the influence of factors such as the geographical location and scale of mulberry garden, the configuration of plant protection machinery and the accuracy, stiffness, bearing capacity and dynamic characteristics of the body are facing new problems and requirements. It is urgent to study the structure of a new spraying plant protection robot.

Mulberry trees in the mulberry garden are mostly planted as shrubs. Although the requirements of mulberry growth environment are not high and the adaptability is strong, in order to improve the yield of mulberry, we must strengthen the protection of mulberry, and adopt scientific and reasonable mulberry protection measures to promote the growth of mulberry in the direction of high yield and high quality. We should not only strengthen

M. A. Jan and F. Khan (Eds.): BigIoT-EDU 2022, LNICST 467, pp. 513–522, 2023.
https://doi.org/10.1007/978-3-031-23944-1_55

the management of fertilizer and water, but also do a good job in the prevention and control of diseases and pests and weeding.

In order to improve the yield of mulberry and get high-quality mulberry, the problems of fertilization, weeding and pest control must be solved. These problems can be solved manually, but the use of labor efficiency is low, labor intensity is high, and the cost is also higher. In order to liberate labor, reduce costs and achieve high efficiency at the same time, it is of great significance to develop a practical and reliable mulberry spraying robot or device in the mulberry planting industry.

In recent decades, scholars at home and abroad have done more research on agricultural spraying plant protection robot. Abroad, Japan [2] developed a spraying equipment induced by cable, which can realize unmanned operation and avoid pesticide poisoning and noise hazards of spraying operators. Liu and other [3] people developed variable sprayer, which can extract target plants online by laser sensor and realize precise variable spray of nozzle. Roberto Oberti [4] developed a fully automatic grape spraying robot crops based on r-g-rin multispectral imaging. Yuichi Ogawa [5] and others developed a spraying robot for grape production in the form of crawler mobile chassis and mechanical arm, which improved the spraying efficiency. Martinez-Guanter J and other [6] studies put forward a new practical program installed on unmanned aerial vehicles to achieve spraying of ultra-high density olives and citrus orchards, and to evaluate the efficiency of spray deposition. Y. Rajaa Vikhram Gand others [7] designed an automatic weed detection and intelligent weeding robot, which uses the way of connecting the water pump and the nozzle. After identifying the weeds, it sends a signal to the motor driver IC to control the water pump motor to spray the agent on the weeds. The advantage is that it can spray drugs at fixed points, reducing the waste of drugs. Meshram Ashish T and others [8] analyzed the latest progress in the development of autonomous pesticide spraying robots, which are divided into four categories: platform mobility and steering, positioning and navigation control, sensing and target detection, and pesticide spraying layout. They also focused on effective methods that can be used in the future to enhance pesticide spraying operations in agriculture. In order to reduce the excessive use of toxic pesticides, a navigation control algorithm suitable for platform motion and an efficient trajectory planning algorithm for the shortest link motion are also designed. The algorithm covers the shortest distance and can access all target pests on plants.

In China, Shi Zengjia [9] refitted the three rod seedling belt spray mechanism. The biggest advantage of the seedling belt spray mechanism is that it saves pesticides and has good weed control effect. The mechanism has the advantages of simple structure, less materials, easy modification, not easy to damage the original model, and makes full use of the original parts, with good leak proof effect of the nozzle. The disadvantage is that the spray bar is welded with angle iron, which is heavy. Liu [9] designed and studied a new rocker reversing nozzle. The reversing mechanism of the nozzle is composed of a reversing box and reversing components. The spray elevation is 27°, and the fan-shaped adjustment range is between 20° and 340°. When the reversing mechanism is disengaged, 360° circumferential spray can be made. The advantages are that the reversing is light and flexible, the large flow channel is long and stable, the water flow resistance is small, and the spray distance is long. The spray needle is installed in the front end of the nozzle, and the spray distance and atomization degree can be adjusted according to needs. The disadvantage is indiscriminate spraying, which wastes water. Before that, the whole process of domestic agricultural spray machinery operation requires manual participation, so that the operator can not get rid of the infringement of toxic agents, which limits the labor efficiency. This study does not need human intervention, improves working conditions and has high efficiency; However, the disadvantage is that the technology is just starting, which is not very reliable. There is no human intervention during operation, which increases the risk of failure. There is no function of carrying medicine, and the operation area is small. Chen Yong [10] studied the weeding robot based on the direct application method. The computer collects the ground image information from the camera to identify weeds, controls the action of the mechanical arm through the servo controller, and the end effector cuts weeds and smears herbal medicine. The research has the advantages of reducing the dosage of weeding agents and eliminating the phenomenon of FOG drift, and protecting the ecological environment. The disadvantages are simple structure and unstable driving. There are burrs on the surface of the gear, which can cut weeds. A layer of sponge is wrapped on the outside of the roller to absorb herbicides. Driven by the gear hobbing motor, the weeds are cut off, and then the roller applies the herbicide stored in the sponge on the cut of the weeds to achieve more thorough weeding. Zhang Yiming designed a three degree of freedom spray robot, using harmonic gear as the joint transmission mechanism, servo motor as the system drive, using Monte Carlo method and MATLAB software to select the largest workspace as the joint angle range. This paper only designs the basic framework of the robot, the disadvantage is that there is no in-depth study of the end effector (nozzle), and there is no protection of the flexible wheel of the harmonic gear in the design process. Zhang Yan studied the multi-function operation of plant protection robot. Through the design of the system, the accuracy and stability of spraying and topping operations have been greatly improved, the operation efficiency has been improved, and the operation can be carried out in a harsh environment. The disadvantage is that the experimental verification of the multi-function operation control system is completed in the test field, and there is no actual operation experimental verification, and the current human-computer interaction interface design is not perfect, and the most concise and practical interface scheme can not be completely adopted according to the needs of operators. Cao Weixin [11] of Anhui Agricultural University designed a remote controlled spraying robot for hilly and mountainous terrain. Machi [12] of southwest university designed a spraying system with automatic target targeting and automatic spraying function for citrus orchards in Hilly and mountainous areas. In the study of grape sprayer, Dong Xiang [13] et al. With wind assisted spray technology, the small droplets sprayed by the medicine pump and the spray head were blown to the canopy of fruit trees, so as to achieve the effect of preventing pests and diseases of fruit trees. Chen [14] et al. Aimed at the original design defects of the spray boom structural dynamics characteristics, a multivariable optimization method based on genetic algorithm is proposed, which greatly reduces the vibration displacement response of the boom. According to the unique maneuver mode of four rotor UAV, Yuan Ye [15] of halbin University of technology designed a new path planning method to solve the problems of route deviation, repeated spraying and missed spraying in the spraying process of UAV. Yang Yi [16] of Gansu Agricultural University designed a self-propelled remote control spraying vehicle with sensitive steering, stable driving and good spraying plant protection effect.

So far, there is little research on the mechanism of specific mulberry spraying plant protection robot, which seriously restricts the development and application of mulberry spraying plant protection robot. The configuration design of mulberry spraying plant protection robot is studied. Based on the innovative configuration design of mulberry spraying plant protection robot, the structure of parallel mulberry spraying plant protection robot is constructed. The kinematics simulation of plant protection robot is analyzed and studied. Based on ADAMS simulation software, the forward kinematics and inverse kinematics simulation of the robot are realized. It provides a valuable reference for the application of mulberry spraying plant protection robot.

2 Configuration Design of Plant Protection Robot

2.1 Establishment of Structural Solution Model of Plant Protection Robot

Because of its single configuration and consistent performance, the traditional spraying plant protection machinery cannot face the large-scale management operation of mulberry management, which seriously restricts the efficiency of mulberry management and wastes a lot of human, material and financial resources. Secondly, the manual hand-held spray bar spraying of pesticides is a random operation, and the spraying accuracy is difficult to ensure, which is easy to cause pesticide waste and environmental pollution. However, the traditional spraying plant protection mechanical equipment has limited carrying capacity, which has a huge impact on the efficiency of spraying operation, and is not suitable for popularization and application in large-scale mulberry management. In addition, manually holding the spray bar is easy to cause pesticide poisoning accidents and endanger the lives of workers, so it is urgent to study the spraying plant protection machinery.

Due to its adaptability and controllability, robots are especially suitable for large-scale mulberry management tasks. Mulberry garden management spraying plant protection machinery is mainly used to accurately spray pesticides on mulberry trees in the mulberry garden. Therefore, the controllable mechanism is applied to the spraying plant protection machinery to construct a new type of multi degree of freedom controllable mechanism mulberry garden management spraying plant protection robot. It has new topological structure, novel functional performance, multiple degrees of freedom and other characteristics. It can carry out the movement of the mechanism according to the task of mulberry spraying. It has the advantages of fast output change, high work efficiency, strong adaptability and so on. It is especially suitable for the requirements of operations in the field of mulberry plant protection.

The structure solution model of mulberry spraying plant protection robot includes robot function, effect, process action, execution action and robot topology [17, 18], as shown in Fig. 1. The function of the robot shows the design requirements for mulberry spraying; The effect describes the working mechanism of the plant protection robot; Process action engineering is an action process of working mechanism; Execution action is the decomposition of process; Robot topology is the whole mechanism model of plant protection robot.

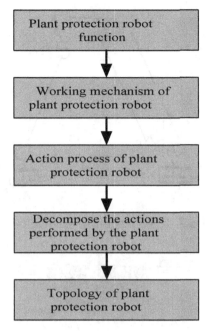

Fig. 1. Structural solution model of mulberry robot

2.2 Modeling of Plant Protection Robot Structure

Mulberry garden spraying plant protection robot is mainly used in large-scale, automatic and intelligent mulberry garden management mode to replace manual management of mulberry garden, protect workers' health and improve management efficiency. At present, the mulberry plant spraying plant protection machinery is mostly semi-automatic product. Taking manual backpack sprayer as an example, its working mechanism is that the pressure rises inside the chamber by swinging up and down the rocker component, and the liquid is ejected from the bottom of the box through the water pipe and the spray rod, and finally by the sprinkler. Therefore, the drug spraying mode determines the movement characteristics in the nozzle space. When designing the mulberry spraying plant protection robot mechanism, the movement trajectory of the spray gun is inverted "Z", so as to complete the task of mulberry spraying.

According to the analysis of the solution model, the structural diagram of mulberry spraying plant protection robot is constructed, as shown in Fig. 2. The robot mechanism consists of a moving platform, a fixed platform and two branch chains. The drive pair is located at A_1, A_2 and B_2 points, so as to realize the movement of two translation and one rotation of the robot mechanism with three degrees of freedom. Figure 3 is the three-dimensional model diagram of the parallel spraying robot.

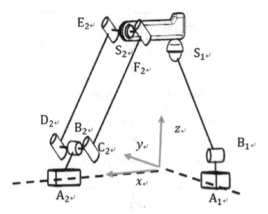

Fig. 2. Structure of parallel spraying robot

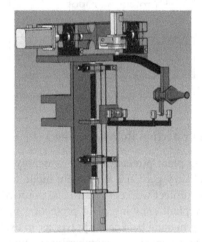

Fig. 3. 3D model of parallel spraying robot

3   Kinematics Simulation Analysis of Plant Protection Robot

The purpose of kinematics simulation analysis is to study the motion performance index of components and whether component interference occurs in the process of motion. The modeled parallel mulberry garden spraying plant protection robot is imported into Adams analysis software. The position of the spray gun is determined by three driving motors on the fixed platform, and the motion characteristic parameters such as displacement, velocity and acceleration of the spray gun of the mulberry garden plant protection robot can be obtained.

3.1   Forward Kinematics Simulation

The forward kinematics simulation of mulberry spraying plant protection robot. The active arm of the mechanism is driven, and the function about time is defined by the function generator provided by the software to construct the motion in the X, y and Z directions. The simulation analysis time is set to 1.5 s, and the displacement simulation curve, velocity simulation curve and acceleration simulation curve of spray gun are shown in Fig. 4, Fig. 5 and Fig. 6 respectively.

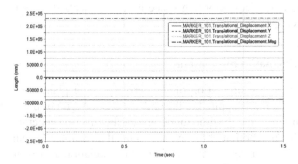

Fig. 4. Displacement curve of spray gun in each direction

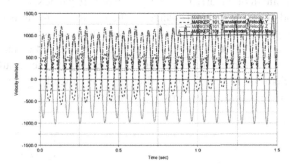

Fig. 5. Velocity curve of spray gun in each direction

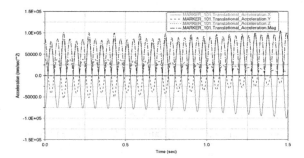

Fig. 6. Acceleration curve of spray gun in each direction

From the above parameter curve data chart, due to the mutual cooperation between the drives, the active arm can realize regular movement, and the spray gun at the end of the mechanism has different trajectory output, so as to realize the flexible and flexible output of the spray gun. It can also be concluded from the figure that the spraying trajectory meets the preset requirements in the *x*, *y* and *z* directions, and the spray gun moves in space. The whole working space basically meets the needs of conventional spray gun spraying.

3.2   Inverse Kinematics Simulation

The inverse kinematics simulation of mulberry spraying plant protection robot. The point motion excitation is applied to the end of the spray gun of the mulberry spraying plant protection robot, and the time function uses the function generator provided by the software to define the motion of the excitation in all directions. The simulation analysis time is set to 1.5 s, and Fig. 6 and Fig. 7 are the simulation curves of angular velocity and angular acceleration of B_2F_2 driving rod respectively.

Figure 7 and Fig. 8 are the simulation curves of angular velocity and angular acceleration of the end point m of the driving rod, respectively. It can be seen that the velocity of point m at the end of the mechanism changes in the *x*, *y* and *z* directions from the starting point, and the angular velocity in the *y*-axis direction changes as a periodic function. On the whole, the change of the end position of the driving rod changes periodically, which meets the work of mulberry spraying plant protection. The simulation curves of the angular acceleration of the driving rod change periodically, which shows that the driving change process of the active arm is relatively gentle.

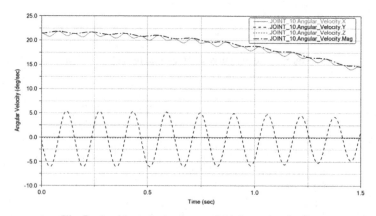

Fig. 7.   Angular velocity curve of driving rod end point

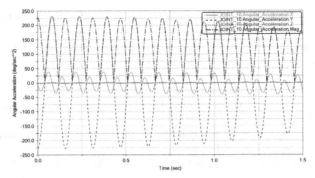

Fig. 8. Angular acceleration curve of driving rod end point

4 Conclusion

(1) The structure solution model of mulberry spraying plant protection robot is established. The structure of mulberry spraying plant protection robot is obtained by solving the model through robot function analysis, and the modeling of spraying plant protection robot is completed.

(2) Through the forward kinematics and inverse kinematics simulation data of mulberry spraying plant protection robot, it is concluded that the parallel mulberry spraying plant protection robot has good kinematics characteristics and can better complete the mulberry spraying plant protection operation.

References

1. He, X.: Research progress of plant protection machinery and pesticide application technology in China. J. Pestic. Sci. **21**(z1), 921–930 (2019)
2. Liu, K.: Development status of agricultural aviation industry in Russia, Japan and South Korea. Times Agric. Mach. **42**(07), 169 (2015)
3. Liu, H., Zhu, H.: Evaluation of a laser scanning sensor in detection of complex-shaped targets for variable-rate sprayer development. Trans. ASABE **59**(5), 1181–1192 (2016)
4. Oberti, R., Marchi, M., Tirelli, P., et al.: Selective spraying of grapevines for disease control using a modular agricultural robot. Biosyst. Eng. **146**, 203–215 (2016)
5. Liu, X.: Path planning and simulation of intelligent mobile robot. Master's thesis of Nanjing University of Technology, Nanjing (2004)
6. Martinez-Guanter, J., Agüera, P., Agüera, J., Pérez-Ruiz, M.: Spray and economics assessment of a UAV-based ultra-low-volume application in olive and citrus orchards. Precision Agric. **21**(1), 226–243 (2019). https://doi.org/10.1007/s11119-019-09665-7
7. Vikhram, G.R., Agarwal, R., Uprety, R., Prasanth, V.N.S.: Automatic weed detection and smart herbicide sprayer robot. Int. J. Eng. Technol. **7**(3.6), 115–118 (2018)
8. Meshram Ashish, T., Vanalkar Anil, V., Kalambe Kavita, B., Badar Avinash, M.: Pesticide spraying robot for precision agriculture: a categorical literature review and future trends. J. Field Robot. **39**(2), 153–171 (2021)
9. Shi, Z.: Refit the three rod seedling belt spray mechanism. Mod. Agric. **45**(03), 23–25 (1984)

10. Chenzhiqing: Development of spray robot control system. China Agricultural University (2002)
11. Cao, W., Zhang, J., Li, D., et al.: Design of remote control intelligent orchard spraying robot. Hubei Agric. Sci. **57**(08), 114–116 + 122 (2018)
12. Ma, C., Li, G., Li, X., et al.: Development of multi-directional automatic spraying device for citrus orchards in Hilly and mountainous areas. J. Agric. Eng. **35**(03), 31–41 (2019)
13. Dong, X., Zhang, T., Yan, M., et al.: 3WPZ-4 wind driven grape sprayer design and experiment. J. Agric. Mach. **49**(S1), 205–213 (2018)
14. Chen, C., Xue, X., Gu, W., et al.: Optimization and test of spray nozzle structure shape and section size. J. Agric. Eng. **31**(09), 50–56 (2015)
15. Yuan, Y.: Design of track planning of four rotor UAV for farmland spraying. Harbin University of Technology (2019)
16. Yang, Y., Zhang, F., Song, X., et al.: Design of self-propelled remote control spraying vehicle. Agric. Equi. Veh. Eng. **59**(01), 46–49 (2021)
17. Zhang, Q., Zou, H., Liao, W.: Generalized mechanism and its conceptual design. Mech. Des. Res. **18**(6), 3 (2002)
18. Cai, G., Pan, Y., Wang, H., et al.: Comprehensive research on new type of loader based on functional analysis. J. Mech. Eng. **50**(11), 50–59 (2014)

Design of Elevated Silkworm Frame Leaf Feeding System

Mengji Chen[✉], Bo Wang, Zhengjie Lu, and Yunshi Yu

School of Artificial Intelligence and Smart Manufacturing, Hechi University, Yizhou,
Hechi 546300, China
782723236@qq.com

Abstract. With the development of silkworm economy in Yizhou, the trend of intensive sericulture is becoming more and more obvious, and the demand for agricultural machinery and equipment in sericulture is increasing. Therefore, in order to correspond to the intensive elevated sericulture road in Yizhou, there are higher requirements for leaf feeding system. Based on the research of leaf feeding system and its similar devices at home and abroad, the existing mechanical equipment is optimized. This subject designs an elevated silkworm frame leaf feeding system. Mainly through the analysis of the existing automatic silkworm frame leaf feeding system, aiming at the problem of uneven leaf distribution of the existing automatic silkworm frame leaf feeding system, the leaf distribution uniformity of different structures is studied, The optimized and improved design scheme is obtained. Finally, PLC is used for program development. After optimizing and improving the design, the mulberry spreading mechanism is changed to roller feeding mechanism, which significantly improves the leaf spreading uniformity of the elevated silkworm frame leaf feeding system and reduces the labor force. This topic mainly analyzes the structure of the existing automatic silkworm frame leaf feeding system, and finally completes the optimization and improvement design of the structure through the UG modeling and analysis results.

Keywords: Elevated sericulture · PLC · Optimize and improve the design · Roller feeding mechanism

1 Introduction

In the economic system of Yizhou District of Hechi City, sericulture economy occupies a very important position. The mulberry garden area and cocoon yield of Yizhou District maintain the first position in the county all year round. Intensive sericulture is the development trend of modern sericulture economy. It is very necessary to develop large-scale and intensive sericulture production. Intensive sericulture can solve the problems of lack of sericulture labor force, masculinity and aging in rural areas. Silkworm rearing in Yizhou is basically a ground silkworm rearing mode, which requires farmers

© ICST Institute for Computer Sciences, Social Informatics and Telecommunications Engineering 2023
Published by Springer Nature Switzerland AG 2023. All Rights Reserved
M. A. Jan and F. Khan (Eds.): BigIoT-EDU 2022, LNICST 467, pp. 523–534, 2023.
https://doi.org/10.1007/978-3-031-23944-1_56

to prepare a large area of production plants, and the utilization rate of space is not high. Yizhou District lacks technological innovation on the road to intensive sericulture. There are few strong silkworm automation machinery R & D institutions in Yizhou district. In terms of mulberry planting and sericulture, the technical innovation problems of efficient integration of supporting automation technology, labor-saving technology and machines and tools are still in a difficult stage [1].

2 Scheme Design of Elevated Silkworm Frame Leaf Feeding System

The traditional leaf feeding system only sprinkles mulberry leaves on the silkworm cultured on the ground of the plant. This ground silkworm breeding mode covers a large area and has low utilization rate of space. In order to improve the space utilization of silkworm breeding, the intelligent silkworm breeding system with elevated silkworm frame was put into operation. As shown in Fig. 1, the silkworm rearing frame is removed from the silkworm frame overhead through the silkworm frame lifting transportation system, and then transported to the leaf feeding system and disinfection system. After the completion of leaf feeding and disinfection, it is transported back to the overhead. This paper studies the silkworm frame leaf feeding system used in conjunction with silkworm frame transportation system and disinfection system in a complete set of elevated intelligent silkworm rearing system. Silkworm frame leaf feeding system plays an important role in the whole elevated intelligent silkworm rearing system. Its function is to evenly lay mulberry leaves in the silkworm rearing frame transported from the elevated, so as to achieve good feeding effect [2].

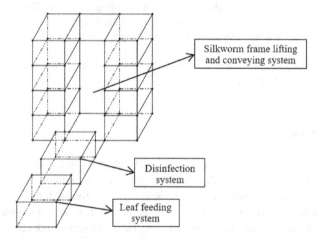

Fig. 1. Intelligent silkworm rearing system with elevated silkworm frame

The working process of the elevated silkworm frame leaf feeding system is very simple. Firstly, the feeding conveyor belt of the mulberry feeding mechanism transports the mulberry leaves of the two silkworm frames to the mulberry storage mechanism, waits for the two silkworm frames with silkworms to reach below the output mechanism, rolls the two roller shafts of the roller feeding device of the mulberry laying mechanism, and the silkworm rearing frame moves at a certain speed, The mulberry leaves in the mulberry storage mechanism are evenly scattered in the silkworm rearing frame to feed the silkworm.

The mulberry feeding mechanism transports the amount of mulberry leaves of two silkworm frames to the mulberry storage mechanism each time. The amount of mulberry leaves in the two silkworm frames changes according to the age of the silkworm and the number of days raised in a single age. For example, the amount of mulberry leaves given to the silkworm in the first two days and the second two days of the 5th instar silkworm should be strictly controlled, and the silkworm should have enough mulberry leaves to eat in the middle time. After clicking the mulberry spreading start button, when the silkworm rearing frame triggers the first limit switch, the PLC control system obtains the signal, sends the operation command to the mulberry conveying belt and transmits the mulberry leaves to the mulberry storage mechanism. When the sensor in the mulberry storage mechanism detects that the amount of mulberry leaves is met, the PLC control system obtains the signal, sends the stop operation command to the mulberry conveying belt and suspends the transportation of mulberry leaves to the mulberry storage mechanism [3, 4].

The mulberry storage mechanism is divided into two parts. The mulberry storage mechanism before the mulberry delivery mechanism is used for the storage of a large number of mulberry leaves, and the mulberry storage mechanism above the mulberry spreading mechanism is used to connect the mulberry delivery mechanism and the mulberry spreading mechanism, and plays a buffer role between the mulberry delivery mechanism and the mulberry spreading mechanism. After clicking the mulberry spreading start button, when the silkworm rearing frame reaches the lower part of the mulberry spreading mechanism and triggers the second limit switch, the PLC control system obtains a signal and sends a command to open the diaphragm to the mulberry storing mechanism, so that the mulberry leaves stored in the mulberry storing mechanism fall to the roller feeding device of the mulberry spreading mechanism, When the silkworm rearing frame reaches the lower part of the mulberry spreading mechanism and triggers the third limit switch, the PLC control system obtains the signal and sends the closing diaphragm command to the mulberry storing mechanism to form a buffer between the mulberry feeding mechanism and the mulberry spreading mechanism.

3 Structure and Transmission Design of Blade Feeding System

3.1 Structural Design of Mulberry Feeding Mechanism

The high-low stand is mainly used as the support frame of the mulberry feeding mechanism [5]. The baffles on both sides of the conveyor belt are mainly used to prevent the mulberry leaves from falling from both sides of the conveyor belt when transporting the mulberry leaves. The conveyor belt is mainly used to transport the mulberry leaves to the mulberry storage mechanism. The conveying roller shaft is divided into driving roller shaft and driven roller shaft. The driving roller shaft is connected with the motor to transmit power for the conveyor belt. The driven roller shaft and the driving roller shaft support the conveyor belt. The motor is connected to the drive roller shaft to provide power for the conveyor belt. As shown in Fig. 2.

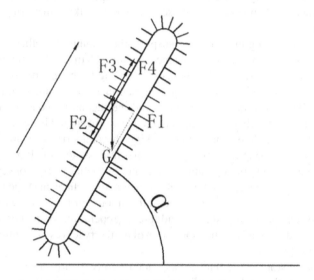

Fig. 2. Conveyor belt movement diagram

3.2 Structural Design of Mulberry Storage Mechanism

The problems needing attention in feeding silkworm mulberry leaves are:

(1) Fresh mulberry leaves are very easy to dry, while silkworms don't eat dry mulberry leaves. Silkworms only like fresh mulberry leaves;
(2) Mulberry leaves fed to silkworms must be free of ash and moisture;
(3) The amount and time of feeding mulberry leaves to silkworms need to be determined according to the demand of silkworms for mulberry leaves and the time of starvation.

Therefore, before putting the mulberry leaves into the mulberry storage mechanism, the mulberry leaves must be washed and then dried. In summer and autumn when the temperature is high and the climate is dry, you can add 5 ml fermentation broth to a kilogram of water, and then spray it to wet the mulberry leaves, which can keep the mulberry leaves for a whole day.

The movement diagram of the diaphragm of the mulberry storage mechanism is shown in Fig. 3 below.

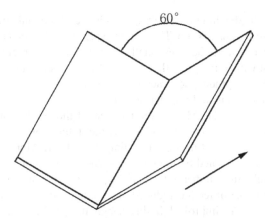

Fig. 3. Diagram of diaphragm movement

There are two inward inclined diaphragms between the mulberry storage mechanism above the mulberry spreading mechanism and the mulberry spreading mechanism. When the two diaphragms are combined, they are used to separate the mulberry storage mechanism and the mulberry spreading mechanism, so that the mulberry leaves will not enter the mulberry spreading mechanism directly after entering the mulberry storage mechanism from the mulberry feeding mechanism, so as to play a buffer role [6]. When mulberry leaves directly enter the mulberry spreading mechanism from the mulberry feeding mechanism, a small amount of mulberry leaves may fall directly from the mulberry spreading mechanism into the silkworm rearing frame, thus affecting the uniformity of mulberry spreading. After the two diaphragms are opened, make the falling position of mulberry leaves face between the opposite roll shafts of the mulberry spreading mechanism, so that when the mulberry leaves fall from the mulberry storage mechanism to the mulberry spreading mechanism, there will be no mulberry leaves left on both sides of the opposite roll shafts of the mulberry spreading mechanism. Adding a partition between the mulberry storage mechanism and the mulberry spreading mechanism is conducive to improve the uniformity of mulberry spreading. In order to store enough mulberry leaves and cooperate with the mulberry spreading mechanism, the length of the two diaphragms is designed as 0.94 m and the inclination angle is designed as 0.48 m. One fixed diaphragm is 0.48 m wide and the other movable diaphragm is 0.8 m wide. A gear rack is installed on the movable diaphragm, and the transmission of the gear rack drives the movement of the diaphragm.

4 Transmission Design

Given the belt speed and the required circumferential force of the transmission drum, the shaft power of the transmission drum can be calculated as:

$$P_A = F_u \cdot v \tag{1}$$

The motor driving power calculated according to formula (1) is:

$$P_m = k_0 \cdot k \cdot P_A \tag{2}$$

In this design, the diaphragm transmission scheme of the mulberry storage mechanism adopts gear strip transmission. The gear is made of 45 steel or 41Cr4 and quenched and tempered, and the surface hardness shall be above 56hrc. In order to reduce the mass, the shell is die cast with aluminum alloy. Due to the low speed of the steering gear, it is a general machinery, so grade 7 accuracy is selected.

Selection of modulus m and number of teeth Z:

Taking the pinion module M = 4, the increase of the number of teeth of the gear can increase the coincidence degree and improve the stability of transmission. However, for this design, the strength of the gear is mainly considered. Moreover, in this design, the smaller the space occupied by the gear rack, the better the tooth surface hardness. Therefore, the smaller the number of teeth of the pinion is, the more suitable the number of teeth is. If the number of teeth is reduced, the module can be increased, The bending strength of the gear can be improved. In this design, the number of teeth of the pinion is z = 20.

The design speed of the rack is 100 mm/s, and the rotation speed of the gear is 100 mm/s, i.e. v = 100 mm/s:

$$V = \frac{\pi dn}{60} \tag{3}$$

$$d = mz \tag{4}$$

When the pressure angle increases, the tooth thickness of the dangerous section of the tooth increases and the bending force arm decreases. Therefore, the strength of the tooth root increases, but with the increase of the pressure angle, the fillet radius of the tooth root decreases, the stress concentration factor increases, and the coincidence degree also decreases, so that the upper boundary point of the single pair of teeth meshing area is far away from the tooth root, and the bending force arm increases, which is unfavorable to the bending strength.

5 Analysis and Optimization of the Key Structure of Mulberry Branch Crusher

5.1 Introduction to Finite Element Method

The finite element analysis process is mainly divided into three steps, namely pre-processing, solution and post-processing. The general flow of each step is shown in Fig. 4:

At present, finite element analysis software mainly includes ANSYS, ABAQUS, simulation and other software. This design uses simulation to carry out finite element simulation analysis and optimization of the key parts of mulberry twig crusher. Simulation has different packages to realize various analysis functions, mainly including static analysis, thermal stress analysis and modal analysis.

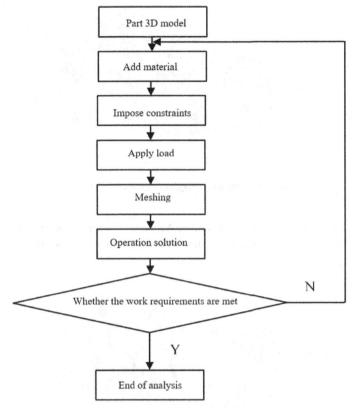

Fig. 4. Finite element analysis flow chart

5.2 Static Analysis of Cutter

According to relevant data, the force exerted by mulberry branches on the cutter can be divided into radial and axial directions, and the resultant force on the cutter can be calculated according to formula 5:

$$F_{\max} = \sqrt{(F_{x\,\max})^2 + (F_{y\,\max})^2} \times \cos 31^{\circ} \tag{5}$$

Open the established cutter model and create a new calculation example. You will see the analysis options such as static stress analysis, frequency, thermal, linear dynamic, etc. This analysis only studies whether the strain, stress and displacement of the cutter meet the strength requirements. Bei chooses the static stress analysis and names it "cutter static stress analysis" to define the material properties. For engineering analysis in any field, materials must be defined, otherwise finite element analysis cannot be carried out. The defined material can be obtained from the solid works material library, or the material can be defined in the modeling module in advance. The material of the cutter is defined as "65Mn steel".

Since the cutter is fixed by bolts in practice, you can select the fixed geometry in simulation, and the schematic diagram of adding constraints is shown in Fig. 5.

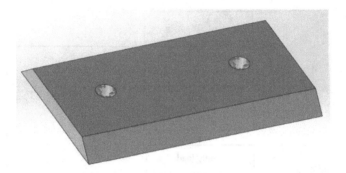

Fig. 5. Schematic diagram of cutter constraint

Apply a load on the blade of the cutter. According to the result, the cutter receives about 4493.8n at the blade. The stress diagram of the cutter is shown in Fig. 6.

Fig. 6. Loading diagram of cutter

The selected grid type is standard grid. The higher the accuracy of mesh generation, the higher the requirements for computer configuration. After comprehensive considera- tion, set the size of the mesh to 5 mm and the tolerance to 0.25 mm. The mesh generation effect is shown in Fig. 7.

After solving the example, the stress, displacement and strain distribution diagram is obtained. The stress distribution is shown in Fig. 8. It can be seen from the figure that the maximum stress is 1.329×108 N/m^2, the maximum yield force that the cutter can bear is 4.3×108 N/m^2, the maximum stress is less than the maximum yield stress, then the design meets the requirements from the point of view of stress. The displacement distribution diagram is shown in 8. After receiving 4493.8 N force, the maximum dis- placement of the cutter is 3.299×10^{-2} mm, the maximum deformation occurs at the middle and lower edge of the blade surface, and the minimum deformation is almost 0, which occurs at both sides of the blade surface (Fig. 9).

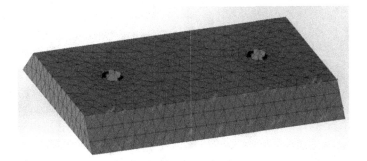

Fig. 7. Cutter mesh rendering

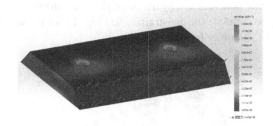

Fig. 8. Cutter stress distribution diagram

Fig. 9. Cutter displacement distribution

The strain distribution diagram is shown in 10, and the maximum cutter strain is 4.703×10^{-4}, the minimum strain is 2.206×10^{-7}. It can be seen from the figure that the magnitude of the strain is directly proportional to the stress (Fig. 10).

5.3 Static Analysis of Hammer Frame Plate

Open the established hammer frame plate model and create a new example in simulation. It only studies whether the strain, stress and displacement of the cutter meet the strength requirements, so the static stress analysis is selected, and the analysis is named "static stress analysis of hammer frame plate".

The defined material is obtained from the solid works material library, or the material can be defined in the modeling module in advance. The material of the hammer frame plate is defined as "Q235 steel".

Fig. 10. Cutter strain distribution

The hammer frame plate is fixed by the main shaft and the pin shaft, and then select the fixed geometry to simulate the constraints. See Fig. 11 for the schematic diagram of adding bundles to the hammer frame plate.

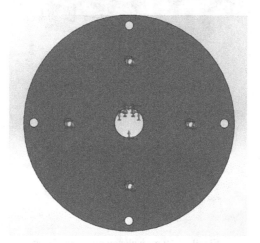

Fig. 11. Schematic diagram of restraint applied by hammer frame plate

Apply load on the four pin holes. According to the calculation, a single pin hole receives about 0.705 mpa. The load diagram of the cutter is shown in Fig. 12.

The mesh type selected in simulation is standard mesh. The higher the accuracy of mesh generation, the closer the results are to reality. Considering the computer performance and the actual situation, the size of the mesh is set to 8 m with a tolerance of 0.4 mm. The mesh generation effect is shown in Fig. 13.

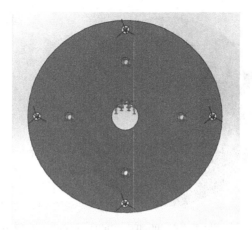

Fig. 12. Loading diagram of hammer frame plate

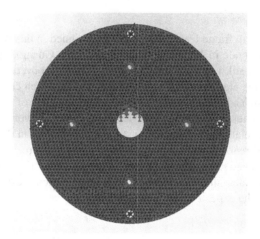

Fig. 13. Rendering of grid division of hammer frame plate

The strain distribution diagram is shown in Fig. 14, and the maximum value of cutter strain is 5.104×10^{-6}, the minimum strain is 3.656×10^{-10}. It can be seen from the figure that it is related to the stress distribution. The strain is larger where the stress is larger, and the strain is smaller where the stress is smaller.

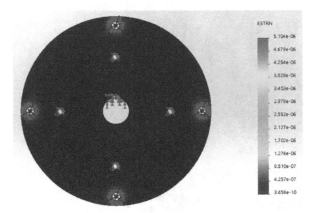

Fig. 14. Strain distribution diagram of hammer frame plate

6 Conclusion

The elevated silkworm frame leaf feeding system designed in this paper is aimed at the silkworm breeding mode in Yizhou District, Hechi City, Guangxi, which can develop faster to the intensive silkworm breeding mode, and quickly convert the ground silkworm breeding mode to the elevated silkworm breeding mode, which can make efficient use of rural resources in Yizhou District and improve the efficiency of silkworm breeding in Yizhou district. Because the existing overhead automatic silkworm rearing machinery and equipment are relatively few, there are still some problems in the existing overhead automatic silkworm rearing machinery and equipment. Therefore, it is necessary to study and design the overhead silkworm frame leaf feeding system. In the continuous research and design, the elevated silkworm frame leaf feeding system designed in this subject can basically meet the expected design requirements.

References

1. Zhou, Z., Tan, L.: Present situation and prospect of large-scale and intensive development of sericulture in China. Agric. Outlook **16**(02), 53–57 (2020)
2. Wang, D.: Research and application of simple intensive sericulture technology system Ankang college, Shaanxi Province, October 2010
3. "Industrialized sericulture" subverts the traditional sericulture mode. Friends Farmers **38**(07), 35 (2019)
4. Luo, M.: Study on the development of silkworm industrialization in Hechi City. Guangxi University (2019)
5. Ohura, M.: Development of an automated warehouse silkworm rearing system for production of useful materials. J. Insect Biotechnol. Sericol. **72**(3), 163–169 (2003)
6. Ou, X.: New feeder and feeder. Foreign Plast. **24**(05), 74 (2005)

Design of English Teaching Resource Management System Based on Collaborative Recommendation

Mingming Ding[✉]

Henan University of Animal Husbandry and Economy, Zhengzhou 450000, Henan, China
1377960836@qq.com

Abstract. This study uses a system approach by relying on collaborative recommendation to provide teachers and students with the best information. The system is designed by using various tools such as LMS, e-learning platform and different types of software. It provides an integrated environment that helps provide users with a better learning experience. These systems are based on the concept of collaborative recommendation, and everyone can contribute to everyone involved in this process. This tool is used by many schools and universities around the world. The main goal is to determine how to make recommendations, how teachers use them, and what factors will affect their use. The design collaboration recommendation system requires us to first determine who will participate in making suggestions (designers), and then develop the process of design suggestions (developers). We need to understand the roles and responsibilities of the two groups so that we can ensure that the work of each group complements the efforts of the other. In addition, it is important to know what kind of information will be collected.In view of the current English teaching resources "lost" and "waste" problem.. In order to realize the system, the use case of the system is analyzed firstly. Based on the use case analysis, the function and overall architecture of the system are designed respectively, and the collaborative recommendation module is designed. In order to improve the accuracy of recommendation, combined with the professional attributes and other attributes of old users, the hybrid recommendation algorithm is used to complete the recommendation of learning resources.

Keywords: Collaborative recommendation · Resource management · English language teaching

1 Introduction

In the process of English education, English education resources are not effectively used or the allocation of resources is unreasonable. Many students suffer from lack of good English learning channels or good learning methods to acquire English knowledge, and their English level is not improved, which makes them feel tired of learning. Moreover, most school teaching methods allow students to accept passively and lack of interaction and communication between teachers and students in teaching activities, Teachers rarely know what kind of teaching means students need. In the teaching process, many teachers only deal with one class, which is more difficult for students to accept [1]. This makes English learning a "death spot" for many students, which is their biggest headache, thus hindering the reform of Vocational English education?. The significance of active and rational use of English teaching resources can help teachers establish the awareness of teaching resources, establish a new concept of teaching resources, improve the knowledge level of teachers, help improve the personal quality of teachers, improve the teaching effect, and help students create an English learning environment. In this environment, students can fully perceive and experience English and the use of English, so that students can be happy physically and mentally, At the same time, it can help some students reduce their anxiety, eliminate their inferiority complex and improve their English quality effectively [2].

With the growth of modern information in Pb level, it is the focus of current computer research and thinking to strengthen the mining of these information to improve the efficiency of data utilization. In the context of massive data growth, education departments and academic institutions have accumulated a large number of teaching resources. For English education institutions, how to recommend these resources to different learners so that learners can combine their own needs and improve the application value of different teaching resources is the focus of the relevant departments of English education institutions [3]. At the same time, the problems of "resource overload" and "resource lost" are seriously troubling educational institutions. Therefore, it is urgent to introduce modern intelligent recommendation algorithm to complete the personalized recommendation of different English teaching resources in combination with English learners' interests and other actual situations, so as to improve the use efficiency of English teaching resources. In order to enable learners to quickly find resources that meet their own requirements and hobbies, Wang Linlin (2017) built an interest model and selected personalized recommendation algorithm according to English learners' interests to complete the recommendation of teaching resources. Liu Haitao (2017) combined the characteristics of users and teaching resources and adopted a hybrid recommendation method, In order to promote the efficiency of students' use of teaching resources. Based on the previous research, this paper constructs an intelligent recommended English teaching resource platform from the perspective of software design, and designs it in detail [4]. Figure 1 below shows the construction of the recommended English teaching resource platform.

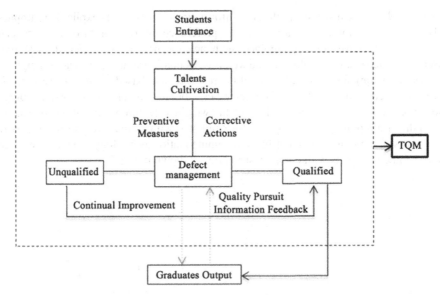

Fig. 1. Construction of recommended English teaching resource platform

2 Collaborative Recommendation Technology

2.1 Introduction of Collaborative Recommendation Technology

Foreign famous recommendation systems include GroupLens, Ringo, Amazon, etc. GroupLens is a collaborative filtering system applied to Usenet news, which is divided into client and server. It allows users to collaborate together and discover what they are interested in from a large number of Usenet news. Ringo is a music recommendation system designed by MIT. The system requires users to evaluate musicians first, then calculate the similarity of users according to the evaluation results, and then classify users. Users of the same category recommend music to each other. Amazon e-commerce website applies a typical recommendation method based on collaborative filtering. It recommends products that users may like through the user's purchase history, product evaluation and personal attributes of customers [5].

The domestic personalized recommendation is better: Douban's Douban guess. It analyzes the users' read, want to read, read and evaluation behaviors every day, and selects the content that users are interested in from the massive data to make recommendations. The more users use it, the more accurate its recommendation will be. Dangdang has also done a good job in personalized recommendation. Many other websites have introduced recommendation technology to provide users with a good user experience. The application of recommendation technology in e-commerce has increased the sales volume of products, increased the income of the website and the number of user visits, and improved the reputation and user viscosity of the website [6].

Collaborative filtering recommendation is not only the most successful recommendation technology, but also the most researched recommendation technology. Its basic idea is to obtain the historical preference information of target users explicitly or implicitly. The information is compared with the preference information of other users, and other users who have similar preferences with the target user are found, and these similar users are called nearest neighbors. The weighted evaluation value of the nearest neighbor is used as the target user's evaluation of the resource, and based on this, the resource is recommended to the target user [7]. Because collaborative recommendation technology does not use the user interest model, nor the weighted feature vector of resources, but from the user's point of view, looking for neighbors with similar preferences, there are no many shortcomings in content-based recommendation technology, which can be used to recommend objects with complex structure, as shown in Fig. 2.

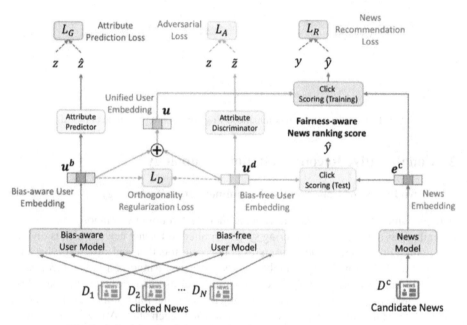

Fig. 2. Principle of collaborative filtering recommendation technology

Collaborative recommendation technology has the following advantages.

① Because collaborative recommendation technology is from the user's point of view, it does not need to build complex weighted eigenvectors for resources, which reduces the system's manpower and time costs.

② Collaborative recommendation technology is based on the preferences of the nearest neighbor to recommend resources for the target user, so it can recommend some new and interesting resources that the target user does not consider. This is different from content-based recommendation, which can only recommend resources in the defined resource types in the user interest model for users.

③ Collaborative recommendation technology can make use of the feedback information of the target user and the feedback information of the nearest neighbor, so it can quickly modify the recommendation content and accelerate the speed of personalized learning [8].

2.2 Implementation Process of Collaborative Recommendation Technology

Collaborative filtering technology adopts the method based on the interest direction of neighbor users. It uses other users' preferences for resource items to obtain the similarity of users, or predicts a user's evaluation of a resource through the common likes and dislikes of similar users for some resources. The system can make personalized recommendations with high accuracy based on these data. Collaborative filtering technology is a personalized recommendation technology which has been researched more and more at present. Using it for recommendation has high personalization and obvious effect.

The basic idea of collaborative filtering is very intuitive: in daily life, people often make some choices (shopping, reading, music, etc.) according to the recommendations of friends and relatives. Collaborative filtering technology is to apply this idea to information recommendation, and recommend certain information to certain users based on the evaluation of other users. Collaborative filtering technology is the most researched and widely used recommendation system, and it is also a personalized recommendation technology with high recommendation efficiency.

Because it is difficult to collect user's historical preference information implicitly, most of the existing collaborative recommendation systems use the display method to obtain user's preference information by collecting user's score of items. All users' scores of all items constitute a user item score matrix, and each item in the matrix represents a user's score of a certain item. The recommendation process for target users is to get the nearest neighbor by using the score in this matrix, and then get the recommendation result for target users by using the neighbor's score [9]. Therefore, collaborative recommendation has three main steps: user information representation, nearest neighbor selection and recommendation result generation, as shown in Fig. 3.

According to Pearson similarity, the predicted score of user U_i and teaching resource D_m can be obtained.

$$P(i,j) = \overline{R}_i \frac{\sum_{n \in Ni} sim(i, N) \bullet (R_{n,j} - \overline{R}_N)}{\sum_{n \in Ni} sim(i, N)} \qquad (1)$$

Thus, through the above prediction, we can get a recommendation set, and finally recommend it to users.

3 Analysis of English Teaching Resource Management System

3.1 Principles of Using English Teaching Resources

The use of English teaching resources is not arbitrary and needs to be regulated according to certain principles. The reason is that the connotation of English teaching resources is extremely rich and there are many kinds of English teaching resources. The use of English curriculum resources is also a huge scientific and systematic work. Therefore, we should follow the following principles in the practice of using English teaching resources:

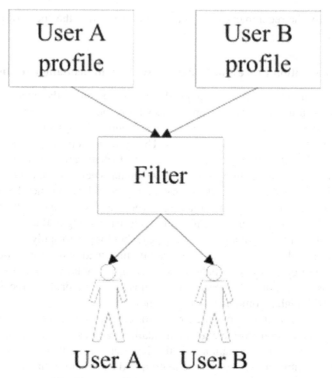

Fig. 3. Model of collaborative recommendation

(1) Pertinence principle

The use of English teaching resources must, on the premise of clarifying the curriculum objectives, carefully analyze all kinds of English curriculum resources related to the curriculum objectives, and understand and master their respective properties and characteristics. The use of English teaching resources should be based on the actual situation of the local and the school, give play to the regional advantages, highlight the English characteristics of the school should be based on the situation of the students, and meet the interests and development needs of the students should consider the situation of the teachers.

(2) Openness principle

The principle of openness means that in the process of using English teaching resources, we should actively absorb other people's valuable achievements, so as to absorb all human civilization achievements with an open mind. We should try our best to develop and study all the things around us that are conducive to English teaching, so as to truly achieve the goal of combining practice with teaching, instead of focusing on teaching materials as shown in many teaching activities at present, which is not conducive to improving students' enthusiasm for learning English.

(3) Adaptability principle

The principle of adaptability mainly includes three aspects. The first is to meet the needs of students. The development of teaching resources should meet the interests of students and be consistent with the scope of students' learning abilities. The next step is to adapt to the teaching level of teachers. The teaching resources that teachers can't control are of no use value, so teachers should make corresponding efforts to improve their teaching level, so as to adapt to the continuous development of the times and technology. The last is to adapt to the school's own conditions and characteristics. There are many kinds of teaching resources needed by students, and there are differences in personality. Schools can not meet the different needs of each student. Therefore, the school should base on its own actual situation, give priority to the needs of the majority of students, and seek teaching resources suitable for their development, so as to truly improve the overall level of students. The use of teaching resources should pay attention to the use of English in different disciplines, and pay attention to the relationship between English and social development, real life, scientific and technological progress [10]. At the same time, the use of English teaching resources should be able to adapt to the exploration and research activities of students. It should be conducive to students to find and put forward problems, so that students can learn by "using" or "doing", and focus on cultivating students' ability to solve practical problems in English.

(4) Developmental principle

The development of teaching resources should first promote the development of students' English level. Through the development of teaching resources, students can make better use of resources to learn, explore and practice. The second is to promote the development of teachers. The development of curriculum resources poses new challenges to teachers, so that teachers should constantly improve their own quality to meet the overall education level of the times. Because the quality and teaching level of teachers determine the identification scope, development and utilization of curriculum resources and the level of exerting benefits. Therefore, curriculum resources should also be able to promote the development of teachers, so as to form a virtuous circle between teachers and curriculum resources.

(5) Economic principle

The premise of the use of English teaching resources must be suitable for the school strength of the school. While developing English teaching resources, we must follow the principle of economy, because our goals of using educational technology are roughly three aspects: expanding the scale of education, improving the quality of teaching and improving the efficiency of teaching. While pursuing the goal, we must also achieve "more, faster, better and less". Otherwise, it will exceed the economic burden of the school. No matter how important this resource is, regardless of its cost, it is useless. Therefore, the principle of economy is one of the most basic and important principles of teaching technology. No matter what English teaching resources are used, as long as it can promote English teaching and improve students' English level. If we have neglected the principle of economy in the past, we must pay enough attention to it now.

3.2   System Design

Overall architecture: using B / S structure mode to build, the overall architecture of the system is divided into three layers: application layer, logic layer and data layer. The overall framework system is shown in Fig. 4.

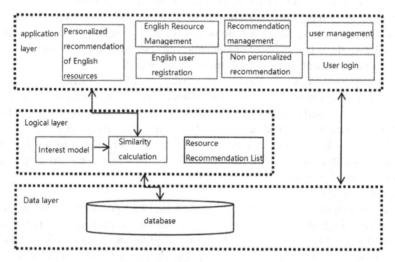

Fig. 4. Overall system architecture

In the application layer of this system, there are personalized recommendation and non personalized recommendation.

For logic layer, it mainly includes application server and personalized recommendation model. The application server mainly responds to the user's operation request. After receiving the user's request from the client, the system sends the response to the database server and sends the response result back to the client for display in front of the user's eyes.

In the process of English teaching, there are abundant extra-curricular English resources. These English resources are vivid and interesting. They can most stimulate students' interest in learning English and make them feel the charm of English. They include newspapers, magazines, literary works, film and television works and daily life English that students usually read. These English resources are an indispensable part of students' learning English, It can create a relaxed, free and happy class learning environment for students, stimulate students' thirst for knowledge, and expand the space of personality, which is conducive to the improvement of students' language ability. In the teaching process, teachers should make use of the positive influence and role of English extra-curricular resources to carry out subconscious language thinking teaching. By providing students with language materials for English construction, reasonably arranging time, effectively organizing extra-curricular teaching, finding ways to create an interactive atmosphere, meeting students' practical needs, encouraging students to actively participate in and deeply experience the language learning process inside and outside the class, and then through communication and cooperation, exploring and practicing, Build the corresponding knowledge, promote the formation and development of students' good English skills and stimulate their interest in improving their practical English application ability.

4 System Implementation

In order to verify whether the above hybrid recommendation algorithm can achieve the expected recommendation effect, based on the data set generated after the system has been used for a period of time, with the accuracy of recommendation as the evaluation standard, 2000 user records visiting the English website during this period are randomly selected, and their score records are exported, a total of 60000.

Thus, the result shown in Fig. 5 is obtained.

Through the above results, we can see that the hybrid recommendation algorithm used in this paper has a slightly higher accuracy than the traditional collaborative recommendation algorithm under different proportions of test machine and training set, which shows the advantages of this algorithm.

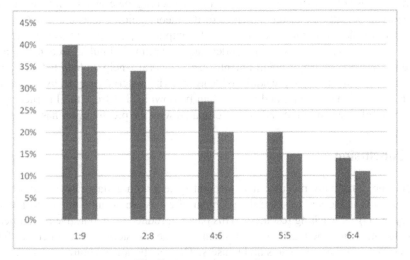

Fig. 5. Accuracy comparison

With the continuous progress of science and technology, the teaching technology has also been improved. Various advanced teaching equipment have been introduced into schools one after another, and the position and role of information technology in English teaching activities have become increasingly important. Because the teaching level of schools is inseparable from the increasingly updated knowledge with the outside world, especially for the students majoring in Business English in vocational schools, And accumulate the professional English required in future work. It can be said that information technology is the backbone of promoting English teaching reform. It provides the largest platform for global knowledge sharing and provides rich information resources for different regions. At the same time, the application of information technology in English teaching has great potential to improve the quality of English teaching environment. The rational use of information resources is of great help to help teachers enrich their teaching contents and promote students' motivation to learn English. It also plays a great role in promoting students' intellectual development and broadening their horizons. It is most appropriate to describe the great influence of information resources with the saying "scholars do not go out, but can know the world". Research shows that information technology in English teaching can more effectively stimulate students' visual and auditory systems, make students remember the knowledge they have learned more deeply, save classroom teaching time, add more rich teaching contents in a limited time, and improve teaching efficiency. Moreover, diversified information channels bring many new things, and can enhance students' curiosity and thirst for knowledge, The English knowledge required for one's major can be expressed through the real language environment, which is more effective than the teachers' simple lecture analysis in the classroom. This real language environment is not only conducive to the teachers' reserve of information resources in teaching and the accumulation of knowledge in students' learning, but also meets the needs of students' personalized learning.

The integration of information resources and teaching materials is of great help to the rational use of teaching resources other than teaching materials. Under the guidance of theory, especially under the guidance of the theory guiding teachers' teaching, it is necessary to take information resources with computers and networks as the core as an important tool to promote students' independent learning, stimulate students' sensory systems, enrich the teaching environment, Teachers can also help students to find learning materials and effectively serve students' learning. The materials needed by students for listening, speaking, reading and writing can be downloaded from the Internet, which saves a lot of costs and time and effort compared with the previous purchase.

5   Conclusion

To sum up, a teaching resource management system with collaborative recommendation function is the key to solve the problem of excessive accumulation and low efficiency of current teaching resources. This paper introduces collaborative recommendation algorithm into the teaching resource management system to recommend different types of teaching resources to suitable users. The collaborative recommendation teaching resource management system is composed of personal space management, resource management, recommendation module and system management to meet the different functional requirements of different users, In order to improve the sharing and utilization of teaching resources.

References

1. Yan, Q.: Design of teaching video resource management system in colleges and universities based on Microtechnology. Secur. Commun. Netw. (2021)
2. Yuan, X.: Design of college English teaching information platform based on artificial intelligence technology. J. Phys: Conf. Ser. **1852**(2), 022031 (2021)

3. Huang, Y.: Design of personalised English distance teaching platform based on artificial intelligence. J. Inf. & Knowl. Manag. (2022)
4. Zhu, M.: Research on English teaching model with computer aid. In: CIPAE 2021: 2021 2nd International Conference on Computers, Information Processing and Advanced Education (2021)
5. Zhou, X., Li, X., Su, N.: Design and internet of things development of network teaching resource base system for educational technology. J. Phys: Conf. Ser. **1769**(1), 012005 (2021)
6. Hendy, N.T.: The effectiveness of technology delivered instruction in teaching Human Resource Management. Int. J. Manag. Educ. **19**(2), 100479 (2021)
7. Nie, A.: Design of English interactive teaching system based on association rules algorithm. Secur. Commun. Netw. (2021)
8. Lin, H., Wei, Y.: Design and implementation of college English multimedia aided teaching resources. Int. J. Electr. Eng. Educ., 2021:002072092098351
9. Chen, C.: A method of digital English teaching resource sharing based on artificial intelligence. J. Inf. & Knowl. Manag. **21**(Supp02) (2022)
10. Tan, Q., Shao, X.: Construction of college English teaching resource database under the background of big data. J. Phys: Conf. Ser. **1744**(3), 032004 (2021)

Discusses the Relationship Between the First Excitation Energy of the Nucleus and the Magic Number

Yin Long and Peng Jinsong[(✉)]

Hechi University, Hechi 546300, Guangxi, China
311073@qq.com

Abstract. The greater the first excitation energy of the nucleus, the higher the relative stability of the nuclide. When the number of nuclei is magical, the nuclei are particularly stable. It can be seen that there must be some correlation between the first excited energy of the nucleus and the magic number. Through the nudat30 library of the International Atomic Energy Agency's Nuclear Data Center, the experimental data on the first excitation energy of 2175 nuclides were statistically analyzed, and a large number of experimental data showed that it was those nuclei with the number of nuclei equal to the magic number that had the largest first excitation energy. Therefore, the positive correlation between the first excitation energy of the nucleus and the stability of the nuclide indicates the correctness of the magic number model.

Keywords: Atomic nucleus · First excite energy · Magic numbers

1 Introduction

The atomic nucleus is a finite quantum multibody system composed of protons and neutrons, which is an important level of the structure of matter and has a very rich content. The beginning of nuclear physics began with the discovery of natural radioactivity in Becquerel in 1896 [1, 2]. Before the 1930s, through early research, the nucleus and nuclear decay were established, nuclear reactions were observed, and protons were discovered. 30) In the 1950s, there were major experimental discoveries such as neutrons, positrons, artificial radioactivity, fission, and fusion phenomena [1, 2]. Theoretically, there are developments from composite nuclear models to direct reaction theory, especially the establishment of shell models and collective models of nuclear structure, which fully demonstrate that nuclear physics has become a booming emerging discipline and shows the prospects for huge nuclear energy applications.

The atomic nucleus is a central issue in the physics of the atomic nucleus, an important level of the structure of matter, an important field of study in itself, and a bridge between atomic physics and particle physics. Basic research on atomic nuclei and their applications is one of the important frontiers in the development of physics and its interdisciplinary disciplines today [1]. At present, there are more than 3 100 kinds of

© ICST Institute for Computer Sciences, Social Informatics and Telecommunications Engineering 2023
Published by Springer Nature Switzerland AG 2023. All Rights Reserved
M. A. Jan and F. Khan (Eds.): BigIoT-EDU 2022, LNICST 467, pp. 546–556, 2023.
https://doi.org/10.1007/978-3-031-23944-1_58

nuclides in nature and experimental synthesis, and the theory predicts more than 9 000 nuclides [2], showing that there are still many basic problems in the atomic nucleus that need to be further studied. The theory of the structure of the nucleus mainly studies the properties of the ground state of the nucleus and a series of excited states, and clarifies the reasons for these properties. Among them, the ground state properties include the binding energy of the nucleus, the radius of charge, the energy level of the single particle, the resonance state, the magnetic moment, the halo phenomenon, etc.; The properties of the excited state include various properties of the excited state energy level of the nucleus (including excitation energy, energy level width, spin, universe and decay characteristics of each energy level, etc.), magnetic rotation, collective rotation, collective vibration, quantum phase transition, etc. [3–5]. The nuclear energy level diagram measured by the experiment is one of the most basic bases for the theory of nuclear structure. According to the basic laws of conservation of energy and conservation of space, the highly excited state of the nucleus will generally be deexcitated to the low excited state or ground state through γ. In particular, light nuclei, many excitation levels emit light particles in addition to γ de-excitation, becoming a new residual nuclear ground state or excited state [6–20]. The general rule of nuclear energy levels is that the higher the energy level, the smaller the spacing between their energy levels. The first excited state energy level is the most important energy level of all excited state energy levels, and the spacing between it and the ground state (that is, the size of the energy of the first excited energy level, referred to as the first excited energy E1), spin, universe and energy level width have a great impact on the nuclear structure and nuclear reaction properties, and even directly reflect the stability of the nuclide to a certain extent. As early as 1953, Goldharber [21] calculated the 125 dual nuclei measured experimentally at that time, and found that the first excitation energy changed relatively smoothly with the number of protons or neutrons of the nucleus, and reached the maximum value at the closed shell layer; In the rare earth region and the nuclear region heavier than thorium, the first excitation energy is relatively low, and the single-particle model of the odd A nucleus is likely to no longer be applicable. Since then, there have been few articles devoted to the first excited state. It was not until 2002 that Kanungo et al. [22] analyzed the first excited state of the even-even nucleus in the lighter neutron nucleus region and concluded that it was possible to have new magic numbers at $Z = 14, 16, 32$. More than 2,000 nuclears in the excited state have been experimentally measured, and the information is included in the NuDat2 library of the International Atomic Energy Agency (IAEA) nuclear data center.

With the rapid development of experimental technology, the measured nuclide region is getting closer and closer to the drop line, and the measurement of various structural data such as excitation energy, spin cosmology, and energy level width of atomic nuclei has become more and more accurate Since the mid-1940s, nuclear physics research has developed rapidly [24]. At present, more than 3100 nuclides exist in nature and are synthesized experimentally, and the theory predicts more than 9000 nuclides [25, 26]. Atoms in the ground state absorb the conditions for quantization γ photon energy and transition from the ground state to the first excited state. The energy absorbed in this process is called the first excitation energy of the nucleus. The greater the first excitation energy of the nucleus, indicating that more energy needs to be provided to excite the nucleus from the ground state to the first excited state. Such nuclei are relatively stable. Therefore, the stability of nuclides can be judged by the experimental data of the first excitation energy of the nucleus.

A large number of experimental facts in nuclear physics show that when the number of protons or neutrons in the nucleus is 2, 8, 20, 28, 50, 82, and the number of neutrons is 126, the nucleus is particularly stable and exhibits many strange properties. These numbers are known as the magic numbers of the nucleus. If the number of protons and neutrons is both a magic core, for example, $^{16}_{8}O$ is called a double magic core, and they are more stable. Scientists have imagined the existence of a shell structure in the nucleus of an atom. They successfully explained the mechanism of the magic numbers 2, 8, and 20 by using a single-particle shell structural model [28]. In 1949, German physicists discovered that the energy levels of spin and shell were divided into two identical orbitals,[82 and 126] that were successfully derived from the action of spin and shell in 1949.

It is conceivable that there should be some correlation between the first excitation energy of the nucleus and the magic number. Through an analysis of the IAEA Nuclear Data Centre, nudat3's statistical analysis of experimental data on the first excitation energy of 2175 nuclides in the library [30] showed that it was those nuclei whose number of nuclei equal to the magic number had the largest first excitation energy value, which clearly demonstrated the correctness of the phantom model.

The first excitation energy of 2 125 nuclides was collected from the NuDat2 library and the latest literature for analysis, and the contour plot is shown in Fig. 1. The red dotted line indicates the position of the nuclide corresponding to the number of neutrons and protons, respectively, the traditional magic numbers 20, 28, 50, 82 and the neutron number is 126. As can be clearly seen from Fig. 1, the first excitation energy of the nuclide corresponding to the traditional phantom position is significantly higher than that of the neighboring nuclide, which is consistent with the case of single neutron separation energy, binon separation energy, single proton separation energy, biproton separation energy, and α decay energy [29]. For isotope chains and homonynous chains with proton numbers and neutron numbers of 20, 28, 50, 82 and neutron numbers of 126, the first excitation energy of the even-dual nucleus is significantly higher than that of other nuclides, which is consistent with the properties of the various coarse blocks of the nucleus [29]. It is worth noting that for the homonyn element chain with neutron number $N = 20$, the average value of the first excitation energy is 2.36 meV, while the average of its even nucleus is only 2.20 meV, mainly the first excitation energy of the parity nucleus 43 23V is as high as 8.25 meV. If 43 23V is excluded, the first excitation energy of the homonynical neutron chain $N = 20$ is 1.91 meV, which is still lower than the corresponding mean of the even-even kernel. It can be seen that the properties of parity 43 23V are very unique (its ground state has a half-life of 79.3 ms), and its first excited state is considered to be the isotopic similar state (Isobaric Analog State, IAS) of the 43 24Cr ground state of the parity nucleus [30].

The existence of the phantom number is a reflection of the "shell structure" of the protonucleus, and the homogeneous particles constituting a combined state in the form of a cluster will show a certain order and determine the nature of the protonucleus. In 1949, german nuclear physicist Meyer and others used a new interaction, that is, orbital and spin interaction, to explain this phenomenon and established a "shell pattern".

The mass of the protonuclear nucleus of atoms with different elements is different from that of protons and neutrons in the proton nucleus. When the number of protons, the number of neutrons is a specific value, or both, the stability of the protonucleus is greater than the average. These values are called "magic numbers".

The extensive study of science tells us that to date, the numbers of illusions known to date are 2, 8, 2 0, 2 8, 5 0, 8 2, 1 2 6. For example, helium, oxygen, calcium, nickel, tin, and lead, which are widely present in nature, correspond to the number of protons or neutrons corresponding to the values of 2 to 82, respectively. Elements with both proton and neutron numbers of 12 6 have not been found, but lead 2 08 (isotopes of lead) with a proton number of 82 and a neutron number of 1 26 also exist in nature.

2 The Statistical Law of the Correlation Between the First Excitation Energy of the Nucleus and the Magic Number

2.1 A Statistical Law of Correlation Between Nuclear Excitation Energy and Isotope Magic Numbers

Calculate the first excitation energy of the nucleus of each isotope, as shown in Figs. 1, 2, 3, 4, 5 and 6 below. The abscissa is the number of neutrons n, and the ordinate is the first excitation energy of the nucleus, in MeV.

1. As shown in Fig. 1, for nuclei with 2 protons ($z = 2$) and 2 neutrons ($n = 2$), the first excitation energy of the helium nucleus is 20.21 meV, which is the maximum first excitation energy of all nuclides; And 2 is the magic number. Note that it is still a dual magic core.

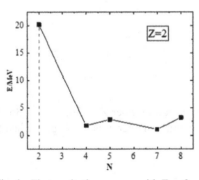

Fig. 1. First excitation energy with $Z = 2$, n = 2.

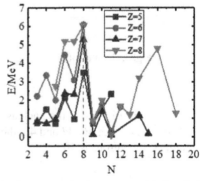

Fig. 2. First excitation energy with $Z = 5, 6, 7, 8$, n = 8.

2. As shown in Fig. 2, for the nuclei of proton number Z = 5, 6, 7 and 8, when the neutron number n = 8, the first excitation energy is the largest, which is a magic number. The first excitation energy is 6.0494 meV. $^{16}_{8}O$

3. As shown in Fig. 3, for the nucleus of the proton number Z = 14, 15, 16, 17, 18, 19 and 23, the first excitation energy is greatest when the number of neutrons is 20.

4. As shown in Fig. 4, for nuclei with proton numbers Z = 20, 21, 24, 26 and 28, the first excitation energy is greatest when the number of neutrons is 28. Among them, it is a double magic core, and the first excitation energy is 3.83172 meV, which is also the largest of the five cores. $^{48}_{20}Ca$

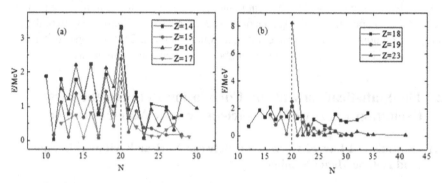

Fig. 3. First excitation energy with Z = 14, 15, 16, 17, 18, 19 and 23, n = 20.

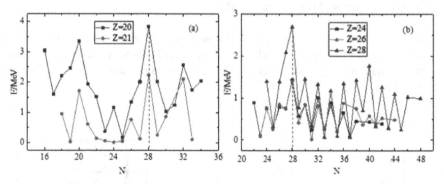

Fig. 4. First excitation energy with Z = 20, 21, 24, 26 and 28, n = 28.

5. As shown in Fig. 5, for the nucleus of the proton number Z = 30, 32, 34, 36, 38, 39, 40, 42, 44, 45, 46, 47 and 48, the first excitation energy is the largest when the number of neutrons is 50.

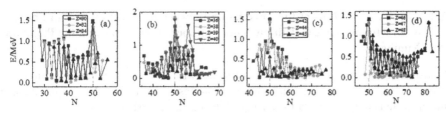

Fig. 5. First excitation energy with Z = 30, 32, 34, 36, 38, 39, 40, 42, 44, 45, 46, 47 and 48, n = 50.

6. As shown in Fig. 6, for the nucleus of the proton number Z = 50, 52, 53, 54, 55, 56, 58, 60, 62, 64, 66, 67, 68, 70 and 72, the first excitation energy is the largest when the number of neutrons is 82. Among them, it is a double magic core, the first excitation energy is 4.04120 meV, which is also the largest of the 15 nuclei. $^{132}_{50}Sn$

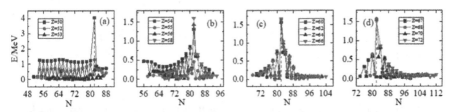

Fig. 6. First excitation energy with Z = 50, 52, 53, 54, 55, 56, 58, 60, 62, 64, 66, 67, 68, 70 and 72, n = 82.

7. As shown in Fig. 7, for the nucleus of the proton number Z = 78, 79, 80, 82, 83, 84, 85, 86, 88, 89, 90 and 91, the first excitation energy is the largest when the neutron number is 126. Among them, it is a double magic core, and the first excitation energy is 2.614522meV, which is the largest excitation energy of the 12 nuclei. $^{208}_{82}Pb$

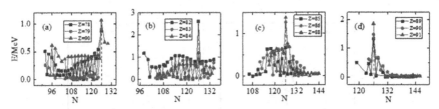

Fig. 7. First excitation energy with Z = 78, 79, 80, 82, 83, 84, 85, 86, 88, 89, 90 and 91, n = 126.

Count the nuclides with proton numbers from 1 to 113. There were 57 nuclides found. When the number of neutrons is the magic numbers 2, 8, 20, 28, 50, 82, and 126, the first excitation energy is the largest and the nucleus is the most stable.

2.2 The Statistical Law of the Correlation Between the First Excitation Energy of an Atomic Nucleus with the Same Number of Neutrons and the Phantom Number

Statistics on the first excitation energy of nuclei with the same number of neutrons are shown in Figs. 8, 9, 10, 11, 12 and 13 below. The abscissa is the number of protonS, and the ordinate is the first excitation energy of the nucleus, in MeV.

1. As shown in Fig. 8, when the number of protons n = 2 in the nucleus is the magic number 2, the first excitation energy is the largest. Where are the double magic cores. $^{4}_{2}He$

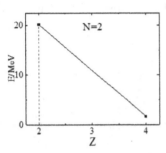

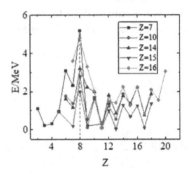

Fig. 8. The first excitation energy of nuclei with the same number of neutrons with n = 2.

Fig. 9. The first excitation energy of nuclei with the same number of neutrons with n = 7, 10, 14, 15, and 16.

2. As shown in Fig. 9, for nuclei with neutron numbers n = 7, 10, 14, 15, and 16, the first excitation energy is greatest when the number of protons is the phantom number 8.

3. As shown in Fig. 10, for the nuclei of neutron number n = 17, 18, 19, 28, 29, 31, 33 and 34, the first excitation energy is the greatest when the number of protons is 20. Among them, it is a double magic core, and the first excitation energy is 3.83172meV, which is also the largest of the eight cores. $^{48}_{20}Ca$

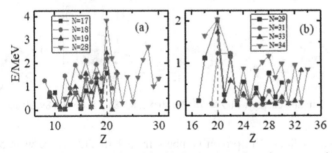

Fig. 10. The first excitation energy of nuclei with the same number of neutrons with n = 17, 18, 19, 28, 29, 31, 33 and 34.

4. As shown in Fig. 11, for the nuclei of neutron number n = 24, 26, 27, 30, 39, 40, 42, 44 and 46, when the proton number is 28, the first excitation energy is the largest.

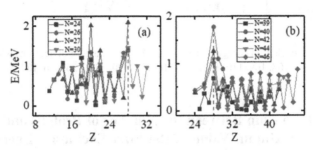

Fig. 11. The first excitation energy of nuclei with the same number of neutrons with n = 24, 26, 27, 30, 39, 40, 42, 44 and 46.

5. As shown in Fig. 12, for the nuclei of neutron number n = 54, 58, 60, 62, 64, 65, 66, 68, 70, 72, 74, 76, 78, 80, 82 and 88, when the proton number is 50, the first excitation energy is the largest. There is a double magic core, and the first excitation energy is 4.0412meV, which is the largest of the 16 nuclei. $^{132}_{50}Sn$

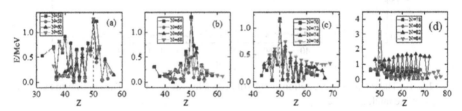

Fig. 12. The first excitation energy of nuclei with the same number of neutrons with n = 54, 58, 60, 62, 64, 65, 66, 68, 70, 72, 74, 76, 78, 80, 82 and 88.

6. As shown in Fig. 13, for nuclei with neutron numbers n = 98, 100, 101, 102, 104, 106, 108, 109, 110, 112, 114, 116, 118, 120, 122, 125, 126, 127, 128, 129, 132 and 134, the first excitation energy is greatest when the proton number is 82. Among them, it is a double magic core, and the first excitation energy is 2.614522meV, which is also the largest of the 23 nuclei. $^{208}_{82}Pb$

Collect nuclides with neutron counts between 1 and 163. It was found that when the proton numbers are phantom numbers 2, 8, 20, 28, 50, and 82, 62 nuclides have the largest first excitation energy and the most stable nuclei.

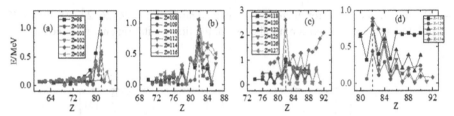

Fig. 13. The first excitation energy of nuclei with the same number of neutrons with n = 98, 100, 101, 102, 104, 106, 108, 109, 110, 112, 114, 116, 118, 120, 122, 125, 126, 127, 128, 129, 132 and 134.

3 The Relationship Between the Number of Protons and Neutrons and the Maximum Value of the First Excitation Energy of the Nucleus

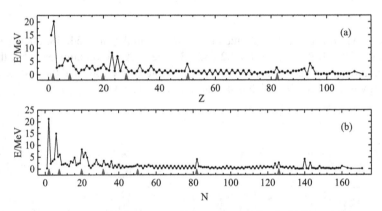

Fig. 14. (a) The maximum excitation energy of the nucleus at Z = 1. (b) The maximum excitation energy of the nucleus n = 2.

Compare the maximum value of the first excitation energy of the nucleus in the isotope. For example, ^4_1H the first excitation energy of the nucleus ^5_1H ^6_1H ^7_1H is 0.31 meV, 3.1 meV, 4.1 meV and 15 meV, respectively, so the maximum excitation energy of the nucleus at Z = 1 is 15 meV. Figure 14a. This is the one with the largest excitation energy of the first excitation in the isotope nucleus, z = 1, e = 15 meV. As can be seen from the figure, when the proton numbers are 2, 8, 20, 50, and 82, the first excitation energy of the nucleus is greater than the nearby value, and they are double magic nuclei, such as ^4_2He $^{16}_8O$ $^{48}_{20}Ca$ $^{132}_{50}Sn$ $^{208}_{82}Pb$.

The maximum value of the first excitation energy of the nuclei with the same number of neutrons is then compared. For example, the ^4_2He first excitation energy of the nucleus with, ^6_4Be is 20.21 meV and 1.67 meV, respectively, so the maximum excitation energy of the nucleus n = 2 is 20.21 meV, as shown in Fig. 14b, it is a nucleus with the same neutron element, and the first excitation energy is the largest. The figure shows that when n = 2, e = 20.21 meV. As can be seen from the figure, when the number of neutrons is 2, 8, 20, 28, 50, 82 and 126, the first excitation energy value of the nucleus is greater than nearby, and the maximum at 2. Their corresponding nuclei are mostly double magic nuclei, such as $_{2}^{4}He$ $_{2}^{4}He_{20}^{48}Ca_{50}^{132}Sn_{82}^{208}Pb$.

4 Analysis and Interpretation of Statistical Laws

In this paper, the first excitation energy of 110 isotopes is calculated. The statistical results show that there are 57 nuclei. When the number of protons is a magic number, the first excitation energy is the greatest (there is no magic number after z = 93); Calculate the first excitation energy of 161 nuclei with the same number of neutrons. Statistics show that there are 62 nuclei. When the neutron number is a magic number, the first excitation energy is the greatest (there is no magic number after n = 135). It can be seen from the relationship between the number of protons, the number of neutrons and the first excitation energy of the nucleus, when the number of protons or neutrons is a magic number, the first excitation energy of the nucleus is greater than the neighboring value, because the greater the first excitation energy of the nucleus, the more stable the nuclide, so when the number of nucleons is a phantom number, the more stable the nuclide. That is, when the number of nucleons is a magic number, the first excitation energy of the nucleus is greater and the nucleus is more stable.

At the same time, it can also be seen from Fig. 13 above that when the number of nuclei is small, the first excitation energy of the nucleus is also relatively large. It can be assumed that this is because when the number of nucleons is small, the nuclear force between them is relatively small, and the structure between the nucleons is relatively loose. At this time, the ground state energy will be relatively low, so it may be very different from the energy of the first excited state, that is, the first excited energy is larger. However, when the number of nuclei is large, because the nuclear force is very complex, there are many factors affecting nuclear energy, so when the first excitation energy is the greatest, the number of nuclei is not magical.

5 Conclusion

Through the statistical analysis of the experimental data of the first excitation energy of the nucleus, it is found that when most nuclei, especially the number of nuclei with fewer nuclei, are magic, the first excitation energy of the nucleus is the largest, and the nucleus is more stable, which indicates the correctness of the magic number model. Of course, there are also some nuclei. When the first excitation energy is greatest, the number of nucleons is not a magic number. This is because there are many factors affecting the size of the first excitation energy of the nucleus, and sometimes the situation is more complicated, which requires further analysis and research from the nuclear force and other aspects.

References

1. Guo, B., Wang, N.Y.: Sci Sin-Phys Mech Astron **60**(10), 102031 (2017)
2. Xia, X.W., Lin, Y., Zhao, P.W., et al.: At Data Nucl DataTables, 121–122 (2017)
3. Yang, C.Z.: Acta Physica Sinica **18**(6), 275 (1962) (in Chinese)
4. Meng, J., Guo, J.Y., Li, J., et al.: Progress in Physics **31**(4), 199 (2011) (in Chinese)
5. Meng, J.: Sci Sin-Phys Mech Astron **46**(1), 012001 (2016) (in Chinese)
6. Zhang, J.S., Han, Y.L.: Commun Theor Phys **36**(04), 437 (2001)
7. Zhang, J.S., Han, Y.L.: Commun Theor Phys **37**(04), 465 (2002)
8. Duan, J.F., Zhang, J.S., Wu, H.C., et al.: Phys Rev C **80**(6), 064612 (2009)
9. Duan, J.F., Zhang, J.S., Wu, H.C., et al.: Commun TheorPhys **54**(01), 129 (2010)
10. Zhang, J.S.: Commun Theor Phys **39**(04), 433 (2003)
11. Zhang, J.S.: Commun Theor Phys **39**(01), 83 (2003)
12. Zhang, J.S., Han, Y.L., Gao, LG.: Nucl Sci Eng **133**(2), 218 (1999)
13. Sun, X.J., Duan, J.F., Wang, J.M., et al.: Commun TheorPhys **48**(03), 534 (2007)
14. Sun, X.J., Qu, W.J., Duan, J.F., et al.: Phys Rev C **78**(5), 054610 (2008)
15. Yan, Y.L., Duan, J.F., Sun, X.J., et al.: Commun Theor Phys **44**(01), 128 (2005)
16. Zhang, J.S., Han, Y.L., Fan, X.L.: Commun Theor Phys **35**(05), 579 (2001)
17. Duan, J.F., Yan, Y.L., Wang, J.M., et al.: Commun TheorPhys **44**(04), 701 (2005)
18. Duan, J.F., Yan, Y.L., Sun, X.J., et al.: Commun Theor Phys **47**(01), 102 (2007)
19. Sun, X.J., Zhang, J.S.: Phys Rev C **92**(06), 061601(R) (2015)
20. Sun, X.J., Zhang, JS.: Phys Rev C **93**(1), 014609 (2016)
21. Goldhaber, G.S.: Phys Rev **90**(4), 587 (1953)
22. Kanungo, R., Tanihata, I., Ozawa, A.: Phys Lett B **528**(1–2), 58 (2002)
23. http://www.nndc.bnl.gov/nudat2/
24. Yang, F.: Atomic Physics, 3rd edn., p. 290. Higher Education Press, Beijing (2019)
25. Xia, X., Lin, Y., Zhao, P., et al.: Datasheet in Data Nucl, 121–122 (2017)
26. Long, Y., Xiaojun, S., Haiyuan, P.: The statistical law of the first excitation energy of atomic nuclei. Nucl. Phys. Rev. **36**(4), 408–413 (2019)
27. Clarification of Nuclear Physics, p. 190. Atomic Energy Press, Beijing (2000)
28. Several Milestones in Nuclear Structure Research of the Nuclear Structure Professional Committee of the Chinese Nuclear Physics Society and 20 Years of Nuclear Structure Research in China. High Energy Physics and Nuclear Physics, 2006, 30, Supplement II:1 – 13
29. Jijun, Z., Gang, C., Shuyong, L.: Mrs. Meyer and the Core-Shell Model. Physics of Colleges and Universities 25 (6), 40–43 (2006)
30. http://www.nndc.bnl.gov/nudat2/.
31. Wang, M., Audi, G., Kondev, F.G., et al.: Chinese Physics
32. Singh, B., Chen, J.: Nuclear Data Sheets, **126**(3), 138 (2015)

Design and Implementation of English Grammar Error Correction System Based on Deep Learning

Ning Chong[✉]

Department of Basic Courses, Modern College of Northwest University, Xi'an 710130, Shanxi, China
chongning1028@163.com

Abstract. The purpose of this project is to develop an English grammar error correction system based on deep learning. The system will be able to recognize grammatical errors and automatically correct them using machine learning technology. The main goal of the project is to build an efficient and accurate grammar error detection tool, which can detect and correct the errors made by users when inputting in English, Chinese and other languages. Grammar error detection system using deep learning technology: grammar correction is a technology that can identify and correct written English grammar errors. The system uses deep learning techniques to identify grammatical errors and correct them. It is used in conjunction with an algorithm for identifying errors and then generates a corrected sentence from which you can learn how to write correctly. The system also learns your writing style by observing how your writing changes over time, so it will be able to detect more errors. When using this tool, you don't have to remember any rules or patterns, because it will automatically detect problems and suggest corrections based on your knowledge of English grammar rules.

Keywords: Deep learning · Grammar correction · Automatic detection system

1 Introduction

Grammatical error correction (GEC) is a sub field of NLP. It has been applied in many scenes that directly interact with the general public, such as search query error correction, voice error correction, public opinion text error correction and so on. Under the background that deep learning is widely used, researchers have proposed a variety of methods to solve the problem of syntax error correction, such as the method of Feature Engineering Based on sequence annotation fusion.

The first is a distributed word vector based on co-occurrence matrix [1]. This method mainly establishes a word context matrix according to the text, each row represents a word, and each column represents a text or context. In the semantic analysis task, the co-occurrence matrix of words and text is counted, and the calculation method of matrix decomposition is used to obtain the word distributed vector. In addition, there

M. A. Jan and F. Khan (Eds.): BigIoT-EDU 2022, LNICST 467, pp. 557–562, 2023.
https://doi.org/10.1007/978-3-031-23944-1_59

are also examples of other scholars using co-occurrence matrix. Among them, the most famous glove model is one of the distributed word vectors generated based on co-occurrence matrix; The second is distributed word vector based on clustering. Among them, the most interesting is the Brownian clustering method, which is mainly used to solve the context of words. Then, researchers proposed several training methods using Brownian clustering; The third is distributed word vector based on neural network. Using neural network to train word embedding vector, word2vec word embedding vector is the most outstanding representative. Based on the previous research on vector embedding, this paper improves the vector embedding model [2]. Compared with traditional text representation, distributed coding has many advantages: 1) distributed coding describes the relevant information between semantics to a certain extent, such as calculating the semantic distance between words through cosine similarity and other methods, so as to carry more information; 2) The distributed coding method can set the dimension independently according to the individual hardware equipment, model structure, task requirements, etc. at the same time, it also alleviates the problem of dimension disaster to a certain extent. Based on this, this paper studies the design and implementation of English grammar error correction system based on deep learning.

2   Related Work

2.1   Deep Learning Algorithm

With people's higher and higher expectations of computer science, the problems required to be solved by it are becoming more and more complex. Beating a small monster is far from meeting people's demands. $1 + 1$ is easy to calculate, and $1 + 2$ is not difficult. These problems that can be solved are not listed below for the time being. The problem domain to be solved is becoming more and more complex. Even if it is the same problem, it faces more and more scenarios. We can't let the coder find the switch every time a new scene comes out, and then add another case before default [3]; There are thousands of scenes in the world. How many cases do you have? If you kill a yard farmer and sacrifice to heaven, there will be problems. Then what shall I do? So someone put forward a new idea - can the machine learn by itself without making it difficult for the coder (the person who put forward this concept must have been a coder)?

In comparison, deep learning is a relatively new concept. It is after 00. Strictly speaking, it was put forward in 2006. It is a machine learning technology used to establish and simulate the neural network of human brain for analytical learning, and simulate the mechanism of human brain to interpret data. Its basic feature is to try to imitate the mode of transmitting and processing information between brain neurons. The most significant applications are in the field of computer vision and natural language processing (NLP). Obviously, "deep learning" is strongly related to "neural network" in machine learning, and "neural network" is also its main algorithm and means [4]; Or we can call "deep learning" as "improved neural network" algorithm. Figure 1 below shows the framework of deep learning algorithm.

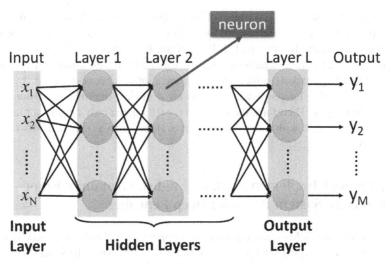

Fig. 1. Deep learning algorithm framework

Deep learning is divided into convolutional neural networks (CNN) and deep belief networks (DBN). Its main idea is to simulate human neurons. Each neuron receives information and transmits it to all adjacent neurons after processing. So it seems that the processing method is a bit like the following figure (students who want to know more can Google by themselves).

2.2 English Grammar Correction

Syntax error correction in this method, the prediction results of the classification model module can output error categories and corrected words, and add mechanical errors to the error categories, including punctuation, spelling and capitalization. Make full use of supervised and unsupervised models to locate and correct some basic errors in this step, so as to make the input of subsequent MT models as accurate and effective as possible [5]. Through the two-stage model fusion, we can combine the advantages of the two models to improve the effect: the classification method can summarize and identify the categories of single errors, and the effect of dealing with some limited types of errors is better; The machine translation method learns from parallel data without linguistic knowledge input, and is better at correcting complex errors.

This is an obvious conclusion. It would be better for MT to correct it after it is corrected based on the classify module. In at least one simple idea, first use the limited error class set to realize classification and positioning, complete the correction of limited class errors, and then input it into the NMT model, which not only makes the semantics more perfect and accurate, but also carries out operations such as error location marking, error type marking, error weighting representation, error loss weighting and so on to realize model optimization. Therefore, this kind of model idea of multi-mode integration is worthy of further exploration.

Although the rule-based error correction method has high error correction accuracy and can provide effective feedback for users, this rule-based automatic error correction method still has many limitations [6]. First of all, these methods rely on manual rule base, and the construction of manual rule base often requires the contribution of a large number of language experts, which will consume a lot of labor cost. Secondly, because English is a complex language with various error modes, the rule base often can not cover all error types. Therefore, the rule-based method can only correct some specific types, but can not deal with more complex error types, such as syntax errors involving context content.

3 Design and Implementation of English Grammar Error Correction System Based on Deep Learning

Statements with multiple syntax errors usually cannot be perfectly corrected by general seq2seq inference (single round inference). In the GEC problem, the source language is the same as the target language. This feature allows us to infer multiple editing statements through the multi round model, which leads to the multi round error correction promotion inference process based on fluency [7].

Specifically, the error correction seq2seq model first takes the primitive sentence XR as the input and outputs the hypothesis xo1. Then, the fluency improvement inference will use xo1 as the input to generate the next output xo2, rather than using xo1 directly as the final prediction. Unless xot can no longer improve the fluency of xot-1, the process will not end, that is, the intermediate results are recorded and can be paired as input until the fluency is not improved.

We use the number of occurrences of words in the data as the weight to construct the Huffman tree. The larger the weight value, the closer it is to the root node. In the Huffman tree structure, its root node corresponds to the word embedding vector mapped by the model, the leaf node is equal to the neuron of the model output layer, and the number of leaf nodes is equal to the length of the dictionary [8]. In Huffman tree, the training process of neural network model is not completed at one time through matrix operation, but goes down gradually along the tree structure until the target vocabulary is found. In the word2vec word vector model, the model judges whether to walk along the left subtree or the right subtree through the calculation method of binary logical regression.

$$J_c = \sum_{i=1}^{k} \sum_{p \in C_1} \|p - M_i\|^2 \tag{1}$$

$$J\left(\prod, W\right) = \sum_{k=1}^{K} \sum_{x \in \pi} \sum_{d=1}^{D} (x_{id} - v_{kd})^2 \tag{2}$$

Generally speaking, if you go to the left, it defaults to negative class (Huffman tree code is 1) and if you go to the right, it defaults to positive class (Huffman tree code is 0). Therefore, the probability of a word can be calculated according to its path in the binary tree. This hierarchical softmax method can reduce the number of calculations from O (n) to o (logn) [9]. Moreover, because the Huffman tree is a high-frequency word close to the root node, the high-frequency word will be found in less time, which is in line with the greedy optimization idea. The arrangement of English grammar bytes is shown in Fig. 2 below.

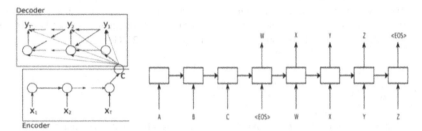

Fig. 2. English grammar byte arrangement

Compared with the rule-based error correction method, this method can well alleviate the pressure of manual annotation. Like the rule-based error correction method, this method can not cover all error types of English grammar. It can only correct specific error types (such as closed errors such as articles and prepositions). With the continuous improvement of computer hardware performance and the development of deep learning related theories, the research on sequence to sequence model is becoming more and more sophisticated. Researchers began to consider the English grammar error correction task as a sequence to sequence generation task, that is, the error correction process as a process of translating a wrong sentence into a correct sentence [10]. The grammar error correction algorithm based on neural machine translation can recognize all types of grammatical errors in sentences without exhausting all English grammar rules, which gets rid of the limitations of the traditional rule-based and statistical classification based error correction algorithms.

4   Conclusion

Deep learning is a kind of machine learning, which uses deep neural network to learn complex functions, such as image recognition, speech and text processing. The model learns by itself without any human intervention. Deep learning is one of the most popular types of artificial intelligence (AI). The system aims to correct errors in English grammar. The error correction system is based on deep learning technology and can be used in any language. The working principle of the system is to analyze the sentence and then correct the grammatical errors of the sentence. It also provides a list of words that may be wrong if they reappear later in the same text or document. How does this work? This type of error correction works by understanding how sentences are constructed, so it can understand the causes of errors and then provide advice on how to fix them without having to read through each word again.

Acknowledgements. This work was supported by:

1) "the 14th Five-year Plan" Education Scientific Research Project of Shaanxi Province in 2021, a Research on "Half-flipped Classroom" Model in College English Teaching for Students Majoring in Art (SGH21Y0492).

2) the New Liberal Arts Research and Reform Practice project of Shaanxi Province in 2021, a Practice and exploration of "Blended-learning" model and "First-class Course" construction based on online self-built courses.

3) the Key education and teaching reform research project of Modern College of Northwest University, The Construction, Development and Reform of College English School-based Online Courses in Media Colleges based on online Teaching Platform (21JG02).

References

1. Zhang, G.: A study of grammar analysis in English teaching with deep learning algorithm. Int. J. Emerg. Technol. Learn. (iJET) **15**(18), 20 (2020)
2. Hu, L., Tang, Y., Wu, X., et al.: Considering optimization of English grammar error correction based on neural network. Neural Comput. Appl. **17** (2021)
3. Saglam, B., Duran, E., Cicek, D.C., et al.: Estimation Error Correction in Deep Reinforcement Learning for Deterministic Actor-Critic Methods (2021)
4. Zhang, J.: A Review of Grammar Corrective Feedback: The Learning Experience in China's English Classes (2020)
5. Julien, E., Tim, V., Joscha, M., et al.: Deep learning-based forward and cross-scatter correction in dual-source CT. Med. Phys. (2021)
6. Li, A., Du, C., Pan, Y.: Deep-learning-based motion correction in OCT angiography. J. Biophotonics (2021)
7. Khadem-Hosseini, M., Ghaemmaghami, S., Abtahi, A., et al.: Error correction in pitch detection using a deep learning based classification. In: IEEE/ACM Transactions on Audio, Speech, and Language Processing, PP(99):1–1 (2020)
8. Zhou, S., Liu, W.: English Grammar error correction algorithm based on classification model. Complexity, 2021 (2021)
9. Puig, O., Henriksen, O.M., Andersen, F.L., et al.: Deep-learning-based attenuation correction in dynamic [15O]H2O studies using PET/MRI in healthy volunteers. J. Cereb. Blood Flow Metab. **41**(12), 3314–3323 (2021)
10. Zhou, D.: The efficacy of oral grammar error correction in classroom. In: 2020 Conference on Education, Language and Inter-cultural Communication (ELIC 2020) (2020)

Design of Children and Adolescents' Physical Health Intervention System Based on Genetic Algorithm

Haibo Dou[✉]

Xianyang Normal University, Xianyang 712000, Shaanxi, China
douhaibo1111@126.com

Abstract. Childhood and adolescence generally refers to the age stage from preschool to puberty, which is an important stage of life. Children and adolescents are also a generation that governments have always been very concerned about. Their physique and health status directly affect the future national physique and health level of a country, and it is also an important aspect to measure a country's comprehensive national strength. The child and adolescent health intervention system based on genetic algorithm is a computer-based application program, which can be used to help people make health decisions. It uses information from the patient's medical history, family history, lifestyle, and environment to recommend appropriate treatment plans. The system also provides information on treatment outcomes to inform future decisions. Genetic algorithm (GA) is a mathematical technology, which has been used by scientists and engineers as a tool to solve complex problems for many years, such as designing new drugs or improving aircraft design.

Keywords: Children and adolescents · Genetic algorithm · Physical health · Intervene

1 Introduction

Childhood and adolescence generally refers to the age stage from preschool to puberty, which is an important stage of life. Children and adolescents are also a generation that governments have always been very concerned about. Their physique and health status directly affect the future national physique and health level of a country, and it is also an important aspect to measure a country's comprehensive national strength. The physical health problems of children and adolescents in China have always been paid great attention by the party and the government. Since 1979, under the organization and leadership of the Ministry of health, the Ministry of education and the State General Administration of sports, China has carried out eight large-scale surveys on students' physical health, learned about students' physical health level, and formulated a series of plans and guidelines to promote the development of children and adolescents' physical health [1].

M. A. Jan and F. Khan (Eds.): BigIoT-EDU 2022, LNICST 467, pp. 563–569, 2023.
https://doi.org/10.1007/978-3-031-23944-1_60

Physique refers to the quality of the human body. The physique of different individuals has obvious differences. At the same time, the physique of the same individual has different characteristics in different stages of development. At the Tai'an conference in 1982, Chinese experts and scholars put forward clear regulations on the boundary of physique, and agreed that physique is a comprehensive and comprehensive physical quality, morphological structure, psychological factors, physiological functions, sports ability and other aspects of the human body on the basis of heredity and acquired Relatively stable characteristics. Genetic factors, natural environment, nutrition, social economy, physical exercise and other aspects will have an impact on human physical condition, which is still quite important [2]. The evaluation of physical condition should also be carried out comprehensively from the five aspects of physical function, morphological structure, physical quality, sports ability and psychological factors contained in the connotation of physical fitness [3].

In the past 20 years since 1979, China has conducted seven large-scale tests, investigations and studies on students' physical health, and conducted seven tests and reports on students' physical health in 1979, 1985, 1991, 1995, 2000, 2002 and 2005. The Chinese students and health research group, as the host institution, systematically studied the physical health status of Chinese students from 1979 to 2005 and predicted the future development trend [4]. The survey shows that the growth level of students' body shape has been greatly improved, such as: height, weight, chest circumference and other morphological development indicators continue to grow; The growth rate of physical function growth level is not obvious. However, some age groups also have negative growth, which obviously lags behind the growth of physical form growth level. Experts also summarized the physical condition of teenagers as "hard, soft and stupid", that is, hard joints, soft muscles and uncoordinated movements. Accompanied by the decline of physical fitness is the adverse trend of teenagers' psychological status, such as poor emotional adjustment ability, inappropriate frustration response, weak psychological tolerance, etc. while adult diseases such as myopia, diabetes, hypertension, etc. also come to teenagers prematurely [5]. Therefore, the adolescent health problem has become a problem that the society, schools and parents must pay attention to.

2   Related Work

2.1   Constitution

Constitution is the quality of human body. Constitution is a relatively stable feature of human organism in form and function on the basis of genetic variation and acquired.

Constitution consists of three aspects: physique, physical fitness and adaptability.

Physique refers to the form and structure of the human body, the level of human growth and development, the overall index and proportion of the body and the posture of the body. Physical ability refers to the ability of the functions of human organs and systems in muscle activities. Adaptability refers to the functional ability of people to adapt to the external environment and the embodiment of the body's ability to resist diseases. Therefore, physique refers to the material basis of people's working ability and life activities [6]. Briefly speaking, constitution refers to the quality of the human body itself, which is a relatively stable feature of the human body in morphology, biochemistry, physiology and behavior.

The factors that affect the physical strength are also determined in many aspects. It has a close relationship with heredity, environment, nutrition, physical exercise and so on. Heredity only provides the possibility or prerequisite for the condition and development of physique. The strength of physique is affected by acquired environment, nutrition, health and physical exercise. Therefore, scientific exercise in a planned and purposeful way is the most active and effective means to enhance physical fitness and a good choice to improve physical fitness.

2.2 Physical Exercise

"Life lies in sports". Physical exercise is one of the most important factors to promote physical development and enhance physical health. Physical exercise can promote the metabolic process in the body. With physical exertion, catabolism accelerates and heat production increases. The movement not only strengthened the dissimilation process, but also strengthened the assimilation process under the proper nutrition guarantee; And under normal circumstances, the assimilation process generally exceeds the dissimilation process, so that the accumulation of nutrients in the body significantly exceeds the consumption, thus promoting the growth and development. Physical exercise can effectively promote the development of the respiratory system of young students and improve their functional level. During exercise, the carbon dioxide produced by muscle activity stimulates the respiratory central system, accelerates and deepens respiration, and promotes carbon dioxide emission and oxygen inhalation [7]. Therefore, those who often take physical exercise have developed respiratory muscles, enlarged chest circumference, significantly enhanced respiratory depth, lung ventilation and vital capacity, improved resistance to the invasion of various bacteria, and significantly reduced the incidence of upper respiratory infectious diseases. Physical exercise can promote the development of cardiovascular system and improve the functional level of cardiovascular system. During exercise, the workload of the heart increases, the blood flow increases, and the heart rate increases, so that the myocardium gets sufficient nutrition. In the long run, it will increase the volume of the heart and thicken the ventricles. The heart muscle gets exercise, the blood circulation of the whole body and the coronary artery are improved. It is found that the volume, longitudinal diameter and transverse diameter of the heart of young athletes aged 14 to 17 who have participated in amateur sports school training for more than one year are larger than those of their ordinary peers; Because the contractility of the heart is enhanced, that is to say, the stroke output of the heart is also increased, so the quiet heart rate of young athletes is lower than that of ordinary teenagers. Physical exercise can significantly promote the development of the motor system (including nerves, bones and muscles) [8]. Participating in physical exercise can master a variety of motor skills, improve the coordination of muscle work, improve motor ability, and also significantly improve the function and development of the nervous system. When taking part in physical exercise, the human body accelerates the blood circulation around the body, so that the bone tissue in the osteogenesis period can get rich blood supplement, get more nutrients, and speed up the process of osteogenesis. The stress borne by bones in running, jumping, jumping and stretching can stimulate the growth of cartilage plate and promote the proliferation of cartilage plate. In addition, sunlight exposure during outdoor activities can promote the production of vitamin D in the body, accelerate the process of bone calcification, and make the bone more solid.

Therefore, the average height of teenagers who often participate in exercise is often higher than those who do not exercise or rarely exercise. During exercise, the muscles work nervously. In order to ensure their needs for oxygen and nutrients, the number of open capillaries in the muscles increases greatly, and the blood supply increases exponentially. In this way, muscle fibers become thicker, larger and more elastic, and endurance and muscle working ability will be improved accordingly. In the long run, it can also make joint ligaments stronger and stronger, increase joint flexibility, and significantly improve the physical quality of teenagers [9]. Physical exercise under the guidance of science is an important means to control body weight, regulate body composition and improve body function. After long-term exercise, adolescents' lean weight increases significantly, but their weight does not change significantly. The main reason is that the fat content in their weight decreases correspondingly. Physical exercise can also effectively regulate endocrine and promote the normal development of adolescence.

3   Children and Adolescents' Physical Health Intervention System Based on Genetic Algorithm

3.1   Genetic Algorithm

Genetic algorithm is an adaptive global optimization probability search algorithm, which simulates the genetic and evolutionary processes of organisms in the natural environment. It was first proposed by Professor Holland of the University of Michigan in the United States. It originated from the research on natural and artificial adaptive systems in the 1960s. In the 1970s, de Jong carried out a large number of pure numerical function optimization experiments on the computer based on the idea of genetic algorithm. On the basis of a series of research work, Goldberg summarized it in the 1980s and formed the basic framework of genetic algorithm. The problems that genetic algorithm can solve involve various fields, such as function optimization, combinatorial optimization, production scheduling, automatic control, robotics, image processing, artificial life and so on [10]. This paper mainly applies genetic algorithm to optimize an objective function whose value is related to the fitness of its decision variable (independent variable):

$$\begin{cases} \max, f(X) \\ s.t. X \in R \\ \quad R \subseteq U \end{cases} \tag{1}$$

In genetic algorithm, the decision variable x constitutes the solution space of the problem. The search for the optimal solution of the problem is realized through the search process of chromosome X, so all chromosomes X constitute the search space of the problem.

The evolution of organisms is dominated by groups. Correspondingly, the operation object of genetic algorithm is a set composed of m individuals, which is called population. Similar to the natural evolution process of biological generations, the operation process of genetic algorithm is also a process of repeated iteration. The population of generation t is recorded as Pt. After one generation of heredity and evolution, the population of generation t + 1 is obtained. They are also a set composed of multiple individuals, which is recorded as P (t + 1). This population continues to undergo genetic and evolutionary operations, and each time it inherits more individuals with high fitness to the next generation according to the rule of survival of the fittest. In this way, an excellent individual x will be finally obtained in the population, and its corresponding phenotype x will reach the optimal solution x*. The genetic algorithm process is shown in Fig. 1.

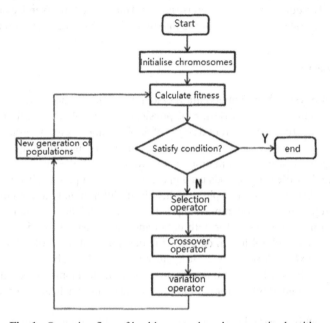

Fig. 1. Operation flow of health system based on genetic algorithm

3.2 Prescription Design of Extracurricular Physical Exercise

In order to ensure the smooth progress of the students participating in the training according to the research plan, this training will strictly determine the type, intensity, frequency and time of exercise in the form of exercise prescription. At the same time, the whole exercise prescription implementation process will take the form of collective training. Under the guidance of several experts and after reading a large number of training books, the experiment carefully formulated the training plan and physical exercise prescription. At the same time, the strict training frequency, intensity and time were formulated. In strict accordance with the principle of scientific training, no training accident occurred in the training process, ensuring the smooth progress of the experiment and achieving the ideal effect for the success of the experiment and the research effect.

The physical exercise prescription is:

(1) The purpose of physical exercise is to improve the physical health level of the experimenter.
(2) Types of physical exercise: endurance sports mainly include aerobic sports, such as basketball, running, mountaineering, rope skipping, step jumping coordination training and strength training, so that students can truly achieve the best effect of comprehensive exercise.
(3) Exercise frequency, exercise time and exercise intensity: exercise frequency 3 times a week; The duration of each exercise is 45–60 min; Moderate exercise intensity (the target heart rate is 65%–75% of the maximum heart rate, i.e. 125–160 beats/min).

4   Conclusion

The design of physical health intervention system for children and adolescents is a study aimed at determining the best design of physical activity plan for children and adolescents. In evaluating the different designs of adolescent exercise programs, including aerobic training, strength training or aerobic strength combined training. The research project will provide useful information on how to design an effective exercise program by evaluating the different methods used in the development process. To study the comprehensive evaluation system of physical health of children and adolescents, establish a scientific, representative, operable and practical index evaluation system, and provide an evaluation method suitable for both urban and rural areas, which is the demand of the development of school health care and the development trend of school education in China from examination oriented to quality-oriented. It is also a new professional requirement put forward by social development and the development of children's and children's health undertakings for our children's and children's health workers.

Acknowledgements. Special Project of Scientific Research Plan from Department of Education in Shaanxi Province (19JK0915); Special Funds for Scientific Research Project of Xianyang Normal University (XSYK17047).

References

1. Shah, K., Mann, S., Singh, R., et al.: Impact of COVID-19 on the mental health of children and adolescents. Cureus **12**(8) (2020)
2. Wilson, B., Barnett, L.M.: Physical activity interventions to improve the health of children and adolescents in out of home care—a systematic review of the literature. Child. Youth Serv. Rev. **110**, 104765 (2020)
3. Pavlyshyn, H., Kovalchuk, T., Furdela, V., et al.: Parents' perception of health-related quality of life in healthy children and adolescents. Paediatr. Croat. **64**(3), 151–158 (2021)
4. Luijten, M., Muilekom, M., Teela, L., et al.: The impact of lockdown during the COVID-19 pandemic on mental and social health of children and adolescents (2021)
5. Pinto, J., Cruz, J., Pinho, T., et al.: Health-Related Physical Fitness of Children and Adolescents in Portugal. Children and Youth Services Review **117**, 105279 (2020)

6. Moran, R., Gutman, L.M.: Mental health training to improve communication with children and adolescents: a process evaluation. J. Clin. Nurs. (2020)
7. Zwi, K., Sealy, L., Samir, N., et al.: Asylum seeking children and adolescents in Australian immigration detention on Nauru: a longitudinal cohort study. BMJ Paediatr. Open **4**(1), e000615 (2020)
8. Sarafis, I., Diou, C., Papapanagiotou, V., et al.: Inferring the spatial distribution of physical activity in children population from characteristics of the environment. In: 2020 42nd Annual International Conference of the IEEE Engineering in Medicine and Biology Society (EMBC) in Conjunction with the 43rd Annual Conference of the Canadian Medical and Biological Engineering Society. IEEE (2020)
9. Salussolia, A., Montalti, M., Marini, S., et al.: Preliminary data on physical well-being of children and adolescents during the SARS-CoV-2 pandemic. Eur. J. Public Health **31**, 164–215 (2021)
10. Ares, G., Bove, I., Vidal, L., et al.: The experience of social distancing for families with children and adolescents during the coronavirus (COVID-19) pandemic in Uruguay: difficulties and opportunities (2021)

Application of Fuzzy Data Mining Algorithm in Human Resource Management of Power Industry

Fengting Zheng[1](), Sentao Song[2], Yu Xia[2], and Yan Zhang[3]

[1] ZheJiang Hua Yun Electric Power Industrial Group Co., Ltd., Hangzhou 310000, Zhejiang, China

[2] ZheJiang HuaYun Information Technology Co., Ltd., Hangzhou 310000, Zhejiang, China
[3] ZheJiang HuaYun Electric Power Engineering Design and Construction Co., Ltd., Hangzhou 310000, Zhejiang, China

Abstract. The main purpose of this study is to provide the application of fuzzy data mining algorithm in the process of human resource management in power industry. 1. It is used to find the best candidate for the position, and it can also be used to find the right candidate for a specific position according to his / her performance. 2. Apply fuzzy set theory to evaluate the quality of information received from employees, customers, suppliers, etc., and then further process these information through decision trees, neural networks and other algorithms. These results will help make decisions about future actions, which may include employee promotion or demotion, setting up new positions or changing existing positions.

Keywords: Fuzzy data mining algorithm · Human resources · Power industry

1 Introduction

In today's increasingly fierce market competition, the competitors faced by the power industry are no longer limited to regions, not only the same ethnic power industry under the same local politics, but also multinational corporations and multinational groups with strong economic strength from all over the world. In such an environment, the power industry can not survive and develop without its core competitiveness - talent. As the core position of "talents" in the market competition is more and more widely recognized, the power industry also pays more attention to the absorption and training of "talents" [1].

In the era of economic globalization and informatization, with the popularization of network and the development of database technology, the power industry is facing a large number of human resource information that is changing rapidly. Scientifically and accurately grasp the massive and dynamic human resource information faced by human resource management, conduct efficient data analysis, extract valuable information, and find the connections and patterns among them, so as to make the use of a large amount

M. A. Jan and F. Khan (Eds.): BigIoT-EDU 2022, LNICST 467, pp. 570–576, 2023.
https://doi.org/10.1007/978-3-031-23944-1_61

of data more scientific and effective, and provide strong decision support for human resource management, which has become the key to human resource management in the power industry.

Human resource data is ability data, including both quantitative and qualitative indicators. The given value of the corresponding indicators is subjective. In order to reduce the deviation of the results caused by subjectivity and reduce the error rate as much as possible, most of the data mining work focuses on deblurring and uncertainty. Undoubtedly, fuzzy algorithm, rough set theory and other methods are of great help to solve uncertain problems, but these methods are not ideal when applied in human resource management. The reason is that the basic concepts are inconsistent. This kind of method, with the basic purpose of transforming the uncertainty of information into certainty, although it helps to classify, summarize and refine human resource data, it does not directly affect human resource management.

However, fuzzy data mining algorithms, which are basically consistent with the concept of human resource management, lack of discussion on the uncertainty problem on the one hand; On the other hand, most studies directly use the traditional fuzzy data mining algorithm, but do not improve or only partially improve the specific problem of human resource management, resulting in problems such as weak local optimization ability, difficult retention of dominant individuals, samples limited to the internal power industry, which are quite different from the actual situation of human resource management.

2 Related Work

2.1 Current Situation of Power Human Resources

Human resource management is very important and necessary for any power industry. For the power industry, brain drain is a huge loss, and some core talents carry a lot of professional knowledge and skills, and master the information and technology within the power industry. If this part of core talents drain, it may cause the leakage of core technology or machine secrets, and the consequences are unimaginable. In addition, the power industry has invested a lot of human and material resources in the talent training stage, such as training costs, recruitment costs, etc. after the brain drain, the human resource development costs invested by the power industry will be wasted. In addition, the new economic environment and the development environment of the power industry are also forcing the power industry to strengthen human resource management [2].

The development of the power industry is inseparable from the continuous contribution of talents. Doing a good job in human resource management can help the power industry establish a standardized management system, excavate and cultivate potential talents in the power industry, and provide core talent support for the development of the power industry. With the development of many power industries, the scale of employees is gradually expanding. At this moment, a large number of complex human resources problems make the HR of the power industry unable to deal with them in time, which seems to be in a dilemma. At this time, using human resource system to solve these problems can effectively improve the efficiency of human resource management in the power industry.

For a power industry, the sustained economic growth of the power industry is insepa-rable from the efficient human resource management operation within the power industry, and an efficient human resource management system can bring long-term and sustainable effects to the power industry, such as helping the power industry establish a standardized and reasonable management system, and helping the power industry to tap and cultivate potential talents in the power industry, Build its own strategic talent echelon in the power industry and lay a good foundation for the development of the power industry.

2.2 Fuzzy Data Mining Algorithm

Big data technology can be understood as a practical application technology covering all kinds of big data platforms and big data index system. In the face of this large data set, it is almost impossible to use traditional data calculation tools. Then the emergence of big data technology solves this problem. Big data technology can collect and clean up all kinds of strange data, save high-quality data for storage, and conduct data analysis and statistics. Simple report statistics can use SQL and hive statistics, and complex ones can use spark and storm. Finally, data visualization can provide reference data for decision-making [3].

With the development of the data age, people are more and more curious about big data, but their cognition is vague, and they do not have a correct understanding of what big data is. Then let me answer your doubts.

The first is the theoretical level. Although practice produces true knowledge, theory is the basis of practice and the only way to get true knowledge. In the theoretical level, big data is defined as having strong decision-making power, keen insight and discovery power and process optimization ability. Through these capabilities, we can adapt to massive, high growth rate and diverse and complex information assets.

Secondly, at the technical level, technology is a necessary means to reflect the value of big data. Here we can use some technical tools, such as basic tools such as VBA, Excel, and advanced tools such as python, to collect, process, store and form the final results of information data.

Finally, the practical level, only through practice can we test the truth. Here, big data from the Internet, big data from the government, big data applications from enterprises, and small applications from personal data have shown a good picture and future of big data applications in modern society. Due to the incompleteness, contradiction and inconsistency of data, we cannot fuse data into the form we want in one step. Therefore, data fusion is usually a hierarchical complex system composed of multiple modules [4]. According to the different functions and characteristics of each module, the data fusion architecture mainly includes the following: Joint directors of laboratories (JDL): as shown in Fig. 1 below, JDL data fusion architecture includes five data processing levels and three supporting components, and the data processing process is one-way hierarchical.

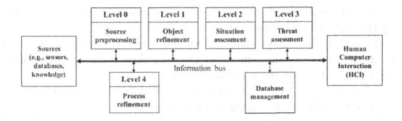

Fig. 1. Joint directors of laboratories (JDL)

3 Application of Fuzzy Data Mining Algorithm in Human Resource Management of Power Industry

Another important function of the human resource system is to analyze the human resource data of the power industry as a whole, or by organization Departments and individuals to analyze. The traditional manual analysis method takes a long time to collect the data of each department, and then analyze it, while the human resources system can call the relevant data in real time, process the data almost every second, and present the analysis report [5]. According to the human resource data report, we can analyze the human resource allocation, cost, performance output, etc. of the Organization Department, reasonably optimize human resources, and give full play to the maximum efficiency of the Department.

In addition to solving transactional problems, the human resources system can also help the power industry conduct talent inventory, excavate potential talents in the power industry, and then cultivate potential talents as a strategic talent reserve for the power industry. The human resources system can conduct comprehensive analysis based on employee file information and employee project experience, training experience, performance data, personality characteristics and other factors, identify talents with high potential, and provide core talent reserves for the strategic development of the power industry.

The basic idea of fuzzy data mining algorithm is "survival of the fittest, elimination of the fittest", which is basically consistent with the idea of enterprises in talent screening. Only the talents suitable for the enterprise are what the enterprise needs.

Talent planning can be carried out according to different industries and the current situation of the enterprise, with strong portability.

The most important thing of fuzzy data mining algorithm is the design of fitness function. As long as the target solution is set, the direction of evolution will be towards the target. This determines that even if the same fuzzy data mining algorithm steps and procedures, as long as the design of fitness function is different, different solutions can be obtained, which solves the problem of different requirements in human resource management in all walks of life and even in all enterprises.

On the one hand, the introduction of fuzzy data mining algorithm is to realize the "survival of the fittest" of posts, find out the most suitable candidates for each post and provide corresponding implementation strategies; On the other hand, it is to realize fast search in massive data. The grey correlation analysis is mainly used to solve the uncertainty of information and realize the quantitative analysis of the development trend of the dynamic process of human resources data [6].

Because in an organization, different jobs require employees to have different ability contents and levels, even if the ability characteristics of employees in the same job are different in different organizations and industries.

Therefore, this paper first establishes the competency index system of the corresponding position, obtains the matching index through the grey correlation analysis, then establishes the fitness function combined with the corresponding weight, and finally applies it to data mining. The processing and execution process of HR algorithm is shown in Fig. 2 below.

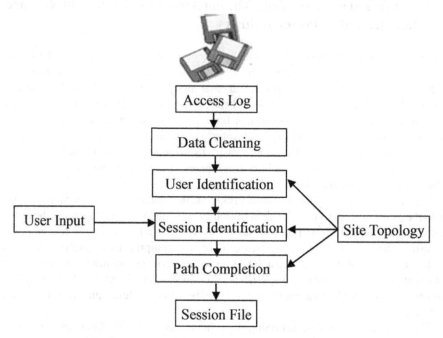

Fig. 2. Processing and execution process of HR algorithm

4 Simulation Analysis

The general model established here has a certain sense of universality, that is, enterprises generally need to consider these aspects in personnel adjustment. However, when matching personnel for a specific position, the corresponding indicators of the model should be increased or decreased to better select talents suitable for the position [7].

(1) Determine the evaluation value

After the competency model is established, corresponding evaluation values should be given to each index. The evaluation value can be objective data, such as work quantity. It can also be an objective evaluation value, such as initiative. However, it should be noted that the evaluation value must be the value after quantification. Qualitative data can be quantified by sorting and scoring.

After the evaluation value is obtained, the index values are normalized. The normalization formula used in this paper is as follows:

$$f(x_{ij}) = \begin{cases} C_1, x_{ij} = 5 \\ C_2, x_{ij} = 4 \\ C_3, x_{ij} = 3 \\ C_4, x_{ij} = 2 \\ C_5, x_{ij} = 1 \end{cases} \tag{1}$$

Take the normalized series Xij as the reference series, which can be the optimal value of each index in M evaluation units, or the evaluation standard recognized in the industry (generally speaking, if only the promotion of talents from within the company, there is no need to adopt the industry recognized standard) [7]. Calculate the correlation coefficient according to the normalized matrix X, and the corresponding calculation formula is:

$$AVF(x_i) = \frac{1}{m} \sum_{f=1}^{m} f(x_{ij}) \tag{2}$$

Based on the characteristics of human resource data and its application in personnel recruitment and enterprise organizational structure, this paper proposes a more suitable coding method for human resource data after referring to a variety of coding technologies.

(1) Simple binary coding is adopted for small numerical data.
(1) For large numerical data or non numerical data, 1-bit or 3-bit binary coding is used to indicate the consistency between personnel information and the information required by the enterprise. In 1-bit binary, "0" means no, "1" means yes. In 3-bit binary, the first bit

"O" of "0" indicates that it is not far exceeded, "1" indicates that the capacity exceeds the requirements of the enterprise; The "O" in the second place means that it does not meet the requirements of the enterprise.

Ask, "1" means to achieve; "O" in the third place means no, "1" means slightly. And when the second bit is 0o, the first bit cannot be 1 [7].

For example, 110 indicates that a person's ability in a certain aspect is higher than the ability required by the enterprise; 001 indicates that someone has certain ability in a certain aspect but has not yet met the requirements of the enterprise.

5 Conclusion

This paper will discuss the application of fuzzy data mining algorithm in human resource management of power industry. The main purpose is to make an important contribution to the development of fuzzy data mining algorithm and its application in human resource management in power industry. Using these methods, we analyze the relevant cases of human resource management in the power industry. Fuzzy data mining algorithm is used to identify hidden patterns in data. It helps to find out the relationship between different variables and predict future results based on these relationships. The main objective of this study is to propose a new human resource management model in the power industry, which can be used as a decision support tool for managers of power generation companies.

References

1. Wei, F.: Performance evaluation of tourism human resource management based on fuzzy data mining. J. Math. (2022)
2. Tv, V., Manikandan, V.: Design and development of adaptive fuzzy control system for power management in residential smart grid using bat algorithm. Technol. Econ. Smart Grids Sustain. Energy 3, 1–5 (2018)
3. Wang, H.M.: Research on data mining algorithm in power marketing analysis. In: Journal of Physics: Conference Series, vol. 1635, no. 1, 012002 (6 p.) (2020)
4. Rs, A., Mm, B.: Generalized fuzzy logic based performance prediction in data mining - ScienceDirect. In: Materials Today: Proceedings (2020)
5. Xu, M., Li, C.: Data mining method of enterprise human resource management based on simulated annealing algorithm. Security and Communication Networks (2021)
6. Bo, Z.: Application analysis of big data in the human resource management of power supply enterprises. Power Systems and Big Data (2018)
7. Qinghua, H.A.N., Minghai, P.A.N., Wucai, Z., Zhiheng, L., et al.: Time resource management of OAR based on fuzzy logic priority for multiple target tracking. J. Syst. Eng. & Electron. 29, 742–755 (2018)

Using Deep Convolution Neural Network to Detect the Wrong Movement in Physical Education Teaching and Training

Shi Yan[⊠]

BoHai University, Shandong 121000, China
Cidy1979@163.com

Abstract. In order to reduce the error rate of sports teaching and training error action detection and improve the detection effect, a sports teaching and training error action detection method based on deep convolution neural network is studied. The main idea of this method is to detect errors in physical training based on deep convolution neural network. The error detection process can be divided into two parts: first, we need to find out whether the physical exercise data is correct; Second, if they are wrong, we need to find out where they are wrong. Therefore, our model is designed as a combination of traditional and new methods, such as deep learning and other machine learning techniques.

Keywords: Physical education · Convolutional neural network · Deep learning · Training · Motion detection

1 Introduction

At this stage, with the continuous improvement of hardware computing power, the continuous development of machine learning and pattern recognition theory, artificial intelligence has once again become a hot topic in the academic and business circles. Artificial intelligence and computer vision technology are inseparable. This upsurge of artificial intelligence is the first to set off in the field of computer vision. The main driving force comes from the deep learning represented by convolutional neural network [1]. Thanks to the high-performance computing graphics card, Professor Hinton of the University of Toronto and his students successfully trained a deep-seated convolutional neural network in 2012, and made great progress in object classification tasks, overcoming the difficulty of neural network training. After that, deep learning technologies such as convolutional neural network have been rapidly applied to various research topics in the field of computer vision, and achieved better results than traditional machine learning methods [2]. At this stage, convolution neural network and recurrent neural network (RNN) 2 introduce new elements on the basis of traditional artificial neural network, such as convolution, nonlinear activation unit, dropout, time gate, etc. the theoretical framework is more perfect. With the strong promotion of academia and business circles,

© ICST Institute for Computer Sciences, Social Informatics and Telecommunications Engineering 2023
Published by Springer Nature Switzerland AG 2023. All Rights Reserved
M. A. Jan and F. Khan (Eds.): BigIoT-EDU 2022, LNICST 467, pp. 577–582, 2023.
https://doi.org/10.1007/978-3-031-23944-1_62

deep learning technology is more and more widely used in practice[3]. At the same time, deep learning technology is also rapidly extended to speech recognition, natural language processing and other fields. In some specific tasks, such as large-scale image classification, artificial intelligence playing go, etc., computers have the same or even higher intelligence level as human beings.

Deep learning is a branch of machine learning, but it is different from traditional machine learning methods. Traditional machine learning methods rely on good manual features. A key problem in using machine algorithms is how to design features suitable for specific problems. The quality of feature selection has a great impact on the results. The starting point of deep learning is to let the machine automatically learn good features without manual feature design process. The traditional machine learning method is generally a shallow model with only a single hidden layer, and the ability of feature expression is limited. Under limited samples and computing units, the ability of shallow model to represent complex functions is limited, and its generalization ability for complex classification problems is restricted [4]. Convolutional neural network and other deep learning models use multiple hidden layers, the output of each layer is used as the input of the next layer, and the hierarchical expression method obtains more abstract feature representation. Deep learning combines low-level features to form more abstract high-level representation attribute categories or features to discover the distributed feature representation of data. Through the nonlinear structure, the deep convolution network can approximate and realize complex functions, establish complex input-output mapping relationships, and perform much better than the traditional shallow model in large-scale classification and detection tasks.

2   Introduction

2.1   Composition Unit of Convolutional Neural Network

Convolutional neural network is derived from traditional artificial neural network, which is different from artificial neural network. The introduction of convolution structure and sampling structure greatly simplifies the complexity of the network, reduces the number of parameters connected between each layer of the network, reduces the risk of over fitting, and makes the network easier to train. The reduced parameters of convolution structure are reflected in two aspects. On the one hand, it is local perception. Convolution structure makes the connection between neurons no longer global connection but local connection [5]. Corresponding to an image pixel and the surrounding local pixels are closely related to each other. It is not necessary to perceive all image pixels, and then connect the neurons with local information at the high level to obtain neurons with a larger sensing range. The other is parameter sharing, that is, in local perception, a set of parameters are shared at different locations, which means that a fixed size convolution check has only one set of parameters when the whole graph is convoluted. The sampling structure directly maps a local area neuron to a value, and achieves efficient spatial dimensionality reduction. Local sensing, weight sharing and sampling in time or space make the convolutional neural network invariant in deformation, displacement and scale to a certain extent [6].

A deep convolution network can be composed of a multi-layer structure. Each layer structure is the input of the characteristic map obtained from the above layer, and the new characteristic map is output through the calculation of this layer. It is generally believed that the information expressed by the feature map at the bottom is close to the gradient, color, edge and other features of the image, while the information expressed by the feature map at the top is more abstract and global, which is compounded by the features at the bottom, has stronger expression ability, and is more closely related to specific tasks. Convolutional neural network can have a variety of layer structure configurations, and different layers can be connected in a variety of different ways, so convolutional network can have a variety of deformations [7]. However, the constituent elements of the network foundation are similar, which are generally composed of convolution layer, sampling layer, activation layer, normalization layer and full connection layer, as shown in Fig. 1.

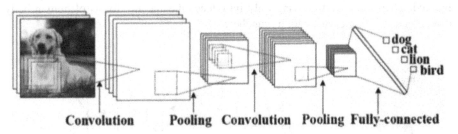

Fig. 1. Convolutional neural network unit

2.2 Action Detection Related Work

Gkioxira et al. Proposed the task of action detection and explained in detail the differences between action recognition and action detection. They applied convolutional neural network to these two tasks. The specific method is to propose a multi task convolutional neural network based on RCNN, which can jointly carry out human motion recognition, human body detection, pose estimation, etc. For different tasks, different branches are constructed in the network, and the loss function corresponding to the task is used to train the RCNN network. Different task branches share the convolution layer parameters of RCNN basic network, which can speed up the detection process. In addition, human detection task and motion recognition task are interrelated. The human detection branch and motion recognition branch of joint training network can help each other to a certain extent, and improve the effect of motion recognition [8]. Experiments on Pascal VOC motion recognition data set have achieved better performance than other methods, and verified the good performance of RCNN network in human posture estimation and motion classification. RCNN is a complete and unified detection algorithm, which only needs to train one component detector. Unlike many previous detection algorithms, for example, DPM needs to train multiple components or component models when detecting objects, poselet combines a series of supervised component detectors to obtain better detection results.

The network structure diagram used is shown in Fig. 2. According to the process of RCNN algorithm, input an image, generate candidate regions by selective search, normalize each region to a unified size, and give it to the intermediate basic network alexnet for feature calculation. The obtained features are distributed to different task branches and learned by using different loss functions. In this paper, three branches are constructed, which correspond to three tasks: human detection, pose estimation and motion classification. Although the network structure of the multiple branches is a complete network, the losses of the corresponding branches are superimposed as the final loss function during the joint training of multiple tasks, from which the joint gradient is calculated and the parameters of the network are updated by back propagation [9]. But not all tasks must be trained together. Task branches that do not participate in joint training actually only need to set the corresponding stacking weight to 0 when stacking the loss function, so that the branch can not work in the training phase. In motion detection, the attitude estimation branch does not need to participate in joint training and can be ignored. Therefore, the following only introduces the specific forms of human body detection and action classification branches.

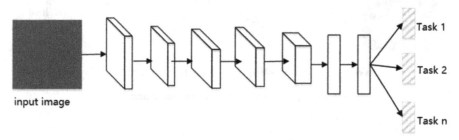

Fig. 2. Action detection structure diagram

3   Wrong Movement Detection in Physical Education Teaching and Training Based on Deep Convolution Neural Network

3.1   End to End Video Motion Detection

Xu et al. Proposed r-c3d network, referring to the two-stage target detection algorithm fast RCNN. This network consists of three parts: 3D convolution network to extract features, timing candidate box extraction network and action classification and fine tuning network. The timing extraction network is similar to the RPN in the fast RCNN in that it extracts anchor frames that may contain targets. Here, it extracts video clips that may contain action proposal frames. The action proposal frames obtained by the timing extraction network are rough. Then, through a 3droi pooling operation, the characteristics of the output of the timing extraction network are unified to the same scale, which is convenient for the subsequent fully connected network. Finally, the action classification and fine tuning network are used to predict the action category and modify the rough action candidate box obtained from the timing extraction network [10]. 3D convolution neural network takes the original video frame as input and calculates convolution features. These are entered into the proposal subnet, which proposes a variable length action proposal box and a confidence score. The classification subnet filters candidate boxes, merges fixed size features, and then predicts action labels and subdivision boundaries.

The basic structure of r-c3d is 3D convolutional neural network, as shown in Fig. 3. It mainly refers to the C3d network structure, and the size of input data is $3L \times H \times W$ (h = w = 112 is the size of the image in the video, l is the time length of the video, and the value is affected by the specific use of device memory). Through the C3d network structure, the dimension of the output feature is $512 \times L/8 \times h/16 \times w/16$, where 512 is the number of channels for the output feature.

Fig. 3. Convolution network feature extraction module

3.2 Feature Extraction and Test Result Output

The improvement of the detection accuracy of wrong movements in physical training depends on the depth of the neural network. There is a positive correlation between the characteristics and the representation ability. The depth neural network will calculate the characteristics of all wrong movement data. The deeper the final output, the stronger the feature extraction ability. In the process of deepening the depth of the network, the gradient is easy to disappear, resulting in the decline of the network performance. In order to solve this problem, resnet101 is used as the basic network when using deep convolution neural network to extract features, which can extract the subtle features of physical education teaching and training sample data faster and better. The normalization layer and residual blocks are added in batch through RESNET between the convolution layer and the pool layer, so as to speed up the network training speed and adjust the data transmission strategy, so as to further optimize the network performance.

Batch normalization algorithm is applied in batch normalization layer, which integrates the processing operation of network layer input into the wrong action detection of physical education teaching and training, and processes the wrong action samples of physical education teaching and training through micro batch normalization.

Batch normalization is expressed as:

$$
\begin{aligned}
\Delta u_{k+1}(t) &= u_d(t) - u_{k+1}(t) = u_d(t) - (u_k(t) + L(t)(\dot{e}_{k+1}(t) + e_{k+1}(t))) \\
&= u_d(t) - u_k(t) - L(t)(\dot{e}_{k+1}(t) + e_{k+1}(t)) \\
&= \Delta u_k(t) - L(t)\big(\dot{C}(t)\Delta x_{k+1}(t) + C(t)\Delta \dot{x}_{k+1}(t) + C(t)\Delta x_{k+1}(t)\big) \quad (1)
\end{aligned}
$$

4 Conclusion

Because the traditional methods can not accurately obtain the wrong action character-istics of physical education teaching and training, resulting in the decline of detection accuracy, this paper proposes a wrong action detection method of physical education teaching and training based on deep convolution neural network. Experiments show that this method can effectively detect the wrong actions of sports personnel in the process of physical education teaching and training. The detection accuracy is high, and the detec-tion error can be effectively controlled in time, Accurately judge the wrong action. In the future application of this method, we need to pay attention to the analysis of training sample data, and use other methods to improve the detection speed, so as to provide strong technical support for the detection of wrong movements in physical education training.

References

1. Wu, N., Weng, S., Chen, J., et al.: Deep convolution neural network with weighted loss to detect rice seeds vigor based on hyperspectral imaging under the sample-imbalanced condition. Comput. Electron. Agric., **196**, 106850 (2022)
2. Salih, T.A., Ali, A.J., Ahmed, M.N.: Deep learning convolution neural network to detect and classify tomato plant leaf diseases. Open Access Libr. J. **7**(5), 1–12 (2020)
3. Wang, B., Xu, B.: A feature fusion deep-projection convolution neural network for vehicle detection in aerial images. PLOS ONE, **16**, e0250782 (2021)
4. Bui-Ngoc, D., Bui-Tien, T., Nguyen-Tran, H., et al.: Structural Health Monitoring Using Handcrafted Features and Convolution Neural Network (2021)
5. Hui, W.L., Ooi, C.P., Aydemir, E., et al.: Decision support system for major depression detection using spectrogram and convolution neural network with EEG signals. Expert. Syst., e12773 (2021)
6. Abbasi, A.A., Hussain, L., Awan, I.A., et al.: Detecting prostate cancer using deep learning convolution neural network with transfer learning approach. Cogn. Neurodynamics **14**(1), 1–11 (2020)
7. Liu, X.: The application of deep convolution neural network to building extraction in remote sensing images. World Sci. Res. J., **6**(3), 136–144 (2020)
8. Shah, R.: Face mask detection using convolution neural network (2021)
9. Kotecha, K.: An efficient deep convolutional neural network approach for object detection and recognition using a multi-scale anchor box in real-time. Fut. Internet **13** (2021)
10. Yektai, H., Manthouri, M.: Diagnosis of lung cancer using multiscale convolutional neural network. Biomed. Eng. Appl. Basis Commun., **32**(5), 2050030 (2020)

Design of Vocabulary Query System in Computer Aided English Translation Teaching

Lijuan Guan[✉] and Yayun Wang

Wuhan Railway Vocational College of Technology, Hubei 430205, China
erkeqianbei@126.com

Abstract. Analysis of association rule algorithm in College English Teaching "Internet + education" has become a development trend, bringing new opportunities and challenges to college English teaching and learning. Association rule analysis algorithm is a statistical technique that helps to find the most important words or phrases in a given text. It helps identify patterns and relationships between different words, phrases, sentences, and paragraphs. In this way, it helps to identify the key concepts or ideas in the text, so the analysis of association rule algorithm is helpful to make changes to improve the quality of written language. The main idea behind using association rule analysis algorithm is that when we read any text, we tend to look at some parts rather than others. It is of great value to students' learning and teachers' teaching to use data mining technology to analyze students' learning data and establish relevant models to explore the correlation between English tests and various elements.

Keywords: Association rule algorithm · English teaching · Teaching analysis

1 Introduction

In China, as a foreign language, College English teaching is an indirect way to carry out multicultural education to a certain extent (because we can mainly understand the culture of English-speaking countries). According to the College English syllabus over the years, we can see the goal of cultivating students' cultural literacy. After the reform and opening up, China has produced three college English syllabus, namely, the 1986 syllabus, the 1999 syllabus and the 2004 curriculum and teaching requirements. Among them, there is no cultural training requirement for students in the 1986 syllabus; The 1999 syllabus stipulates that "the purpose of College English teaching is to cultivate students' strong reading ability… Improve their cultural literacy, so as to meet the needs of social development and economic construction." In 2004, the Higher Education Department of the Ministry of Education issued the College English teaching requirements, aiming to meet the needs of the country and Society for talent training in the new era [1]. The goal of College English teaching is to cultivate students' English level, improve their comprehensive cultural quality, and adapt to the needs of China's social development and

M. A. Jan and F. Khan (Eds.): BigIoT-EDU 2022, LNICST 467, pp. 583–587, 2023.
https://doi.org/10.1007/978-3-031-23944-1_63

international exchanges. The cultivation of Comprehensive English ability depends on the comprehensive development of students' language skills, language skills, emotional attitudes, learning strategies and cultural awareness. Cultural awareness includes cultural knowledge, cultural understanding and cross-cultural communication skills. This is the guarantee of correct use of language. Cultural knowledge and understanding, including cultural knowledge of China and English speaking countries, and understanding of Chinese culture and English speaking countries [2].

The design of vocabulary query system in computer-aided English translation teaching is the process of designing a system that can help students learn and use vocabulary. The main purpose of this study is to design a new software for learning English and its related vocabulary [3]. This research work involves the design, implementation, testing and evaluation of a prototype based on artificial intelligence technology for learning and memorizing word lists. The main goal behind this research work is to develop an intelligent tool to help students learn words from a given list. Research methods: the methods used in this study include literature review and experimental analysis [4].

2 Related Work

2.1 Construction of Association Rule Mining

Association rule mining is to find interesting connections in data items and decide which things will be one From. Association rule mining is a data mining method that has been studied more in recent years. The discovery of association rules, which is the most widely used in various data mining methods, can be divided into two steps: first, find all frequent itemsets, and then use these frequent itemsets to generate strong association rules. Apriori algorithm is a classical algorithm for generating frequent itemsets, which plays a milestone role in data mining. Its basic idea is to use an iterative method of hierarchical sequential search to generate frequent itemsets, that is, use k-itemsets to generate - itemsets, and use candidate itemsets CK to find frequent itemsets LK [5]. This method requires multiple scans of potentially very large transaction databases. The scale of the transaction database used for association rule mining is usually very large, so the cost is very large. Under the limited memory capacity, the system i/o load is quite large, and the time of scanning the database each time will be very long, so its efficiency is very low.

The task of association rule mining is to find strong association rules with the minimum support and confidence given by users in the transaction database. The itemsets corresponding to strong association rules must be frequent itemsets, and the confidence of association rules derived from frequent itemsets can be calculated by the support rate of the sum of frequent itemsets [6]. Therefore, association rule mining can be decomposed into the following two steps:

Step 1: find all frequent itemsets in D according to the minimum support.
Step 2: generate strong association rules based on frequent item sets and minimum confidence.

In the above two steps, the task of step 1 is to quickly and efficiently find all the frequent itemsets in D. the overall performance of association rule mining is determined by this step.

Therefore, all current association rule mining algorithms focus on step one. Step 2 is relatively easy to implement. First, for each frequent itemset L, all non empty subsets of 1 are generated. Then, for each non empty subset S of 1, if, the rule "s = > (1-s)" is output

$$S(i) = \frac{b(i) - a(i)}{\max\{a(i), b(i)\}} \tag{1}$$

2.2 The Process of Data Mining

In principle, data mining can be applied to any type of data It can be commercial data, data generated by social science and natural science processing or data observed by satellites. The data forms and structures are also different. They can be hierarchical, network and relational databases, object-oriented and object-relational advanced database systems, databases for special applications, such as spatial databases, time series databases, multimedia data, and web information. Of course, the difficulty and technology of data mining vary with the data storage system.

access, analyze, act, auto; The semma of SAS adopts the following processes: sample, explore, modify, model, access, etc. [7]. These mining process models have their own merits, but they are all related to their own products and lack of trafficability. Therefore, some regional organizations or multinational companies actively support and promote the research of data mining process in view of the commercial application prospect of data mining technology. This topic mainly adopts "data mining cross industry standard process", divides data mining tasks from the perspective of data mining technology application, closely combines data mining technology with application, and pays more attention to the quality of data mining model and how to combine it with business problems. Because using the mining model is the most concerned problem of data mining users [8]. The basic steps include business understanding, data understanding, data preparation, modeling, evaluation and implementation, as shown in Fig. 1.

3 Analysis of College English Teaching Based on Association Rule Algorithm

3.1 Analysis of College English Teaching System Based on Association Rule Algorithm

In order to adapt to the development of society, College English teaching has made great reforms in the selection of syllabus and teaching materials, as well as in the content, form, focus and level of teaching. English level should be steadily improved during their college study. Students' ability to exchange information in English should be cultivated. so as to achieve the optimal teaching effect Graphics, etc. are organically integrated with animation, taking learners as the center, giving full play to learners' enthusiasm and

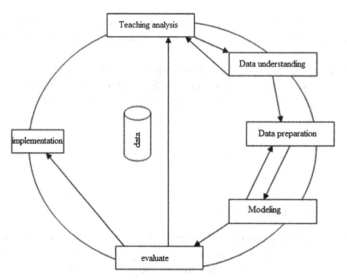

Fig. 1. Data mining process model for College English Teaching

initiative, taking into account learners' individual differences, exercising learners' ability of independent self-study, giving better play to teachers' guiding role, and realizing personalized education of teaching according to materials [9, 10]. At the same time, hypermedia and hypertext have a variety of convenient jumps and connections, as well as a network of knowledge structure, which makes multimedia foreign language learning more suitable for people's divergent thinking. In addition, the stimulation in the form of multimedia can greatly improve the efficiency and interest of foreign language learning, and better realize the teaching principle of "teaching in fun".

3.2 Result Analysis

The design of vocabulary query system in computer-aided English translation teaching is a tool that can help students learn English as a foreign language. It helps students understand the meaning of words and phrases in the context by providing them with relevant examples. The software is based on the concept of "contextualization", which means that it presents words or phrases and their contexts (i.e., sentences, paragraphs, chapters) to users so that they can better understand the meaning and usage of these terms / phrases. As for "students' self-assessment scores" and "students' mutual assessment scores", the two variables are assessed from the perspective of students' speaking or writing. Students' mutual assessment scores have more influence on the prediction results than self-assessment scores. "Test paper mode", "question type category 1" and "question type category 2" have no effect on whether students can pass the exam. The design of vocabulary query system in computer-aided English translation teaching is a set of tools to help teachers design vocabulary query for students. It provides a way for teachers to create their own custom queries and then use them for the whole class or individual learners. This tool can help teachers to ask their own questions according to the needs of learners, which is more effective than the questions raised by other teachers. The tool also helps teachers monitor students' progress through the built-in reporting function, and provides feedback to them on how to improve teaching strategies. The purpose of this study is to develop a prototype of a vocabulary query system, which can be used as an auxiliary tool for foreign language teaching in English translation courses. This study adopts the method of questionnaire survey, in which 25 questions are asked to four groups: ten students in each group and five students in the other group. The results showed that all participants agreed with their views on what they thought were good features or elements in the vocabulary query system, but there were some differences between them.

4 Conclusion

Although the research on the data analysis in College English teaching based on associa-tion rule algorithm has preliminarily realized the construction of students' teaching data, and can use the logistic regression model, enhanced decision tree model and the model after the integration of logistic regression model and enhanced decision tree model to predict the passing situation of students' examination results, in the actual work pro-cess, due to personal theoretical level Due to the limitations of objective conditions such as development ability and insufficient data dimensions in the system, follow-up researchers need to conduct more in-depth research in order to provide valuable ref-erence information for English teaching and learning through the use of data mining technology.

References

1. Du, J.: Application of computer multimedia technology in the design of english education curriculum. In: International Conference on Machine Learning and Big Data Analytics for IoT Security and Privacy. Springer, Cham (2022)
2. Wang, Y., Zhang, L.: Design of computer information system integration based on metadata. J. Phys. Conf. Ser. **1992**(2), 022085 (2021)
3. Bluche, T., Primet, M., Gisselbrecht, T.: Small-Footprint Open-Vocabulary Keyword Spotting with Quantized LSTM Networks. arXiv (2020)
4. Naderhirn, M.: Computer-Assisted Design of Mechatronic Systems to Comply with Textual System Description, US20200320233A1[P] (2020)
5. Yuan, G.: Computer Digital Technology in the Design of Intangible Cultural Heritage Protection Platform (2021)
6. Mao, H., et al.: Discussion on top-level design of the environmental monitoring standard sys-tem based on the changes of 109 method standards for surface water. Meteorologic. Environ. Res. **13**(2), 5 (2022)
7. Samrat, G., Gennady, B.: Detection of Gaps Between Objects in Computer Added Design Defined Geometries, EP3627277A1 (2020)
8. Sun, Y.: Design of information system for accounting file management based on computer technology (2022). https://doi.org/10.1155/2022/7908112
9. Wang, Q., Zhang, S., Liu, W.: Design and simulation of computer aided chinese vocabulary evaluation system. Comput. Aided Design Appl. **18**(S3), 1–11 (2020)
10. Rahmadani, R.G., Sumitra, I.D.: Design of enterprise architecture information system practicum scheduling in computer laboratory STMIK WIDYA CIPTA DHARMA Samarinda using TOGAF ADM method. IOP Conf. Ser. Mater. Sci. Eng. **879**, 012095 (2020)

Application of Data Mining Technology in University Education Management

MinYan Gong[✉]

College of Marxism, Xianyang Normal University, Xianyang 712000, Shannxi, China
gongmy@163.com

Abstract. University education management has a great impact on the quality of education, so in order to ensure the quality, this paper will focus on data mining technology research, first introduces the basic concept of data mining technology, education management application advantages, and then puts forward the technology application methods. The research proves that data mining technology has high application value in the educational management of colleges and universities, and can solve the problems of the previous educational management, so that the educational management can play a role and improve the quality of education.

Keywords: Data mining · Education management

1 Introduction

Modern university education management work very seriously, but the quality of university education management work for a long time didn't meet expectations, the reason is that the existing education management relies heavily on artificial and real environment, so the artificial capacity limitations and realistic environment of space and time limit, cannot do the elaborating management, is difficult to improve the quality of management. This case, the modern university presents its own appeal, want to be able to use technical means to make up for the inadequacy of the current management system, colleges and universities in this field thought can use data mining technology to achieve the purpose, the existing research has confirmed that, but how to apply data mining technology in the education management is a problem to be solved, so it is necessary to expand related research.

2 Basic Concepts of Data Mining Technology and Advantages of Educational Management Application

2.1 Basic Concepts

Data mining technology is a kind of data processing technology, the main function is an analysis of the characteristics of the data, combined with the characteristics of each data

M. A. Jan and F. Khan (Eds.): BigIoT-EDU 2022, LNICST 467, pp. 588–595, 2023.
https://doi.org/10.1007/978-3-031-23944-1_64

are defined, at the same time also can according to the definition, features of the data to find the connection between the data, according to the data link to construct data relation model, this model can reveal the relationship between the data form, correlation, etc. [1–3]. The another big characteristic of data mining technology is capable of handling huge amounts of data, the growth in all areas of modern data are very large, under the accumulating data level already amounts of level, large amount of data makes artificial unable to deal with, but data mining technology can be processed to this, the reason is that as a technical tool, there is no human limitations, so you can process data quickly [4]. It can be seen that data mining technology can do in-depth data processing, and data processing efficiency is very fast. It is worth noting that the data mining technology can further data processing, because the artificial neural network, namely if the simple pursuit of efficiency of data processing, conventional technology can do, but regular data means cannot both efficiency and the data processing depth, in contrast, the data mining technology, its under the blessing of artificial neural network, it can be analyzed by a kind of artificial machine logic, so it can be processed in depth [5]. There are many forms of artificial neural network in data mining technology, and various forms of neural network have different functions, so they should be carefully selected when used. Table 1 introduces common forms of artificial neural network for selection. Figure 1 shows the operation flow of data mining technology.

Table 1. Common forms of artificial neural networks in data mining

In the form of	Characteristics of the
Feedforward model	It is composed of input layer, hidden layer and output layer, with logical flow forward and no interaction between each layer. It is a typical one-way neural network model
Feedback type	It is composed of input layer, hidden layer and output layer, and the logical process is repeated. Input layer and hidden layer will constantly interact to form feedback, and the output result will be only after all nodes have completed the interaction. It is a typical interactive neural network model

Combined with Fig. 1, the data mining technology begin from data import, then put all need mining data import it second to establish data set, in view of the data set for feature extraction using technology analysis the relationships and data operation, need to compute the data of the relationships in the data, the correlation between calculation method has a lot of, the more common is association rule mining algorithm, the algorithm is expressed in Formula (1) [6–8]. Through the above steps, the characteristics of single data, data relationship model and correlation degree will be output as the results, according to which the real things can be accurately judged or predicted.

$$suPP(X) = \frac{|\{t \in D, X \in t\}|}{|D|} \tag{1}$$

where, X is the target ratio, D is the data set, and t is a data item in D.

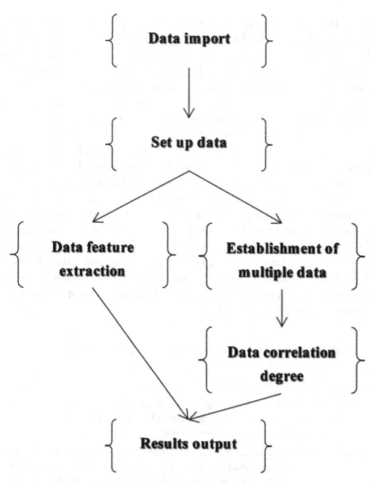

Fig. 1. Operation flow of data mining technology

2.2 Application Advantages

In the past, college education management depended on artificial and realistic environment, so there were many defects in the actual work: First, combined with the ideal results of education management, teachers need to fully understand the specific situation of each student, and then carry out targeted management, so as to achieve the ideal results, but in fact, due to human limitations, teachers can not always know the situation of each student. Make teachers in the implementation of education management work can only take some unified, superficial methods, such as simple to students put forward unified requirements, let students comply with, but in fact, students may not comply with, at the same time, it is difficult for teachers to find students to comply with the requirements of the behavior, so that management often loopholes; Secondly, affected by the realistic environment, many teachers can't the first time after the discovery of the problem in management, it also causes many students to carry out the relevant behavior without constraint, or a stroke of luck in carrying out some irregularities, such as some students think teachers can't the first time found that has not stopped so individual behavior [9]. These defects lead to the poor quality of education management in many colleges and universities, which not only affects the quality of education, but also is not conducive to the physical and mental development of students.

In reaction to the phenomenon, and related fields have long put forward the theory of higher education quality management method, is to let the teacher know students situation, and the first time in view of the problems in management, but want to use this method in practical education management work, we must solve the two problems, first is to handle all of the students' learning data, followed by the integration of data, build relationships, however, teachers cannot do this by themselves or by conventional technical means, which makes the method slow to implement. From this perspective, the data mining technology can solve the above problem, making method, namely the technology of data mining technology tool, there is no human limitations, at the same time it has similar to human logic, thus to further integration of the data, to dig deep as a result, teachers only need to make management decisions or preventive judgment according to the results, therefore, data mining technology has great advantages in college education management and is worth popularizing [10].

3 Technical Application Methods of Higher Education Management

3.1 System Design

In order to use data mining technology in college education management and give full play to the role of this technology, it is necessary to design the system around the technology first. This paper has carried out relevant work on this, and the overall framework of the system designed is shown in Fig. 2.

Combined with Fig. 2, the system first obtain student learning data through data collection, these data will become a dataset summary to the database, the data set in the second database is import to data preprocessing layer, the layer to the data processing, improve the quality of the data itself, through high quality data, can get high quality results. Finally, the pre-processed data will be used for data mining, and the results will be sent to teachers, who can make decisions and make predictions according to the results. In addition, the core of the supporting system and teacher-side equipment is various communication networks. Table 2 introduces common communication networks, all of which can be used and can be selected according to the actual situation.

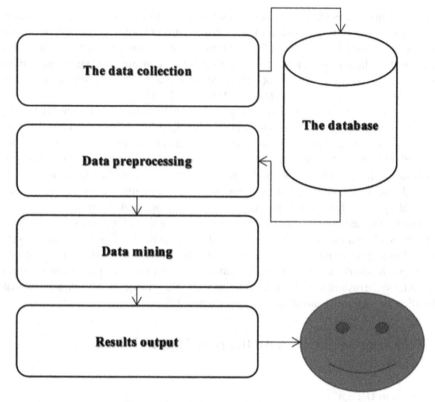

Fig. 2. Overall framework of the system.

Table 2. Common communication networks

Common communication network	Characteristics
Ethernet	Small range, only applicable to campus internal communication, the advantage is high security
The Internet	Large range, in any case can achieve device communication, but there are security risks
Mobile	Large range, and support mobile devices, so the convenience is very high, but there are also security risks

According to Table 2, if the Internet or mobile network is selected, network security protection work should be done, while Ethernet is generally not required to carry out this work. However, Ethernet has a relatively small communication range, so it is not recommended to choose Ethernet in general.

3.2   System Implementation

Combined with the system design results, the system needs to be implemented in college education management, so that data mining technology can be applied. Therefore, the implementation methods of each part of the system will be discussed below.

(1)   Data collection

There is a special method to realize the data collection function of the system in college education management, that is, in most cases, data collection needs to find the corresponding data channel first, and then collect the scattered data in each channel together. However, the relevant data in college education management itself is very centralized. All of them are centralized in the online learning platform and teacher education records, and the channels are clear, so they can be collected directly. Combined with this, the two steps of finding channels and centralizing and dispersing data in conventional data collection can be removed, and data can be collected directly on the platform or recorded by teachers manually. According to this method, the realization methods of data collection function are as follows: First, the communication protocol of Internet or mobile network is adopted to realize the communication connection between the online learning platform and the system (teachers manually input without communication), so that all existing and newly generated data in the platform will be automatically sent to the system; Secondly, in order to store the data sent and import the data into the system database, it is necessary to establish a temporary database in the online learning platform, whose function is to store the data sent and send the expired data to the system database, so as to realize data collection.

(2)   Database

System database is an important part of the system to store data acquisition data and transfer these data to the pretreatment layer, so it must be designed. Different from the temporary database of data collection, the system database needs to store a large amount of data permanently, so the capacity of the database must be as large as possible. At the same time, considering the continuous growth of data in education management, the database also needs to have good capacity expansion. Combining the two, this paper chose the cloud database, the reason is that the ordinary database for the physical database, although there are large capacity, but is always limited, in the case of increasing data can appear the problem of insufficient capacity, and its expansion method is complicated, need to build a new, complete physical server, and the method the cost is very high, in contrast, cloud databases do not have these defects, that is, the capacity is unlimited, generally need not expand, in special cases only need to increase virtual resources to achieve expansion. It can be seen that the cloud database is currently one of the few databases to meet the needs of the system, it should be introduced into the system.

(3)   Data preprocessing

Because directly collected data may have quality problems, such as incomplete data, data repetition, etc., direct use of these data for data mining is likely to lead to inaccurate final results, so in order to avoid this situation, data preprocessing design is needed. Data preprocessing is mainly realized by various preprocessing tools, that is, because data preprocessing needs exist in various fields, and has aroused people's attention for a long time, so the relevant fields have developed mature preprocessing tools, directly select the relevant tools, and then use the module technology to load the flux. The data preprocessing tools selected by this system are de-duplication tool and matching supplement tool, which can solve the problem of incomplete data and repeated data. In addition, new data preprocessing tools can be developed in the Java language if there is a special need.

(4) Data mining

After data pretreatment, data can be mined. In order to enable the system to have this function, it is necessary to construct the technical operation process according to Fig. 1, and then build the corresponding artificial neural network model. Because most of the problems in the management of education is not complicated, so choose type feed forward artificial neural network model can be directly, after the completion of the establishment of association rule mining algorithm model, blend in the artificial neural network model to realize the data mining layer, the layer will be shown in Fig. 1 in accordance with the process of data mining, the result will be generated in the system, ready to export.

(5) Result Output

The preliminary mining results generated in the system cannot be read directly, so it is necessary to make the results output correctly through design. The method adopted in the design of this paper is data visualization. Data visualization is a data interpretation program, which can transform the data initially in electronic code format into text, image, curve and other forms, and the results of these forms can be read by people.

4   Conclusion

To sum up, the educational management of colleges and universities is very important, and its quality must be guaranteed. Therefore, colleges and universities should actively introduce data mining technology, with the help of this technology to break through the limitations of human resources and the influence of realistic factors, improve the precision of educational management, so as to do a good job in in-depth management and achieve ideal results.

References

1. Raut, A.R., Khandait, S.P.: Review on data mining techniques in wireless sensor networks. In: IEEE Sponsored 2nd International Conference On Electronics And Communication System (ICECS 2015). IEEE (2020)
2. Cheng, N., et al.: Workflow model mining based on educational management data logs. In: 2019 Chinese Control And Decision Conference(CCDC) (2019)
3. Zheng, C., Zhou, W.: Research on information construction and management of education management based on data mining. J. Phys. Conf. Ser. **1881**(4), 042073(6pp) (2021)
4. Jk, A., Jak, A.: IT and data mining in decision-making in the organization.education management in the culture of late modernity. Procedia Comput. Sci. **176**, 1990–1999 (2020)

5. Maphosa, M., Maphosa, V.: Educational data mining in higher education in sub-saharan africa:a systematic literature review and research agenda. In: ICONIC: 2020 International Conference on Intelligent and Innovative Computing Applications (2020)

6. Moscoso-Zea, O., et al.: A hybrid infrastructure of enterprise architecture and business intelligence & analytics for knowledge management in education. IEEE Access. **7**, 38778–38788 (2019)

7. Rodrigues, R.L., et al.: Forecasting students' performance through self-regulated learning behavioral analysis. Int. J. Dist. Educ. Technol. **17**(3), 52–74 (2019)

8. Trakunphutthirak, R., Cheung, Y., Lee, V.: A study of educational data mining: evidence from a Thai University. Proc. Conf. AAAI Artif. Intell. 33, 734–741 (2019)

9. Nguyen, A., Gardner, L., Sheridan, D.P.: Data analytics in higher education: an integrated view. J. Inf. Syst. Educ. **31**(1), 61–71 (2020)

10. Tan, C., Xue, L.: Application research of big data mining in personalized teaching of internet education platform. J. Phys. Conf. Ser. **1992**(2), 022120(4pp) (2021)

Exploration of Course Teaching Reform Based on the Construction of Teaching Resource Base Under Neural Network

Ying Zhang[✉]

Shenyang University, Shenyang 110044, Liaoning, China
zying02090@163.com

Abstract. The construction of network teaching resource database is an important content of school education information construction and quality education reform in the information age. The construction of teaching resource database based on neural network is a method of automatic classification of teaching resources. Classification is done by using data collected from various sources, such as the Internet, books, periodicals and other resources. The classification process involves identifying patterns in these datasets. These patterns are then used to build a model that can be used to predict the category to which any new resource belongs. Although this approach has some limitations, it cannot identify all possible categories of any given resource. It also requires manual curation and validation before it can be used in practice.

Keywords: Teaching resource library · Neural network · Teaching reform

1 Introduction

The information technology revolution that arose in the 1970s has deeply influenced and is changing human life. The human world has entered the information age represented by multimedia and Internet technology from the era of industrialization. Information technology has penetrated into all aspects of human life, and education is no exception. The support of information technology, the establishment of Internet platform, the comprehensive application of multimedia and the formation of learning society have all created good conditions for the rise of network education. The digital learning environment created by modern information technology is changing people's educational thoughts and concepts, and thus providing a broader space for the development of education [1]. The arrival of the information age not only provides opportunities for the development of education, but also poses new challenges to contemporary education. The first feature of the information age is that knowledge is being updated at an unprecedented speed. In a short period of several decades, human beings have created more knowledge than the total amount of knowledge created in the past few thousand years. The changing and updating of knowledge has led to higher requirements for talent specifications in the information age [2]. Yesterday's knowledge has become obsolete today. As an educatee,

M. A. Jan and F. Khan (Eds.): BigIoT-EDU 2022, LNICST 467, pp. 596–603, 2023.
https://doi.org/10.1007/978-3-031-23944-1_65

students urgently need to arm their minds with the latest knowledge. As an educator, we have the responsibility and obligation to provide students with the latest knowledge reflecting the development of the times. The teaching material system and structure are relatively stable, It limits the provision of knowledge that reflects the latest development of the times to students. Therefore, people pay more and more attention to the development of network teaching resources to make up for the defects and deficiencies of teaching materials. The dynamic and open nature of network teaching resources can enable students to contact the latest knowledge in the shortest time [3].

Another feature of the information age is the Internet of the world. The Internet brings the world into the classroom and provides us with the opportunity to sit in the classroom and touch the world. All countries in the world are gradually promoting the construction of educational informatization [4]. At present, the state attaches great importance to the application of the network in the process of education and teaching, and it has become a social consensus to drive the modernization of education with informatization. The Ministry of education has decided to basically popularize information technology education in primary and secondary schools nationwide in about 5–10 years from 2001, fully implement the "school to school" project, drive the modernization of education with informatization, and strive to realize the leapfrog development of basic education. In 5–10 years, we will strengthen the construction of information infrastructure and information resources so that about 90% of the country will become independent The established primary and secondary schools can be connected with the network, so that every primary and secondary school teacher and student can share online education resources, improve the teaching quality of all primary and secondary schools, and make all teachers generally accept the continuing education aimed at improving the level and ability of implementing quality education [5]. The specific goal is to ensure that by 2005, primary and secondary schools in cities above the county level in the eastern region and in cities above the middle level in the central and western regions can access the Internet, and secondary schools at or below the county level and Township Central Primary Schools in the western region and remote and poor areas in the central region will generally establish distance education receiving stations. By 2010, we will strive to make more than 90% of the country's independent primary and secondary schools have access to the Internet. A few primary and secondary schools with poor conditions can also be equipped with multimedia teaching equipment and educational and teaching resources.

2   Related Work

2.1   Convolutional Neural Network CNN

The convolution neural network model is similar to the shallow neural network model, which uses the forward propagation to calculate the output value, and the back propagation to adjust the weight and offset; However, the neurons of two adjacent layers in convolutional neural network are connected by partial connection, rather than by full connection in shallow neural network, which is the most significant difference between them. At the same time, convolutional neural network is a deep neural network, which will not appear in the traditional shallow neural network.

The convolution neural network can directly extract the features of the two-dimensional image of the input model, and optimize the parameters of the model by using the optimization algorithm. Compared with the general traditional neural network, the convolution neural network shows its unique advantages in image recognition: (1) in order to avoid the complex preprocessing process, the convolution neural network can directly take the two-dimensional image as the input; (2) Convolutional neural network can combine pattern classification and feature extraction at the same time. After continuous optimization, the required parameters are obtained. Finally, the results are given in the output layer; (3) By means of weight sharing and sparse connection, the number of parameters to be trained in convolutional neural network is far less than that of traditional neural network, which has stronger generalization [6]. In essence, convolutional neural network is an input-output mapping. It can learn a large number of mapping relationships between output and input without any accurate mathematical expression. When the convolutional neural network is trained with known patterns, the network has the ability to map the input to the output.

The template value of the convolution kernel in the convolution layer is set randomly at the beginning. One goal of the convolution neural network is to train a suitable convolution kernel so that the training image can get the desired output through this convolution kernel. In computer vision, convolution kernel is often used to identify important attributes in digital images. In a convolution neural network, it needs to go through multi-layer convolution. The main purpose is: after the first convolution, the learned features are local features, while the second convolution is to convolute again on the basis of the first layer convolution, so it will develop towards the global trend [7]. After multiple such convolutions, the learned features will become more and more global. Figure 1 shows the structure of convolution kernel of convolution layer.

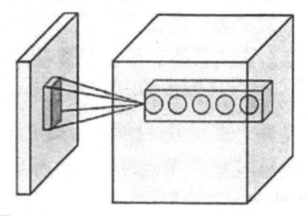

Fig. 1. Structure diagram of convolution kernel of resource library

2.2 Problems in Teaching Resource Database

Through the analysis of the research status of the network teaching resource database, it is found that the current research related to the construction of the network teaching resource database is mostly focused on the management system, and the research on the construction of resources is less concerned. The development of network teaching resources plays a very important role in the construction of network teaching resources, and it is the primary problem to be overcome in the construction of network teaching resources. The problems existing in the construction of network teaching resource database mainly focus on resources.

(1) The production of resource data is nonstandard and nonstandard. This is not conducive to data sharing and exchange, resulting in repeated construction of resources, and also brings great difficulties to data update. Fortunately, this situation has attracted the attention of relevant departments [8]. The Ministry of education has published the technical specifications for the construction of educational resources on the basis of analyzing the research results of relevant foreign parties, as a reference system for the development of online teaching resources. At the same time, the Ministry of education has also set up a relevant group to draft relevant documents. This element must be taken into account in the process of resource design and development.

(2) Resources are only "massive" but not practical. In terms of quantity, At present, most educational and teaching resources are in the form of "libraries", ranging from tens of gigabytes to hundreds of gigabytes, which will As a selling point of the resource library. However, in the process of building the database, developers did not really design and develop resources from the needs of teachers and students, ignoring the practicality of resources, so that the content of resources still lags behind the actual needs of teaching [9]. The reason for this is that there is no suitable resource design and development model to follow in the process of building the database.

(3) The resource library only provides resources without corresponding resource editing tools. "In many resource databases, except for providing a resource search tool, no other information editing tools are provided. Therefore, primary and secondary school teachers need to edit the obtained materials according to the actual situation of students after obtaining the materials, such as web page making tools, multimedia presentation software, etc. to combine the information, which increases the workload of teachers and inevitably reduces the utilization rate of the resource database. Many teachers feel inconvenient and have a problem Therefore, it affects their interest and enthusiasm in the use of the resource pool and reduces the role of resources in teaching. The resources provided by the network teaching resource library are only resources that meet the standards of resource developers. It is necessary to have a processing process to transform them into software that meets the needs of teaching. Therefore, the network teaching resource library should provide teachers with resource editing tools as a part of the resources of the network teaching resource library.

(4) The organization clue and classification method of resources are single. In the process of consulting some network teaching resource databases, the author found that most of the network teaching resource databases organize resources according to the classification method of "discipline chapter knowledge point", and classify resources according to their physical attributes. It only considers the target teachers of the network teaching resource database, but does not take into account the

differences of students. The network teaching resource database should provide the organization clues and classification methods of various resources according to the characteristics of students.

3 Construction of Teaching Resource Base Based on Neural Network

3.1 The Function of Network Teaching Resource Database System

The Internet and Intranet endow the network teaching resource library with unique functions such as shared browsing, reconstruction and development, retrieval and navigation, two-way transmission, etc. The construction of network teaching resource database injects new educational concepts, teaching models and rich teaching resources into subject teaching. The construction of network teaching resource database mainly has the following functions in subject teaching:

(1) Applied to teachers' lesson preparation. The sharing of teaching resources through the Internet or intranet is a major advantage of the network teaching resource library. The same resource can accommodate a large number of teachers to browse and download at the same time. In the process of preparing lessons, teachers can make use of the network teaching resource database, from finding the latest reference materials of subject teaching, searching various media materials related to teaching content to applying the online lesson preparation system and tools to integrate and make teaching materials suitable for the teaching design of this course. At the same time, teachers can also upload the prepared teaching materials to the resource database for backup, and constantly enrich the content of the network teaching resource database. The whole process can be guaranteed by any client terminal on the Internet. The resource database provides teachers with rich teaching resources (including local network and remote network) for lesson preparation, and provides favorable conditions for teachers to optimize teaching design [10]. At the same time, the two-way transmission advantage is used to provide storage for the prepared textbooks, and can be used as a supplementary resource base for new resources.

(2) It is applied to centralized classroom teaching. In the multimedia teaching environment equipped with network, teachers can call various media information and teaching materials (including teaching courseware independently constructed by teachers and stored in the Library) of the resource library through the classroom teaching application system, so as to create a multi-dimensional learning space for students and provide strong support for multimedia combination and optimization teaching.

(3) Apply and create rich and vivid learning situations. The new chemistry textbooks for junior middle school compiled according to the chemistry curriculum standards incorporate quite a lot of content related to society and science and technology. The teaching of these course contents involves a large number of production, life, social and other information resources. Without the help of extensive information technology, it is difficult to achieve the expected results of the course standards.

Information resources enable these contents related to production and life to be presented to students in a real and vivid form.

(4) Open online learning and instant evaluation. At present, due to the lack of educational funds and the poor self-control of middle school students, it is unrealistic to require middle school students to surf the Internet at home or in Internet cafes after class. However, as an educational institution, under the existing conditions, the school should provide students with the most possible effective help, and actively guide and organize students to surf the Internet in the school. The establishment of network teaching resource database makes it easier for students to use this kind of online education resources, so as to improve students' learning efficiency. At the same time, the network is timely feedback, which can timely feed back the test and evaluation results to students, and give them instant reinforcement.

3.2 Structure of Network Teaching Resource Database System

Resources are the core and soul of the network teaching resource database, through which the function of the resource database can be realized. At the same time, in order to better support students' learning, resources must be scientifically managed and organized, which requires a management platform. In order to make better use of the advantages of the network, the network teaching resource library should also be connected with the campus network or the Internet, so as to maximize the function of the network teaching resource library and give full play to its advantages. Therefore, based on the existing research results, the characteristics of the network teaching resource library and the functions of the network teaching resource library, the author also divides the network teaching resource library into two parts, and realizes the connection between the network teaching resource library and the campus network and the Internet through the network port. The overall structure of the network teaching resource library is shown in Fig. 2:

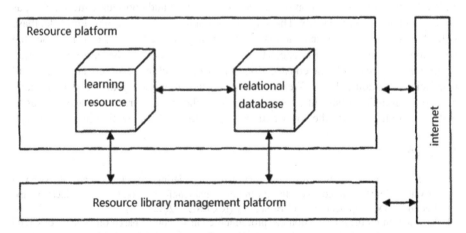

Fig. 2. Structure diagram of network teaching resource database system

The resource database management platform is the supporting system of the network teaching resource database. The educational resource management system is a functional facility for managing, maintaining and updating the educational resources stored in the resource database media. Through the resource database management platform, the scientific and reasonable composition and management of the network teaching resource database can be realized, which is conducive to giving full play to the advantages of the network teaching resource database, and then conducive to the teaching and learning of disciplines and the development of students. The main function of the resource database management platform is to provide communication and exchange between resource providers and resource users. Therefore, a scientific resource management platform is essential for the network teaching resource database. Resources are the soul and core of the network teaching resource pool. The full play of the functions and advantages of the network teaching resource pool depends on the network teaching resources stored in it. If the resource pool management platform is the trunk, then the resource platform is the soul. The network teaching resource pool without the soul will only have a body, which cannot give full play to its own advantages and functions. Resources are the direct carrier to achieve the curriculum objectives, promote subject teaching and learning, and promote the development of students. The quality of resources and the quality of resource organization will directly affect the quality of the whole network teaching resource database. At the same time, the network teaching resource database can not only become the accumulation of network teaching resources, but must process and organize the resources according to certain clues according to the needs of teachers and students, that is, certain data processing clues are necessary.

4 Conclusion

The construction of network teaching resource database is an important content in the construction of educational informatization. It is of great significance to carry out the integration of information technology and subject teaching, carry out long-distance teaching, and cultivate students' information literacy, cooperation and communication ability, as well as students' inquiry ability. The construction of network teaching resource database will certainly become an unavoidable problem in school education reform under the conditions of the information age. However, as a hot issue in the current education informatization research, the construction of network teaching resource database is still insufficient in guiding theory. We all need to continue to work together, and at the same time, we can make persistent efforts to transform theory into practical results, so as to make our contribution to the construction of education informatization in our country!

References

1. Li, L.: Exploration on the course construction of "engineering project management" based on private undergraduate colleges. In: 4th International Conference on Culture, Education and Economic Development of Modern Society (ICCESE 2020) (2020)
2. Exploration on the construction of "procedural control" course based on concept of CDIO and online-offline hybrid teaching mode. Creat. Educ. Stud. **09**(1), 1–9 (2021)
3. Luan, G., Kong, L., Chen, L.: Exploration and practice on the construction of teaching staff for a plan for educating and training outstanding engineers based on engineering education accreditation. In: WSSE 2020: 2020 The 2nd World Symposium on Software Engineering (2020)

4. Xlab, C., et al.: Methodological exploration on the construction of a traditional Chinese medicine nursing expert consensus based on evidence—taking stroke as an example. J. Tradit. Chin. Med. Sci. **9**, 128–134 (2022)
5. Kang, J.: Reform and exploration of stamping process and die design course based on flipped classroom. Int. J. Soc. Sci. Educ. Res. **3**(5), 101–106 (2020)
6. Wang, L., Zhang, E.: Exploration and practice of teaching reform of industrial robot course based on application ability training. IOP Conf. Ser. Mater. Sci. Eng. **780**, 032017 (2020)
7. Li, Y., Zhao, B.: Construction of the university's intelligent teaching model based on mobile technology-take the reform of english curriculum at Chengdu Neusoft College as an example. In: Innovative Computing, pp. 77–84 (2020)
8. Liu, S., Li, S., Pang, L., et al.: Autonomous exploration and map construction of a mobile robot based on the TGHM algorithm. Sensors **20**(2), 490 (2020)
9. Zhang, W.: The exploration of Chinese rhetoric teaching under the logic of "course thinking and politics " construction. In: 2020 3rd International Conference on Humanities Education and Social Sciences (ICHESS 2020) (2020)
10. Xiao, Q., Zhang, L., Li, J.: Exploration on the Teaching System of Artificial Intelligence Practice Course (2021)

Research on Sales Simulation Teaching System Based on Data Mining

Guiyun Chen, Qingchen Peng, Xinru Luo, and Gao Wang[✉]

Changsha Medical University, Changsha, Hunan, China
p15608485878@163.com

Abstract. The research on sales simulation teaching system based on data mining is a research aimed at using data mining technology to improve the quality of sales simulation training. The main objective of this study is to develop and apply an effective learning management system that will allow students, teachers and trainers to manage their knowledge about sales simulation by creating a database that contains all the information they need to learn from it. The application of data mining technology in this case is accomplished by applying machine learning algorithms (such as decision trees) to a large number of data collected from different sources. The main purpose of this study is to understand whether there are any differences in the learning outcomes of students who use different types of sales simulation professors, and how these differences affect their performance in this field. This research will also help us understand which types of sales simulations are most effective for teaching, which should be used more frequently, and why they are better than other simulations.

Keywords: Data mining · Sales simulation · Teaching system

1 Introduction

Someone said, "engaging in the sales industry is a process of cultivation. You must break yourself up and reshape a new mode of thinking." Therefore, sales is a very challenging job, but you can get more wealth, whether it is material wealth or spiritual wealth. Many sales Xiaobai who have just entered the industry will look for many sales training courses to enrich their sales knowledge and improve their sales ability.

Sales simulation teaching in universities is a lesson worth listening to and learning. The current trend tells us that it is really necessary to master one more skill. The whole society and the world need talents with multiple talents. Learning should not be confined to a certain field. We should expand our knowledge and talents. If you don't know what to do, you might as well look at the materials of the course. Knowledge is the method and know-how to solve things. Of course, some people will ask why we need to learn these things [1]. In fact, the answer is very simple. We are not satisfied with our current life. We have the courage to try to break through ourselves and try to climb higher mountains. In this study, the author tries to find out the relationship between sales simulation teaching

M. A. Jan and F. Khan (Eds.): BigIoT-EDU 2022, LNICST 467, pp. 604–610, 2023.
https://doi.org/10.1007/978-3-031-23944-1_66

system and data mining. The author takes the sales simulation teaching system based on data mining as an example. The reason for using the case study is that all students can easily understand it because they are already familiar with the topic. The study also includes a comparison between sales simulation teaching system (sssts) and data mining to show how the two technologies work together to achieve better results than each technology used independently. Based on this, this paper studies the sales simulation teaching system based on data mining.

2 Related Work

2.1 Data Mining

Simply put: data mining is to find hidden rules from massive data. Generally, the goal of data analysis is relatively clear. At present, big data is hot and everyone must have heard of data mining, but laymen know little about the more specific algorithms of data mining [2]. Data mining is mainly divided into three categories: classification algorithms, clustering algorithms and association rules. These three categories basically cover all the needs of the current commercial market for algorithms. These three categories contain many classical algorithms. Figure 1 below shows the data mining application.

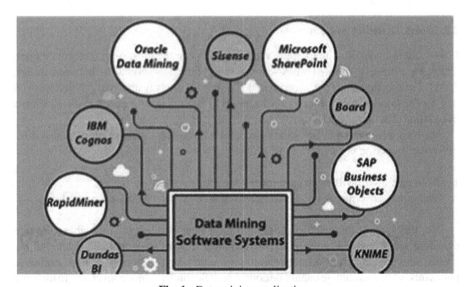

Fig. 1. Data mining applications

The focus of "data analysis" is to observe data, while the focus of "data mining" is to discover "knowledge discovery in database" KDD (knowledge discovery in database) from data.

The conclusion of "data analysis" is the result of human intelligence activities, while the conclusion of "data mining" is the knowledge rules discovered by machines from learning sets (or training sets, sample sets).

The application of "data analysis" to draw conclusions is human intellectual activity, and the knowledge rules found by "data mining" can be directly applied to prediction [3].

"Data analysis" can not establish a mathematical model and needs manual modeling, while "data mining" directly completes the mathematical modeling. For example, the essence of traditional cybernetics modeling is to describe the functional relationship between input variables and output variables. "Data mining" can automatically establish the functional relationship between input and output through machine learning. According to the "rules" obtained by KDD, given a group of input parameters, a group of output quantities can be obtained.

Data analysis: through the observation of the data, we found that 82% of the poor people did not pay in time. Therefore, the conclusion is that people with low income often do not pay in time. The conclusion is that the tariff should be reduced.

Data mining: find deep-seated reasons by writing algorithms [4]. The reason may be that people living outside the Fifth Ring Road do not pay in time due to the remote environment. Conclusion it is necessary to set up more business halls or self-service payment points.

2.2 Sales Teaching System

If we want to understand marketing, we must start with the most original form of sales. The most primitive form of sales - that is, the equivalent exchange between things. Today, I grabbed a rabbit, and you picked 10 apples. I don't want to eat rabbits, and you don't want to eat apples either. Let's discuss whether we should eat them instead? So a transaction was completed.

We have observed that this kind of equivalent exchange between things must meet two basic conditions:

1. Both parties are willing to exchange;
2. The goods are equivalent (at least the exchange parties consider it equivalent).

But this kind of barter efficiency is too low! First of all, it is impossible to ensure that both sides have the willingness to exchange. I want to exchange apples, but the people who collect apples do not want to exchange rabbits, but only want to exchange pheasants, so this exchange cannot be completed; Second, it is not convenient to measure the equivalence of exchange items. In order to solve this problem, man invented the general equivalent and its advanced version - money. The emergence of money perfectly solves the problems of exchange willingness and the measurement of the value of goods [5]. It allows the exchange parties to divide into two groups according to the different Holdings:

- Currency holder—buyer
- commodity holder—seller.

The ultimate goal of training students is to make students face the society and go to their posts. Therefore, it is necessary to develop a business simulation teaching and sales system that is more conducive to students' understanding of the real operation process of enterprises. Enterprises need students to understand the business process of enterprises, but it should not be limited to the content in books. It should be combined with the actual process of enterprises and be in line with the development status of the market and enterprises. Therefore, the function setting of the simulation system should keep pace with the times, so as to truly reflect the latest sales concept and market status, and enable students to have a basic understanding of the current sales management mode of enterprises. By using this system, students can experience the whole process of enterprise operation in a series of activities such as market analysis, demand forecasting, strategy formulation, overall marketing, customer analysis, and deeply understand the management idea of ERP, so as to better cultivate the talents that enterprises really need.

3 Research on Sales Simulation Teaching System Based on Data Mining

Life cycle theory also plays an important role in sales forecasting. For example, what is the difference between making sales forecasts for Li Ning and for an online red brand with a history of only 5 years, just in terms of the life cycle? The predictions here refer to how their growth rates differ. For example, two brands also predict the sales in 2022. Do you think the growth rate of Li Ning in the past 30 years is higher, or the 5-year online popular brand may be higher? This is the meaning of life cycle analysis. You should take this difference into account when making predictions for an old enterprise and a new brand.

In the highly competitive environment of the information age, more and more enterprises realize that in order to survive and develop, they must use scientific methods to sort out data, extract business rules, and make correct and timely decisions, which makes data mining technology widely used in enterprise sales forecasting and analysis [6]. In order to give students a more realistic enterprise environment, this system makes up for the lack of sales forecasting function of the current simulation system, and uses data mining technology to build a sales forecasting model system.

The emerging data mining technology can find some unknown and valuable rules from the massive data, which undoubtedly provides a strong support for providing personalized sales simulation teaching services. Combined with database, data warehouse and other technologies, the use of data mining technology will make full use of students' academic records, browsing patterns, online records and other data to obtain students' learning characteristics, and turn teachers' teaching experience into strategic rules that can be operated by computers. In this way, it is possible to establish a more successful personalized sales simulation teaching system that meets the requirements [7].

In the simulation system, the overall market demand of the product is fixed and has a certain change law, which is arch linear distribution according to the length of simulation time. The market share is determined by the annual advertising investment and total sales. The advertising investment in the early stage determines the order in which the contestants choose the order. The contestants who choose the order first can choose the order with large quantity and high price as much as possible according to their own production capacity and inventory status, so as to occupy the most market share and lay a solid foundation for the future simulation process.

$$\|e_{k+1}(t)\| = \|C(t)\| \|\Delta x_{k+1}(t)\| \tag{1}$$

$$e_j = -k \sum_{i=1}^{n} f_{ij} ln f_{ij} \tag{2}$$

Advertising investment. In the simulation system, it does not involve the specific conditions such as the mode of advertising communication and the advertising receiving group, but only considers the impact of advertising costs on the order acquisition of enterprises. The market mechanism module in the background of the system determines the ownership of the "market leader" according to the advertising input of each participant and the evaluation rules [8]. The "market leader" can get the priority of orders. The party who gives priority to the order can select the order that is beneficial to itself according to its own production capacity and sales plan.

4 Simulation Analysis

The system establishes a multi-dimensional data cube based on OLAP. Users can query and analyze the data in the data warehouse from multiple angles and levels through the system operation, store common data in multiple dimensions in a way that users can easily understand, and provide users with a multi-dimensional data cube, so that users can view the data from different angles without knowing the storage structure of the database [9], Query and analysis operations are carried out in a multidimensional data structure similar to its sales activities, which improves the situation of cumbersome data conversion and complex table relationship links when using traditional relational databases to query data. Users can be liberated from the massive data without direction and distribution rules. They can interactively and quickly observe information from all levels, deeply understand the data, better analyze problems from the perspective of sales business, and master the changes of sales activities [10]. As shown in Fig. 2 below, the main code for database establishment is shown.

```
>> function [C,L,L1,l]=lagran1 (X,Y)
m=length(X);L=ones(m,m);
for k=1:m
    V=1;
    for i=1:m
    if k~=i
        V=conv(V,poly(X(i)))/(X(k)-X(i));
    end
end
L1(k,:)=V;1(k,:)=poly2sym(V)
end
C=Y*L1;L=Y*1;x=[0.4,0.5,0.6,0.7,0.8];
y=[ -0.756291,-0.443147,-0.150826,0.133325,0.416856];
[c,L,L1,l]=lagran1 (x,y)
??? function [C,L,L1,l]=lagran1 (X,Y)
  |
Error: Function definitions are not permitted at the prompt or in scripts.
```

Fig. 2. Main codes for database establishment

5 Conclusion

The research of sales simulation teaching system based on data mining is to develop and implement a sales simulation learning system, which can promote the skills of salespeople using various tools. The main purpose of this study is to promote the development of salespeople by using computerized simulation, which is more effective than traditional methods. Data mining is a technology used in information retrieval and data analysis. In this technique, data is analyzed to find the relationship between patterns or variables. The results of these analyses can be used to predict future behavior, and then can be tested against real-life events. Data mining is a process of discovering patterns from a large amount of data by analyzing their structures and relationships. The goal is to find useful information from the data that can be used for decision-making or prediction.

References

1. Shang, Y.J., Suo, D.D.: Design of dance action simulation teaching system based on cloud computation. In: International Conference on E-Learning, E-Education, and Online Training. Springer, Cham (2021)
2. Du, X., Jiang, B., Zhu, F.: A new method for vehicle system safety design based on data mining with uncertainty modeling (2021)
3. Chen, L., Wang, L., Zhou, Y.: Research on Data Mining Combination Model Analysis and Performance Prediction Based on Students' Behavior Characteristics. Mathematical Problems in Engineering, 2022 (2022)
4. Zhang, S.Y., Chen, X., Han, P.J.: Design of management accounting online teaching system based on virtual simulation technology. In: International Conference on E-Learning, E-Education, and Online Training. Springer, Cham (2021)
5. Lu, L., Zhou, J.: Research on Mining of Applied Mathematics Educational Resources Based on Edge Computing and Data Stream Classification. Mob. Inf. Syst. **2021**(7), 1–8 (2021)

6. Li, X., Cheng, K., Huang, T., et al.: Equivalence analysis of simulation data and operation data of nuclear power plant based on machine learning. Ann. Nucl. Energy **163**(1), 108507 (2021)
7. Zhang, Y., Huang, W.: Design of Intelligent Diagnosis System for Teaching Quality Based on Wireless Sensor Network and Data Mining. 2020
8. Ma, X., Qiu, X..: Simulation Analysis of Building Energy Consumption Based on Big Data and BIM Technology (2021)
9. Hao, Z.: Emotion recognition simulation of Japanese text based on FPGA and neural network. Microprocess. Microsyst. **6**, 103384 (2020)
10. Zhong, S., Guo, Y., Li, Y., et al.: Research on Optimization of Mining Substitution in Wangzhuang Mine Based on System Dynamics. Advances in Civil Engineering (2021)

Visual Monitoring Method of Digital Computer Room Based on Digital Twin

Huang Chao[(⊠)], Zhang Chen, Liao Rongtao, Dong Liang, Dai Dangdang,
and Guo Yue

Information and Communication Branch, Huber EPC, Wuhan 430074, Hubei, China
chaohuangum@163.com

Abstract. With the rapid development of the Internet of things, big data, artificial intelligence and other new generation information technologies, more and more information technologies are applied in actual production activities. The powerful computing and analysis capabilities of the new generation of information technology have rapidly promoted the digitalization and intelligence of the industry. Visual monitoring is used to monitor the status of the system. It is also called a visual inspection method, because it involves the use of a microscope, magnifying glass or binoculars and other visual tools to observe the system. The main purpose of this method is to obtain an overall view of all components and their functional relationships, so as to identify any fault conditions that may occur on them. Visual monitoring method can be applied to control room, machine room and other different fields, including many types of equipment, such as PLC (programmable logic controller), HMI (human machine interface), SCADA (monitoring and data acquisition) system.

Keywords: Digital computer room · Digital twinning · Visual monitoring

1 Introduction

With the development of modern computer technology and the continuous improvement of social informatization, many universities and enterprises need a large number of computers and servers to store and manage massive data information in the process of operation. Most of these data involve internal technology, daily work, capital flow, personnel privacy and other important contents. Therefore, the equipment for storing data is usually placed in a special data center computer room for unified management [1]. The normal operation of various electronic equipment in the computer room requires that the temperature and humidity in the environment be kept within a certain range. When the range is exceeded, such as ignoring the problem of high temperature and humidity for a long time, it will cause accelerated aging of components in the equipment, affect the normal function of components, and even affect the operation of the whole equipment. When the equipment in the computer room breaks down or goes down directly, it will affect the normal operation of all departments of the unit [2]. When the equipment in

M. A. Jan and F. Khan (Eds.): BigIoT-EDU 2022, LNICST 467, pp. 611–618, 2023.
https://doi.org/10.1007/978-3-031-23944-1_67

the computer room breaks down due to environmental impact, leading to the loss of important data, it will cause unpredictable losses. In serious cases, major accidents such as fire may occur [3]. Therefore, the monitoring of the computer room environment is an important part of the daily management of the computer room. It is necessary to ensure that the equipment in the computer room operates in a stable environment.

At present, the computer room management mainly adopts the all-weather shift system, with special staff regularly inspecting the environment in the computer room. This management method not only aggravates the supervision task of managers, but also fails to find and eliminate faults at the first time. To solve these problems, we must monitor and predict the key environmental parameters in the computer room through more efficient methods, including the temperature, humidity, smoke concentration, equipment potential and ground water level of the computer room, view all parameter information in real time, quickly locate and eliminate hidden dangers, ensure the safe and stable operation of the computer room, and improve the efficiency and scientificity of management [4].

Digital twin (DT) is a new technical term put forward in the era of the fourth industrial revolution. It is the core technology to vigorously develop intelligent manufacturing. In order to better interact and integrate the physical world and the information world, the concept of digital twin came into being. Digital twinning refers to the construction of a physical entity or system in the information space. It is a complete life cycle process that uses the physical prototype, sensor collection, historical operation data and other information to realize the mirror mapping of the physical prototype working process in the virtual space, and can reflect the status and behavior of the physical prototype [5]. The digital virtual twin has two distinct characteristics. One is that the mapping of physical entities is comprehensive and complete, which not only reflects the geometric characteristics and physical behavior, but also reflects the operating rules; Secondly, the digital virtual entity evolves synchronously according to the running data of the entity, and analyzes the data through the simulation system, which in turn helps the physical entity to make decisions and improve.

2 Related Work

2.1 Research Status of Computer Room Environment Monitoring

With the development and rise of the Internet of things, big data, cloud computing and other new generation information technologies, more industries choose to carry out digital transformation. In this process, the amount of data that each processing terminal needs to process and store grows exponentially. The construction of the data center computer room is becoming increasingly important in production and life. It has become an essential component to support the work and operation of major universities, enterprises and institutions [6]. However, the electronic equipment in the computer room has high requirements for the stability of environmental parameters (temperature and humidity, computer room water level, smoke concentration, etc.), and the relevant parameters must be kept within a certain range in accordance with the regulations, otherwise it will affect the operation of the equipment and even damage the equipment [7]. Therefore, improving the level and ability of computer room environmental monitoring is a research topic of practical significance.

The rudiment of the computer room monitoring system appeared in the 1980s. It took the industrial computer mode as the core and presented the scattered monitoring subsystem through the single chip microcomputer and PC; In the 1990s, the computer room monitoring system mainly used the industrial computer as the data acquisition host, and realized the overall software based monitoring under the local area network; Until 1997, a working conference on computer room environment diagnosis and monitoring was held in the United States. Teams from Stanford and MIT demonstrated the demonstration system for computer room environment diagnosis and monitoring, which opened the research on modern computer room environment monitoring system. Since then, experts and scholars at home and abroad have done a lot of research work [8].

Lihuasong et al. Designed and implemented a centralized power environment monitoring system for the computer room, which centrally monitors various information on the same platform, including UPS equipment, precision air conditioning, environmental parameters and on-site video. For the first time, the "prism" principle and "error prevention alarm" logic technology were brought into the system design, which has the advantages of unity, openness and integration; Liudongdong et al. Optimized the current monitoring methods of 3D visual computer room, intelligently de noised the monitoring images of computer room through time domain de-noising algorithm, solved the problems of poor effect and long response time of traditional de-noising methods, and explored the visual presentation method of computer room environmental parameters.

2.2 Research Status of 3D Visualization Technology

Visualization technology began to appear and develop in the late 1980s. It is an information technology that combines computer data processing and image display for practical application. With the rapid development of virtual reality technology, visualization technology has broken the traditional two-dimensional plane situation and began to develop to three-dimensional. 3D visualization technology realizes visualization, scene and real-time data by combining 3D virtual reality technology and data real-time rendering technology [9]. It can truly reproduce the physical world, and users can more intuitively obtain data information. Because 3D visualization technology can be more close to the real world in the way of visual display, 3D visualization technology is gradually applied to various fields of life and industrial production, such as medical treatment, transportation, military and other fields.

In foreign studies, palkovics et al. Used 3D visualization technology to simulate the intraosseous periodontal model, and used automatic threshold algorithm to reconstruct the 3D intraosseous periodontal model for diagnosing the damage of the intraosseous periodontal. Stylianost et al. Used building information model (BIM) and 3D visualization to develop 3D model of building tunnel and predict the settlement risk caused by tunnel construction.

In domestic research, 3D visualization has achieved good results in education and training due to its good interactivity and immersion. Chen Tao and others applied the computer three-dimensional visualization technology to medical education. By using the three-dimensional, authentic and interactive characteristics of the technology, they fully restored the human anatomical structure and the operation process, increased students' interest in surgery learning, and thus improved the teaching quality. Liuzhiqi from

Nanchang University has developed a three-dimensional visual interactive weather forecasting system, which makes the public more intuitive and fast access to weather conditions, so as to make better decisions. The system greatly improves the user experience. Yumingzheng, a student of Dalian Maritime University, has developed a container ship stowage system by using the three-dimensional visualization technology to visually display good data in the form of three-dimensional visualization [10]. At the same time, he can timely find the problems of ship stability and container transfer that may occur in the process of container handling operations, so as to improve the safety of port operations.

At present, there are many ways to realize 3D visualization technology, such as the earlier flash technology, the more popular SVG (scalable vector graphics), HTML, etc. However, the applications developed with these three-dimensional visualization technologies require users to install plug-ins, which is more troublesome.

3 Digital Twin Theory

3.1 Digital Twin Concept

In 2003, the embryonic form of the concept of digital twins appeared. Professor Michael grieves put forward the concepts of virtual space and real space in his courses. Each real space carries a system model and is connected through data and information flow. However, this idea was initially named "mirror space model" and later referred to as the concept of "digital twins". Subsequently, in 2012, NASA gave a detailed description of the concept of digital twinning. The key core of digital twinning technology is to realize virtual real mapping, that is, mapping physical systems to digital models. It makes full use of physical systems, numerous sensors, operation history and other data to build three-dimensional models and analyze data of physical systems, and integrates multi-disciplinary, multi-scale and multi probability simulation processes. Based on the basic state of the physical entity, the digital twin model is dynamically established in real time. The twin model and the collected data are simulated and analyzed for the monitoring, prediction and optimization of the physical entity. As a technical means integrating model, data and intelligence, it is a bridge connecting physical entities and virtual entities, and provides real-time and intelligent control services.

In order to understand digital twin technology more comprehensively and accurately, it is necessary to interpret its connotation from the perspective of digital twin application. At present, digital twin is widely used in product R&D, equipment manufacturing, condition monitoring, fault diagnosis, health management and other fields. Intelligent workshop and Aerospace Science and technology are widely used in China. This paper adopts the characteristics of digital twin technology, replaces physical entities with virtual models, collects the operating data of the computer room environment, and monitors the equipment status and environmental status of the computer room more intuitively through three-dimensional modeling.

3.2   Basic Composition of Digital Twins

In 2011, Professor Michael grieves formally proposed the digital twin, which mainly includes three parts: physical products in physical space, virtual products in virtual space, and data links between virtual and real products. The physical product of physical space is the object of digital twin technology service, which needs real-time and accurate description and update of its characteristics, behavior, formation process and performance; Virtual products in virtual space are also called digital twins. Because virtual products are exactly the same model as physical products in the real world, they can simulate the behavior and state of physical products in real time; Data link provides access, integration and conversion functions for product digital interfaces. Its goal is to achieve full traceability, real-time two-way sharing and information exchange throughout the product life cycle and value chain.

Tao Fei and others from Beijing University of Aeronautics and Astronautics put forward the digital twin five-dimensional model, including physical equipment (PE), virtual equipment (VE), connection (CN), dtdata (DD) and services (SS). The relationship between the dimensions is shown in Fig. 1.

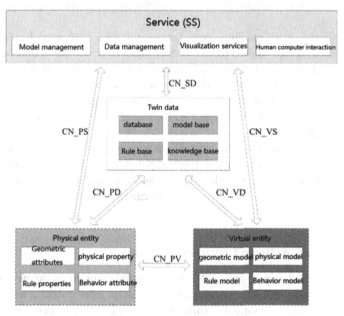

Fig. 1. Digital twin structure model

4 Visual Monitoring Method of Digital Computer Room Based on Digital Twin

4.1 Virtual Machine Room Construction Requirements

The modeling of virtual machine room shall meet the following requirements:

(1) Organizational hierarchy.
The virtual machine room is composed of different models, including more three-dimensional equipment models. Therefore, it should have a clear organizational hierarchy, realize the rapid management of the model, and facilitate the developers to adjust the model in the use and maintenance process.
(2) Interactivity.
Virtual machine room is the main window for the twin machine room visual monitoring system to interact with users. Users can control the models in the system and get corresponding feedback. Users can intuitively understand the operation status of equipment in the computer room, and realize scene roaming in the computer room. The system can also timely feed back prompt information and alarm information to users. Through strong human-computer interaction to improve the user's sense of experience.
(3) Balance.
In the modeling of virtual machine room, because there are many models, rendering and material processing are required for the models, and a large number of data transmission and calculation processing behaviors are generated in the data drive, higher requirements are required for the performance of the computer. Therefore, when the virtual machine room is actually modeled, it should be optimized as far as possible to reduce the burden of computer GPU and CPU while ensuring the real effect of the virtual machine room.
(4) Behavioral characteristics.
During the modeling process of the virtual machine room, it should be consistent with the real machine room environment as much as possible, and follow the physical rules of the real machine room. For example, when the scene roams, it cannot directly cross the equipment model. Real behavior characteristics can improve users' sense of experience and immersion.

4.2 Virtual Machine Room Construction Process

According to the real mapping characteristics of digital twins, the computer room digital model is the digital twin of the computer room physical objects. This chapter uses blender and three, JS to design the virtual machine room model. The process of virtual machine room modeling is shown in Fig. 2.

Blender is a lightweight 3D animation software released by blender foundation. Because of its open source advantages, blender has become the preferred modeling software for many developers. The biggest reason for choosing blender software in this article is that it can support JSON file format. You only need to install three The JS exporter plug-in can export the file format of the model to JSON type, which can reduce the resources occupied by the model and improve the rendering speed.

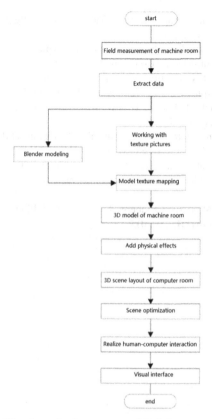

Fig. 2. Visual monitoring process of digital computer room

5 Conclusion

With the changes of times and technological progress, all industries have entered a digital era. In this context, the monitoring and management of data has become a crucial thing. Aiming at the problems of poor visualization, poor real-time performance and low management efficiency in the current computer room, this paper introduces the digital twin technology and applies it to the computer room monitoring system, and designs and implements the computer room three-dimensional visual monitoring system based on the digital twin.

References

1. Zhuang, C., Miao, T., Liu, J., et al.: The connotation of digital twin, and the construction and application method of shop-floor digital twin. Robotics and Computer-Integrated Manufacturing **68**, 102075 (2021)
2. Wang, C., Sha, Z., Jia, L.: Research on digital resource system construction of smart library based on computer network and artificial intelligence. J. Phys: Conf. Ser. **1952**(4), 42018 (2021)

3. Moore, S.F.: Computer-Implemented Method Of Digital Music Composition US20210272543A1 (2021)
4. Jamie, F.C.: Rules for mediated romance: a digital exploration of how couples negotiate expectations. J. Comput.-Mediat. Commun. **3**, 3 (2022)
5. Torres, P.E., Ulrich, P.I.N., Cucuiat, V., et al.: A systematic review of physical-digital play technology and developmentally relevant child behaviour (2021)
6. Carpenter, C.: Artificial Intelligence Transforms Offshore Analog Fields Into Digital Fields. J. Petrol. Technol. **72**(1), 71–72 (2020)
7. Herz, E.M. System and Method for Dynamically Regulating Order Entry in an Electronic Trading Environment: US, US8606689 B2 (2020)
8. Finnegan, M.E., Konicek, J.C., Lisa, S.G.: Realtime, interactive and geographically defined computerized personal identification and payment matching methods: US, US20130066731 A1 (2020)
9. Astete, N.L., Brethorst, A.B., Goldberg, J.M., et al.: Multitenant hosted virtual machine infrastructure US10817318B2 (2020)
10. Hager, P.M.: Methods and systems for correcting transcribed audio files US10861438B2 (2020)

A Survey of Trendy Financial Sector Applications of Machine and Deep Learning

Nur Indah Lestari[1](✉), Walayat Hussain[1,2](✉) (iD), Jose M. Merigo[1], and Mahmoud Bekhit[1,3] (iD)

[1] Faculty of Engineering and Information Technology, University of Technology Sydney, Ultimo, Australia
Nurindah.lestari@student.uts.edu.au,
{Jose.Merigo,Mahmoud.bekhit}@uts.edu.au
[2] Victoria University Business School, Victoria University, Melbourne 3000, Australia
Walayat.Hussain@vu.edu.au
[3] Kent Institute Australia, Sydney, Australia

Abstract. In the field of finance, machine learning encompasses a number of disciplines, including pattern recognition, financial econometrics, statistical computing, probabilistic programming, and dynamic programming. Machine learning (ML) is causing a revolution in the financial industry as more and more companies use ML-automated operations to make better decisions, increase productivity, and achieve other business goals. Machine learning algorithms are being utilised by financial institutions, including banks, fintech companies, insurance brokers, and other suppliers of financial services, in order to forecast financial risk, automate repetitive processes, and gain real-time investment advice. Because of the very nature of their operations, financial institutions generate enormous amounts of data that are often complex. This creates the ideal setting for machine learning, which requires vast datasets from which machines can learn. This research investigates the impact of machine learning, deep learning, and statistical approaches on key financial principles, including fraud detection, money laundering prevention, and credit risk assessment. To investigate the impact of these methodologies on financial indicators, secondary data sources such as books and peer-reviewed journals were analysed.

Keywords: Machine learning · Deep learning · Statistical models · Finance · Risk management · Fraud detection & money laundering prevention

1 Introduction

Machine learning is a branch of artificial intelligence that lets computers learn new skills by looking for patterns in data and getting more and more practice.

© ICST Institute for Computer Sciences, Social Informatics and Telecommunications Engineering 2023
Published by Springer Nature Switzerland AG 2023. All Rights Reserved
M. A. Jan and F. Khan (Eds.): BigIoT-EDU 2022, LNICST 467, pp. 619–633, 2023.
https://doi.org/10.1007/978-3-031-23944-1_68

A model automatically interprets this information using natural language processing techniques after being fed data samples by machine learning algorithms. Then, it learns to look for patterns and make guesses when given similar data it hasn't seen before. Machine learning has a lot of potential in an industry that creates a lot of important data. Using machine learning in finance can help cut costs by automating routine tasks, increase revenue by making decisions faster and better, improve customer satisfaction by automatically putting the most important issues at the top of the list, and improve security by making it easier to spot fraud and other suspicious activities.

When it related to the implementation of a machine learning solution, companies have the option of either purchasing a software as service (SaaS) product or using open-source libraries to develop their own machine learning software. The development of software for machine learning might take several months, and significant up-front expenses are required (like hiring a team of data science experts and developers). If you decide to purchase cloud-based AI tools, the process will go much more quickly, and the platform will supply you with a set of tools that have already been trained, so you can get started right away [1,2]. SaaS solutions are not only cost-effective but also can be put into place in a matter of weeks, which enables financial services to quickly acquire important insights from unstructured data.

The aim of this article is to explore the recent advancements of the machine learning, deep learning, and statistical methods in the fields of finance e.g., learning rate and activation functions. The rest of this paper is organized as follows. The definition of machine, deep learning systems and statistical methods in the field of finance were discussed in Sect. 2. In Sect. 3, several finance applications that utilized systems are reviewed. Finally, the conclusion of the paper is presented in Sect. 4.

2   Background

2.1   Machine Learning

The three basic subfields that lie under the umbrella of machine learning are reinforcement learning, supervised learning, and unsupervised learning. Supervised learning examples include categorization and regression (e.g., reward-based). This paper is primarily concerned with the first subfield of machine learning, supervised learning. The ultimate objective of the field of machine learning is to develop models and programmes that enable computer systems to duplicate the human learning process using accessible data. This will be accomplished by imitating human learning. There are three parts that make up any machine learning-based system: the data, the models, and the learning. The most important step in the process of creating an ML system is to tune the model's hyperparameters in order to fit the data to the model. This job is referred to as model training, and it is completed with the help of hypotheses that are derived from performance criteria. The goal of a process known as hyperparameter optimization is to identify a machine learning model's optimum collection of the hyperparameters that correspond to it.

Finding the appropriate configuration of hyperparameter values for a predictive model has a direct impact on the performance of the models as well as the datasets on which they are tested. Although tuning of hyperparameters is an essential part of the process of training a model, which is necessary to ensure that an application of machine learning will be successful, this process requires a significant amount of computational power. This is due to the enormous number of testable combinations and the required computer resources [3]. The task of regression in the field of machine learning is considered to be one of the essential tasks. In order to design an ML-based regressor, one must make use of several mathematical techniques in order to make a prediction regarding the value of the continuous output variable Y based on the value of one or more of the input variables X. For the purpose of forecasting future results on the basis of previously collected information, the simplest kind of regression analysis is linear regression. Because of this, the process of making a machine learning model has four main steps: picking the training data, picking the target function, picking the representation for the target function, and picking a method for getting close to the target function.

Random Forest. Random forest, which is also called RF, is a helpful technique for machine learning that can be applied to a wide range of problems. It is a collection of tree predictors that may be used to predict trees and is a mechanism for aggregating the findings of individual tree predictors. In terms of observations or attributes, each tree predictor has a random subsample of the entire dataset. A more precise forecast can be obtained by using the random forest model, which incorporates the results of various estimators. A tree is formed by combining or combining attributes at each node in a random manner. The ensemble design of the random forest enables it to generalise effectively to data it has not seen before, including data with missing values. This helps the random forest to compensate for the unknown data and perform well. In addition to this, random forests effectively manage enormous datasets with high dimensionality and a variety of different feature types. Random forests are effective at solving classification problems, but they are only somewhat effective at solving regression problems. In contrast to a linear regression model, a random forest regressor cannot make predictions that go beyond what its training data shows. In contrast to other more conventional machine learning techniques, it is difficult to examine the inside of a random forest classifier and grasp the reasoning behind its judgments. In addition to this, they can be slow to train and run, and the file sizes they create can be rather enormous. Whenever a data scientist is constructing a new machine learning model, random forests are often their first point of contact. This is due to the fact that random forests are incredibly robust, simple to implement, effective with heterogeneous types of data, and have several hyperparameters. Even though the ultimate answer does not use a random forest, random forests help data scientists to gain a fast understanding of the precision that can be reasonably achieved for a specific issue.

Decision Trees. One of the key objectives of the Decision Trees (DT) methodology is to place the most crucial splits between the nodes of the tree, hence enhancing the classification of the data. To accomplish this, the proper decision rules should be applied to the data collected, which has a significant impact on the performance of the algorithm [4]. The DT method makes use of Information Gain (IG) since the purpose of a decision tree model is to identify the optimal split node that guarantees high accuracy. The IG method seeks out the most pertinent nodes that provide the most information, which may be measured using the Entropy factor. The Entropy factor is used to quantify a system's level of disorder.

Support Vector Machine. Support vector machine (SVM) is defined as a statistical learning theory in order to establish the optimal decision boundaries for class separation. Initially, SVMs were developed to address problems with two classes (binary). There must be a multiclass method when several classes are involved. In multiclass circumstances, 'one versus one' and 'one against the others' techniques are frequently utilised.

Linear Regression. The most fundamental type of regressor is known as linear regression or LR. The fundamental concept behind it is to locate a function that can convert the input to the output. The fact that the coefficients always maintain a linear property is where the term "linear" derives from. While this is carrying on, the feature may have a non-linear order. When all the features of an equation are linear, the linear regression model is represented by nothing other than a linear line. Changing the order of the feature from linear to non-linear can make it possible to improve the function curvature as it just better fits the form of the data. In this perspective, linear regression can be understood as a method of curve fitting. In linear regression, the data should be divided into two sets, which are referred to as the training set and the test set. The shape of the curve is determined by the training data, while the accuracy of the model is evaluated by determining the distance between the data points in the test set and the curve. When its presumptions are verified, the linear regression method can be utilised. The following are considered to be true: normalcy, independence, linearity, and homoscedasticity.

2.2 Deep Learning-Based Prediction: GRU (Gated Recurrent Units)

Deep learning techniques, in particular recurrent neural networks (RNNs), have been shown to be effective in a range of applications, including time series forecasting, where they have been utilised [5–7]. RNN is a robust model that can learn a wide range of complex associations from an arbitrarily long set of data and has been used effectively to solve a number of problems. It has also been used to address many other problems effectively [8–10]. However, as a result of the depth of the RNN, two difficulties that are already well-known arose: the bursting and the vanishing gradient. In order to overcome the challenges that were outlined before, two distinct variants of the recurrent model-namely, GRU [11] and Long Short-Term Memory (LSTM) were developed. Each GRU and LSTM architectures have gating strategies for controlling the flow of data through the unit, and both have a design that is comparable to the other. Despite this, the requires a significant amount of time to both train and converge due to its complex structure [12]. GRU-DNN is easier to understand and has an architecture that is not as complex as LSTM. Because of this, it can be trained more quickly than LSTM can. Recurrent units are what identify patterns and dependencies across different periods in the GRU model. In contrast to the LSTM cell, the GRU does not have a dedicated memory gate. As a result, it is capable of learning data much more quickly and efficiently.

The benefit of using Deep learning (DL) is that DL is being utilised in nearly all industries. As a consequence of this, many people refer to this method as a universal learning method. DL is being utilised in a variety of contexts that could benefit from the application of machine intelligence. Some examples of these contexts include navigation on Mars, which does not have a human expert available, vision, speech recognition, language understanding, and biometrics and the personalisation of solutions for specific cases. The DL method is now occasionally referred to as universal learning as it is proven to be a valuable technique in practically any application field. The method "universal learning" was created to describe this trend. Robust deep learning approaches do not require a specific design feature in order to function well. Instead, its robustness comes from a method that allows it to automatically learn and represent the best features for any given task. Because the deep learning methodology is adaptable, it is possible to use the same DL method with various datasets and in a number of different contexts. A different name for this method is "transfer learning." In addition, this method is helpful in cases where there is inadequate data to support the problem. The DL method is very scalable concerning both the amount of data and the computation it requires. In addition to this, there are a lot of obstacles to overcome in DL, such as combining big data analytics with DL. The many principles of big data, such as velocity, volume, and veracity, as well as the benefits of using DL with large data, are described in this article. Scalability in DL approaches refers to the ability to produce significant data even when appropriate information is not readily available for the purpose of learning the system.

2.3   Statistical Predictive Models

A substantial quantity of literature has explored the most effective time series forecasting approaches. The results indicate that these methods can be classified into two distinct macrocategories, namely statistical and machine-learning methods. The auto-regressive moving average (ARMA) model is a generalisation of the model that is appropriate for describing non-stationary time series. Specifically, the principal advantage of utilising the ARIMA model is to turn a non-stationary series into a series without seasonality or trend by applying finite data point differencing [13]. A time series is stationary by description if its statistical features remain constant throughout time. If a stationary series lacks a trend, the amplitude of its deviations around the mean is constant. In addition, the autocorrelations of time series remain consistent across time. On the basis of these assumptions, this sort of time series can be considered a mixture of signal and noise. The signal is managed by isolating it from the noise using an ARIMA model. The output of the ARIMA model, after reducing noise from the input, is the signal step-ahead for forecasting.

Using the ARIMA and GARCH models, the authors of study [14] investigated the problem of producing reliable predictions of stock market time series data. On the other hand, they show that these traditional methods were adopted by a significant body of literary works in order to solve difficulties involving anticipating one step further in the future. The aforementioned model does not perform accurately when attempting to make a forecast that is several steps or N steps into the future. In particular, the authors have expressed worry regarding the decline in accuracy as well as the absence of any upkeep of the trend or dynamics of the data. A linear hybrid model that combines ARIMA and GARCH was offered as a solution in order to circumvent these restrictions. First, in order to separate the stock market time series into two distinct series, they used a straightforward moving average filter on the data. The ARIMA model and the GARCH model are both being used to model one of these data streams respectively.

Time series modelling is an exciting area of study that aims to gather and evaluate data from previous time series in order to create modelling that precisely captures the fundamental structure of the series being modelled. This model is then used to predict future values of the series being modelled. After that, the model is utilised to make projections regarding the future values of the series while keeping in mind that accurate model fitting is essential for producing accurate time-series forecasts. For the past few decades, researchers have concentrated their efforts on linear models due to the ease with which these models can be understood and applied. When using linear models, one must restrict the future values to being linear functions of the historical data. One of the most well-known and often employed linear stochastic time series models is the autoregressive integrated moving average (ARIMA) model. The Autoregressive n (AR) model, the Moving Average (MA) model, and the Autoregressive Moving Average (ARMA) model are all subclasses of the ARIMA model. Other models such as the Moving Average (MA) model and the Autoregressive Moving Average (ARMA) model. Non-stationary behaviour can be seen in a great deal of different time series, including those associated with socioeconomics and business. Non-stationary time series also include those that exhibit trends and seasonal patterns. The ARMA model can only be applied to data belonging to a stationary time series; it is not adequate to accurately describe non-stationary time series. As a direct consequence of this, the ARIMA model was developed to account for non-stationarity.

3   Finance Applications

3.1   Process Automation

The progress made in data science, machine learning, and artificial intelligence needs us to reconsider this subject continually. One of these advancements is called robotic process automation, or RPA. The term "Robotic Process Automation" (RPA) is a concept that applies to software applications that simulate human activities on the user interface of many other computer systems. The goal of RPA is to eliminate the need for people by automating processes in an "outside-in" fashion. In contrast to the traditional "inside-out" strategy for improving information systems, this one works from the outside in. In contrast to more conventional workflow technologies, the information system has not been modified in any way.

Robotic Process Automation (RPA) is described in the following way by Gartner: "RPA tools conduct [if, then, else] statements on structured data, often making use of a combination of user interface interactions or by connecting to APIs in order to drive client servers, mainframes, or HTML code. The operation of an RPA tool consists of mapping a process into the RPA tool language for the software robot to follow, with runtime being assigned to execute the script by a control dashboard." [15] Therefore, the purpose of RPA tools is to relieve workers of the repetition and simplicity of routine jobs [16].

The demand for RPA products from commercial providers has recently increased significantly. In addition, several new businesses have entered the market during the course of the past two years. This should not come as a surprise, given that the majority of firms are still searching for methods to save expenses and rapidly integrate together legacy applications. RPA is currently considered a means to generate a high return on investment in a short amount of time (RoI). Some companies solely sell RPA software, such as AutomationEdge, Automation Anywhere, Blue Prism, Kryon Systems, Softomotive, and UiPath. Other dedicated RPA vendors include AutomationEdge and Automation Anywhere [15,17]. There are also a great number of other companies that offer a variety of tools or software that have incorporated robotic process automation features into their products (not just RPA). The purpose of this editorial is to explore the difficulties associated with RPA research for the BISE community and to reflect on the recent advancements that have taken place. People who work in finance and insurance spend more than half of their time collecting and analysing data. By using machine learning tools, companies can automate a lot of their routine and time-consuming tasks, which can boost productivity, save money, and free up workers to focus on more valuable tasks. For example, the finance sector uses AI and machine learning to automate client onboarding, which is a complicated and time-consuming process that usually involves collecting, revising, and processing a large amount of data from various departments. Through intelligent automation, the Bank was able to cut the time it took to open an account from 23 days to less than 5 min.

3.2 Document Analysis

Text analysis tools utilise machine learning in order to make sense of unstructured data. These tools assist businesses in the financial sector in gaining value from their data quickly and cost-effectively while simultaneously lowering the likelihood of errors caused by human intervention. Applications range from automatically classifying data found in emails, contracts, and reports to extracting important information from legal documentation, statements, and bills. In 2007, JP Morgan Chase implemented a software called COIN, which is based on machine learning, with the goal of reducing the amount of time it takes to analyse paperwork and the number of mistakes it makes when servicing loans for new wholesale contracts. The software is able to identify recurring clauses within contracts and place each of those phrases into one of approximately 150 different categories.

3.3 Algorithmic Trading

Trading based on algorithms provides a natural setting for the application of machine learning. The premise that trading decisions should be based on facts rather than intuition is at the core of the algorithmic trading approach. As a result, it ought to be possible to automate this decision-making process by utilising an algorithm, either one that is stated or one that is learned. Some of the benefits of algorithmic trading include the ability to recognise complicated market patterns, reduce errors caused by humans, and test strategies using historical data [18, 19]. Recent years have seen a dramatic increase in both the practicability and the capacity of algorithmic trading thanks to the digitisation of an increasing amount of formerly analogue information.

Numerous machine learning techniques are non-linear as well as semi-parametric or non-parametric, and as a result, they prove to be complementary to existing econometric models. With the help of a feedforward neural network, we will construct a straightforward momentum portfolio strategy in this example. We limit ourselves to the S&P 500 stock universe and assume that we know the daily close price for each stock throughout the course of the past decade. The use of algorithms in trading enables companies to create trading choices much more quickly and accurately. Machine learning algorithms can uncover trading potential by recognising patterns and behaviours in historical data. These algorithms are trained to do this. Since of this, businesses have an advantage over their competitors because they are able to concurrently monitor and analyse vast amounts of data in real-time, which is something that is beyond the capability of humans. The use of algorithms could also help reduce the amount of error caused by humans. When it comes to financial decisions, human beings are frequently guided by their feelings. On the other hand, the algorithms used in machine learning do not have any inherent biases, which makes them a valuable ally in the financial industry.

3.4 Digital Assistants

Customer service and support can be a crucial differentiation for many retail clients, particularly when it comes to issues regarding technology, products, or just general inquiries. According to a 2014 J J.D. Power survey on U.S. retail banking satisfaction, the main reason clients change banks was lousy customer service. The awareness of customers, products, and systems is vital in customer support. However, this component of the operation is viewed as a costly approach to serve the customer in the long term [20]. Consequently, banks are progressively shifting to 'self-service' even in the physical branch. Support that combines precision, practical assistance, and good interpersonal skills may be the most beneficial for clients. Therefore, the retail banking business is heading towards 'augmented A.I.' where the activities of the contact centre representative are boosted by technology, chatbots and eventually automation, all of which will be analytically linked.

The use of machine learning bots is gaining popularity in the banking business. These bots help companies improve the service experience while simultaneously reducing the amount of money they spend on call centres. Chatbots, for example, come equipped with algorithms for machine learning and are trained to handle frequent and non-critical client enquiries around the clock. This helps scale support and improves customer satisfaction. In addition, virtual assistants are being employed to automate a variety of duties, such as the search for historical transaction data and the collection of client contact information.

3.5 Risk Management

The first aim of investors is to develop a portfolio that would provide them with the maximum potential return on their starting capital, especially because banks no longer offer interest and safety. There are thousands of portfolios on the market from which an investor can choose, making portfolio selection a not-so-simple but rather involved process. In addition to the portfolio's arithmetic average return, the standard deviation of its returns is a crucial component that an investor should consider when evaluating the quality of a portfolio.

The application of machine learning to solve traditional quantitative finance problems, such as return forecasting, risk modelling, and optimal portfolio creation, has seen widespread use in recent years. Throughout this work, we mainly focus on its application cases for financial risk management, which encompasses either risk modelling (the effort of measuring and forecasting risk) or risk mitigation (challenge of reducing risk by constructing a portfolio with optimal risk management or hedging). Risk modelling is the task of determining how much risk there is, and risk mitigation is the task of predicting how much risk there will be in the future.

According to the article [21], risk is defined as the probability of loss, while exposure is defined as the possibility of loss. The acceptance of certain levels of risk is frequently essential to the successful operation of a corporation. The foundation of FRM is the process of identifying risk and exposure. Due to the fact that risk and exposure are experienced differently in various fields, the ways in which they are measured also vary. The finance business is fraught with numerous types of risk, including market risk, regulatory risk, credit risk, operational risk, and many others. Financial institutions have been increasingly integrating AI and machine learning to better risk management throughout the past few years. These technologies have assisted these institutions in detecting and quantifying risks, as well as in making the appropriate judgments Algorithms that learn through machine learning are able to continuously monitor and examine massive volumes of data, which enables them to identify trends and patterns and provide crucial information in real-time.

3.6   Fraud Detection and Money Laundering Prevention

In 2011, the financial industry lost around 80$ billion yearly due to fraudulent fraud (Consumer Reports, June 2011). The Global Economic Crime Survey conducted by PwC in 2016 found that 46% of respondents working in the Financial Services industry reported having been victims of financial fraud in the preceding 24 months. This figure represents a slight increase from the 45% of respondents who reported being targets in 2014. 16% of individuals who reported being victims of financial fraud had experienced more than 100 cases, and 6% had experienced over 1,000 cases. According to the data collected from the survey, the top five types of economic crime are

- asset misappropriation (60%, which is a decrease from 67% in 2014),
- cybercrime (49%, which is an increase from 39% in 2014)
- bribery and corruption (18%, which is a decrease from 20% in 2014)
- money laundering (24%, which is the same as in 2014)
- Accounting fraud (18%, down from 21% in 2014).

One of the oldest and most practical applications of machine learning in the financial services business is identifying fraudulent financial activity. Authors of [22] provides a concise introduction of some traditional methods, including logistic regression, naive Bayes, and support vector machines. New types of financial fraud and market manipulation have emerged due to the expansion of electronic trading. Several exchanges are exploring the use of deep learning to combat spoofing.

The analysis of user-generated online content, such as Twitter conversations or YouTube videos, can also be aided by machine learning with the help of sentiment analysis technique [23–27]. These techniques can be Despite this, the sector continues to exercise caution, and the application of these technologies has, up until this point, been more experimental than systematic [28].

Machine learning plays a crucial role in the ongoing fight against fraudulent transactions and money laundering. This technology can detect anomalies in big historical sets of data and monitor activity in real-time for suspicious transactions, thereby alerting financial services in real-time to security concerns and criminal actions. Stripe Radar, for instance, is a suite of machine learning tools that assist businesses in detecting and preventing fraud. It analyses every card payment, combines data into behavioural patterns that are predictive of fraud, and rejects payments if there is a high likelihood that they are fraudulent.

3.7 Financial Inclusion

According to the research that has been done, many academics have come up with a variety of definitions of "financial inclusion" [29]. According to the definition provided by [30], the process of financial inclusion is the delivery of banking services in such a way that they become affordable to many disadvantaged groups, particularly those with low incomes. [31] has proposed a definition of financial inclusion. According to this definition, financial inclusion is the process through which formal financial institutions make it possible for disadvantaged groups to obtain financial services at prices that are within their means. The second definition of "financial inclusion" was provided by [32]. According to this definition, "financial inclusion" is the practise of ensuring that all people in an economy have easy access to formal financial services and that those services are readily available to them. Authors also defined "financial inclusion" as "the art of making sure that there is the availability of formal financial services."

Arun and Kamath [33] pointed out another important aspect of financial inclusion, which is that it should be understood as a circumstance in which individuals have access to high-quality financial services and products that are also low-cost and offer a convenient experience, all while maintaining their dignity. [31] defined financial exclusion as the inability or unwillingness of groups of people in a society to utilise mainstream financial services. The lack of access to mainstream financial services is another definition of financial exclusion. According to [34], financial exclusion encompasses any conditions that prevent people or parts of society from gaining access to low-cost, fair, and secure financial products and services from official financial service providers. He describes these circumstances as "anything that prevents groups or parts of society from accessing low-cost, fair, and secure financial products and services."

Another goal of financial inclusion is to make sure that financial systems and institutions can keep running, as well as to encourage and support healthy levels of competition. The end goal is to offer customers a wide range of products and services at prices they can afford [29].

3.8 Credit Risk Assessments

It is imperative for lending organisations to have effective credit-risk assessment since defaulting debtors can result in significant financial losses for the institution. As a direct result of this, statistical tools that are capable of accurately measuring and analysing credit risk are becoming increasingly crucial.

The probability that a potential borrower will not fulfil their commitments in accordance with the terms that were agreed upon is the definition of credit risk. Most financial institutions analyse and manage risk to increase the bank's rate of return after taking into account the risk. This is accomplished by ensuring that the bank's credit risk exposure remains within the prescribed limits. The efficient management of credit risk is one of the essential components of risk management and it is essential for the sustained prosperity of any financial institution. Loans are considered the primary and most obvious source of credit risk by many financial institutions, including but not limited to banks and other credit-providing firms.

[35] concludes that the main causes of banking problems are, among other things, loose credit standards for borrowers and counterparties and bad portfolio risk management. Other problems include not paying enough attention to changes in the economy that can hurt the credit standing of a bank's counterparties. In addition, authors stated that one of the major causes of banking problems is a lack of attention to the economic changes that can compromise the credit standing of a company. According to [35], some of these experiences are especially prevalent in G-10 nations, while others are most prevalent in non-G-10 nations. As a result of the challenges caused by a lack of information, certain groups of people in many emerging countries are prevented from participating in the mainstream formal financial markets. Some of these individuals, such as young people, small business owners, and women, may not have a credit history, and in some cases, they do not have collateral security, which limits their ability to obtain credit. Information asymmetry is the term used by academics to describe this issue. Some people also think that AI might be able to help find a solution to this problem.

3.9 Information Asymmetry

A scenario known as "information asymmetry" occurs when different agents do not have access to the same amount of information [29,36,37]. Information asymmetry has been defined by [38] as the study of human decisions that were made in circumstances when one individual has more information than another human being. This is referred to as the study of decision making under information asymmetry. When it comes to certain markets, such as the credit market and the labour market, as well as other contexts, having unequal access to information is not always ideal [39].

As described by the winner of the Nobel Prize in Economics, Michael Spence, information asymmetry is not desired in the labour market when interviews are being conducted. This is especially true in situations in which the prospective employer demands more knowledge about the possible employee [36,40].Both sides must cooperate in a procedure known as the signal for the potential employer to collect as many details as possible. Throughout this phase, the prospective employer signals to the employee to expose as much information as possible. The potential employee signals information such as their competencies to the potential employer in order to convey that they are qualified for the role.

According to [37], the problem of information asymmetry can potentially cause some problems in the loan market. It is considered that debtor claims are sometimes in a vulnerable situation due to a lack of correct data on the financing project. In addition, the financial institution is unable to analyse credit risk since it lacks precise information. Both of these factors contribute to the situation. In order for the bank to avoid suffering losses, it must make every effort to reduce the amount of credit risk it takes on. When a bank is ready to receive credit applications, the credit risk that it takes on depends on how well it can collect and process the information that comes with those application.

According to [38,41,42] machine learning can help to solve the problem of information asymmetry, which could go a long way towards improving the big developmental problem of financial exclusion, especially in the credit market. This is something that has been articulated by [41,42]. Signaling, as well as the application of big data and deep learning, are the primary avenues via which machine learning might contribute to the resolution of the issue of information imbalance. The problem of social networks, which are powered by machine learning to such an extent that they are able to signal information in a lot more accurate manner than what a human agent is capable of doing, was one example that was provided by [42]. In this approach, it is said that machine learning could contribute to the solution of the problem of not having enough information in many places, including the loan market.

4 Conclusion

One of the obstacles that the researchers needed to overcome was the process of analysing financial data. Because of the recent reevaluation of the foundations upon which financial markets are built, there is an immediate need for the development of original models to comprehend financial assets. Researchers in the last few decades have presented several methods based on traditional methodologies such as ARIMA and smoothing models with exponential decay in order to design a precise data representation. Despite being effective, existing methods have a number of limitations, the most significant of which is that they are not very good at handling massive amounts of data that are complex, have a significant proportion of dimensions, and have casual dynamics. In addition, these methods are not appropriate for comprehending the hidden dependencies and relationships that exist amongst the data. This study provides a comprehensive assessment of new machine learning techniques in quantitative finance, demonstrating that these ways prove to be more effective than conventional methods. Unobtrusive research methods, such as conceptual analysis, were applied to authoritative sources in order to contextualise the impact of machine learning, deep learning, and statistical methods on a wide range of financial concerns.

References

1. Hussain, W., Hussain, F.K., Saberi, M., Hussain, O.K., Chang, E.: Comparing time series with machine learning-based prediction approaches for violation management in cloud slas. Futur. Gener. Comput. Syst. **89**, 464–477 (2018)
2. Gao, H., Huang, J., Tao, Y., Hussain, W., Huang, Y.: The joint method of triple attention and novel loss function for entity relation extraction in small data-driven computational social systems. IEEE Trans. Comput. Soc. Syst. **9**, 1725–1735 (2022)

3. Hussain, W., Merigo, J.M., Gao, H., Alkalbani, A.M., Rabhi, F.A.: Integrated AHP-IOWA, POWA framework for ideal cloud provider selection and optimum resource management. IEEE Trans. Serv. Comput. (2021)
4. Raza, M.R., Hussain, W., Varol, A.: Performance analysis of deep approaches on airbnb sentiment reviews. In: 2022 10th International Symposium on Digital Forensics and Security (ISDFS), pp. 1–5, IEEE (2022)
5. Alameer, Z., Fathalla, A., Li, K., Ye, H., Jianhua, Z.: Multistep-ahead forecasting of coal prices using a hybrid deep learning model. Resour. Policy **65**, 101588 (2020)
6. Hussain, W., Gao, H., Raza, M.R., Rabhi, F.A., Merigo, J.M.: Assessing cloud QoS predictions using OWA in neural network methods. Neural Comput. Appl. **34**, 14895–14912 (2022)
7. Hussain, W., Raza, M.R., Jan, M.A., Merigo, J.M., Gao, H.: Cloud risk management with OWA-LSTM predictive intelligence and fuzzy linguistic decision making. IEEE Trans. Fuzzy Syst. **30**, 4657–4666 (2022)
8. Xiao, L., Zhang, Y., Li, K., Liao, B., Tan, Z.: A novel recurrent neural network and its finite-time solution to time-varying complex matrix inversion. Neurocomputing **331**, 483–492 (2019)
9. Chen, C., Li, K., Teo, S.G., Zou, X., Wang, K., Wang, J., Zeng, Z.: Gated residual recurrent graph neural networks for traffic prediction. In: Proceedings of the AAAI Conference on Artificial Intelligence, vol. 33, pp. 485–492 (2019)
10. Quan, Z., Lin, X., Wang, Z.-J., Liu, Y., Wang, F., Li, K.: A system for learning atoms based on long short-term memory recurrent neural networks. In: 2018 IEEE International Conference on Bioinformatics and Biomedicine (BIBM), pp. 728–733. IEEE (2018)
11. Cho, K., et al.: Learning phrase representations using RNN encoder-decoder for statistical machine translation. arXiv preprint arXiv:1406.1078 (2014)
12. Ravanelli, M., Brakel, P., Omologo, M., Bengio, Y.: Light gated recurrent units for speech recognition. IEEE Trans. Emerg. Topics Comput. Intell. **2**(2), 92–102 (2018)
13. Box, G.E., Jenkins, G.M., Reinsel, G.: Time series analysis: forecasting and control holden-day san francisco. BoxTime Series Analysis: Forecasting and Control Holden Day 1970 (1970)
14. Williams, B.M., Hoel, L.A.: Modeling and forecasting vehicular traffic flow as a seasonal Arima process: theoretical basis and empirical results. J. Transp. Eng. **129**(6), 664–672 (2003)
15. Tornbohm, C., Dunie, R.: Gartner market guide for robotic process automation software. Report G00319864. Gartner (2017)
16. Aguirre, J.M., El cine como arte cinéticamente modularizado. Comunicación: estudios venezolanos de comunicación **179**, 65–71 (2017)
17. Le Clair, C., Cullen, A., King, M.: The forrester wave^TM: robotic process automation, q1 2017. Forrester Res. (2017)
18. Wang, J., Wang, Y., Yang, J.: Forecasting of significant wave height based on gated recurrent unit network in the taiwan strait and its adjacent waters. Water **13**(1), 86 (2021)
19. Hussain, W., Merigó, J.M., Raza, M.R., Gao, H.: A new QoS prediction model using hybrid IOWA-ANFIS with fuzzy c-means, subtractive clustering and grid partitioning. Inf. Sci. **584**, 280–300 (2022)
20. Boobier, T.: AI and the Future of Banking. Wiley, Chichester (2020)
21. Horcher, K.A.: Essentials of Financial Risk Management. Wiley, Hoboken (2011)

22. Gottlieb, O., Salisbury, C., Shek, H., Vaidyanathan, V.: Detecting corporate fraud: an application of machine learning. A publication of the American Institute of Computing, pp. 100–215 (2006)
23. Ahmad, S., Asghar, M.Z., Alotaibi, F.M., Awan, I.: Detection and classification of social media-based extremist affiliations using sentiment analysis techniques. HCIS **9**(1), 1–23 (2019)
24. Cunliffe, E., Curini, L.: Isis and heritage destruction: a sentiment analysis. Antiquity **92**(364), 1094–1111 (2018)
25. García-Retuerta, D., Bartolomé, Á., Chamoso, P., Corchado, J.M.: Counter-terrorism video analysis using hash-based algorithms. Algorithms **12**(5), 110 (2019)
26. Raza, M.R., Hussain, W., Tanyıldızı, E., Varol, A.: Sentiment analysis using deep learning in cloud. In: 2021 9th International Symposium on Digital Forensics and Security (ISDFS), pp. 1–5. IEEE (2021)
27. Raza, M.R., Hussain, W., Merigó, J.M.: Cloud sentiment accuracy comparison using RNN, LSTM and GRU. In: 2021 Innovations in Intelligent Systems and Applications Conference (ASYU), pp. 1–5. IEEE (2021)
28. Gombár, M., Vagaská, A., Korauš, A.: Analytical view on legalization of crime proceeds in context of European union. Economics, Politics and Management in Times of Change, p. 30 (2021)
29. Mhlanga, D.: Financial inclusion and poverty reduction: evidence from small scale agricultural sector in Manicaland Province of Zimbabwe. Ph.D. thesis, North-West University (South Africa) (2020)
30. Leeladhar, V.: Taking banking services to the common man-financial inclusion. Reserve Bank of India Bulletin **60**(1), 73–77 (2006)
31. Ambarkhane, D., Singh, A.S., Venkataramani, B.: Measuring financial inclusion of Indian states. Int. J. Rural. Manag. **12**(1), 72–100 (2016)
32. Sarma, M.: Index of financial inclusion. Technical report, Working paper (2008)
33. Arun, T., Kamath, R.: Financial inclusion: policies and practices. IIMB Manag. Rev. **27**(4), 267–287 (2015)
34. Mohan, R.: Economic growth, financial deepening and financial inclusion. Reserve Bank of India Bulletin, vol. 1305 (2006)
35. Witzany, J.: Credit risk management. In: Credit Risk Management. PMSBFI, pp. 5–18. Springer, Cham (2017). https://doi.org/10.1007/978-3-319-49800-3_2
36. Marwala, T.: Impact of artificial intelligence on economic theory. arXiv preprint arXiv:1509.01213 (2015)
37. Tfaily, A.: Managing Information Asymmetry And Credit Risk A Theoretical Perspective. In: Proceedings of the International Management Conference **11**, 652–659 (2017)
38. Marwala, T., Hurwitz, E.: Artificial intelligence and asymmetric information theory. arXiv preprint arXiv:1510.02867 (2015)
39. Hussain, W., Merigo, J.M.: Onsite/offsite social commerce adoption for SMES using fuzzy linguistic decision making in complex framework. J. Ambient Intell. Humanized Comput. 1–20 (2022)
40. Spence, M.: Job market signaling. Q. J. Econ. **87**(3), 355–374 (1973)
41. Moloi, T., Marwala, T.: Advanced information and knowledge processing (2020)
42. Moloi, T., Marwala, T.: Artificial Intelligence in Economics and Finance Theories. AIKP, Springer, Cham (2020). https://doi.org/10.1007/978-3-030-42962-1

Author Index

Printed in the United States
by Baker & Taylor Publisher Services